The Harlem Renaissance 1920–1940

Series Editor

Cary D. Wintz
Texas Southern University

A Garland Series

Contents of the Series

Black Writers
Interpret the
Harlem Renaissance

Edited with introductions by

Cary D. Wintz
Texas Southern University

GARLAND PUBLISHING, INC.
New York & London
1996

Library of Congress Cataloging-in-Publication Data

Black writers interpret the Harlem Renaissance / edited with introduc-
    tions by Cary D. Wintz.
        p.   cm. — (The Harlem Renaissance, 1920–1940 ; 3)
    Includes bibliographical references.
    ISBN 0-8153-2214-3 (alk. paper)
        1. American literature—Afro-American authors—History and
    criticism.   2. American literature—New York (State)—New York—
    History and criticism.   3. Afro-Americans—New York (State)—New
    York—Intellectual life.   4. American literature—20th century—
    History and criticism.   5. Harlem (New York, N.Y.)—Intellectual
    life—20th century.   6. Afro-American arts—New York (State)—
    New York.   7. Harlem Renaissance.   I. Wintz, Cary D., 1943–
    II. Series.
    PS153.N5B564   1996
    810.9'896073—dc20   96-16938
                                                                 CIP

Printed on acid-free, 250-year-life paper
Manufactured in the United States of America

Contents

Autobiographical and Historical Sketches

Series Introduction

The Harlem Renaissance was the most significant event in African American literature and culture in the twentieth century. While its most obvious manifestation was as a self-conscious literary movement, it touched almost every aspect of African American culture and intellectual life in the period from World War I to the Great Depression. Its impact redefined black music, theater, and the visual arts; it reflected a new more militant political/racial consciousness and racial pride that was associated with the term "New Negro"; it embodied the struggle for civil rights that had been reinvigorated by the founding of the N.A.A.C.P. and the ideology of W.E.B. Du Bois; and it was an aspect of the urbanization of African Americans that first attracted public attention in the early twentieth century with the black migration.

Within this context it is difficult to pinpoint the chronological limits of the Harlem Renaissance. Generally the consensus among scholars is that the Harlem Renaissance was an event of the 1920s, bounded on one side by World War I and the race riots of 1919 and on the other side by the 1929 stock market crash. Some, however, have either greatly expanded or sharply restricted the time span of the movement. In 1967 Abraham Chapman wrote that he saw elements of the Renaissance in Claude McKay's poetry of 1917 and even in W.E.B. Du Bois's poem, "The Song of the Smoke," which was published in 1899.[1] Nathan Huggins argued that the Renaissance began during the years between the beginning of World War I and 1920, when the center of power in the African American community shifted from Tuskegee to Harlem, and he saw the Harlem Riots of 1935 as the end of the movement.[2] John Hope Franklin, on the other hand, wrote as late as 1980 that the Harlem Renaissance extended into the 1960s; more recently he has modified that concept, and now speaks of a first and second phase of the Harlem Renaissance, with the latter phase extending into the 1940s and beyond; he also observes that African American literary creativity was not confined to Harlem, but spread across the entire country[3] Benjamin Brawley, the preeminent African American literary historian contemporary to the Harlem Renaissance, downplayed the concept of the "so-called Negro literary renaissance," which he felt was centered around the publication of Carl Van Vechten's *Nigger Heaven* in 1926 and which he argued had no significant positive influence on African American literature.[4] Finally, Sterling Brown, one of the Harlem Renaissance poets and later a literary scholar, denied that Harlem was ever the center of a black literary movement.[5]

For the purposes of this collection the Harlem Renaissance is viewed primarily as a literary and intellectual movement. While theater, music, and the visual arts are looked at briefly, the focus is on African American literature, the assessment and criticism of this literature, and the relation of this literature to the political and social issues confronting African Americans in the early twentieth century.

The Harlem Renaissance was a self-conscious movement. That is, the writers and poets who participated in the movement were aware that they were involved in a literary movement and assumed at least partial responsibility for defining the parameters and aesthetics of the movement; black scholars and intellectuals were also aware of the Harlem Renaissance (even if they railed against it) and attempted to define the movement in terms both of literature and the political and social implications of that literature. While it was self-conscious, the Harlem Renaissance lacked a well-defined ideological or aesthetic center. It was more a community of writers, poets, critics, patrons, sponsors, and publishers than a structured and focused intellectual movement. It may be best conceptualized as an attitude or a state of mind—a feeling shared by a number of black writers and intellectuals who centered their activities in Harlem in the 1920s and early 1930s. The men and women who participated in the movement shared little but a consciousness that they were part of a common endeavor—a new awakening of African American culture and creativity; other than that what bound them together was a pride in their racial heritage, an essentially middle-class background, and the fact that all, to a greater or lesser degree, were connected to Harlem at the time that Harlem was emerging as the cultural, intellectual, and political center of black America.

Within this context, the Harlem Renaissance may best be conceptualized as a group of black writers and poets, orbiting erratically around a group of black intellectuals positioned in the N.A.A.C.P., the Urban League, and other African American political and educational institutions. These older intellectuals supported the movement, criticized it, attempted with varying success to define it, and served as liaison between the writers and the white publishers, patrons, and critics who dominated the business of literature in the United States in the 1920s. Complicating and enriching this mix was the fact that the lines between the various types of participants were not clearly drawn. James Weldon Johnson, for example, was a major promoter of the movement and a poet and novelist in his own right; Jessie Fauset, the most prolific novelist of the period, also served as literary editor of *The Crisis* and actively promoted the careers of young black writers; Countee Cullen, Sterling Brown, and Gwendolyn Bennett wrote regular literary columns, while Wallace Thurman, Langston Hughes, and several other writers attempted to publish literary magazines; and Carl Van Vechten, a white promoter of African American literature, worked closely with the Knopfs to publish black literature, authored the best-known novel of Harlem life, and almost singlehandedly created the white fascination with Harlem and African American life that characterized the 1920s.

With this definition it becomes a little easier to define the parameters of the movement. The Harlem Renaissance began in the early 1920s, when Jean Toomer published *Cane* and African American writers and intellectuals began to realize that something new was happening in black literature. The movement extended well into the 1930s and included the works of Zora Neale Hurston, Claude McKay, and Langston Hughes that were published in that decade. As long as they and other writers consciously identified with the Renaissance, the movement continued. It did not, however, encompass the younger writers like Richard Wright, Frank Yerby, or Ralph Ellison, who emerged in the 1930s and 1940s. Like so much else, these boundaries are not exact. Antecedents to the Harlem Renaissance are clear in the first two decades of the twentieth century; likewise it is easy to place some of Langston Hughes's work from the 1940s and 1950s in the Renaissance.

The goal of this series is to reprint articles and other materials that will delineate a clear picture and foster an understanding of the Harlem Renaissance. Three types of materials are included in this series. First, and most important, are the critical and interpretive materials on the Harlem Renaissance written by participants in and contemporaries of the movement. These firsthand accounts will assist readers in understanding the efforts of Harlem Renaissance writers, poets, and critics to define the movement and enable readers to glimpse the dynamics of the movement. Second, this series includes a retrospective look at the Harlem Renaissance through the eyes of participants and contemporaries, as well as by writers and critics who were involved in post-Renaissance black literature. Finally, the series presents a sample of the scholarly analysis and criticism of the movement from the 1950s through the early 1990s. The selections come from articles, essays, columns, and reviews in periodical literature; selections from memoirs, novels, histories, and books of criticism; and essays from scholarly journals. These materials are supplemented by a selection of previously unpublished materials, including letters, speeches, and essays. Not included are the literary works of the Harlem Renaissance. There are a number of anthologies of African American literature that already serve that purpose well.

This series also reflects one of the major problems confronting the study of the Harlem Renaissance in particular and African American history in general—the difficulty of accessing needed source materials. For years the study of African American history was handicapped by the fact that many of its primary sources had not been preserved or were not made available to scholars. If they had been preserved, they were housed in scattered collections and often incompletely processed and catalogued. The sharp increase in interest in African American history during the last thirty years has improved this situation enormously, but problems still persist. This series is in part an effort to make material related to one aspect of African American history more available to students and scholars. Unfortunately, it also suffers from the problem that some resources, even when located, are not readily available. For this reason a number of items by James Weldon Johnson had to be excluded; likewise, a very valuable retrospective on the Harlem Renaissance that was published initially in *Black World* is missing here. In the future, perhaps these and other barriers that impede research in African American history will be lifted.

As in any project of this nature there are scores of persons who have provided valuable support and assistance; it is impossible to name them all here. I want to especially thank Leo Balk and Carole Puccino of Garland Publishing. Leo with patience and firmness guided this series to completion; Carole worked diligently to arrange permissions for the publication of the material that appears here. In addition, I want to thank Paul Finkelman, who played a key role in helping me conceptualize the scope and nature of this project. Wolde Michael Akalou, Howard Beeth, Merline Pitre, and my other colleagues and students at Texas Southern University provided valuable feedback as the project developed. I also had wonderful assistance from the staff at the libraries

xii   SERIES INTRODUCTION

I visited while collecting the material for this series. I want to especially acknowledge the staff at the Harry Ransom Humanities Research Center at the University of Texas at Austin, the Beinecke Library at Yale University, and the Heartman Collection at the Robert J. Terry Library at Texas Southern University; in addition, librarians at the Fondren Library at Rice University, the M.D. Anderson Library at the University of Houston, the Perry Casteñeda Library at the University of Texas at Austin, and the library at the University of Houston, Clear Lake helped me track down the copies of the more elusive journals and periodicals used for this collection. I also want to thank Kathy Henderson and and Barbara Smith-Labard, who helped arrange for permission to publish previously unpublished materials from the collections at the Harry Ransom Humanities Research Center. Finally, research for this project was supported in part by a Travel to Collections grant from the National Endowment for the Humanities.

  Cary D. Wintz

Notes

  1. Abraham Chapman, "The Harlem Renaissance in Literary History," *CLA Journal* 11 (September 1967): 44–45.
  2. Nathan Irvin Huggins, ed., *Voices from the Harlem Renaissance* (New York: Oxford University Press, 1976), 6–10.
  3. John Hope Franklin, *From Slavery to Freedom: A History of Negro Americans*, 5th ed. (New York: Alfred Knopf, 1980), 383; John Hope Franklin and Alfred A. Moss, Jr., *From Slavery to Freedom: A History of African Americans*, 7th ed. (New York: McGraw–Hill, Inc., 1994), 379–80.
  4. Benjamin Brawley, *The Negro Genius: A New Appraisal of the American Negro in Literature and the Fine Arts* (New York: Dodd, Mead, 1937), 231–68.
  5. Sterling Brown, "The New Negro in Literature (1925–1955)." In *The New Negro Thirty Years Afterward*, ed. by Rayford W. Logan, Eugene C. Holmes, and C. Franklin Edwards (Washington, D.C.: Howard University Press, 1955).

Further Reading

Cooper, Wayne F. *Claude McKay: Rebel Sojourner in the Harlem Renaissance*. Baton Rouge: Louisiana State University Press, 1987.
Douglas, Ann. *Terrible Honesty: Mongrel Manhattan in the 1920s*. New York: Farrar, Straus, and Giroux, 1995.
Ferguson, Blanche E. *Countee Cullen and the Negro Renaissance*. New York: Dodd, Mead, 1966.
Hemenway, Robert E. *Zora Neale Hurston: A Literary Biography*. Urbana: University of Illinois Press, 1977.
Huggins, Nathan Irvin. *Harlem Renaissance*. New York: Oxford University Press, 1971.
———, ed. *Voices from the Harlem Renaissance*. New York: Oxford University Press, 1976.
Hull, Gloria T. *Color, Sex, and Poetry: Three Women Writers of the Harlem Renaissance*. Bloomington: Indiana University Press, 1987.
Kerman, Cynthia Earl, and Richard Eldridge. *The Lives of Jean Toomer: A Hunger for Wholeness*. Baton Rouge: Louisiana State University Press, 1987.
Levy, Eugene. *James Weldon Johnson: Black Leader, Black Voice*. Chicago: University of Chicago Press, 1973.
Lewis, Dadid Levering. *W.E.B. Du Bois: Biography of a Race, 1868–1919*. New York: Henry Holt, 1993.
———. *When Harlem Was in Vogue*. New York: Vintage Books, 1981.
Marable, Manning. *W.E.B. Du Bois: Black Radical Democrat*. Boston: Twayne Publishers, 1986.
Rampersad, Arnold. *The Life of Langston Hughes*. Vol 1. *I, Too, Sing America: 1902–1941*. New York: Oxford University Press, 1986.
———. *The Life of Langston Hughes*. Vol 2. *I Dream a World: 1942–1967*. New York: Oxford University Press, 1988.
Singh, Amritjit. *The Novels of the Harlem Renaissance: Twelve Black Writers, 1923–1933*. University Park: The Pennsylvania State University Press, 1976.
Sundquist, Eric J. *To Wake the Nations: Race in the Making of American Literature*. Cambridge: Harvard University Press, 1993.
Tillery, Tyrone. *Claude McKay: A Black Poet's Struggle for Identity*. Amherst: The University of Massachusetts Press, 1992.
Wintz, Cary D. *Black Culture and the Harlem Renaissance*. Houston: Rice University Press, 1988.

Volume Introduction

One of the interesting features of the Harlem Renaissance was the degree to which black writers and poets were involved in promoting and analyzing their own literary movement. One of the formative events of the Harlem Renaissance was the 1926 attempt by Wallace Thurman, Langston Hughes, and a handful of other young black writers to publish a literary magazine, *Fire!!* This was the first of several similar efforts by black writers to establish literary journals. While these efforts failed, several African American periodicals used black writers to review and analyze black literary efforts. Countee Cullen, Eric Walrond, Gwendolyn Bennett, and Jessie Fauset served at one time or another on the editorial staff of *Opportunity* or *The Crisis*, and Wallace Thurman served briefly on the editorial staff of *The Messenger* before attempting to establish his own literary magazine. In addition, Cullen, Bennett, and Sterling Brown wrote regular literary columns for *Opportunity*.

African American writers also contributed to efforts to understand and analyze the Harlem Renaissance by producing autobiographies and historical works, editing anthologies, and going on the road to conduct lectures and readings from their books. For example, in 1926 Countee Cullen edited a "Negro Poets" number of the avant-garde literary magazine *Palms*, while Langston Hughes spent several months in the fall and winter of 1931–1932 touring black college campuses in the South, reading selections from his poems and promoting black literature. In the early 1930s, Hughes also helped Nancy Cunard identify potential contributors to her anthology on black literature and art.

This volume opens with two efforts spearheaded by Wallace Thurman to create literary magazines for the Harlem Renaissance. In November, 1926 the first and only issue of *Fire!!*, "a quarterly devoted to the younger Negro artists," appeared in Harlem. Like the Harlem Renaissance itself, *Fire!!* attempted to blend a somewhat militant and avowedly independent, bohemian outlook with a rather moderate attempt to achieve literary success and middle-class recognition and respectability. Wallace Thurman edited the magazine, in association with Langston Hughes, Zora Neale Hurston, Richard Bruce, John Davis, Gwendolyn Bennett, and Aaron Douglas. Two years later, in November, 1928, Thurman tried again with the inaugural issue of *Harlem*. Like its predecessor, *Harlem* included illustrations by Harlem artist Aaron Douglas; its tone, however, was less flamboyant and less militant. Essays by Alain Locke and Walter White insured a level of respectability, but attacks on W.E.B. Du Bois and his efforts to confine Harlem artists to "respectable" subject matter guaranteed that the new magazine would be as controversial as its predecessor. It also was equally short-lived.

The second section of this volume includes a complete collection of the *Opportunity* literary columns of Gwendolyn Bennett, Countee Cullen, and Sterling Brown. Bennett and Cullen published their columns almost simultaneously with Bennett beginning first in August, 1926 and continuing to May, 1928, while Cullen began a few months later in December, 1926, and continued until September, 1928. Almost three years later, in January, 1931, Sterling Brown inaugurated the five-year run of his column. Each of these columns obviously reflected the interests and personality of its creator; together the three provide insight to the efforts of black poets to understand and evaluate the literary and cultural developments in black America during the Harlem Renaissance.

In addition to their work with black periodicals, a number of persons involved in the Harlem Renaissance interpreted the movement in their autobiographical and historical writings. Selections that focus on the Harlem Renaissance from the autobiographies of Walter White, Claude McKay, Zora Neale Hurston, and Langston Hughes provide an interesting perspective on the movement. Equally revealing are the selections on the Renaissance from the history of Harlem written by Claude McKay. Finally, this volume concludes with a selection from Wallace Thurman's rather bitter satirical novel of the Harlem Renaissance, *Infants of the Spring*. In this novel, Thurman depicts, in thinly disguised caricature, the major players in the "niggerati," Thurman's euphemism for the literary and intellectual establishment of the Harlem Renaissance.

Read—

Some Southern Snapshots
by

GEORGE S. SCHUYLER

in the December issue of

NEW MASSES

In this article Mr. Schuyler, a Negro writer, gives short sketches of Negro-white incidents in various Southern states. Negro boys and girls, men and women, insulted, arrested, hounded out of town, beaten, molested, and killed for imaginary, or at the most, ridiculously small and superficial acts. New details of the same old stories.

See the November and December issues of
NEW MASSES
for our Special Christmas Book Offers
25 CENTS A COPY

Rip This Off and Mail

NEW MASSES,
39 West Eighth Street, New York.

Enclosed find $\left\{\begin{array}{l}\$2.00 \\ \$1.00\end{array}\right\}$ for a $\left\{\begin{array}{l}\text{year's} \\ \text{6 months'}\end{array}\right\}$ subscription to the NEW MASSES:

Name..

Address..

....

Please send sample copies to:

1. *Name*..

   Address..

   ....

2. *Name*..

   Address..

   ....

~~~~~~~~~~~~~~~~~~~~~~~~~~~~~~~~

Foreword

FIRE . . . *flaming, burning, searing, and penetrating far beneath the superficial items of the flesh to boil the sluggish blood.*

FIRE . . . *a cry of conquest in the night, warning those who sleep and revitalizing those who linger in the quiet places dozing.*

FIRE . . . *melting steel and iron bars, poking livid tongues between stone apertures and burning wooden opposition with a cackling chuckle of contempt.*

FIRE . . . *weaving vivid, hot designs upon an ebon bordered loom and satisfying pagan thirst for beauty unadorned . . . the flesh is sweet and real . . . the soul an inward flush of fire. . . . Beauty? . . . flesh on fire—on fire in the furnace of life blazing. . . .*

> *"Fy-ah,*
> *Fy-ah, Lawd,*
> *Fy-ah gonna burn ma soul!"*

~~~~~~~~~~~~~~~~~~~~~~~~~~~~~~~~

FIRE!

A Quarterly Devoted to the Younger Negro Artists

Wishes to Thank the Following Persons
Who Acted as Patrons
For the First Issue

MAURINE BOIE, *Minneapolis, Minn.*
NELLIE R. BRIGHT, *Philadelphia, Pa.*
ARTHUR HUFF FAUSET, *Philadelphia, Pa.*
DOROTHY HUNT HARRIS, *New York City*
ARTHUR P. MOOR, *Harrisburg, Pa.*
DOROTHY R. PETERSON, *Brooklyn, N. Y.*
MR. AND MRS. JOHN PETERSON, *New York City*
E. B. TAYLOR, *Baltimore, Md.*
CARL VAN VECHTEN, *New York City*

Being a non-commercial product interested only in the arts, it is necessary that we make some appeal for aid from interested friends. For the second issue of FIRE we would appreciate having fifty people subscribe ten dollars each, and fifty more to subscribe five dollars each.

We make no eloquent or rhetorical plea. FIRE speaks for itself.

Gratefully,
THE BOARD OF EDITORS.

FIRE!!

A Quarterly Devoted to the Younger Negro Artists

Premier Issue Edited by
WALLACE THURMAN

In Association With

Langston Hughes	Zora Neale Hurston
Gwendolyn Bennett	Aaron Douglas
Richard Bruce	John Davis

Table of Contents

Volume One   Number One

EDITORIAL OFFICES

314 West 138th Street, New York City

Price $1.00 per copy   Issued Quarterly

DEVOTED TO YOUNGER NEGRO ARTISTS

Cordelia the Crude

Physically, if not mentally, Cordelia was a potential prostitute, meaning that although she had not yet realized the moral import of her wanton promiscuity nor become mercenary, she had, nevertheless, become quite blasé and bountiful in the matter of bestowing sexual favors upon persuasive and likely young men. Yet, despite her seeming lack of discrimination, Cordelia was quite particular about the type of male to whom she submitted, for numbers do not necessarily denote a lack of taste, and Cordelia had discovered after several months of active observation that one could find the qualities one admires or reacts positively to in a varied hodge-podge of outwardly different individuals.

The scene of Cordelia's activities was The Roosevelt Motion Picture Theatre on Seventh Avenue near 145th Street. Thrice weekly the program changed, and thrice weekly Cordelia would plunk down the necessary twenty-five cents evening admission fee, and saunter gaily into the foul-smelling depths of her favorite cinema shrine. The Roosevelt Theatre presented all of the latest pictures, also, twice weekly, treated its audiences to a vaudeville bill, then too, one could always have the most delightful physical contacts . . . hmm. . . .

Cordelia had not consciously chosen this locale nor had there been any conscious effort upon her part to take advantage of the extra opportunities afforded for physical pleasure. It had just happened that the Roosevelt Theatre was more close to her home than any other neighborhood picture palace, and it had also just happened that Cordelia had become almost immediately initiated into the ways of a Harlem theatre chippie soon after her discovery of the theatre itself.

It is the custom of certain men and boys who frequent these places to idle up and down the aisle until some female is seen sitting alone, to slouch down into a seat beside her, to touch her foot or else press her leg in such a way that it can be construed as accidental if necessary, and then, if the female is wise or else shows signs of willingness to become wise, to make more obvious approaches until, if successful, the approached female will soon be chatting with her baiter about the picture being

shown, lolling in his arms, and helping to formulate plans for an after-theatre rendezvous. Cordelia had, you see, shown a willingness to become wise upon her second visit to The Roosevelt. In a short while she had even learned how to squelch the bloated, lewd faced Jews and eager middle aged Negroes who might approach as well as how to inveigle the likeable little yellow or brown half men, embryo avenue sweetbacks, with their well' modeled heads, stickily plastered hair, flaming cravats ,silken or broadcloth shirts, dirty underwear, low cut vests, form fitting coats, bell-bottom trousers and shiny shoes with metal cornered heels clicking with a brave, brazen rhythm upon the bare concrete floor as their owners angled and searched for prey.

Cordelia, sixteen years old, matronly mature, was an undisciplined, half literate product of rustic South Carolina, and had come to Harlem very much against her will with her parents and her six brothers and sisters. Against her will because she had not been at all anxious to leave the lackadaisical life of the little corn pone settlement where she had been born, to go trooping into the unknown vastness of New York, for she had been in love, passionately in love with one John Stokes who raised pigs, and who, like his father before him, found the raising of pigs so profitable that he could not even consider leaving Lintonville. Cordelia had blankly informed her parents that she would not go with them when they decided to be lured to New York by an older son who had remained there after the demobilization of the war time troops. She had even threatened to run away with John until they should be gone, but of course John could not leave his pigs, and John's mother was not very keen on having Cordelia for a daughter-in-law — those Joneses have bad mixed blood in 'em—so Cordelia had had to join the Gotham bound caravan and leave her lover to his succulent porkers.

However, the mere moving to Harlem had not doused the rebellious flame. Upon arriving Cordelia had not only refused to go to school and refused to hold even the most easily held job, but had also victoriously defied her harassed parents so frequently when it came to matters of discipline that she soon found herself with a mesmerizing lack of home restraint, for the stress of trying to maintain themselves and their family in the new environment was far too much of a task for Mr. and Mrs. Jones to attend to facilely and at the same time try to control a recalcitrant child. So, when Cordelia had refused either to work or to attend school, Mrs. Jones herself had gone out for day's work, leaving Cordelia at home to take care of their five room railroad flat, the front room of which was rented out to a couple "living together," and to see that the younger children, all of whom were of school age, made their four trips daily between home and the nearby public school—as well as see that they had their greasy, if slim, food rations and an occasional change of clothing. Thus Cordelia's days were full—and so were her nights. The only difference being that the days belonged to the folks at home while the nights (since the folks were too tired or too sleepy to know or care when she came in or went out) belonged to her and to—well—whosoever will, let them come.

Cordelia had been playing this hectic, entrancing game for six months and was widely known among a certain group of young men and girls on the avenue as a fus' class chippie when she and I happened to enter the theatre simultaneously. She had clumped down the aisle before me, her open galoshes swishing noisily, her two arms busy wriggling themselves free from the torn sleeve lining of a shoddy imitation fur coat that one of her mother's wash clients had sent to her. She was of medium height and build, with overly developed legs and bust, and had a clear, keen light brown complexion. Her too slick, too naturally bobbed hair, mussed by the removing of a tight, black turban was of an undecided nature, i.e., it was undecided whether to be kinky or to be kind, and her body, as she sauntered along in the partial light had such a conscious sway of invitation that unthinkingly I followed, slid into the same row of seats and sat down beside her.

Naturally she had noticed my pursuit, and thinking that I was eager to play the game, let me know immediately that she was wise, and not the least bit averse to spooning with me during the evening's performance. Interested, and, I might as well confess, intrigued physically, I too became wise, and played up to her with all the fervor, or so I thought, of an old timer, but Cordelia soon remarked that I was different from mos' of des' sheiks, and when pressed for an explanation brazenly told me in a slightly scandalized and patronizing tone that I had not even felt her legs . . . !

At one o'clock in the morning we strolled through the snowy bleakness of one hundred and forty-fourth street between Lenox and Fifth Avenues to the walk-up tenement flat in which she lived, and after stamping the snow from our feet, pushed through the double outside doors, and followed the dismal hallway to the rear of the building where we began the tedious climbing of the crooked, creaking, inconveniently narrow stairway. Cordelia had informed me earlier in the evening that she lived on the top floor—four flights up east side rear—and on our way we rested at each floor and at each half way landing, rested long enough to mingle the snowy dampness of our respective coats, and to hug clumsily while our lips met in an animal kiss.

Finally only another half flight remained, and instead of proceeding as was usual after our amourous demonstration I abruptly drew away from her, opened my overcoat, plunged my hand into my pants pocket, and drew out two crumpled one dollar bills which I handed to her, and then, while she stared at me foolishly, I muttered good-night, confusedly pecked her on her cold brown cheek, and darted down into the creaking darkness.

⤎❍

Six months later I was taking two friends of mine, lately from the provinces, to a Saturday night house-rent party in a well known whore house on one hundred and thirty-fourth street near Lenox Avenue. The place as we entered seemed to be a chaotic riot of raucous noise and clashing color all rhythmically merging in the red, smoke filled room. And there I saw Cordelia savagely careening in a drunken abortion of the Charleston and surrounded by a perspiring circle of handclapping enthusiasts. Finally fatigued, she whirled into an abrupt finish, and stopped so that she stared directly into my face, but being dizzy from the calisthenic turns and the cauterizing liquor she doubted that her eyes recognized someone out of the past, and, visibly trying to sober herself, languidly began to dance a slow drag with a lean hipped pimply faced yellow man who had walked between her and me. At last he released her, and seeing that she was about to leave the room I rushed forward calling Cordelia?—as if I was not yet sure who it was. Stopping in the doorway, she turned to see who had called, and finally recognizing me said simply, without the least trace of emotion,—'Lo kid. . . .

And without another word turned her back and walked into the hall to where she joined four girls standing there. Still eager to speak, I followed and heard one of the girls ask: Who's the dicty kid? . . .

And Cordelia answered: The guy who gimme ma' firs' two bucks. . . .

WALLACE THURMAN.

Color Struck

A Play in Four Scenes

Time: Twenty years ago and present.   *Place: A Southern City.*

PERSONS

JOHN - - - - - - - - *A light brown-skinned man*
EMMALINE - - - - - - - - - *A black woman*
WESLEY - - - - - - - *A boy who plays an accordion*
EMMALINE'S DAUGHTER - - - - - - *A very white girl*
EFFIE - - - - - - - - - - *A mulatto girl*
       A RAILWAY CONDUCTOR   A DOCTOR
Several who play mouth organs, guitars, banjos.
Dancers, passengers, etc.

SETTING.—*Early night. The inside of a "Jim Crow" railway coach. The car is parallel to the footlights. The seats on the down stage side of the coach are omitted. There are the luggage racks above the seats. The windows are all open. They are exits in each end of the car—right and left.*

ACTION.—*Before the curtain goes up there is the sound of a locomotive whistle and a stopping engine, loud laughter, many people speaking at once, good-natured shrieks, strumming of stringed instruments, etc. The ascending curtain discovers a happy lot of Negroes boarding the train dressed in the gaudy, twdry best of 1900. They are mostly in couples—each couple bearing a covered-over market basket which the men hastily deposit in the racks as they scramble for seats. There is a litle friendly pushing and shoving. One pair just miss a seat three times, much to the enjoyment of the crowd. Many "plug" silk hats are in evidence, also sun-flowers in button holes. The women are showily dressed in the manner of the time, and quite conscious of their finery. A few seats remain unoccupied.*

Enter Effie (*left*) *above, with a basket.* ONE OF THE MEN (*standing, lifting his "plug" in a grand manner*). Howdy do, Miss Effie, you'se lookin' jes lak a rose.

(*Effie blushes and is confused. She looks up and down for a seat.*) Fack is, if you wuzn't walkin' long, ah'd think you *wuz* a rose—(*he looks timidly behind her and the others laugh*). Looka here, where's Sam at?

EFFIE (*tossing her head haughtily*). I don't know an' I don't keer.

THE MAN (*visibly relieved*). Then lemme scorch you to a seat. (*He takes her basket and leads her to a seat center of the car, puts the basket in the rack and seats himself beside her with his hat at a rakish angle.*)

MAN (*sliding his arm along the back of the seat*). How come Sam ain't heah—y'll on a bust?

EFFIE (*angrily*). A man dat don't buy me nothin tuh put in *mah* basket, ain't goin' wid *me* tuh no cake walk. (*The hand on the seat touches her shoulder and she thrusts it away*). Take yo' arms from 'round me, Dinky! Gwan hug yo' Ada!

MAN (*in mock indignation*). Do you think I'd look at Ada when Ah got a chance tuh be wid you? Ah always wuz sweet on you, but you let ole Mullet-head Sam cut me out.

ANOTHER MAN (*with head out of the window*). Just look at de darkies coming! (*With head inside coach.*) Hey, Dinky! Heah come Ada wid a great big basket.

(*Dinky jumps up from beside Effie and rushes to exit right. In a moment they re-enter and take a seat near entrance. Everyone in coach laughs. Dinky's girl turns and calls back to Effie.*)

GIRL. Where's Sam, Effie?

EFFIE. Lawd knows, Ada.

GIRL. Lawd a mussy! Who you gointer walk de cake wid?

EFFIE. Nobody, Ah reckon. John and Emma gointer win it nohow. They's the bestest cake-walkers in dis state.

ADA. You'se better than Emma any day in de week. Cose Sam cain't walk lake John. (*She stands up and scans the coach.*) Looka heah, ain't John an' Emma going? They ain't on heah!

(*The locomotive bell begins to ring.*)

EFFIE. Mah Gawd, s'pose dey got left!

MAN (*with head out of window*). Heah they come, nip and tuck—whoo-ee! They'se gonna make it! (*He waves excitedly.*) Come on Jawn! (*Everybody crowds the windows, encouraging them by gesture and calls. As the whistle blows twice, and the train begins to move, they enter panting and laughing at left. The only seat left is the one directly in front of Effie.*)

DINKY (*standing*). Don't y'all skeer us no mo' lake dat! There couldn't be no cake walk thout y'all. Dem shad-mouf St. Augustine coons would win dat cake and we would have tuh kill 'em all bodaciously.

JOHN. It was Emmaline nearly made us get left. She says I wuz smiling at Effie on the street car and she had to get off and wait for another one.

EMMA (*removing the hatpins from her hat, turns furiously upon him*). You wuz grinning at her and she wuz grinning back jes lake a ole chessy cat! JOHN (*positively*). I wuzn't.

EMMA (*about to place her hat in rack*). You wuz. I seen you looking jes lake a possum.

JOHN. I wuzn't. I never gits a chance tuh smile at nobody—you won't let me.

EMMA. Jes the same every time you sees a yaller face, you *takes* a chance. (*They sit down in peeved silence for a minute.*)

DINKY. Ada, les we all sample de basket. I bet you got huckleberry pie.

ADA. No I aint, I got peach an' tater pies, but we aint gonna tetch a thing tell we gits tuh de hall.

DINKY (*mock alarm*). Naw, don't do dat! It's all right tuh save the fried chicken, but pies is *always* et on trains.

ADA. Aw shet up! (*He struggles with her for a kiss. She slaps him but finally yields.*)

JOHN (*looking behind him*). Hellow, Effie, where's Sam?

EFFIE. Deed, I don't know.

JOHN. Y'all on a bust?

EMMA. None ah yo' bizness, you got enough tuh mind yo' own self. Turn 'round!

(*She puts up a pouting mouth and he snatches a kiss. She laughs just as he kisses her again and there is a resounding smack which causes the crowd to laugh. And cries of "Oh you kid!" "Salty dog!"*)

(*Enter conductor left calling tickets cheerfully and laughing at the general merriment.*)

CONDUCTOR. I hope somebody from Jacksonville wins this cake.

JOHN. You live in the "Big Jack?"

CONDUCTOR. Sure do. And I wanta taste a piece of that cake on the way back tonight.

JOHN. Jes rest easy—them Augustiners aint gonna smell it. (*Turns to Emma.*) Is they, baby?

EMMA. Not if Ah kin help it.

Somebody with a guitar sings: "Ho babe, mah honey taint no lie."

(*The conductor takes up tickets, passes on and exits right.*)

WESLEY. Look heah, you cake walkers—y'all oughter git up and limber up yo' joints. I heard them folks over to St. Augustine been oiling up wid goose-grease, and over to Ocala they been rubbing down in snake oil.

A WOMAN'S VOICE. You better shut up, Wesley, you just joined de church last month. Somebody's going to tell the pastor on you.

WESLEY. Tell it, tell it, take it up and smell it. Come on out you John and Emma and Effie, and limber up.

JOHN. Naw, we don't wanta do our walking steps—nobody won't wanta see them when we step out at the hall. But we kin do something else just to warm ourselves up.

(*Wesley begins to play "Goo Goo Eyes" on his accordian, the other instruments come in one by one and John and Emma step into the aisle and "parade" up and down the aisle—Emma holding up her skirt, showing the lace on her petticoats. They two-step back to their seat amid much applause.*)

WESLEY. Come on out, Effie! Sam aint heah so you got to hold up his side too. Step on out. (*There is a murmur of applause as she steps into the aisle. Wesley strikes up "I'm gointer live anyhow till I die." It is played quite spiritedly as Effie swings into the pas-me-la—*)

WESLEY (*in ecstasy*). Hot stuff I reckon! Hot stuff I reckon! (*The musicians are stamping. Great enthusiasm. Some clap time with hands and feet. She hurls herself into a modified Hoochy Koochy, and finishes up with an ecstatic yell.*)

There is a babble of talk and laughter and exultation.

JOHN (*applauding loudly*). If dat Effie can't step nobody can.

EMMA. Course you'd say so cause it's her. Everything she do is pretty to you.

JOHN (*caressing her*). Now don't say that, Honey. Dancing is dancing no matter who is doing it. But nobody can hold a candle to you in nothing.

(*Some men are heard tuning up—getting pitch to sing. Four of them crowd together in one seat and begin the chorus of "Daisies Won't Tell." John and Emma grow quite affectionate.*)

JOHN (*kisses her*). Emma, what makes you always picking a fuss with me over some yaller girl.

10

What makes you so jealous, nohow ? I don't do nothing.

(*She clings to him, but he turns slightly away. The train whistle blows, there is a slackening of speed. Passengers begin to take down baskets from their racks.*)

EMMA. John! John, don't you want me to love you, honey?

JOHN (*turns and kisses her slowly*). Yes, I want you to love me, you know I do. But I don't like to be accused o' ever light colored girl in the world. It hurts my feeling. I don't want to be jealous like you are.

(*Enter at right Conductor, crying "St. Augus-*

tine, St. Augustine." *He exits left. The crowd has congregated at the two exits, pushing good-naturedly and joking. All except John and Emma. They are still seated with their arms about each other.*)

EMMA (*sadly*). Then you don't want my love, John, cause I can't help mahself from being jealous. I loves you so hard, John, and jealous love is the only kind I got.

(*John kisses her very feelingly.*)

EMMA. Just for myself alone is the only way I knows how to love.

(*They are standing in the aisle with their arms about each other as the curtain falls.*)

⤙⤙∝⤚⤚

SCENE II

SETTING.—*A weather-board hall. A large room with the joists bare. The place has been divided by a curtain of sheets stretched and a rope across from left to right. From behind the curtain there are occasional sounds of laughter, a note or two on a stringed instrument or accordion. General stir. That is the dance hall. The front is the ante-room where the refreshments are being served. A "plank" seat runs all around the hall, along the walls. The lights are kerosene lamps with reflectors. They are fixed to the wall. The lunch-baskets are under the seat. There is a table on either side upstage with a woman behind each. At one, ice cream is sold, at the other, roasted peanuts and large red-and-white sticks of peppermint candy.*

People come in by twos and three, laughing, joking, horse-plays, gauchily flowered dresses, small waists, bulging hips and busts, hats worn far back on the head, etc. People from Ocala greet others from Palatka, Jacksonville, St. Augustine, etc.

Some find seats in the ante-room, others pass on into the main hall.

Enter the Jacksonville delegation, laughing, pushing proudly.

DINKY. Here we is, folks—here we *is*. Gointer take dat cake on back tuh Jacksonville where it belongs.

MAN. Gwan! Whut wid you mullet-head Jacksonville Coons know whut to do wid a cake. It's gointer stay right here in Augustine where de *good* cake walkers grow.

DINKY. Taint no 'Walkers' never walked till John and Emmaline prance out—you mighty come a tootin'.

Great laughing and joshing as more people come in. John and Emma are encouraged, urged on to win.

EMMA. Let's we git a seat, John, and set down.

JOHN. Sho will—nice one right over there. (*They push over to wall seat, place basket underneath, and sit. Newcomers shake hands with them and urge them on to win.*)

(*Enter Joe Clarke and a small group. He is a rotund, expansive man with a liberal watch chain and charm.*)

DINKY (*slapping Clarke on the back*). If you don't go 'way from here! Lawdy, if it aint Joe.

CLARKE (*jovially*). Ah thought you had done forgot us people in Eatonville since you been living up here in Jacksonville.

DINKY. Course Ah aint. (*Turning.*) Looka heah folks! Joe Clarke oughta be made chairman uh dis meetin'—Ah mean Past Great-Grand Master of Ceremonies, him being the onliest mayor of de onliest colored town in de state.

GENERAL CHORUS. Yeah, let him be—thass fine, etc.

DINKY (*setting his hat at a new angle and throwing out his chest*). And *Ah'll* scorch him to de platform. Ahem!

11

(*Sprinkling of laughter as Joe Clarke is escorted into next room by Dinky.*)

(*The musicians are arriving one by one during this time. A guitar, accordian, mouth organ, banjo, etc. Soon there is a rapping for order heard inside and the voice of Joe Clarke.*)

JOE CLARKE. Git yo' partners one an' all for de gran' march! Git yo' partners, gent-mens!

A MAN (*drawing basket from under bench*). Let's we all eat first.

(*John and Emma go buy ice-cream. They coquettishly eat from each other's spoons. Old Man Lizzimore crosses to Effie and removes his hat and bows with a great flourish.*)

LIZZIMORE. Sam ain't here t'night, is he, Effie.

EFFIE (*embarrassed*). Naw suh, he aint.

LIZZ. Well, you like chicken? (*Extends arm to her.*) Take a wing!

(*He struts her up to the table amid the laughter of the house. He wears no collar.*)

JOHN (*squeezes Emma's hand*). You certainly is a ever loving mamma—when you aint mad.

EMMA (*smiles sheepishly*). You oughtn't to make me mad then.

JOHN. Ah don't make you! You makes yo'self mad, den blame it on me. Ah keep on tellin' you Ah don't love nobody but you. Ah knows heaps uh half-white girls Ah could git ef Ah wanted to. But (*he squeezes her hard again*) Ah jus' wants you! You know what they say! De darker de berry, de sweeter de taste!

EMMA (*pretending to pout*). Oh, you tries to run over me an' keep it under de cover, but Ah won't let yuh. (*Both laugh.*) Les' we eat our basket!

JOHN. Alright. (*He pulls the basket out and she removes the table cloth. They set the basket on their knees and begin to eat fried chicken.*)

MALE VOICE. Les' everybody eat—motion's done carried. (*Everybody begins to open baskets. All have fried chicken. Very good humor prevails. Delicacies are swapped from one basket to the other. John and Emma offer the man next them some supper. He takes a chicken leg. Effie crosses to John and Emma with two pieces of pie on a plate.*)

EFFIE. Y'll have a piece uh mah blueberry pie —it's mighty nice! (*She proffers it with a timid smile to Emma who "freezes" up instantly.*)

EMMA. Naw! We don't want no pie. We got cocoanut layer-cake.

JOHN. Ah—Ah think ah'd choose a piece uh pie, Effie. (*He takes it.*) Will you set down an' have a snack wid us? (*He slides over to make room.*)

EFFIE (*nervously*). Ah, naw, Ah got to run

on back to mah basket, but Ah thought maybe y'll mout' want tuh taste mah pie. (*She turns to go.*)

JOHN. Thank you, Effie. It's mighty good, too. (*He eats it. Effie crosses to her seat. Emma glares at her for a minute, then turns disgustedly away from the basket. John catches her shoulder and faces her around.*)

JOHN (*pleadingly*). Honey, be nice. Don't act lak dat!

EMMA (*jerking free*). Naw, you done ruint mah appetite now, carryin' on wid dat punkin-colored ole gal.

JOHN. Whut kin Ah do? If you had a acted polite Ah wouldn't a had nothin' to say.

EMMA. Naw, youse jus' hog-wile ovah her cause she's half-white! No matter whut Ah say, you keep carryin' on wid her. Act polite? Naw Ah aint gonna be deceitful an' bust mah gizzard fuh nobody! Let her keep her dirty ole pie ovah there where she is!

JOHN (*looking around to see if they are over-heard*). Sh-sh! Honey, you mustn't talk so loud.

EMMA (*louder*). Ah-Ah aint gonna bite mah tongue! If she don't like it she can lump it. Mah back is broad—(*John tries to cover her mouth with his hand*). She calls herself a big cigar, but I kin smoke her!

(*The people are laughing and talking for the most part and pay no attention. Effie is laughing and talking to those around her and does not hear the tirade. The eating is over and everyone is going behind the curtain. John and Emma put away their basket like the others, and sit glum. Voice of Master-of-ceremonies can be heard from beyond curtain announcing the pas-me-la contest. The contestants, mostly girls, take the floor. There is no music except the clapping of hands and the shouts of "Parse-me-lah" in time with the hand-clapping. At the end Master announces winner. Shadows seen on curtain.*)

MASTER. Mathilda Clarke is winner—if she will step forward she will receive a beautiful wook fascinator. (*The girl goes up and receives it with great hand-clapping and good humor.*) And now since the roosters is crowin' foah midnight, an' most of us got to git up an' go to work tomorrow, The Great Cake Walk will begin. Ah wants de floor cleared, cause de representatives of de several cities will be announced an' we wants 'em to take de floor as their names is called. Den we wants 'em to do a gran' promenade roun' de hall. An' they will then commence to walk fuh de biggest cake ever baked in dis state. Ten dozen eggs—ten pounds of flour —ten pounds of butter, and so on and so forth.

Now then—(*he strikes a pose*) for St. Augustine—
Miss Lucy Taylor, Mr. Ned Coles.
(*They step out amid applause and stand before stage.*)
　For Daytona—
Miss Janie Bradley, Enoch Nixon
(*Same business.*)
　For Ocala—
Miss Docia Boger, Mr. Oscar Clarke
(*Same business.*)
　For Palatka—
Miss Maggie Lemmons, Mr. Senator Lewis
(*Same business.*)
And for Jacksonville the most popular "walkers" in de state—
Miss Emmaline Beazeby, Mr. John Turner.
(*Tremendous applause. John rises and offers his arm grandiloquently to Emma.*)
　EMMA (*pleadingly, and clutching his coat*). John let's we all don't go in there with all them. Let's we all go on home.
　JOHN (*amazed*). Why, Emma?
　EMMA. Cause, cause all them girls is going to pulling and hauling on you, and—
　JOHN (*impatiently*). Shucks! Come on. Don't you hear the people clapping for us and calling our names? Come on!
　(*He tries to pull her up—she tries to drag him back.*)
　Come on, Emma! Taint no sense in your acting like this. The band is playing for us. Hear 'em? (*He moves feet in a dance step.*)
　EMMA. Naw, John, Ah'm skeered. I loves you —I—.
　(*He tries to break away from her. She is holding on fiercely.*)

　JOHN. I got to go! I been practising almost a year—I—we done come all the way down here. I can walk the cake, Emma—we got to—I got to go in! (*He looks into her face and sees her tremendous fear.*) What you skeered about?
　EMMA (*hopefully*). You won't go it—You'll come on go home with me all by ourselves. Come on John. I can't, I just can't go in there and see all them girls—Effie hanging after you—.
　JOHN. I got to go in—(*he removes her hand from his coat*)—whether you come with me or not.
　EMMA. Oh—them yaller wenches! How I hate 'em! They gets everything they wants—.
　VOICE INSIDE. We are waiting for the couple from Jacksonville—Jacksonville! Where is the couple from—.
　(*Wesley parts the curtain and looks out.*)
　WESLEY. Here they is out here spooning! You all can't even hear your names called. Come on John and Emma.
　JOHN. Coming. (*He dashes inside. Wesley stands looking at Emma in surprise.*)
　WESLEY. What's the matter, Emma? You and John spatting again? (*He goes back inside.*)
　EMMA (*calmly bitter*). He went and left me. If we is spatting we done had our last one. (*She stands and clenches her fists.*) Ah, mah God! He's in there with her—Oh, them half whites, they gets everything, they gets everything everybody else wants! The men, the jobs—everything! The whole world is got a sign on it. Wanted: Light colored. Us blacks was made for cobble stones. (*She muffles a cry and sinks limp upon the seat.*)
　VOICE INSIDE. Miss Effie Jones will walk for Jacksonville with Mr. John Turner in place of Miss Emmaline Beazeley.

SCENE III—*Dance Hall*

Emma springs to her feet and flings the curtains wide open. She stands staring at the gay scene for a moment defiantly ,then creeps over to a seat along the wall and shrinks into the Spanish Moss, motionless.
Dance hall decorated with palmetto leaves and Spanish Moss—a flag or two. Orchestra consists of guitar, mandolin, banjo, accordian, church organ and drum.

　MASTER (*on platform*). Couples take yo' places! When de music starts, gentlemen parade yo' ladies once round de hall, den de walk begins. (*The music begins. Four men come out from behind the platform bearing a huge chocolate cake. The couples are "prancing" in their tracks. The men lead off the procession with the cake—the contestants make a grand slam around the hall.*)
　MASTER. Couples to de floor! Stan' back, ladies an' gentlemen—give 'em plenty room.

　(*Music changes to "Way Down in Georgia." Orchestra sings. Effie takes the arm that John offers her and they parade to the other end of the hall. She takes her place. John goes back upstage to the platform, takes off his silk hat in a graceful sweep as he bows deeply to Effie. She lifts her skirts and curtsies to the floor. Both smile broadly. They advance toward each other, meet midway, then, arm in arm, begin to "strut." John falters as he faces her, but recovers promptly and is perfection in his style.* (*Seven to nine minutes to curtain.*) *Fervor of spectators grows until all are taking part in some way—either hand-clapping or singing the words. At curtain they have reached frenzy.*)

QUICK CURTAIN

~

(*It stays down a few seconds to indicate ending of contest and goes up again on John and Effie being declared winners by Judges.*)

MASTER (*on platform, with John and Effie on the floor before him*). By unanimous decision de cake goes to de couple from Jacksonville! (*Great enthusiasm. The cake is set down in the center of the floor and the winning couple parade around it arm in arm. John and Effie circle the cake happily*

and triumphantly. *The other contestants, and then the entire assembly fall in behind and circle the cake, singing and clapping. The festivities continue. The Jacksonville quartet step upon the platform and sing a verse and chorus of "Daisies won't tell." Cries of "Hurrah for Jacksonville! Glory for the big town," "Hurrah for Big Jack."*)

A MAN (*seeing Emma*). You're from Jacksonville, aint you? (*He whirls her around and around.*) Aint you happy? Whoopee! (*He releases her and she drops upon a seat. She buries her face in the moss.*)

(*Quartet begins on chorus again. People are departing, laughing, humming, with quartet cheering. John, the cake, and Effie being borne away in triumph.*)

~

SCENE IV

Time—present. The interior of a one-room shack in an alley. There is a small window in the rear wall upstage left. There is an enlarged crayon drawing of a man and woman—man sitting cross-legged, woman standing with her hand on his shoulder. A center table, red cover, a low, cheap rocker, two straight chairs, a small kitchen stove at left with a wood-box beside it, a water-bucket on a stand close by. A hand towel and a wash basin. A shelf of dishes above this. There is an ordinary oil lamp on the center table but it is not lighted when the curtain goes up. Some light enters through the window and falls on the woman seated in the low rocker. The door is center right. A cheap bed is against the upstage wall. Someone is on the bed but is lying so that the back is toward the audience.

ACTION—As the curtain rises, the woman is seen rocking to and fro in the low rocker. A dead silence except for the sound of the rocker and an occasional groan from the bed. Once a faint voice says "water" and the woman in the rocker arises and carries the tin dipper to the bed.

WOMAN. No mo' right away—Doctor says not too much. (*Returns dipper to pail.—Pause.*) You got right much fever—I better go git the doctor agin.

(*There comes a knocking at the door and she stands still for a moment, listening. It comes again and she goes to door but does not open it.*)

WOMAN. Who's that?

VOICE OUTSIDE. Does Emma Beasely live here?

EMMA. Yeah—(*pause*)—who is it?

VOICE. It's me—John Turner.

EMMA (*puts hands eagerly on the fastening*). John? did you say John Turner?

VOICE. Yes, Emma, it's me.

(*The door is opened and the man steps inside.*)

EMMA. John! Your hand (*she feels for it and touches it*). John flesh and blood.

JOHN (*laughing awkwardly*). It's me alright, old girl. Just as bright as a basket of chips. Make a light quick so I can see how you look. I'm crazy

to see you. Twenty years is a long time to wait, Emma.

EMMA (*nervously*). Oh, let's we all just sit in the dark awhile. (*Apologetically.*) I wasn't expecting nobody and my house aint picked up. Sit down. (*She draws up the chair. She sits in rocker.*)

JOHN. Just to think! Emma! Me and Emma sitting down side by each. Know how I found you?

EMMA (*dully*). Naw. How?

JOHN (*brightly*). Soon's I got in town I hunted up Wesley and he told me how to find you. That's who I come to see, you!

EMMA. Where you been all these years, up North somewheres? Nobody round here could find out where you got to.

JOHN. Yes, up North. Philadelphia.

EMMA. Married yet?

JOHN. Oh yes, seventeen years ago. But my wife is dead now and so I came as soon as it was decent to find *you*. I wants to marry you. I couldn't die happy if I didn't. Couldn't get over you—couldn't forget. Forget me, Emma?

EMMA. Naw, John. How could I?

JOHN (*leans over impulsively to catch her hand*). Oh, Emma, I love you so much. Strike a light honey so I can see you—see if you changed much. You was such a handsome girl!

EMMA. We don't exactly need no light, do we, John, tuh jus' set an' talk?

JOHN. Yes, we do, Honey. Gwan, make a light. Ah wanna see you.

(*There is a silence.*)

EMMA. Bet you' wife wuz some high-yaller dickty-doo.

JOHN. Naw she wasn't neither. She was jus' as much like you as Ah could get her. Make a light an' Ah'll show you her pictcher. Shucks, ah gotta look at mah old sweetheart. (*He strikes a match and holds it up between their faces and they look intently at each other over it until it burns out.*) You aint changed none atall, Emma, jus' as pretty as a speckled pup yet.

EMMA (*lighter*). Go long, John! (*Short pause*) 'member how you useter bring me magnolias?

JOHN. Do I? Gee, you was sweet! 'Member how Ah useter pull mah necktie loose so you could tie it back for me? Emma, Ah can't see to mah soul how we lived all this time, way from one another. 'Member how you useter make out mah ears had done run down and you useter screw 'em up agin for me? (*They laugh.*)

EMMA. Yeah, Ah useter think you wuz gointer be mah husban' then—but you let dat ole—.

JOHN. Ah aint gonna let you alibi on me lak dat. Light dat lamp! You cain't look me in de eye and say no such. (*He strikes another match and lights the lamp.*) Course, Ah don't wanta look too bossy, but Ah b'lieve you got to marry me tuh git rid of me. That is, if you aint married.

EMMA. Naw, Ah aint. (*She turns the lamp down.*)

JOHN (*looking about the room*). Not so good, Emma. But wait till you see dat little place in Philly! Got a little "Rolls-Rough," too—gointer teach you to drive it, too.

EMMA. Ah been havin' a hard time, John, an' Ah lost you—oh, aint nothin' been right for me! Ah aint never been happy.

(*John takes both of her hands in his.*)

JOHN. You gointer be happy now, Emma. Cause Ah'm gointer make you. Gee Whiz! Ah aint but forty-two and you aint forty yet—we got plenty time. (*There is a groan from the bed.*) Gee, what's that?

EMMA (*ill at ease*). Thass mah chile. She's sick. Reckon Ah bettah see 'bout her.

JOHN. You got a chile? Gee, that great! Ah always wanted one. but didn't have no luck. Now we kin start off with a family. Girl or boy?

EMMA (*slowly*). A girl. Comin' tuh see me agin soon, John?

JOHN. Comin' agin? Ah aint gone yet! We aint talked, you aint kissed me an' nothin', and you aint showed me our girl. (*Another groan, more prolonged.*) She must be pretty sick—let's see. (*He turns in his chair and Emma rushes over to the bed and covers the girl securely, tucking her long hair under the covers, too—before he arises. He goes over to the bed and looks down into her face. She is mulatto. Turns to Emma teasingly.*) Talkin' 'bout *me* liking high-yallers—yo husband musta been pretty near *white*.

EMMA (*slowly*). Ah, never wuz married, John.

JOHN. It's alright, Emma. (*Kisses her warmly.*) Everything is going to be O.K. (*Turning back to the bed.*) Our child looks pretty sick, but she's pretty. (*Feels her forehead and cheek.*) Think she oughter have a doctor.

EMMA. Ah done had one. Course Ah cain't git no specialist an' nothin' lak dat. (*She looks about the room and his gaze follows hers.*) Ah aint got a whole lot lake you. Nobody don't git rich in no white-folks' kitchen, nor in de washtub. You know Ah aint no school-teacher an' nothin' lak dat.

(*John puts his arm about her.*)

JOHN. It's all right, Emma. But our daughter is bad off—run out an' git a doctor—she needs one. Ah'd go if Ah knowed where to find one—you kin git one the quickest—hurry, Emma.

EMMA (*looks from John to her daughter and back again*). She'll be all right, Ah reckon, for a while. John, you love me—you really want me sho' nuff?

JOHN. Sure Ah do—think Ah'd come all de way down here for nothin'? Ah wants to marry agin.

EMMA. Soon, John?

JOHN. Real soon.

EMMA. Ah wuz jus' thinkin', mah folks is away now on a little trip—be home day after tomorrow—we could git married tomorrow.

JOHN. All right. Now run on after the doctor —we must look after our girl. Gee, she's got a full suit of hair! Glad you didn't let her chop it off. (*Looks away from bed and sees Emma standing still.*)

JOHN. Emma, run on after the doctor, honey. (*She goes to the bed and again tucks the long braids of hair in, which are again pouring over the side of* the bed by the feverish tossing of the girl.) What's our daughter's name?

EMMA. Lou Lillian. (*She returns to the rocker uneasily and sits rocking jerkily. He returns to his seat and turns up the light.*)

JOHN. Gee, we're going to be happy—we gointer make up for all them twenty years (*another groan*). Emma, git up an' gwan git dat doctor. You done forgot Ah'm de boss uh dis family now—gwan, while Ah'm here to watch her whilst you're gone. Ah got to git back to mah stoppin'-place after a while.

EMMA. You go git one, John.

JOHN. Whilst Ah'm blunderin' round tryin' to find one, she'll be gettin' worse. She sounds pretty bad—(*takes out his wallet and hands her a bill*)—get a taxi if necessary. Hurry!

EMMA (*does not take the money, but tucks her arms and hair in again, and gives the girl a drink*). Reckon Ah better go git a doctor. Don't want nothin' to happen to *her*. After you left, Ah useter have such a hurtin' in heah (*touches bosom*) till she come an' eased it some.

JOHN. Here, take some money and get a good doctor. There must be some good colored ones around here now.

EMMA (*scornfully*). I wouldn't let one of 'em tend my cat if I had one! But let's we don't start a fuss.

(*John caresses her again. When he raises his head he notices the picture on the wall and crosses over to it with her—his arm still about her.*)

JOHN. Why, that's you and me!

EMMA. Yes, I never could part with that. You coming tomorrow morning, John, and we're gointer get married, aint we? Then we can talk over everything.

JOHN. Sure, but I aint gone yet. I don't see how come we can't make all our arrangements now.

(*Groans from bed and feeble movement.*)

Good lord, Emma, go get that doctor!

(*Emma stares at the girl and the bed and seizes a hat from a nail on the wall. She prepares to go but looks from John to bed and back again. She fumbles about the table and lowers the lamp. Goes to door and opens it. John offers the wallet. She refuses it.*)

EMMA. Doctor right around the corner. Guess I'll leave the door open so she can get some air. She won't need nothing while I'm gone, John. (*She crosses and tucks the girl in securely and rushes out, looking backward and pushing the door wide open as she exits. John sits in the chair beside the table. Looks about him—shakes his head. The girl on*

the bed groans, "water," "so hot." John looks about him excitedly. Gives her a drink. Feels her forehead. Takes a clean handkerchief from his pocket and wets it and places it upon her forehead. She raises her hand to the cool object. Enter Emma running. When she sees John at the bed she is full of fury. She rushes over and jerks his shoulder around. They face each other.*)

EMMA. I knowed it! (*She strikes him.*) A half white skin. (*She rushes at him again. John staggers back and catches her hands.*)

JOHN. Emma!

EMMA (*struggles to free her hands*). Let me go so I can kill you. Come sneaking in here like a pole cat!

JOHN (*slowly, after a long pause*). So this is the woman I've been wearing over my heart like a rose for twenty years! She so despises her own skin that she can't believe any one else could love it!

(*Emma writhes to free herself.*)

JOHN. Twenty years! Twenty years of adoration, of hunger, of worship! (*On the verge of tears he crosses to door and exits quietly, closing the door after him.*)

(*Emma remains standing, looking dully about as if she is half asleep. There comes a knocking at the door. She rushes to open it. It is the doctor. White. She does not step aside so that he can enter.*)

DOCTOR. Well, shall I come in?

EMMA (*stepping aside and laughing a little*). That's right, doctor, come in.

(*Doctor crosses to bed with professional air. Looks at the girl, feels the pulse and draws up the sheet over the face. He turns to her.*)

DOCTOR. Why didn't you come sooner. I told you to let me know of the least change in her condition.

EMMA (*flatly*). I did come—I went for the doctor.

DOCTOR. Yes, but you waited. An hour more or less is mighty important sometimes. Why didn't you come?

EMMA (*passes hand over face*). Couldn't see.

(*Doctor looks at her curiously, then sympathetically takes out a small box of pills, and hands them to her.*) Here, you're worn out. Take one of these every hour and try to get some sleep. (*He departs.*)

(*She puts the pill-box on the table, takes up the low rocking chair and places it by the head of the bed. She seats herself and rocks monotonously and stares out of the door. A dry sob now and then. The wind from the open door blows out the lamp and she is seen by the little light from the window rocking in an even, monotonous gait, and sobbing.*)

Flame From the Dark Tower

A Section of Poetry

From the Dark Tower

e shall not always plant while others reap
The golden increment of bursting fruit,
Nor always countenance, abject and mute,
That lesser men should hold their brothers cheap;
Not everlastingly while others sleep
Shall we beguile their limbs with mellow flute,
Not always bend to some more subtle brute;
We were not made eternally to weep.

The night whose sable breast relieves the stark,
White stars is no less lovely being dark,
And there are buds that cannot bloom at all
In light, but crumple, piteous, and fall.
So in the dark we hide the heart that bleeds,
And wait, and tend our agonizing seeds.

Countée Cullen.

A Southern Road

Yolk-colored tongue
Parched beneath a burning sky,
A lazy little tune
Hummed up the crest of some
Soft sloping hill.
One streaming line of beauty
Flowing by a forest
Pregnant with tears.
A hidden nest for beauty
Idly flung by God
In one lonely lingering hour
Before the Sabbath.
A blue-fruited black gum,
Like a tall predella,
Bears a dangling figure,—
Sacrificial dower to the raff,
Swinging alone,
A solemn, tortured shadow in the air.

HELENE JOHNSON.

19

Jungle Taste

There is a coarseness
In the songs of black men
Coarse as the songs
Of the sea.
There is a weird strangeness
In the songs of black men
Which sounds not strange
To me.

There is beauty
In the faces of black women,
Jungle beauty
And mystery.
Dark, hidden beauty
In the faces of black women
Which only black men
See.

Finality

Trees are the souls of men
Reaching skyward.
And while each soul
Draws nearer God
Its dark roots cleave
To earthly sod:
    Death, only death
    Brings triumph to the soul.
    The silent grave alone
    Can bare the goal.
    Then roots and all
    Must lie forgot—
    To rot.

                    Edward Silvera.

20

The Death Bed

All the time they were praying
He watched the shadow of a tree
Flicker on the wall.

There is no need of prayer.
He said,
No need at all.

The kin-folk thought it strange
That he should ask them from a dying bed.
But they left all in a row
And it seemed to ease him
To see them go.

There were some who kept on praying
In a room across the hall
And some who listened to the breeze
That made the shadows waver
On the wall.

He tried his nerve
On a song he knew
And made an empty note
That might have come,
From a bird's harsh throat.

And all the time it worried him
That they were in there praying
And all the time he wondered
What it was they could be saying.

WARING CUNEY.

Elevator Boy

I got a job now
Runnin' an elevator
In the Dennison Hotel in Jersey,
Job aint no good though.
No money around.
    Jobs are just chances
    Like everything else.
    Maybe a little luck now,
    Maybe not.
    Maybe a good job sometimes:
    Step out o' the barrel, boy.
Two new suits an'
A woman to sleep with.
    Maybe no luck for a long time.
    Only the elevators
    Goin' up an' down,
    Up an' down,
    Or somebody else's shoes
    To shine,
    Or greasy pots in a dirty kitchen.
I been runnin' this
Elevator too long.
Guess I'll quit now.

LANGSTON HUGHES.

Railroad Avenue

Dusk dark
On Railroad Avenue.
Lights in the fish joints,
Lights in the pool rooms.
A box car some train
Has forgotten
In the middle of the block.
A player piano,
A victrola.
    942
    Was the number.
A boy
Lounging on the corner.
A passing girl
With purple powdered skin.
    Laughter
    Suddenly
    Like a taut drum.
    Laughter
    Suddenly
    Neither truth nor lie.
    Laughter
Hardening the dusk dark evening.
    Laughter
Shaking the lights in the fish joints,
Rolling white balls in the pool rooms,
And leaving untouched the box car
Some train has forgotten.

        LANGSTON HUGHES.

Length of Moon

Then the golden hour
Will tick its last
And the flame will go down in the flower.

A briefer length of moon
Will mark the sea-line and the yellow dune.

Then we may think of this, yet
There will be something forgotten
And something we should forget.

It will be like all things we know:
A stone will fail; a rose is sure to go.

It will be quiet then and we may stay
Long at the picket gate,—
But there will be less to say.

                                        ARNA BONTEMPS.

Little Cinderella

Look me over, kid!
I knows I'm neat,—
Little Cinderella from head to feet.
Drinks all night at Club Alabam,—
What comes next I don't give a damn!

Daddy, daddy,
You sho' looks keen!
I likes men that are long and lean.
Broad Street ain't got no brighter lights
Than your eyes at pitch midnight.

Streets

Avenues of dreams
Boulevards of pain
Moving black streams
Shimmering like rain.

LEWIS ALEXANDER.

Wedding Day

His name was Paul Watson and as he shambled down rue Pigalle he might have been any other Negro of enormous height and size. But as I have said, his name was Paul Watson. Passing him on the street, you might not have known or cared who he was, but any one of the residents about the great Montmartre district of Paris could have told you who he was as well as many interesting bits of his personal history.

He had come to Paris in the days before colored jazz bands were the style. Back home he had been a prize fighter. In the days when Joe Gans was in his glory Paul was following the ring, too. He didn't have that fine way about him that Gans had and for that reason luck seemed to go against him. When he was in the ring he was like a mad bull, especially if his opponent was a white man. In those days there wasn't any sympathy or nicety about the ring and so pretty soon all the ringmasters got down on Paul and he found it pretty hard to get a bout with anyone. Then it was that he worked his way across the Atlantic Ocean on a big liner—in the days before colored jazz bands were the style in Paris.

Things flowed along smoothly for the first few years with Paul's working here and there in the unfrequented places of Paris. On the side he used to give boxing lessons to aspiring youths or gymnastic young women. At that time he was working so steadily that he had little chance to find out what was going on around Paris. Pretty soon, however, he grew to be known among the trainers and managers began to fix up bouts for him. After one or two successful bouts a little fame began to come into being for him. So it was that after one of the prize-fights, a colored fellow came to his dressing room to congratulate him on his success as well as invite him to go to Montmartre to meet "the boys."

Paul had a way about him and seemed to get on with the colored fellows who lived in Montmartre and when the first Negro jazz band played in a tiny Parisian cafe Paul was among them playing the banjo. Those first years were without event so far as Paul was concerned. The members of that first band often say now that they wonder how it was that nothing happened during those first seven years, for it was generally known how great was Paul's hatred for American white people. I suppose the tranquility in the light of what happened afterwards was due to the fact that the cafe in which they worked was one in which mostly French people drank and danced and then too, that was before there were so many Americans visiting Paris. However, everyone had heard Paul speak of his intense hatred of American white folks. It only took two Benedictines to make him start talking about what he would do to the first "Yank" that called him "nigger." But the seven years came to an end and Paul Watson went to work in a larger cafe with a larger band, patronized almost solely by Americans.

I've heard almost every Negro in Montmartre tell about the night that a drunken Kentuckian came into the cafe where Paul was playing and said:

"Look heah, Bruther, what you all doin' ovah heah?"

"None ya bizness. And looka here, I ain't your brother, see?"

"Jack, do you heah that nigger talkin' lak that tah me?"

As he said this, he turned to speak to his companion. I have often wished that I had been there to have seen the thing happen myself. Every tale I have heard about it was different and yet there was something of truth in each of them. Perhaps the nearest one can come to the truth is by saying that Paul beat up about four full-sized white men that night besides doing a great deal of damage to the furniture about the cafe. I couldn't tell you just what did happen. Some of the fellows say that Paul seized the nearest table and mowed down men right and left, others say he took a bottle, then again the story runs that a chair was the instrument of his fury. At any rate, that started Paul Watson on his siege against the American white person who brings his native prejudices into the life of Paris.

It is a verity that Paul was the "black terror." The last syllable of the word, nigger, never passed the lips of a white man without the quick reflex action of Paul's arm and fist to the speaker's jaw. He paid for more glassware and cafe furnishings in the course of the next few years than is easily imaginable. And yet, there was something likable about Paul. Perhaps that's the reason that he stood in so well with the policemen of the neighborhood. Always some divine power seemed to intervene in his behalf and he was excused after the payment of a small fine with advice about his future conduct. Finally, there came the night when in a frenzy he shot the two American sailors.

They had not died from the wounds he had given them hence his sentence had not been one of death but rather a long term of imprisonment. It was a pitiable sight to see Paul sitting in the corner of his cell with his great body hunched almost double. He seldom talked and when he did his words were interspersed with oaths about the lowness of "crackers." Then the World War came.

It seems strange that anything so horrible as that wholesale slaughter could bring about any good and yet there was something of a smoothing quality about even its baseness. There has never been such equality before or since such as that which the World War brought. Rich men fought by the side of paupers; poets swapped yarns with dry-goods salesmen, while Jews and Christians ate corned beef out of the same tin. Along with the general leveling influence came France's pardon of her prisoners in order that they might enter the army. Paul Watson became free and a French soldier. Because he was strong and had innate daring in his heart he was placed in the aerial squad and cited many times for bravery. The close of the war gave him his place in French society as a hero. With only a memory of the war and an ugly scar on his left cheek he took up his old life.

His firm resolutions about American white people still remained intact and many chance encounters that followed the war are told from lip to lip proving that the war and his previous imprisonment had changed him little. He was the same Paul Watson to Montmartre as he shambled up rue Pigalle.

Rue Pigalle in the early evening has a sombre beauty—gray as are most Paris streets and otherworldish. To those who know the district it is the Harlem of Paris and rue Pigalle is its dusky Seventh Avenue. Most of the colored musicians that furnish Parisians and their visitors with entertainment live somewhere in the neighborhood of rue Pigalle. Some time during every day each of these musicians makes a point of passing through rue Pigalle. Little wonder that almost any day will find Paul Watson going his shuffling way up the same street.

He reached the corner of rue de la Bruyere and with sure instinct his feet stopped. Without half thinking he turned into "the Pit." Its full name is The Flea Pit. If you should ask one of the musicians why it was so called, he would answer you to the effect that it was called "the pit" because all the "fleas" hang out there. If you did not get the full import of this explanation, he would go further and say that there were always "spades" in the pit and they were as thick as fleas. Unless

you could understand this latter attempt at clarity you could not fully grasp what the Flea-Pit means to the Negro musicians in Montmartre. It is a tiny cafe of the genus that is called *bistro* in France. Here the fiddle players, saxophone blowers, drumbeaters and ivory ticklers gather at four in the afternoon for a porto or a game of billiards. Here the cabaret entertainers and supper musicians meet at one o'clock at night or thereafter for a whiskey and soda, or more billiards. Occasional sandwiches and a "quiet game" also play their parts in the popularity of the place. After a season or two it becomes a settled fact just what time you may catch so-and-so at the famous "Pit."

The musicians were very fond of Paul and took particular delight in teasing him. He was one of the chosen few that all of the musicians conceded as being "regular." It was the pet joke of the habitues of the cafe that Paul never bothered with girls. They always said that he could beat up ten men but was scared to death of one woman.

"Say fellow, when ya goin' a get hooked up?"

"Can't say, Bo. Ain't so much on skirts."

"Man alive, ya don't know what you're missin' —somebody little and cute telling ya sweet things in your ear. Paris is full of women folks."

"I ain't much on 'em all the same. Then too, they're all white."

"What's it to ya? This ain't America."

"Can't help that. Get this—I'm collud, see? I ain't got nothing for no white meat to do. If a woman eva called me nigger I'd have to kill her, that's all!"

"You for it, son. I can't give you a thing on this Mr. Jefferson Lawd way of lookin' at women."

"Oh, tain't that. I guess they're all right for those that wants 'em. Not me!"

"Oh you ain't so forty. You'll fall like all the other spades I've ever seen. Your kind falls hardest."

And so Paul went his way—alone. He smoked and drank with the fellows and sat for hours in the Montmartre cafes and never knew the companionship of a woman. Then one night after his work he was walking along the street in his queer shuffling way when a woman stepped up to his side.

"Voulez vous."

"Naw, gowan away from here."

"Oh, you speak English, don't you?"

"You an 'merican woman?"

"Used to be 'fore I went on the stage and got stranded over here."

"Well, get away from here. I don't like your kind!"

"Aw, Buddy, don't say that. I ain't prejudiced like some fool women."

"You don't know who I am, do you? I'm Paul Watson and I hate American white folks, see?"

He pushed her aside and went on walking alone. He hadn't gone far when she caught up to him and said with sobs in her voice:—

"Oh, Lordy, please don't hate me 'cause I was born white and an American. I ain't got a sou to my name and all the men pass me by cause I ain't spruced up. Now you come along and won't look at me cause I'm white."

Paul strode along with her clinging to his arm. He tried to shake her off several times but there was no use. She clung all the more desperately to him. He looked down at her frail body shaken with sobs, and something caught at his heart. Before he knew what he was doing he had said:—

"Naw, I ain't that mean. I'll get you some grub. Quit your cryin'. Don't like seein' women folks cry."

It was the talk of Montmartre. Paul Watson takes a woman to Gavarnni's every night for dinner. He comes to the Flea Pit less frequently, thus giving the other musicians plenty of opportunity to discuss him.

"How times do change. Paul, the woman-hater, has a Jane now."

"You ain't said nothing, fella. That ain't all. She's white and an 'merican, too."

"That's the way with these spades. They beat up 'll the white men they can lay their hands on but as soon as a gang of golden hair with blue eyes rubs up close to them they forget all they ever said about hatin' white folks."

"Guess he thinks that skirt's gone on him. Dumb fool!"

"Don' be no chineeman. That old gag don' fit for Paul. He cain't understand it no more'n we can. Says he jess can't help himself, everytime she looks up into his eyes and asks him does he love her. They sure are happy together. Paul's goin' to marry her, too. At first she kept saying that she didn't want to get married cause she wasn't the marrying kind and all that talk. Paul jus' laid down the law to her and told her he never would live with no woman without being married to her. Then she began to tell him all about her past life. He told her he didn't care nothing about what she used to be jus' so long as they loved each other now. Guess they'll make it."

"Yeah, Paul told me the same tale last night. He's sure gone on her all right."

"They're gettin' tied up next Sunday. So glad it's not me. Don't trust these American dames. Me for the Frenchies."

"She ain't so worse for looks, Bud. Now that he's been furnishing the green for the rags."

"Yeah, but I don't see no reason for the wedding bells. She was right—she ain't the marrying kind."

. . . and so Montmartre talked. In every cafe where the Negro musicians congregated Paul Watson was the topic for conversation. He had suddenly fallen from his place as bronze God to almost less than the dust.

The morning sun made queer patterns on Paul's sleeping face. He grimaced several times in his slumber, then finally half-opened his eyes. After a succession of dream-laden blinks he gave a great yawn, and rubbing his eyes, looked at the open window through which the sun shone brightly. His first conscious thought was that this was the bride's day and that bright sunshine prophesied happiness for the bride throughout her married life. His first impulse was to settle back into the covers and think drowsily about Mary and the queer twists life brings about, as is the wont of most bridegrooms on their last morning of bachelorhood. He put this impulse aside in favor of dressing quickly and rushing downstairs to telephone to Mary to say "happy wedding day" to her.

One huge foot slipped into a worn bedroom slipper and then the other dragged painfully out of the warm bed were the courageous beginnings of his bridal toilette. With a look of triumph he put on his new grey suit that he had ordered from an English tailor. He carefully pulled a taffeta tie into place beneath his chin, noting as he looked at his face in the mirror that the scar he had received in the army was very ugly—funny, marrying an ugly man like him.

French telephones are such human faults. After trying for about fifteen minutes to get Central 32.01 he decided that he might as well walk around to Mary's hotel to give his greeting as to stand there in the lobby of his own, wasting his time. He debated this in his mind a great deal. They were to be married at four o'clock. It was eleven now and it did seem a shame not to let her have a minute or two by herself. As he went walking down the street towards her hotel he laughed to think of how one always cogitates over doing something and finally does the thing he wanted to in the beginning anyway.

⤽

Mud on his nice gray suit that the English tailor had made for him. Damn—gray suit—what did he have a gray suit on for, anyway. Folks with black faces shouldn't wear gray suits. Gawd, but it was funny that time when he beat up that cracker at the Periquet. Fool couldn't shut his mouth he was so surprised. Crackers—damn 'em—he was one nigger that wasn't 'fraid of 'em. Wouldn't he have a hell of a time if he went back to America where black was black. Wasn't white nowhere, black wasn't. What was that thought he was trying to get ahold of—bumping around in his head—something he started to think about but couldn't remember it somehow.

The shrill whistle that is typical of the French subway pierced its way into his thoughts. Subway —why was he in the subway—he didn't want to go any place. He heard doors slamming and saw the blue uniforms of the conductors swinging on to the cars as the trains began to pull out of the station. With one or two strides he reached the last coach as it began to move up the platform. A bit out of breath he stood inside the train and looking down at

what he had in his hand he saw that it was a tiny pink ticket. A first class ticket in a second class coach. The idea set him to laughing. Everyone in the car turned and eyed him, but that did not bother him. Wonder what stop he'd get off—funny how these French said descend when they meant get off—funny he couldn't pick up French—been here so long. First class ticket in a second class coach! —that was one on him. Wedding day today, and that damn letter from Mary. How'd she say it now, "just couldn't go through with it," white women just don't marry colored men, and she was a street woman, too. Why couldn't she have told him flat that she was just getting back on her feet at his expense. Funny that first class ticket he bought, wish he could see Mary—him a-going there to wish her "happy wedding day," too. Wonder what that French woman was looking at him so hard for? Guess it was the mud.

GWENDOLYN BENNETT.

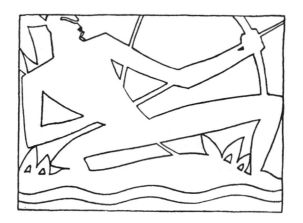

Three Drawings

Aaron Douglas

Smoke, Lilies and Jade

*e wanted to do something . . . to write or draw . . . or something . . . but it was so comfortable just to lay there on the bed . . . . . . his shoes off . . . and think . . . think of everything . . . short disconnected thoughts—to wonder . . . to remember . . . to think and smoke . . . why wasn't he worried that he had no money . . . he *had* had five cents . . . but he had been hungry . . . he *was* hungry and still . . . all he wanted to do was . . . lay there comfortably smoking . . . think . . . wishing he were writing . . . or drawing . . . or something . . . something about the things he felt and thought . . . but what did he think . . . he remembered how his mother had awakened him one night . . . ages ago . . . six years ago . . . Alex . . . he had always wondered at the strangeness of it . . . she had seemed so . . . so . . . so just the same . . . Alex . . . I think your father is dead . . . and it hadn't seemed so strange . . . yet . . . one's mother didn't say that . . . didn't wake one at midnight every night to say . . . feel him . . . put your hand on his head . . . then whisper with a catch in her voice . . . I'm afraid . . . sh don't wake Lam . . . yet it hadn't seemed as it should have seemed . . . even when he had felt his father's cool wet forehead . . . it hadn't been tragic . . . the light had been turned very low . . . and flickered . . . yet it hadn't been tragic . . . or weird . . . not at all as one should feel when one's father died . . . even his reply of . . . yes he is dead . . . had been commonplace . . . hadn't been dramatic . . . there had been no tears . . . no sobs . . . not even a sorrow . . . and yet he must have realized that one's father couldn't smile . . . or sing any more . . . after he had died . . . every one remembered his father's voice . . . it had been a lush voice . . . a promise . . . then that dressing together . . . his mother and himself . . . in the bathroom . . . why was the bathroom always the warmest room in the winter . . . as they had put on their clothes . . . his mother had been telling him what he must do . . . and cried softly . . . and that had made him cry too but you mustn't cry Alex . . . remember you have to be a little man now . . . and that was all . . . didn't other wives and sons cry more for their dead than that . . . anyway people never cried for beautiful sunsets . . . or music . . . and those were the things that hurt . . . the things to sympathize with . . . then out into the snow and dark of the morning . . . first to the undertaker's . . . no first to Uncle Frank's . . .why did Aunt Lula have to act like that . . . to ask again and again . . . but when did he die . . .

when did he die . . . I just can't believe it . . . poor Minerva . . . then out into the snow and dark again . . . how had his mother expected him to know where to find the night bell at the undertaker's . . . he was the most sensible of them all tho . . . all he had said was . . . what . . . Harry Francis . . . too bad . . . tell mamma I'll be there first thing in the morning . . . then down the deserted streets again . . . to grandmother's . . . it was growing light now . . . it must be terrible to die in daylight . . . grandpa had been sweeping the snow off the yard . . . he had been glad of that because . . . well he could tell him better than grandma . . . grandpa . . . father's dead . . . and he hadn't acted strange either . . . books lied . . . he had just looked at Alex a moment then continued sweeping . . . all he said was . . . what time did he die . . . she'll want to know . . . then passing thru the lonesome street toward home . . . Mrs. Mamie Grant was closing a window and spied him . . . hallow Alex . . . an' how's your father this mornin' . . . dead . . . get out . . . tch tch tch an' I was just around there with a cup a' custard yesterday . . . Alex puffed contentedly on his cigarette . . . he was hungry and comfortable . . . and he had an ivory holder inlaid with red jade and green . . . funny how the smoke seemed to climb up that ray of sunlight . . . went up the slant just like imagination . . . was imagination blue . . . or was it because he had spent his last five cents and couldn't worry . . . anyway it was nice to lay there and wonder . . . and remember . . . why was he so different from other people . . . the only things he remebered of his father's funeral were the crowded church and the ride in the hack . . . so many people there in the church . . . and ladies with tears in their eyes . . . and on their cheeks . . . and some men too . . . why did people cry . . . vanity that was all . . . yet they weren't exactly hypocrites . . . but why . . . it had made him furious . . . all these people crying . . . it wasn't *their* father . . . and he wasn't crying . . . couldn't cry for sorrow altho he had loved his father more than . . . than . . . it had made him so angry that tears had come to his eyes . . . and he had been ashamed of his mother . . . crying into a handkerchief . . . so ashamed that tears had run down his cheeks and he had frowned . . . and some one . . . a woman . . . had said . . . look at that poor little dear . . . Alex is just like his father . . . and the tears had run fast . . . because he *wasn't* like his father . . . he couldn't sing . . . he didn't want to sing . . . he didn't want to sing . . . Alex blew a cloud of smoke . . . blue smoke . . . when they had taken his father from the vault three weeks later . . . he had grown beautiful . . . his nose had become perfect and clear . . . his hair had turned jet black and glossy and silky . . . and his skin was a transparent green . . . like the sea only not so deep . . . and where it was drawn over the cheek bones a pale beautiful red appeared . . . like a blush . . . why hadn't his father looked like that always . . . but no . . . to have sung would have broken the wondrous repose of his lips and maybe that was his beauty . . . maybe it was wrong to think thoughts like these . . . but they were nice and pleasant and comfortable . . . when one was smoking a cigarette thru an ivory holder . . . inlaid with red jade and green . . . .

he wondered why he couldn't find work . . . a job . . . when he had first come to New York he had . . . and he had only been fourteen then was it because he was nineteen now that he felt so idle . . . and contented . . . or because he was an artist . . . but was he an artist . . . was one an artist until one became known . . . of course he was an artist . . . and strangely enough so were all his friends . . . he should be ashamed that he didn't work . . . but . . . was it five years in New York . . . or the fact that he was an artist . . , when his mother said she couldn't understand him . . . why did he vaguely pity her instead of being ashamed . . . he should be . . . his mother and all his relatives said so . . . his brother was three years younger than he and yet he had already been away from home a year . . . on the stage . . . making thirty-five dollars a week . . . had three suits and many clothes and was going to help mother . . . while he . . . Alex . . . was content to lay and smoke and meet friends at night . . . to argue and read Wilde . . . Freud . . . Boccacio and Schnitzler . . . to attend Gurdjieff meetings and know things . . . Why did they scoff at him for knowing such people as Carl . . . Mencken . . . Toomer . . . Hughes . . . Cullen . . . Wood . . . Cabell . . . oh the whole lot of them . . . was it because it seemed incongruous that he . . . who was so little known . . . should call by first names people they would like to know . . . were they jealous . . . no mothers aren't jealous of their sons . . . they are proud of them . . . why then . . . when these friends accepted and liked him . . . no matter how he dressed . . . why did mother ask . . . and you went looking like that . . . Langston was a fine fellow . . . he knew there was something in Alex . . . and so did Rene and Borgia . . . and Zora and Clement and Miguel . . . and . . . and . . . and all of them . . . if he went to see mother she would ask . . . how do you feel Alex with nothing in your pockets . . . I don't see how you can be satisfied . . . Really you're a mystery to me . . . and who you take after . . . I'm sure I don't know . . . none of my brothers were lazy and shiftless . . . I can never remember the time when they weren't sending money home and your father was your age he was supporting a family . . . where you get your nerve I don't know . . . just because you've tried to write one or two little poems and stories that no one understands . . . you seem to think the world owes you a living . . . you should see by now how much is thought of them . . . you can't sell anything . . . and you won't do anything to make money . . . wake up Alex . . . I don't know what will become of you . . . .

it was hard to believe in one's self after that . . . did Wildes' parents or Shelly's or Goya's talk to them like that . . . but it was depressing to think in that vein . . . Alex stretched and yawned . . . Max had died . . . Margaret had died . . . so had Sonia . . . Cynthia . . . Juan-Jose and Harry . . . all people he had loved . . . loved one by one and together . . . and all had died . . . he never loved a person long before they died . . . in truth he was tragic . . . that was a lovely appellation . . . The Tragic Genius . . . think . . . to go thru life known as The Tragic Genius . . . romantic . . . but it was more or less true . . . Alex turned over and blew another cloud of smoke . . . was all life like that . . . smoke . . . blue smoke from an ivory holder . . . he wished he were in New Bedford . . . New Bedford was a nice place . . . snug little houses set complacently behind protecting lawns . . . half open windows showing prim interiors from behind waving cool curtains . . . inviting . . . like precise courtesans winking from behind lace fans . . . and trees . . . many trees . . . casting lacey patterns of shade on the sun dipped sidewalks . . . small stores . . . naively proud of their psuedo grandeur . . . banks . . . called institutions for saving . . . all naive . . . that was it . . . New Bedford was naive . . . after the sophistication of New York it would fan one like a refreshing breeze . . . and yet he had returned to New York . . . and sophistication . . . was he sophisticated . . . no because he was seldom bored . . . seldom bored by anything . . . and weren't the sophisticated continually suffering from ennui . . . on the contrary . . . he was amused . . . amused by the artificiality of naivety and sophistication alike . . . but may be that in itself was the essence of sophistication or . . . was it cynicism . . . or were the two identical . . . he blew a cloud of smoke . . . it was growing dark now . . . and the smoke no longer had a ladder to climb . . . but soon the moon would rise and then he would

clothe the silver moon in blue smoke garments . . .
truly smoke was like imagination . . . .

Alex sat up . . . pulled on his shoes and went out
. . . it was a beautiful night . . . and so large . . . the
dusky blue hung like a curtain in an immense arched
doorway . . . fastened with silver tacks . . . to wander in the night was wonderful . . . myriads of in-
quisitive lights . . . curiously prying into the dark
. . . and fading unsatisfied . . . he passed a woman
. . . she was not beautiful . . . and he was sad because
she did not weep that she would never be beautiful
. . . was it Wilde who had said . . . a cigarette is
the most perfect pleasure because it leaves one unsatisfied . . . the breeze gave to him a perfume stolen
from some wandering lady of the evening . . . it
pleased him . . . why was it that men wouldn't use
perfumes . . . they should . . . each and every one of
them liked perfumes . . . the man who denied that
was a liar . . . or a coward . . . but if ever he were
to voice that though. . . . express it . . . he would be
misunderstood . . . a .ine feeling that . . . to be misunderstood . . . it made him feel tragic and great
. . . but may be it would be nicer to be understood
. . . but no . . . no great artist is . . . then again
neither were fools . . . they were strangely akin
these two . . . Alex thought of a sketch he would
make . . . a personality sketch of Fania . . . straight
classic features tinted proud purple . . . sensuous
fine lips . . . gilded for truth . . . eyes . . . half
opened and lids colored mysterious green . . . hair
black and straight . . . drawn sternly mocking back
from the false puritanical forehead . . . maybe he
would made Edith too . . . skin a blue . . . infinite
like night . . . and eyes . . . slant and grey . . . very
complacent like a cat's . . . Mona Lisa lips . . . red
and seductive as . . . as pomegranate juice . . . in
truth it was fine to be young and hungry and an
artist . . . to blow blue smoke from an ivory holder
. . . .

here was the cafeteria . . . it was almost as tho it
had journeyed to meet him . . . the night was so
blue . . . how does blue feel . . . or red or gold or
any other color . . . if colors could be heard he could
paint most wondrous tunes . . . symphonious . . .
think . . . the dulcet clear tone of a blue like night
. . . of a red like pomegranate juice . . . like Edith's
lips . . . of the fairy tones to be heard in a sunset
. . . like rubies shaken in a crystal cup . . . of the
symphony of Fania . . . and silver . . . and gold . . .
he had heard the sound of gold . . . but they weren't
the sounds he wanted to catch . . . no . . . they must
be liquid . . . not so staccato but flowing variations
of the same caliber . . . there was no one in the
cafe as yet . . . he sat and waited . . . that was a

clever idea he had had about color music . . . but
after all he was a monstrous clever fellow . . .
Jurgen had said that . . . funny how characters in
books said the things one wanted to say . . . he
would like to know Jurgen . . . how does one go
about getting an introduction to a fiction character
. . . go up to the brown cover of the book and knock
gently . . . and say hello . . . then timidly . . . is
Duke Jurgen there . . . or . . . no because if entered
the book in the beginning Jurgen would only be a
pawn broker . . . and one didn't enter a book in the
center . . . but what foolishness . . . Alex lit a cigarette . . . but Cabell was a master to have written
Jurgen . . . and an artist . . . and a poet . . . Alex
blew a cloud of smoke . . . a few lines of one of
Langston's poems came to describe Jurgen . . . . .

    Somewhat like Ariel
    Somewhat like Puck
    Somewhat like a gutter boy
    Who loves to play in muck.
    Somewhat like Bacchus
    Somewhat like Pan
    And a way with women
    Like a sailor man . . . .

Langston must have known Jurgen . . . suppose
Jurgen had met Tonio Kroeger . . . what a vagrant
thought . . . Kroeger . . . Kroeger . . . Kroeger . . .
why here was Rene . . . Alex had almost gone to
sleep . . . Alex blew a cone of smoke as he took
Rene's hand . . . it was nice to have friends like Rene
. . . so comfortable . . . Rene was speaking . . .
Borgia joined them . . . and de Diego Padro . . .
their talk veered to . . . James Branch Cabell . . .
beautiful . . . marvelous . . . Rene had an enchanting
accent . . . said sank for thank and souse for south
. . . but they couldn't know Cabell's greatness . . .
Alex searched the smoke for expression . . . he . . .
he . . . well he has created a phantasy mire . . . that's
it . . . from clear rich imagery . . . life and silver
sands . . . that's nice . . . and silver sands . . .
imagine lilies growing in such a mire . . . when they
close at night their gilded underside would protect
. . . but that's not it at all . . . his thoughts just
carried and mingled like . . . like odors . . . suggested but never definite . . . Rene was leaving . . .
they all were leaving . . . Alex sauntered slowly
back . . . the houses all looked sleepy . . . funny
. . . made him feel like writing poetry . . . and about
death too . . . an elevated crashed by overhead scat-
tering all his thoughts with its noise . . . making
them spread . . . in circles . . . then larger circles
. . . just like a splash in a calm pool . . . what had
he been thinking . . . of . . . a poem about death . . .

but he no longer felt that urge . . . just walk and think and wonder . . . think and remember and smoke . . . blow smoke that mixed with his thoughts and the night . . . he would like to live in a large white palace . . . to wear a long black cape . . . very full and lined with vermillion . . . to have many cushions and to lie there among them . . . talking to his friends . . . lie there in a yellow silk shirt and black velvet trousers . . . like music-review artists talking and pouring strange liquors from curiously beautiful bottles . . . bottles with long slender necks . . . he climbed the noisy stair of the odorous tenement . . . smelled of fish . . . of stale fried fish and dirty milk bottles . . . he rather liked it . . . he liked the acrid smell of horse manure too . . . strong . . . thoughts . . . yes to lie back among strangely fashioned cushions and sip eastern wines and talk . . . Alex threw himself on the bed . . . removed his shoes . . . stretched and relaxed . . . yes and have music waft softly into the darkened and incensed room . . . he blew a cloud of smoke . . . oh the joy of being an artist and of blowing blue smoke thru an ivory holder inlaid with red jade and green . . .

the street was so long and narrow . . . so long and narrow . . . and blue . . . in the distance it reached the stars . . . and if he walked long enough . . . far enough . . . he could reach the stars too . . . the narrow blue was so empty . . . quiet . . . Alex walked music . . . it was nice to walk in the blue after a party . . . Zora had shone again . . . her stories . . . she always shone . . . and Monty was glad . . . every one was glad when Zora shone . . . he was glad he had gone to Monty's party . . . Monty had a nice place in the village . . . nice lights . . . and friends and wine . . . mother would be scandalized that he could think of going to a party . . . without a copper to his name . . . but then mother had never been to Monty's . . . and mother had never seen the street seem long and narrow and blue . . . Alex walked music . . . the click of his heels kept time with a tune in his mind . . . he glanced into a lighted cafe window . . . inside were people sipping coffee . . . men . . . why did they sit there in the loud light . . . didn't they know that outside the street . . . the narrow blue street met the stars . . . that if they walked long enough . . . far enough . . . Alex walked and the click of his heels sounded . . . and had an echo . . . sound being tossed back and forth . . . back and forth . . . some one was approaching . . . and their echoes mingled . . . and gave the sound of castenets . . . Alex liked the sound of the approaching man's footsteps . . . he walked music also . . . he knew the beauty of the

narrow blue . . . Alex knew that by the way their echoes mingled . . . he wished he would speak . . . but strangers don't speak at four o'clock in the morning . . . at least if they did he couldn't imagine what would be said . . . maybe . . . pardon me but are you walking toward the stars . . . yes, sir, and if you walk long enough . . . then may I walk with you I want to reach the stars too . . . perdone me senor tiene vd. fosforo . . . Alex was glad he had been addressed in Spanish . . . to have been asked for a match in English . . . or to have been addressed in English at all . . . would have been blasphemy just then . . . Alex handed him a match . . . he glanced at his companion apprehensively in the match glow . . . he was afraid that his appearance would shatter the blue thoughts . . . and stars . . . ah . . . his face was a perfect compliment to his voice . . . and the echo of their steps mingled . . . they walked in silence . . . the castanets of their heels clicking accompaniment . . . the stranger inhaled deeply and with a nod of content and a smile . . . blew a cloud of smoke . . . Alex felt like singing . . . the stranger knew the magic of blue smoke also . . . they continued in silence . . . the castanets of their heels clicking rythmically . . . Alex turned in his doorway . . . up the stairs and the stranger waited for him to light the room . . . no need for words . . . they had always known each other . . . . as they undressed by the blue dawn . . . Alex knew he had never seen a more perfect being . . . his body was all symmetry and music . . . and Alex called him Beauty . . . long they lay . . . blowing smoke and exchanging thoughts . . . and Alex swallowed with difficulty . . . he felt a glow of tremor . . . and they talked and . . . slept . . .

Alex wondered more and more why he liked Adrian so . . . he liked many people . . . Wallie . . . Zora . . . Clement . . . Gloria . . . Langston . . . John . . . Gwenny . . . oh many people . . . and they were friends . . . but Beauty . . . it was different . . . once Alex had admired Beauty's strength . . . and Beauty's eyes had grown soft and he had said . . . I like you more than any one Dulce . . . Adrian always called him Dulce . . . and Alex had become confused . . . was it that he was so susceptible to beauty that Alex liked Adrian so much . . . but no . . . he knew other people who were beautiful . . . Fania and Gloria . . . Monty and Bunny . . . but he was never confused before them . . . while Beauty . . . Beauty could make him believe in Buddha . . . or imps . . . and no one else could do that . . . that is no one but Melva . . . but then he was in love with Melva . . . and that explained that . . . he would like Beauty to know

Melva . . . they were both so perfect . . . such compliments . . . yes he would like Beauty to know Melva because he loved them both . . . there . . . he had thought it . . . actually dared to think it . . . but Beauty must never know . . . Beauty couldn't understand . . . indeed Alex couldn't understand . . . and it pained him . ,. . almost physically . . . and tired his mind . . . Beauty . . . Beauty was in the air . . . the smoke . . . Beauty . . . Melva . . . Beauty . . . Melva . . . Alex slept . . . and dreamed . . . . .

he was in a field . . . a field of blue smoke and black poppes and red calla lilies . . . he was searching . . . on his hands and knees . . . searching . . . among black poppies and red calla lilies . . . he was searching pushed aside poppy stems . . . and saw two strong white legs . . . dancer's legs . . . the contours pleased him . . . his eyes wandered . . . on past the muscular hocks to the firm white thighs . . . the rounded buttocks . . . then the lithe narrow waist . . . strong torso and broad deep chest . . . the heavy shoulders . . . the graceful muscled neck . . . squared chin and quizzical lips . . . grecian nose with its temperamental nostrils . . . the brown eyes looking at him . . . like . . . Monty looked at Zora . . . his hair curly and black and all tousled . . . and it was Beauty . . . and Beauty smiled and looked at him and smiled . . . said . . . I'll wait Alex . . . and Alex became confused and continued his search . . . on his hands and knees . . . pushing aside poppy stems and lily stems . . . a poppy . . . a black poppy . . . a lilly . . . a red lilly . . . and when he looked back he could no longer see Beauty . . . Alex continued his search . . . thru poppies . . . lilies . . . poppies and red calla lilies . . . and suddenly he saw . . . two small feet olive-ivory . . . two well turned legs curving gracefully from slender ankles . . . and the contours soothed him . . . he followed them . . . past the narrow rounded hips to the tiny waist . . . the fragile firm breasts . . . the graceful slender throat . . . the soft rounded chin . . . slightly parting lips and straight little nose with its slightly flaring nostrils . . . the black eyes with lights in them . . . looking at him . . . the forehead and straight cut black hair . . . and it was Melva . . . and she looked at him and smiled and said . . . I'll wait Alex . . . and Alex became confused and kissed her . . . became confused and continued his search . . . on his hands and knees . . . pushed aside a poppy stem . . . a black-poppy stem . . . pushed aside a lily stem . . . a red-lily stem . . . a poppy . . . a poppy . . . a lily . . . and suddenly he stood erect . . . exhultant . . . and in his hand he held . . . an ivory holder . . . inlaid with red jade . . . and green . . . .

and Alex awoke . . . Beauty's hair tickled his nose

. . . Beauty was smiling in his sleep . . . half his face stained flush color by the sun . . . the other half in shadow . . . blue shadow . . . his eye lashes casting cobwebby blue shadows on his cheek . . . his lips were so beautiful . . . quizzical . . . Alex wondered why he always thought of that passage from Wilde's Salome . . . when he looked at Beauty's lips . . . I would kiss your lips . . . he *would* like to kiss Beauty's lips . . . Alex flushed warm . . . with shame . . . or was it shame . . . he reached across Beauty for a cigarette . . . Beauty's cheek felt cool to his arm . . . his hair felt soft . . . Alex lay smoking . . . such a dream . . . red calla lilies . . . red calla lilies . . . and . . . what could it all mean . . . did dreams have meanings . . . Fania said . . . and black poppies . . . thousands . . . millions . . . Beauty stirred . . . Alex put out his cigarette . . . closed his eyes . . . he mustn't see Beauty yet . . . speak to him . . . his lips were too hot . . . dry . . . the palms of his hands too cool and moist . . . thru his half closed eyes he could see Beauty . . . propped . . . cheek in hand . . . on one elbow . . . looking at him . . . lips smiling quizzically . . . he wished Beauty wouldn't look so hard . . . Alex was finding it difficult to breathe . . . breathe normally . . . why *must* Beauty look so long . . . and smile *that* way . . . his face seemed nearer . . . it was . . . Alex could feel Beauty's hair on his forehead . . . breathe normally . . . breathe normally . . . could feel Beauty's breath on his nostrils and lips . . . and it was clean and faintly colored with tobacco . . . breathe normally Alex . . . Beauty's lips were nearer . . . Alex closed his eyes . . . how did one act . . . his pulse was hammering . . . from wrists to finger tip . . . wrist to finger tip . . . Beauty's lips touched his . . . his temples throbbed . . . throbbed . . . his pulse hammered from wrist to finger tip . . . Beauty's breath came short now . . . softly staccato . . . breathe normally Alex . . . you are asleep . . . Beauty's lips touched his . . . breathe normally . . . and pressed . . . pressed hard . . . cool . . . his body trembled . . . breathe normally Alex . . . Beauty's lips pressed cool . . . cool and hard . . . how much pressure does it take to waken one . . . Alex sighed . . . moved softly . . . how does one act . . . Beauty's hair barely touched him now . . . his breath was faint on . . . Alex's nostrils and lips . . . Alex stretched and opened his eyes . . . Beauty was looking at him . . . propped on one elbow . . . cheek in his palm . . . Beauty spoke . . . scratch my head please Dulce . . . Alex was breathing normally now . . . propped against the bed head . . . Beauty's head in his lap . . . Beauty spoke . . . I wonder why I like to look at some things Dulce . . . things like smoke and cats . . . and you . . . Alex's pulse no longer hammered from . . . wrist to finger tip . . . wrist to finger tip . . . the rose dusk had become blue night . . . and soon . . . soon they would go out into the blue . . . .

the little church was crowded . . . warm . . . the rows of benches were brown and sticky . . . Harold was there . . . and Constance and Langston and Bruce and John . . . there was Mr. Robeson . . . how are you Paul . . . a young man was singing . . . Caver . . . Caver was a very self assured young man . . . such a dream . . . poppies . . . black poppies . . . they were applauding . . . Constance and John were exchanging notes . . . the benches were sticky . . . a young lady was playing the piano . . . fair . . . and red calla lilies . . . who had ever heard of red calla lilies . . . they were applauding . . . a young man was playing the viola . . . what could it all mean . . . so many poppies . . . and Beauty looking at him like . . . like Monty looked at Zora . . . another young man was playing a violin . . . he was the first real artist to perform . . . he had a touch of soul . . . or was it only feeling . . . they were hard to differentiate on the violin . . . and Melva standing in the poppies and lilies . . . Mr. Phillips was singing . . . Mr. Phillips was billed as a basso . . . and he had kissed her . . . they were applauding . . . the first young man was singing again . . . Langston's spiritual . . . Fy-ah-fy-ah-Lawd . . . fy-ah's gonna burn ma soul . . . Beauty's hair was so black and curly . . . they were applauding . . . encore . . . Fy-ah Lawd had been a success . . . Langston bowed . . . Langston had written the words . . . Hall bowed . . . Hall had written the music . . . the young man was singing it again . . . Beauty's lips had pressed hard . . . cool . . . cool . . . fy-ah Lawd . . . his breath had trembled . . . fy-ah's gonna burn ma soul . . . they were all leaving . . . first to the roof dance . . . fy-ah Lawd . . . there was Catherine . . . she was beautiful tonight . . . she always was at night . . . Beauty's lips . . . fy-ah Lawd . . . hello Dot . . . why don't you take a boat that sails . . . when are you leaving again . . . and there's Estelle . . . every one was there . . . fy-ah Lawd . . . Beauty's body had pressed close . . . close . . . fy-ah's gonna burn my soul . . . let's leave . . . have to meet some people at the New World . . . then to Augusta's party . . . Harold . . . John . . . Bruce . . . Connie . . . Langston . . . ready . . . down one hundred thirty-fifth street . . . fy-ah . . . meet these people and leave . . . fy-ah Lawd . . . now to Augusta's party . . . fy-ahs gonna burn ma soul . . . they were at Augusta's . . . Alex half lay . . . half sat on the floor . . . sipping a cocktail . . . such a dream . . . red calla lilies . . .

Alex left . . . down the narrow streets . . . fy-ah . . . up the long noisy stairs . . . fy-ahs gonna bu'n ma soul . . . his head felt swollen . . . expanding . . . contracting . . . expanding . . . contracting . . . he had never been like this before . . . expanding . . . contracting . . . it was that . . . fy-ah . . . fy-ah Lawd . . . and the cocktails . . . and Beauty . . . he felt two cool strong hands on his shoulders . . . it was Beauty . . . lie down Dulce . . . Alex lay down . . . Beauty . . . Alex stopped . . . no no . . . don't say it . . . Beauty mustn't know . . . Beauty couldn't understand . . . are you going to lie down too Beauty . . . the light went out expanding . . . contracting . . . he felt the bed sink as Beauty lay beside him . . . his lips were dry . . . hot . . . the palms of his hands so moist and cool . . . Alex partly closed his eyes . . . from beneath his lashes he could see Beauty's face over his . . . nearer . . . nearer . . . Beauty's hair touched his forehead now . . . he could feel his breath on his nostrils and lips . . . Beauty's breath came short . . . breathe normally Beauty . . . breathe normally . . . Beauty's lips touched his . . . pressed hard . . . cool . . . opened slightly . . . Alex opened his eyes . . . into Beauty's . . . parted his lips . . . Dulce . . . Beauty's breath was hot and short . . . Alex ran his hand through Beauty's hair . . . Beauty's lips pressed hard against his teeth . . . Alex trembled . . . could feel Beauty's body . . . close against his . . . hot . . . tense . . . white . . . and soft . . . soft . . . soft . . . .

they were at Forno's . . . every one came to Forno's once maybe only once . . . but they came . . . see that big fat woman Beauty . . . Alex pointed to an overly stout and bejeweled lady making her way thru the maize of chairs . . . that's Maria Guerrero . . . Beauty looked to see a lady guiding almost the whole opera company to an immense table . . . really Dulce . . . for one who appreciates beauty you do use the most abominable English . . . Alex lit a cigarette . . . and that florid man with white hair . . . that's Carl . . . Beauty smiled . . . The Blind bow boy . . . he asked . . . Alex wondered . . . everything seemed to . . . so just the same . . . here they were laughing and joking about people . . . there's Rene . . . Rene this is my friend Adrian . . . after that night . . . and he felt so unembarrassed . . . Rene and Adrian were talking . . . there was Lucricia Bori . . . she was bowing at their table . . . oh her cousin was with them . . . and Peggy Joyce . . . every one came to Forno's . . . Alex looked toward the door . . . there was Melva . . . Alex beckoned . . . Melva this is Adrian . . . Beauty held her hand . . . they talked . . . smoked . . . Alex loved Melva . . . in

Forno's . . . every one came there sooner or later . . . maybe once . . . but . . . .

⌒

up . . . up . . . slow . . . jerk up . . . up . . . not fast . . . not glorious . . . but slow . . . up . . . up into the sun . . . slow . . . sure like fate . . . poise on the brim . . . the brim of life . . . two shining rails straight down . . . Melva's head was on his shoulder . . . his arm was around her . . . poise . . . the down . . . gasping . . . straight down . . . straight like sin . . . down . . . the curving shiny rail rushed up to meet them . . . hit the bottom then . . . shoot up . . . fast . . . glorious . . . up into the sun . . . Melva gasped . . . Alex's arm tightened . . . all goes up . . . then down . . . straight like hell . . . all breath squeezed out of them . . . Melva's head on his shoulder . . . up . . . up . . . Alex kissed her . . . down . . . they stepped out of the car . . . walking music . . . now over to the Ferris Wheel . . . out and up . . . Melva's hand was soft in his . . . out and up . . . over mortals . . . mortals drinking nectar . . . five cents a glass . . . her cheek was soft on his . . . up . . . up . . . till the world seemed small . . . tiny . . . the ocean seemed tiny and blue . . . up . . . up and out . . . over the sun . . . the tiny red sun . . . Alex kissed her . . . up . . . up . . . their tongues touched . . . up . . . seventh heaven . . . the sea had swallowed the sun . . . up and out . . . her breath was perfumed . . . Alex kissed her . . . drift down . . . soft . . . soft . . . the sun had left the sky flushed . . . drift down . . . soft down . . . back to earth . . . visit the mortals sipping nectar at five cents a glass . . . Melva's lips brushed his . . . then out among the mortals . . and the sun had left a flush on Melva's cheeks . . . they walked hand in hand . . . and the moon came out . . . they walked in silence on the silver strip . . . and the sea sang for them . . . they walked toward the moon . . . we'll hang our hats on the crook of the moon Melva . . . softly on the silver strip . . . his hands molded her features and her cheeks were soft and warm to his touch . . . where is Adrian . . . Alex . . . Melva trod silver . . . Alex trod sand . . . Alex trod sand . . . the sea *sang* for her . . . Beauty . . . her hand felt cold in his . . . Beauty . . . the sea *dinned* . . . Beauty . . . he led the way to the train . . . and the train dinned . . . Beauty . . . dinned . . . dinned . . . her cheek *had* been soft . . . Beauty . . . Beauty . . . her breath *had* been perfumed . . . Beauty . . . Beauty . . . the sands *had* been silver . . . Beauty . . . Beauty . . . they left the train . . . Melva walked music . . . Melva said . . . don't make me blush again . . . and kissed him . . . Alex stood on the steps after she left him and the night was black . . . down long streets to . . . Alex lit a cigarette . . . and his heels clicked . . . Beauty . . . Melva . . . Beauty . . . Melva . . . and the smoke made the night blue . . .

Melva had said . . . don't make me blush again . . . and kissed him . . . and the street had been blue . . . one *can* love two at the same time . . . Melva had kissed him . . . one *can* . . . and the street had been blue . . . one *can* . . . and the room was clouded with blue smoke . . . drifting vapors of smoke and thoughts . . . Beauty's hair was so black . . . and soft . . . blue smoke from an ivory holder . . . was that why he loved Beauty . . . one *can* . . . or because his body was beautiful . . . and white and warm . . . or because his eyes . . . one *can* love . . . .

RICHARD BRUCE.

. . . *To Be Continued* . . .

Sweat

It was eleven o'clock of a Spring night in Florida. It was Sunday. Any other night, Delia Jones would have been in bed for two hours by this time. But she was a washwoman, and Monday morning meant a great deal to her. So she collected the soiled clothes on Saturday when she returned the clean things. Sunday night after church, she sorted them and put the white things to soak. It saved her almost a half day's start. A great hamper in the bedroom held the clothes that she brought home. It was so much neater than a number of bundles lying around.

She squatted in the kitchen floor beside the great pile of clothes, sorting them into small heaps according to color, and humming a song in a mournful key, but wondering through it all where Sykes, her husband, had gone with her horse and buckboard.

Just then something long, round, limp and black fell upon her shoulders and slithered to the floor beside her. A great terror took hold of her. It softened her knees and dried her mouth so that it was a full minute before she could cry out or move. Then she saw that it was the big bull whip her husband liked to carry when he drove.

She lifted her eyes to the door and saw him standing there bent over with laughter at her fright. She screamed at him.

"Sykes, what you throw dat whip on me like dat? You know it would skeer me—looks just like a snake, an' you knows how skeered Ah is of snakes."

"Course Ah knowed it! That's how come Ah done it." He slapped his leg with his hand and almost rolled on the ground in his mirth. "If you such a big fool dat you got to have a fit over a earth worm or a string, Ah don't keer how bad Ah skeer you."

"You aint got no business doing it. Gawd knows it's a sin. Some day Ah'm gointuh drop dead from some of yo' foolishness. 'Nother thing, where you been wid mah rig? Ah feeds dat pony. He aint fuh you to be drivin' wid no bull whip."

"You sho is one aggravatin' nigger woman!" he declared and stepped into the room. She resumed her work and did not answer him at once. "Ah done tole you time and again to keep them white folks' clothes outa dis house."

He picked up the whip and glared down at her. Delia went on with her work. She went out into the yard and returned with a galvanized tub and sit it on the washbench. She saw that Sykes had kicked all of the clothes together again, and now stood in her way truculently, his whole manner hoping, *praying,* for an argument. But she walked calmly around him and commenced to re-sort the things.

"Next time, Ah'm gointer kick 'em outdoors," he threatened as he struck a match along the leg of his corduroy breeches.

Delia never looked up from her work, and her thin, stooped shoulders sagged further.

"Ah aint for no fuss t'night Sykes. Ah just come from taking sacrament at the church house."

He snorted scornfully. "Yeah, you just come from de church house on a Sunday night, but heah you is gone to work on them clothes. You aint nothing but a hypocrite. One of them amen-corner Christians—sing, whoop, and shout, then come home and wash white folks clothes on the Sabbath."

He stepped roughly upon the whitest pile of things, kicking them helter-skelter as he crossed the room. His wife gave a little scream of dismay, and quickly gathered them together again.

"Sykes, you quit grindin' dirt into these clothes! How can Ah git through by Sat'day if Ah don't start on Sunday?"

"Ah don't keer if you never git through. Anyhow, Ah done promised Gawd and a couple of other men, Ah aint gointer have it in mah house. Don't gimme no lip neither, else Ah'll throw 'em out and put mah fist up side yo' head to boot."

Delia's habitual meekness seemed to slip from her shoulders like a blown scarf. She was on her feet; her poor little body, her bare knuckly hands bravely defying the strapping hulk before her.

"Looka heah, Sykes, you done gone too fur. Ah been married to you fur fifteen years, and Ah been takin' in washin' fur fifteen years. Sweat, sweat, sweat! Work and sweat, cry and sweat, pray and sweat!"

"What's that got to do with me?" he asked brutally.

"What's it got to do with you, Sykes? Mah tub of suds is filled yo' belly with vittles more times than yo' hands is filled it. Mah sweat is done paid for this house and Ah reckon Ah kin keep on sweatin' in it."

She seized the iron skillet from the stove and struck a defensive pose, which act surprised him greatly, coming from her. It cowed him and he did not strike her as he usually did.

"Naw you won't," she panted, "that ole snaggle-toothed black woman you runnin' with aint comin' heah to pile up on *mah* sweat and blood. You aint paid for nothin' on this place, and Ah'm gointer stay right heah till Ah'm toted out foot foremost."

"Well, you better quit gittin' me riled up, else they'll be totin' you out sooner than you expect. Ah'm so tired of you Ah don't know whut to do. Gawd! how Ah hates skinny wimmen!"

A little awed by this new Delia, he sidled out of the door and slammed the back gate after him. He did not say where he had gone, but she knew too well. She knew very well that he would not return until nearly daybreak also. Her work over, she went on to bed but not to sleep at once. Things had come to a pretty pass!

She lay awake, gazing upon the debris that cluttered their matrimonial trail. Not an image left standing along the way. Anything like flowers had long ago been drowned in the salty stream that had been pressed from her heart. Her tears, her sweat, her blood. She had brought love to the union and he had brought a longing after the flesh. Two months after the wedding, he had given her the first brutal beating. She had the memory of his numerous trips to Orlando with all of his wages when he had returned to her penniless, even before the first year had passed. She was young and soft then, but now she thought of her knotty, muscled limbs, her harsh knuckly hands, and drew herself up into an unhappy little ball in the middle of the big feather bed. Too late now to hope for love, even if it were not Bertha it would be someone else. This case differed from the others only in that she was bolder than the others. Too late for everything except her little home. She had built it for her old days, and planted one by one the trees and flowers there. It was lovely to her, lovely.

Somehow, before sleep came, she found herself saying aloud: "Oh well, whatever goes over the Devil's back, is got to come under his belly. Sometime or ruther, Sykes, like everybody else, is gointer reap his sowing." After that she was able to build a spiritual earthworks against her husband. His shells could no longer reach her. *Amen.* She went to sleep and slept until he announced his presence in bed by kicking her feet and rudely snatching the cover away.

"Gimme some kivah heah, an' git yo' damn foots over on yo' own side! Ah oughter mash you in yo' mouf fuh drawing dat skillet on me."

Delia went clear to the rail without answering him. A triumphant indifference to all that he was or did.

The week was as full of work for Delia as all other weeks, and Saturday found her behind her little pony, collecting and delivering clothes.

It was a hot, hot day near the end of July. The village men on Joe Clarke's porch even chewed cane listlessly. They did not hurl the cane-knots as usual. They let them dribble over the edge of the porch. Even conversation had collapsed under the heat.

"Heah come Delia Jones," Jim Merchant said, as the shaggy pony came 'round the bend of the road toward them. The rusty buckboard was heaped with baskets of crisp, clean laundry.

"Yep," Joe Lindsay agreed. "Hot or col', rain or shine, jes ez reg'lar ez de weeks roll roun' Delia carries 'em an' fetches 'em on Sat'day."

"She better if she wanter eat," said Moss. "Syke Jones aint wuth de shot an' powder hit would tek tuh kill 'em. Not to *huh* he aint."

"He sho' aint," Walter Thomas chimed in. "It's too bad, too, cause she wuz a right pritty lil trick when he got huh. Ah'd uh mah'ied huh mah-seff if he hadnter beat me to it."

Delia nodded briefly at the men as she drove past.

"Too much knockin' will ruin *any* 'oman. He done beat huh 'nough tuh kill three women, let 'lone change they looks," said Elijah Mosely. "How Syke kin stommuck dat big black greasy Mogul he's layin' roun' wid, gits me. Ah swear dat eight-rock couldn't kiss a sardine can Ah done thowed out de back do' 'way las' yeah."

"Aw, she's fat, thass how come. He's allus been crazy 'bout fat women," put in Merchant. "He'd a' been tied up wid one long time ago if he could a' found one tuh have him. Did Ah tell yuh 'bout him come sidlin' roun' *mah* wife—bringin' her a basket uh pee-cans outa his yard fuh a present? Yessir, mah wife! She tol' him tuh take 'em right straight back home, cause Delia works so hard ovah dat washtub she reckon everything on de place taste lak sweat an' soapsuds. Ah jus' wisht Ah'd a' caught 'im 'roun' dere! Ah'd a' made his hips ketch on fiah down dat shell road."

"Ah know he done it, too. Ah sees 'im grinnin' at every 'oman dat passes," Walter Thomas said. "But even so, he useter eat some mighty big hunks uh humble pie tuh git dat lil' 'oman he got. She wuz ez pritty ez a speckled pup! Dat wuz fifteen yeahs ago. He useter be so skeered uh losin' huh, she could make him do some parts of a husband's duty. Dey never wuz de same in de mind."

"There oughter be a law about him," said Lindsay. He aint fit tuh carry guts tuh a bear."

Clarke spoke for the first time. "Taint no law on earth dat kin make a man be decent if it aint in 'im. There's plenty men dat takes a wife lak dey do a joint uh sugar-cane. It's round, juicy an' sweet when dey gits it. But dey squeeze an' grind, squeeze an' grind an' wring tell dey wring every drop uh pleasure dat's in 'em out. When dey's satisfied dat dey is wrung dry, dey treats 'em jes lak dey do a cane-chew. Dey thows 'em away. Dey knows whut dey is doin' while dey is at it, an' hates theirselves fuh it but they keeps on hangin' after huh tell she's empty. Den dey hates huh fuh bein' a cane-chew an' in de way."

"We oughter take Syke an' dat stray 'oman uh his'n down in Lake Howell swamp an' lay on de rawhide till they cain't say 'Lawd a' mussy.' He allus wuz uh ovahbearin' niggah, but since dat white 'oman from up north done teached 'im how to run a automobile, he done got to biggety to live—an' we oughter kill 'im." Old Man Anderson advised.

A grunt of approval went around the porch. But the heat was melting their civic virtue and Elijah Moseley began to bait Joe Clarke.

"Come on, Joe, git a melon outa dere an' slice it up for yo' customers. We'se all sufferin' wid de heat. De bear's done got *me!*"

"Thass right, Joe, a watermelon is jes' whut Ah needs tuh cure de eppizudicks," Walter Thomas joined forces with Moseley. "Come on dere, Joe. We all is steady customers an' you aint set us up in a long time. Ah chooses dat long, bowlegged Floridy favorite."

"A god, an' be dough You all gimme twenty cents and slice away," Clarke retorted. "Ah needs a col' slice m'self. Heah, everybody chip in. Ah'll lend y'll mah meat knife."

The money was quickly subscribed and the huge melon brought forth. At that moment, Sykes and Bertha arrived. A determined silence fell on the porch and the melon was put away again.

Merchant snapped down the blade of his jack-knife and moved toward the store door.

"Come on in, Joe, an' gimme a slab uh sow belly an' uh pound uh coffee—almost fuhgot 'twas Sat'-day. Got to git on home." Most of the men left also.

Just then Delia drove past on her way home, as Sykes was ordering magnificently for Bertha. It pleased him for Delia to see.

"Git whutsoever yo' heart desires, Honey. Wait a minute, Joe. Give huh two botles uh strawberry soda-water, uh quart uh parched ground-peas, an' a block uh chewin' gum."

With all this they left the store, with Sykes reminding Bertha that this was his town and she could have it if she wanted it.

The men returned soon after they left, and held their watermelon feast.

"Where did Syke Jones git dat 'oman from nohow?" Lindsay asked.

"Ovah Apopka. Guess dey musta been cleanin' out de town when she lef'. She don't look lak a thing but a hunk uh liver wid hair on it."

"Well, she sho' kin squall," Dave Carter contributed. "When she gits ready tuh laff, she jes' opens huh mouf an' latches it back tuh de las' notch. No ole grandpa alligator down in Lake Bell ain't got nothin' on huh."

⤙⤚

Bertha had been in town three months now. Sykes was still paying her room rent at Della Lewis' —the only house in town that would have taken her in. Sykes took her frequently to Winter Park to "stomps." He still assured her that he was the swellest man in the state.

"Sho' you kin have dat lil' ole house soon's Ah kin git dat 'oman outa dere. Everything b'longs tuh me an' you sho' kin have it. Ah sho' 'bominates uh skinny 'oman. Lawdy, you sho' is got one portly shape on you! You kin git *anything* you wants. Dis is *mah* town an' you sho' kin have it."

Delia's work-worn knees crawled over the earth in Gethsemane and up the rocks of Calvary many, many times during these months. She avoided the villagers and meeting places in her efforts to be blind and deaf. But Bertha nullified this to a degree, by coming to Delia's house to call Sykes out to her at the gate.

Delia and Sykes fought all the time now with no peaceful interludes. They slept and ate in silence. Two or three times Delia had attempted a timid friendliness, but she was repulsed each time. It was plain that the breaches must remain agape.

⤙⤚

The sun had burned July to August. The heat streamed down like a million hot arrows, smiting all things living upon the earth. Grass withered, leaves browned, snakes went blind in shedding and men and dogs went mad. Dog days!

Delia came home one day and found Sykes there before her. She wondered, but started to go on into the house without speaking, even though he was standing in the kitchen door and she must either stoop under his arm or ask him to move. He made no room for her. She noticed a soap box beside the steps, but paid no particular attention to it, knowing that he must have brought it there. As she was stooping to pass under his outstretched arm, he suddenly pushed her backward, laughingly.

"Look in de box dere Delia, Ah done brung yuh somethin'!"

She nearly fell upon the box in her stumbling, and when she saw what it held, she all but fainted outright.

"Syke! Syke, mah Gawd! You take dat rattlesnake 'way from heah! You *gottuh.* Oh, Jesus, have mussy!"

"Ah aint gut tuh do nuthin' uh de kin'—fact is Ah aint got tuh do nothin' but die. Taint no use uh you puttin' on airs makin' out lak you skeered uh dat snake—he's gointer stay right heah tell he die. He wouldn't bite me cause Ah knows how tuh handle 'im. Nohow he wouldn't risk breakin' out his fangs 'gin yo' skinny laigs."

"Naw, now Syke, don't keep dat thing 'roun' heah tuh skeer me tuh death. You knows Ah'm even feared uh earth worms. Thass de biggest snake Ah evah did see. Kill 'im Syke, please."

"Doan ast me tuh do nothin' fuh yuh. Goin' 'roun' tryin' tuh be so damn asterperious. Naw, Ah aint gonna kill it. Ah think uh damn sight mo' uh him dan you! Dat's a nice snake an' anybody doan lak 'im kin jes' hit de grit."

The village soon heard that Sykes had the snake, and came to see and ask questions.

"How de hen-fire did you ketch dat six-foot rattler, Syke?" Thomas asked.

"He's full uh frogs so he caint hardly move, thass how Ah eased up on 'm. But Ah'm a snake charmer an' knows how tuh handle 'em. Shux, dat aint nothin'. Ah could ketch one eve'y day if Ah so wanted tuh."

"Whut he needs is a heavy hick'ry club leaned real heavy on his head. Dat's de bes 'way tuh charm a rattlesnake."

"Naw, Walt, y'll jes' don't understand dese diamon' backs lak Ah do," said Sykes in a superior tone of voice.

The village agreed with Walter, but the snake stayed on. His box remained by the kitchen door with its screen wire covering. Two or three days later it had digested its meal of frogs and literally came to life. It rattled at every movement in the kitchen or the yard. One day as Delia came down the kitchen steps she saw his chalky-white fangs curved like scimitars hung in the wire meshes. .This time she did not run away with averted eyes as usual. She stood for a long time in the doorway in a red fury that grew bloodier for every second that she regarded the creature that was her torment.

That night she broached the subject as soon as Sykes sat down to the table.

"Syke, Ah wants you tuh take dat snake 'way fum heah. You done starved me an' Ah put up widcher, you done beat me an Ah took dat, but you done kilt all mah insides bringin' dat varmint heah."

Sykes poured out a saucer full of coffee and drank it deliberately before he answered her.

"A whole lot Ah keer 'bout how you feels inside uh out. Dat snake aint goin' no damn wheah till Ah gits ready fuh 'im tuh go. So fur as beatin' is concerned, yuh aint took near all dat you gointer take ef yuh stay 'roun' *me.*"

Delia pushed back her plate and got up from the table. "Ah hates you, Sykes," she said calmly. "Ah hates you tuh de same degree dat Ah useter love yuh. Ah done took an' took till mah belly is full up tuh mah neck. Dat's de reason Ah got mah letter fum de church an' moved mah membership tuh Woodbridge—so Ah don't haftuh take no sacrament wid yuh. Ah don't wantuh see yuh 'roun' me atall. Lay 'roun' wid dat 'oman all yuh wants tuh, but gwan 'way fum me an' mah house. At hates yuh lak uh suck-egg dog."

Sykes almost let the huge wad of corn bread and collard greens he was chewing fall out of his mouth in amazement. He had a hard time whipping himself up to the proper fury to try to answer Delia.

"Well, Ah'm glad you does hate me. Ah'm sho' tiahed uh you hangin' ontuh me. Ah don't want yuh. Look at yuh stringey ole neck! Yo' rawbony laigs an' arms is enough tuh cut uh man tuh death. You looks jes' lak de devvul's doll-baby tuh *me.* You cain't hate me no worse dan Ah hates you. Ah been hatin' *you* fuh years.

"Yo' ole black hide don't look lak nothin' tuh me, but uh passle uh wrinkled up rubber, wid yo' big ole yeahs flappin' on each side lak up paih uh buzzard wings. Don't think Ah'm gointuh be run 'way fum mah house neither. Ah'm goin' tuh de white folks bout *you,* mah young man, de very nex' time you lay yo' han's on me. Mah cup is done run ovah." Delia said this with no signs of fear and Sykes departed from the house, threatening her, but made not the slightest move to carry out any of them.

That night he did not return at all, and the next day being Sunday, Delia was glad that she did not have to quarrel before she hitched up her pony and drove the four miles to Woodbridge.

She stayed to the night service—"love feast"—which was very warm and full of spirit. In the emotional winds her domestic trials were borne far and wide so that she sang as she drove homeward,

"Jurden water, black an' col'
Chills de body, not de soul
An' Ah wantah cross Jurden in uh calm time."

She came from the barn to the kitchen door and stopped.

"Whut's de mattah, ol' satan, you aint kickin' up yo' racket?" She addressed the snake's box. Complete silence. She went on into the house with a new hope in its birth struggles. Perhaps her threat to go to the white folks had frightened Sykes! Perhaps he was sorry! Fifteen years of misery and suppression had brought Delia to the place where she would hope *anything* that looked towards a way over or through her wall of inhibitions.

She felt in the match safe behind the stove at once for a match. There was only one there.

"Dat niggah wouldn't fetch nothin' heah tuh save his rotten neck, but he kin run thew whut Ah brings quick enough. Now he done toted off nigh on tuh haff uh box uh matches. He done had dat 'oman heah in mah house, too."

Nobody but a woman could tell how she knew this even before she struck the match. But she did and it put her into a new fury.

Presently she brought in the tubs to put the white things to soak. This time she decided she need not bring the hamper out of the bedroom; she would go in there and do the sorting. She picked up the pot-bellied lamp and went in. The room was small and the hamper stood hard by the foot of the white iron bed. She could sit and reach through the bedposts—resting as she worked.

"Ah wantah cross Jurden in uh calm time." She was singing again. The mood of the "love feast" had returned. She threw back the lid of the basket almost gaily. Then, moved by both horror and terror, he spring back toward the door. *There lay the snake in the basket!* He moved sluggishly at first, but even as she turned round and round, jumped up and down in an insanity of fear, he began to stir vigorously. She saw him pouring his awful beauty from the basket upon the bed, then she seized the lamp and ran as fast as she could to the kitchen. The wind from the open door blew out the light and the darkness added to her terror. She sped to the darkness of the yard, slamming the door after her before she thought to set down the lamp. She did not feel safe even on the ground, so she climbed up in the hay barn.

There for an hour or more she lay sprawled upon the hay a gibbering wreck.

Finally she grew quiet, and after that, coherent thought. With this, stalked through her a cold, bloody rage. Hours of this. A period of introspection, a space of retrospection, then a mixture of both. Out of this an awful calm.

"Well, Ah done de bes' Ah could. If things aint right, Gawd knows taint mah fault."

She went to sleep—a twitchy sleep—and woke up to a faint gray sky. There was a loud hollow sound below. She peered out. Sykes was at the wood-pile, demolishing a wire-covered box.

He hurried to the kitchen door, but hung outside there some minutes before he entered, and stood some minutes more inside before he closed it after him.

The gray in the sky was spreading. Delia descended without fear now, and crouched beneath the low bedroom window. The drawn shade shut out the dawn, shut in the night. But the thin walls held back no sound.

"Dat ol' scratch is woke up now!" She mused at the tremendous whirr inside, which every woodsman knows, is one of the sound illusions. The rattler is a ventriloquist. His whirr sounds to the right, to the left, straight ahead, behind, close under foot—everywhere but where it is. Woe to him who guesses wrong unless he is prepared to hold up his end of the argument! Sometimes he strikes without rattling at all.

Inside, Sykes heard nothing until he knocked a pot lid off the stove while trying to reach the match safe in the dark. He had emptied his pockets at Bertha's.

The snake seemed to wake up under the stove and Sykes made a quick leap into the bedroom. In spite of the gin he had had, his head was clearing now.

"Mah Gawd!" he chattered, "ef Ah could on'y strack uh light!"

The rattling ceased for a moment as he stood paralyzed. He waited. It seemed that the snake waited also.

"Oh, fuh de light! Ah thought he'd be too sick"—Sykes was muttering to himself when the whirr began again, closer, right underfoot this time. Long before this, Sykes' ability to think had been flattened down to primitive instinct and he leaped—onto the bed.

Outside Delia heard a cry that might have come from a maddened chimpanzee, a stricken gorilla. All the terror, all the horror, all the rage that man possibly could express, without a recognizable human sound.

A tremendous stir inside there, another series of animal screams, the intermittent whirr of the reptile. The shade torn violently down from the window, letting in the red dawn, a huge brown hand seizing the window stick, great dull blows upon the wooden floor punctuating the gibberish of sound long after the rattle of the snake had abruptly subsided. All this Delia could see and hear from her place beneath the window, and it made her ill. She crept over to the four-o'clocks and stretched herself on the cool earth to recover.

She lay there. "Delia, Delia!" She could hear Sykes calling in a most despairing tone as one who expected no answer. The sun crept on up, and he called. Delia could not move—her legs were gone flabby. She never moved, he called, and the sun kept rising.

"Mah Gawd!" She heard him moan, "Mah Gawd fum Heben!" She heard him stumbling about and got up from her flower-bed. The sun was growing warm. As she approached the door she heard him call out hopefully, "Delia, is dat you Ah heah?"

She saw him on his hands and knees as soon as she reached the door. He crept an inch or two toward her—all that he was able, and she saw his horribly swollen neck and is one open eye shining with hope. A surge of pity too strong to support bore her away from that eye that must, could not, fail to see the tubs. He would see the lamp. Orlando with its doctors was too far. She could scarcely reach the Chinaberry tree, where she waited in the growing heat while inside she knew the cold river was creeping up and up to extinguish that eye which must know by now that she knew.

ZONA NEALE HURSTON.

Intelligentsia

Of all the doughty societies that have sprung up in this age of Kluxers and Beavers the one known by that unpronounceable word, "Intelligentsia," is among the most benighted. The war seems to have given it birth, the press nurtured it, which should have been warning enough, then the public accepted it, and now we all suffer.

Of course no one would admit that he is a member of the Intelligentsia. Modern civilizing influences do not develop that kind of candor. But it is just as easy to spot a member of the genus as it is to spot a Mississippian or a Chinese: the marks are all there.

According to the ultra-advanced notions of the great majority of this secret order if it were not for the Intelligentsia this crippled old world would be compelled to kick up its toes and die on the spot. Were it not for these super-men all the brilliance of the ages and the inheritance which is so vital to the maintenance of the spark of progress would vanish and pass away. In other words if the Intelligentsia were to stick their divinely appointed noses a little higher into the ethereal regions and withdraw themselves completely from the tawdry field of life that field would soon become a burial ground for the rest of humanity.

This is the rankest folly. The world owes about as much to the rank and file of this society as a Negro slave owes to Georgia. Besides a few big words added to the lexicon and one or two hifalutin' notions about the way the world should be run, the contribution of Intelligentsia to society is as negligible as gin at a Methodist picnic. This is not to discount the many notable contributions by really intelligent men and women who didn't know that such a society existed until insignificant nincompoops with their eyes set towards enhancing their own positions in society, made them honorary members.

What is intelligence anyway? If you ask a member of the Intelligentsia he will probably sneer at you and ask who wants to know. The Intelligentsia are very particular about observing the admonition against putting a herd of swine on an oyster diet, so particular in fact that they have become much more adept at discovering pigpens than they are at digging pearls. But if you ask a truly intelligent person he will tell you in a jiffy that intelligence is simply the ability to solve a new problem, nothing more, nothing less.

Now that is just what the average member of the Intelligentsia does not do. He does not solve new problems, he makes them; then he leaves it to the true intellectuals to solve them. Sift the chaff out of Intelligentsia and you will find that the residuum is about fifty-six one hundredths of one per cent. For the rest, the society is made up of non-producers and bloodsuckers who feed voraciously on the bones which the true intellectuals pass on to them to pick over.

47

The average member of Intelligentsia comes as near being a true intellectual as the proverbial hot water in which resides a cabbage leaf comes to being stew. His earmarks are abundant information about the most recent literature, an obsession for the latest shows, wild notions about art in general, along with a flair for disdaining Babbits, and for feigning spiritual chumminess with the true intellectuals who are accomplishing things.

He reads H. L. M. and George Jean Nathan, knows his Freud from cover to cover, and has an ability for spotting morons which is positively as uncanny as the ability of a Texas bloodhound to sniff a nigger. If he's a man he is as incapable of attending to his own affairs and doing something once in a while, as a hobo is incapable of paying a month's rent. All this goes for the feminine Intelligentsia, with this added distinction—they sneer at every homely virtue, including taking care of babies and frying eggs without breaking the yolks.

Far be it from me to sing paens to the days when men amused themselves with dominoes and the fair sex waded through enough dishwater to make a Jordan. Those days and their folk hold no illusions for me. But it is high time that a halt is called on these snobbish sycophantish highbrow hero-worshippers who, having got a smattering of wisdom from one of the fifty-seven hundred purveyors of this rare article in America, deign to damn with their sneers and jibes any activity, institution, or mortal it strikes their fancy to treat in such a manner.

These are the folk who talk Bolshevism in their parlors and wouldn't go to Russia if it were placed, like milk for cats, in saucers on their doorsteps. They slur Beethoven or Tennyson and extol Stravinsky and Whitman when they are hardly able to grasp such simple minded folk as Leybach or Longfellow, or even Eddie Guest himself.

They mull over best sellers and can call authors' names by the scores. Literature for them is measured by its mystic qualities or its pornographical settings; music by its aberrations from generally accepted forms; art by its illusiveness.

Anything that is plain or clear or clean comes under the suspicion of these folk if not actually beneath their contempt. They who themselves do almost nothing by way of contributing to the nation's artistic development set themselves up as the struggling workman's severest critics. Ofttimes they are actually proud of their non-accomplishment: it shows their artistic temperament, they boast. Good God deliver us from their art!

One can admire truly intellectual types like Sinclair Lewis, Dreiser, H.L.M., and Shaw, men who are in every respect creative critics and thinkers. What one cannot swallow is this carrion prostrated at the altar of Liberalism when as a matter of fact their lying hearts are as faint as they are insipid. Their pelts are as mangy as Main Streeters' and their sentiments as hypocritical as those of the most pious Kluxer in the Bible Belt. They are by far more to be despised than the "morons" whom they single out with such avidity; for the latter do at least make an attempt to earn their salt, and to express themselves honestly, while the Intelligentsia steal all they can get away with and never do anything unless it be in the attitude of a dethroned prince who suddenly has to go to work.

These folk have no more right to become associated with true artistic spirits than Knights of Columbus have to drink the Grand Kleagle's health. They simply give art and artists a black eye with their snobbery and stupidity; and their false interpretations and hypocritical evaluations do more to heighten suspicion against the real artist on the part of the ordinary citizen than perhaps any other single factor in the clash of art and provincialism.

Certainly there is more excuse for innocent idiocy and moronesia than there is for the sophisticated bigotry of these fair folk who, in the secret recesses of their inner consciousness, lay claim to membership in the Intelligentsia.

ARTHUR HUFF FAUSET.

Fire Burns

A Department of Comment

ome time ago, while reviewing Carl Van Vechten's lava laned Nigger Heaven I made the prophecy that Harlem Negroes, once their aversion to the "nigger" in the title was forgotten, would erect a statue on the corner of 135th Street and Seventh Avenue, and dedicate it to this ultra-sophisticated Iowa New Yorker.

So far my prophecy has failed to pan out, and superficially it seems as if it never will, for instead of being enshrined for his pseudo-sophisticated, semi-serious, semi-ludicrous effusion about Harlem, Mr. Van Vechten is about to be lynched, at least in effigy.

Yet I am loathe to retract or to temper my first prophecy. Human nature is too perverse and prophecies do not necessarily have to be fulfilled within a generation. Rather, they can either be fulfilled or else belied with startling two-facedness throughout a series of generations, which, of course, creates the possibility that the fulfillments may outnumber the beliements and thus gain credence for the prophecy with posterity. Witness the Bible.

However, in defending my prophecy I do not wish to endow Mr. Van Vechten's novel (?) with immortality, but there is no real reason why Nigger Heaven should not eventually be as stupidly acclaimed as it is now being stupidly damned by the majority of Harlem's dark inhabitants. Thus I defiantly reiterate that a few years hence Mr. Van Vechten will be spoken of as a kindly gent rather than as a moral leper exploiting people who had believed him to be a sincere friend.

༄

I for one, and strange as it may sound, there are others, who believe that Carl Van Vechten was rendered sincere during his explorations and observations of Negro life in Harlem, even if he remained characteristically superficial. Superficiality does not necessarily denote a lack of sincerity, and even superficiality may occasionally delve into deep pots of raw life. What matter if they be flesh pots?

In writing Nigger Heaven the author wavered between sentimentality and sophistication. That the sentimentality won out is his funeral. That the sophistication stung certain Negroes to the quick is their funeral.

The odds are about even. Harlem cabarets have received another public boost and are wearing out cash register keys, and entertainers' throats and orchestra instruments. The so-called intelligentsia of Harlem has exposed its inherent stupidity. And Nigger Heaven is a best seller.

༄

Group criticism of current writings, morals, life, politics, or religion is always ridiculous, but what could be more ridiculous than the wholesale condemnation of a book which only one-tenth of the condemnators have or will read. And even if the book was as vile, as degrading, and as defamatory to the character of the Harlem Negro as the Harlem Negro now declares, his criticisms would not be considered valid by an intelligent person as long as the critic had had no reading contact with the book.

The objectors to Nigger Heaven claim that the author came to Harlem, ingratiated himself with Harlem folk, and then with a supercilious grin and a salacious smirk, lolled at his desk downtown and dashed off a pornographic document about uptown in which all of the Negro characters are pictured as being debased, lecherous creatures not at all characteristic or true to type, and that, moreover, the author provokes the impression that all of Harlem's inhabitants are cabaret hounds and thirsty neurotics. He did not tell, say his critics, of our well bred, well behaved church-going majorities, nor of our night schools filled with eager elders, nor of our brilliant college youth being trained in the approved contemporary manner, nor of our quiet, home loving thousands who hardly know what the word cabaret connotes. He told only of lurid night life and of uninhibited sybarites. Therefore, since he has done these things and neglected to do these others the white people who read the book will believe that all Harlem Negroes are like the Byrons, the Lascas, the Pettijohns, the Rubys, the Creepers, the Bonifaces, and the other lewd hussies and whoremongers in the book.

It is obvious that these excited folk do not realize that any white person who would believe such poppy-cock probably believes it anyway, without any additional aid from Mr. Van Vechten, and should such a person read a tale anent our non-cabareting, church-going Negroes, presented in all their virtue and glory and with their human traits, their human hypocrisy and their human perversities glossed over, written, say, by Jessie Fauset, said person would laugh derisively and allege that Miss Fauset had not told the truth, the same as Harlem

49

Negroes are alleging that Carl Van Vechten has not told the truth. It really makes no difference to the race's welfare what such ignoramuses think, and it would seem that any author preparing to write about Negroes in Harlem or anywhere else (for I hear that DuBose Heyward has been roundly denounced by Charlestonian Negroes for his beautiful Porgy) should take whatever phases of their life that seem the most interesting to him, and develop them as he pleases. Why Negroes imagine that any writer is going to write what Negroes think he ought to write about them is too ridiculous to merit consideration. It would seem that they would shy away from being pigeon-holed, so long have they been the rather lamentable victims of such a typically American practice, yet Negroes would have all Negroes appearing in contemporary literature made as ridiculous and as false to type as the older school of pseudo-humorous, sentimental white writers made their Uncle Toms, they Topsys, and their Mammies, or as the Octavius Roy Cohen school now make their more modern "cullud" folk.

One young lady, prominent in Harlem collegiate circles, spoke forth in a public forum (oh yes, they even have public forums where they spend their time anouncing that they have not read the book, and that the author is a moral leper who also commits literary sins), that there was only one character in Nigger Heaven who was true to type. This character, the unwitting damsel went on, was Mary Love. It seems as if all the younger Negro women in Harlem are prototypes of this Mary Love, and it is pure, poor, virtuous, vapid Mary, to whom they point as a typical life model.

Again there has been no realization that Mary Love is the least life-life character in the book, or that it is she who suffers most from her creator's newly acquired seriousness and sentimentality, she who suffers most of the whole ensemble because her creator discovered, in his talented trippings around Manhattan, drama at which he could not chuckle the while his cavalier pen sped cleverly on in the same old way yet did not—could not spank.

But—had all the other characters in Nigger Heaven approximated Mary's standard, the statue to Carl Van Vechten would be an actualized instead of a deferred possibility, and my prophecy would be gloriously fulfilled instead of being ignominiously belied.

WALLACE THURMAN.

PRINTED BY JOSEPH LEVENTHAL, NEW YORK CITY

HARLEM

A FORUM
OF NEGRO LIFE

Vol. I   NOVEMBER, 1928   No. 1

Twenty-five Cents per Copy

51

You Can Still Save Money if You Join the Guild NOW!

Membership is FREE!

MORE than 50,000 men and women now enjoy free membership in The Literary Guild. They subscribed for twelve of the year's best books in advance of publication for a single fee—a great deal less than the total retail value of the books they receive. *Now the price is going up!* Circumstances beyond the control of the Guild executives have made a price advance necessary.

For a limited time only you can subscribe at the old rate and assure your-self Guild books for a year at the same amazingly low price.

You know how the Guild plan works —how Carl Van Doren and the Editorial Board choose one book each month from publisher's manuscripts *before* publication—and how that book is issued in a special binding and special edition *for Guild members only* on the same date that the trade edition is distributed to the stores. You receive your copy of each book postpaid, before your friends have discovered it and urged you to read it. You are an *insider* in constant touch with the latest and best in American letters.

Quality Is Not Sacrificed

The beauty of Guild books has continued to amaze members and non-members alike. No economy is exercised in the production of Guild selections. The best paper and binding materials are always used, specially chosen types and artistically designed covers and title pages are features of the Guild editions. BLACK MAJESTY, one of the most popular Guild books issued, was illustrated throughout with three-color, full page pictures and other decorations by Mahlon Blaine.

Both TRADER HORN and that famous old adventurer's second book, HAROLD THE WEBBED, have been Guild selections. The much-discussed BAD GIRL was the Guild book for April. These are books you *want*, books you will read whether you are a member of the Guild or not. Join the Guild at once and realize a considerable saving on twelve chosen books a year. Get full information *now* before the price is advanced.

Mail the coupon at once for your copy of WINGS absolutely *free!*

The Literary Guild of America, Inc.
Dept. 54, H. M. M.
55 Fifth Avenue   New York City

Send for WINGS —Free

HARLEM

A FORUM OF NEGRO LIFE

wishes

Articles on Current Events

Debates on Racial and Non-Racial Issues

Short Stories

Poems

Literary Essays   Illustrations and Cartoons   Economic Studies
Reviews of Worthwhile Books

There are no editorial restrictions on subject matter or manner of treatment. Harlem is a magazine of free expression—independent and alive.

54

HARLEM
A Forum of Negro Life

Volume I NOVEMBER, 1928 Number 1

Table of Contents

PUBLISHED MONTHLY AT 25c. PER COPY, ANNUAL SUBSCRIPTION $2.50, THE H. K. PARKER PUBLISHING COMPANY, 2376 SEVENTH AVENUE, NEW YORK CITY. WALLACE THURMAN, EDITOR; AARON DOUGLAS, ART EDITOR; S. PACE ALEXANDER, MANAGING EDITOR. COPYRIGHTED, 1928, BY THE H. K. PARKER PUBLISHING CORPORATION.

55

HARLEM

A Forum of Negro Life

| Volume I | NOVEMBER, 1928 | Number 1 |

For Whom Shall the Negro Vote?

By WALTER WHITE

ILL you write an article for the first issue of HARLEM, the editor of that magazine writes me, concerning "the dilemma of Negro voters today—surveying the attitude of the old guard toward loyalty to the Republican party and the attitude of another group which is openly advocating a bolt from the traditional party of our fathers."

As fulfillment of such an assignment is being done some three weeks before election day and as the words commanded by the editor of HARLEM will hardly appear in print before the issue between Herbert Hoover and Alfred E. Smith is decided, the difficulties of such a task are apparent. Whatever may be written, therefore, which deals with the dilemma of the Negro voter in 1928 will be of importance, if any, only in so far as it may bear upon future elections in which Negroes may participate.

The reasonably detached observer of Negro activities in the 1928 presidential election can find ample material for Gargantuan laughter. Neither candidate has done any one striking thing nor uttered a single phrase which would, inspire enthusiasm in Negro breasts. Those Negroes who are supporting either candidate have dredged the careers and utterances of both men seeking for some solace or some tangible material indicative of friendly or even perfunctory interest in the problems which face black men in American life today. When one reads the printed material or listens to the speeches of the Negroes supporting Smith or Hoover, one at first may be inclined to laugh, but on more sober reflection the thoughtful reader or auditor will realize how pathetic is the position of the Negro voter in American life.

Consider Al Smith, for example, who undoubtedly had a vast amount of enthusiastic support among Negro voters prior to the Democratic convention in Houston in June. These Negroes saw in Smith a new type of leader who

offered promises of Negro emancipation from slavish and increasingly unprofitable devotion to the Republican party. The Ku Klux Klan, Tom Heflin of Alabama, and all of the combined forces of bigotry, prejudice and intolerance seemed united against Al Smith because of his religion, and, more mildly, because of his Tammany Hall connection and his views on prohibition. Thoughtful Negroes imagined that they saw in Smith a champion, who would wrest control of the Democratic party from the hands of southern bourbons and vest that control once more as it was in the days of Grover Cleveland in the hands of the north and east. Most of these hopes died aborning. The Democratic convention paid sinful tribute to the reactionary south by nominating a shrewd and Negro-hating politician as Smith's running mate. Pat Harrison of Mississippi, demanded and secured a loud voice in the conducting of the Democratic campaign. Cole Blease of South Carolina, and Carter Glass of Virginia, were not far behind their Mississippi senatorial confrere. Even these political barnacles would not have alienated so much Negro support from Smith as they did, had Smith himself had the same courage on the Negro question as he demonstrated on such issues as prohibition and religion. Not one word has he uttered which directly or indirectly would attract honest and intelligent Negro voters. A semi-official Negro organization was established to cultivate Negro support, but, laboring against the odds already mentioned, it has been woefully unsuccessful in attracting thoughtful, influential and respected Negroes to its ranks.

When one turns to the Republican side, the picture is equally, if not more, depressing. The Negro supporters of Hoover have striven valiantly to make out a case for him. The chief contentions have been the usually negative emphasis on Democratic perfidy phrased most fre-

5

quently, "better a passive friend than an active enemy"; and discreet playing up of Hoover's order abolishing segregation in the Department of the Interior. The discretion was doubtless due to orders from higher up because this same issue has been most viciously used against Hoover in the south, the criticism there being so virulent that white Hooverites have lustily been denying in the south that Hoover even issued such an order.

The counts against Hoover have more than offset many arguments in his favor which would appeal to the Negro. He has been as silent as Smith on the Negro question. In his speech of acceptance he timidly did declare that "equality of opportunity is the right of every American, rich or poor, foreign or native born, irrespective of sect or color." But the assertion has been shown to be as empty as the proverbial vacuum by the obvious yielding of the Republican party to the lily whites of the south.

One need hold no brief for Perry Howard, the Negro Republican National Committeeman of Mississippi, or Ben Davis of Georgia, to see how thoroughly dishonest the Republican party is in its appeal for Negro support. Mrs. Mabel Walker Willebrandt, the stormy petrel of the Republican party, passed through Virginia on her way from Washington to Mississippi to participate actively in the indictment of Perry Howard for alleged sale of patronage. In that same state of Virginia the big boss of the Republican party, the swarthy white man, Bascom Slemp, not only as Republican boss but as Secretary to Calvin Coolidge had dealt actively in the sale of post offices and his acts had been spread on the pages of the Congressional Record. Perry Howard, the black man, was indicted on *charges* of dealing in post offices; Bascom Slemp, the deeply brunette white man, known to be guilty of such sales, was given a high position in the management of the Hoover campaign.

What, if any, are the chances for hope by Negroes that in 1932 their dilemma is going to be any less perplexing? The answer to that rests almost solely with the Negro himself. There are in 1928 ten states in which the Negro vote unquestionably holds or very nearly holds an absolute balance of power between the two major parties. If the Negro in those and other states refuses to bestir himself until another presidential year he is going to face not only as hopeless a choice in 1932 as he does today, but the situation is almost certain to be even more depressing. If, on the other hand, intelligent, decent, self-respecting and honest

Negro men and women start some racial housecleaning and throw into the discard all of those Negroes, both men and women, who are no better than the average run of white politicians in selling out their honor and everything else to the highest bidder, there is going to be some lightening of the clouds which hang over the Negro voter today. I know personally of the cases of a large number of Negroes who in 1928 decided whether or not they would be Republicans or Democrats only after they had learned out of which party the largest sum could be squeezed.

A movement which has just been born in Harlem may offer an example of this new leadership. Judge Olvany, boss of Tammany Hall, during the presidential campaign, expressed in a private conversation his lack of respect for or interest in Negro voters in Harlem, declaring that out of that Negro population which approximates a quarter of a million, only twenty-three thousand were registered voters. One of the men to whom Olvany made this statement possessed more garrulity than discretion. On a street corner in Harlem this man told half a dozen persons of Olvany's statement. The next issues of various Harlem newspapers spread Olvany's words over the greater portion of their front pages.

The result served effectively to stir resentment among Negroes who had self-respect, but who also had been cursed with slothfulness. An independent movement was born, taking the name of Ferdinand Q. Morton, to build up a large body of intelligent, active Negro voters who expressed their determination to control the political destinies of the areas in which Negroes are numerous. If this movement has the courage, the honesty and the clearness of vision which is voiced in their declaration of political independence it can revolutionize not only the Negro's political situation in Harlem, but in all parts of the United States. If, on the other hand, the movement degenerates into a narrow-visioned, selfish organization it will do nothing but fasten more securely the shackles on the Negro's hands.

The call for new leaders is an old one but one which does not lose its potency by reason of the fact that Negroes have heard it ever since the Civil War. It is so obvious that it is a truism that as long as political bosses can safely start their campaigns by eliminating all consideration of the Negro because he is known to be incapable of voting any but one ticket,

(Continued on page 45)

Langston Hughes

Luani of the Jungles

By LANGSTON HUGHES

"NOT another shilling," I said. "You must think I'm a millionaire or something. Here I am offering you my best hat, two shirts, and a cigar case, with two shillings besides, and yet you want five shillings more! I wouldn't give five shillings for six monkeys, let alone a mean-looking beast like yours. Come on, let's make a bargain. What do you say?"

But the African, who had come to the wharf on the Niger to sell his monkey remained adamant. "Five shillin' more," he said. "Five shillin'. Him one fine monkey!" However, when he held up the little animal for me to touch, the frightened beast opened his white-toothed mouth viciously and gave a wild scream. "Him no bite," assured the native. "Him good."

"Yes, he's good all right," said Porto Rico sarcastically. "We'll get a monkey at Burutu cheaper, anyhow. It'd take a year to tame this one."

"I won't buy him," I protested to the native. "You want too much."

"But he is a fine monkey," an unknown voice behind us said, and we turned to see a strange, weak-looking little white man standing there. "He is a good monkey," the man went on in a foreign sort of English. "You ought to buy him here. Not often you get a red monkey of this breed. He is rare."

Then the stranger, who seemed to know whereof he spoke, told us that the animal was worth much more than the native asked, and he advised me softly to pay the other five shillings. "He is like a monkey in a poem," the man said. Meanwhile the slender simian clung tightly to the native's shoulder and snarled shrilly whenever I tried to touch him. But the very wildness of the poor captured beast with the wire cord about his hairy neck fascinated me. Given confidence by the stranger, for one old hat, two blue shirts, a broken cigar case, and seven shillings, I bought the animal. Then for fear of being bitten, I wrapped the wild little thing in my coat, carried him up the gang-plank of the "West Illana" and put him into an empty prune box standing near the galley door. Porto Rico and the stranger followed and I saw that Porto Rico carried a large valise, so I surmised that the stranger was a new passenger.

The "West Illana," a freight boat from New York to West Africa, seldom carried passengers other than an occasional trader or a few poor missionaries. But when, as now, we were up one of the tributaries of the Niger, where English passenger steamers seldom came, the captain sometimes consented to take on travelers to the coast. The little white man with the queer accent registered for Lagos, a night's journey away. After he had been shown his stateroom he came out on deck and, in a friendly sort of manner, began to tell me about the various methods of taming wild monkeys. Yet there was a vague far-off air about him as though he were not really interested in what he was saying. He took my little beast in his hands and I noticed that the animal did not bite him nor appear particularly alarmed.

It was late afternoon then and all our cargo for that port,—six Fords from Detroit and some electric motors,—had been unloaded. The seamen closed the hatch, the steamer swung slowly away from the wharf with a blast of the whistle and began to glide lazily down the river. Soon we seemed to be floating through the heart of a dense sullen jungle. A tangled mass of trees and vines walled in the sluggish stream and grew out of the very water itself. None of the soil of the river bank could be seen,—only an impenetrable thickness of trees and vines. Nor were there the brilliant jungle trees one likes to imagine in the tropics. They were rather a monotonous grey-green confusion of trunks and leaves with only an occasional cluster of smoldering scarlet flowers or, very seldom, the flash of some bright-winged bird to vary their hopelessness. Once or twice this well of ashey vegetation was broken by a muddy brook or a little river joining the larger stream and giving, along murkey lengths, a glimpse into the further depths of this colorless and forbidding country. Then the river gradually widened and we could smell the sea, but it was almost dinner time before the ship began to roll slowly on the ocean's green and open waters. When I went into the salon to set the officers' table we were still very near the Nigerian coast and the grey vines and dull trees of the delta region.

After dinner I started aft to join Porto Rico and the seamen, but I saw the little white man seated on one of the hawser posts near the

7

LUANI OF THE JUNGLES
AARON DOUGLAS

handrail so I stopped. It was dusk and the last glow of sunset was fading on the edge of the sea. I was surprised to find this friend of the afternoon seated there because passengers seldom ventured far from the comfortable deck chairs near the salon.

"Good evening," I said.

"Bon soir," answered the little man.

"Vous êtes francais?" I asked, hearing his greeting.

"Non," he replied slowly. "I am not French, but I lived in Paris for a long while." Then he added for seemingly no reason at all, "I am a poet, but I destroy my poems."

The gold streak on the horizon turned to orange.

There was nothing I could logically say except, "Why?"

"I don't know," he said. "I don't know why I destroy my poems. But then there are many things I don't know. . . . I live back in that jungle." He pointed toward the coast. "I don't know why."

The orange in the sunset darkened to blue.

"But why," I asked again stupidly.

"My wife is there," he said. "She is an African."

"Is she?" I could think of nothing other to say.

The blue on the horizon greyed to purple now.

"I'm trying to get away," he went on, paying no attention to my remark. "I'm going down to Lagos now. Maybe I'll forget to come back —back there." And he pointed to the jungles hidden in the distant darkness of the coast. "Maybe I'll forget to come back this time. But I never did before,—not even when I was drunk. I never forgot. I always came back. Yet I hate that woman!"

"What woman?" I asked.

"My wife," he said. "I love her and yet I hate her."

The sea and the sky were uniting in darkness.

"Why?" was again all I could think of saying.

"At Paris," he went on. "I married her at Paris." Then suddenly to me, "Are you a poet, too?"

"Why, yes," I replied.

"Then I can talk to you," he said. "I married her at Paris four years ago when I was a student there in the Sorbonne." As he told his story the night became very black and the stars were warm. "I met her one night at the Bal Bulier,—this woman I love. She was with an African student whom I knew and he told me

that she was the daughter of a wealthy native in Nigeria. At once I was fascinated. She seemed to me the most beautiful thing I had ever seen,—dark and wild, exotic and strange, —accustomed as I had been to only pale white women. We sat down at a table and began to talk together in English. She told me she was educated in England but that she lived in Africa. 'With my tribe,' she said. 'When I am home I do not wear clothes like these, nor these things on my fingers.' She touched her evening gown and held out her dark hands sparkling with diamonds. 'Life is simple when I am home,' she said. 'I don't like it here. It is too cold and people wear too many clothes.' She lifted a cigarette holder of platinum and jade to her lips and blew a thin line of smoke into the air. 'Mon dieu!' I thought to myself. 'A child of sophistication and simplicity such as I have never seen!' And suddenly before I knew it, crazy young student that I was, I had leaned across the table and was saying, 'I love you.'

"'That is what he says, too,' she replied, pointing toward the African student dancing gaily with a blonde girl at the other end of the room. 'You haven't danced with me yet.' We rose. The orchestra played a Spanish waltz full of Gypsy-like nostalgia and the ache of desire. She waltzed as no woman I had ever danced with before could waltz, — her dark body close against my white one, her head on my shoulder, its mass of bushy hair tangled and wild, perfumed with a jungle-scent. I wanted her! I ached for her! She seemed all I had ever dreamed of; all the romance I'd ever found in books; all the lure of the jungle countries; all the passions of the tropic soul.

"'I need you,' I said. 'I love you.' Her hand pressed mine and our lips met, wedged as we were in the crowd of the Bal Bulier.

"'I'm sailing from Bordeaux at the end of the month,' she told me as we sat in the Gardens of the Luxemburg at sunset a few days later. 'I'm going back home to the jungle countries and you are coming with me.'

"'I know it,' I agreed, as though I had been planning for months to go with her.

"'You are coming with me back to my people,' she continued. 'You with your whiteness coming to me and my dark land. Maybe I won't love you then. Maybe you won't love me, —but the jungle'll take you and you'll stay there forever.'

"'It won't be the jungle making me stay,' I protested. 'It'll be you. You'll be the ebony goddess of my heart, the dark princess who saved me from the corrupt tangle of white civilization, who took me away from my books into life, who discovered for me the soul of your dark countries. You'll be the tropic flower of my heart.

"During the following days before our sailing, I made many poems to this black woman I loved and adored. I dropped my courses at the Sorbonne that week and wrote my father in Prague that I would be going on a journey south for my health's sake. I changed my account to a bank in Lagos in West Africa, and paid farewell calls on all my friends in Paris. So much did I love Luani that I had no regrets on taking leave of my classmates nor upon saying adieux to the city of light and joy.

"One night in July we sailed from Bordeaux. We had been married the day before in Paris.

"In August we landed at Lagos and came by river boat to the very wharf where you saw me today. But in the meantime something was lost between us,—something of the first freshness of love that I've never found again. Perhaps it was because of the many days together hour after hour on the boat,—perhaps she saw too much for me. Anyway, when she took off her European clothes at the Liberty Hotel in Lagos to put on the costume of her tribe, and when she sent to the steel safe at the English bank there all of her diamonds and pearls, she seemed to put me away, too, out of her heart, along with the foreign things she had removed from her body. More fascinating than ever in the dress of her people, with the soft cloth of scarlet about her limbs and the little red sandals of buffalo hide on her feet,—more fascinating than ever and yet farther away she seemed, elusive, strange. And she began that day to talk to some of the servants in the language of her land.

"Up to the river town by boat, and then we travelled for days deep into the jungles. After a week we arrived at a high clear space surrounded by bread-fruit, mango, and cocoanut trees. There a hundred or more members of the tribe were waiting to receive her,—beautiful brown-black people whose perfect bodies glistened in the sunlight, bodies that shamed me and the weakness under my European clothing. That night there was a great festival given in honor of Luani's coming,—much beating of drums and wild fantastic dancing beneath the moon,—a festival in which I could take no part for I knew none of their ceremonies, none of their dances. Nor did I understand a word of their language. I could only stand aside and look, or sit in the door of our hut and sip the palm wine they served me. Luani, wilder than any of the others, danced to the drums, laughed and was happy. She seemed to have forgotten me sitting in the doorway of our hut drinking palm wine.

"Weeks passed and months. Luani went hunting and fishing, wandering about for days in the jungles. Sometimes she asked me to go with her, but more often she went with members of the tribe and left me to walk about the village, understanding nobody, able to say almost nothing. No one molested me. I was seemingly respected or at least ignored. Often when Luani was with me she would speak no French or English all day, unless I asked her something. She seemed almost to have forgotten the European languages, to have put them away as she had put away the clothes and customs of the foreigners. Yet she would come when I called and let me kiss her. In a far-off, strange sort of way she still seemed to love me. Even then I was happy because I loved her and could hold her body.

"Then one night, trembling from an ugly dream, I suddenly awoke, sat up in bed and discovered in a daze that she was not beside me. A cold sweat broke out on my body. The room was empty. I leaped to the floor and opened the door of the hut. A great streak of moonlight fell across the threshold. A little breeze was blowing and the leaves of the mango trees rustled dryly. The sky was full of stars. I stepped into the grassy village street,—quiet all around. Filled with worry and fear, I called, 'Luani!' As far as I could see the tiny huts were quiet under the moon and no one answered. I was suddenly weak and afraid. The indifference of the silence unnerved me. I called again, 'Luani!' A voice seemed to reply: 'To the palm forest, to the palm forest. Quick, to the palm forest!' And I began to run toward the edge of the village where a great cocoanut grove lay.

"There beneath the trees it was almost as light as day and I sat down to rest against the base of a tall palm, while the leaves in the wind rustled dryly overhead. No other noise disturbed the night and I rested there wide awake, remembering Paris and my student days at college. An hour must have passed when, through an aisle of the palm trees, I saw two naked figures walking. Very near me they came and then passed on in the moonlight,—two ebony bodies close together in the moonlight. They were Luani and the chief's young son, Awa Unabo.

"I did not move. Hurt and resentment,

anger and weakness filled my veins. Unabo, the strongest and greatest hunter of the tribe, possessed the woman I loved. They were walking together in the moonlight, and weakling that I was, I dared not fight him. He'd break my body as though it were a twig. I could only rage in my futile English and no one except Luani would understand. . . . I went back to the hut. Just before dawn she came, taking leave of her lover at my door.

"Like a delicate statue carved in ebony, a dark halo about her head, she stood before me, beautiful and black like the very soul of the tropics, a woman to write poems about, a woman to go mad over. All the jealous anger died in my heart and only a great hurt remained and a feeling of weakness.

"I am going away, back to Paris, I said.'

"'I'm sorry,' she replied with emotion. 'A woman can have two lovers and love them both.' She put her arms around my neck but I pushed her away. She began to cry then and I cursed her in foreign, futile words. That same day, with two guides and four carriers, I set out through the jungles toward the Niger and the boat for Lagos. She made no effort to keep me back. One word from her and I could not have left the village, I knew. I would have been a prisoner,—but she did not utter that word. Only when I left the clearing she waved to me and said, 'You'll come back.'

"Once in Lagos, I engaged passage for Bordeaux, but when the time came to sail I could not leave. I thought of her standing before me naked that last morning like a little ebony statue, and I tore up my ticket! I returned to the hotel and began to drink heavily in an effort to forget, but I could not. I remained drunk for weeks, then after some months had passed I boarded a river boat, went back up the Niger, back through the jungles,—back to her.

"Four times that has happened now. Four times I've left her and four times returned. She has borne a child for Awa Unabo. And she tells me that she loves him. But she says she loves me, too. Only one thing I do know,—she drives me mad. Why I stay with her, I do not know any longer. Why her lover tolerates me, I do not know. Luani humiliates me now, —and fascinates me, tortures me and holds me. I love her. I hate her, too. I write poems about her and destroy them. I leave her and come back. I do not know why. I'm like a mad man and she's like the soul of her jungles, quiet and terrible, beautiful and dangerous, fascinating and death-like. I'm leaving her again, but I know I'll come back. . . . I know I'll come back."

Slowly the moon rose out of the sea and the distant coast of Nigeria was like a shadow on the horizon. The "West Illana" rolled languidly through the night. I looked at the little white man, tense and pale, and wondered if he were crazy, or if he were lying.

"We reach Lagos early in the morning, do we not?" he asked. "I must go to sleep. Good night." And the strange passenger went slowly toward the door of the corridor that led to his cabin.

I sat still in the darkness for a few moments, dazed. Then I suddenly came to, heard the chug, chug, of the engines below and the half-audible conversation drifting from the fo'c's'ls, heard the sea lapping at the sides of the ship. Then I got up and went to bed.

❧❧❧❧❧

CUI BONO?

She sat all day and thought of love.
She lay all night and dreamed it.
Our romance stricken little dove
Grew truly quite anaemic.

But one day Fate was satiate
Of her continuous pleading
And sent her down a passionate
Young knight to do her heeding.

And tho directly did she know
Their hearts were truly mated,
His eagerness she thought was so. . .
And so . . . she hesitated.

"If, if," she argued helplessly,
Alighting from his carriage
To hitch hike home respectably,
"If he had offered marriage—"

"I wish I'd let him kiss me tho.
Oh, just the merest peck.
I wish—I wish—I wish, but no,
I'd lose my self-respect."

And so she sits and thinks of love.
And all night long she dreams it.
And with regret our little dove
Continues quite anaemic.

HELENE JOHNSON

63

Art or Propaganda?

By Alain Locke

ARTISTICALLY it is the one fundamental question for us today,—Art or Propaganda. Which? Is this more the generation of the prophet or that of the poet; shall our intellectual and cultural leadership preach and exhort or sing? I believe we are at that interesting moment when the prophet becomes the poet and when prophecy becomes the expressive song, the chant of fulfillment. We have had too many Jeremiahs, major and minor,—and too much of the drab wilderness. My chief objection to propaganda, apart from its besetting sin of monotony and disproportion, is that it perpetuates the position of group inferiority even in crying out against it. For it leaves and speaks under the shadow of a dominant majority whom it harangues, cajoles, threatens or supplicates. It is too extroverted for balance or poise or inner dignity and self-respect. Art in the best sense is rooted in self-expression and whether naive or sophisticated is self-contained. In our spiritual growth genius and talent must more and more choose the role of group expression, or even at times the role of free individualistic expression,—in a word must choose art and put aside propaganda.

The literature and art of the younger generation already reflects this shift of psychology, this regeneration of spirit. David should be its patron saint:—it should confront the Phillistines with its five smooth pebbles fearlessly. There is more strength in a confident camp than in a threatened enemy. The sense of inferiority must be innerly compensated, self-conviction must supplant self-justification and in the dignity of this attitude a convinced minority must confront a condescending majority. Art cannot completely accomplish this, but I believe it can lead the way.

Our espousal of art thus becomes no mere idle acceptance of "art for art's sake," or cultivation of the last decadences of the over-civilized, but rather a deep realization of the fundamental purpose of art and of its function as a tap-root of vigorous, flourishing living. Not all of our younger writers are deep enough in the sub-soil of their native materials,—too many are pot-plants seeking a forced growth according to the exotic tastes of a pampered and decadent public. It is the art of the people that needs to be cultivated, not the art of the coteries. Propaganda itself is preferable to shallow, truckling imitation. Negro things may reasonably be a fad for others; for us they must be a religion. Beauty, however, is its best priest and psalms will be more effective than sermons.

To date we have had little sustained art unsubsidized by propaganda; we must admit this debt to these foster agencies. The three journals which have been vehicles of most of our artistic expressions have been the avowed organs of social movements and organized social programs. All our purely artistic publications have been sporadic. There is all the greater need then for a sustained vehicle of free and purely artistic expression. If HARLEM should happily fill this need, it will perform an honorable and constructive service. I hope it may, but should it not, the need remains and the path toward it will at least be advanced a little.

We need, I suppose in addition to art some substitute for propaganda. What shall that be? Surely we must take some cognizance of the fact that we live at the centre of a social problem. Propaganda at least nurtured some form of serious social discussion, and social discussion was necessary, is still necessary. On this side; the difficulty and shortcoming of propaganda is its partisanship. It is one-sided and often prejudging. Should we not then have a journal of free discussion, open to all sides of the problem and to all camps of belief? Difficult, that, —but intriguing. Even if it has to begin on the note of dissent and criticism and assume Menckenian scepticism to escape the commonplaces of conformity. Yet, I hope we shall not remain at this negative pole. Can we not cultivate truly free and tolerant discussion, almost Socratically minded for the sake of truth? After Beauty, let Truth come into the Renaissance picture,—a later cue, but a welcome one. This may be premature, but one hopes not,— for eventually it must come and if we can accomplish that, instead of having to hang our prophets, we can silence them or change their lamentations to song with a Great Fulfillment.

❧❧❧❧❧

DEAD AND GONE

Allison Davis

"Son, I'm pas' eighty, but I still
Mus' grub an' swing er hoe
Ter keep my roof'. I sometime fill
My pipe, and think of dem so
Long daid here, what use' ter be
'Fraid of dis berr'in' groun' befo'.
Deaf stopped der fears an' slav'ry.

"Den mem'ries lak de mo'nful ho'n
Of hunters come down on me
Ter throddle hope—Dese hab no stone,
But I doan need er mark' fur
All dat pas' is rooted ter our bone."

 Lak my soul, sun a-burnin'.
  Fallin'.
 Lak my soul, moon 'll be droppin'
  Blood-red
 Behin' de berr'in' groun'
 Unseen ter her settin'
  Lonely, neah her time.

"De ol' folks an' deir hoodoo-doctor,
Daddy Jim wuz glad ter shout
Deir lesson time dat little Brer
Wuz th'own here in de co'ner wifout
Mo'ners, frenzied by er mocc'sin's bite
An' daid in fury. Brer wux 'bout
Our dancin'est boy an' fust ter fight,
Or sing de songs he allus made
Fur break-downs. Late ev'ry night
In quarters miles aroun' he laid
De seed fur Massa's reapin',
Sons sowed fur slav'ry.

  "Brer paid,
De ol' folks said, fer all his creepin'
Time dat de rice swamp turned his breaf
Ter fever. He kep on leapin'
Tell de mocc'sin let him dance fur Deaf."

 Lonely ez de listener, Lawd,
  Still listener, Lawd.
 Fur de long cry frum de houn'
 Lonesome when I'm thinkin', Lawd,
  Of dat stoneless burr'in' groun';
  Know I'm ready's ever goin' ter be
  Ready's I'm ever goin' ter be.

"She wuz de putties' an' bes'
Beloved of all our gals, but Bef
Wuz kep' ter eaze young Massa's nes'.
Dose in de fiels all wished her place,
Tell Massa sent her home ter res'."

Glide, glide, glide,
Water lily's white, wild rose red,
Missis singin' by my side,
'Gaters playin' daid.

Singin' softly ter de sweep,
Crane an' bittern cryin';
Missis sings her chile ter sleep,
Knows my own chile's sighin'.

Ben' yo' back, boy, pull dis one fur home;
Water cryin' lonely ez de sun flames low,
River rollin' out'ard ter de great sea foam,
Ben' a-gen it, boy, pull dis one fur home.

"Maum Sue was broken by de pace
Dey set her in de rows of co'n,
Between chile-bearin's; but her face
Wuz strong an' taut, firm lak de tone
Struck from tight banjers. Ev'ry year
She gave new birth, an' laid her moan
At night in all her pangs, ter fear
De sick-house wif its ha'nts unlaid.

"Sue loved her own enough ter fight
Fur dem an' try ter cook an' sew
When she had lef' de fiel's at night.
She thought de weren't a speck below
White Missis' babes, an' wondered how
Bef could love white chillun so."

 Oh, go 'lang, ox,
 Down de row;
 Dawn ter sunset
 We gots ter go,
 You an' me,
 In dis row.

Co'n, co'n, co'n an' cotton
Till I die;
Walkin' in de mo'nin' dew,
Singin' ter de sky,
Lovin' you. Lawd,
Lovin' you.

"When I see some u' us shrink an' cow
An' 'spise our blood-won liberty,
My min' goes back ter Sam'el Pryer,
Massa's foreman fur us, who
Knew had got from Massa his desiah
Fur knowledge, with its power an'
Punishment. His hopes like fish
Burnt in his eyes, tell all wuz spen'.

13

His stren'th wuz crushed, while weakness
Made us strong.

       "In youth he had ben
Whupped, when he had done his bes'
Ter reach de no'th, an' torn by
Dogs, till Massa saved his son, jes
Fur his price. Dough he would never cry,
De white folks every day could see
In him what dey denied—man's high
Immo'tal soul in slav'ry.

"De songs he make brought him some

Peace, songs dat gives us heavenly
Calm, an' far-off hopes fur freedom."

When de mo'nin' trumpets soun',
I'll be sleepin' in de mountain;
   Lak Moses, Lawd!
My ol' Mammy say day foun'
Her by de Mountains of de Moon,
   Slavers, my Lawd!
So, doan burry me in dis burr'in' groun'
Where de skeeters sing deir tune,
But berry me in a mountain, Lawd,
   Lak Moses.

THE YOUNG VOICE CRIES

To Alice Dunbar Nelson

MAE COWDERY

Can you not hear us?
Or are you deaf
To our pleading . . .
Can you not see us?
Or are you blind
To our weeping . . .
We yearn to hear
The beauty of truth
From your lips.
As rain drips
From trees
On the budding flowers
'Neath its feet.
We look to see
The naked loveliness
Of things . . . thru your eyes
A barren cliff . . . made
A crimson rise
Of earth's breast
Against the sky!

But
We must be the roots
Of the tree
And push up alone
Thru earth
Rocky with prejudice
And foul with smirking
Horrors . . .
Until at last
We thrust our rough virile
Bodies into the sun
And lift verdant arms in prayer
That we might drip soft rain
On the budding flowers
'Neath our feet.

And when we look
To see the naked loveliness
Of things
There is only a barren cliff
Veiled in ugly mists
Of dogmas and fear.
But we will send our singing into
The wind . . . and blow the mists away
That those who still are in the valley
May see it . . . A crimson rise
Of earth's breast against the sky!

O! You who bore us in pain and joy
To whom God entrusted our souls . . .
Be not deaf to our pleading
Nor blind to our silent weeping!
Look not down in frowning anger!
Else tired of futile tears . . .
We blaze a new path into depths you
Cannot enter . . . and only from afar
Will you see the naked loveliness of things
And the simple beauty of truth
To which time has blinded and defended
    you!

The young voice cries
For the pagan loveliness.
Of a moon
For the brazen beauty
Of a jazz song . . .
The young voice
Is hushed
In silent prayer
At beauty's shrine . . .

Holes

ROY DE COVERLY

SHE was not beautiful, but God had given her eyes. No, I lie. God had taken two holes—bottomless, black holes—and in them He had cast with a prodigal hand, that with which He savors His cosmos. Then He had filled those holes with the ink with which He draws the storm-clouds on the canvas of the skies, and, pleased with His work, had dropped in two moons, one in each.

People stared, agape, and said that her eyes were marvellous. But they were not eyes. I knew better.

As if to atone for the sweet, black misery of these holes, her other features were plain. No, they were homely. No, they were ugly. But that did not matter, for one could not see them. The black radiance from those sinister holes over-shadowed all her face. Still, I knew that her mouth was terrible. I knew that it was like the broken mouth of an obscene, leering gargoyle, but with perfect ivory teeth that laughed in one's face. I knew, because I had often felt those edged pearls laughing at me when I was struggling to keep my head above the pools of ink that filled the black holes.

Such people should not be. But then, she was not a person, but an ironic, cruel enchantress, who did not yet know where to find her wand.

But this was not all. God had taken desire-stuff—plenty of it—and woven it into silken strands; then He had dropped it into the ink in the holes and forgotten it for a thousand years. He then had taken an imp—oh, yes, God sometimes employs Satan's children—and placed him to live forever in this desire-stuff. He crowned her head with it, and also placed it where He places eyelashes and eyebrows on His other creatures.

People said that her hair was wonderful. They lied. It was not hair. It was desire-stuff with a grinning imp living among its strands.

I first saw her in a gin-mill. I had gone there because I wanted to look upon ugly things, and to hear ugly sounds. I have what one might call spells, sometimes. I am a painter.

She sat alone at a table, drinking gin, which she poured from a flat, blue-cloudy bottle. She was almost drunk, but that night she never seemed to fall entirely under the influence. Her clothes were shabby, and they seemed none too clean. There was a ladder on one of her stockings, and her shoes were run over.

I sat across the room from her, ordered whiskey, then looked in her direction. She raised the lids that had half-covered the holes, and I pitched, head foremost, into their bottomless, ink-filled depths. At that moment the imp that lived in the strands of the desire-stuff laughed. I heard his dry, creaky snicker, and there was no blood in my face for many seconds. Then the moons that floated in the ink glimmered for a moment, and I knew that her teeth laughed at me through the broken, leering cleft that was her mouth.

I knew that I must paint her, and I prayed to the God that had fashioned her to keep me from drowning in the inky perdition of those holes. I did not talk to her. One cannot talk when one's throat is full of black God's-ink, and one struggles to keep from sinking in bottomless holes with moons floating in them. I waited, using my drink sparingly, because I was afraid. One does not become drunk——

Presently she rose. With an effort I raised my shoulders above the surface of the ink and placed my arms across the brink of the holes. I should have raised myself higher, but the imp stirred, and his dry hiccough tumbled across the space that separated us and rolled up against my face. My arms weakened, and I spat out the ink that filled my mouth when I sank again. Storm-ink, God's ink.

So, when she went, she carried me with her. Diana, had she seen her walk to the door of the place, through the lewd stares of intoxicated men, would have shot an arrow through her in jealousy.

I followed her to a lobscouse tenement, and mounted the steps into a filthy hall-way. She stopped and turned to face me. The moons had sunk deep into the depths of the holes, and the imp was silent. "Two dollars," she muttered, and her mouth was horrible while her perfect ivory teeth laughed in my face. The imp was silent. There was ink in my mouth, black God's ink, thick and viscous. I tried to speak, and the sound of my voice was strange to my ears. "Come to my apartment," I said. "You may stay as long as you want. It is quite comfortable."

There were ripples on the surface of the ink, and the imp was peeping out at me, with a

15

strand of desire-stuff caught in his little yellow teeth. The moons were still sunken. Silent, she turned and led the way to the door. I was glad she did not speak.

It was about three o'clock in the morning. There was a pale, watery moon whose face was scarred with strings of ragged clouds, dark-tinted with ink—God's-ink. The streets were deep gorges with black heaving sides that closed in on one's consciousness, and stained one's very soul with the black God's-ink with which they dripped. The hoarse roar of a passing taxicab startled me for a moment, then I hailed it, opened the door and motioned her to enter. I could not speak, and I was very thankful that she did not.

I sat beside her, cold and hot by turns, as we drove to my rooms. I longed to turn my head and look at the broken gargoyle's mouth, but I knew that the beady, black eyes of the imp peeped out at me from the depths of the desire-stuff, and that if I moved, his dry hiccough would smite my face with its hoarse revilings. She walked into my studio, and stood in the middle of the room, a creature of blackness with the body of Diana; a fiercely vindictive enchantress enwrapped in a cloud of evil; a fascinating, grimly beautiful Circe, with the mouth of a gargoyle fashioned by a raving, half-devil of a stone-cutter. God, I was her slave. But I would paint her; oh, how I would paint her.

Daylight seemed aeons away. My fingers itched for the brushes. I knew that when I commenced to paint I would no longer be afraid. The imp might thrust his head out of the desire-stuff and leer at me, but I would only laugh in his face and blend the yellow of his teeth, the vermillion of his mouth into my pigments and paint them into the clouds of desire-stuff that would float on my canvas. But I must wait for the light, and, in the meantime, we would sleep.

Daylight streamed into the room with a yellow, luminous burning. A broad, dusty ray settled on the dais and spilled burnt gold on the black draperies. With the morning came reassurance. Black God's-ink in the daylight would surely be only black God's-ink, and not a seething styx of evil boilings. I was sure I could paint her, and I would take advantage of the yellow radiance that filled the room.

Three days later I struggled to the surface of the ink, belched a burning, choking stream of it from my straining throat, and looked at what I had done. Her head was on my canvas. Evil, at once seductive and repellant, her face was there. I had drawn it well. The blue-black shadow cast by the desire-stuff I had painted superbly; the broken cleft of a gargoyle-mouth laughed at me in perfect counterfeit, but,—God help me—I could not paint the holes.

I had tried, fighting madly to clear from my eyes the cloggings of that cursed ink, to draw them in my picture. They were bottomless, black holes of swirling God's-ink—they had no shape. How could I draw what had no shape? Frantic, I had seized a brush, and with black paint, and shades of yellow, of green, of blue, I had tried to imprison their bitter-sweet malevolence on my canvas. I had failed. I could not see to paint them. The moons glistened and dazzled my sight, and then I would sink into the black, surging God's-ink. I could not paint those holes.

In the moment of realizing my failure, I realized also that I must paint them. If, after limning their sweetly evil radiance on my canvas, I sank and drowned in their inky perdition, I would not care. But I must paint them. I would not be foiled by the eyes of a creature of the streets; a common prostitute of a lobscouse tenement; an ignorant, evil-cloaked Circe. But I knew she was none of these. She was a glorious caprice of an all-powerful Creator; a colossal satire, superbly carved in flesh by the omnipotent Sculptor; a Venus, endowed in a moment of levity with the eyes of a Medusa. I was her slave, and she was necessary to my further existence.

A week later, my canvas held a gloriously painted mask. I knew that no painter could have done better work. Something had possessed me. But where the eyes should be were stark, empty spaces that were almost as terrible as the ink-filled, moon-inhabited holes that should have been painted there. As I dropped my brushes in sheer exhaustion, I heard the derisive cackle of the imp in the desire-stuff, and I knew that I was drowning fast in inky deepness.

The whisky that I had been drinking continously had shattered my nerves. My hands trembled. I would never paint again. But neither would any other misguided artist try to paint her.

That night, as she and her loathsome imp slept, I strangled her with my shaking, paint-spattered hands.

I must have fallen into a stupor of drunkenness and exhaustion. When next I was conscious of my surroundings, it was late evening. The bit of sky I could see from my windows

(Continued on page 45)

Woof

George S. Schuyler

"AH WANT you people to understan' that Ah'm First Sergeant of 'H' Company." Thus William Glass, Top Sergeant, veteran of the Spanish American War and the Philippine Insurrection, proud possessor of seven "Excellent" certificates of discharge from the U. S. Army and a non-commissioned officer for nearly twenty years. It was during my first meal with the company that I thus heard the "sound off." Just re-enlisted, and knowing of the reputation the company had for rigid discipline, I had come to it as a change from a rather happy-go-lucky or "ragtime" outfit in another battalion. It was said all over the regiment that if you could "make the time" in "H" Company, you could do so anywhere. Such organizations have a certain fascination. They put a fellow on his mettle. It is something of an adventure, this business of seeing how long you can stay out of the guardhouse.

Woof, as Glass was nicknamed by his men, was a Kentuckian of medium height, the color of chocolate; stocky, with powerful shoulders and arms, and short sturdy legs. He had a square head, determined jaw and little piggish eyes that smouldered from under heavy brows and corrugated forehead, while his close-cropped mustache hid a hard, stern mouth. Though generally hated by the men because of the rigid discipline he maintained, yet he was feared and respected. He knew his duty thoroughly, and what was worse for the incompetent's, he knew everybody else's. He could tell every one just what was his particular duty, and he never lost an opportunity to do so. There was just one way to do a thing, and that was—according to "The Book." Thus there was never any debate about what was right. Always his counsel was "What does the regulations say?"

In most companies the departure of the commissioned officers from the vicinity of the barracks is the signal for a let-up in tension and a certain tolerance toward minor infractions; but not so in *that* company. As long as Woof was about—and he always *was* about—it was just the same as if the Colonel, the Major, the Captain and the Lieutenants were there. Any infraction of rules or violation of orders, no matter how slight, was reported religiously and with great accuracy to the Company Commander. It was the custom in some "ragtime" companies, after an unusually arduous field exercise, to march back to the barracks and scatter to the gun racks after a perfunctory "dismissed" from the weary Top Soldiers. None of that for Woof. No matter how tired the men might be from "Chasing Will" (an expression from the command, "Fire at Will") ; no matter how their throats and eyes might be filled with the red, volcanic dust of the Hawaiian roads, Woof followed the regulations. "Company, Attention. Squads right, march. Compan-e-e, halt. Port, arms. Inspection, arms. Now you people, etc., etc., dismissed!"

Everyday after First Sergeant's Call, when the Top Soldiers of the regiment repaired to headquarters for Morning Reports and new orders, Woof returned immediately to the company, entered the mess hall and invariably interrupted the midday meal to deliver a lecture. One could always be sure that even if there were no orders from headquarters, there would be some from him. Striding to the center of the mess hall, he would startle the men in the midst of their "chow" by loudly blowing "attention" upon his whistle. Then he would "sing the blues" for at least five minutes. There had been some infraction of rules, the lawns were not being carefully policed, the beds were not being properly lined for inspection, some of the men had soiled mosquito bars, the barracks were "filthy" (meaning that he had probably found a couple of match stems lying around), there was too much noise in the barracks after Tattoo, and non-commissioned officers were not properly performing their duties, or any of a hundred other complaints. Always the foreword and afterword ran something like this: "Ah want you people to understan' that Ah'm First Sergeant of 'H' Company, and Ah'm gonna run 'H' Company. You people either gotta do right or face the consequences. Ah'm gettin' sick and tired tellin' you people the same thing every day. This ain't no summer resort; you gotta soldier here. There's gotta be more pep on that parade ground, too; Ah'm gettin' sick and tired of seein' people that call themselves soldiers comin' out to drill and draggin' round like a whore after a hard Saturday night."

It was "H" Company that was the best drilled. It was "H" Company that had the largest number of expert riflemen, sharpshooters and marksmen. It was "H" Company that had the most quiet and orderly mess hall, recreation room and barracks. It was "H" Company that held the straightest line on parade. It was "H" Company that had the largest number of men depositing part of their monthly pay. It was "H" Company that had the cleanest equipment. It was "H" Company that won tent-pitching contests. And it was "H" Company that had the smallest number of drunks the morning after pay day. You couldn't gamble there and you'd better not be caught bringing liquor into the barracks. It was a company, run as the big red-faced Captain from Tennessee used to say, "According to Hoyle." And Woof was as exacting on himself as on the other men. He was always immaculate; his room was always ready for inspection; he knew his drill thoroughly; he never made mistakes in his reports and duty rosters; he was never late on or absent from a formation, and, as was quite fitting, he was an Expert Rifleman and the best pistol shot in the company.

And yet this height of military perfection was not appreciated by the majority of his men. To repeat, they hated him. There was hardly a member of the outfit, private or non-commissioned officer, who would say a good word for him. On one occasion some of the rougher element plotted to plant a bomb under the orderly room. At another time an undiscovered enemy fired a ball cartridge at him during the annual manoeuvers. The most delightful pastime to large numbers of the privates was to lie on their bunks after drill and talk of what they would do to Woof if they ever caught him "on the outside," i. e., in civil life. The punishments they proposed ran all the way from blackjacking to decapitation.

Once, a tall, black, evil-looking Negro from Florida, goaded to desperation by the rigid discipline, sat down and wrote a long anonymous letter to the Secretary of War protesting against the "tyranny" existing in the company. In due time the letter was returned to the Company-Commander through the usual "military channels," decorated with a dozen indorsements. Woof was furious and set about to discover the culprit. An excellent judge of men, he pondered only a short while before he reduced the suspects to three, all of whom were pretty well schooled, among them being the private from Florida. Two or three days later he casually notified the three to report to the orderly room. Upon arrival, he artfully informed them that the Company Commander had decided to have a man in training to take the place of the Company Clerk in the event of sickness, death or dismissal, and that he had chosen them as the three most likely candidates. It would, of course, be necessary he said, for him to submit samples of their work to the Captain. Accordingly he had all three to do various examples in arithmetic and to write sample letters. When the three had departed he compared their handwriting with that on the troublesome anonymous letter. Soon he emitted a gloat of triumph, and rushing to the telephone, requested the Captain to come down immediately. The Captain arrived, and the gentleman from Florida was confronted with the two letters. Next day he was courtmartialed by Old Tremble, the summary court officer and given a short sentence in the guard house. He preceded Woof from the Summary Court-room and as that worthy came along to deliver his usual noonday lecture, he leaped at him with a drawn knife. With great agility Woof hurtled a low fence, sped across "H" Company's velvety lawn closely pursued by the irate private, and leaped upon the porch where an ice axe leaned against the wall. Gratefully he seized this respectable weapon and immediately turned the tables. Instead of serving a couple of months, the letter writer served several years.

Woof would brook no rivalry. Aspirants for his job were squelched or got rid of in numerous ways. If a non-commissioned officer had a better education than Woof, which was not infrequently the case, he was viewed with suspicion. Even if the more intellectual soldier was not seeking Woof's job, that worthy was still suspicious. It happened once that a very light-colored man, nicknamed Lily-White, a college graduate and former clergyman who had been corporal and company clerk for a long time, was rather suddenly appointed Supply Sergeant. This was a very responsible position having to do with the food and equipment of the company. Woof didn't like that at all. Lily-White was now next in importance to him. Moreover, he was a "yallah nigger." Nearly all of Woof's non-commissioned officers were very obviously Negroes because he was the one that recommended them to the Captain for appointment, and without his endorsement, it was next to impossible to get a non-commissioned officer's warrant. Only great necessity would cause him to recommend a "yallah nigger." Well from the time the new Supply Sergeant was appointed, Woof carried on continuous warfare against him, and it wasn't always above board, either. Finally, the relations between them became so strained that it drew the attention of Sniff-snuff, as the Captain was nicknamed because of his nasal catarrh. He tried to patch up the difference, but to no avail. Finally the octaroon sergeant was got rid of by the fortuitous circumstances of promotion to Battalion Sergeant Major. A darker man of more limited intellectual gifts was appointed in his stead, and Woof was happy once more.

He was always "taking the joy out of life." For example, there was the incident at Waianae whence we had hiked from our barracks. These two points are only about nine miles apart across a volcanic mountain ridge and connected by a military road that winds through the windswept Kole Kole Pass. On this occasion, however, the company had marched by a circuitous route; through dusty pineapple plantations and vast seas of sugar cane, around the end of the mountain chain and thence up the coast to the little plantation town. It was a journey of well over thirty miles in the tropical sun, and there were no trees to shade the tired column enroute. It goes without saying that the men, burdened with full field equipment, caked with dust and wet with perspiration, were terribly weary. The sun was dipping into the Pacific as they trudged into camp.

In many companies after such an arduous day, the buying of a little strong drink from the wholesaler liquor-house hard by would have been winked at by those in authority. Not so in "H" Company. Despite his weariness, Woof was, as ever, on the alert. This evening several of the prominent liquorterians, including Big Fairy, Whiskey, Bear, Squareface and Dip, chipped in enough money to purchase a huge demijohn of dago red and a quart of elephant gin. Knowing Woof, they did not bring their cargo in through the gate of the pasture in which the company was camped, but attempted to smuggle it in by way of a field of waving sugar cane that bordered on the rear. The strategy was eminently successful. The whole gang was bagged along with the precious liquor and placed under close arrest. With a chuckle of triumph, Woof retired for the night.

What annoyed the men more than anything else was the fact that there was no way to "get anything" on Woof. He didn't drink, didn't smoke, didn't gamble and didn't run after women, although his wife, whom he well cared for, was far away in Kentucky. He was not a victim of any of the sexual vices to which single men in barracks often fall heir, and he read his Bible every night. As a tall, black, sardonic private known for his wisdom as Dip (short for

The Diplomat), used to say, "How the hell can you get anything on a man like that—he ain't human." Only once did Woof fall from grace, and then only the Captain's "Dog Robber" (servant) and I knew about it. This "Dog Robber," quite accurately nicknamed Handsome, had several comely lady friends in Honolulu, among whom was a Portuguese charmer named Marie. Thinking to make himself solid with the First Sergeant, he conceived the brilliant idea of arranging a liaison between the two. At first Woof was indifferent to these blandishments, but after considerable urging from both of us, coupled with glowing descriptions of the Caucasian maid's beauty, he decided to pay a visit to town. As he almost never went on pass, his going occasioned much comment and surmise.

After two days he returned, radiant and enthusiastic, and confided to me the highly satisfactory result of his mission. "Dog Robbers" in other outfits got special privileges such as exemption from certain formations and often from guard duty, but not in "H" Company. It had, therefore, been the desire to get some of these privileges that had impelled Handsome to introduce Woof to his girl. Accordingly, the next morning after that gentleman's return, Handsome absented from Reveille. But he suffered bitter and immediate disillusionment, for, after receiving the report of his squad leaders, Woof turned to the Officer of the Day and snapped out, " 'H' Company, one private absent."

Nor could even close friendliness stand between Woof and his duty. Once his company clerk and confidant, somehow gained the erroneous impression that Woof might ignore minor violations on his part. But he was soon disillusioned. Returning off pass in town one day, this young man brought along a quart of Johnny Walker. The company being on police and guard duty, there was no one around the barracks except a couple of fellow non-commissioned officers. Together they consumed the Scotch, and, when the bottle yielded no more, the clerk glided to one of the windows, glanced carefully up and down, and then thrust the "dead soldier" into a trash-box on the porch. Alas, he had reckoned without Sergeant Glass, who always seemed to be everywhere. This time he happened to be standing in the door of the orderly room, looking down the 200-foot veranda.

Next morning when the clerk went to the office to do some work before drill time, the empty bottle sat on Woof's desk and that worthy was wearing a look of triumph. The clerk's heart sank. When Sniff-snuff came in after drill, Woof related the story, dwelling with great emphasis on the fact that the corporal had "eased" the bottle down into the trash-box instead of nonchalantly tossing it in as an innocent man would have done. The clerk, a smart fellow, adroitly lied out of it to the satisfaction of the Old Man, but much to Woof's disgust. Numerous times afterwards when Woof thought the clerk was off his guard he would ask with a clumsy attempt to be jocular, "Now didn't you really have that bottle of liquor that day?" But the man knew him too well to confess.

If Woof had been a coward as well as a martinet, it is doubtful whether his men would have hated him so, though they might well have respected him less. But the man was brave as a lion. One Saturday morning before the weekly inspection when the entire company was busy cleaning rifles, brushing equipment, lining beds, arranging trunks, folding blankets, shining shoes and putting buttons in freshly laundered khaki coats, a man went insane. He had concealed about him a clip of ball cartridges. These he shoved into the magazine of his Springfield and began firing indiscriminately in the crowded barracks. At the first shot everybody started in alarm. At the second shot the company deserted the building via windows and doors. Then Woof came on the scene. His little eyes red with anger, his lips drawn back in Rooseveltian style, exposing his magnificent teeth, he came running down the veranda, the lather streaming from one side of his face. "Why don't some of you people stop that man?" he breathlessly scolded. "Why don't you stop him," somebody yelled from under the barracks. Woof did. Leaping through the door nearest to the lunatic, he snatched the loaded rifle from his hands as the third shot was fired and knocked him unconscious with the rifle butt. Then, after the ambulance had taken the fellow to the Post Hospital, Woof yelled down through the barracks: "All right! You people hurry up and get ready for inspection!"

Another time, the company barber, crazed from drinking Bay Rum cocktails, locked himself in his shop, and, surrounded with his large assortment of razors, defied anyone to enter. The assembled crowd held back. Then two non-commissioned officers lunged against the door, broke the lock and prepared to rush the fortress—but they also stopped short. Inside the sagging door stood the erstwhile peaceful barber, a wild look in his booze-reddened eyes and a bright blade in his hand. The non-coms fell back in respect. At this juncture Woof rushed up. Thrusting the crowd aside, he lunged forward and almost broke the barber's jaw with his huge fist, saying at the same time, "Whatta you *mean;* causin' all this disturbance?"

When the government finally decided to join the crusade for democracy in April, 1917 orders came to the regiment for some eighty non-commissioned officers to be sent to Uncle Sam's jim crow officers' training camp. When the contingent left in June, Woof was in it. Four months later he became a captain in the National Army. No one strutted more proudly. No officer looked more imposing. Then he went on leave to visit his wife in Louisville and immediately created a disturbance there. White soldiers avoided him to escape saluting a black officer. This dodge was not lost on Woof. One day two Nordic sergeants deliberately turned their backs on him and gazed unconcernedly into a shop window. In a fury, Woof accosted them, bawled them out and made them salute. "You people ain't salutin' *me,*" he informed them fiercely. "You're salutin' my rank." The incident was observed by hundreds of outraged Nordic passersby. A great hubbub arose and the newspapers carried considerable comment. Everything blew over, however, when an old Confederate general spoke out and said that the captain had done his duty. That was sufficient for any Southern town.

You probably expect to hear that Woof died in France leading his company over the top. He didn't. When his thirty years in harness were almost up, he resigned his commission, re-enlisted, and was retired on First-Sergeant's pay. Learning that his wife had violated her marriage vows while he was busy soldiering, he promptly divorced her, married again and settled down in an Arizona town. In his letters to me he dwelt at length on the ease of his life. "I've got the Bear muzzled," he wrote once, and then went on to tell how he liked to lie abed mornings, with the rain beating on the window panes, and "spell out" the newspapers while his buxom wife was getting breakfast. Then the letters stopped. Soon afterward a mutual friend wrote to me that Woof had been killed by a Ford.

EDITORIAL

IN the past there have been only a few sporadic and inevitably unsuccessful attempts to provide the Negro with an independent magazine of literature and thought. Those magazines which have lived throughout a period of years have been organs of some philanthropic organization whose purpose was to fight the more virulent manifestations of race prejudice. The magazines themselves have been pulpits for alarmed and angry Jeremiahs spouting fire and venom or else weeping and moaning as if they were either predestined or else unable to do anything else. For a while this seemed to be the only feasible course for Negro journalists to take. To the Negro then the most important and most tragic thing in the world was his own problem here in America. He was interested only in making white people realize what dastards they were in denying him equal economic opportunities or in lynching him upon the slightest provocation. This, as has been said, was all right for a certain period, and the journalists of that period are not to be censored for the truly daring and important work they did do. Rather, they are to be blamed for not changing their journalistic methods when time and conditions warranted such a change, and for doing nothing else but preaching and moaning until they completely lost their emotional balance and their sense of true values. Every chord on their publicist instrument had been broken save one, and they continued raucously to twang this, unaware that they were ludicrously out of tune with the other instruments in their environment.

Then came the so-called renaissance and the emergence of the so-called new (in this case meaning widely advertised) Negro. As James Weldon Johnson says in the current issue of Harper's magazine: "The Negro has done a great deal thru his folk art creations to change the national attitudes toward him; and now the efforts of the race have been reinforced and magnified by the individual Negro artist, the conscious artist. Overnight, as it were, America became aware that there were Negro artists and that they had something worthwhile to say. This awareness first manifested itself in black America, for, strange as it may seem, Negroes themselves, as a mass, had had little or no consciousness of their own individual artists." Naturally these new voices had to be given a place in Negro magazines and they were given space that hitherto had been devoted only to propaganda. But the artist was not satisfied to be squeezed between jeremiads or have his work thrown haphazardly upon a page where there was no effort to make it look beautiful as well as sound beautiful. He revolted against shoddy and sloppy publication methods, revolted against the patronizing attitudes his elders assumed toward him, revolted against their editorial astigmatism and their intolerance of new points of view. But revolting left him without a journalistic asylum. True, he could, and did, contribute to the white magazines, but in doing this almost exclusively he felt that he was losing touch with his own group, for he knew just how few Negroes would continually buy white magazines in order to read articles and stories by Negro authors, and he also knew that from a sense of race pride, if nothing more, there were many Negroes who would buy a Negro magazine.

The next step then was for the artist himself to produce this new type of journal. With little money but a plethora of ideas and ambition he proceeded to produce independent art magazines of his own. In New York, *Fire* was the pioneer of the movement. It flamed for one issue and caused a sensation of which had never been known in Negro journalism before. Next came *Black Opals* in Philadelphia, a more conservative yet extremely worthwhile venture. Then came *The Quill* in Boston which was to be published whenever its sponsors felt the urge to bring forth a publication of their own works for the benefit of themselves and their friends. And there were other groups of younger Negroes in Chicago, Kansas City and Los Angeles who formed groups to bring out independent magazines which never became actualities.

This last development should have made someone realize that a new type of publication was in order. The old propagandistic journals had served their day and their generation well, but they were emotionally unprepared to serve a new day and a new generation. The art magazines, unsoundly financed as they were, could not last. It was time for someone with vision to found a wholly new type of magazine, one which would give expression to all groups, one which would take into consideration the fact that this was a new day in the history of the American Negro, that this was a new day in the history of the world and that new points of views and new approaches to old problems were necessary and inescapable.

Harlem hopes to fill this new need. It enters the field without any preconceived editorial prejudices, without intolerance, without a reformer's cudgel. It wants merely to be a forum in which all people's opinions may be presented intelligently and from which the Negro can gain some universal idea of what is going on in the world of thought and art. It wants to impress upon the literate members of the thirteen million Negroes in the United States the necessity of becoming "book conscious," the necessity of reading the newer Negro authors, the necessity of realizing that the Negro is not the only, nor the worst mistreated minority group in the world, the necessity of sublimating their inferiority complex and their extreme race sensitiveness and putting the energy, which they have hitherto used in moaning, and groaning, into more concrete fields of action. To this end Harlem will solicit articles on current events, essays of the more intimate kind,

short stories and poetry from both black and white writers; the only qualification being that they have sufficient literary merit to warrant publication. Harlem will also promote debates on both racial and non-racial issues, giving voice to as many sides as there seem to be to the question involved. It will also be a clearing house for the newer Negro literature, striving to aid the younger writers, giving them a medium of expression and intelligent criticism. It also hopes to impress the Negro reading public with the necessity for a more concerted and well-balanced economic and political program. It believes that the commercial and political elements within the race are just as in need of clarification as the literary element and will expend just as much energy and time in the latter fields as in the former.

This is Harlem's program, its excuse for existence. It now remains to be seen whether the Negro public is as ready for such a publication as the editors and publishers of Harlem believe it to be.   WALLACE THURMAN.

FOREST FIRE

And I have seen a forest fire;
God, it was an awful thing!
It crept with scarlet tongues,
Fire!
Higher.
It lapped at the soft white rim
Of the dogwood blooms;
It flung orange and black
Scarves to hang in a mocking wrack,
That made green leaves shrivel and curl in
     despair;

Pointed ironic fingers here and there
In the cool caverns of moss,
Turning the gold of foliage to dross;
Till the forest, panting in shame,
Gave its virginal beauty to the flame
That left it a stark, black hag
Stripped
Of soul and beauty and love,
Whipped
By the Forest Fire!
     ALICE DUNBAR-NELSON

FICTION

Ah! love!
I shall not seek to penetrate
Your webbed gauze
Nor tease my heart
By queries deep,
But hold you tenderly;
The day is evening,
And I must cull my flowers
'Ere dark.
     GEORGIA DOUGLAS JOHNSON.

Backstage Glamour

Theophilus Lewis

SHOW folks are great believers in luck. If you ask the average actor to relate the story of his success, if any, the chances are ten-to-one that he will ignore such elements as pluck and perseverance and describe his career as a series of "breaks." By the "breaks" the actor means those unpredictable vagaries of fortune which advance or retard success, and it is the constant anticipation of the breaks which gives show business most of its color and glamour.

The pre-production and between-performance drill of an actor is hard and monotonous work. The neophyte hoofer performs labors in rehearsal that would break a stevedore's heart if not his legs. And the latter's pay envelope is fatter and more dependable. Backstage drudgery has driven many a would-be chorus girl back to the laundry. Only a girl that's pure in heart can make the front line. But the stevedore does not live in anticipation of the stroke of luck that will take him off the dock and put him in the office. He knows that if he is ever promoted to straw boss it will be because he demonstrates his ability to handle freight and handle men. On the other hand the fledgling hoofer, and the veteran hoofer as well, is constantly on the lookout for the big break that will put his name in electric lights. The chorine is buoyed up by the hope that even if the break does not bring her professional preferment it will at least make her look appealing to the eye of some gay dog with a fat bankroll and a fat head, who will elevate her to the status of a cocotte.

The universal anticipation of the breaks in the show world keeps its denizens, tyros and patriarchs alike, perpetually sensitive and alert. Backstage and in the outside haunts of actors the atmosphere is continuously charged with the enthusiasm of folks overflowing with great expectations. No actor who has not yet made the the grade ever has the slightest doubt that Fortune will ultimately smile on him. It never occurs to him that the jade may continue to laugh in his face. Stick around and the break is sure to come, is the universal belief. It may be long delayed, but it is inevitable. If an outsider is bold enough to express a hint of skepticism he is immediately overwhelmed with case examples from the careers of the reigning and departed great, each of whom, it seems, was catapulted

to the peaks, as it were, by a stroke of luck.

A classic break was the incident which veteran performers declare started the team of Williams and Walker on the road to fame. One of the partners of the team, Bert Williams, rose to be the leading American low-comedian of his time. Walker became famous, too, but years before either of them tasted success they were just another pair of actors playing the small-time houses of Chicago and having a hard time keeping in contact with their meals. They were staying in Chicago only because they could not get enough money ahead to pay their railroad fare anywhere else. Their outlook was as black as Bert's face when he appeared in makeup. Instead of getting better their luck got worse until there came a week when they were the only unengaged team in Chicago. Although they did not know it, being out of work just at that time was the break.

While they were waiting for something to turn up a booking agent got a rush order to send an act to West Baden, Indiana. The agent did not think much of the colored team but as it was the only act available he sent it along. It happened that the act was needed to fill a gap in a show being staged for the entertainment of a convention of the Show Managers of America. Oddly enough, the team which had been knocking about the small time houses without creating much comment went over big with the critical audience composed of men who knew, or were supposed to know, the show racket from every angle. But that was only half the break.

During the performance a New York manager received a telegram which informed him that one of his shows in the big city had opened to a cold house. The manager had just seen Williams and Walker and without waiting to see the rest of the bill he went to their dressing-room and engaged them for an immediate appearance in New York. Their addition to the New York show changed the production which had been a flop to a sensational hit and "made" the team of Williams and Walker. The rest was gravy.

Sometimes the break for a coming actor is the illness or temperamental disposition of some reigning star. Florence Mills got a chance to appear before a Broadway audience as a result of a disagreement between the man-

23

agement of "Shuffle Along" and the leading lady, Daniel Haynes, who had never been on the stage before, was given a leading role when Charles Gilpin fell ill three days before the opening. The play, "The Inside of the Cup," was short lived; but it gave Haynes his hour in the limelight. Subsequently he was given the leading male role in "Earth," a play which had a longer run, and still later he appeared in "Rang Tang." Recently he understudied Jules Bledsoe in "Show Boat." At present he is working for King Vidor in "Halleluiah," the first colored talking picture.

Frank Wilson, who plays the title role in "Porgy," was also the beneficiary of a star's fit-of-temperament. The play was "In Abraham's Bosom" and Wilson was understudying the leading part but entertaining no hope of ever playing it. The play moved from the Provincetown Theatre to more commodious quarters on Broadway and Julius Bledsoe, now "Jules" Bledsoe, chose that time to exhibit his temperament. He failed to show up for a performance, and after delaying the curtain to the last possible moment the management sent Wilson in to take the lead. Wilson's portrayal of the part, according to the critics, surpassed that of the original star and the management decided to worry along without Mr. Bledsoe for the remainder of the run.

Clever actors have been known to make their own breaks. An instance of this kind was the exploit of a colored actor, who, because of the nature of the case, I will call Mr. X. This Mr. X. was in the gallery of a New Orleans theatre when a prominent white actor introduced the Texas Tommy in that town. After carefully noting the climax of each step Mr. X went home and arranged a Texas Tommy of his own which consisted of all climaxes. A few weeks later both actors were booked in Chicago at the same time. The Texas Tommy, while not new in that city, was still a popular dance, and the white actor got a big hand at every performance. At another theatre a few blocks away Mr. X. was stopping the show.

Backstage romance is another element that keeps show life glowing with color. Every actor who has been in the profession long enough to gather memories includes among them several fetching stories of how professional interest has led to tenderer relations.

Love almost wrecked the old Lafayette Players at the beginning of their career. A leading member of the company, who subsequently achieved national fame, fell in love with one of the least-talented women and refused to accept a part for himself unless his inamorata was also given a conspicuous role. The result was that both the star and his flame were forced to sever their connections with the company; but they were married shortly afterward and for years they have lived an ideal wedded life.

The tender passion also united the careers of the late George and Aida Walker. A tobacco company had engaged Williams and Walker to pose for some Cake Walking pictures to be used in advertising their product. Walker, who was without a dancing partner at the time, requested one Stella Wiley to get a girl friend who could dance and meet himself and Williams at the studio. Miss Wiley happened to meet Aida Walker, at that time Aida Reed, and induced her to complete the foursome. Aida earned twenty dollars posing for the pictures and returned home without paying any special attention to George; at least so the story goes.

Some time later the manager of Williams and Walker saw the Cake Walk pictures in a store window. He decided to produce the dance on the stage, but to obtain the benefit of the tobacco advertising he insisted on the same costumes and the same girls. When Walker sent for Miss Reed this time she refused to come. She had been on the stage before and her experience had not been any too pleasant. When his messenger returned with Aida's refusal Walker decided to go see her himself. Several visits were required to persuade her to join the show, and then she agreed to remain with the company only so long as it ran in New York.

The Cake Walk was a huge success. It is said it was the first act in America to be forced to play two houses a night—Coster and Biel's in New York and Beaman's in Brooklyn. Before the New York run of the show was concluded Miss Reed must have changed her mind about not leaving town with the company. Perhaps she made her remaining with the show conditional. At any rate she went with the company on the road—as Mrs. Walker.

What Price Glory in Uncle Tom's Cabin

RICHARD BRUCE

I WAS sitting in at the professional matinee of "Goin' Home." Rialto to the left of me, Rialto to the right. Stock actors. Broadway and the provinces well represented. Numerous and multi-colored representatives from Broadway's sepia productions. Blackbirds' and Porgy-ites. I was bowing to people whose names I could not recall and telling them how much I liked (or disliked) their performances which I *could* remember. A string quintet playing from one of the boxes silenced me. The lights grew dim and the curtain rose.

What Price Glory in Uncle Tom's Cabin?

I watched Madam Du Bois receive, in the absence of her husband, the concentrated praise of all France. I witnessed M. Du Bois, in an Indian makeup, trying hard to shuffle (all Negroes of the type he was portraying shuffle) as a nigger would. I witnessed some superb acting. Not flawless, of course, but excepting the Indian makeup and nigger shuffle of the many-times-decorated M. Du Bois and the obviously stagey comedy of one Mr. Bailey, a Negro soldier, very creditable acting. I listened with much interest to the unwinding of an excellent plot. And I saw with regret the curtain fall on the first act. I applauded loud and long, until stopped by the hostile eyes of two swart beauties sitting before me. It then occurred to me that the word *nigger* had been used and that I was a Negro. I hastened to the lobby. A cigarette. I met four or five friends and we chatted about plays in general, about this one in particular. I praised the acting of the Southern Major rather highly. I spoke favorably of the honorable M. Du Bois. We were warned that the curtain was about to rise on the second act. There were handshakes and promises to meet at next intermission. As I passed into the theatre I was conscious of contemptuous eyes level at me. I recognized the swart beauties, reenforced now by three gentlemen of color. Indeed, extreme color. Under their stare I may have colored (can I?) for I realized that in my criticisms to my friends in the lobby, I had been guilty of using, numberless times, the words Nigger and Cracker. I really must maintain a better hold on my tongue in the future. It was with some forebodings and dire misgivings that I returned to my seat.

Several times during the second act I caught myself in time to prevent outbursts of applause for certain bits of worthwhile effort that happened to cloak bits of propaganda; propaganda at least to the propaganda-seeking beauties before me. It would *never* do to applaud, say, the cracker entering the bedroom of the Negro's wife with intent to rape. Thank my stars *I could* applaud the clownings of the Negro soldiers. I did. Then Samba Sar's dance. His gyrations, his whoops, the brandishings of his knife, the steady boom-boom-boom of the upturned wooden bucket used as a tom-tom, all got into me. My foot was pounding (to the evident disgust of my self-appointed censors), pounding time to the intoxicating rhythm. I was worked to a frenzy when the climax was reached. When the major entered from the bedroom insolently buttoning his clothes. I held tight as Du Bois reminded him that France was not New Orleans; when he leveled a gun at the Major with intent to kill and Samba Sar, taking his friend's insult upon himself, lept toward the Southerner with his knife. Samba Sar was about to settle his friend's debt when Du Bois shot him. Curtain.

I wandered rather limply to the lobby. I met my friends and we rehashed the last act. And then I saw those baleful condemning eyes again. Hastily and with a splutter, *nigger* became Negro, and *cracker* was elevated (God forgive me) to the status of Southerner. And still those condemning contemptuous eyes. It was then that I realized the magnitude of my crime. At each intermission the friends with whom I had discussed the play had been *White.* The people before whom I had used the word nigger had been *White.* Well, please God, I could not help it. I *knew* them. I did not know the Blackbirds and things, except as an audience knows its paid entertainers. And the Porgies, well, I saw them much too often to expect a new view in anything from the majority of them. They would like the Negroes in the play and the favorable propaganda. No more. Acting was only incidental. The play would, of course, be bad because the nigger (pardon) Negro, was an handkerchief-head. No views except time worn and familiar prejudices and I wanted new views or at least new angles on old prejudices. And I had unconsciously drifted to the people frank enough to voice their's plainly and boldly.

The eyes still condemned. My reaction was ludicrous. Du Bois became instead of 'soft Negro,' loud nigger and the Major fell back in his proper title, cracker. I no longer needed the subconscious corroboration that such was their actual relationship. That it cannot be cracker and Negro because they do not balance. That it cannot be cracker and Negro merely to salve raw wounds. There *are* crackers and there are *niggers* and anyhow . . . . The lights warned us of the last act.

I left the theatre gratified. A good show. Play weak in construction, strong lines, excellent individual psychology and acting. And I was happy. I had dodged the contemptuous eyes.

Happy too soon. After dinner I was talking of the play with certain Porgy-ites, and happened to criticize the performance of one of the Negro actors. I said that, my opinion was that he, having a (to race conscious Negroes) sympathetic part, should have appeared to a much better advantage than he had. That he was

stiff. Fathers protect me. I should have known better. They were all personal friends of his and they were Negroes as was he. I was assailed on all sides. Who was I to call this acclaimed actor (Negro) stiff? Mr. Dale, Mr. Woollcott had not thought so. What did I know about acting. And when I called attention to the fact that the acclaimed gentlemen had possibly been too engrossed criticizing the *acting* in the play to notice him, that, in other words, they may possibly not have considered him worthy of strict criticism, or that possibly being a Negro, which they were not, I might possibly be more aware of the delicate shadings and nuances of the part psychologically and therefore able (maybe) to render a word or two of criticism, that in a word my opinion was mine, I was booed and put to shame. "It had to be me." "Always belittling my own race." "Just like a nigger." Someone shouted from a dressing room. "If you all like that you like 'The Birth of a Nation'." So, after all, What Price Glory in Uncle Tom's Cabin?

꙾꙾꙾

MEMORABILIA

EFFIE LEE NEWSOME

There are hoarded in my mind
Little detached memories
That to me have the beauty and value
Of jewels—
A Sonora dove under the limpid drip
Of pepper tree leaves
With tender fringe of blue green rain
That never falls.
A spider web at dawn,
Woven to angles evanescent as wishes
And jeweled with green sweet dew.
The ashy blue green of millet,
The wistful blue green of millet,
The nest that some oriole has left
For the winter's stare;
The wan basket waved by the winds,
Like the door of a deserted cabin.
A deserted cabin
With swelling sorrel broom tides

That sweep toward the untrodden step
And threshold.
The austere grace of Anunciation lilies.
The cold tender purity of a violet
That though low on the earth
Lifts and lifts one,
Purging the soul like velvet fire
The dainty subtlety that Romney
Gave to the mouths of women.
The ineffable epochs
That Leonardo hid there.
Leonardo's rocks,
Leonardo's waters.
Chopin's restless spirit
Stirring in his music,
The detached wing of a butterfly
With silver gems upon it.
The music in the movement of a gull,
Riding, riding, riding!

Two Dollars

By George W. Little

THE Dew Drop Inn was masked behind an innocent window front. A passer-by would have noticed only a solitary Negro leaning back in a chair against the wall, and a dusty unused bootblack stand. To the right of the chair and its occupant was a door. This was the entrance to the Inn.

The Inn was an L shaped affair. The long part of the L contained the tables, a space for dancing and at the rear a bar. The short part of the L was partitioned off into a shrine devoted to the fickle goddess of chance.

The ceiling of the main room was hung with red and white streamers of crepe paper—dust covered and faded. From the center of the room depended a bowl-shaped frosted light; red crepe paper had been stuffed into the bowl to dim the radiance of the light. An orchestra consisting of a trap drum and a piano occupied the left side of the room. Beyond this and a step down was the bar, a small place about six feet in length. On one end of the counter was a cash register, on the other a barrel.

Happy and Mary arrived when affairs were at their height. Almost every table was filled. The waiters were busy carrying hooch, chicken, ginger ale and pig's feet to the patrons. A plump brown skin girl with protruding front teeth, thick lips and straightened hair sticking out ludicrously, was playing the piano without sheet music for a guide, while at her right a trap drummer with a sloping forehead and skin black as night, rolled a cigar stub between his thick and flabby lips and nodded his head in time with the music, now and then coming in with a roll on the small drum or a thump on the large one as his fancy dictated.

The entertainer was singing "I Wonder Where My Sweetie Is Tonight." She was almost black, her head was small and well shaped. She wore her hair long and caught back in a roll at her neck. She was slightly above medium height and had a figure in which suppleness and voluptuousness were combined to a pleasing degree. Her calves and ankles were exquisitely proportioned—a delight to the eye. She had a voice of strength and clarity. She sang without effort. She moved her body in rhythm with her song. After she had finished singing she lifted the curtain on an exquisite scene of chiffon lingerie and blond hose and danced the Charleston. Her efforts were abetted by exclamations from the patrons such as,

"Ah, play wid it!"

"Stan' up in there!"

"Do that thing!"

"Now do it!"

The girls secured a table and looked for Mom. Finally they located her near the orchestra—a dowdy little brown skin woman approaching stout middle age. Her hair was streaked with grey, her hat perched precariously on top of her head as if undecided which way to fall, the pince nez with long gold chain which Mom always affected stood out in austere and dignified contrast to her abandoned gestures. Mom was voicing sweet nothings such as, "I'll love you all over the world! My lover! My big handsome man! My brownskin papa!" The object of her adoration watched her hat in a fascinated sort of way as she made these slobbering expressions. Having failed to quiet her he was trying to drink himself into a state of unconsciousness.

People at the other tables laughed and commented now and then encouragingly, spurring the love sick lady to further declarations.

The two girls laughed heartily and watched the play. Finally Mom, casting a scorching glance at her escort, said, "Let's go, dear one, where we can be alone."

The man, before replying, drained the half-full half-pint into a glass and gulped it down. "Yes, woman, let's go, for cryin' out loud!"

The crowd laughed only as Negroes can laugh—heartily and unrestrainedly. Mom and her man left.

The waiter came for the girls' order.

"Two straight eights and two bottles of ginger ale," said Mary.

He glided through the tables to the bar behind which presided a baldheaded old man with the face of a mischievous pickaninny, all the more ludicrous because of an artificial eye which stared steadily and unwinkingly when he gazed at anyone.

The order was taken and two half-pints of amber colored fluid were laid flat on the tray—they gave off a pungent and somewhat fetid odor. The old man sighed as he recalled the days of rot-gut whiskey and temperance.

"Mary," said Happy, after the second drink, "I'm goin' in and see what that nigger of mine is doin'."

27

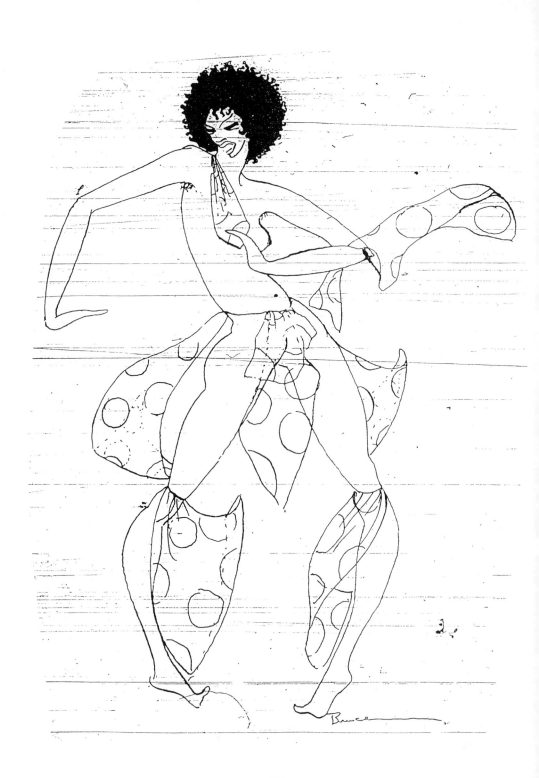

"Ah, let him alone. A man don't want no woman draggin' after him all the time."

"Well, I'm goin' anyhow," and she suited her actions to the words.

There were two tables in the backroom. A medium sized wooden table around which were men playing cards, and a pool table. The pool table was the center of attraction. Above it hung a light protected by a conical tin shade painted black. The light illuminated every crevice on the table, then, spent and subdued, was reflected back on the faces of those who crowded about the table. On one side of the table was a man who cut the game. He was seated on a high stool. He was a smooth skinned brown man, his hair cut so close as to give the scalp a shaved appearance. His skull slanted backward, the occiput coming almost to a peak. Below this were two transverse lines of fat which marred the beginning of his neck. He was heavy jowled and loose mouthed. He looked like a brown slug.

Opposite him a raw-boned youth of darker brown, wearing a dirty cap and shirt open at the neck, with shabby shoes and trousers to complete his outfit, caught the dice after each pass was made, called out the numbers and gave each man the dice as his turn came. He also threw the fat man a nickel for each bet, this was the "cut" the house got.

"Five and a tray—his point is eight!"

A Jew rattled the dice and flicked them across the mid line of the table. The speckled cubes raced neck to neck, struck the rubber cushion opposite and came to a stop.

"Five and two—crap! Next! What's the bet—dollar—five. The gentleman's point is nine!"

The gentleman was Slim, who had been breaking even for the last two hours. Happy watched him. He was good looking, she thought, and he could love. He was just a spoilt child, that was all. She couldn't turn him loose. If he wins he'll feel better and won't act so tight and mean . . . .

"Nine right! Gentleman shoots all!"

The tide had changed. Slim won consistently. Happy dared not speak to him or touch him. The winning went into two figures, then into three. The battle concentrated between Slim and the Jew. Slim continued to win until the Jew called upon the God of his fathers, but that deity was either out or busy or deaf, for Slim continued to hold the dice.

Finally Slim, with his pockets full of crumpled bills left the room. He was drunk and blind with elation.

She followed him shortly afterwards, rejoicing in his good fortune. She would not let know she had been present. She would let him think he was surprising her. The Slovak's two dollars which she had given him had been lucky. . . .

She returned to the cabaret and looked about. Mary was talking to some man who was seated at the table. Slim was nowhere in sight. She accosted a waiter.

"Where's Slim?"

"Just went out this minute," he answered, hurrying past.

Going home to tell me, Happy thought. She hastened homeward. The house could be reached in ten minutes' walk. She would pretend that she had gone to the movies or had just stepped out to the store. Maybe they would tell him she had gone to the cabaret, but she could say she changed her mind. She opened the door and saw Babe lying in the window seat.

"Where's Slim?"

"Damn if I know. I tho't he was over at the Inn."

"Oh, isn't he here?"

"No——."

She went to her room somewhat disconsolate. Well—perhaps he went to get something to eat. Three hours passed. She heard Mary come in and finally she could stand it no longer. She dressed and walked outside. It was that period just before dawn when even inanimate things seem to sleep. Occasionally the sky took on an evil red glare from the distant mills, and during this time the steel rails of tracks running parallel to the street gleamed and the shabby houses, the uneven paving and all the squalor of the street flashed into view.

Happy saw a cab cross the tracks and pull up to the curb. She walked toward it, half hoping it was he. She reached the corner and halted, drawing back into the shadow of the walk. It was Slim. He was talking to some one in the cab. She could not see who it was. At last the cab pulled away and then the occupant looked through the back window and waved to Slim. It was a woman.

"Tomorrow!" he called after her.

Happy's first impulse was to rush out and catch the cab. She wanted to tear the grinning face to shreds, but she controlled the impulse. Her hate turned toward the man. He was singing to himself as he turned the corner. "A man gets tired, yes, mighty tired, of one woman all the time. . . ."

Happy clinched her teeth and let him pass. She waited long enough to make sure he was in the house, then followed him.

Slim was undressing when she came in. He didn't look at her but crawled into bed and composed himself for sleep. Being wise in the ways of a woman he knew she would soon break the silence. He was not wrong. She tossed her hat in the corner, tore loose her dress and then turned to him.

At last she spoke, slowly and with a forced calm.

"You dirty rat—you've struck me for the last time. I know everything that's happened to-night. You've double-crossed me long enough. You think I'm a fool, don't you? Well I have been. I've treated you too damn nice but now I'm gonna make you pay for it."

Slim laughed contemptuously. He had heard talk like that before. "Aw, dry up woman and sleep it off."

"You think I'm bluffin', don't you?"

She flung herself at him and before he could recover from his surprise her hands were at his throat. Her fingers contracted viciously, the long nails sinking into his flesh. He realized she meant to kill him and fought desperately, striking at her head and body. Her face was close to his—she reached down and sank her teeth into his cheek. He tried to scream but only made a hoarse croaking sound. His struggles became weaker—a body weakened by debauchery and disease was too fragile to withstand such an onslaught—his tongue lolled out and his eyes protruded. She straightened up and looked into his face. The cheek she had bitten was swollen and bloody. The face was dusky, the lips thick and dry. He gave a little moaning sound and coughed, a bloody froth came to his lips.

Her anger had burnt itself out. She had punished him.

"Now I guess you know I ain't bluffin'."

No answer.

"Slim! Slim!!!"

He was not breathing. She felt for his heart. There was no sign of life.

She gave a shriek.

"My God, my daddy's dead!"

She put the bed clothes over the corpse in futile hope of warming it and then as that disfigured face, still wearing a look of stupid amazement at the sudden advent of death, stared up at her she shrieked again and again.

The door opened and Mom, clad in a silk dressing gown which betrayed the devastation that wear and tear of time had wrought on her

figure, rushed into the room in a state of despair. With eyes bleared by her recent debauch she did not at once comprehend the tragedy.

"Why don't you niggers keep quiet, do you want us raided?"

"He's dead—" Happy gasped.

"Dead—dead?" then stark reality caused Mom to wring her hands and give vent to her feelings. "My God, we're all ruined, we're all ruined! Look what you've done! You damned fool! You've got us all in trouble! Well, you'll pay for it, by God you'll pay for it—" she shoved the fainting girl away from her.

By this time the house was aroused and soon all of the occupants were in the room in various states of excitement and undress. The greyness of fear was on every face. They stood and stared at Slim, who lay there with the mute indifference of the dead.

Happy rose to her feet from where she had been lying, her face buried in her hands after Mom had shoved her. The paroxysm of rage and grief had passed, leaving the calm of resignation.

"Well, I done it an' I don't give a damn, and as for you—" she turned toward Mom who was moaning furiously—"I ain't asked nothing of you and never intend to. Call the wagon and let me ride. It's all on me—I'm paying for it."

As if in response to her summons there was the noise of a motor without and a pounding on the door. The officer on the beat had been rudely awakened by the shrieks of Happy and sagely realizing that there was safety in numbers, and also being too modest to take credit by handling the situation alone, had called the wagon. Babe opened the door.

"What the hell's the matter—" queried the sergeant pointedly.

"Happy's killed a guy upstairs."

The squad of six men stirred uneasily.

"You needn't be afraid, she just told us to call the wagon."

"Who the hell's afraid, you nigger wench!" he growled. "Put her in the wagon, Mac-Clancy. You watch the back and you the front," he detailed two men, "and the rest of you officers come with me." The intrepid sergeant, followed by his fearless retainers ascended the stairs cautiously. Mom met them in the hallway.

"Oh, sergant, sergant, oh, oh!"

"Take care of her, Sweeny." Sweeny promptly put on handcuffs. The sergeant entered the

(Continued on page 45)

High, Low, Past and Present

Wallace Thurman

The Walls of Jericho, by Rudolph Fisher (Alfred Knopf: $2.50)
Quicksand, by Nella Larsen (Alfred Knopf: $2.50)
Adventures of an African Slaver, by Captain Canot (Albert & Charles Boni: $4.00)

I HAD already written a review of *The Walls of Jericho* and was about to send it into the printer when I chanced to open a copy of *The Crisis* for November, and found therein a review of the same work by W. E. B. Du Bois. The following paragraph set my teeth on edge and sent me back to my typewriter hopping mad. Listen to this:

"Mr. Fisher does not yet venture to write of himself and his own people; of Negroes like his mother, his sister and his wife. His real Harlem friends and his own soul nowhere yet appear in his pages, and nothing that can be mistaken for them. The glimpses of better class Negroes which he gives us are poor, ineffective make-believes. One wonders why? Why does Mr. Fisher fear to use his genius to paint his own kind, as he has painted Shine and Linda? Perhaps he doubts the taste of his white audience although he tries it severely with Miss Cramp. Perhaps he feels too close to his own to trust his artistic detachment in limning them. Perhaps he really laughs at all life, and believes nothing. At any rate, here is a step upward from Van Vechten and McKay —a strong, long, interesting step. We hope for others."

The more I reread the above lines the more angry and incoherent I became. I was not so much worried about the effect such a narrow and patronizing criticism would have on Mr. Fisher or on any other of Dr. Du Bois' audience who might take it seriously, as I was concerned for what it tokened for the reviewer himself. Were he a denizen of "Striver's Row," scuttling hard up the social ladder, with nothing more important to think about than making money and keeping a high yellow wife bleached out and marcelled, one would laugh at such nonsense and dismiss it from one's mind. But Dr. Du Bois is not this. He is one of the outstanding Negroes of this or any other generation. He has served his race well; so well, in fact, that the artist in him has been stifled in order that the propagandist may thrive. No one will object to this being called a noble and necessary sacrifice, but the days for such sacrifices are gone. The time has come now when the Negro artist can be his true self and pander to the stupidities of no one, either white or black.

Anyone with a knowledge of literature and the people who write it should know that when the truly sincere artist begins to write he does not take into consideration what the public might say if his characters happen to be piano movers or his wife and sister. He is drawn toward certain characters and certain situations which interest him and which seem worth writing about. There happens to be no Will Hays or Judge Landis of literature to say: "Nay, nay, dear scribe. Don't you dare write about such and such a situation or such and such a character. They're not nice. What will the best people in the community think?" It happens that most writers have all been able and brave enough to say, "To hell with what the best people in the community think," because they know that generally speaking, the best people in the community do not think at all. The entire universe is the writer's province and so are all the people therein, even lower class Negroes, and if they happen to attract the writer there is no reason why he shouldn't write about them. Nor is it implied here that all Negro writers should write only of "the half world above 125th Street," for such an implication would be just as ridiculous as the one being constantly made by Dr. Du Bois.

The Walls of Jericho is a disappointing book from the standpoint that Mr. Fisher's short stories, published off and on for the past three years, have led one to believe that his first novel would be a more unusual piece of work. And it *is* unusual in one respect, being the first novel written by a Negro wherein the author handles his theme and writes with enviable ease; the first novel written by a Negro which does not seem to be struggling for breath because the author insists upon being heavy handed either with propaganda as in *Dark Princess* or with atmosphere as in *Home to Harlem*. Mr. Fisher keeps his proportions well, almost too well, and despite what Dr. Du Bois says, does not give us any "ineffectual make believes" when a "better class Negro" appears on the

31

scene. But after that what have you? Some brilliant bits of authentic dialogue, some biting caricatures, viz; Miss Cramp, but no sustained characterizations or anything vital, truely indicative of the gifts Mr. Fisher so ably displayed in one of the best short stories of Negro life ever written: *The City of Refuge.*

Had this novel been written by some of the lesser lights, or greater ones for that matter, among Negro authors, one's applause would be less constrained. But here is the case where the author lays himself open to criticism not because he has not been good, but because he has not been good enough. However, I am glad that Mr. Fisher has this off his chest, glad that he has proven that it is not necessary for a Negro writer to moan and groan and sweat through a book simply because he is a Negro, and I hope he comes across in the near future with something that will not be a let-down from the man who could write the remarkable short story mentioned above. More, I even hope he takes Dr. Du Bois' suggestion and applies his artistic detachment to his own kind and I hope he includes Dr. Du Bois in his gallery of characters. Then the fun will really begin, and I know of no one better than Mr. Fisher to do this as it should be done.

The author of *Quicksand* no doubt pleases Dr. Du Bois for she stays in her own sphere and writes about the sort of people one can invite to one's home without losing one's social prestige. She doesn't give white people the impression that all Negroes are gin drinkers, cabaret hounds and of the half world. Her Negroes are all of the upper class. And how! Nevertheless, one has to admit that the performance here is a little less impressive than Mr. Fisher's. Not because of her people or because of the milieu in which they move, but purely because the author seems to be wandering around lost, as lost as her leading character who ends up by doing such an unexpected and inexplainable thing that I was forced to reread the book, wondering, if in my eagerness to reach the end, I had perhaps skipped a hundred pages or so. But no, such had not been the case. Helga does get blown into the gutter and Helga does let herself be carried away by a religious frenzy to the point where she marries a Southern minister and spends the rest of her life having babies. This would have been all right for anyone except the Helga to whom Miss Larsen had introduced us, and even then it would have been all right had the author even as much as hinted that some day her char-

acter might do either the expected or the unexpected. But for the most part all Helga ever does is run away from certain situations and straddle the fence; so consistently, in fact, that when she does fall on the dark side the reader has lost all interest and sympathy, nor can he believe that such a thing has really happened.

Captain Canot was a jolly old soul and in this narrative almost convinces one that the slave trader was a much maligned and noble creature. It wasn't his fault that there was a slave trade. Could he help it that Nordic and Latin tradesmen fomented civil strife among African tribes and bought the vanquished from the victors with brilliantly colored cloth, German glass, English rum and American tobacco? Not at all. He was just an ambitious man out in a hard world trying to make a living and having a good time while doing so. You even suspect that Captain Canot had a good time writing this narrative and can almost hear the reverberation of what Walter Winchell would call his belly laughs, as he thought of the gullibility of the human race in general and of the readers of this book in particular.

This is a book that almost anyone could enjoy, even a bitter twentieth century Negro, for it contains a wealth of information and makes good and interesting reading despite the rather turgid and bombastic style. The drawings by Covarrubias alone are worth the price of the book. If Captain Canot makes the crossing of the slaves in the middle passage seem like a luxurious and interesting event Covarrubias makes one realize just what a brutal and indescribable experience it really must have been, and what is more interesting, his delineation of African types is no less than masterful.

Captain Canot, were he alive now, would probably be a guiding spirit among rum runners, for he would never be content to participate in any but a lawless pursuit. It would please him to exchange shots with the revenue cutter, please him to drop a boat load of liquor into the ocean rather than have it taken by government officers. He did as much with slaves and despite his holy protestations that he was always kind and generous to those with whom he was entrusted, the reader can easily sense that a load of contraband slaves were to him of no more human consequence than would be a load of contraband liquor.

Yet there is no doubt much truth in what he says. Students in this field have long known that no one was more assiduous in selling their brethren into slavery than certain African

Have the best new books come to your home by mail

Get only those you want, and pay only for those you keep...
Find out how the Book-of-the-Month Club prevents over
80,000 people from missing the new books they want to read.

AGAIN and again you miss outstanding books you want to read. Through oversight or because you are too busy, you just "never get around to it." Take the Book-of-the-Month Club service—it does not cost you a cent!—and this need never happen again! How is it prevented?

The plan is simplicity itself. The publishers of the country submit their books to us in advance of publication. Every month a distinguished group of five critics chooses the most readable and most important ones—fiction and nonfiction. They also choose what they consider the "outstanding" book every month. This we call the "book-of-the-month."

Before you get the book-of-the-month, you receive a full report about it, a month before it is published. If you judge, from this report, that you want it, you let it come to you. You receive it by mail, on or shortly after the publication date, so that you can't miss it.

If one of the other books reported upon appeals to you more strongly, you specify that that one be sent. And if none of them appeal to you in any month, you take none at all!

Moreover, whenever you take a book on the recommendation of our selecting committee, you are guaranteed against dissatisfaction. If you don't like it, you may exchange it for some other book you prefer.

Over 80,000 of the most notable people in this country—in every line of endeavor—now guard themselves, by means of this service, against missing the new books they want to read. Why don't you try it? You can join this organization, and obtain the many benefits of its service, and yet take as few as four books a year. You may take more if you please, but you don't have to.

Moreover, the cost is—nothing! There are no fees, no dues, no extra charges of any kind. You pay only for the books you keep, and for them you pay the same price as if you got them from the publisher himself by mail!

Surely, among the 150 or more books our judges will report upon in 1928, there will be at least four you will be very anxious not to miss. Find out how this service will absolutely prevent you from missing them. Mail the coupon below for complete information. Your request will involve you in no obligation.

Henry Seidel Canby *Chairman*   Heywood Broun   Dorothy Canfield   Christopher Morley   William Allen White

THE SELECTING COMMITTEE OF THE BOOK-OF-THE-MONTH CLUB

tribes. It was their means of punishment to the criminal, their means of ridding the tribe of its enemies and of the unfit, their means of making away with recalcitrant parents, husbands, wives and children. And one also cannot deny that there is much truth in the author's statement that the better the slaves were cared for on their voyage the more money they would draw at the auction block. At any rate slave trading was a profitable and adventurous business and one can hardly condemn a man of Captain Canot's calibre for entering into it with so much zeal and enthusiasm. He at least made the most of his opportunities and we most certainly thank him for this book. Can one say more?

❦❦❦❦❦

Conjure Men and Black Sirens

H. Van Weber

Magie Noire (Grasset, 12 fr.), Paul Morand
La Maitresse Noire (Les Editions De France, 12 fr.), Louis Charles Royer

I

SEVERAL years ago my father told me of a South Carolina root doctor whom he had known when a boy. This root doctor could cast charms and spells on men and animals alike. Ferocious dogs refused to bite him, ran from him as from the rabies and lost their minds. People who opposed him died in mysterious accidents. Even his son could work wonders. The boy killed chickens by plucking a mysterious wing feather. That was apparently all that he did yet the chickens dropped to the ground fluttering and jumping, then died. Later I met a man who was generally supposed to be a conjurer or root doctor. He was a tall spare man. His skin was the color of a faded walnut and his shoulders were slightly stooped as though continual peering at the ground had curved them permanently. He lived in a large drab-colored house. The magnolia, oak and chestnut trees that grew around the place kept it cool and dark. Here, it was rumored, the white business men of the town came stealthily at night to peer into the future and to secure demoniac aid for their mundane endeavors. Then again in New York I boarded for a while at the home of a woman who devoutly believed in witchcraft and sorcerers. She was always going to some seance or trying out some charm that was supposed to bring good luck. She even read the Bhagavad Gita. All of these things excited my interest, contempt, or curiosity; so it was indeed interesting to find M. Paul Morand writing in "Magie Noire" or Black Magic, a collection of short stories, all on the motif of black magic.

Upon this framework Morand paints vivid and colorful pictures of the Negroes of Haiti, Louisiana, Charleston, Syracuse of the Ivory Coast of Liberia and of the Soudan. In the introduction to this book Morand tells us that before writing "Magie Noire" he travelled fifty thousand kilometres and visited twenty-eight Negroid countries. This is a large and broad canvas on which he paints his Negroes and it needs must present many different aspects and views; but the thread that unifies this book, that runs throughout the labyrinth of countries and the islands of the sea is the mystic thread of black magic. Nearly all of these Negroes either believe in or practice some occult rite. Thus on a background of picturesque Negro life and folkways, here in America, in Haiti and in Africa, Morand depicts the root doctors, the papalois, the sorcerers, portraying the future, working charms and casting spells.

The conjurer or witch doctor has always played an important part in savage life and here in civilized America, the root doctor, the West African scientist and herbist and the spiritualist, are his prototype. However, patent these practises may have been in a jungle environment, however important psychologically in Africa, South America and the islands of the Caribbean, they are certainly out of mode and impotent nowadays. The witch doctor can't compete with the trader, the missionary and the banker. His charms are futile against the persuasive machine gun and hand grenade. His knowledge of poisons is useless with invaders who live on canned food and his power over the soul comes to naught against the Nordic entrepreneur who neither believes in souls or possesses any.

As long as such papers as the *Negro World*

is filled with advertisements of companies selling black cat bones, lodestones, lucky roots, luck crystals, love rings, lucky oils, lucky salts, Oriental luck bags and such trash, we need a powerful antidote to keep us remembering that these things are useless, that black magic hasn't a ghost of a show with science or as Caruso, a Harlem street speaker, used to tell his tormentors on Seventh Avenue, that "Ignorance and superstition can't compete with intelligence." This book may not be such a powerful antidote, but in several of the stories this effect is reached.

"Congo" is a typical example of the eight short stories in this book. It tells the story of Sophie Taylor, a Creole emigré living in Paris whose nickname is Congo. At one of her fetes, while looking in a mirror, Congo notices a small black spot under her ear. Like many mulattoes she abhors blackness, so she immediately runs to invoke the aid of a voodoo doctor who holds his weird court in a bar. There, due to the influence of black magic, she sees in a vision, her old grandmother, Lizzie Dejoyé in a boat on the Mississippi near Baton-Rouge. Only this grandmother can aid her so she leaves Paris for the States and rushes South only to find her grandmother dead.

Morand's treatment of the funeral certainly would never receive a prize at any Baptist convention because he paints it in all of its ridiculous lights. The minister preaches on the famous text of "Dry-bones in the valley." He perspires and pants, imitates the bell of the locomotive, fires questions at his audience, jumps upon a chair, yelps, squeaks and in general makes a fool of himself just as the average Methodist or Baptist preacher does today, especially in the South. When he has settled the state of sister Lizzie Dejoyé's soul and placed it in heaven beyond the reach of any devil, six of the deaconesses fall to the floor with staring eyes and foaming mouths, yelling and shrieking so loudly that they frighten the mules on the farthest plantations. When this emotional frenzy abates, a song of deliverance arises. A hallelujah floats out towards the sky breathing a relief so great, so spontaneous and with a spirit so pure that one would thing it sung by prisoners who had suddenly been unchained. With all of her soul Congo shares in the passionate zeal of her black brothers, in the enthusiasm of these primitive folk, who, having skirted the borders of hell, suddenly find for the first time since the world began a god ready to help them. Her veneer of sophistication is stripped off. She forgets Broadway and the boulevards of Paris. All of the spangle and glitter of her life falls away and she sings with them, a little daughter of Ham, of the race that has been exploited, sold, beaten, martyrized, who has not deserved this fate and who can only hope for happiness in death. Leaving the funeral she is drowned while crossing the Mississippi in a ferryboat.

Morand shows in this story that he can really write beautiful and impassioned prose, and if the pious would condemn him for his cynicism in laughing at the antics of these religious zealots, they would have to admit that he only pokes fun at the ludicrous and that behind the wild emotional orgies he senses the terrible travails of body and soul that are mirrored there.

II.

In "La Maitresse Noire" M. Louis-Charles Royer has written a book around two hypotheses that most of us have always either known or believed to be true. First, that Negroes are more passionate than white people, and second that there is a strong attraction between black and white people. Royer has done for French Colonial Africa what needs to be done for Charleston, South Carolina, New Orleans, Louisiana and the United States as a whole. In spite of their different and (according to Anglo-Saxon standards) ugly features, their peculiar and distinctive odor, their predilection for pilfering the belongings of others, their lack of intelligence and ambition, the Negro has always had a potent charm for the Nordics. The number of mulattoes in this country eloquently testifies to the antipathy that every Nordic knows exists between the white and black people; and also to the fundamental, ineradicable and unescapable difference that divides the two races.

La Maitresse or The Black Mistress tells a story of the relations that exist in the Soudan between the native Africans and the whites. Robert de Coussan, a young Frenchman with a penchant for gambling on horse races, becomes involved in debt and is sent to the Soudan by his friend, Bourdier, who hopes that in Africa de Coussan will redeem himself and retrieve his money and position.

En route to Bamako he has an affair with a French woman, Mme. Colomba, then later at Bamako he spends an amorous night with Mme. Heliet, the white wife of a cotton planter. But Mme. Heliet likes Africans in general and her servant Gorko in particular so well, that when the young Frenchman leaves, she repeats with Gorko all of the fondling and caressing that she had previously gone through with Robert and ends by practically raping Gorko. Shades of Vardemann, Blease and Heflin! Whoever heard of such a thing before?

Robert goes through the initial feelings of disgust, antipathy, curiosity, and desire for the African women. On every side he sees white Frenchmen living with these African women much as the white southern planters used to live with their Negro women. He visits the home of his chief, Kervelen and watches his mousso, Matjonda, admires her beautiful eyes, large and calm as the pure water of a lake, her lovely, slender arms, in fact he thinks her ravishing. He listens to M. Bresse, a fellow Frenchman on whose barge he travels to Kambara and who has come to believe that it is the blacks who have the intelligence, opposed to the stupidity of the whites and their sterile activities. "I came to be their teacher," he tells Robert, "to civilize them. Civilization? What a good humbug. We give them our vices without relieving them of theirs." He offers one of his two moussos to Robert for the duration of their voyage and, after a slight protest, Robert shows his wisdom by selecting the one who is less beautiful, but, according to Bresse, more passionate than the other. He causes no tumult to arise in her breast for she responds to his amorous caresses without any apparent emotion but with the heredity science which the Mussulman woman have for satisfying their masters. However, on their last night aboard, when Robert, fatigued and impotent from the love making of the preceeding days is tardy in taking his pleasure, all of her sleeping emotion and lust is aroused and she draws him to her in a vice-like embrace, her thick lips open and a long tremor runs over her entire body. When she retires to her mat where she sleeps, apart from him, he is so ensnared with her charms that he leaps from his bed, throws himself alongside her and holds her in his arms until morning. He finally settles his sex problems by buying Mouk, a beautiful African girl, who is the sister of Aissatou, his friend Ligniere's mousso. Mouak is a virgin with beautiful eyes and the grace and charm of some wild forest animal. Does Robert make love to her with the gentle grace and polished technique of a cultured Frenchman? Not at all. He is so aflame with desire that he pulls her down on the sand behind a bush, tears her garments from her and slakes his desire in a savage fashion. Her sister, Aisston, comes up after they are ready to begin their march anew and pale with emotion shows de Coussan that she has given him a virgin and tells him that he is now her husband,

then she takes from Mouk the white band that she had worn as the symbol of her virginity.

Mouk and de Coussan live happily at Bamako in spite of the attempt of Mme. Heliet to ensnare Mouk in a Lesbian love affair. When his vacation time comes Robert leaves for Paris and falls in love again with his former sweetheart Yvonne. He takes her back to Africa with him but Yvonne's pink and white beauty doesn't find the hot African sun very kind nor does it improve her disposition.

Mouk is living with another Frenchman who loads her with presents and frequently de Coussan meets her standing quietly watching him or passing him with her long undulating walk.

Yvonne becomes more and more jealous and disagreeable as she discovers that Robert has had a love affair with Mme. Heliet and Mme. Colomba and has lived with an African Negro woman. Finally he leaves her in disgust and returns to Mouk. The Black Venus has won back her lover.

One night Gorko brings Yvonne a letter, presumably from Mme. Heliet, that tells her to follow him if she doesn't fear the truth. Gorko leads her to the cabin where Robert and Mouk spend their nights together. With her own eyes she sees her lover lying at ease in the house of this African woman. Yvonne walks home in a daze, lies down on the divan and arouses to feel in the dark room, someone who has touched her with his hand. It is the thoughtful Gorko who has returned to cheer her loneliness. His relations with Mme. Heliet seem to have given him a taste for French women. Gorko is evidently a broth of a boy when it comes to raping for he shows the finished technique of a master. When Yvonne screams in fright he slaps her on the mouth and without more ado makes violent love to her. At first frightened out of her wits, Yvonne, as the savage caresses awaken her passion, abandons herself to the persuasive Gorko and the brute perhaps did not know the pleasure that he had given her. When he leaves she falls into the depths of despair. She has lost Robert, all of her romance is shattered so she leaves the following day for Paris.

Mouk has changed from the simple, naive girl that she was at first. Experience has given her more sophistication and greater desires. She no longer goes out in her bare feet, but wears fine sandals of red leather. She has developed expensive tastes and in trying to satisfy them Robert falls into debt. At last he disgraces himself when he is caught tampering with the bids in Kervelen's office. He is sent to Sankoro as a last resort. Here there is no white man for him to plunder or to gamble with. Only the natives and his mousso Mouk. He lives an animal life until he loses Mouk to a passing Frenchman who seduces her with promises of fame and money made tangible by moving pictures of Parisian scenes. Robert follows her to Paris where she is dancing in a cafe. He finds her there and cuts her throat.

This is one of the best written and most colorful of the books that have been written about colonial Africa. Not since René Maran won the Goncourt prize with Batouala have we seen another book that paints with such clarity and fidelity the life of the natives and the French Colonists. It deserves a translation and will probably be used as a model when the first honest and courageous novelist decides to brave the scorn and indifference of the great American public by writing a worthwhile novel on the life of the South.

Now—where is this courageous novelist?

Three Poems

LANGSTON HUGHES.

MAZIE DIES ALONE IN THE CITY HOSPITAL

I hate to die this way with the quiet
Over everything like a shroud.
I'd rather die where the band's a-playin'
Noisy and loud.

I'd rather die in the way I lived,—
Drunk and rowdy and gay!
God! why did you ever curse me
Makin' me die this way?

HURT

Who cares
About the hurt in your heart?

Make a song like this
For a jazz band to play:

Nobody cares.
Nobody cares.

Make a song like that
From your lips.

Nobody cares.

LADY IN CABARET

She knows
The end of the evening will come,—
It has come before.
And if it should never come again,
Well,—
Just that much more
A bore.

Langston Hughes

90

On Warped Minds

JAMES EGERT ALLEN

A DEMOCRACY depends upon free speech. The degree in which free speech is limited is the degree that designates the limitations of a Democracy. Ancient Athens and antiquated Rome, lacking the ready influence of the printed page, relied upon the forensic gladiators to keep unscathed, the principle of open and unbiased discussion.

How this principle has deteriorated!

In this age of political corruption, racial hatred, bigoted education, tainted religion and Pharisaical society, free speech has been cruelly sacrificed and its exponents mercilessly crucified.

Rarely do we read a book, hear an address, or peruse a journal but that the spirit of narrowness is predominant. It seems that the mind of America is warped. Long years of tradition and standardized teaching have resulted in a one-sided view-point—a single track mind. All colors blend into one before our astigmatic vision. All unexperienced actions are labeled immoral. All new thoughts and ideas are dubbed radical and dangerous.

The pages of HARLEM are dedicated to individual freedom. Readers are not expected nor will they be asked to agree with the cullings of persons, high and low in the intellectual, moral, social and economic scale of our Literati. Rather are they asked to view the sayings with tolerance and mutual respect.

When Dean Inge of St. Paul's Cathedral, London shocked the ecclesiastical world with his ideas of liberal religion, why should he be held in contempt by some devout Episcopalian? Recently, Bishop William Montgomery Brown, the modern heretic, was unfrocked because he dared to give vent to his communistic philosophy. Should he be held up to scorn and mockery because ripe experience has taught him to believe in an unorthodox form of Christianity? Why become disgruntled, ye Baptists, because Dr. Harry Emerson Fosdick is dynamic rather than immersive in his chosen faith? Has Catholicism affected your feeling for Governor Smith? Election Day may result in Roosevelt being elected Governor of New York State merely because Ottinger comes of Jewish stock.

Over the head of Clarence Darrow, the Negro clergy has hung the Damoclean sword. Perhaps they are still more infuriated since the *Forum* magazine exposed his views on the "Myth of the Soul." Society's elite hold no brief for Oswald Garrison Villard since his vivid portrayal of their hypocrisy in his recent article, "The Blue Menace" that graces the October issue of *Harpers*. Our own W. E. B. Du Bois typifies a red flag in the estimation of the sainted, tainted D. A. R.

The liberal divine, Dr. John Haynes Holmes has lately given the world his broad attitude on "Marriage and Divorce." A letter to the magazine editor, commenting on this article brought forth this reply:

"Thank you for your cooperation with my request relative to Dr. Holmes' article, 'Marriage and Divorce.'

"So many of the reactions to this article have proved to be intolerant and biased that it is a satisfaction to know there are some who can look at it from its broader aspects, picking out the worthwhile and discarding that which seems to them unsatisfactory."

This extract pictures forcibly and vividly the warped mind of many Americans on marital relationship. In spite of the Renos, the Hollywoods and the ever increasing divorce evils, we are too biased to take the broader viewpoints that might remedy many unfortunate situations.

Because of his firm conviction, Judge Lindsey and his enviable judicial record were violently repudiated by his next door neighbors. Modern methods to regulate birth control mark Margaret Sanger as a moral leper. The sainted Jane Addams of Hull House fame is just as much misunderstood due to her efforts raise unchancy women.

A kaleidoscopic view of the trend of Mr. Average American's mind reveals a sad picture. It presents the basic cause for confusion, ignorance and deviltry. It produces narrow class groups, the closed-door idea of Christianity, the party cliques, the Ku Klux Klan, the fanatics of all descriptions and the slow, staid, impeding conservatives.

The warped mind draws the heavy line of demarcation between North and South, East and West, Catholic and Protestant, Republican and Democrat, Negro and Nordic, Jew and Gentile. To it, fellowship and reconciliation are complete strangers. It knows no creed but the creed of "Ego" and worships no god but the god of self.

Warped minds sent Alexander Meiklejohn from the confines of the East to work out his educational policies in Wisconsin. They drove Kerlin from his Pennsylvania classroom just as they are driving the heroine of Nella Larsen's *Quicksand* from many southern colleges and institutes today.

What of the future of our civilization? Men like Will Durant, H. L. Mencken, James Harvey Robinson and Charles A. Beard are expressing their opinions frequently. They agree in toto that civilization and progress are handicapped due to the distorted minds of our Republic. Unless a more liberal attitude is assumed, the future looms up before us filled with foreboding and gloom.

An open mind is the first and most essential thing in intellectual development. Tolerance must prevail in this polyglot combination of American life. If the spirit of individual evolution is to survive, one eye must always be able to envisage the deeds of the other fellow and one ear ever ready to hear the experiences of our brother in white, black or brown.

The joy of life comes from playing the game "fair and square." Warped minds can produce neither fairness nor squareness. They produce only intolerance and confusion.

Look out upon the broad expanse of the vast mental reservation with a free, unbiased, tolerant mind. Then drink in the undreamed-of pleasures, the ecstatic delights, the scintillating charms and the generous reactions that are the inevitable heritages of the sweet-spirited soul that has not defiled itself or "bent its knee before Baal."

A MISSIONARY BRINGS A YOUNG
NATIVE TO AMERICA

HELENE JOHNSON

All day she heard the mad stampede of feet
Push by her in a thick unbroken haste.
A thousand unknown terrors of the street
Caught at her timid heart, and she could taste
The city grit upon her tongue. She felt
A steel-spiked wave of brick and light submerge
Her mind in cold immensity. A belt
Of alien tenets choked the songs that surged
Within her when alone each night she knelt
At prayer. And as the moon grew large and white
Above the roof, afraid that she would scream
Aloud her young abandon to the night,
She mumbled Latin litanies and dreamed
Unholy dreams while waiting for the light.

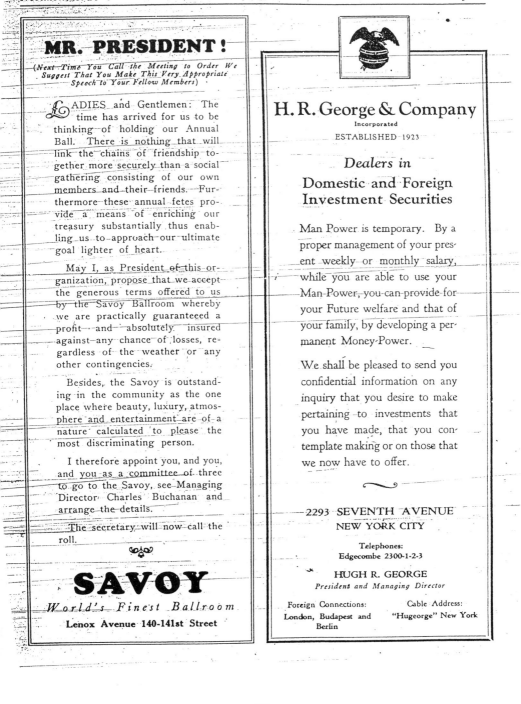

DEEP HARLEM

A STUDY IN SEPIA, BY LEON NOYES

Harlem Directory

Where To Go And What To Do When In Harlem

⟨✦⟩

THERE are four main attractions in Harlem: the churches, the gin mills, the restaurants, and the night clubs. It is not necessary here to define what churches are so we will proceed to give a list of those which attract the largest congregations:

St. Mark's A.M.E., 138th Street and St. Nicholas Avenue.
St. Philip's Episcopal, 133rd Street, between 7th and 8th Avenue.
Abyssinian Baptist, 138th Street, between Lenox and 7th.
Mother Zion, 136th Street, between Lenox and 7th.
Salem M.E., 129th Street and 7th Avenue.
Metropolitan Baptist, 128th Street and 7th Avenue.
St. Mark's Catholic, 138th Street and Lenox Avenue.
Mt. Olivet Baptist, 120th Street and Lenox Avenue.
Grace Congregational, 139th Street, between 8th Avenue and Edgecombe Avenue.

And there are innumerable smaller churches and missions, countless spiritualists' rooms, a synagogue, a mosque, and a great number of Holy Roller refuges, the most interesting of which is at 1 West 137th Street.

Gin mills are establishments which have bars, family entrances, and other pre-Volstead luxuries. For reasons best known to ourselves and the owners of these places we will not give the addresses and even were these reasons not personal, there are far too many gin mills to list here. As a clue to those of our readers who might be interested we will tell them to notice what stands on every corner on 7th, Lenox, and 8th Avenues. There are also many such comfort stations in the middle of the blocks.

The best restaurants to go to in Harlem are Tabb's, located at 140th Street and Lenox Avenue, where you can get a good chicken dinner in the Grill Room and have ragtime music while you eat. The Marguerite, on 132nd Street between Lenox and Seventh Avenues, guarantees you a full stomach. Johnny Jackson's at 135th Street and Seventh Avenue; St. Luke's on 130th Street, between Lenox and Seventh. The Venetian Tea Room on 135th Street, between Seventh and Eighth Avenues, and the Blue Grass at 130th Street and Seventh Avenue, are also good bets. If you are broke and want only coffee and rolls or a piece of pie, there are Coffee Pots next to every gin mill or if you should wish vino with your dinner there is the La Rosa on Seventh Avenue near 139th Street.

Among the best known Harlem night clubs are the Cotton Club at 142nd Street and Lenox Avenue; the Lenox Avenue Club on Lenox Avenue, between 142nd and 143rd Streets; Cairo's on 125th Street, between Lenox and Fifth Avenues; the Sugar Cane at 135th Street and 5th Avenue; Small's at 135th Street and 7th Avenue; Barron's at 134th Street and 7th Avenue; Connie's Inn at 131st Street and 7th Avenue; Club Harlem at 129th Street and Lenox Avenue, and the Bamboo Inn at 139th Street and 7th Avenue. Most of these places with the exception of The Cotton Club and Connie's Inn are fairly reasonable and are generally packed, but if you really desire a good time, make friends with some member on the staff of HARLEM and have him take you to Mexico's or to Pod and Jerry's or to the Paper Mill. We warn you that only the elect and the pure in heart are admitted to these places.

96

FOR WHOM SHALL THE NEGRO VOTE?
(Continued from page 6)

just so long is the Negro's hopeless political outlook going to continue.

There can be no doubt that dreams of a labor or liberal or other third party in the United States are visionary and unlikely of achievement for many years to come. It is probable that for years to come the only hope which the Negro or any other minority group may have politically rests in the presence in the United States of two poliical parties of approximately the same strength. Such a condition enables the Negro to trade ballots for justice, doing so in the most unselfish manner. This enlightened selfishness can and will bring worthwhile results as has already been seen in states and cities where Negroes have broken away from blind devotion to the Republican party. It is also becoming less important each year for the Negro and other minority groups to pay much attention to what parties shall control national affairs or who shall be President of these United States. The Negro must continue to make his ballot an uncertain quantity, pay no attention whatever to party labels and vote for men and measures which careful study of records convinces the Negro mean most to him as a race. The choice of members of both Houses of Congress and of state legislatures, and of county and city officials mean much more to minority groups than who shall sit in the White House. In the words of James Waldon Johnson, "It is worth a great deal more for a Negro in Mississippi to help elect the sheriff, the prosecuting attorney, the police judge, the board of education and the various other local officers than it is to help elect the President of the United States."

More intelligence and honesty among Negroes can and will definitely affect the political complexion of the Congress to be elected two years from now and of state and city officials. Out of the election of 1928 there seems likely a shaking if not a breaking of the solid south. The Negro himself, with his new economic, political and cultural strength, must answer the question as to whether or not he is going to remain the one hopelessly backward political group in the American electorate.

HOLES
(Continued from page 6)

was blue-black; one small wisp of cloud was reddish as with a blood-stain, and there was a stain of ink on its ragged edge. God's ink.

I walked slowly across the room to look at the Thing across the bed. The lids had lifted from the bottomless holes, and my mouth and throat burned as I sank into their swirling, moon-filled depths.

I am almost at the end of this account. The open gas-jet in the fire-place is hissing steadily. There is a daze before my eyes, but I can still see the form across my bed. I do not smell the gas now; I have become used to it. My head is very light. It takes more and more effort to write. I seem to be floating. It has become quite dark. I wonder if she is waiting? I am very tired. I am floating, I——

TWO DOLLARS
(Continued from page 30)

room. Seeing that all was quiet he cast a fierce look at Happy.

"Well, what ya got to say?"

"I done it."

"Yuh did, eh? Yuh did? Come along, and the rest of you too—" He made a perfunctory examination of the corpse, spat in disgust and hustled them out of the room.

The wagon was filled to capacity. A crowd had accumulated with great rapidity. There was much jostling and chattering and stretching of necks and gaping of mouths. The sergeant himself escorted Happy to the city conveyance and a silence fell on the crowd. They were disappointed, for she was apparently calm and unmoved.

III.

Two Slovaks were walking down the track to work. The older one said, "Those places no good—raise too much hell all the time, eh?"

The younger one sighed reminiscently as he thought of two dollars he had spent the night before. "Well, maybe; I dunno," he replied.

CONJURE MAN
By WILLIAM HILL

Morning, noon and all night thru,
Conjure doctor stirs his brew—
A black bat's wool, a black cat's maw
Herbs, bones, a baboon's paw,
Thrice around the cauldron pass
Magic wand and crystal glass.
Imprecations, vulgar chants—
Than a naked tribal dance.
Now a drum of magic potion,
Agonizing, writhing motion,
Cold, congealing purple hue,
Conjure doctor's fee is due.

Our Contributors

WALTER WHITE is the Assistant Secretary of the N. A. A. C. P. He is also the author of two novels of Negro life, "Fire in the Flint" and "Flight." He has just recently returned from a year of writing abroad.

LANGSTON HUGHES is a senior at Lincoln University. He is the author of two books of verse,—"The Weary Blues" and "Fine Clothes to the Jew."

AARON DOUGLAS, the Art Editor of *Harlem* magazine, was formerly a student of Winold Reiss and had a Fellowship last year at the Barnes Foundation. He did the illustrations for "God's Trombones" by James Weldon Johnson.

HELENE JOHNSON, Mae Cowdery, Alice Dunbar Nelson, Effie Lee Newsome, Georgia Douglas Johnson, are among the outstanding Negro poets.

ALISON DAVIS is professor of English at Hampton Institute.

ALAIN LOCKE is professor of philosophy at Howard University. He edited "The New Negro" and "Plays of Negro Life."

ROY DE COVERLY was educated in England and is now living in New York devoting his time to writing.

THEOPHILUS LEWIS is the best known Negro critic of the drama. He was formerly connected with *The Messenger*. At the present time he is busy preparing his first novel for publication.

GEORGE S. SCHUYLER has contributed several articles to *The American Mercury*. He was formerly editor of *The Messenger* and is now the editorial head of a new Negro newspaper syndicate.

RICHARD BRUCE is contributing editor of *Harlem*. At the present time he is travelling with "Porgy" and finding time to write and draw between acts.

H. VAN WEBBER is a graduate of Lincoln University and a linguist. He is devoting his time to writing.

JAMES EGBERT ALLEN is a teacher in the New York City School system. He will contribute a monthly digest of magazine writing to every issue.

LEON NOYES is a young artist living in New York.

99

WALL DECORATIONS   REVUE STAGED

BY   BY

AARON DOUGLAS   FRANK MONTGOMERY

ATTENTION
Agents and Newsdealers!

HARLEM is to be a national magazine. We
want representatives in every community. An
unprecedented opportunity awaits you. The
advance inquiries from all over the country
indicate that HARLEM will be an indispensable addition to your monthly magazine stock.

For information write:

S. Pace Alexander, Managing Editor, The H. K. Parker Pub. Co.

2376 Seventh Avenue, New York City

100

101

THE growth of Negro literary groups throughout the country and their manifest concern about the activities of other writers prompts the introduction this month of a column carrying informal literary intelligence. It begins under the hand of Gwendolyn Bennett, one of the most versatile and accomplished of our younger group of writers. The title for her column, *The Ebony Flute,* is an exceptionally engaging one and she is in position to provide interest in plenty for those who enjoy the lighter side of Negro letters. Miss Bennett is a poet and a teacher of art at Howard University. She has recently returned from a year's study in Paris on a scholarship provided by the Delta Sigma Theta Sorority. Several of her poems have been carried in OPPORTUNITY, and her *Song* will appear in the new edition of *The New Negro.*

The Ebony Flute

The Ebony Flute

By GWENDOLYN BENNETT

IN searching about for a heading that would make a fit label for literary chit-chat and artistic what-not I stumbled upon "The Ebony Flute." So lovely a name it is that I should like to have made it myself, but I didn't. I say "stumbled" advisedly. Reading again William Rose Benet's poem, Harlem, in the *October Theatre Arts Magazine* I was struck by the exceeding great beauty of his use of the "ebony flute" as an instrument upon which one could "sing Harlem." An ebony flute ought to be very effective for most any sort of singing for that matter. Ebony, black and of exquisite smoothness. . . . And a flute has that double quality of tone, low and sweet or high and shrill, that would make of Harlem or any other place a very human song. No better instrument then for the slim melody of what book one has read or who is writing what new play than an ebony flute . . . speaking of Benet's *Harlem*, what a lovely thing it is! It opens with:

> *I want to sing Harlem on an ebony flute*
> *While trap-drums ruffle to a crash and blare,*
> *With a clear note*
> *From a sylvan throat*
> *Of a clarinet—of a clarinet!*
> *God and brute, black god and brute*
> *Grinning, brooding in the murk air,*
> *Moons of flame and suns of jet,*
> *Hurricane joy and dumb despair.*
>
> *Vermillion, black and peacock blue,*
> *Pink, plum-purple, zig-zag green—*
> *I want to sing Harlem with a paint-box too,*
> *Shaking out color like a tambourine,*
> *Want a red*
> *Like a furious fire;*
> *Want a black*
> *Like midnight mire;*
> *Want a gold*
> *Like golden wire;*
> *Want a silver*
> *Like Heaven entire*
> *And God a-playing at his own front door*
> *On a slide trombone with a conical bore!*

And on through line on line of beauty that coins a Harlem as a poet would see it, lush and colorful . . . fertile like rich earth. On and on to its close which ends with the crooning of his "Mammy Earth. . . ."

> *O child of the wild, of the womb of the night,*
> *Rest, and dream, my dark delight!*

Tropic Death, a book of short stories by Eric Walrond will come out in October. Boni and Liveright are the publishers. I can scarcely wait for this book to be on the market. . . . Few of the Negro writers that are being heralded on all sides today can begin to create the color that fairly rolls itself from Mr. Walrond's facile pen. *Tropic Death* ought to have that ripe color that is usually the essence of Mr. Walrond's writing . . . and also a simple forcefulness that the author often achieves. . . . A new magazine is added to the Chicago list of Negro publications: *American Life Magazine,* Moses Jordan editing . . . the same Mr. Jordan whose book, *The Meat Man,* was published a few years back. The June issue, Volume One— Number One, carried "From Venice to Vienna" by Jessie Redmon Fauset and "Pale Lady" by Langston Hughes. I have not seen the July issue of this magazine but look forward to seeing the future copies that will come out. . . . Maude Cuney Hare has an article on *Creole Folksongs* in the July number of the *Musical Observer.* Needless to say, Mrs. Hare's article is adequate . . . certainly there are few people more authoritative in their speaking of Creole folksongs than she.

Aaron Douglas is doing the illustrations for Carl Van Vechten's *Nigger Heaven* which will appear August the twentieth. *The Publisher's Weekly* says that Mr. Douglas' advertisement for this book in the current magazines is the best for the month of June . . . but by far the most important thing about Mr. Douglas these days is his new wife. He married Miss Alta Sawyer of Kansas City, Missouri, on Friday June eighteenth. . . . The English edition of Langston Hughes' *Weary Blues* came out on July ninth . . . the second edition of *The New Negro* will be out in the fall. . . . The Negro writers must not let the first of September slip up on them without having their manuscripts ready for the Albert and Charles Boni contest. The address for sending the novels to the judges is 66 Fifth Avenue. . . . Thinking of novels makes me recall what Simeon Strunsky of the *New York Times Book Review* said not so long ago about beautifully written books. . . . "The beautifully written book as a rule is the over-written book. One sinks into beauty ankle-deep." He goes to quite some trouble to poke fun at the elegant conservatism of what is called beautiful prose today. But even in the face of Mr. Strunsky's caustic remarks on the question of beautiful writing, properly so-called, I should be ever so happy to see some of that ankle-deep beauty in the things that come out of the Boni contest . . . what of it, if some Negro should write a *Marie Chapdelaine* with its wistful but perfect simplicity or perhaps an "Ethan Frome. . . ." Mr. Strunsky rambles on to the amazing consolation that "We still have our newspapers. In them are the reservoirs of simple health upon which we can draw when the English language threatens to cave in under heavy doses of beauty between bound covers" . . . and we can do little else but wonder how any one can live in New York and see the rife yellow journalism of the daily news sheets and speak of them as the salvation of the English language . . . nor even the aridity of the *New York Times* could be set on the pinnacle that had been built for "beautiful writing."

"George Sand Reigns Again For A Day" in the *Times* for June twenty-seventh made me think of a young newspaper writer I knew in Paris who was always breaking into any conversation that chanced to be going on at the time with the information that he lived in the back part of a house the front part of which had belonged to George Sand . . . and I always think within myself that I could see in that about as much claim to fame as any. . . . F. Fraser Bond in reviewing *The Best Love Stories of 1925*: "Something has come over the American love story. . . . It seems to have grown up. No longer does it find its chief concern in the billings and cooings of tepid adolescents" . . . he goes on further to observe that "Peter Pan has put on long trousers." Can't you see some E. E. Cumings-John V. Weaver person coming forward with a "Come out of it Lovers" to scare away that something that has "come over" the love story of today. . . .

Hall Johnson's Negro operetta, *Goophered;* with the libretto by Garret is to have in it three lyrics by Langston Hughes: *Mother to Son; The Midnight Blues;* and *Song for a Banjo.* This operetta is for early fall or late summer production. Mr. Johnson is the winner of the third prize of the music section of the OPPORTUNITY Contest . . . and by the way, Zora Neale Hurston and Langston Hughes are collaborating on an operetta the libretto of which is to be by Miss Hurston and the lyrics by Mr. Hughes . . . they are also writing a musical comedy together. . . . Mentioning musical comedies of a' dusky character reminds me of the ill-fated *My Magnolia* which ran for a single week at the Mansfield Theater.

Jean Toomer, author of *Cane*, is spending the summer at the Gurdjieff Institute in Fountainbleau, France. . . . Countee Cullen and his father, Reverend Cullen, are traveling through Europe for the summer months . . . they will make many interesting stops chief among them a pilgrimage to the Holy Land. . . . Arthur Huff Fauset whose "Symphonesque" won first prize in the short story section of the OPPORTUNITY contest is to be a member of their party. . . . Dr. Rudolph Fisher has very endearingly nick-named his new baby "the new Negro."

Friday, July sixteenth, the annual reception for summer school students was given at the 135th Street Library. Mr. Johnson of OPPORTUNITY spoke on the OPPORTUNITY contests and what they had meant to the younger school of writers. When Mr. Johnson had finished his speech he called on several of the prize winners of the first and second OPPORTUNITY contests who chanced to be in the audience and asked them to read. . . . "Golgatha Is A Mountain" was never so lovely for me until I heard Mr. Arna Bontemp read it himself. He reads with a voice as rich in its resonance as his prize-winning poem is in its imagery and beauty. It was good to see so many

of the people who are writing and doing things together . . . Zora Neale Hurston, Bruce Nugent, John Davis . . . Langston Hughes who talked a bit about blues and spirituals and then read some of the new ones he had been doing . . . and just before he sat down he read a poem called "Brass Spittoons" . . . as lovely as are many things with much more delectable names.

Horace Liveright is busy casting his play *Black Boy* for its fall production. Paul Robeson is to play the lead which I understand is to be a prize-fighter. I heard Mr. Liveright say the other night that he was having difficulty in finding an actress for the role of Irene who plays in the lead opposite Mr. Robeson. This part is difficult to fill since the heroine is supposed all during the play to be white and is discovered at the end to be a colored girl who "passes." Remembering the harmful publicity that attended the opening of *All God's Chillun* because of a white woman's playing opposite a Negro, Mr. Liveright has been leaving no stone unturned to find a Negro girl who can take the part. There are hundreds who are fitted for the physical requirements of the piece but few whose histrionic powers would measure up to the standard of Broadway production.

Clarissa Scott of Washington dropped into the office the other day on her first trip in the interest of the new social investigation work she is to be doing in New York this summer . . . the same Clarissa Scott whose *Solace* won a prize in the OPPORTUNITY contest for last year . . . and it was good to see her again and to know that she would be in New York all the summer . . . sandwiched between talk of what was happening in Washington and at Howard the question arose as to what was the most beautiful line of poetry written by a Negro . . . her first thought was:

> *Dark Madonna of the grave she rests;*
> *Lord Death has found her sweet.*

from Countee Cullen's *A Brown Girl Dead* . . . strange how discussions of this sort get started, isn't it? I had never thought in terms of the best or most beautiful or the greatest or first line of Negro poetry before . . . there are several that come in line for the distinction now that I come to think of it . . . without thinking too long my first choice is from Langston Hughes' new blues poem called *The Railroad Blues.* . . .

> *A railroad bridge is a sad song in de air*

or

> *Where twilight is a soft bandanna handkerchief*

. . . or perhaps Lewis Alexander's

> *A body smiling with black beauty* . . .

or Jean Toomers

> *Above the sacred whisper of the pines,*
> *Give virgin lips to cornfield concubines,*
> *Bring dreams of Christ to dusky, cane-lipped throngs.*

We wonder what William Stanley Braithwaite would say . . . or Claude McKay . . . or Jessie Fauset. . . . But all that resolves itself into the hopelessness of deciding what the greatest of anything is . . . nothing is really greatest but greatness itself. . . .

The Ebony Flute

By Gwendolyn Bennett

WITH timely alacrity Langston Hughes has thrown his hat into the intellectual ring with the pretty compliment of one poet to another. . . . I think Countee's lines,

> *The dead are wisest for they know*
> *How deep the roots of roses grow.*

is very beautiful." . . . There has been a goodly response to the question as to what is the greatest or most beautiful line of poetry written by a Negro. . . . It is of incident interest that Robert Frost says the finest lines submitted to the 1926 OPPORTUNITY contest are from Helene Johnson's *The Road*, namely:

> *Ah, little road, brown as my race is brown,*
> *Your trodden beauty like our trodden pride,*
> *Dust of the dust, they must not bruise you down.*

Kinckle Jones suggests that his favorite is:

> *Yet would we die as some have done:*
> *Beating a way for the rising sun.*

from Arna Bontemps' *The Daybreakers*. . . . And Aaron Douglas chooses from Jean Toomer's *Georgia Dusk* these lines:

> *A feast of moon and men and barking hounds,*
> *An orgy for some genius of the South*
> *With blood-hot eyes and cane-lipped scented mouth,*
> *Surprised in making folk-songs from soul sounds.*

. . . speaking of poetry calls to mind the announcement of William Stanley Braithwaite's *Anthology for 1926.* It is to have a larger scope this year. It is to be divided into four parts, i.e., The Poetry of the United States, Anthology of Poems 1926, Yearbook of American Poetry, and A Biographical Dictionary of Poets in the United States. The first section includes articles by Jessie B. Rittenhouse, Glenn Hughes, James Southall Wilson, Dawson Powell, Willard Johnson, George Sterling, Thomas Walsh, Henry Harrison, Alain Locke, Josel Washington Hall, Marianne Moore, Joseph Auslander, and E. Merrill Root. . . . There will be many of the younger Negro writers represented in his coming volume. *Golgotha is a Mountain*, by Arna Bontemps; *No Images*, by Waring Cuney; *Northboun'*, by Lucy Ariel Williams; *Tragedy of Pete*, by Joseph Cotter; *Lines to Elders, Scornful Lady* and *Confession*, by Countee Cullen; *Magula, Fulfillment* and *Calla Bella*, by Helene Johnson . . . these are to be among those printed this year . . . they are either prize or mention winners in the 1926 OPPORTUNITY Contest . . . the book will be ready October twenty-first and its price is to be four dollars. . . . William Rose Benet writes me ever so pleasant a letter in which he says: "I am flattered that you like "Harlem," and glad that you should use the term "The Ebony Flute" for a heading to your column, which column seems to me an excellent idea." . . .

Bruce Nugent, whose *Sahdji* appeared in the *New Negro*, has finished his first novel. As yet he has not named it . . . by the way, *Nigger Heaven*, by Carl Van Vechten, is to be on the stands the twentieth of August. However, the review copies are out and I was fortunate enough to see and read one of them. For me it is a splendid book. Mr. Van Vechten has done what I choose to call a perfect piece of research work . . . of it Isabel M. Paterson says in "Turns With a Bookworm"; "It is going to occupy much the same position this coming autumn as *The Green Hat* did last year." . . . We also had the rare privilege of glancing hurriedly over the proof for *Tropic Death*, Eric Walrond's book . . . it certainly has "flights of bright delight." He weaves the warm magic of the tropics with simple words and bright colors. *Drought*, which appeared in the London *New Age*, is heavy with its weight of heat and aridity. The author's careful description leaves the reader's lips parched and dry. This excerpt fairly bakes with white heat:

"*The sun had milked the land of its moisture—pressed it dry. Star apples, sugar apples, husks, transparent on the dry sleepy trees. Savagely prowling through the orchards blackbirds stopped at nothing . . . turtle doves rifled the pods of green peas and purple beans and even the indigestible Brazilian bonavis. Potato vines yellow as the leaves of autumn severed from their roots by the pressure of the sun, stood on the ground, the winds eager prey. Undug, stemless—peanuts, carrot—seeking balm, relief, the caress of a passing wind,—shot dead unlustered eyes up through sun etched cracks in the withering earth. The sugar corn went to the birds. Ripening prematurely breadfruits fell swiftly on the hard naked soil, half ripe, good only for fritters . . . fell in spatters . . . and the hungry dogs, anticipating the children, lapped up the mellow fruit.*"

And we have much cause for being glad that Langston Hughes has won the 1926 Witter Bynner Contest. The prize was awarded for a group of five poems called *"A House in Taos."* The prize is $150 . . . the judges were Rose O'Neill, Vachel Lindsay and Witter Bynner. There were six hundred entries from forty-nine colleges in twenty-six states . . . the contest is for undergraduates in American colleges. . . . Tenth honorable mention was awarded to Waring Cuney, who won a half of the first prize of the OPPORTUNITY poetry contest for his poem *No Images.* Both Mr. Hughes and Mr. Cuney are students at Lincoln University. This year the prize winner was to have received a year's tuition to a Mexican University, with carfare from the United States border into Mexico. . . . Mr. Hughes is rejecting this part of the winnings and allowing it to pass on to the first honorable mention which goes to Josephine Jackson of Mt. Holyoke College. He puts it very nicely—"You see this way it makes it possible for two people to win prizes."

Contests grow thickly about us as the summer wears on. . . . The Survey Associates Incorporated offers a prize of $250 for the best account of the "most interesting thing you know about plays for grown-ups." . . . The manuscripts must not be less than 1,000 nor more than 2,500 words in length, typewritten, double spaced, and on one side of the paper . . . the last date is September thirteenth and the address is—Jury, Harmon-Survey Award 3, care of *The Survey,* 112 East 19th Street, New York City. . . . *College Humor* offers $10,000 in prizes for the best novel or story adaptable to magazine and motion picture production. . . . Midnight, February first, 1927, is the last date and the address is: Contest Editor, *College Humor,* 1050 La Salle Street, Chicago, Illinois.

Which reminds me that Donald J. Hayes is said to be at work on a new literary monthly of the Negro race, called *Vision* . . . to be published from Atlantic City . . . the editors characterize their hopes for the magazine in these words: "In contrast to other Negro magazines, it will have no chip on its shoulder, but will attempt to win friends by giving the Negro writer opportunity for development and by presenting work of distinction. The magazine will be published with white cooperation." . . . It pleases me to see that *American Life,* which had its *premiere* in June, is still in the running.

John Matheus' *Fog* is being translated into German by Dr. Herman Muller for a syndicate which supplies matter for literary publications in Germany. . . . O'Brien has written asking Arthur Huff Fauset for a hundred and fifty word biography of himself for this year's "Best Short Stories" . . . that means that *Symphonesque* goes in this year's honor roll. . . . Countee Cullen writes from Paris that it is the "only city" and that he'd like to stay ever so much. . . .

The Krigwa Little Theater has decided upon the plays that it will produce in the fall. . . . *Blue Blood,* by Georgia Douglas Johnson, which was awarded honorable mention in the play section of the OPPORTUNITY Contest; *Her,* by Eulalia Spence; *No 'Count Boy,* by Paul Green, which was produced in New York by the Dallas Little Theater in 1925 and was awarded the Belasco Cup in the National Little Theater Tournament . . . this movement plans working up a repertoire of both Negro and general plays which will be given alternately during the season. Aaron Douglas is decorating the walls of the Krigwa Little Theater which holds its meetings in the basement of the 135th Street Public Library.

Rudolph Fisher has had two stories accepted by the

Cosmopolitan Magazine. . . . *Fire By Night* and *The Back-slider* are their names. Edwin Morgan's *Prayer* is to appear in *The Bookman* . . . he is spending his summer in Europe. Frank Horne, winner of the second prize of the *Crisis* Literary Contest for 1925, is assistant director of the Boys' Camp Welcome Hall which is situated at Saltaire, Fire Island . . . his *To Chick* from *Letters Found by a Suicide* is to appear in Braithwaite's *Anthology.*

I am particularly interested in reading *Beyond the Rockies,* by William Augustus Banks, published by Dorrance and Company in Philadelphia . . . it is a book of poetry written by a young man who has had an unbelievably hard time of it . . . in fact his struggle for a livelihood has been almost of a story-tale quality . . . the verse is carefully done and I find much of it worthy of special note . . . this particular verse has a wistful quality that pleases me: . . .

> *When January locks me in*
> *Cool mists come dimming down.*
> *The winter is suggesting then*
> *The cool of Twilight Town.*

. . . two other books of poetry have come to n notice recently: . . . *Gems of Inspiration,* by A. R. Schooler; *Poems* by Sarah C. Fernandis.

Richard Reid is doing a portrait of Reverend John Haynes Holmes, pastor of the Community Church. . . . Mr. Reid is the artist whose work was in last year's Exhibit of Independent Artists.

Yone Noguchi is criticizing the Japanese themes as presented by Lewis Alexander . . . he lives in Japan and had a book of *Hokku* published in 1920 by the Four Seas Company. . . . This poem, *To Countee Cullen,* appeared in the *Chicago Tribune* in the column entitled *Line o'Type or Two* by The Faun:

> *It matters not if your skin is dark*
> *As the midnight jungle track,*
> *I thrill to the beat of the song you sing*
> *Feeling the torture and rack*
> *That sundered the souls of your broken slaves*
> *For hundreds of dead years back.*
>
> *Under the march of your musical lines,*
> *Under the tread of their feet,*
> *I hear the wind in the jungle pines*
> *And the drone of the tom-tom's beat,*
> *With ebon savage under the sun*
> *In the shimmering tropic heat.*
>
> *Chance gave you the 'soul of a minstrel fair*
> *Housed in a blackamoor's frame,*
> *With your heart tuned high to the upper air*
> *Though a scion of scorn and shame,*
> *Refusing a outcast's usual lot*
> *And turning it into fame!*

. . . So the talk of this and that comes to a close. . . . I wonder how the manuscripts for the *Boni Contest* are coming along . . . and hope that there will be a novel come out of it worthy of the name of *the Negro novel.* . . .

The Ebony Flute

By GWENDOLYN BENNETT

COMES first a very charming letter from Washington and from Georgia Douglas Johnson her very self, saying: "I like the Ebony Flute. . . . I like those lines of Alexander's very much myself. He is now in Philadelphia working at the Exposition. He will be so happy to know that his poem has been cited . . . then, too, a letter from William Stanley Braithwaite wherein he pays us the delightful compliment of saying: "You have made *The Ebony Flute* attractive and interesting and I am looking forward to each month as a sort of personal chat with you about books and things." Eugene Gordon of Boston makes the pleasing gesture of an enthusiasm which calls forth two letters . . . he throws us this delicious sweetmeat: "Helene Johnson is a member of the *Saturday Evening Quill Club* (of which I happen to be president), as is also Dorothy West, whose story was printed in the July OPPORTUNITY. These girls are cousins and are both so modest that they do not speak of their work even at *Quill Club* meetings, where such matters are supposed to be discussed, until formal demand had been made upon them. I was both surprised and delighted to note according to *The Ebony Flute* that Helene Johnson is to have three poems in *Braithwaite's Anthology."*

This *Quill Club* interests me . . . here we have such people as Helene Johnson of such rare talent chatting with Eugene Gordon whose articles on the *Negro Press* have appeared in many magazines including the *American Mercury.* He, by the way, is writing a series of articles for the *Fourth Estate* published at 25 West 43rd Street, New York City, . . . he will discuss the *Negro Press and Publications.* The first two appeared in the issues for July 24th and 31st. Dorothy West, whose *Typewriter* was awarded the second prize in the Short Story Section of the *Opportunity Literary Contest* for 1926, is also a member . . . she has been contributing short stories to the *Boston Post* and has developed quite a following. . . . We who clink our cups over New York fire-places are wont to miss the fact that little knots of literary devotees are in like manner sipping their "cup o' warmth" in this or that city of the "provinces." Which reminds me that I have heard Georgia Douglas Johnson say that there is a *Saturday Nighters Club* in Washington, too.

Well now that the *Boni Contest* is closed what have we? Certainly the breathless waiting until the awards are announced will keep us keyed up to the proper pitch that should greet the coming of this prize-winning novel by a Negro. Speaking of novels, I bethink me of all the people I have heard say they were going to write novels in the coming year. Eugene Gordon sets the pace at two which he plans completing by May 1st. . . . Frank Horne, hailing from "the islands," tells us that he has piles of notes that deal with his cerebral youngling. . . .

Which reminds us to what extent the vogue for *Nigger Heaven* has set its tentacles upon Negro readers. I have seen the pale blue jacket with its discreet white printing in more brown arms than I have ever seen any one other book. Is it that we like so much reading about ourselves or are we particularly interested in Mr. Van Vechten's reaction to

us whom he has known so well? With the critics of the New York journals giving it a friendly pat on the back and the dark readers of the town consumed either by interest or curiosity, *Nigger Heaven* ought to make of its author a wealthy as well as a wiser man.

Other contests descend upon us . . . there is the new edition of the *Opportunity Contest* for this coming year with Mr. Holstein holding out a gracious hand to the new Negro . . . the *Crisis* awards to be made in a comparatively short time . . . a $500 reward for the most convincing proof as to who was the author of *The Yarn of a Yankee Privateer*—the date is January 1st; the address is Funk and Wagnalls Company, 354-360 Fourth Avenue, New York . . . there will be Sesqui-Centennial Awards to be given to the best poems taken from the *Braithwaite Anthology* . . . prizes of $100, $50 and $25 will be given to the three best poems. . . . The donor of these prizes is unknown. The biggest catch by way of prizes is that offered by *The Woman's Home Companion*—John Day Company. $50,000 in two prizes; $25,000 for the best novel by a man and $25,000 for the best novel by a woman. A competitor may submit more than one manuscript and any author is eligible "regardless of nationality." The date for the manuscript to be in the hands of the judges is July 1, 1927. The address is The John Day Company, 25 West 45th Street, New York City. It seems that with all this causeway one or two of our younger writers ought to be able to procure the means of a mere sustenance at any rate.

The question as to the finest, most beautiful or best line of poetry written by a Negro is still of moment. Miss Mary P. Burrill, teacher of Dramatics at Dunbar High School, says: "I was interested in the discussion of the finest lines by a Negro poet. To me these lines by Claude McKay have a beauty that no Negro poet has equaled; in fact few poets of any race or clime have surpassed them"—

Her voice was like the sound of blended flutes
Blown by black players on a picnic day.

Frank Horne flashes his lance in the fray with these words: "Interested in your quest for the best lines of poetry by a Negro. It is no doubt true that most of the lines of sheer beauty must be sought among the 'very' moderns. But this line from Paul Lawrence Dunbar's poem is always beauty for me—

Ere sleep comes down to soothe the weary eyes—

a line pregnant with soft sounds and vast mystery of infinite space. . . . And this from Claude McKay's *Harlem Shadows*—

Through the long night until the silver break
Of day the little gray feet know no rest;

utterly gorgeous expression of the poignant gray restlessness of a race, from dawn through eternal night. . . . From James Weldon Johnson I always recall the last line from his little poem, *If I Were Paris,* in which he extols "the woman sweetly ripe"—

And utterless longings in her eyes. . . .

And this ecstatic cry out of Jean Toomer's lush collection in *Cane*—

*Her skin is like dusk on the Eastern horizon
. . . before the sun goes down.*

And from Jessie Fauset's *Noblesse Oblige* this gorgeous bit:—

*I must jest while sorrow's knife
Stabs in ecstasy.*

. . . which brings me ultimately to the two masters —these lines from Countee Cullen's *Brown Girl*—

*That brown girl's swagger gives a twitch
To beauty like a queen;*

. . . to crown these scattered jewels, this diadem from Langston Hughes—

*Beat the drums of tragedy for me,
And let the white violins whir thing and slow.*

—besides knowing lovely things when he sees them Dr. Horne also has a loud voice of praise for his fellow poets . . . and from poems by Negroes it is but a thought's span to poems about dusky folks. . . . This poem reprinted in the Sunday edition of the *New York World* for September 5th from *Gypsy: a Cincinnati All Poetry Magazine*—

DARK DANCER

*You are a black rose
Slowly bending
Against the crying red of sunset.*

*Only the pools of the forests
Know eyes that hold such depth;
Only the wind
Such birdlike swiftness.*

*You are slender
Like a reed at midnight;
(Midnight with no moon!)
You are carven of ebony—
Cold like black marble.*

*Only the sea
Knows the swirl of the scarves
About you—
Only the wind
Such bird-like swiftness.*

J. P. McEvoy now turns from the Nordic vagaries in *Americana* to the soft loam of Harlem's material for a revue, . . . if its title presages anything *Hallelujah, Get Hot* ought to be a musical revue whose color and snap would make even the hectic intricacies of the erstwhile popular Charleston become the retarded movement of some pale and forgotten race. Miss Fredricka Washington, formerly of the Club Alabam', plays Irene opposite Paul Robeson in *Black Boy*, the Liveright play. . . . I am reminded of a letter that appeared in the *Herald-Tribune* for September 5th. Katherine Metcalf Roof blunders through answer ta Anne Lawrence who it seems has written a calcitrant letter over *Lulu Belle's* being taken as a prototype of the darker race. Miss Roof comes to the amazing conclusion that Miss Lawrence must be a West Indian and stumbles onto this conclusion:

The West Indians may feel bitterly about such productions as "Shuffle Along" and "Blackbirds of 1926" —I understand that they do—but if I were a Negro I would rather have the talents of Florence Mills, Charles Gilpin, Johnny Hudgins and that priceless person who played the Chinese coolie in "Blackbirds," than have all the solemn education of their universities, or be president of one of their island republics.

And right here we are moved to ask what being a West Indian and a Negro has to do with going to college or dancing a "wicked" Charleston or presiding over an island republic . . . who ever heard of Negroes having an island republic, anyway? I think it is for some such impracticable dream that one Marcus Garvey is singing *Water Boy* at present. Katherine Roof worries on to this awe-inspiring close:

Far from implying inferiority, such dramatic gifts are the very genius of the colored race; and artists like Harry Burleigh, Paul Lawrence Dunbar, Booker T. Washington, John Tanner—a really great painter —or for the matter of that Paul Robeson and Taylor and Johnson are far too wise to release their hold upon them with higher education. These arrived artists appreciate too profoundly the soul-stirring beauty and subtle humor of the music and folk lore of their race.

This is, of course, a pretty gesture on the part of Miss Roof but we see now that neither she nor Miss Lawrence is talking about the same thing and certainly neither of them feel the way a true artistic critic should feel about Negroes in modern drama. Certainly they don't wish to be put in the class with folks who say *Nigger Heaven* was written by a white man to prove that all Negroes think cabarets are a Paradise nor with people that say *Lulu Belle* is propaganda . . . at any rate I wonder whether Katherine Roof knows how educated and "college spoiled" some of the folks she listed are. . . . Harry Burleigh would not be so flattered to be called untrained . . . and Paul Robeson's Phi Beta Kappa key and law degree have been subject for much newspaper and editorial comment. I don't know of John Tanner but I imagine he might be a relative of H. O. Tanner, the famous painter of whom we as a race are so proud. . . . H. O. Tanner is ever so well trained and educated as an artist. But why battle about thinks like this . . . so long as black is black and the moon comes up on the left we have people who measure art by a rule of thumb and begs by the length of a word. By the by, Cecil De Mille is going to do *Porgy* with the hope of having Charles Gilpin as Porgy and Robeson as Cross . . . *and Porgy lived in a Golden Age*—and it most surely is a Golden Age when you can have a Gilpin and a Robeson at one and the same time. . . .

And from Paris, the city of dreams come true, this lovely word from Countee Cullen . . .

"And how foolish I feel with all this traveling and nothing done save one lone sonnet written at Keat's grave in Rome: while your column fairly shrills with all the ambitious projects on foot by the younger and newer Negro. I must begin looking for gray hairs, for I fear my day is in the sere, the yellow leaf. *The Ebony Flute* shall hear from me when I return early in September."

. . . and how eagerly we shall wait for some more of those silver tones from a throat that knows right well the God in music!

The Ebony Flute

By Gwendolyn Bennett

GOLD October has now given way to the crisp call of November and with acceleration akin to that which goes surging through our blood these sharp autumn days the news about Negroes and what they are doing, as well as what is being done about them, piles higher and higher. . . . *Deep River,* the all-American opera or rather operetta, as some of our more fastidious musical critics would have it, has appeared on Broadway in one and the same week with *Black Boy* . . . both of these two vehicles feature the Negro. . . . There is a deal of satisfaction in the fact that New York news sheets have given so much space to the discussion of the former, although little or nothing has been said of the fact that most of the players in the piece are Negroes. Some meagre praise is given to Julius Bledsoe, *whose rich voice is a*

very benison over the stage whenever he stands forth —to quote Gilbert Gabriel of the *New York Sun.* Most of the critiques are given over to the fact of *Deep River's* being a purely native product as well as to the fact that Laurence Stallings wrote the book. Due praise is given Mr. Stallings for having recaptured in his libretto some of the brittle beauty of Lafcadio Hearn's New Orleans . . . the New Orleans of the fabled 1830's. We wonder though whether an author can be any greater than the emotion he inspires in his audience . . . most people are of the opinion that *Deep River* is fairly dull entertainment. Rose McClendon in the third act receives rare commendation. . . . Alexander Woollcott says in the *New York World* for October tenth:

When "Deep River" was having its trial flight in

110

Philadelphia Ethel Barrymore slipped in to snatch what moments she could of it. "Stay till the last act if you can," Arthur Hopkins whispered to her, "and watch Rose McClendon come down those stairs. She can teach some of our most hoity-toity actresses distinction."

It was Miss Barrymore who hunted him up after the performance to say, "She can teach them all distinction."

Mrs. McClendon will be remembered for her appearance with Charles Gilpin in *Roseanne* several years ago. Gladys White, wife of Walter F. White, author of *Fire in the Flint* and *Flight*, plays the minor part of Julie in *Deep River*.

As for *Black Boy* . . . Jim Tully and Frank Dazey seem to have misused material that was destined for a fine plot. New York critics are of an opinion that the authors have concocted a rather cheap, tawdry sort of play. However, its star, Paul Robeson, is with one acclaim said to play his part with distinction and beauty. One knew, of course, even before the play went into rehearsal that, if *Black Boy* was to be played by Paul Robeson, this good-natured, fame-drunk pugilist would sing with those mellow organ tones that few songsters achieve . . . and right here we think again of that faulty, over-advertised piece, *All God's Chillun* . . . in it Robeson sang *Sometimes Ah Feel Lak a Motherless Chile* offstage with melting beauty and simplicity. Alexander Woollcott says: *There are times when the play is just pushed aside while Robeson sings, and it is the kind of a play wherein such interludes are not unwelcome. That Black Boy should have a golden voice was as inevitable as the curious talent for giving imitations which developed in the heroine of Mr. Zangwill's "Serio Comic Governess" when Cissie Loftus undertook that comedy long ago.*

And so we have the native American opera which has as its subject the Negro or rather the Creole who is in part Negro . . . in the same instant we have the furor that is being created by the "mustard colored" *Lulu Belle* . . . close on the heels of both of these comes *Black Boy* with a colored star and just in the offing we have J. P. McEvoy's *Hallelujah, Get Hot,* for which Zora Neale Hurston is writing some of the scenes. Which reminds us that the Actors' Theatre announces that it will produce a dramatization of *Porgy* by Dubose Heyward. I understand that Mrs. Heyward assisted her husband in preparing it for the stage. The piece is to be called *Catfish Row* for the stage on the ground that the dramatic production deals more with the group of people who live in this turbulent neighborhood than with Porgy as a single, outstanding personality. So far little is known of the cast save the fact that the players will all be Negroes. It has been characterized by the producers as *a study of the old-fashioned Negro as opposed to the numerous scenes of more sophisticated life in the cabarets of Harlem.*

The Negro as a factor in dramatic art is not confined to New York alone. . . . *Popoplikahu,* an African play by Georgia Douglas Johnson and Bruce Nugent, is being rehearsed by Barrington Guy for the President Theatre in Washington, D. C. Barrington Guy is the son of the famous Nathaniel Guy. Mrs. Johnson is also the author of *Blue Blood,* one of the OPPORTUNITY Contest prize-winning plays, which is to be included in Frank Shay's *Fifty Contemporary One-Act Plays* which is to be brought out by *Appleton and Company.* Mr. Shay also plans getting together a collection that will be labeled *Fifty Contemporary*

Plays by Negroes . . . speaking of Mrs. Johnson reminds me of the perfectly delightful chat I had with her after she had come back from Chicago where she was graciously received by Harriet Monro of the *Poetry* staff . . . and of how Carl Sandburg did speak with her of this and that thing about Negroes and their work . . . while in the "Windy City" she saw Fenton Johnson who it seems constantly bemoans the fact that he is not in New York City.

Hand in hand with the Negro's position as a figure in American Drama goes our continued importance in literature. *Tropic Death* has been on the market several weeks now . . . reviewers are of the opinion that Mr. Waldrond knows his subject well and presents his material with ability and assurance. *Nigger Heaven* has been and still is a best seller. Langston Hughes' new book of poems, *Fine Clothes to the Jew,* will be published by Alfred Knopf in the Spring. . . . Aaron Douglas has been commissioned to design the wrapper for this as well as three other Knopf books. The information has leaked through that Joseph Hergesheimer is at work on a new novel which deals with the Negro. The scene is to be laid in Charleston and its name ot this writing is to be *Sulphur Rose.*

If Mr. Van Vechten has done nothing else in writing *Nigger Heaven,* he has at least made one more contribution to the vernacular. . . . Sightseers, visitors and other strangers that might find themselves within the limits of Harlem for a space are said to be "vanvechtening" around . . . however, there is one other effect that *Nigger Heaven* has had that is of distinct value to our race history—the Librarian of the Queen's University in Canada has written to James F. Drake, the New York rare book dealer, that he has become so interested in Charles W. Chesnutt, through reading *Nigger Heaven,* that he wants a complete list of his books for the Queen's Library. *The Literary Lovers* of Washington, D. C., of whom E. C. Williams is chairman, met on Sunday, October third, to discuss Mr. Van Vechten's last book . . . a composite opinion was reached that it was a rather fine thing, although not exactly after the style of their own community.

Comes now three new volumes of the *Encyclopedia Britannica* which will add a modern slant to the already meaty collection of information that this set holds. And with it this fact goes upon the shelves of posterity:

The only dance that has survived the American invasion is the valse. . . . The valse continued to dominate the English Ballroom until the arrival of the American dances in 1912. The new dances, which were of Negro origin, were of a two-four rhythm and this change of time from the valse and the attractive lilt of the American dance bands immediately captivated the upper class ballrooms. Their popularity increased year by year until every class in England had its own rendezvous for dancing.

In 1925 there arose an entirely new type of ballroom dancing known as the Charleston. Negroid in origin, its peculiar and strenuous steps aroused some misgivings on the part of the medical profession as to the danger to the body caused by excessive strain on the muscles subjected to constant distortion. Public endurance contests were often the scene of complete breakdown on the part of the participants, sometimes with permanent injury. The Charleston was taken up to some extent in England, but the dance was too ungracefully violent to remain popular either there or in the United States for very long and in 1926 was already dying out.

. . . and somehow I wish that along with the record of Negro dances in the Twentieth Century could go the story of Negro music . . . high up in the pages of its glory I would write the name of Edmund T. Jenkins, composer and musician, *Associate to the Royal Academy of Music* in England, and member of the *Society of Musicians and Composers* in Paris. He was born in Charleston, S. C., and I wonder a bit sadly whether that proud southern city knows that one of her talented sons has died. But thirty years of age, Jenkins' life was snapped short after an acute attack of appendicitis. . . . I shudder to think of the genius the race has lost! In last year's OPPORTUNITY *Contest* his *African War Dance* won the first prize. One had but to sit a while in his tiny studio on rue Pasquier in Paris and hear him play bits of this or that composition on which he was at work to realize that here was a musician of rare talent, a poet with a sensitive soul. At the time that he was taken ill he was at work on a descriptive epic for the symphony orchestra. He had finished the composition and orchestration of four movements of it . . . it was to be in five movements and its name was *The Gully*. The steady thump-thump of the left hand chords will now resound through the years with the last agonized beatings of his noble heart . . . he was my friend and in the rush of what Negroes are writing or doing and the songs they are singing I should like to pipe one shrill note on a flute of ebony to his memory . . . and as a hope to the Negroes who will come after this generation with music in their hearts I dedicate this month's column to Edmund T. Jenkins.

THE EBONY FLUTE

By GWENDOLYN BENNETT

NEW YORKERS have a way of thinking that after Gotham nothing is. I suppose because the city itself is the very door of the Nation, even the name of the place becomes the synonym for the center of the world . . . evident then that we should come to think of New York as the great book-publishing, book-consuming ogre. Needless to say, gossip of this and that thing concerning books and their makers would tend by centripetal force alone to precipitate into what groups in the great Metropolis are doing and thinking . . . it is ever so refreshing to be brought sharply up against the fact that here and there in other less motley cities are little knots of people writing, and reading . . . perhaps hoping and certainly thinking. So when came a letter from Emma Lue Sayers of Los Angeles, California—
"This is just a line from the Far West to tell you how much we enjoy the *Ebony Flute*. And when I say 'we' I mean a Saturday noon writers' organization, which Charles S. Johnson was good enough to help us form, when he was in Los Angeles a few weeks ago. We call ourselves the *Ink Slingers.*" . . . And from Boston comes the word that Thomas L. G. Oxley's *Souls of Colored Poets* soon to be on the market including three hundred poems selected from eighty-five poets. . . . Mr. Oxley is the Director of the Colored Poetic League of the World . . . also one of the *Quill Club* devotees . . . which reminds me that Dorothy West and Helene Johnson are spending the winter in New York. . . . I believe they are studying Journalism at Columbia University.
This month's geographical check-up presents an interesting aspect. . . . Jean Toomer off for Chicago for Gurdjieff work; Abram Harris in New York . . . he is now assisting Dr. Melville Herskovits; Frank Horne gone down Georgia-way to dip his intellectual finger into the publicity of the Hunt Industrial School. . . . Langston Hughes divides his time very nicely between Lincoln University and New York City; Countee Cullen permanently located in the "City of Skyscrapers" is now the Assistant Editor of OPPORTUNITY . . . which, by the way, gives me a splendid opportunity to extend to him the right hand of fellowship and welcome upon the advent of his column, *Thoughts from a Dark Tower*. Both of these two last named young men deserted their several ways around the twenty-first of November to go to Columbus, Ohio, where they read at a meeting similar to the one held in New York called *The New Negro Speaks.*
Just to show you how marvelous is this nothing-new-under-the-sun idea . . . I was browsing around among the *Literary Digest* clippings when I came across this poem:

THE BLACK FLUTE

The music of the black flute dances
With jigging Negro feet. It chances
The labyrinth of violin
And thrusts its polished figure in.

Meanwhile the drum oracular
Keeps philosophic thud and jar,
An elephantine tread that nears
The piccolo's hysteric jeers.

The saxophone with sullen moans
Will wring its hands and shake its bones
Observing that sadistic brute,
The bass horn, chase the little flute.

But round and round and in and out
The dodging flute will shrilly shout,
Until tired out, it seeks a nap
In the astonished cello's lap.

. . . which pleased me very much being a whimsical thing to add to my ever-growing attributes for a flute.
With the passing of *Deep River* and *Black Boy* we have the arrival of the Negro concert season. . . . Roland Hayes again holds American audiences motionless and breathless with music silver sweet; again Paul Robeson's immense voice shall boom forth to the delight of his listeners. . . . Rosamond Johnson and Taylor Gordon are again at team-work on the spirituals; from the warm suns of Southern France comes Lillian Evanti who after a tour of the United States will return to Europe, there to begin a continental tour in December. So music will go close on the slinking heels of mimicry and drama. Louis Gruenberg, a young white American composer living in Paris, has made a setting of James Weldon Johnson's poem *The Creation*. This was performed for the first time at a concert of the League of Composers given at the Town Hall on November twenty-seventh. The Conductor was Koussevitzky, who conducts the Boston Symphony Orchestra.
With surprising surety American Negroes who go to the European capitals as entertainers in the fashionable night clubs and cafes become endeared to the French pleasure-seeker. *The Chocolate Kiddies, La Revue Negre*, Josephine Baker, and Florence Mills . . . each caught and held the admiration of first Paris and later other cities on the continent. At the opening of *Les Nuits du Pardo*, the most chic cabaret Paris has yet seen, Nora Holt Ray entertained in inimitable way . . . she accompanies herself at the piano and her voice has a touching appeal in it . . she was immediately engaged to sing in Monte Carlo . . . and now has come the offer to be starred by the Champs Elysee management . . . this theater is accepted as one of the best Music Halls in Europe . . . the French are in happy consternation over the miracle of *La Blonde Negresse* . . . strange, we live here side by side by many members of the black race whose skins are fairer than some of their white neighbors.
Braithwaite's Anthology is out. It is a full volume and an interesting one with many selections therein by Negroes. . . . It would be a peculiar fate should one of the contributions by a Negro win the special awards that are to follow the publishing of the book itself. Speaking of anthologies, I bethink me of how Arthur Fauset's story, *Symphonesque*, will be reprinted in the O'Brien Selection of the *Best Short Stories for 1926* . . . and also in the *O. Henry Memorial Awards Collection.*
By a sweet token the library shelves are full of books about and by Negroes. The *Second Book of Spirituals* is well on the road to success; *Color* should by this time be nearing its sixth edition; and *The Weary Blues* is in the third edition. And with a rush has come *Tropic Death* by Eric Walrond, *The Negro in American Life* by Jerome Dowd, *Denatured Africa* by Daniel W. Streeter, and *Tom-Tom* by John W. Vandercook . . . which book I take to be one of the most vivid things I have ever read.

113

THE EBONY FLUTE

TIME is guilty of a certain atavistic tendency. We are caught up in the whirl of doing things and thinking others so that it always comes as a shock that at one and the same moment Father Time has snipped short the days of one year and redoubled upon himself so that we find ourselves confronting the miracle of another year. Certainly it has been a brief span since the Christmas of 1925 when *Color* was happily in the book-marts and *The Weary Blues* was going through the process of being printed. With amazing alacrity 1926 gave birth to *Flight*, *The New Negro*, *Tropic Death*, and the *Second Book of Negro Spirituals* . . . . . to say nothing of the myriad books about and around Negroes by those who are not of the group themselves. It is scarcely believable that *Color* and *The Weary Blues*, books of poetry by Negro poets, have in a sense revolutionized the accepted idea of what happens to a first book of verse. . . . . The tale of the Negro in drama, although of a very scintillating quality, enjoyed no such lasting good fortune during the past year. True, *Lulu Belle* has jazzed its melodramatic way through several successful months . . . . . however, we must remember the unfortunate fate of *My Magnelia*, *Black Boy*, and *Deep River*. Nevertheless, we can still cherish the memory of Paul Robeson's splendid interpretation and the impressive beauty of Rose McClendon's acting . . . . . which recollection sends me scurrying from browsing about among the ashes of yesteryear to the bright prospects of the tomorrow—Rose McClendon is said to be in the running fora part in the cast of *Abraham's Bosom* that powerful tragedy that was so simply and exquisitely written by Paul Green. Julius Bledsoe, late star of *Deep River* in the role of the Voodoo King, is to play the central part in Paul Green's play. It is to be produced by the *Provincetown Players* . . . . . Mr. Bledsoe's rugged stature and deep bass voice are well fitted for the part of Abraham McCraine. At the same time preparations are being made for the production of Frank Wilson's play, *Sugar Cane*, on Broadway. It will be remembered that this play was awarded the first prize in the *Opportunity Contest* for 1926. . . . . . Jack Goldberg is the producer. The play has been lengthened to three acts. Speaking of our place in the theater-world reminds me that there was a very good article on the *Negro Theater* in the October issue of the *Theatre Arts Magazine*. Dr. Locke, editor of *The New Negro*, was its author.

But to go back to the rich literary harvest the Negro has garnered during 1926. . . . . The magazine situation with regards to the Negro has been most encouraging. *Opportunity* and the *Crisis* have gone on record as fosterparents of the young Negro writer . . . . . which gives us a chance to remind young Negro writers that they must not forget forth-coming literary contests of both of these magazines—*The Messenger* too has had its place in the literary tendencies of the race . . . . Of no small importance was the Negro issue of *Palms* which was edited by Countee Cullen. By the same token of progress has come the appearance of *Fire*, the new literary venture of the newer Negroes. This magazine is a quarterly and its advent has been hailed with enthusiasm. To Wallace Thurman goes the praise for the editorship of this first number./ William Stanley Braithwaite's *Sesqui-Centennial Anthology of Magazine Verse* has also created a stir among readers of poetry and its critics . . . . . none less than a full page was given over to the discussion of this book by its author

in the Book Section of the *Boston Evening Transcript*.

Comes now the announcement of the *Harmon Awards* in which Countee Cullen adds one more laurel to his already ample crown. . . . . He was awarded the first place in literature for his book of poems, *Color*. The award is $400 and a gold medal. James Weldon Johnson was named for the second award in literature for his splendid editorial work on Negro spirituals and their interpretation. . . . . . I was particularly interested in the fact that a practically unknown artist won the painting award — Palmer C. Hayden was given the award in Art for five oil paintings of water scenes. . . . . And speaking of Art calls to mind that Miss Mabel Brooks, artist, is now studying in New York . . . . she will exhibit with the *Independent Artists* at the Waldorf Astoria in March of the coming year. A painting called *Opportunity* by the same artist will be on exhibition at the *Salons of America, Anderson Galleries*. While we are talking about exhibitions I would remind you that Frans Masereel, a Belgian artist who has lived for years in France, will soon be showing his paintings in New York . . . . . this hanging, I understand, includes several beautifully wrought pictures with Negroes as the subject. Masereel is one of France's accepted artists of the day . . . . besides being a painter he is also famed for the extreme beauty of his wood-blocks with which he has illustrated many of the finer editions of French books. . . . . Aaron Douglas grows in popularity as a designer of jackets for the new books. Along with the outer cover for *Fine Clothes to the Jew*, Langston Hughes' new book, he has done the jackets for *Little Pitchers* by Isa Glenn, the author of *Heat*, James Weldon Johnson's forthcoming volume of Negro sermons in verse, and *Max Havelaar* or *The Coffee Sale of the Netherlands Trading Co.* by Multatuli . . . . . these latter two are very beautiful in color and will be for sale in the book-shops in February. . . . . . The book of Negro sermons in verse will most likely be off press sometime in April. There are to be seven sermons done after the manner of the *Creation* which has so recently been set to music.

Speaking of Mr. Johnson's book of verse brings to mind the fact that *The Autobiography of an Ex-Colored Man*, which was published anonymously by *Sherman, French and Co.* in 1912, will be reissued by *Knopf* during September of 1927 in the *Blue Jade Library*. It might be interesting to go back to a clipping from the *Crisis* files for 1912. The following itemized account appeared in the December issue:

In account with the Old Year

Credits

Full fifty years of freedom and celebrations planned in Pennsylvania and New Jersey. * Defeat of "Grandfather Clause" in Arkansas. * Enfranchisement of 50,000 colored women. * The Independent political vote. * Several civil rights cases won. * Large new Y. M. C. A. buildings planned in Chicago and Indianapolis and finished in Washington. * Census reports showing reduction of our illiteracy to 30 per cent. * Combined increase in property holding thruout the nation. * Promotion of Major Young. * Promotion of Lt. of Police Childs.

IN ARTS AND LETTERS

Two Doctors of Philosophy

Two artists

"Autobiography of an Ex-colored Man."

. . . . . . our eyes scarcely believe themselves when they

read this and certainly our mind takes small hold on the surprising truth of this statement. Little over a dozen years ago in the hurry and flurry of modern American life the contribution to Arts and Letters by the Negro was so small that it could be told so briefly.

In a recent poetry contest conducted by the *United Daughters of the Confederacy* (North Carolina Division) a prize for the best sonnet was awarded to George Leonard Allen, a Negro, for his poem *To Melody*. This I consider one of those unaccountable twists of Fate which sometimes come in the tides and times of man . . . . the sponsors, judges, and what-not were, of course, white . . . . as yet they are unacquainted with the fact that they have awarded a prize to a Negro. Daughters of the Confederacy honoring a *Negro*—mirabile dictu! I oftimes stop short on such occasions as this smitten by the utter probabilities of lions and adders and lambs and so forth munching from a common morsel. But then that analogy means little for in that millenium these reptiles and more or less docile animals will be quite conscious of the fact that a spade is a spade . . . . so beautiful life and living shall be in that far day that the more fortunate of the species will not mind a spade's being a spade and a very nice spade at that. But that has nothing to do with the fact that Mr. Allen teaches at Kendall Institute, Sumpter, North, Carolina, and himself gets a deal of fun out of the abnormality in which he finds himself.

Helene Johnson has just sold *Bottled*, a poem, to *Vanity Fair Magazine*. We think it very interesting that Miss Johnson is only eighteen years old and has written so many lovely poems . . . . and is from Boston and is now studying with Professor John Erskine at Columbia.

On February 19th Crystal Bird is to be the guest of the *Twentieth Century Club* in Boston. She is going to give a talk on *Nigger Heaven*. Mr. Van Vechten, the author, will be present at the meeting. *The Twentieth Century Club* is one of the smartest clubs in the country and is composed of 250 men.

It seems that the Netherlands are particularly interested in Negro music. . . . An Amsterdam Journalist brings the information that all of the Dutch know the blues singing of Bessie and Clara Smith. . . . . . In fact Mengelberry, conductor of the *New York Philharmonic Orchestra*, in possession of all the records either of these two artists have made and thinks them the finest of fine music. And by the by, Ethel Waters has been playing to the *Princess Theater* in Chicago. . . . . . *The Chicago Evening Post* carries this commendation:

"Ethel Waters is the star of *Miss Calico*—a tall, slender, Negro girl with a full-throated voice as soft as velvet. This voice she has under magnificent control.

She can glide easily from the lofty heights of a Hebrew chant to the witty obscenities of a Harlem cabaret. Always she appears to be far from the end of her resources—always she gives the impression of having a reservoir of reserve power. Emotionally poised she is a superb actress. She has been compared with Raquel Meller and with good cause—an astonishing ease and simplicity. She has an added fire—something akin to the animating spirit of Mary Garden."

. . . . . and I call that right royal praise. By the happiest of surprises Evelyn Preer of the *Lulu Belle* caste made a record for one of the phonograph companies— singing blues! The record was so good and its popularity so far assured that the vogue for Miss Preer as a blues singer has spread so that she has now made records for several companies. It comes to light at the same time that she has done this sort of thing before—and more marvelous still on the stage. It seems that she has toured the South with small companies over a period of years . . . . . which of course makes a pretty compliment to her great versatility as an actress.

. . . . . and for no reason at all we are reminded of having read in H. L. Mencken's *Hiring a Hall*:

"Poetry is simply a mellifluous statement of the obviously not true. The two elements are both important and perhaps equally. It is not sufficient that the thing be said with a certain grace—it must soothe the ear while it debauches the mind. And it is not sufficient that it be voluptuous; it must also offer a rock and a refuge from the harsh facts of everyday. All poetry embodies a lie."

. . . . Dr. W. E. B. Du Bois was a guest of the *Literary Lovers* of Washington, D. C., at a dinner Saturday night, December the eleventh. . . . . A dramatic group has been formed among the Washingtonians—they are calling themselves the Washington edition of the *Krigwa Players* . . . . among them are numbered such well-known writers as Willis Richardson, May Miller and Lewis Alexander.

Mary, Mother of Christ, a poem by Countee Cullen has been set to music for Christmas. . . . . I understand that it is set up in form suitable for Yuletide greeting usage.

And so 1926 martials its files of books, magazines, plays, et al. . . . . Comes 1927 with the January Atlantic Monthly carrying *The Promised Land* by Rudolph Fisher and the promise of *Blades of Steel* to be published at a subsequent date. . . . . . Langston Hughes' new book of poetry to come out Feb. 10th and Countee Cullen's *Anthology of Negro Verse* to come in the Fall of 1927. And so Negro books go on . . . .and stay . . . and hope . . . . and a Happy New Year to all!   *Gwendolyn Bennett.*

THE EBONY FLUTE

BY the same token that American Negroes are writing new books and publishing new magazines, Negroes in other parts of the world are throwing their literary caps into the reading public's ring . . . a new magazine has been published in Paris, France, by Negroes from the French Colonies. Its name is *Le Voix des Negres* . . . it was formed by a number of political and literary leaders in Paris. The committee announces its aims as follows:

> "The preservation of the colored race; to combat calumny and prejudices, and to tighten the attachment of the Negro colonies to France."

. . . the editors of the magazine are proclaiming that Negroes are proud to be Negroes. This is in direct line with the new race consciousness among colored people of intelligence in America.

At one and the same time Paris continues to laud the terpsichorean arts of Josephine Baker, colored star of the *Folies Bergere*. The Magazine Section of the *New York World*, for January 9th, carries a full-page article on Miss Baker, entitled *How an Up-to-date Josephine Won Paris*, by Carl de Vidal Hunt. There is much tom-foolery in the article about her undying belief in the power of a rabbit's foot and a good deal of misstatement about the company with which she first appeared in Paris, but even this rather uninformed writer arrives at this beautiful conclusion about a Negro girl, whose rise to envied stardom in the music halls of Europe, has been so phenomenal:

> . . . Her lithe, young body, looking like a Venetian bronze come to life, seemed to incarnate the spirit of unrestrained joy. It is a wild thing, yet graceful and harmonious—a demon unchained, yet delicate in its sleek, symmetrical beauty.

Miss Baker is barely over twenty years old and full of all the youthful enthusiasms that such an age usually carries with it. She loves clothes . . . it seems a divine twitch of Fate that at present she wears only clothes designed by Paul Poiret, one of the world's greatest designers for women. . . . There is also another very famous Negro woman who is dancing for Europeans. Djemil Anik, one of France's colonists, is at present one of that country's most famous interpretive dancers. . . . She has made an extensive study of Indo-Chinese and Javanese dances and costumes and it is said that she has one of the finest collections of dancing costumes in Europe. Mlle. Anik is a very beautiful gold-colored woman with a stature that is at once strong and of a graceful litheness. She speaks not one word of English. . . . At present her tour takes her to the largest theater in Munich . . . which reminds me that *Black People*, an all-colored review, recently opened in Berlin, Germany, at the *Metropole Theatre*. It is being sponsored by Lonidoff and Sirota, Russian producers, who took the *Chocolate Kiddies* abroad. Maud De Forest, who went to Europe in the same company with which Josephine Baker left America, is the star. Here's hoping that this new company will not suffer the misfortunes of the ill-fated *Chocolate Kiddies* who were stranded in a small Russian village.

Fine Clothes to the Jew, Langston Hughes' new book of poems, is off the press. The greater portions of the book are given over to his studies in *blues* rhythms. He has been un-afraid in his coining new things from old rhythms and ageless things from new ryhthms. However, there are those who will not like his blues poems . . . for them there are poignant slices from life with which he has concerned himself. To those who do not see poetry in *blues* and *spirituals*, I recommend *The Sport*, which I would say was one of the finest poems I had ever read anywhere. If this book by Mr. Hughes is as warmly received by the reading public as was his first, *The Weary Blues*, which is now in its fourth edition, his name as one of the accepted modernists in the field of poetry will be unquestioned. The book is dedicated to Carl Van Vechten, the author of *Nigger Heaven*. . . . Distinct praise has gone to *Symphonesque*, the short story by Arthur Huff Fauset, which won the OPPORTUNITY Short Story Contest last year. Frederic Taber Cooper, in a review of *The Best Short Stories of 1926*, by Edward J. O'Brien, pays this compliment in *Brentano's Book Review*:

> "By far the most signal achievement in this collection is *Symphonesque*, by Arthur Huff Fauset. It is a Negro story by a Negro author, a study of primitive reactions to the stirrings of religion and of love. Cudjo is a natural-born pagan, and his desires are simple and primary. His greatest desire is for Amber Lee. . . . And the story—no, technically, it isn't a story, it is rather a verbal symphony—tells of his desire, his temptation, and his final conquest of self. And it tells it in a passionate, cadenced prose that beats and throbs like the primitive beat of heathen drums in an African jungle, sweeping the reader along in a breathless, aching sympathy, a tense sharing in exotic, primeval emotions such as hark back to just one other book in my own range of memories: Haldane McFall's *House of the Sorcerer*. Arthur Huff Fauset is a name to be carefully registered on the tablets of memory, for he is bound to do some surprising work in the near future."

. . . This endorsement reads exceedingly well when coupled with the splendid send-off Mr. O'Brien, himself, gave to *Symphonesque* in the preface to *The Best Short Stories of 1926* . . . right here it might be well to drop a gentle hint that some of our writers finish up that novel they have started and send it in to *The Woman's Home Companion—John Day Company Novel Contest* . . . the outside date is July first . . . the address—25 West 45th Street, New York City . . . there are no internal phrases to the subject matter nor the contestants. Of particular note is the item that the *Boni Novel Contest* closing date, which was originally fixed for last August thirtieth, has been re-opened until July first. . . . By the way, we understand that *The Fire in the Flint* will shortly be published in French . . . and that Nella Imes is now lengthening a rather good novel for Knopf. But to go back to literary contests and their awards. . . . *Harper Brothers* is offering its annual *Intercollegiate Literary Contest*. The closing date is March fifth and prizes of $500, $300 and $200 are to be given to the best piece of English prose written by an under-graduate in any American college or university . . . and since the inhabitants of Great Britain maintain that we, as a people (i. e., *the great American people*) do not speak English, this contest is the equivalent of a thesis in Russian or French . . . the judges of this contest are Henry Seidel Canby, Elinor Wiley and William McFee. . . . One easily remembers here Countee Cullen's and Langston

Hughes' having won the Witter Bynner Under-graduate Contest during consecutive years. . . . The *American Caravan* has extended the time limit for the submitting of manuscripts for its first annual issue to March first. . . . The *Macaulay Company* is fostering the plan . . . they are going to branch out in several unfrequented directions . . . there ought to be a place in these ramifications for the young Negroes . . . and there is *Overtures*, a new magazine of verse.

F. E. Syphax writes me from Boston of *The Garret Paint Pot*, a club composed of twelve members all of whom are students at recognized art schools in and around Boston .. . . the name is taken from its meeting place, which chances to be an attic in a community house . . . they held an exhibit just after Thanksgiving in connection with Educational Week at the *Aristo Club*. The show opened on the Fine Arts night. . . . Meta Warwick Fuller spoke and students from the Conservatory gave musical selections. In commenting on this opening, the *Boston Post* said that it had genuine merit. . . . We've been meaning to say for some time that Malcolm Dodson, last year's editor-in-chief of the C. C. N. Y. *Mercury*, besides being a teacher of Art at the Thomas Jefferson High School, has been at work for the *Chicago Dupont Corporation* . . . he does illustrating for magazines and periodicals of the *College Life* genre. It interests me to know that this corporation's chief illustrator is Elmer Campbell and that he is colored.

In Abraham's Bosom has been highly praised by the critics . . . with the note that Julius Bledsoe makes a splendid actor. And it is now a fact that Paul Robeson is going to play in the coming production of *Show Boat* . . . he will have a part in which he may sing. To me it bespeaks the type of artistry for which Mr. Robeson is striving that he has just refused splendid offers for vaudeville production.

I was rummaging over some old copies of *The Literary Review* of the *New York Times* when I came across an article, entitled *Negro's Art Lives in His Wrought Iron* . . . a discussion of the beautiful iron work that has been found in New Orleans, which was fashioned by Negro workers. From the article I have taken this interesting bit:

> *Did they sing songs as they wrought? There must have been songs for the rhythm of every labor. Did the rhythm of the hammer on the anvil strike new syncopations to his sensitive ear, unlike the anvil songs of Europe? The rhythms and the songs, too, have faded into the silence of forgetfulness. So forgotten are those craftsmen that northern connoisseurs dismiss the idea with a smile.*

which adds one more interesting detail to our history of rhythms. . . . The Fisk Jubilee Singers have had many ovations in Spain, but chief among them is the news of their having sung before the Marquis de Bandana . . . which reminds me of a quip that I will not make.

The editors of *Fire* were happily received at the *Civic Club* for tea on Sunday, January second. Several of the board read to quite an ample audience after tea had been served. . . . James Weldon Johnson presided at a meeting at the *Civic Club* on Friday evening, January twenty-first . . . the subject of the meeting was *Should the So-called Art Magazines Be Barred from the Press* . . . but a short time ago Langston Hughes read some of his poems at this same club, on the evening when Eda Lou Walton and Margaret Larkin read also.

John Vandercook, who wrote *Tom Tom*, was at one time an actor and a newspaper man before he became an explorer and anthropologist. Recently, he has been spending some time in Haiti.

And so let us turn from literary wanderings to "the miracle of every-dayness." . . .

GWENDOLYN BENNETT.

THE EBONY FLUTE

A S we passed a window on our way to this very type-writer to write this very "Black Piccolo," as one of our friends so delightfully called our stint, we saw no less than a host of buds pushing their way through the indignant bark of winter . . . so if we seem a bit frolicsome and inclined to gambol a bit wantonly over literary meads, do be patient with us for there is so much of Spring in this early March day. . . .

It is with seasonal timeliness that Julia Peterkin's new novel, *Black April* makes its advent into the book stalls . . . . a tale of Negro life, as Isabel Paterson puts it, "at the opposite extreme from Van Vechten's *Nigger Heaven*—" there are only Negroes in this new book by the author of *Green Thursday* and they are a folk nurtured and versed in the life of a remote Carolina plantation. Mrs. Peterkin ought to write well just such a novel, being born and bred on a Carolina plantation like to the one around which her story is woven. To us it smacks of *Little Colonel* days that this woman, who is one of the present-day writers who "count," owns and manages a real honest-to-goodness plantation. . . . Speaking of *Nigger Heaven* reminds us that Carl Van Vechten, its author, has returned from a trip to Hollywood, where he no doubt took a note or two on what cinema actors and actresses do in their spare time. Harry Salpeter writes a very enthusiastic account of an interview with Mr. Van Vechten for the *New York World* of March sixth. To me a more significant fact than Carl Van Vechten's having been to Hollywood is that in his cross-country jaunt he looked in on Indian life in New Mexico. . . . Taos, with its aura of Indian legend and history coupled with its present-day movement towards Art and Beauty, ought to furnish fine stuff for a novel of atmosphere as well as psychological research. He makes this cogent observation on the problem of at least two darker races and their adaptability to New World civilization:

The Negro is progressive and adaptable. The Indian's civilization is based on repetition. As soon as the Indians leave school they run back to the pueblo and are Indians again. It may be hard for a white man to understand the Indian, but it is impossible for an Indian to understand white civilization.

Mr. Salpeter makes the comment that Mr. Van Vechten, contrary to custom, continues to be interested in *Nigger Heaven* even after its important birth. We can readily understand this. . . . There are many who would accuse Van Vechten of mere exploitation in his relations with Negroes prior to the appearance of his book about them. This is not true, for Mr. Van Vechten can cite example after example of Negroes for whom he has a lasting friendliness . . . . . there are, too, a goodly number of Negroes to whom he has rendered invaluable service towards the achievement of those things their hearts have held dear. His has been a rather intimate knowledge of this little understood people—small wonder his interest in their chronicle, fashioned by his own hand, should linger a while. *Nigger Heaven* is now in its tenth American edition, while it is being published serially in the *Frankfurter Zeitung* in Germany. It is also to appear in France and in Sweden. . . . Mr. Van Vechten brings back the news from Hollywood that Cecil de Mille plans including Paul Robeson—if he is willing—in his cast of

Porgy. Speaking of Paul Robeson, he is now on concert tour in the South. He will be heard in the nation's capital on March thirtieth at the Auditorium. Surely there ought be place even in the breast of southern white people for the warm kindness of Paul Robeson's beautiful voice.

Paul Robeson's name doesn't necessarily call to mind *Black Boy,* the play in which he appeared not so long ago . . . however, Jim Tully, its author, recently spoke to the *Inkslingers,* a literary group of Negroes in Los Angles . . . we understand that he spoke to them about the play—we have no idea what he could have said about it except perhaps that it had been.

And about Negroes and plays and things . . . In *Abraham's Bosom,* which moved from the Village to the Garrick Theatre, had a brief triumphant run . . . . . Stark Young, however, in the *New Republic,* for March second, reviews the play with acrimony. He has little of praise to offer for either actors or the show as an entirety . . . however, in the very middle of his acidity this confession is more or less squeezed from him:

As I ponder this play it seems moving and profound. Certainly the course of its struggle is full of tragic despair, this poor, confused, high-souled creature beating out his life in vain against circumstance. There is, too, a certain wise balance of parts in the dramatic elements; the white people mean to be kind, but they are as lost in the midst of a race situation as the Negro is; they are moved now by human or affectionate impulses and now by blind racial instinct and an arbitrary, desperate sense of self-preservation. The climaxes in the play are strong and bold. I seem, as I think of it to have been present at a full, passionate story, told by a poet. Certainly this material that Mr. Green attempts is ambitious of power and devastation and beauty; we are in deep waters with such subject matter as he employs.

—so much for the words of a critic who comes to the final conclusion that he does not like this play, which most of his fellow-critics have given the high-sign of praise. . . . I feel particularly lucky to have been allowed to peep into a letter written Mr. Charles S. Johnson by Mr. Paul Green, the author of *In Abraham's Bosom* . . . . . and more than lucky to be allowed to quote therefrom:

"Many thanks for your interest in the Provincetown production of *Abraham.* I'm glad that you find the play written with sympathy and understanding of one of our snarls of being alive. There are many, of course, but this particular one must affect you with pessimism more often than it does me, since you are keeping so much more closely in touch than I with the general changeful activity of the Negro in America. Still it doth afflict me most grievously, too. I hope that the fact that the South is beginning to be dimly aware of the truth that, as Abraham haltingly says, 'It's the man that count'—I hope that this fact is of some significance to us all. May I express thanks for the excellent magazine you are editing. Personally, I think it is one of the most interesting now appearing in the country. The way each month's library copy is worn here would surprise you."

—so much for a gentleman who is from the South and has a talent and a soul.

By the by, the application of the Krigwa Players to present a one-act play in the coming Belasco Tournament has been cordially accepted. This tournament is a competitive presentation of one play each by twenty of the leading little theater groups throughout the country. The showing is scheduled for the week of May third at a Broadway theater whose name has not yet been announced. . . . Dr. Alain Leroy Locke has been host at the Primitive African Art Exhibit. . . . *Theatre Arts Monthly* presents this collection — the Blondiau collection. This group of fine pieces was assembled by a Belgian collector over a period of twenty-five years. It is said to be one of the best private collections of Congo Art there are. From the brochure which announces this exhibition comes this forceful truism about African art: *Africa's art creed was Beauty in use. No tool of daily living was too small or too unimportant to be made with grace and with imagination* . . . and a far cry there is from this world-old art to the very interesting work by two Negro students from Boston (whose names for the moment slip me) which is now on exhibition at the Whitney Studio Club.

Dr. Locke is preparing a pamphlet on four Negro poets: Jean Toomer, Claude McKay, Countee Cullen and Langston Hughes. . . . This is for Simon and Schuster, publishers of a series of *Pamphlet Poets*—I think Carl Sandburg, Natalie Crane and Edwin Markham are among some of the poets who have already been brought out. These publishers were fortunate enough to see the glitter of gold in the Cross-word Puzzle Fad and then by a more serious lodestone they were drawn into the publishing of Will Durant's *Story of Philosophy*, which has gone irretrievably into its hundred and forty-seventh thousand . . . but before it gets away from us—*Theatre Arts Magazine* is getting out a volume on world drama made up largely of essays having appeared in its issues. Dr. Locke's two articles on the Negro in the field of drama are being welded into one for this volume.

And about Claude McKay:—This quotation from a rather wistful letter written in the sun-drenched South of France:

"I suffered a big loss when my suitcase of manuscripts (containing all of the poems I have written during the last four years, dictionaries, reference books, etc.) was stolen at Marseilles last summer. Luckily I had in a satchel the novel I was writing and some short stories.

"At present I am devoting all my spare time to prose. I find poetry such an inadequate means of saying the things I have to say."

We are ever so thankful for the God-given satchel that saved the novel and short stories, however we cannot but tremble at the thought of the beauty that may have been lost in the ill-fated suitcase. We are a little awed before the immensity of Claude McKay's outlook when he can say poetry is too small a medium for the expression of his thoughts . . . he who has so beautifully wooed and won the Muse of Poetry.

Speaking of novels, I wonder whether it makes very much difference that Albert and Charles Boni, publishers, did not award to anyone their thousand-dollar prize for the best Negro novel . . . we could be very wounded about it and make a perfect fool of ourselves, but as it is we are prone to be quite sensible and say that there was without doubt no one worthy of the prize. I should have liked to have seen some Negro write a novel worthy of this prize, but if there were no novels of merit, I am more than glad that the judges and publishers did not award the prize to a mediocre novel. That would have been an irreparable mistake . . . as it is, the great Negro writer may yet be given his just dues without first having to clean a historical blot from his escutcheon. . . . I hear that Rudolph Fisher is at work on a novel—Hear! Hear!

Langston Hughes' new book of poems has been receiving very good reviews . . . as an appropriate send-off for the book there comes the announcement of his having been awarded the *John Keats Prize* of twenty-five dollars by *Palms Magazine* for his group of poems, *A House in Taos*. Mark Van Doren was the judge. It will be remembered that this poem was the one that was awarded the *Witter Bynner Undergraduate Poetry Prize* for 1926. And this is about as good a time as any to remind young Negro poets who are still in college that there will be another award of the same prize for 1927 . . . for the past two years Negroes have won it. Poems must be mailed before May 15, 1927, to Witter Bynner, Box 1061, Santa Fe, New Mexico.

A new jazz symphony is to be performed at the Composers Concert at Carnegie Hall on April tenth. The symphony is by George Antheil, who for years has lived abroad. Mr. Antheil believes that Negro musicians are best adapted for the interpretation of his work and the W. C. Handy Orchestra will play it with the composer at the piano. On the same evening, Mr. Antheil will conduct his *Ballet Mecanique* . . . some critics have called his music noise . . . we don't know . . . perhaps it was the primitive in our soul that rose within us when we heard the crashing thunder of what Mr. Antheil had to say . . . anyhow . . . we liked it.

And so Spring comes creeping over the hill and the Urban League Conference meets in St. Louis . . . and we hope that a copy of the magazine will stray into the midst of the midlanders . . . perhaps if we call this month's pipings the middle-western tune . . . oh, just perhaps we may make one or two literary finds . . . at any rate, Greetings!

GWENDOLYN BENNETT.

119

THE EBONY FLUTE

GO Down Death—a poem-sermon by James Weldon Johnson, is given two pages in the April issue of *The American Mercury* . . . this poem is one of a collection that appears in a volume entitled *God's Trombones* that is now off the press. Although these poem-sermons are written in the manner of the natural ebullitions that arose from the souls of Negro preachers during slavery times, Mr. Johnson does not use dialect in them. He very ably defends this in the preface to the volume as follows:

"At first thought, Negro dialect would appear to be the precise medium for these old-time sermons; however, as the reader will see, the poems are not written in dialect. My reason for not using the dialect is double. First, although the dialect is the exact instrument for voicing certain traditional phases of Negro life, it is, and perhaps by that very exactness, a quite limited instrument. Indeed, it is an instrument with but two full stops, pathos and humor. This limitation is not due to any defect of the dialect as dialect, but to the mold of convention in which Negro dialect in the United States has been set, to the fixing effects of its long association with the Negro only as a happy-go-lucky or a forlorn figure. . . . The second part of my reason for not writing these poems in dialect is the weightier. The old-time Negro preachers, though they actually used dialect in their ordinary intercourse, stepped out from its narrow confines when they preached. They were all saturated with the sublime phraseology of the Hebrew prophets and steeped in the idioms of King James English, so when they preached and warmed to their work they spoke another language, a language far removed from traditional Negro dialect. It was really a fusion of Negro idioms with Bible English; and in this there may have been, after all, some kinship with the innate grandiloquence of their old African tongues. To place in the mouths of the talented old-time preachers a language that is a literary imitation of Mississippi cotton-field dialect is sheer burlesque."

This preface is not only important because of its direct bearing on the poetry that Mr. Johnson, himself, has written, but it is a very timely commentary on all attempts at doing justice to Negro dialects . . . most white writers coin a set, invariable speech that in no way resembles the soft, fluid, ever-changing talk of the Negroes themselves. . . . The poem that appears in *The American Mercury* is strangely beautiful . . . may we be allowed the indulgence of quoting one stanza that we think is particularly lovely?

And Death heard the summons,
And he leaped on his fastest horse,
Pale as a sheet in the moonlight.
Up the golden street Death galloped,
And the hoofs of his horse struck fire from the gold,
But they didn't make no sound.
Up Death rode to the great, white throne,
And waited for God's command.

. . . the *Viking Press* is going to bring out a new edition of *Fifty Years and Other Poems* by James Weldon Johnson . . . . This, together with the Fall appearance of *The Autobiography of an Ex-Colored Man* in The

Blue Jade Library, will bring about the very happy condition of having all Mr. Johnson's works again in print.

Nella Imes has written a novel called *Quick Sands* which is to be published by Knopf under her own name, Nella Larsen . . . . in the words of one of the contemporary white novelists, "It's pretty darned marvelous!" . . . . Dr. Rudolph Fisher has half finished his novel and has a contract with Knopf for it when it is finished. Knopf has been very sympatheticly inclined towards Negro authors; anent—*The Weary Blues, Fine Clothes To the Jew, Fire in the Flint, Flight* and now Nella Imes, Rudolph Fisher and James Weldon Johnson. I understand that *Harper and Bros.* has accepted a novel by Claude McKay.

From San Francisco, California comes a charming note written us by Julian E. Bagley in which he encloses a clipping from the *San Francisco Daily News* . . . . in unqualified praise Arthur S. Garbett says:—of the first J. Rosamond Johnson-Taylor Gordon recital of Negro spirituals:—

The sheer beauty of the music carries him (Johnson) along, and the magical blend of humor and pathos in these works has in him an ideal interpreter, and in Taylor Gordon he himself has an ideal disciple. A sort of ecstacy drives these artists, and it rings true. The homely words often achieve a divine yet sophisticated symbolism to which the simple melodies add a mystic touch. The hushed voices in "Same Train" crooned pianissimo make the song expressive of a universal futility that transcends racial limits. And in "Roll the Old Chariot Along" again, we were made to feel the deep inner meaning latent in the words. And so it was in all they did.

. . . . in *Child Life* for February Henry Purmort Eames, L.L.B., writes an article on *Music of the Black Folk* in which he says:—

The Negro sang in a peculiarly fascinating harmony—not the harmony taught in books but harmony taught by their own hearts. Not a note or a word was written down, and many a song was composed on the spur of the moment when great joy or deep sorrow inspired the singer.

I find this a simple and beautiful legend to be instilled in the young mind . . . . Henry Eames is a Doctor of Music, a composer, a piano-lecturer, recitalist, teacher of piano and lecturer at the American Conservatory of Music in Chicago, and President of the Society of American Musicians. Speaking of educating the youth Roy L. French has written a text-book entitled *Recent Poetry for High Schools* in which he quotes poems by Negroes without stating the fact that they are Negroes . . . . it seems that he is concerned solely with the idea of their being poets regardless of race or color . . . . he says that James Weldon Johnson's *Creation* is the finest religious poem that has been written in America.

Porter Grainger has set one of Langston Hughes' blues to music and it is to be recorded on the New Brunswick records . . . .

Which reminds us that we have not kept our travelogue up to date . . . Zora Neal Hurston is now in Florida doing some research work for Dr. Boaz of Columbia University . . . Du Bose Heyward, author of *Porgy* is now in Europe where he is to complete his new book entitled *Mamba's Daughter* . . . Frank Horne is still in Georgia . . . and Langston Hughes is going South this summer . . . I believe he has some sort of romantic idea about sailing down the Mississippi River—that ought to bring forth some new poems full of the chugging rhythm of the old steamboat.

Helene Johnson's poem, *Bottled*, appeared in the May issue of *Vanity Fair* . . . *The Carolina Magazine*, the official organ of North Carolina University, is to appear as a Negro number in its next issue . . . one cannot help marveling at the fine liberality of thought this school exhibits.

Charles Cecil Cohen gave a piano recital in Washington on March thirty-first . . . his program was well-balanced and splendidly rendered to a very appreciative audience . . .

Arthur Ficke writes to Carl Van Vechten about *Fine Clothes To the Jew*, Langston Hughes's new book of poems and says:—

> Langston Hughes, whose earlier poems had such great promise, here fulfills every vestige of that promise. He is a great artist; he never yields to the obvious temptation to comment on his themes, but produces the theme, stark and stripped, for the reader to feel and vibrate to. With a devastatingly ironic sense of the possible comic quality of some of his material, he accepts that limitation and writes poetry that is usually as beautiful as it is tragic . . . Hughes stands at the other pole from the clever verse-writer. His technical cleverness is enormous; yet he does not exploit it. He knows—only too well—that poetry is the result of some catastrophic agony of the spirit—and he seems rarely to write from any more trivial level of experience.

. . . the mention of Carl Van Vechten reminds us that Paul Morand is to write the preface to the French edition of *Nigger Heaven* . . . Morand is the author of *Open All Night* and several other modern novels in French.

And so another moon has passed and *the world do move* . . .

Gwendolyn B. Bennett.

THE EBONY FLUTE

AT this writing there are many things, there are ever and ever so many things more rare than this particular "day in June" . . . . a gentle rain patters its way down upon the city roofs . . . . for some unknown reason I am reminded of a spiritual that I heard a young Negro student sing a few nights ago . . . *Keep Your Hand Upon the Plow* . . . for me it was a new spiritual and oh such a beautiful one. In a recent issue of *The Town Crier* there appeared an editorial entitled *Old Spirituals* . . . lavish applause was showered upon the Negro as a songster. The following paragraph carries the gist of the entire article:

> The Negro is becoming articulate. There was a time when he was known only as the singer of other men's ballads. That was the day of Jubilee Singers, long before an Old Spiritual had even a name. Every one went to hear them, much in the same spirit that every one went to see the freaks in the sideshows. Even then the Negro carried himself with a dignity which disarmed the most prejudiced . . . It would seem that they might have a message for the world. It has been sung on the road up from slavery and with a poignancy that has lain beneath an exterior of carefree indolence, now dimly understood as being something in the nature of camouflage. There must have always existed a toughness of fibre which would not permit the surrender of individuality to those who dominated them. In a way, they were captains of their souls if not masters of their fate.

Edward J. O'Brien, compiler and editor of the best short story series, a volume which is issued annually, has written to Eugene Gordon, the Boston newspaper man, a request for a biographical sketch to be inserted in the *Best Short Stories of 1927*. This means that *Rootbound*, winner of the fourth prize in the short story division of last year's *Opportunity* Contest, has been designated by Mr. O'Brien as one of the stories printed in 1926 which in his opinion may fairly claim a position in American literature, and which is to be listed in the *Roll of Honor* in his volume. It is also to be indicated in that part of the volume known as the yearbook by three asterisks affixed to its title. Blanche Colton Williams in her *O. Henry Memorial Award Volume of Short Stories for 1926* also picked *Rootbound* as an outstanding story, along with Dorothy West's *The Typewriter*, which with a story by Zora Neale Hurston, *Muttsy*, won second prize in *Opportunity*'s contest last year.

The Saturday Nighters of Washington, D. C., met on June fourth at the home of Mrs. Georgia Douglas Johnson. Mr. Charles S. Johnson was the guest of honor. It was particularly pleasing to see and talk with Miss Angelina Grimke. She is a beautiful lady with ways as softly fine as her poems. The company as a whole was a charming medley. . . . E. C. Williams with his genial good-humor; Lewis Alexander with jovial tales of this thing and that as well as a new poem or two which he read; Marieta Bonner with her quiet dignity; Willis Richardson with talk of "plays and things" . . . and here and there a new poet or playwright . . . and the whole group held together by the dynamic personality of Mrs. Johnson . . . some poems by Langston Hughes were read.

. . . he, by the way, is in the Southland. Dr. Locke tells us that his trip is to cover much of the "Land of Cotton" . . . and while we are tracing our travelogue let us say that Frank Horne is spending the summer in Chicago after a winter in Fort Valley, Georgia. Dr. Locke is again returning to Europe. . . . Jean Toomer will again be in Fountainbleau, France, at the Gurjieff Institute. . . . Eric Walrond, who has been in Panama, has now returned to New York. And so Negroes go hither and thither and yon, writing about this and that. . . .

We have at hand the May number of the *Carolina Magazine*, which is devoted to articles and poems by Negro authors. The magazine is well set up with a noble list of truly artistic contributors . . . Arna Bontemps, Aaron Douglas, Charles S. Johnson, Arthur Huff Fauset, Helene Johnson and Eulalie Spence. If all white colleges were so liberally inclined, the combined artistic expression of the darker and fairer groups might arrive at a truly great Art. This issue of the *Carolina Magazine* was one more brave step toward this Utopian communion of spirit. In accord with this general urge to "render unto Caesar what is Caesar's" *The Midland, A Magazine of the Middle West* carries as the first article in its May issue a piece entitled *The Harlem Poets*.

Recently Mr. Benjamin Brawley, Professor of English Literature at Shaw University, wrote a paper entitled *The Negro Literary Renaissance* which appeared in *The Southern Workman*. Mr. Brawley had little or no high praise to spare for the "younger Negro" . . . there was an almost venomous sting in the severity of his criticism of those young black throats that have dared to sing a new song. I have come by a copy of a letter which Mr. Carl Van Vechten wrote in answer to Mr. Brawley's paper and incidentally in defense of the younger Negro. This question is of too great moment for the letter to be hidden from the public eye and so I shall take the liberty to print it here:

> My dear Mr. Brawley:
>
> I have read with interest your paper entitled the *Negro Literary Renaissance,* in the *Southern Workman.* Your opinions are your own, and although I do not share them you are entitled to them. I think, however, that in such a paper, written by a college professor, one might expect a meticulous niceness in regard to matters of fact. You write: "When Mr. Hughes came under the influence of Mr. Carl Van Vechten and *The Weary Blues* was given to the world," etc. *The Weary Blues* had won a prize before I had read a poem by Mr. Hughes or knew him personally. The volume, of which this was the title poem, was brought to me complete before Mr. Hughes and I had ever exchanged two sentences. I am unaware even to this day, although we are the warmest friends and see each other frequently, that I have had the slightest influence on Mr. Hughes in any direction. The influence, if one exists, flows from the other side, as any one might see who read my first paper on the *Blues,* published in *Vanity Fair* for August, 1925, a full year before *Nigger Heaven* appeared, before, indeed, a line of it had been written. In this paper I quoted freely Mr. Hughes' opinions on the sub-

ject of Negro folk song, opinions which to my knowledge have not changed in the slightest.

I might say a word or two apropos of the quotableness of the verse of Countee Cullen. Suffice to say that the fact is that he is quoted more frequently, with two or three exceptions, than any other American poet. I myself quoted four lines as a superscription to *Nigger Heaven*, and two other lines later in the book, I think the concluding lines of his beautiful sonnet, *Yet Do I Marvel*, I have seen printed more often (in peri-odicals in other languages than English, more-over) than any other two lines by any contempo-rary poet.

I beg to remain yours very sincerely,

(Signed)   CARL VAN VECHTEN.

. . . And at this juncture I am moved to quote H. G. Wells: *Art that does not argue nor demonstrate nor discuss is merely the craftsman's impudence.*

Gwendolyn B. Bennett.

THE EBONY FLUTE

AS I go about this month's mental gymnastics I am in quite a festive mood . . . just one year ago this very month "we" came into being . . . I say this "we" in the true Lindberghian fashion . . . and so this month I, in the role of a fond parent, am celebrating the first anniversary of my brain-child, *The Ebony Flute*. At birth this instrument was destined to be a "literary chit-chat and artistic what-not" . . . fate has not as yet played us too foul and we are still keeping up the what-not side of the bargain. This has been an eventful year for my child and me what with the appearance of *Tropic Death*, by Eric Walrond; Braithwaite's *Anthology of Magazine Verse; The Second Book of Negro Spirituals* by James Weldon Johnson and J. Rosamond Johnson; *Fine Clothes to the Jew* by Langston Hughes; *The Pamphlet of Negro Poets* by Alain Leroy Locke and *God's Trombones* by James Weldon Johnson . . . to say nothing of *Black Boy, My Magnolia, Deep River, In Abraham's Bosom* and *Lulu Belle* in the realm of the drama. Then too, *Nigger Heaven, Tom-Tom,* and *Black April* have cast intelligent light on the subject by artists of the other group. We have tried to keep our tune in a staccato time with only now and then a melodic break in the shrill purpose of our song. It has been an exhilarating task to chronicle the gossip of Negro writers, singers and players. And by the way, while I am dancing a jig over this first birthday I don't want to forget the godfather of this column . . . for the benefit of those who were not among my audience last summer let me say that there appeared in the *Theatre Arts Magazine* for October, 1926, a poem entitled "Harlem" by William Rose Benet in which the line, *I want to sing Harlem on an ebony flute*, occurred . . . and so I called this column the "ebony flute" and it was not but recently that I reminded Mr. Benet that he was the godfather of my column . . . he took the relationship very graciously and I gleaned further that he is still reading what we have to say here each month which is no faint praise coming from a godfather who himself writes a literary column.

As for the contests et al there are a few juicy morsels for this month: *The Penn Publishing Company* at 925 Filbert Street, Philadelphia, Pa., will offer their annual play contest again this year. The closing date for the manuscripts to arrive in that office is December first of this year . . . there are to be five prizes—First: $1,000; Second: $500; Third: $250; Fourth: $150; Fifth: $100 . . . the royalties for production are to be divided equally between the authors and the publisher. In view of the *Krigwa Players* having won a $200 prize at the Belasco Tournament this year this contest might be an interesting try for an aspiring Negro playwright . . . Miss Eulalie Spence wrote *Fool's Errand*, the play which was awarded one of the Samuel French prizes. But to go back to the prizes . . . A fund has been donated by Paderewski for the purpose of encouraging serious creative effort among musicians in the United States . . . the contest is open to anyone who is an American-born citizen or born abroad of American parents . . . There will be two awards—one of $1,000 for the best orchestral work not exceeding fifteen minutes in performance; the other of $500 for the best piece of chamber music. The judges are to be George W. Chadwisk, Frederick S. Converse and Henry Hadley . . . the address for the manuscripts is Mrs. Elizabeth C. Allen, Secretary, 296 Huntington Avenue, Boston, Mass.

Whenever I mention or think of music in terms of competitions or encouragement for creative effort my thought turns inadvertently to Edmund Jenkins who died last fall . . . he should have lived to have won just such a prize as this to have put him permanently before the public eye.

Much hullabaloo is being raised in England about the *Elgin marbles*. Greece, where they originally graced the Parthenon, has asked for their return. Again we have the hopeless mechanism of "the law" and "the people" at work to hinder the progress of art . . . these marbles cannot be returned to Greece without the consent of the British people through parliament . . . I'd be willing to wager that not fifty per cent of the English people nor even fifty per cent of the English parliament have truly seen the *Elgin marbles* . . . it will be of small surprise to me if parliament feels no sentiment about these beautiful works of art being returned to the place they rightfully belong. Lord Elgin went to Greece and saw these marbles and without a legal purchase had them moved to England at his own expense and there gave them to the English government . . . and now when Greece has the nicety to request their return instead of claiming her ownership the English people must put it to a vote . . . and so the machine works.

In Abraham's Bosom, the play written by Paul Green which won the Pullitizer Prize for the Drama this year, will be revived by the *Provincetown Players* about the end of August . . . this play is to be put into the permanent reportoire of these players. Which reminds me that *Plumes* by Georgia Douglas Johnson has been accepted for publication by French and Company . . . this was the prize-winning play of this year's *Opportunity* contest. The Negro musical play is again making its onslaught upon Broadway . . . June 27th *Bottomland* opened at the *Princess Theater* . . . of it Alison Smith of the *New York Morning World* says:

> A Negro company which to this time had been imprisoned in Okeh records suddenly burst out of its phonograph last night and bounced onto the stage of the Princess Theater.

. . . and that is literally what happened. The New York critics give this new piece but scant praise . . . however, they all admit that a Negro chorus always has speed, if not beauty and organization. And as we go to press *Rang Tang*, boasting of Miller and Lyles and Flournoy Preer, is on. Opened at the *Royale* on the twelfth of July. *Africana*, featuring Ethel Waters is due at *Daly's 63rd Street Theater* on the eleventh of July . . . Louis Douglas, who staged Josephine Baker in her colored show in Paris, is to do the same for *Africana*. Prior to directing in Paris Mr. Douglas was dance director at the *Grosse Schauspielhaus* for Max Reinhardt in Berlin . . . speaking of Josephine Baker reminds me that the altogether remarkable "Jo" has done the inimitable again . . . according to the *New York Morning World* for June 27th she has now become Countess d'Albertini . . . in Europe she has been exposed to royalty and in the manner of the true stage darling has captured one of the nobility in matrimony . . . her words on the subject are gems: "He sure is a count—I looked him up in Rome. He's got a great big family there with lots of coats of arms and everything."

My Spirituals, by Eva Jessye, is a beautiful book, if

ever there was one. *Robbins Engel is the publishing house* . . . the book is beautifully illustrated with black and white drawing and the text is lovingly and understandingly written . . . I found therein many spirituals that I had never known existed. Macmillan publishes *A Short History of the American Negro* by Benjamin Brawley. Harper and Brothers will present *Home To Harlem,* a book of short stories by Claude McKay, author of *Harlem Shadows* . . . after this long silence it is a genuine relief to hear that Claude McKay will be on the scene once more . . . Aaron Douglas is to do the jacket design. Alain Locke who is now in Paris will there complete the translation of Rene Maran's new book entitled *Kongo* . . . Aaron Douglas is also to do the illustrations for this book . . . this book by M. Maran is based on his own experiences as a colonial administrator in Equatorial Africa . . . Charles and Albert Boni will be the publishers . . . Rene Maran has also written another book which is a sequel to *Batouala* and is called *Djouma, Chien de Brousse* . . . it was published in France by Albin Michel, M. Maran's old publisher . . . the French critics are proclaiming it a master work . . . Octave Beliard compares it to Kipling at his best and calls it "a Darwinian novel par excellence" . . . of it Romain Rolland of *Jean Christophe* fame writes: *"It is the privilege of great spirits, even in the midst of the tortured present, to live beyond in the future. We have tried, you and I, my dear Maran, to live as "citizens of the future." Djouma, the Jungle Dog* will not be published in English at once although it is being published in Spanish and Russian. M. Maran is extremely interested in the American situation, and is constantly writing in French journals and magazines critical notes on the recent literature and cultural advance of the American Negro. It was his article on Walter White's novel that led to its translation into French by Mademoiselle Margeruite Humbert . . . I remember so well how earnest he was in a conversation we once had in Paris. He brought out a copy of a current French news sheet and showed an article on lynching . . . he, himself, was incensed at the idea of such barbarity and told me that in a like manner the white Frenchmen could in no way understand the toleration of such cruelty in a civilized community . . It was a beautiful thing to note the kindredship that existed in his heart because of the irradicable black of our skins.

. . . and to go on with what new books are to be published . . . Harper and Brothers will also publish an anthology of Negro plays entitled *Plays of Negro Life,* edited by Alain Locke with the collaboration of Montgomery Gregory . . . this volume will contain twenty one-act plays, eleven by white and nine by Negro authors. By the by, Dr. Locke has sailed for Europe where in addition to the translation of M. Maran's book he will make a first hand study of the work of the League of Nations in African reconstruction with particular reference to the administration of the African mandates. The investigation is under the auspices of the Foreign Policy Association and is made possible by a grant from the Pauline Wells McCabe Memorial Fund.

The Sunday World for July third carried a very interesting article on the famous French gourmets . . . the article was punctuated with spicy dishes as one might well imagine, however, the most interesting fact that I got from it was that Alexandre Dumas was one of the greatest gourmets of his day. He told his friends that he wished to close his literary work of five hundred volumes by a book on cookery. Indeed, his last volume was a book on cookery. It is filled with appetizing recipes from all over Europe, including thirty-one ways in which to treat a carp, fifty-six for dressing eggs, a formula for halcyon's nest and dozens of other exotic concoctions.

I wonder if any of my readers know what sort of books one should give in a gift packet to a skeptical white person . . . something say that would tickle his fancy as well as enlighten him. I don't think it ought to be an over-dose . . .

If all the employers should suddenly cease employment and at a stroke donate all former employees a vacation, I should go somewhere—oh! just anywhere, so long as there was a brook that made just a wee bit o'gurgling sound as it went over some rocks . . . I wouldn't bother packing my bag with much other than Stevenson's *Inland Voyage,* John Masefield's *Collected Poems,* and Joseph Conrad's *The Shadow Line* . . . with such rations it wouldn't matter how many books were published in New York per month.

Gwendolyn B. Bennett.

THE EBONY FLUTE

WELL, what's o'clock? Seems to me that this is another one of those *Shuffle Along* seasons on Broadway .... *Rang Tang,* with the well known Miller and Lyles, still holds forth at the *Royale Theatre* while the inimitable Ethel Waters continues to draw enthusiastic audiences at *Daly's* with her revue, *Africana.* A few nights ago I went to see *Africana* .... never have I seen such gorgeous abandon as was exhibited by that chorus nor have I ever seen such a perfectly matched curtain of brownness as hung behind Ethel Waters .... literally there were the sort of "brown girls" about which the poets sing. I grow a little tongue-tied when I begin to speak of Miss Waters, herself. She sings to her audience with the same intimacy that one feels sitting in one's own home listening to one's own gramaphone. The night that I was there the audience clamored for song after song and she delightfully gave them what they knew they wanted. Carl Van Vechten was in the audience and greeted the performance with an enthusiasm that does not seem to dim as the play lasts .... "folks say" *Rang Tang* is a better show and I wonder .... I understand that *Rang Tang* is more after the pattern of the usual Broadway musical show but is that what we want of a Negro revue? I was amused to hear a colored woman comment on *Africana* as she left the theater. In no uncertain terms and certainly not in that soft sweet voice that is so excellent a thing in woman she declared that she surely preferred *Rang Tang* to *Africana.* ..... I think that the sum and substance of her diatribe was that *Rang Tang* was much the *classier* show of the two .... and so I shall live to see this other show, I trust.

If you want to read a very amusing article be sure to hunt out the *Saturday Review of Literature* for August sixth and read *Parnassus in Station* by Marshall McClintock ..... it is a clever slant on what a clerk goes through in one of the new book-stores that also have lending libraries. As Mr. McClintock says he is one of the "young, wide-awake clerks" .... he gives this interesting observation on the readers and buyers of books:

"Another interesting thing is the different way in which men and women handle books. Most men pick up a book as if they were not at all afraid of it, virilely, strongly, securely. They look at the title page, the blurbs on the jackets, and glance over the pages. All very sane, of course. But women drop the book while taking it from the shelves with two fingers, drop two packages while picking up the book, set the book on the table in front of them upside down, poke an umbrella as they turn the book around, then open the volume precisely at a certain page, with hand flat on the open pages. They read intently a few lines, then turn swiftly and certainly to another page as if they had been referred definitely there. This repeated several times. Then, "No, I don't like the looks of this," and set the book upside down on a pile far removed from the place they picked it up. They are very careful to do this every time they examine a book. What they read and why is a mystery to me, and their whole attitude towards the book and handling of it are astounding and incomprehensible."

..... I wonder what the Ruth Hales would say to this ..... probably, "Well, those are that kind of woman." In the *Sunday World* for July tenth Harry Salpeter

wrote a column about Mrs. Julia Peterkin, author of *Green Thursday* and *Black April* ..... the column was entitled "Studies in Color" ..... this dialogue might interest my readers:

"My writing is less a creative thing than an attempt to record people I admire. The Negroes are not beasts; they are human beings." "Why," Mr. Salpeter asked, "did you write *Green Thursday* and *Black April?*" "Because, although much had been written about the Negro, nothing had been written that applied to the Negroes on our plantation. They meet life with a courage and a grace that few people achieve. I like them! they've been my friends; I've learned so much from them."

Will she write of others than Negroes?

"I shall never write of white people; their lives are not so colorful. If the South is going to write, what is it they are going to write about—the Negro, of course."

She then goes on to wonder why it is that so many writers about the Negro live in New York rather than closer to their material. . . . She says a beautiful thing about this aspect of Negro life and living,

"Our people die in the houses in which they are born. Do you know what love of the land is? It is to live on a piece of land which feeds us and to which, when we die, our bodies shall return .... that sounds sentimental but it's what I mean."

..... and speaking of southern white writers I am reminded how this amusing incident in James Branch Cabell's life was brought out in an article entitled "Censored into Fame" written by David Karsner for the magazine section of the *Herald-Tribune* of Sunday, July twenty-fourth. .... He came to New York when a young man and worked as an assistant to the Society Reporter of the *New York Herald* .... he reported a wedding of a family that was not counted among the social *elite* . . . the article was written with so much sparkle and cleverness that he became quite distinguished therefrom .... he was then given an assignment to report the society notes among the Negroes of Harlem . . . this to be run as a smart feature in the *Telegram,* at that time the Herald's fifth wheel ..... Mr. Karsner says: "The editor did not know that he had affronted the young Virginian until he held in his hand Cabell's card, engraved, not merely printed, and saw the youth depart with an injured air. He never came back to New York after that, except as a full-fledged writer" .... and by the by, Octavus Roy Cohen, well-known writer of humorous Negro stories, has been given the degree of Literary Doctor by Birmingham Southern College .... and while we are still speaking of Negroes and their sympathizers and chroniclers of the South, let us say that we read in the magazine section of the *New York Times* for July thirty-first that a bronze statue of an old Negro, "heroic in size," has been recently erected in Natchitoches, Louisiana. It bears this inscription:

Erected by the City of Natchitoches in grateful recognition of the arduous and faithful service of the good darkies of Louisiana—donated by J. L. Bryan.

. . . . I understand that the figure in the Statue looks as if he had just shuffled into the square and recognized some of his white folks . . . . he has just removed his hat and is bowing and smiling his joyous greeting . . . you know, a place like Nachitoches, Louisiana, would be just the sort of city to be bothering itself to do a thing like this . . . . I wonder if its inhabitants know that not only is the Civil War over but also there has been a World War. . . . . .

Benjamin Brawley, of Shaw University, takes up the cudgel in answer to my remarks on his article in the *Southern Workman* and my wanton exposing of the letter Carl Van Vechten wrote in answer thereto . . . he writes this letter to the "editors of OPPORTUNITY":

Gentlemen:

I have seen in your July number the letter addressed me by Mr. Carl Van Vechten. In my personal reply to Mr. Van Vechten some weeks ago I called attention to the facts that he wrote the introduction of Mr. Hughes for *The Weary Blues* and that this young poet later dedicated *Fine Clothes to the Jew* to him, Mr. Hughes certainly seems to be conscious of some indebtedness or influence.

As a matter of fact, however, whether Mr. Van Vechten influenced Mr. Hughes, or Mr. Hughes influenced Mr. Van Vechten, is of minor importance. The chief things I had to say in my article in the *Southern Workman* were that for the most part our young writers seemed to prefer themes unnecessarily sordid and vulgar, and that they frequently showed imperfect mastery of technique. I may be wrong, but I find that a good many people agree with me, and in any case the public will have to be the judge as to whether the points are well taken or not. The evidence is in the stories and books that our young writers produce. Yours very truly,

(Signed) Benjamin Brawley.)

So . . . . If I had been one whit a gentleman I most likely would not have gotten myself in this scrap and certainly I would not say further that a writer or an artist cannot be deemed incompetent simply by the moral aspect of the subject matter he chooses. . . . . I prefer not to sit in judgment on the younger Negro writer or any other writer for that matter . . . . . I wonder whether Professor Brawley would like to say that all the French writers including the right honorable Anatole France were wrong or immoral because certain of their works deal with subjects not freely discussed in drawing rooms or in the presence of the "jeune fille bien elevee" . . . his first act would be to strike from his library that very delightful book, *The Queen Pedauque.*

Speaking of French literature calls to mind a circular I received which announced the coming of *The Negro Courier*, a new magazine first published in French and then translated into English which will appear this month. The founders are Rene Maran, Roggas, Sarrotte, Betton, Bloncourt, Caminade, Faure, Lacombe and Linstant Auguste . . . . . the magazine is planned as an organ for the international cooperation of Negroes . . . . it will be sold only on subscription . . . .the address is care of Courrier des Noirs, 6 rue Royer-Collard, Paris (5ieme) . . . . . I am a little breathless before this new attempt at the unification of Negroes throughout the world . . . . certainly these Negroes in France are a royal crowd with which to be associated . . . . by the way, M. Sylvain, a well-known Haitian writer, is now in this country attending the Pan African Conference in New York . . . . Mr. Johnson was so kind as to allow me to peep in on an article by M. Sylvain which will appear in OPPORTUNITY . . . . without giving its content away I may say that it is entitled *Jan-Jan: a Haitian Idyl* . . . . and literally it is just that and a right lovely one, too . . . . here we have a tale of languorous beauty . . . . . it commences:

On the shore of a tropical sea where the foot sinks lightly in the soft sand, lies indolently the little Haitian port of Archaie. Fringed by deep green islands of mangroves, the Bay of Port-au-Prince stretches westward, blue, calm, at rest—a picture of the hospitable people living on its shores.

If you haven't seen Countee Cullen's new book of poems, *Copper Sun,* published by *Harper and Brothers,* you should rush right out now and buy one . . . . his anthology of Negro poets entitled *Caroling Dusk* will not be far behind it . . . . The illustrations for Copper Sun were done by one Charles Cullen . . . . . Countee Cullen tells an interesting tale of how the father of Charles Cullen is always interested in anyone whose name is Cullen . . .it was in this way that he came to buy *Color,* Countee Cullen's first book, the which he sent to his son Charles . . . it later developed that Charles was an artist . . . . hence these very beautiful drawings which he did for Countee Cullen's book . . . . and truly they are lovely to behold!

More news of our young Negro poets . . . . Langston Hughes writes on July twenty-ninth from Tuskegee Institute in Alabama:

"I am having the time of my life down here. Everybody's fine to me and the South isn't half bad. Tuskegee is wonderful. Jessie Fauset is here, Marie Peterson and gangs of delightful folks. Ran face to face into Zora Neale Hurston in Mobile. She has a little car and is driving around herself. I am going to the country tomorrow for a while and then on to Georgia."

So, the literary Negroes invade the South and drive to the winds . . . and so keep up our travelogue, Lewis Alexander writes from Philadelphia that he is at work in that city and has seen Arthur Huff Fauset here and there as well as Alice Dunbar Nelson . . . . Frank Horne is still a-doctoring eyes in Chicago. . . .

Who should I meet on the steps of the Forty-second Street Library the other day but Eric Walrond? He tells me that now that he has come back from Panama he is writing a book about that country . . . and I said how he surely ought to do just that!

I guess it is the very essence of being passe to add one more comment to the other hundreds that have been made about H. L. Mencken's column in the *Sunday World* of July seventeenth but here goes . . . besides the many other things that Mr. Mencken said and the which were amply discussed by most Negro writers, he says, "No Negro writing short stories rises above the level of the white hacks." I was quite calm until then. Surely even the sardonic Mr. Mencken could not compare Rudolph Fisher and Eric Walrond to white or any other colored hacks . . . .that seems to be falling over backwards to prove a point . . . . after all both these two Negro writers have been well received and criticized by white writers who are not hacks . . . . . but that is that . . . . he ends by saying that Negroes who follow their ministers remain ignorant and ridiculous . . . . "Nothing comes out of them but moans" . . . . after all a moan is a lovely thing when it bursts from the warm throat of a Negro singer.

Gwendolyn B. Bennett.

lives. It was a literal shame to have so much elegance pass under the dank sceptre of the steadily falling rain . . . we had a queer twist of memory as we first beheld the Elks in all their splendor about the streets of Harlem . . . we thought back to Byron's *Destruction of Senacharib* . . . how *the Assyrian came down like a wolf on the fold, and her cohorts were gleaming in purple and gold.* . . .

Quite an interesting article by Wallace Thurman appeared in the *New Republic* for August thirty-first . . . it was entitled *Negro Artist and the Negro.* Mr. Thurman wrote a clear article and a courageous one . . . however, now and then its sincerity was seared by an acid thrust of almost too searching critcism of his fellow writers. . . . We had luncheon with Mr. Thurman at the Civic Club the other day and among many other things he told us that he was to have several articles appear in such magazines as *The Nation* and *The Bookman*, et al . . . and that is that, and I am glad . . . he also tells us that Langston Hughes is in town but that never was needle in any haystack so difficult to find . . . also that Zora Neale Hurston is back in Gotham. . . . Mr. Thurman applied for a position in the cast of *Porgy*, the dramatization of Du Bose Heyward's book that is soon to be presented by the *Theatre Guild* . . . they told him that "he wouldn't do as he was too supercilious" . . . another national attribute of the younger Negro, we take it.

The Nation for September fourteenth carries an article entitled *Is Africa Going White, Black or Brown?* by Wynant Davis Hubbard. . . . The writer lets drop this gem:

"I have the greatest respect for Negroes. I like them personally and collectively. One or two of my old hunters and nurse boys I love as much as I ever loved any white man. But I recognize that the Negro in Africa occupies at present a very distinct place. And most certainly that place is not a place of equality on earth with the white man. I do not know about Heaven. But I do know that I have never seen a missionary eating with an African Negro, sleeping or bathing with one, or doing anything except order him around most imperiously. I have, however, seen missionaries kick Negroes, beat them with bullock straps, and hammer them with canes. Once I saw one force a balky Negro to chew up a mouthful of dry quinine and epsome salts."

And so the march of the Brotherhood of Man goes on . . . and on. . . . Mr. Hubbard finally comes to these considerations and conjectured conclusions:

"I feel that there are three possibilities: first, that Africa will eventually be a black country; second, that the whites will wipe out the blacks; third, that whites and blacks will interbreed and produce a new brown race which will control the wealth of Africa. I am not sure but that I would like to see it. The whites, after all is said and done, have not progressed far beyond the Negroes in the one commodity of life which means much—happiness. In this, in spite of our telephones, subways, electricity, etc., the natives of Africa far excel the vaunted civilized white men. And is not happiness the ultimate aim of our own existence, whether we be white, yellow, brown, or black?"

Mr. Hubbard shares the same views as Mr. Vandercook, author of *Tom-Tom*, about native Africans and their inherent happiness.

The other evening I grew tired of moderns and the things about which they write . . . out of this ennui I turned to reading some of Paul Laurence Dunbar . . . after the present-day "problems" he makes delightful reading. There is a simplicity about his short stories that relieves the heart after the moil of current neurasthenia. The dialect poems flow like sweet, forgotten music into the tired ears

THE EBONY FLUTE
GWENDOLYN BENNETT

NOW that the golden-rod is yellow and the corn is turning brown, we shall get us to this business of what's what among dusky folk. . . . We went to see *Rang-Tang* at the Royale Theatre the other night and were delightfully surprised. . . . we had heard so much about it that we had come to think that it couldn't possibly be as fine as people said it was . . . it *was* beautiful! There was a banjo scene that was about the cleverest chorus trick we had ever seen . . . scores of lovely brown girls filled the stage bearing banjos . . . one could hardly expect that these girls could *really* play the instruments that they bore . . . it would be too much for the male chorus to play the banjos they carried and the girls to play, too . . . there were many clever steps and much mocking at banjo-playing when lo and behold the entire company began playing their banjos just as though they had been hired for their parts on that score alone . . . imagine some fifty banjos going at full tilt with lights, fingers, smiles and feet all keeping "in step" to the tune of *When Sammie Plays on His Old Banjo* . . . on the other hand, about the funniest thing we have ever seen was the spectacle of Miller and Lyles aboard an aeroplane which they had stolen in order to fly to Africa the which had very unceremoniously dropped in mid-ocean . . . and the other colored show, *Africana*, has moved farther down-town. Which reminds me that Witter Bynner, the poet, presented Ethel Waters with a beautifully carved bit of jade at a formal party given for her at the studio of Carl Van Vechten, novelist, who is the author of *Nigger Heaven* . . . Mr. Bynner's collection of jades is world famous and this piece that he presented to Miss Waters was one of his rarest bits.

Many and interesting things have happened in this cosmopolitan city since last we were a-talking here. . . . While the Pan-African Congress held its fourth session in Harlem, the Elks' Annual Convention held full sway throughout the same section of the city . . . never were two totally different gatherings of Negroes so perilously juxtaposed against one another! Negroes from all over the world came to take part in the Pan-African Congress in a serious discussion of ideals and hopes for future Negro life and policy, while colored folk from all parts of the United States swarmed about the streets of Harlem clad in the royal purple of the Improved Benevolent Protective Order of the Elks of the World. We have never seen so many combinations of purple and white before in our

of today . . . while browsing about among the less popular
of his poems I ran across the lines *To a Lady Playing the
Harp* . . .

Thy tones are silver melted into sound,
And as I dream
I see no walls around,
But seem to hear
A gondolier
Sing sweetly down some slow Venetian stream.

Italian skies—that I have never seen—
I see above.
(Ah, play again, my queen;
Thy fingers white
Fly swift and light
And weave for me the golden mesh of love.)

Oh, thou dusk Sorceress of the dusky eyes
And soft dark hair,
'Tis thou that mak'st my skies
So swift to change
To far and strange;
But far and strange, thou still dost make them fair

Now thou dost sing, and I am lost in thee
As one who drowns
In floods of melody.
Still in thy art
Give me this part,
Till perfect love, the love of loving crowns.

According to the modern scheme of things there are too
many "thees and thous", but that is only the change that
comes with years . . . barring these differences of rendition
we have a simple, beautiful love song filled with exquisitely coined phrases. . . . I advise any one who has a
present-day-fag to turn to Dunbar. If you are fortunate
enough to get hold of a copy, *The Life and Works of Paul
Laurence Dunbar* by Lida Keck Wiggins with an introduction by William Dean Howells, published by *J. L. Nichols
and Company*, you will have the added treat of the photographs that illustrate this volume. These pictures have an
aura of other days about them . . . *Dese Eyes o' Mine is
Wringin' Wet* is one of the very fine ones . . . *Dese Little
Boots*, a sensitive photograph of an old mammy looking
fondly at the worn boots of the *po' li'l lam'* who has died,
makes the muscles in one's throat contract queerly. It
seems to me that along with other movements for the
furtherance of Negro art, some publisher ought to become
interested in putting out a new and modern edition of Paul
Laurence Dunbar's poems . . . a beautifully bound edition
of these poems would grace any shelf.

And along this general line, one of my readers has very
kindly offered a copy of Countee Cullen's *Copper Sun* as
a prize for the most beautiful four lines of poetry or single
sentence of prose written by a Negro of "other days" . . .
that will include the immortal Frederick Douglass and
Phyllis Wheatley . . . so there you are . . . something
quite interesting ought to come out of this.

And speaking of prizes, I am reminded that the *Stratford
Magazine*, a periodical for creative readers, offers a hun-
dred-dollar prize for the best poem submitted to their edi-
tor. Further particulars will be found in the current issue
of the magazine . . . a free sample will be sent on request.
The address is: The Ttratford Magazine, 234 Boylston
Street, Boston, Mass. It's a wonder some of the young
Negro writers would not try some of these contests. . . .

And as we go to press the wee kiddies and the summer-
jaded teachers are again starting their year's work . . .
there's bustle in the air on the first day of school . . . but
out in the fields *the golden-rod is yellow and the corn is
turning brown.* . . . Gwendolyn B. Bennett.

THE EBONY FLUTE

EVERYTHING seems all agog among dusky cliff-dwellers these days . . . first and foremost, I believe, is the opening of *Porgy* as a *Theatre Guild* production . . . the dramatization of the novel of the same name by its author, DuBose Heyward and his wife Dorothy Heyward . . . a tale of Negro-life in "Catfish Row" of Charleston, S. C. The novel, which came out two seasons ago, was as beautiful a piece of writing as I have ever seen . . . and this superfluous good-will about it is not only shared by myself; most literary critics have not yet done with grumbling because it did not win the *Pulitzer Prize*. The cast of the play bears in its list the names of Frank Wilson and Rose McClendon. Both have flashed across the proscenium with meteor-like surety and glory. . . . The press has done some pretty capers now that the first night, October tenth, has come and passed . . . Allan Dale of the *New York American* enthusiastically proclaims:—

"Certainly a more unusual and characteristic scene has rarely been staged. It was something new to most of us—may I say, to all of us. And it lived so completely that one forgot that it was a mere Broadway theatre. It was Charleston. It was Catfish Row. It was the colored quarter, seen intimately, graphically, photographically. . . .

"But it was all so beautifully done. It is artistically a gem. It had such thorough understanding, such flashes of remarkable color, such energy and such repression at the same time. The staging by Rouben Mamoulian could not have been finer and the sets by Throckmorton deserve a paragraph all by themselves.

"Among the actors I may mention Westley Hill, who was Jake to the life, Percy Verwayne, Frank Wilson—the Porgy—Evelyn Ellis and Rose McClendon. And I insist on my enthusiastic approval to Leigh Whipper, who played the 'crab man' too gorgeously for words. The entire cast was so excellent that it is difficult to make selections for commendation".

Percy Hammond of the *New York Herald-Tribune*, who by the by but a few months ago voted that Rose McClendon and Frank Wilson should be named the finest actors that last season's Broadway presented writes:—

"No harm has come to Mr. Heyward's novel *Porgy* in its adventure among the perils of the drama. In fact, the story's rich substance and manner have been intensified by their contact with the *Theater Guild*, and even the most devout admirers of the book find their favorite undefiled. Dramatized by the author himself, touched up in the Guild's efficient laboratory and acted faithfully by Negro players, *Porgy* is a fusion of two arts that are usually discordant." He even goes so far as to say as his last rapier thrust:—

"*No doubt it is traitorous to say so, but the fact remains that the only bad actors in 'Porgy' are white*" . . . even the usually sardonic pen of Alexander Woolcott, dramatic critic for *The Morning World*, gives *Porgy* this send-off:—

"Except for the isolated masterpiece *The Emperor Jones* this *Porgy* is the first good job the American Theater has done with the Negro, and certainly it is the first fine performance of a play that I have ever seen given by a Negro troupe. For, with a few exceptions, all the characters of *Porgy* are colored folk and the Guild production uses no burnt cork. . . . The first scene, with a whole chattering, derisive neighborhood peering down on the craps game, deliberately goes out after Mr. Belasco's scalp—and, I might add, comes home with it. For this scene and all of *Porgy* suggests what, in the same hands, *Lulu Belle* might have been.

"There is not enough room here to make mention of all the individuals in the troupe who are good enough. Yet room somehow must be made to say something of the beautiful work of Frank Wilson as Porgy himself, and of Georgette Harvey as Maria. . . There is only just room to tell you that Porgy is pronounced a hard "g" and to say again that the Guild has begun its tenth season magnificently."

And so . . . I chanced to be in the *Club Ebony* on the opening night of *Porgy* when Rose McClendon and a party of her friends came in. I went over to speak to her and ask her "how the opening night went." . . . I found her very gracious and lovely—a person who seems to radiate sincerity and charm. . . . She said that Mr. Heyward and his wife were extremely well-pleased with the opening. She turned with infinite beauty of possession to a handsome gentleman, saying "Do meet my husband" . . . and as I spoke to him I thought to myself how wonderful it must be to be married to so talented and yet simple a woman . . . they each beamed upon the other in a most engaging manner.

And about this *Club Ebony* . . . Mr. Pinckett, one of the co-owners (and by the way, Mr. Lloyd Thomas, the husband of Edna Thomas of the original *Lulu Belle* cast, is the other one) said to me, "I was trying to decide what to name the club when I picked up the *Opportunity Magazine* and saw your column and like a flash I decided to name the club 'ebony' " . . . and so *Club Ebony* it stands. . . . I went up to see the new night club with Aaron Douglas, for he has done the mural decorations . . . and right marvelous they are, indeed. . . . In warm blues, oranges and yellows he has depicted the Negro from jungle days on up to the modern jazz era. The figures are done in the characteristic Douglas manner and are extremely well-suited to the club. I must say that few cabarets or night clubs are more spacious and well ventilated nor have I often heard a better dance orchestra. I have heard many glamorous tales of the opening night and have by this time begun to bite my nails in anguish at not having been there. There were many notables on the first night · . . Carl Van Vechten, Madame A'lelia Walker, Dr. W. E. B. Du Bois, Eric Walrond, Jessie Fauset and goodness knows who else . . . it *is* a beautiful place and one where it ought to be quite easy to have a good-time . . . at any rate, I hope it will be a success. I understand that on Friday, October fourteenth, "the press" is to be entertained by the management . . . and on Wednesday, Octobr nineteenth, there is to be a party there given by the N. A. A. C. P.

Speaking of opening nights, I am reminded that October fifteenth is opening night of the *Dark Tower Tea Room*. . . . Madame A'Lelia Walker is fostering the idea of having an eating place where people who write may gather to discuss their work and topics pertaining thereto . . . and where people who don't write may have a bite to eat among things and folks literary. It seems like a mighty good idea to me. . . .

And now for the greatest bit of information of all—Dr. Du Bois has written another novel which is to be published by *Harcourt, Brace and Company*. I understand that it is to be a tale of Negro life in Harlem · . . surely, this is something to look forward to. . . . As yet the publication date is not given to the public. Speaking of Dr. Du Bois' novel I am reminded of Eric Walrond's new book which is listed among Boni and Liveright's fall publications. . . . It is to be named *Big Ditch* and is a story of Panama . . . conjecturing from the title I arrive at the idea that it might have something to do with the Panama Canal which the Negroes call "a big ditch." . . .

Miguel Covarrubias' *Negro Drawings* is being brought out by Knopf. They ought to be exceedingly clever, if

they follow the line of the caricatures of his that appeared in *Vanity Fair* about 1924 or '25. . . . *Plays of Negro Life* by Alain Locke and Montgomery Gregory is out and indeed is a beautifully printed book. There are some rather wonderful photographs and also some fine decorations by Aaron Douglas. The selection of plays seems a wise one and I look forward to the time when the *Krigwa Players* or some other amateur troupe will have all of these plays in repertoire . . . which reminds me that Doralyne Spence of the *Krigwa Players*, who was the star of the ill-fated *Stigma*, is now playing the role in *Abraham's Bosom* which Rose McClendon played before the opening of *Porgy*. This is proof positive that the little theater movement is an important factor in the artistic development of Negro life.

A day or so ago I had the rare pleasure of visiting the Barnes Foundation in Merion, Pa. . . . I am stricken a bit dumb before the marvelous collection of modern paintings Dr. A. C. Barnes has there. . . . Dr. Barnes is the author of *The Art in Painting* which was published by Harcourt, Brace and Co. His experiments in seeing pictures objectively are by now quite famous but true to the legend about him he is still blazing new paths. . . He has a collection of African art that is both beautiful and rare. . . . I stood for a long time in one of the galleries where the African art is kept—I wanted to bring away something in my mind's eye, a something that would be one with myself and so link me with the selves of Lost or Undiscovered Africa—I looked about, undecided what to choose for my own among all this gorgeous collection of beautiful things . . . my tendency was to choose everything . . . and finally the bust of an African woman separated itself from its companions . . . it was descreetly marked Baoule XIVe Siecle, but surely it was more than that. . . . I've seen the same beautiful droop to an old Negro woman's mouth from South Carolina. . . . I've seen the same luscious haze in the eyes of young Negro girls as they walked the streets of Harlem . . . there must have been the same firm curve to the breasts of the young slave mothers who were torn from their babes by new and harsher masters . . . and yet there was something in the beautifully carved hair, the delicate chiseling of the nose, and the fine sculpturing of the neck that made this piece of age-old wood something of life and breath that belongs to all climes and peoples . . . and I felt that a young white dreamer might have gotten the same beautiful tone chord from what I like to term *my* "Head of an African Woman."

I was reading an account of Balieff's *Chauve Souris* in the *New York Times* the other morning . . . this description of that delightful production struck me very forcibly:—

The fellow has a recipe for smiles and laughter which no mere half-dozen years of commercial exploitation in the hardest-boiled cities of the world have availed to rob of its magic spontaneity or served to dry up its well-spring of joy, or still its throb of leaping life. . . . And I bethought me how well that described the irrepressable, undaunted mirth that has suffused the life of the Negro through many, many sad years. . . .

Gwendolyn B. Bennett.

THE EBONY FLUTE

AS we go to press it is Book Week in America . . . and truly it *is* book week among Negroes with literary leanings. *Caroling Dusk*: *An Anthology of Verse by Negro Poets* edited by Countee Cullen is now to be found in the book-stalls . . . and a right beautiful book it is, too. He has made some pretty courageous selections, and his foreword gives just reason for the book's being. His inclusions range from the gentle sobriety of Arna Bontemps' *Golgotha Is A Mountain* to the sheer simplicity and naivete of Lula Lowe Weeden's *Dance*. . . . One can easily understand a sober-eyed child's saying:

> Down at the hall at midnight sometimes,
> You hear them singing rhymes.
> These girls are dancing with boys.
> They are too big for toys.

. . . Miss Weeden is not yet ten years old. Indeed, Mr. Cullen has done a noble piece of compilation—one that might easily take its place in importance alongside of Braithwaite's *Anthology of Magazine Verse*. Then, too, there is Arthur Huff Fauset's book *For Freedom!* For us this book is one of the most notable achievements of the past decade in Negro history. Here we have the careful assembling of Negro heroes around a Negro Round Table. It is essentially fine that Negro children should have their own dark-skinned heroes; Mr. Fauset has seen this need with clear eyes. . . . He has worked for several years among Negro children and is therefore cognizant of their needs . . . this book has, in the words of John Dewey, a "high simplicity" that is closely kin to sophistication. The book is published by the *Franklin Publishing and Supply Company* at Philadelphia . . . this book is to be used in the Philadelphia Public Schools. One says this in an awe-inspired whisper for truly this is progress. . . . Mr. Fauset will be remembered for the agreeable stir that his short story, *Symphonesque*, caused after the *Opportunity Contest* of 1926. It is quite interesting that Mr. Fauset's book should appear about the same time that Mary White Ovington's *Portraits in Color* has been published. . . . The *Viking Press* is the publisher of the latter. Miss Ovington's book has for its subject Negroes of today who are making important contributions to the arts and sciences . . . they are in a measure "success stories" and as such are important in furthering notice of what Negroes are doing side by side with the whites . . . again brown heroes!

Golden Dawn, an operetta, opened recently in Philadelphia . . . it had been scheduled for a two-week run, but after the ready approval of its audiences it has remained two weeks longer . . . it will no doubt stay at the Philadelphia *Schubert Theatre* until time for its New York opening. . . . Of a cast of one hundred and fifty people fifty-odd are Negroes . . . the scene of the play is laid in Africa. There is an extravagant lushness about this production that fits well the subject matter of the score as well as the material the producers have used. Fifty Negroes in brilliant-colored robes present a beautiful picture as they wander to and fro across the stage . . . and when that same fifty can sing—well, that is too much of another matter. There is beautiful music in *Golden Dawn* . . . it should be successful in New York. It is a bit reminiscent of the bright days when *Mecca* played at the *Century Theatre* . . . *Coquette* in which Abbie Mitchell plays also had its opening in Philadelphia . . . which reminds us that Miss Mitchell's concert at *Steinway Hall* on November sixth was well received . . . here is final and complete justification of many years of playing this or that role or singing this or that part in mediocre productions . . . to realize just how famous Abbie Mitchell was in other days one should hear some of the colored musicians who are either working or stranded in Paris . . . theirs is a story of a beautiful girl whose voice was like molten silver . . . whose voice covered easily an impossible range of tones. . . . I shall never forget hearing Al Johns

tell how Abbie Mitchell used to whistle *Li'l Gal* by Will Marion Cook . . . how her voice easily spanned the extremes of *Red, Red Rose* . . . then in 1925 I heard her sing in concert in Washington, D C. . . . I shall never forget how she sang *The Erlking*. I wondered then why she did not tackle the difficult critics of musical New York . . . and now I am quite content and happy that she has done just that. . . . And, by the way, Florence Cole-Talbert, soprano, gave a recital at the *John Golden Theatre* on Fifty-eighth Street on Sunday afternoon, November twentieth. . . . She has studied in Italy and made her debut in European opera . . . and again I am happy, for ten years ago I heard her sing "The Cows Are In the Clover" and I have never forgotten it. . . . Jules Bledsoe, who first received note in *Deep River* and later in *In Abraham's Bosom*, is to have a part in *Show Boat* by Edna Ferber . . . his is a singing part. And Paul Robeson is at present in Europe. . . . I know that he is elated at the tiny visitor that has come to his home since he left. . . . Paul Robeson is passionately fond of children and Paul, Jr., has just arrived.

In Philadelphia there is a group of Quakers and Negroes who meet together to discuss this and that under the name of *The Fireside Club* . . . on Friday, November eleventh, they had as their guests of honor, Dr. Sylvain, of Haiti, and Dr. Barnes, of Merion, Pa. . . Dr. Barnes gave a delightfully informal talk about the interesting experiments he has carried on for year upon year among the Negroes who are in his employ . . . the conditions under which these Negroes work at his manufacturing plant are well nigh ideal and he has put the high sign of truth on the hope that Negroes and white people might work together in harmony. Dr. Sylvain's talk was also informal . . . he told of Haiti . . . Haiti whose heart is sorely oppressed . . . those who could not understand French must have been charmed by the musical flow of beautiful foreign words from his lips . . . those who could understand his French heard a beautiful discourse full of poetry and color. The *Fireside Club* was the guest of Dr. Barnes at the *Barnes Foundation* in Merion, Pa., on Sunday afternoon, November twentieth . . . Oh, little did they know the rare treat in store for them. Here was a collection of pictures so beautiful that it hurt!

The slender fingers of Death have plucked two rare blossoms from the bosom of the Negro's heart . . . Clarissa Scott Delany and Florence Mills. The one serene and beautiful in the ways of the world . . . poised and with a great surety born of inner truth; the other filled with the verve of life and movement . . . afloat on the crystal wings of song. Not as many people will know and bemoan the death of Clarissa Scott Delany as will weep at the passing of the inimitable Florence for her paths were quiet and still. Never have I known or heard of a person so sure in the essence of beauty as she . . . her thoughts were so beautiful that they struck dumb fear in my heart. The world has passed by the bier of Florence Mills—I feel it a rare privilege to keep quiet sanctuary in my heart for Clarissa Scott Delany . . . she was my friend and I feel better for having known her . . . in my heart I shall remember always her fine enthusiasms: a picture of three dancing girls in the wind; *Of Human Bondage*, by Somerset Mangham, her favorite book; and *The Lake of Innisfree*, by William Butler Yeats, her favorite poem. . . . Out in the crystal clearness where she is she would like for me to quote these lines from this poem she loved so well.

I will arise and go now, and go to Innisfree,

* * * * * *

And I shall have some peace there, for peace comes dropping slow,
Dropping from the veils of the morning to where the cricket sings;
There midnight's all a-glimmer, and noon a purple glow,
And evening full of the linnet's wings.

I will arise and go now, for always night and day
I hear lake water lapping with low sounds by the shore;
While I stand on the roadway, or on the pavements grey,
I hear it in the deep heart's core.

Gwendolyn B. Bennett.

THE EBONY FLUTE

THE fluter has been far afield this month. . . . We had the rare pleasure of attending the *Stock-Taking and Fact-Finding Conference on the American Negro* which was held in Durham, North Carolina, December seventh to ninth. . . . There was an eye-opener, indeed! First of all they actually did find facts at this conference . . . and facts on every phase of Negro life in America—religion, work, wages, business, commerce manufacturing, politics, education, health, the press and the outlook of Negro youth. This latter part of the program showed an interesting departure from accepted conventions and conferences . . . here the race leaders dared to inject new blood into their discussions by inviting some of the fledglings to participate in their stock-taking and fact-finding. Those who know or have heard of Eugene Corbie of New York will know that he did not bite his tongue on the question of religion, politics or education; those who know the calm surety of Allison Davis now at Hampton Institute know that he certainly punctured a few myths in his level, exquisite voice; and those who know John P. Davis, publicity manager of Fisk University, know that with cryptic tongue and his inimitable sang froid he well told the leaders of American Negro life today exactly what he thought of them. The air as well as the discussion was charged with electricity but who can deny the facts found—pleasant or otherwise? But on the other hand the recognized race leaders had their say: Dr. Mordecai Johnson, President of Howard University, caught and held the audience with his eloquent appeal for the faith of our fathers. Eugene Kinckle Jones, Secretary of the National Urban League, stirred the company with the earnestness of his words; W. E. B. Du Bois shattered a few fables with his piercing analysis of existing political systems; W. A. Robinson, State Supervisor of Teacher Training and High Schools in Raleigh, told the bitter truth about Negro education in the South . . . oh, it was a long and noble list of names of people who shared the treasure of their knowledge with those who had come to hear them speak . . . over and above it all was the moving spirit of the men who caused this conference to be . . . W. G. Pearson, C. C. Spaulding, and James E. Shepard . . . and just the mere contemplation of those three names calls forth a flood of memory of the marvelous things they have done for and with the community at Durham . . . for thirty-odd years a group of some twenty-two men in Durham have worked diligently toward the high ideal of establishing a truly beautiful community and these three men have acted somewhat as leaders in the struggle. And right well have they succeeded—here we have Negroes owning $175,473.00 worth of land; $758,218.00 worth of buildings, and $602,-009.00 worth of stock and equipment . . . to say nothing of the fact that they are the sole owners of ninety-five businesses maintaining 2,105 employees. I came away from the Southland with my heart filled with courage and a great, beautiful belief in the Negro race . . . I treasure one rare moment of beauty from the rank and file of my busy days in North Carolina—seldom have I seen anything so beautiful as the hills there as they raised their sleepy heads out of the early mists of the morning . . . It was as though the earth had wrapped so much gauzy tulle of a soft purple hue around her shoulders!

All too soon our trip was over and we came rushing back this way. . . . Philadelphia was all in an uproar Sunday, December eleventh, over the fact of Dr. Barnes having the *Bordentown Singers* at the Foundation. . . . A chorus of thirty-odd voices gave a rare treat to a carefully chosen audience. They were trained and conducted by F. J. Work, formerly of Fisk University. Never have I heard the spirituals so beautifully sung. Mr. Work has done much to preserve the true character of these songs of worship as they were sung in the Negro churches of other years and right well has he succeeded. Mr. Work as done a great deal of research work on the subject of Negro spirituals . . . some of the spirituals that these children sang were new to almost every one present— *Keep Inchin' Along; Good Lord I Done Done What You Told Me to Do;* and *Rise Up Shep.* . . . Mr. Work made a delightful remark about this latter one. He said that his chorus would sing a Christmas Carol that he considered quite as beautiful as any of the famous carols that had been given the world by the English and the German . . . he was indeed right. Dr. Barnes gave a splendid speech introductory to the children's singing, tracing the origin of the spirituals from the beautiful African chants on through their contact with Christianity durng slavery days to their present popularity as a true work of art . . . he made the statement that he considered the spirituals the only true art that had been given the world by America . . . the greater portion of his audience was white, too. No one can doubt Barnes' genuine sympathy and belief in the Negro once they have heard him talk about their spirituals. Then too, Professor John Dewey, dean of American authorities on Education and Psychology, was present and gave a short talk expressing his appreciation for the opportunity of hearing such beautiful music and corroborated Dr. Barnes' statements of the distinction of the Negro's gift to the world.

All this talk about spirituals reminds me that Paul Robeson is making a tremendous success of his European tour . . . it is reported that people are being turned away from his Parisian concerts.

Show-Boat, Florenz Ziegfeld's new musical vehicle featuring Jules Bledsoe, has truly surpassed its fondest hopes of success in the provinces. So well taken was it in Philadelphia that it is to remain over another week. . . . After a glorious run *In Abraham's Bosom* has left Broadway. . . . *Porgy* still draws record-breaking crowds, although moved to *The Republic Theater* . . . which reminds us that the *New York Times* for Sunday, December fourth, carried an able article by Dorothy Heyward, co-author of the dramatic version of *Porgy* . . . it was entitled "Porgy's Native Tongue" and discusses the beautiful but intricate Negro dialect of South Carolina called Gullah . . . folklore redounds with tales about the interesting Negroes who inhabit the islands off the coast of South Carolina and speak this interesting language.

Leslie Pickney Hill has written a dramatic history of *Toussaint L'Ouverture* which is published by *The Christopher Publishing House in Boston* . . . of it Agness Repplier says:—

"No American Negro had hitherto attempted a work of any such range, elevation and artistic merit as this. Mr. Hill has told the story of one of the most stirring and surprising epochs in the history of the western world in his own way . . . a rather new and daring way."

I understand that Rudolph Fisher has completed the manuscript of his novel . . . it is to be called *The Walls of Jericho.*

God's Trombones is listed among the fifty best illustrated books published during the last year. . . . Aaron Douglas did the illustrations.

As we go to press Christmas is in the air and we wish you all a very merry Christmas and a glad New Year.

Gwendolyn B. Bennett.

THE EBONY FLUTE

WELL, we have come deliciously close to the workings of the present day drama in the last day or two..... one of those "big moments" that come only in the life of an actor stalked through our office with almost phantom tread..... Miss Dorothy Embry of the OPPORTUNITY office corps who had for nights upon night, played the part of one of the merry throng in the caste of *Porgy* came into sudden fame when for six glorious performances she played the part of Crown's Bess. . . . Miss Evelyn Ellis, the regular actress in the part, was indisposed for a day or two . . . endless days of rehearsing understudy lines seldom receive their just praise . . . being an understudy is such a thankless job! Upon Miss Ellis' return to the caste *The Theatre Guild* presented Miss Embry with a handsome check as a token of their appreciation for her having played the part in the star's absence. And so we go doggedly about our work for another span after a few tremors of excitement. . . . Gee it must be great to be an actress!!!

Which reminds us that Wallace Thurman of the caste of *Porgy* has written a play of Harlem life. . . . I have heard that it is very good and that negotiations are on foot for its purchase. . . . I understand that it is to be a Broadway production. At this writing a tentative title for the play is *Black Mecca*. Should this play receive a Broadway production a great precedent will be established. namely, that a Negro has a right at least to attempt to portray his own drama of existence.

We were very interested in attending the *Exhibition of Fine Arts by Negro Artists* that was held under the auspices of the Harmon Foundation and the Commission on the Church and Race Relations Federal Council of Churches. One saw there many names one had known before: Laura Wheeler Waring, Aaron Douglas, Alan Freelon, William Edouard Scott and Augusta Savage. For the most part the work exhibited was surprisingly academic with but few new departures from the beaten track of Art as it is taught in the general run of American art schools. Mrs. Laura Wheeler Waring's work stood out for its sheer technical proficiency. . . . Her canvas entitled *Head of a Young Girl* was done in lush, warm color and I wondered that it had not been awarded the prize rather than *Anna Washington Derry* which did receive the award. Mrs. Waring deserved this prize as a fit benison for the years she has toiled relentlessly. Each of Mrs. Waring's seven canvasses were ably painted with a sure hand. By far the most unusual and original work of the entire exhibit was that of Sargent Johnson. . . . The porcelain head entitled *Sammy* was awarded a special prize of two hundred and fifty dollars . . . this charming bit of statuary was sold within a surprisingly short time to Mrs. Alexander. . . . There were one or two very fine etchings by Albert Smith who has been working in Paris for several years . . . and by the way he is in America at this writing . . . his etchings have received high acclaim among art critics in Paris. He has exhibited in several of the noted Paris Salons. *The Schooners* by Palmer C. Hayden was again on exhibit . . . this is the painting which received First Award in Fine Arts of the Harmon Awards for Distinguished Achievement Among Negroes for 1926. . . . Hale W. Woodruff, winner of the second Harmon award in Fine Arts for 1926, writes from Paris that Mr. Hayden has recently had an exhibit there which received very favorable comment.

And books . . . Dr. W. E. B. Du Bois' novel to be published about March fifteenth by *Harcourt, Brace and Company* is to be called *Dark Princess* and is the tale of a young Negro doctor, driven from the country by prejudice, who goes to Germany and there meets a dark Indian princess with whom he falls in love. . . . March fifteen is the date set for several of the books written recently by Negro authors. . . . *Big Ditch* by Eric Walrond will be published on that date. . . . Mr. Walrond's book is not a novel but is a non-fictional study of the history of the Panama Canal. *Home To Harlem*, a full-length novel by Claude McKay, has had its publication date changed from the fall to the early spring, too. Which reminds us that we received but a few days ago a very charming letter from Mr. McKay in which he enclosed a clipping from *Petit Provencal*. "Severine" writes a column entitled *Mon frere Cham* in which she mentions the fact that Rene Maran, author of *Batouala*, wrote a very bitter article for the *Journal du Peuple* in which he retraces the sad but meritorious career of Colonel Martenol who suffered so many injustices because of his color. Severine goes on to trace the race situation in many different countries telling in the course of her article of the lynching of Leonard Wood in Kentucky . . . finally she asks in satirical despair, *Des barbares, ces Americains-la? Ah! certes oui!* However, she concludes that the Europeans may not speak with too much scorn of America's barbarity for have they not the memory of the Congo atrocities and the gruesome tale of the four peasants who were buried alive in Pologne. Severine is one of the best known Parisian journalists.

And to return to books . . . Nella Larsen's *Quicksand* has for its publication date March thirtieth. *In the Valley and Other Carolina Plays* by Paul Green, author of *In Abraham's Bosom* has recently been published by the *Samuel French Publishing Company* . . . among other plays of colored folk this book contains *The No-count Boy*, the play which won first place in the *Belasco Little Theatre Tournament* a year or two ago. *Black and White: An Anthology of Washington Verse*, edited by J. C. Bryars is on the book-stands now . . . this book contains both white and colored poets . . . although it is edited by a white man there are more Negroes in the volume than whites.

There is a goodly assortment of contest announcements this month. . . . *Contemporary Verse*, a monthly, offers Gladys Shaw Erskine Quatrain Prize of ten dollars and a year's subscription to *Contemporary Verse* for the best quatrain on any subject submitted to the magazine before midnight, February first . . . also the Benjamin Musser Prize of twenty dollars for the best poem not over thirty-four lines in any poetic form including free verse on any theme submitted before midnight, April first . . . the address of *Contemporary Verse* is 107 South Mansfield Avenue, Margate, Atlantic City, New Jersey . . . and so, young poets, get busy!

The second issue of *Black Opals*, the voice of the New Negro group in Philadelphia, was out for Christmas. . . . Folks interested in the literary output of the young Negro writers will be glad that this word-child continues to thrive. I had the rare pleasure of being asked to be their guest editor for this issue and so I watched it grow from the first stages of manuscript infancy to its present happy debut before its readers. . . . I understand that the *Black Opals* have been asked to visit the *Quill Club* in Boston in the spring of the year. Such interchange is good . . . and mayhap some year both of these groups with one or two of New York's younger, newer Negroes will get together and go to visit the *Ink Slingers* in California. Which gives us an opportunity to make a pretty bow of thanks for the lovely card with "Greetings from California" which Julian Bagley sent to *The Ebony Flute* for its Christmas.

GWENDOLYN B. BENNETT.

THE EBONY FLUTE

WE hasten to welcome another group of creative workers to the fold. . . . *Book and Bench,* comprising four writers of verse, five prose writers, two composers of music and one painter, has been organized in Topeka, Kansas, since last fall. They plan publishing a year-book, entitled *Urge,* early in May. . . . The number grows. . . . The Quill Club in Boston, The Ink-Slingers in California and Black Opals in Philadelphia . . . to say nothing of the many groups in New York.

Uncle Tom's Cabin, the American cinema featuring James B. Lowe, a Negro, in the part of Uncle Tom, has been enthusiastically received in England. In December it began its run at the *London Pavilion, Piccadilly Circus.* Mr. Lowe appears in person in a prologue to the picture in which there are real Negroes singing spirituals. *The Glasgow Bulletin, The Illustrated Graphic, Cinema, The Daily Chronicle,* and *Reynold's* give unmeasured acclaim to Mr. Lowe's acting. A special benefit performance of this moving picture was held on Sunday, January the twenty-ninth. The proceeds of the performance were given in aid of the Mayor of Westminster's Flood Relief Fund. The program included such internationally known Negro entertainers as The Three Eddies, Noble Sissle, Eubie Blake, The Four Harmony Kings and none other than Josephine Baker who "flew" over from Paris for the occasion.

Lawrence Brown, partner of Paul Robeson and former accompanist of Roland Hayes has left Paris for London where he will give several concerts. Thence he will go to Cannes and Vienna where he will fill several drawing-room engagements.

Forbes Randolph's *Kentucky Jubilee Choir* are to be heard with "Roxy" over Radio Station W.J.Z. on Sunday evenings. The jubilee choir is made up of eight male voices that were picked from an audition of five hundred voices from all over the country. It has been said that the audition for the chorus cost about ten thousand dollars. These singers have seventy-five songs in their repertoire. . . . *The Dixie Jubilee Singers* under the direction of Miss Eva A. Jessye, author of *My Spirituals,* gave concerts on Saturday, Monday and Wednesday during the week of February eleventh to eighteenth at the Wanamaker Store in New York City. Miss Jessye's book will be remembered with delight by those who have seen it. By the way, *Forty Negro Spirituals* by Clarence Cameron White has been published by the Theodore Presser Company in Philadelphia. This book is well edited and many of the arrangements are more charming than those to which we have become accustomed. Clarence Cameron White has just been awarded First Prize for Distinguished Achievement as a Violinist and Composer by the Harmon Foundation. At the same time Dr. Nathaniel Dett was awarded First Prize for Distinguished Achievement in Music . . . the two awards were made because there was no musical award made last year. No longer ago than Sunday afternoon, February nineteenth, we had the pleasure of meeting Dr. Dett. It was at the Barnes Foundation in Merion, Pa. . . . Dr. Albert C. Barnes had invited a small group of people, both colored and white, to the Foundation where he spoke on "African Art". . . . With the beautiful pieces from the Barnes collection as examples of what is best in African art it is quite evident that Dr. Barnes succeeded in convincing his audience that the Africans truly had an art form which bore easy comparison with the best in Greek and Egyptian art. But to go back to our meeting Dr. Dett. . . . We had always just missed him on every occasion so that we were delighted to run upon him in this unexpected fashion. He was with Alan Freelon . . . who, by the way, has just completed the illustrations for a score by Dr. Dett . . . and it is to Mr. Freelon that I owe this glad surprise. Dr. Dett has the simplicity that goes with true greatness. Youth pervades his talking and thinking. He was as avid a searcher into the truths and beauties of plastic art as he must be into the hidden mysteries of music. He paid us the pretty compliment of saying, "The Ebony Flute continues in its even dulcet tones" and of course we were friends right off after that. In the course of our tour around the galleries we mentioned the fact that Edmund T. Jenkins had spoken with such respect and admiration for Dr. Dett's work. . . . Dr. Dett then spoke of what a tremendous loss the race had suffered in losing Jenkins, stating that he was perhaps the only Negro that had done any reputable work with symphony composition. I was pleased to know that Dr. Dett had seen and spent a great deal of time with Mr. Jenkins on that last discouraging trip which Jenkins made to America. In so many words Nathaniel Dett, fellow genius and musician, said that Edmund Jenkins bore the stamp of a divine fire and that his great dream was misunderstood and scorned by those who should have been his friends.

Meek Mose, a drama by Frank Wilson who plays the leading part in the caste of *Porgy,* the Theatre Guild production, opened in New York City at the *Princess Theatre* on Monday, February sixth. There had been a single week's tryout in Philadelphia . . . although most of the Quaker City and Gotham dramatic reviewers gave the play a fair break yet it was quite evident that only an unimportant few of them spoke of it as great drama. The plot was hackneyed . . . here and there the acting was superb . . . the music, arranged and directed by Alston Burleigh was beautiful. But to us the play in itself and its success or failure was unimportant. We were more concerned with the fact that here had arrived the day when the theatre goers of Broadway were willing to attend seriously to the things that Negroes had to say about their own lives . . . then too, here were such players as Charles Moore who had played for nine years with *Williams and Walker* in their hey-day, Laura Bowman who has played for years in Negro stock companies, and J. L. Criner long known as one of the Lafayette Players who were in essence the spirit of the old school in Negro acting and yet they were taking a leading part in the new movement towards true Negro expression upon the American stage. So . . . de sun do move. . . . *Meek Mose* was produced by Lester Walton of the staff of the *New York World.*

Carl Van Vechten, author of *Nigger Heaven,* is nominated for the Hall of Fame in *Vanity Fair* for February. We are very glad for this for whether you are a person who likes *Nigger Heaven* or not you must admit that this book paved the way for a good bit of the writing that Negroes themselves are doing today . . . and goodness knows that is surely something. But then you see we've always liked *Nigger Heaven* regardless of what many of our friends have said or thought about it. *Gwendolyn B. Bennett*

THE EBONY FLUTE

BY far the most important thing that has happened in the literary world during the last month is the marriage of Countee Cullen to Yolande Du Bois. Mr. Cullen is the editor of *The Dark Tower* as well as the author of several volumes of verse. Miss Du Bois is by her own right something of a literateur. And of course there is *Home to Harlem* by Claude Mc Kay, author of *Harlem Shadows*, a book of poetry. Well now here is something! Heralded by loud hurrahs on the lips of all the critics, it has within a month's period achieved a place on the New York *World's* list of best sellers. Mr. Mc Kay has approached his novel with the same sensitiveness that he showed in his poetry. However, it is interesting to note how Negroes, themselves, receive what he has written. I am a bit afraid that they are going to resent the subject-matter of his book and in so doing they will miss the surety of his handling the material he has chosen and the beauty of his touch albeit the tale he tells is not a pretty one. Mr. Mc Kay is at present in Marseille where he has been for some time. This is indeed a gala year for Negro literature. Dr. W. E. B. Du Bois' novel *Dark Princess* ought to be in the book stalls any day now. Nella Larsen's *Quicksand* has just arrived. And let me say that many folks will be interested to hear that this book does not set as its tempo that of the Harlem cabaret—this is the story of the struggle of an interesting cultured Negro woman against her environment. Negroes who are squeamish about writers exposing our worst side will be relieved that Harlem night-life is more or less submerged by this author in the psychological struggle of the heroine—and in the fall Walter White will have returned from southern France where he is now at work. Which reminds me of an interesting tale that James Weldon Johnson tells of how Walter White had thought that he would reside in a villa of romantic French nomenclature only to find that the home in which he at present finds himself goes under the name, *Villa Sweet Home*. But to go back to books— *Black Majesty* by John W. Vandercook, author of *Tom-Tom*, is now on sale in the book shops. Having set his beautiful pace in the writing of *Tom-Tom*, he was hard put to maintain it in this story of Henry Christophe, King of Haiti. One is agreeably surprised to find that *Black Majesty* ably keeps pace with *Tom-Tom*—here is historical fact woven into a sequence that reads like a fairytale. Dr. Odum of the University of North Carolina has given the public *Rainbow Round My Shoulder* which has received glowing tribute by the critics. Dr. Odum, it will be remembered, wrote two books on Negro spirituals as co-author with Guy B. Johnson.

Up From Slavery by Booker T. Washington is to be translated into Turkish and used in the schools of Turkey. This seems to have been a month for art exhibits. Allan R. Freelon of Philadelphia showed thirty paintings in an exhibit given under the sponsorship of the Alpha Kappa Alpha Sorority . . . Albert Smith, formerly of Paris and Madrid, also held an exhibit in New York City . . . Mr. Smith's etchings have received much favorable comment.

Keep Shufflin', another Miller and Lyle production, is holding forth with enviable success at *Dalys 63rd Street*

Theatre . . . *Porgy*, after a brilliant run in New York City has gone on tour . . . at this writing Washington audiences are experiencing this thing of beauty . . . Alexander Woolcott in the *N. Y. World* for Sunday, March the eighteenth, picks this play for the *Pulitzer Prize* with this word of praise:

The performance, in which the tolling from a distant steeple, the boom of fog-horns in the harbor, the rackety laughter of the pickaninies, the humming of the spirituals, the clink of hammer on stone, the rattle of dice in the courtyard, the snores of the drunken and the sorrowing of the heavy-laden have, by a miracle of imaginative direction, been orchestrated into a rhapsody in brown, remains alive and true. Six months of playing have not staled nor dulled it, nor robbed it of the throb of life. And the climax of the first act, when the monstrous nightmare shadows cast by the tossing arms of the mourners, dance a weird and frightening rigadoon on the bare, scrofulous wall of a once gracious room—that climax seems now, as it seemed when it was new, one of the high memorable moments in the history of the American theatre.

This gives us an opportunity to rejoice in the fact that Paul Robeson played Crown in the caste of *Porgy* for a spell . . . this is as it had originally been planned. However, Paul Robeson has now gone to London where he is to appear in the English edition of *Show Boat*. Speaking of Paul Robeson and his singing reminds us that Maude Cuney Hare, the folk-lorist, has just finished giving a group of four lectures on *Negro and Creole Music* at the *Allied Arts Studio* in Boston. William Richardson, baritone, gave the song illustrations that went with these lectures. But to return to the theatre . . . *Meek Mose* has gone by the board . . . the home edition of *Show Boat* continues with Jules Bledsoe singing very beautifully . . . *Coquette* in which Abbie Mitchell plays a minor part goes along evenly. By the by, Abbie Mitchell has given several successful concerts in the last month. Alexander Woolcott goes so far as to predict that there will eventually be a Negro Theatre of which *In Abraham's Bosom* and *Porgy* are the harbingers. The Negro in drama again comes in for another bit of publicity in the *New York Herald Tribune* for Sunday March eighteenth . . . *Color Notes*, a full-length column by William M. Houghton, appears in the dramatic section of that paper. The entire article is devoted to a discussion of the Negro in the American theatre.

On Thursday evening, March twenty-second, *Opportunity Magazine* held forth in a broadcasting hour over Station WABC at *Steinway Hall* . . . Aaron Douglas read a paper on the Negro artist; Countee Cullen, Jessie Fauset and Arna Bontemps read some of their poems; Dr. Albert C. Barnes gave a lecture on African Art; Miss Ernestine Covington played *Nocturne*, *E. Sharp Major* by Chopin and *Humoresque* by Rachmaninoff; Mrs. Lyndon Caldwell sang *Die Lotus Blume* and *Widmung* by Schumann and *Were You There* and *Go Down Moses* by Burleigh. Charles S. Johnson, editor of *Opportunity Magazine*, was the master of Ceremonies . . . he appropriately ended the evening with the quotation of an old African proverb which seems to have a vast prophetic quality. . . . *If you would tell anything to Heaven, tell it to the wind.*

And as we go to press the cherry blossoms are blooming . . . Just the other day I passed the miracle of a magnolia tree alight with blossoming candles.

Gwendolyn B. Bennett.

O PPORTUNITY is pleased to announce the addition to its staff of Countee Cullen, poet and author of COLOR, with whose extraordinary literary competence, particularly in the field of poetry, our readers are already acquainted. Mr. Cullen is not merely a leading Negro poet, but ranks in the first magnitude of the younger American poets. His coming to OPPORTUNITY we regard as both fortunate and significant, a step virtually decreed by the demands of that awakening generation to which this magazine, in many of its interests, has consistently addressed itself. Mr. Cullen will select the poetry and, in his office as assistant to the editor, counsel with that large and growing group of young writers of verse whose work is gradually breaking into light. His opinion on books and events of literary significance will appear regularly as a special new department, and there will be occasional articles and poetry from his pen. He is a graduate of New York University, holder of a Phi Beta Kappa Key, a Master of Arts from Harvard, one who, even as an undergraduate, was a contributor to practically all of the important literary magazines; thus he brings to OPPORTUNITY and its friends, and to the parent organization— the National Urban League, rare gifts and a magnificent capacity for usefulness to the whole cause. There will be a special appropriateness, by way of marking the beginning of Mr. Cullen's formal connection, in carrying, in our next issue, an article by Izetta Winter Robb of the University of Minnesota which, along with its own brilliant appraisal of his work, reflects some measure of those new values in racial understanding at large for which his art and energies are already responsible.

Countee Cullen

The Dark Tower

THE last week of 'White Wings'! Step up, boys and girls, and see how a gay and and gallant gentleman may die'." Thus Miss Edna Ferber, in an open letter to Mr. Alexander Woollcott of the *New York World*, baited the younger generation to a last minute attendance at a play that after an all too brief run was closing because it was too beautiful and rare and gay to be a financial success. Those of us whose nostrils can still quiver in the sulphurous atmosphere of a challenge, went and laughed and applauded, to come away indignant but helpless in a world that, for the most part, lets the fine decline and the stupid flourish like the green bay. To be sure, most of us didn't understand it all right down to the last elusive symbol, but we knew that it was a riotously jubilant and a pitifully whimsical drama of the thing we are in arms against: the attempt of old uncompromising patterns to rule in a world needing the robust and the new, not because they are novel, but because they fit into the shifting grooves of our times. The younger generation went, Miss Ferber, and they laughed at and pitied the stiff-backed Inches; they fought along with Mary Todd; and best of all they appreciated to the fullest Joseph, that marvelous horse of totally unequine parts who could enjoy a joke and tell one, and die that the things which were beating in the womb of time might have a birth. It *was* a gay and gallant death!

On the whole it was a month of catastrophes for performances in which we were more than passingly interested for both *Deep River* and *Black Boy*, which we had expected to hold the boards for a large part of the season, the one because of its inveigling music topped with a most adequate cast that included Julius Bledsoe, Lottice Howell, Frank Harrison and Rose McClendon; the other because we felt that any play could stand for a while that gave Paul Robeson a chance to exercise his vibrant personality, and to sing a stave or two. Paul Robeson can act as well as he can sing; it is even probable that the thespian heritage in him outvalues the melodic, and one would like to see him in another play worthy of his powers. That calls for stalwart writing when you remember *The Emperor Jones*. It is a far cry from Eugene O'Neil to William Shakespeare, but after *The Emperor Jones,* to bill Robeson in anything except *Othello* seems retrogres-

---

PRAYER

Now that I know
  That what I am must be,
Lord, take Thy rod
  And change me to a tree.

Now that I see
  And now the best is known
Lord, wave Thy hand
  And turn me to a stone;

A dull, dumb stone,
  Or a stark old tree,
Thy rain, Thy wind,
  Thy lightning over me.

EDWIN MORGAN in November *Bookman*.

---

sive to us on more points than that of time.

At last we have had explained to our satisfaction the identity of that gay ebony Harlemite whom, at odd moments of the day and night, we have met, with his limping gait and his feet encased in the queerly-patterned shoes, which we now suspect were expressly made to conceal the cloven hooves within them. Witter Bynner in the *New Yorker* has tracked the Prince of Darkness to his lair — Harlem. *Black Lucifer* is the poem.

He was always as blithe, always as black
  As any boy in Harlem:
Light used to glitter on his back
  In heaven as it does in Harlem.
He sang hosannas to the Lord
And watched what he was bowing toward,
Till Lucifer at last was bored
  And came away to Harlem.

And now you can find him any night,
  Glittering in Harlem,
Thanking God that he isn't white
  Like visitors in Harlem.
With a paler skin he might have stayed
And tinkled a harp and sung and prayed.
And where would you rather be on parade—
  In heaven, or in Harlem?

What seems to us the high water mark in race consciousness was exhibited by the gentleman who recently inquired at the new circulating library in Harlem for a copy of *Negro Heaven*. Happily the young lady who served him was not meticulous as far as titles go.

Courage is costly, and in this world a departure from precedent costlier, as Julian S. Starr and R. K. Fowler, erstwhile editor and assistant editor respectively of the *Carolina Magazine*, literary mouthpiece of the University of North Carolina, have undoubtedly learned by now. For they have both been deposed because, in the last edition of the magazine they published a story in which the principal characters were a white girl and a mulatto. And this just after we had been turning double somersaults and triple handsprings because that same issue carried a sketch by Eric Walrond, along with a pronunciamento asking for contributions from people of all races, colors, creeds, and political leanings!

Apparently we belong to a race that with charming inappreciation of the rights due the planter insists upon reaping where it has not sowr.. And once in a while the rightful heir, apparent to all except ourselves, is moved to feeble protest. Some of us fail to see that the various excitements of Negro living can appeal to writers who share no blood relationship with us at all, whose interest in us does not go beyond the perfectly legitimate and dispassionate concern of the artist for his plastic materials. Because Miss Lenore Ulric plays Lulu Belle with an uncanny certainty, and because Miss Lottice Howell in *Deep River* was an entrancing quadroon both visibly and vocally is no reason why the geneses of these actresses should be amiably reconstructed to make them, as it were, to the manner born, as an explanation of their felicitous portrayals of their roles. Nor should the fact that *Porgy,* in our opinion, is to date the best novel woven around Negro characters, subjects its author, Du Bose Heyward, to gratuitous and unwilling adoption into the Negro race. A recent note in the *Saturday Review of Literature* informs us that Mr. Heyward is "more moved than delighted at the question which is being asked about his degree of pigmentation." His friend Hervey Allen is even preparing a brief critical biography of Mr. Heyward which Doran will publish as a booklet, and which "ought to stop any question as to Heyward's color and quality." Long ago Carl Van Vechten was taken into the fold, but we fancy more to his amusement than to his alarm, if any word of his initiation has come to him.

***

We believe that what is being read at the Harlem library is a fair index of what books are most in demand by Negroes, and in a measure indicative of the Negro's literary mind. The list for November is distinguished, almost highbrow. The books, listed according to the number of reservations on them, are: fiction: Dreiser's "American Tragedy", Erskine's "Private Life of Helen of Troy", Ferber's "Show Boat", Fauset's "There is Confusion", Van Vechten's "Nigger Heaven", White's "Flight", and Wren's "Beau Geste" and "Beau Sabreur"; nonfiction: De Kruif's "Microbe Hunters", Dell's "Intellectual Vagabondage", Dorsey's "Why We Behave Like Human Beings," Durant's "Story of Philosophy", Locke's "The New Negro", and Niles' "Black Haiti".

***

Our mind refuses to carry us back to a book by a new writer that has so completely ingratiated itself into our esteem, as has *The Time of Man* by Elizabeth Madox Roberts. (The Viking Press, $2.50), with such a lack of insinuating effort on the part of its author. This first novel by a woman whose fame heretofore was secured only to a discriminating few by her delightful book of children's verses, shows how incontestable is the affiliation between fine prose and fine poetry. The reader cannot turn the most casual page of this book without finding himself confronted by something

unalterably and irrevocably said. The author's style is a heaven-made marriage of words, with no incompatibility of phrase or sentence; divorce would be disastrous to this perfect mating. There has always been room to question the flat assertion frequently encountered that poets never write distinguished prose; now there is more room than ever, with the publication of (*The Time of Man.*) Read the following representative passage describing the marriage of Ellen Chesser, and see if its aloof dignity does not both hurt and heal you, silence you and cause you to sing:

"Then they went, all, into the outer room and stood about the walls. Ellen's eyes followed the child as she slipped in unpremeditated motions from place to place or stood in unfixed quiet. The room became very still as Ellen and Jasper stood beside the man, the brother who had been brought; or the man faced them, and joining their hands, said ceremonial words. His face was thin and set with ceremony, his hands moving rigidly over the words or settling down in hard, firm finality over the said word, fixed and done. Fixed forever, pronounced, finished, said and unrevoked, his words flowed down through the great hardness of his voice, a groundwork on which to lean, a foundation beneath a foundation, the framework of the house set and fixed in timbers and pinned together with fine strong wedges of trimmed hard wood. His voice trembled a little with its own fixity and hardness, but it erected a strong tower. In the end he made a prayer for herself and Jasper, and gave her a paper on which their names were written. The women shook her hand, and then the men came, their handshakes reserved and ceremonious. The child stood beside the wall, her gaze light and aloof, or she tapped her shoulder softly against the door or touched the latch, her look free and her way unhampered, and the beauty of her look came about Ellen as she gave her hand to the men."

This is a book to bow before in humble, breathless acknowledgment. Like the manner in which it is written, the story is simple and close to the earth, concerning one Ellen Chesser whose life seems a series of moving from place to place from the time we first encounter her as a backwoods girl to the time we leave her, a matron with many children, setting out with calm acceptance to accompany her husband in his search for a new home. Of great struggle there is none in the book, but whosoever starts it will end it, and relinquish it feeling that perfect performances are not solely of the past. Do you remember Maria Chapdelaine? You will remember Ellen Chesser also.

For your Christmas book list we recommend William Stanley Braithwaite's *Anthology of Magazine Verse for 1926,* and Elizabeth Madox Robert's *The Time of Man.* We assume that *Tropic Death* is already on your list.

William Stanley Braithwaite's anthologies of magazine verse are a yearly confirmation of what a greater poet than any therein assembled realized when he said "The poetry of earth is never dead." This year's edition (Anthology of Magazine Verse for 1926, B. J. Brimmer Co., Boston, $4.00), the Sesqui-Centennial number and the fourteenth annual issue, is, aside from being an anthology of the best magazine verse of 1926, a survey of American poetry from 1912 to 1926. No serious student of our verse can afford to neglect this volume. If American verse is going the way of all flesh with alarming alacrity, these poems collected by Mr. Braithwaite cannot be arraigned as evidence.

Besides the list of poems honored by inclusion in the anthology, a heady and stimulating symposium is offered in the section *Poetry of the United States,* where some of the most distinguished poets and critics of today discuss American verse somewhat geographically. Of special interest to us were the articles by Jessie B. Rittenhouse on the poetry of New England, that by Marianne Moore on the "New" Poetry since 1912, the caustic essay *On Poetry* in which E. Merrill Root takes up the cudgels for the poets against H. L. Mencken and the article on the Negro Poets of the United States, by our fervent arch-stimulator of the younger generation, Alain Locke.

Some—but these will not be the younger Negro poets—may take exception to Alain Locke's appraisal of the work of Negro poets in this statement: "Therefore I maintain that the work of Negro poets in the past has its chief significance in what it has led up to; through work of admittedly minor

and secondary significance and power a folk consciousness has slowly come into being and a folk tradition has been started on the way to independent expression and development." Truths the most self-evident are rarely accepted with corresponding immediacy.

There can be no question of the growth of expression in Negro poets in the past year or two when we consider that Mr. Braithwaite's anthology, in which poems are reprinted solely on their merits as poetry, contains this year works by no less than twelve Negro poets: Gwendolyn Bennett, Arna Bontemps, Jospeh Cotter, Waring Cuney, Frank Horne, Langston Hughes, Helene Johnson, Georgia Douglas Johnson, Chaliss Silvay, Wallace Thurman, and Lucy Ariel Williams. And with all the respect due our racial magazines from which most of these poets' work is reprinted, it is good to see the horizon widening in that Langston Hughes is reprinted from *The New Republic* and *The New York Herald-Tribune,* and Chaliss Silvay, a newcomer, from *The Will 'O The Wisp.*

Braithwaite's anthology has always been, to quote an appreciative reviewer, "a national institution", but we may for all that be pardoned a bit of selfish pride in this nationally recognized work of one of ours.

COUNTEE CULLEN.

THE DARK TOWER

Tom - Tom

by

MARGARET
VANDERCOOK

posed by

MAURICE
HUNTER

WE have been having an exciting time of it reading John W. Vandercook's *Tom-Tom*. Like the great drum that gave it its name, the book beats its way into the mind and the emotions with a steady insistency that still throbs long after the last word has been scanned and the book laid aside. Legion is not the name of books of descriptive travel creatively written, but Mr. Vandercook has succeeded in entering *Tom-Tom* into that restricted class. Moreover, he may rest in the knowledge that the genuine pleasure one gets in reading his creation does not subjugate the books's provocation to thought. Especially in his preface are we prone to take exception to Mr. Vandercook's assertions, however well-intentioned they may be. We are content to assume the obeisant attitude of the layman in reading the body of his book where we are ushered into the unknown realms of Suriname, definitely established by Mr. Vandercook as the quondam fabulous land of El Dorado; but the preface touches us to the quick, and we must be pardoned a protest or two toward our personal interest. For example, Mr. Vandercook says, "To my mind there is no hope for the modern Negro in the way he is now vainly going. Slavery lasted too long and ended too suddenly for the whites ever to forget and forgive enough to allow the black people into our sancta. Our state, our civilization is our own, for we made it. It is fair, as things in this partial world can be fair, that we should keep it, use it for ourselves, and shut the outcasts that we made away from it." Surely, Mr. Vandercook has made a hasty judgment in saying *our state, our civilization is our own, for we made it,* leaving the Negro no share in this gigantic project. Only a few days ago a southern white publication in Richmond, Virginia, was fairer-minded than that, when it said, "Next to the Anglo-Saxon race the most numerous in this country is the Negro race. Few people realize what that race has meant to this country. They made the south a great agricultural country, and largely because of their labor it is becoming greater each year. The agricultural south has furnished much of the cotton and other products that have

made the New England States a great manufacturing section. Thus the Negro has added wealth and prosperity to both the North and the South." Toward the end of *Tom-Tom,* Mr. Vandercook himself admits that Negro music constitutes the one great American contribution to the artistic world. And no civilization ever rose above its artistic achievements.

Mr. Vandercook has thorough sympathy for the inhabitants of Suriname, giving us a picture of persons far more subtle, intelligent, and proud than we have been wont to deem these people whom we have known only by hearsay, not by the actual contact on which this author has based his observations. Time and time again his briefs for the Bushnegroes are couched in language which is an ambush of amused and covert pricks at both white and colored people in our varying civilization. Here is his interesting comment upon the psychic element in Bushnegro life: "In our country we believe a man is telling the truth if he can bring forward half a dozen reputable people who will testify that they agree with him. In Suriname there are twenty thousand witnesses who will swear upon their life that they *do actually, physically hear the discourse of dead lips.* Yet we whites complacently make an exception to our own law of evidence in this extra-curricula case, and sniff intolerantly." Most Christians will not relish the Bushnegro's attitude toward missionaries as set down in *Tom-Tom:* "All our theology appears utterly illogical and contradictory to the forest black man. Christ, as taught by missionaries, demands everything and gives nothing in exchange—except occasional doles of bad rice and scratchy, undesirable clothes. He is the symbol of all that is oppressive and wrong about the white man's world. Mission work is founded on the self-satisfied premise that the Negroes are an inferior race. Just so long as intelligent Bushnegroes cling to the knowledge that they are superior to stupid priests—mission work will fail in Suriname."

The American Negro with his penchant towards slick hair, bleaching creams, and beauty devices for thinning bulbous lips and straightening flaring noses, comes in for his share of criticism slyly insinuated in this paragraph, which we can imagine Mr. Vandercook writing with infinite approval: "Both the Djoekes and Aucaners are black as the sun can cook them. It is their supreme pride, the perfect proof of their complete superiority to all men of lighter shades. Among them a youth or maiden whose hair is not tightly kinked is cast out of the village to die wandering alone in the forest. There is a test. A heavy iron nail, or, in lack of that, a splinter of very heavy wood, is stuck in the wool just above the center of the forehead. If the kinks do not hold it tightly from that moment on, through every condition and exercise of life, the straight-haired one is put away. The same fate, exile, awaits a child who shows a taint of foreign blood, even if there is no other proof of alien heritage besides the accidental curse of a brownish skin. Each must be black as coal or go."

It occurs to us that Mr. Vandercook may have meant to be satirical in the preface to which we object, but it is the sort of satire that can be easily mistaken by people in our predicament where most things not said openly for us are construed against us. We remember thoroughly delighting in David Garnett's story *The Sailor's Return* until we reached the concluding paragraph where Mr. Garnett spoke of Tulip as "knowing her place" when she returned as a servant to the home in which she had formerly been mistress. It took Carl Van Vechten to jolt us into the realization that Mr. Garnett was being subtle and satirical, all in Tulip's favor and ours.

We are glad to welcome back *The World Tomorrow* under the editorship of Kirby Page and Devere Allen. We can think of no magazine of its kind that is doing work with quite the same magnetism for results. Of especial interest to us is its calm but effective column. *Not in the Headlines*. Truth gets a hearing in *The World Tomorrow*, and we are thankful for it.

[The outstanding birth of the month was that of *Fire*, the new quarterly devoted to work by the younger Negro artists. Its first issue was edited by Wallace Thurman, in association with Langston Hughes, Gwendolyn Bennett, Richard Bruce, Zora Neale Hurston, Aaron Douglas, and John Davis, all members of the Board of Editors. With its startlingly vivid Douglas cover done in red and black, *Fire*, on the whole, represents a brave and beautiful attempt to meet our need for an all-literary and artistic medium of expression. Its contents are, in places, exemplary of the tyro, but in the aggregate there is enough good writing and art in the issue to establish for it a definite *raison d'être*. There seems to have been a wish to shock in this first issue, and, though shock-proof ourselves, we imagine that the wish will be well realized among the readers of *Fire*. However, ample extenuation for what some may call a reprehensible story can be found in the beautifully worded, *Smoke, Lilies, and Jade*, by Richard Bruce. We liked Wallace Thurman's editorial better than we did his story, though why he should have contended for a monument to the author of *Nigger Heaven* is more than we can see. This first issue of *Fire* introduced to us Edward Silvera, probably the youngest of the Negro poets, and a person decidedly worth watching, along with Waring Cuney. Arthur Huff Fauset flays the intelligentsia in sprightly and amusing, even if ineffective, fashion. The laurels of the issue, we think, ought to be divided between Aaron Douglas for his three caricatures and Zora Neale Hurston for her play *Color Struck*. Both these contributions are noteworthy for their method of treating racial subjects in a successfully detached manner. This sort of success, more than any other, augurs good for the development of Negro artists. *Fire* is well worth its price, and it is good to know that another issue is being planned.]

A literary event that we consider worth waiting for is

James Weldon Johnson's book of sermon-poems scheduled for publication next year. We heard Mr. Johnson read two of them recently: "Go Down, Death", a funeral sermon, and "Judgment Day," both as graphic and as gripping as their forerunner, "The Creation", one of the finest poems by a Negro poet. We hope Mr. Johnson will do a special treatment of that old sermon of fire and thunder about the dry bones in the valley, a number in every revivalist repertoire, and, when well done, as striking a reminder of the great day to come as one would want to experience.

"Odes of Worship and Service" by Henry Coffin Fellow is a purposeful book of poems, written with a sincerity and intensity of feeling that atone, in a measure, for the frequent use of the first word and the most imminent imagery. The very titles of the various sections of the book (Worship, Service, War, and Meditation) are exemplary of the author's concern with the vital aspects of living. To us the book as a whole represents the curious instance of the poet's sympathy with, and quick espousal of, the things that matter lost and negatived by an inadequate skill in employing the tools of the trade. A fine flare for the dramatic in such poems as "The Death of Jim" and "Just a Dead Boy" wavers of its mark because of the impoverished language that fails to supplement it. This verbal indigence, however, aids rather than hinders the author in that sort of verse which prospers under just such seriousness and simplicity—poems which, while not hymns themselves, have a hymnlike quality that might well shunt the author's poetic endeavors into that genre with very satisfying results.

The Harlem branch of the New York Public Library lists this month's most popular books, with the reservations on them, as follows: Theodore Dreiser's *American Tragedy*, 23, John Erskine's *Galahad*, 6; his *Private Life of Helen of Troy*, 6; Edna Ferber's *Show Boat*, 11; Carl Van Vechten's *Nigger Heaven*, 58; and Eric Walrond's *Tropic Death*, 7. Non-fiction books most in demand are: Durant's *Story of Philosophy*, 14; Vandercook's *Tom-Tom*, 10; De Kruif's *Microbe Hunters*, 8; Dr. Joseph Collins' *The Doctor Looks at Life and Love*, 7; Browne's *This Believing World*, 4; and Cheyney's *European Background of American History*, 4. For varying reasons, running the gamut from unqualified approval to intense dislike, this column endorses the reading of the following from the list: *Tropic Death, Galahad, The Private Life of Helen of Troy, Tom-Tom, The Story of Philosophy, The Doctor Looks at Life and Love,* and *Nigger Heaven*.

THE DARK TOWER

DESPITE his admission that Josephine Baker's attire in the Folies Bergère in Paris consists of a "get-up" of "a few bananas and not too much jewelry," it was a beautifully phrased tribute that Mr. E. E. Cummings paid this new object of Parisian adulation in last September's issue of *Vanity Fair*. He writes, "As a member of the 'Chocolate Dandies' chorus, she resembled some tall, vital, incomparably fluid nightmare which crossed its eyes and warped its limbs in a purely unearthly manner—some vision which opened new avenues of fear, which suggested nothing but itself and which, consequently, was strictly aesthetic. It may seem preposterous that this terrifying nightmare should have become the most beautiful (and beautiful is what I mean) (*such a parenthetical asseveration by Mr. Cummings, we think, may be taken as either mere emphasis, or a manner of emphasis born of hearing the blues*) star of the parisian stage. Yet such is the case."

"Herself is two perfectly fused things: an entirely beautiful body and a beautiful command of its entirety. Her voice (simultaneously uncouth and exquisite—luminous as only certain dark voices are luminous) is as distinctly a part of this body as are her gestures, which emanate a spontaneousness or personal rigidity only to dissolve it in a premeditation at once liquid and racial."

Josephine Baker's rise, though to her it may have seemed at times tragically laggard in gathering its momentum, has been undeniably meteoric, and now, in Paris at least, her ascendancy far outtwinkles that of her sister stars. Last summer, watching her being lowered from the Folies Bergère roof on the great glass mirror on which she does the Charleston, and remembering vividly the bizarre marionette that pirouetted and jerked in *The Chocolate Dandies*, we could not help but gasp at the transformation. The ugly duckling had really been a swan, and we had never known it. She was like Cinderella touched with the magic wand—only this Cinderella balked at clothes. And Paris is in a state of violent hysterics over her; there are Josephine Baker perfumes, costumes, bobs, statuettes; in fact, she sets the pace. All that remains now is for her to try on the glass slipper and marry the prince.

G. de la Fouchardière, one of the cleverest of French journalists, in *L'Ouevre* writes amiably and impatiently of the New Vogue. His article "La Femme En Serie" is interesting enough to warrant full translation:

It appears that the arbiters of fashion, who are tyrannical dealers, have already decided what type of women shall prevail this winter: they shall be small, brown, and rather plump.

You ask how the women who, in accordance with this summer's vogue, are large, blond, and curveless, will contrive this winter to be plump, small, and brown? Do not trouble yourself about them; they will find a way, because it is the fashion, because it is necessary, because they cannot do otherwise. We have seen many other metamorphoses. And do not claim that these astonishing transformations are due to art: they are natural. Nothing differs more from a caterpillar than a butterfly: all the caterpillars conform to the new mode of spring; for a caterpillar would be ridiculous among butterflies, even as a butterfly would be incongruous among caterpillars.

In the severe sunlight of August, one sees women, who, stretched along the sandy beach, expose to the burning rays in absolute innocence, as much of their skin as it is

decent (strictly speaking) to reveal. For them this is the most absorbing of bathing occupations, and the most heroic because of the long patience which it exacts. The lady thus exposed declares stoically, "No, go have your tea without me; I am busy broiling myself." It is required that on returning to Paris she be perfectly broiled; failing which, she will be given the cold shoulder at dances.

The time is not far past when the Parisian lady, at the sea shore or in the country, had but one concern: to preserve the whiteness of her skin from the attacks of the sun. Sunburn was then a sign of vulgarity; it betrayed the goose-girl and the fish-wife. Women protected themselves from it as from the plague with umbrellas, gloves, hats, with creams sold them by the perfumers, which guaranteed a freshness of complexion. Today the perfumers sell beauty products the virtue of which for the skin is that of the walnut, and the instant application of which is equal to three months at the sea-shore, without the expense and the bother.

In the same manner we have all known the time when a country girl was recognized by having her hair compactly plastered with pommade, glistening, and tightly drawn back behind. Such a coiffure spelled tradition for an actress who playing in vaudeville the role of badly turned out country wench, tried to make the public laugh. It was frightful; it was vulgar. I hasten to add that today it is charming and distinguished. Today it is the country girls, who never being up to date, bear visages framed in vaporous curls. A Parisienne must have glistening locks, well plastered with pommade, and drawn tightly back behind. And as, in addition, the color of the skin must be comparable to that given by a stereotyped plate which has been submitted too long a time to the sun, we can aver that the Parisian ideal is Miss Josephine Baker.

Unfortunately, this is not a bit of pleasantry, Miss Josephine Baker is the initial model which is now being reproduced AD INFINITUM. A woman of fashion must have the coloring of Miss Josephine Baker, the coiffure of Miss Josephine Baker, and bend all her efforts toward imitating the primitive graces of Miss Josephine Baker when she does the Charleston.

And saddest of all, the vogue of Paris is spreading into the provinces. When a distinguished foreigner appears in the comparatively impenetrable salon of a prefect or subprefect of France, he often asks to be presented to the colored lady.

All the charm of the colored lady consists in her not being like the others.

Don't you think that she will lose her interest when all the others are like her?

And the others likewise. . . . . . .

The first annual Youth Contest conducted by *The World Tomorrow*, has resulted in a group of prize essays which if indicative of what young men and women are really thinking today, show that they entertain little satisfaction in the present way of the world. All is far from being right to them. The January World Tomorrow carries a group of these essays, all worth quoting from, but we will content ourselves with two extractions. E. Merrill Root, had you never before read a line by him, you would know immediately for a poet from this section of his article, "From Genesis to Exodus":

"And so we come to the present moment in America; the moment when the disillusion and depression of war approach their flood in the soul, and when the tonic and tocsin of revolution approach their ebb in the soul. Scepticism, despair, the aestheticism of the ivory tower, an attack not upon the causes defeating democracy but upon democracy itself, a general vulgarization of Nietzsche in the interests not of the Superman but of the Hyperman, become the drift and drive in the philosophy of young, thinking America. Philosophers of decadence reign supreme and scarcely challenged—from H. L. Mencken (whom one may define as the brilliant phosphorescence of the corpse of capitalism) to E. Haldeman-Julius, that Main Street Nietzsche, that Chautauqua Voltaire. *The Liberator* has gone out like a brilliant meteor; and *The New Masses* cannot rentender the first fine careless splendor. Men worship a new star whose name is Mercury. Everywhere yea—saying is out of fashion, and faith and love are called sentimental, and creative activity is sneered at as futile. Everywhere men make a creed and a faith of doubt, and are sceptics of all but scepticism."

That is a fierce arraignment, with youth in the stocks. An equally devastating indictment is charged by Miss Eloise Sutherland Thetford, whose background is startling, in the face of her righteous indignation. These are curious words coming from one born in Dallas, Texas, and educated at Southern Methodist University:

"Our treasury is filled with gold; and each year thousands of little children die of hunger. Our orators roll under their tongues the syllables 'democracy'; yet Riverside Drive and Third Avenue never meet. Sheridan Road and Halsted Street are ever strangers. Our preachers wax eloquent as they talk of the 'brotherhood of man,' but we still have the Jim Crow cars and the Ku Klux Klan flourishes.

"We carol 'peace on earth, good will toward men,' and are so embalmed in party politics, so smugly self-satisfied that we refuse to take part in any organization designed to establish harmony among the nations.

Education is the hope of the world, we proclaim, and our schools teach us everything except the one thing that we need most to know—how to live together."

To be appropriately Biblical, Julius Bledsoe has now exemplified the statement which is so curious when taken with its converse, that unto him that hath shall be given. He has allied himself with that group of versatile people (like the Phi Beta Kappa athlete — lawyer — actor —singer Paul Robeson and the three-keyed doctor-author, Rudolph Fisher, and we understand that this young man keeps covered over somewhere a musicianly talent also) who with gracious regularity flash upon us a new facet of genius while we are still blinking in the glare of their last performance. As the protaganist, Abraham McCranie, in Paul Green's play, *In Abraham's Bosom*, now being given at the Provincetown Theater in New York, Bledsoe

rises to histrionic heights that warrant an asterisk of commendation on his new ability. He is ably supported by Rose McClendon as his long-suffering patient wife, and Abbie Mitchell (she also belongs to the versatile tribe) as his aunt, Muh Mack, a combination of irascibility, tenderness, and mouthiness, who has no faith in Abraham's love of books and desire to lift his people.

If there ever was a man of sorrows, acquainted with grief, Paul Green has drawn him in Abraham McCranie. From the first they were against him—the stars and all the planets. Born a bastard—combination of black and white, hating the oil and water mixture in his veins, yearning after knowledge with a frenzy incommunicable to his fellow laborers, even to the members of his family, except his wife (and she understands only in the loyal way that a staunch woman can simulate), he sees tower after tower crash to earth, dream after dream go down, his children die as babes in arms, and the one child who does remain, the boy whom he has baptized Douglas with a sure faith in the name, grow up into a shiftless corner laggard. In the end, Abraham goes to his death, after having killed his white half-brother, still crying for Freedom and Light. He dies deserted by all except his wife, and we wish that a mask might be made of Rose McClendon's face in that last delineation of anguish, and hung up high for growing thespians to see and pattern after.

Paul Green has done a fine and glowing piece of work, and there is no mistaking the sincerity behind it. Depressing it is, from beginning to ending.. But life is like that, nine times out of ten.

The Harlem branch of the New York Public Library reports that the end of last year saw no decrease in the demand for new and worthwhile books. There seems to be an endurance test on for *Nigger Heaven* which heads the list of popular fiction with 66 reserves followed by:

Edna Ferber:	*Show Boat*	25 Reserves
John Erskine:	*Galahad*	14 Reserves
John Erskine:	*The Private Life of Helen of Troy*	8 Reserves
H. G. Wells:	*The World of William Clissold*	7 Reserves
Ellen Glasgow:	*The Romantic Comedians*	6 Reserves
Eric Walrond:	*Tropic Death*	6 Reserves
Percival Wren:	*Beau Geste*	6 Reserves

On the non-fiction list, J. W. Vandercook's *Tom-Tom* leads with 11 reserves. Then come:

Will J. Durant:	*Story of Philosophy*	10 Reserves
Paul De Kruif:	*Microbe Hunters*	6 Reserves
Lewis Brown:	*This Believing World*	5 Reserves
George A. Dorsey:	*Why We Behave Like Human Beings*	5 Reserves

Countee Cullen.

THE DARK TOWER

TWO plays with racial aspects that came and went during the month were *The Bottom of the Cup* by John Tucker Battle and William J. Perlman; and *Stigma*, a play about miscegenation, bv Dorothy Manley and Donald Duff. There is not much that we can say about *The Bottom of the Cup* save that it gave Daniel L. Haynes an opportunity, through the sudden illness of Charles Gilpin, to enact the leading role in a manner which many have acclaimed as first rate. For us, however, the best part of Mr. Haynes' performance was the resonance of his voice and his unmistakable sincerity; beyond that he impressed us as being uncommonly ill at ease on the stage. But it is no small feat to attempt to fill Gilpin's place at the last moment.

Stigma is a play which, despite the united chorus of condemnation by accredited critics, we consider a gallant endeavor. It was quite evident on the evening we attended the play that most of the audience disliked the theme. One white gentleman later remarked that he felt that both races were made uneasy by the subject. If they were it was a silly uneasiness, and one that certainly does not extend to every day living. Mr. Percy Hammond of *The New York Herald-Tribune* felt that it was "not uninteresting to discover that the youthful authors of *Stigma* were sufficiently plucky to take up the cause of reaction and oppose the frenzied advances of progress." *Stigma* seems to have superinduced into the critics a perfect round of misconstruction. If there is anything which the play is *not*, it is reactionary. Mina, the colored girl in the play, does not reject the white father of her unborn child because either he or she is against miscegenation. The pivot of her refusal is that she feels that she as an individual is superior to this clay-footed god. Not one of the critics seems to have an adequate notion what sort of person Mina really was; they all took her at face-value as "a Negro maid of all work" not seeing that she wore a mask to hide and protect her pride and intelligence which would have been objectionable in the South.

With a cast of only four players, *Stigma* made exacting demands on each of them, and each account was settled creditably. Donald Duff as Pierre, the young lover, made all that was possible out of a thankless role in which he was doomed throughout the play to act as a feeder and a lead for the more active roles of his fellow players; Edmond Rickett as the December husband was convincing and natural. The laurels however went to Miss Joanna Roos, who gave a splendid enactment of her part as the young wife, and to Miss Doralyne Spence, who as Mina, made up in dignity what she lacked physically, and established herself as more than an actress of promise.

* * *

Fine Clothes to the Jew, Langston Hughes' new collection of verses, is an array of poetical vestments in which

Doralyne Spence and Donald Duff in "Stigma."

any poet can find more than one garment he would be willing and anxious to wear. With admiration and some pardonable envy we fingered the fine-wrought texture of "Brass Spitoons," "Mulatto," and "Prayer"; and though we cannot clothe ourselves in Hughes' "Song for a Dark Girl," we can quote it, thus catering to a small extent to our particular brand of vanity which covets this vivid robe more than any other:

> *Way down South in Dixie*
> *(Break the heart of me)*
> *They hung my black young*
> *lover*
> *To a crossroads tree.*
>
> *Way down South in Dixie,*
> *(Bruised body high in air)*
> *I asked the white Lord Jesus*
> *What was the use of prayer.*
>
> *Way down South in Dixie,*
> *(Break the heart of me),*
> *Love is a naked shadow*
> *On a gnarled and naked*
> *tree.*

* * *

New stars, especially in the histrionic heavens, swim into our ken with astonishing regularity. In *Abraham's Bosom*, of which we spoke in last month's tower, and called by J. Brooks Atkinson of *The New York Times* "the most penetrating, unswerving tragedy in town, and surely one of the most pungent folk dramas of the American stage" is the vehicle in which Frank Wilson, erstwhile understudy to Julius Bledsoe, now rides to stardom and the unstinted praise of the press. Atkinson in the February 20th issue of *The New York Times* explains the situation in the following manner: "On last Tuesday evening the opportunity for which every muted understudy prays earnestly every day came to Frank Wilson in the cast of *In Abraham's Bosom*. Julius Bledsoe, the leading player in that uncommonly adroit cast, did not appear at the usual hour and did not communicate with the management. Actors and audience both waited patiently for about thirty minutes. Then Mr. Wilson, who had been playing a minor part in the first scene, walked on as Abraham McCranie, and gave a performance not only almost letter perfect, but also swift, direct, and extraordinarily moving. Inasmuch as *In Abraham's Bosom* is the 'biography of a Negro in seven scenes,' the leading player is on the stage almost without interruption, and he sets the key of the entire production. Mr. Wilson suffused the drama with a passionate sincerity that pulled together the scattered scenes and gave a lucid meaning to the theme. He is the sort of understudy that strikes terror in the hearts of leading players. As the result of what the management considered to be Mr. Bledsoe's contractual defection, Mr. Wilson has been given the leading role permanently. His talents richly deserve that mark of confidence."

We have not seen Mr. Wilson's performance yet, but we wish more power both to him and to Mr. Bledsoe, to whose interpretation of Abraham McCranie all who saw

Frank Wilson playing in "In Abraham's Bosom."

him may look back with pride and approval. There is small, if any need to bewail a fortuitous circumstance that raises us up two giants where we had but one. The world is wide; its paths are broad; and there is room and to spare for all.

*   *   *

The initial issue of this column in a comment on William Stanley Braithwaite's *Anthology of Magazine Verse* for 1926 spoke of one Chaliss Silvay as among the Negro poets included in Mr. Braithwaite's year book of American poetry. Subsequent intelligence of a more perdurable sort enforces a retraction upon us: Mr. Silvay does not belong to us in the confining sense of the word. This retraction is doubly painful to us because that same issue attempted the censure of the prevalent tendency to establish a consanguinity with all persons who evince the slightest friendly interest in us. Our error, however, is easily explained. Having found in our files certain poems by Mr. Silvay which we liked, we wrote him, and learned that a certain necessary faith in himself, which had resulted in the acceptance of various of his poems by numerous periodicals, owed its development to encouragement given him in correspondence with Charles S. Johnson. Later both Mr. Johnson and I learned that Mr. Silvay was not of our pigmentary persuasion. But when we consider the extent to which Mr. Johnson's encouragement, given in the normal run of things, spurred Mr. Silvay, the situation assumes a significance deeper than it would have if racially confined. Here follows a list of Mr. Silvay's magazine appearances, "most of which," as he says, "materialized since writing Mr. Johnson: "White Music" in *Poetry* reprinted in *The Christian Science Monitor*; "Landscape" in *The Buccaneer*; "Disillusion" in *Tomorrow*; "Segments" in *The*

Lyric West; "Aristocrat" in *The Guardian*—reprinted in *The Literary Review of the New York Evening Post*; "Even So" in *The Gypsy*; "Nine Poems" in *California Sports*; "Songs" in *The Gammadion*; "Chromatic" in *The Lyric West*; "Grace Notes" in various issues of *Muse and Mirror*; "Words Over a Child Just Dead," Potters Field," "Sonnet for S.," and "Quatrains" in various numbers of *The Echo*; "Rivers" and "Further Instructions" in *The Will of the Wisp*; "Impertinences for Certain Religionists" in *The Minaret*; "Two Poems" in *Hollands*; "Avowal" in *The Overland Monthly*; "Song For a Slight Voice," "Supplication" and "Sonnet" in *The Archive*; "With Child" in *The Harp*; "Grief" in *The Oracle*, and various poems in *The Greenwich Quill*. Thirty odd poems—and, weigh the word as you will, they remain poems—in twenty odd periodicals; surely a creditable record for the author, and reason for a proper pride in us that "one of ours" had a hand in it.

*   *   *

A few nights ago we were a party to one of the most cosmopolitan and delightful gatherings in which we have been privileged to participate in many a day. It was a Goodwill Dinner given by the Greater Boston Federation of Churches. A group of speakers representing many countries, races, and religions brought good will messages to their American well-wishers. There were speakers from Switzerland, Sweden, and Russia; the "unspeakable" Turk was there, eloquently articulate; folk songs of Germany and Syria were sung by natives from these countries; the cause of Nicaragua and her small sister territories was effectively pled by a Colombian professor; a young American born in the heart of China made clear some misty points for us; and Siam had as her ambassador extraordinary a prince of the blood who rallied us kindly for knowing nothing of Siam except white elephants and the Siamese twins, and who informed us that the defensive weapons employed by this small independent country, resting so snugly and peacefully between two world powers, were good will and justice. The listening audience was large, sympathetic and mixed. During the speechmaking, when a colored lady near the head table became faint, a distinguished white clergyman rose, and with the courtesy of his Boston heritage, led her from the hall. When the meeting was opened, a white minister presided; when the urgency of another engagement called him away, he turned his gavel over to a colored colleague who in summing up the spirit of the evening remarked that with all the mingling and confraternity that had prevailed no one had been harmed by the contact.

*   *   *

The report of the Harlem library on books most in demand for the month shows *Nigger Heaven* still in the vanguard with 68 reservations although there are four copies of the book circulating in an effort to meet the demand. The runners-up in fiction are: Theodore Dreiser's *An American Tragedy.* (26); John Erskine's *Galahad* (21); his *Private Life of Helen of Troy* (13); Edna Ferber's *Show Boat* (11); Percival Wren's *Beau Geste* (8); Ellen Glasgow's *The Romantic Comedians* (5); and Kathleen Norris' *Hildegarde* (4). *Tom-Tom* heads the nonfiction list with 13 reservations and is followed by: Durant's *The Story of Philosophy* (11); Browne's *This Believing World* (6); De Kruif's *Microbe Hunters* (5); and Dorsey's *Why We Behave Like Human Beings* (4).

Countee Cullen.

THE DARK TOWER

MARCH brought to the New Playwrights' Theatre in New York, *Earth*, a play based on Negro life by one Em Jo Basshe. It deals with the struggle between voodooism and Christianity, exemplified in the vacillation of Deborah, a Negro matron, whose faith and worship are the bone of contention between the voodooistic rites of Senon, the witch-doctor, and the Christianity of Brother Elijah, the blind village preacher. Acting that reaches the dizziest reaches of art is supplied here and there by Daniel Haynes and William Townsend (many will remember him as the "Babe" Townsend of the former Lafayette Stock Company) and through the entire performance by Inez Clough, who brings to the lowly questioning role of Deborah a dignity and intensity that drew rounds of bravos from an audience, which, dubious as it might be about the general merits of *Earth*, recognized Miss Clough's impeccable delineation. We find that this lady has lost none of the oldtime charm of speech and manner that made her such a favorite when the Lafayette players flourished; it still remains a pleasure to see her walk and to watch the poise of her head, and we can imagine no role so mean that it would not succumb to these attributes in her. Incidental music of a memorable kind has been composed for the play by Hall Johnson. It may sound blasphemous, but the way things are going we think a play about Negroes in which nary a spiritual was sung would be a huge success because of the sheer novelty of the thing.

With the new Negro becoming less and less the fanciful creation of a few dreamers, and more and more a flesh and blood entity, determined, now that he is here, to make the painful process of his birthing a basis for longevity, it is a most pertinent question that Devere Allen asks in his article, "The New White Man," in the March *World Tomorrow*: "But what," he asks, "of the white man. Despite the legend of the Civil War, he has allowed himself to be sold by his desire for dominance into a spiritual slavery. His back is bent beneath the burden of his own weighty supersitions, the load of his self-created fears. His dreams of the future are haunted by dire demons; loss of suprem-

acy; reduction of economic gain, racial intermarriage, and exactly as the ignorant slaves of the South found their way to some famed dream interpreter, these modern bondmen have besought their scientists, so-called, to conjure Nordic strains, and cast the spell of psychological tests in order to free their dreams from goblins. But voodooism and medicine men, whether old style or new, can lure for long none but the ignorant and dull. It is because thus far we whites have not yet had *our* spiritual renaissance that we pay any heed to oracles who but bolster up our prejudices. The white man in our time is still the old white man, holding his hand aloft with the fingers widely spread, and mouthing *still* the old taboos." Mr. Allen realizes that, wide world as it is, this is too small a world to hold in peaceful proximity the new Negro and the old white man, but he tells us, "The new white man will soon become articulate. Even now he is trying to find his voice." Mr. Allen outlines for us the renovating process to which the old white man must subject himself, and we find it surprisingly similar to that through which the old Negro passed! "The new white man will have to burst the bonds of ignorance. He will be aware of Negro achievement and cultural contributions. He will know so many Negroes personally, if he has the good fortune to deserve their friendship, that the experience of association alone will render him immune to the foolish phrases of traditionalism, which often do, alas, get by as 'principles.' . . . . The new white man will burst the bonds of *superstition*. He will scotch them and the basic one on which they rest, the general faith in white supremacy." Other bonds which the writer calls upon the new white man to break are those of *economic dependency* and *fear*. The road mapped out is certainly not unfamiliar to any of us; it is up hill and hard climbing all the way, with the crest as yet still hidden from view. Let us hope that the new Negro and the new white man will soon be able to clasp congratulatory hands at the summit.

"What is the difference between a ballad and a ballade? How many kinds of sonnets are there, and how do they differ from one another? What is the meaning of cliche, cadence, strophe, polyphonic prose, assonance, vers libre, rime royale, villanelle?" No doubt there are many who will consider these questions, so admirably answered with examples in Louis Untermeyer's *The Forms of Poetry* (Harcourt, Brace & Co.) of small moment in the making of poetry. But to those who think the manipulation of the tools of any craft worth study, this book will come as a God-send. It is divided into three main divisions, each carefully treated in a scholarly manner that is enhanced by the fact that Mr. Untermeyer is both critic and creator. The able illustrations by which the author has chosen to exemplify the various poetic forms and expressions will either introduce you to, or reacquaint you with, some excellent poems which still retain their attraction despite the straight-jacket of form they wear. Austin Dobson's chant royal, *The Dance of Death*, after numerous readings remains more a poem than a *tour de force*, as do many of his other examples of the strict English and French forms. Justin Huntley McCarthy's ballade, *I Wonder in What Isle of Bliss*, is still remembered, and Shelley's use of the Spencerian stanza in *Adonais*, and Keats' in *The Eve of St. Agnes* are enduring monuments to form, while no less a

Inez Clough and William Townsend in "Earth."

modern poet than Edwin Arlington Robinson has used the villanelle with telling effect in his poem, *The House on the Hill.* For those who think these are considerations of the past, let me mention just a few of the moderns whom Mr. Untermeyer cites as having this intelligence of poetic form, and making conscious use of it in their poetry: Joseph Auslander, A. E. Housman, Robert Frost, Edwin Arlington Robinson, Amy Lowell, and Edna St. Vincent Millay. *The Forms of Poetry* impresses us as indispesible to both poet and poetry-student; and its perusal would save many a young poet the error of writing twelve-line sonnets, and blank verse poems in which the lines run the gamut from trimeter iambics to pentameter trochees.

Daniel Haynes in "Earth"

Pride and Humility (Harcourt, Brace & Company) an entrancingly beautifully bound book of poems by Amy Spingarn, illustrated by the author, contains for us more titular appeal than we found in the body of the book. For the most part the author is too complacent, too yielding to the blandishments of the obvious word, phrase and rhyme. When we read lines like these:

No human frame can long endure
The strength or power of your lure.

or

But, oh, once more
I feel like balm
The fair fresh promise of fresh calm.

we realize that when it wills there is no greater despot than rhyme. For us the author sounds her clearest notes in those poems which have a racial framework, such as *Wanderers* and the poem beginning "I come of a proud and stiff-necked race." And when she asks "What can a Ghetto give the world?" there is a question to batter down the flood gates of the imagination. A brittle epigrammatic quality lends flavor to some of the verses, such as:

Into dissolute lives
Pain burns,
But it shrives
Till at length,
Born on spearheads of pain,
Blossoms strength.

Through the Aldine Publishing Company of Xenia, Ohio, Hallie Q. Brown has brought out *Homespun Heroines and Other Women of Distinction,* a series of brief biographies of distinguished Negro women, who achieved and overcame despite the rugged way they were forced to travel. The list carries one through the struggles of Catherine Ferguson, founder of the first Sunday School movement in New York City, Phillis Wheatley, Sojourner Truth, Harriet Tubman, who gained for herself the sobriquet of General Tubman, down to those of more recent times such as Mary B. Talbert, preserver of the Frederick Douglas Home, and the late Madam C. J. Walker. While the book does not belong to the class of fine writing, it is a commendable piece of work, showing in Miss Brown a discriminating taste for the essentials of biography, and for what in a past life makes it worthy of being brought to the attention of succeeding generations.

The list of reserved books for the Harlem Library seems to remain the same, with only a slight decrease in the number of requests for new books, due, no doubt, to the lull before the rush of spring books. The following twelve are the most popular. On the fiction list:

Van Vechten—*Nigger Heaven*..63 reserves
Dreiser—*An American Tragedy*........................32 reserves
Erskine—*Galahad* ....22 reserves
Erskine—*The Private Life of Helen of Troy*..14 reserves
Ferber—*Show Boat* .... 9 reserves
Wasserman—*Wedlock* .... 5 reserves
Norris—*Hildegarde*.................................... 5 reserves

NON-FICTION:

Durant—*The Story of Philosophy*....................14 reserves
Vandercook—*Tom-Tom* ....14 reserves
De Kruif—*Microbe Hunters* .... 5 reserves
Dorsey—*Why We Behave Like Human Beings*... 4 reserves
Mantle—*Best Plays of 1925-1926*....................... 4 reserves

Countee Cullen.

THE DARK TOWER

FIRE *Under the Andes,* under the Knopf imprint, a group of American portraits by Elizabeth Shepley Sergeant, would we believe have met the critical approval of that austere evaluator of men and letters, Walter Pater, could it have come under his consideration. "My 'subjects' ", says the author in her introduction, "are all figters, Americans in conflict with something — wtih the age, with evil or gnorance, as they see it,—with themselves, if they are artists. Below that conflict lies the fire under the Ander which gives them their motive force and makes them, however small or great, absorbing to a New Englander who cannot quite do justice to those who take life with too great content ment and bland satisfaction. Here the world is, here we all are, what are we going to do about it? Take something out of life, like coupons cut at the bank, or put something in?" This intense personal interest, a consuming spiriutal kinship, is what enables the author to create for us her fighting subjects in their most agoniz-

Paul Robeson from the statue by Antonio Salemme

by the gadfly." The other subjects in this Olympian survey are: Amy Lowell, Robert Edmond Jones, William Alanson White, Paul Robeson, Eugene O'Neill, Elinor Wylie, Charles Townsend Copeland, Wm. Allen White, Alice Hamilton, Willa Cather, Robert Frost, and Oliver Wendell Holmes, — great spirits all. Miss Sergeant has made each of them live and move individually in the light of her interpretation. Of especial interest to racial readers will be her treatment of Paul Robeson. When she says he is "sublimating the least acceptable of American destinies," we wish the statement were less cryptic, that *least acceptable* were clarified by modification. But it is easy to see that Robeson has waved the magic wand of his personality over her to her happy enthrallment. She is deeply appreciative of the man's background, his intellect, struggles, and accomplishments. A situation is sensed and summed up in a sentence here: "But if the artist, more than any other, must lose his life to find it, it, so must the Am-

ing as well as their most magnificent and towering attitudes. The list is one of brilliant and belligerent contenders, ranging from H. L. Mencken who, Miss Sergeant tells us, "must and will be Titan" at all honest costs and hazards, to Pauline Lord, gentle and ingenue in appearance, but under the surface where the fire rages "one stung erican Negro be born twice into the American universe to live there like a man." Robeson, she finds, has risen to his second birth without that travail which Nicodemus thought necessary and impossible.

What has it done, this world,
With hard fingertips?

might be asked of him as well as of Elinor Wylie. It has not chiselled and curled his lips into inscrutability; a mouth of stone could be no adequate organ for the spirituals and folk songs as sung by Robeson. Rather have those finger-tips found his lips already tuned and moulded beyond any altering by bigotry and ignorance. The world, for all its barbs and stings, must admit, some portion of it grudgingly perhaps, what Miss Sergeant finds such pleasure in noting: "Robeson's singing mouth has no twist of acrid pain. Notes of eternity roll out of it. They are round and whole. They come from the depths of a man who stands rooted in 'the most ancient heavens' ".

Behind the work there is always the man, often severely disappointing when met face to face by his admirers and leveled by the plane of familiarity. Happily, however, Miss Sergeant has chosen to treat personages whose lives have at the core fire that will but blaze the higher under microscopic scrutiny.

Our Youngest Generation Becomes Articulate
(Introducing Lula Lowe Weeden, aged eight)

"On the whole, I like the Youngest Generation. It is going to be vastly more revolutionary than the present Younger Generation, I believe, but with less wobbling, doubting, recanting and uncertainty. The Younger Generation hasn't accomplished much and even that little remains unfinished. The Youngest Generation is going to finish the job. Instead of an era of mere noise it will usher in a constructive peace. From a practical point of view, what we believe is less important than that we believe something which will enable us to work and love and live in understanding unison. The Younger Generation boasts and postures, but the Youngest Generation believes." Believes and does! Chester T. Crowell might have truthfully ended his encomium on the Youngest Generation in the April *American Mercury* on that note of definite accomplishment. For even while our Younger Generation hasn't yet turned its first gray hair, the Youngest Generation is beginning gently but firmly to prod it into the ranks of the former times. The poise and self-sufficiency of the Nathalia Cranes and Daisy Ashfords of our day are attributes to marvel at and to respect. They will not permit their efforts to be circumscribed by age or their ambitions to be curtailed by lack of experience.

Appreciating to the full the seriousness with which they take themselves and demand that others take them, it is altogether meet and proper that we allow our youngest voice to be raised in these columns this month. Lula Lowe Weeden, born in Lynchburg, Virginia, February 4, 1918, has already at the age of nine written a sheaf of some thirty or forty short verses which, while they do not startle us into undue adulation are significant enough for us to call attention to as being indicative of a reassurance that the creative urge of the race will suffer no estoppel with the passing of the present newer and younger generation. The newest and youngest generation of them all will continue to carry on. Miss Weeden's mother sends us the following interesting comment on her daughter: "She is a very close observer. Each flower in my garden, she knows. Sometimes she counts each bloom, lingering over those she likes most . . . . . I have always mixed my night time stories with 'Home spn' ones. I asked Lula why she liked my stories. She said because they seemed to be true, and criticised fairy stories."

Those of us who wail for quiet and leisure hours removed from the disturbing presence of the madding crowd will marvel at this Youngest Generation locked in its retreat of mind and aspiration, and oblivious to all besides: "Lula does most of her writing at night. It is a privilege for her to remain a few minutes after the other children to finish something. Some nights she will write several. She mumbles them to herself before she begins to write and then

keeps saying the words softly. Interruptions don't seem to bother her, as the little ones (remember she herself is the august age of nine) are always saying something to make her laugh. I usually attempt to quiet them, but some of her best things are written with many around."

Undoubtedly it is the aim of the Youngest Generation to grasp Time securely by the forelock as soon as their chubby fingers can approximate a hold, for we learn that at nine, Lula "feels that she has begun to write at a mature age; but consoles herself with this statement: "Stevenson did not begin to write until he was fifteen and wrote very skillful things."

But enough of this interpretation. Let the Youngest Generation speak for itself in these examples of Lula's verse:

Have You Seen It

Have you ever seen the moon
And stars stick together?
Have you ever seen it?
Have you ever seen bad?
Have you ever seen good
And bad stick together?
Have you ever seen it?

Robin Red Breast

Little robin red breast,
I hear you sing your song.
I would love to have you put it into
        my little cage,
Into my little mouth.

Me Alone

As I was going to town,
I saw a King and a Queen.
Such ringing of bells you never heard:
The clerks ran out of the stores;
You know how it was, Me alone.
I was standing as the others were,
"Oh! you little girl," some one said,
"The king want you."
I became frightened
Wondering what he had to say,
Me alone.
Here's what he wanted:
He wanted me to ride in his coach,
I felt myself so much riding in a King's coach,
Me alone.

From Lang Syne Plantation in Fort Motte, South Carolina where we picture Julia Peterkin serenely having her being and writing of Negro life and character with an accuracy and understanding the like of which we have known only once before (we never tire of saying it happened in *Porgy*) comes this note of bewilderment at the crass inability of people to recognize the truth when most clearly seen: "I am constantly amazed and hurt that people right here who should know Negroes as well as I do keep saying to me that the people in both *Green Thursday* and *Black April* are the result of my imagination: that no such folks ever were! Here or anywhere else!"

"My conviction is that the earth here, rich, fever-breeding soil, plays no small part in molding us, whether we are black or white. And it turns us back into its dust, apparently quite careless of our color or circumstances."

Such convictions are those of the clairvoyant, the full-sighted, the understanding, and the doomed to be misunderstood by those whose eyes still bear the weight of scales.

Countee Cullen.

THE DARK TOWER

AMONG the past month's items of interest to which we wish to draw the attention of readers of this column are the following: Boni and Liveright have finally brought out a new edition of Jean Toomer's *Cane*, so that a book containing some of the most colorful writing by a race author is now accessible to those who were not quick enough to see its value on its initial publication. *Current History* for May carries an interesting and well done article by Cleveland G. Allen on "The Contribution to Music by American Negroes". Arthur Huff Fauset of Philadelphia is to emerge as a full-fledged author this spring wtih the publication of his book, *For Freedom*,' under the imprint of the Franklin Publishing Company of Philadelphia. *For Freedom* is a connected series of Negro biographies from the bringing over of the Negro to America down to the present time. It is especially adapted for use in the public schools. Among the figures treated are: Phyllis Wheatley, Crispus Attucks, Frederick Douglas, Booker T. Washington, W. E. B. Du Bois, Alain Locke, and the New Negro group. Also largely through the influence of Mr. Fauset, Philadelphia's young Negro group has launched its first literary bark dubbed *Black Opals*. They plan to make it a quarterly. The first issue contains some highly commendable material, especially two poems, *Longing* by Nellie R. Bright, and *Goal* by Mae V. Cowdery. The *Black Opals* venture is one which we should like to see sweep the country as the Little Theatre movement has done. . . . In the *American Monthly* for March, Wallace Thurman has an article *Harlem* sub-captioned "A Vivid Word Picture of the World's Greatest Negro City." Vivid it is, and riotous with that sharp staccato writing affected by so many modern young writers. But the impression it would give us of Harlem, did we not know our own habitat better, would be one of human checkers automatically moving on a huge crazy-quilt and getting nowhere at all. Witness a typical paragraph: "Poor hall Johnnies in front of the Renaissance Casino watching eagerly for unescorted women to follow through the door. A pregnant woman from Jamaica runs the gauntlet. She wants to see the basket ball game and watch the dancers. Harlem fire has hardened her. A West Indian with a wart on his nose, a misfit top coat obscuring his little form, and an ill-used cane on his arm, flaunts his sartorial inelegance. People laugh and move on, Monkey-chaser. Harlem is the city of refuge and Seventh Avenue is freedman's lane." The May *Midland*, one of the most consistently fine little magazines that we have come across, has in an article on *The Harlem Poets*, by Frank Luther Mott, some very sane, but debatable, remarks on that ever-recurring query as to what the Negro should write about. Mr. Mott says: ". . . the resentment of intelligent Negroes against a morbid and condescending interest in the productions of Negro artists and musicians and writers, which is based chiefly upon a sentimental concern with the 'Negro problem' is natural and justifiable enough. But it is possible to carry this feeling too far. The Negro has materials at his fingers' ends which the white man does not possess, or at least possesses less perfectly. The extraordinary endowment of rich, full-bodied emotion; a certain fearlessness in the face of the primitive; a sympathetic understanding of the facts and circumstances of modern Negro life in America—these things are a heritage which would be too cheaply sold for

the white man's mess of literary pottage. It is bad counsel to advise the Negro to refrain from anything that smacks of propaganda, to threw away Negro dialect, to abandon the materials of Negro life—in short, to forget he is a Negro. Abject imitation is the worst of literary sins; and for the Negro to be contemptuous of his own materials and his own endowment is a sin not only against literature but against his race and against himself. Of course, a writer has the privilege of writing about anything that interests him, but he ought to be interested in the things which, luckily, he stands possessed of here and now. For Negro writers to throw those things away would be as bad as throwing away the old spirituals; they are precious, for racy autochthonous values are not common any more in America." In that excerpt it seems to us that Mr. Mott is concerned more with preservation than creation. And to that extent we agree with him. Only at his dictum that an author *ought*, by virtue of birth or any other circumstance, be interested solely in any *particular* thing do we utter protest. The mind of man has always ridden a capricious wandering nag, that just will not stay reined into a beaten path. Dante's took him catapulting down into the great circles of hell; Browning, for all his English love, found himself galloping into Italy for his dramatic narratives and his magnus opus; Shakespeare went by many a devious route and bypath, and many present-day writers are constantly straying into foreign fields and literary dream lands. The press has been lavish with plaudits for Du Bose Heyward's *Porgy*, Julia Peterkin's *Green Thursday* and *Black April*, and Carl Van Vechten's *Nigger Heaven*.. Few have resented or bewailed their treatment of the lives of Negroes; rather has the material, to a large extent, been responsible for the praise. Let us not then be stricken into such dire lamentation when the Negro writer goes excursioning. Let the test be how much of a pleasant day he himself has had, and how much he has been enabled to impart to us. Incidentally in the May issue (which is the first issue) of the *Home Mission College Review* which he edits, Benjamin Brawley goes off on a fine scholarly picnic in his article, "Is 'The Ancient Mariner' Allegorical?"

Two recent books totally dissimilar in style that we find ourselves linking together are *Latter Day Symphony* (Alfred A. Knopf, publisher) by Romer Wilson and *Ninth Avenue*, (Boni and Liveright) by Maxwell Bodenheim The point of parity between the two is that each represents a treatment both unusual and audacious of the much-mooted color question. In language that is at once economical and distinguished Miss Wilson vividly describes two n'ghts in the lives of a group of highly sophisticated denizens of Mayfair in England. The two main characters are a brillant young Englishman and an American Negro who, *mirabile dictu*, is a person of fine sensibility, poise and language. These two, like many others of less importance in the story, are in love with a beautiful English woman whom neither can possess although it is the young Englishman she loves instead of the magnate to whom she gives her aliegiance. Lindsay Jackson, the Negro suitor in speaking of her says, "It kind of hurts me to think of her, Mr. Russell. If I were not colored, I should give myself a chance with her dark eyes, and take my answer when it came to me. I would lose a very great deal for the melancholy privilege of losing her. I would lose all I have." And (says Miss Romer) "Stephen (the Englishman) looked at Lindsay Jackson. He saw nothing whatever in him but the light coffee shade of his complexion, that would make him come amiss with Mary Linton. In open class, Stephen knew he himself fell a long way short of Jackson's standard, both as an Adonis, an artist—and a gentleman. But —some people would have put Jackson in the Zoo on trust that monkeys and colored men were nearly related. . . ."

Knowing the author of Ninth Avenue primarily as a poet, we miss the poet's touch in this novel. There is, to be sure, enough and to spare of the Bodenheim deft acerbity. But one does expect a poet to handle words with some degree of care. The amazing part of this story of an ambitious lower class white girl, hampered by a coarse family that does not understand her and does not care to, is that she finally hopes of her own volition to find her happiness by marrying a Negro. To be sure he is fair enough to pass, but before he revealed his racial kinship to her, Blanche said in no uncertain tones, "I don't want to be narrow-minded, but I don't see how they can love each other—they must be lying to themselves. The races just weren't meant to have physical relations with each other. There's something, something in their flesh and blood that stands between, like . . . like a warning signal. That's it."

But "As she spoke, though, she had the sensation of uttering sentences which she had borrowed from books and other people, and which did not decisively express her opinions."

Both Latter Day Symphony and Ninth Avenue are well worth reading.

Even though we deplore general conditions in the South, there are a few things for which we can be grateful. On of those oases in that barren land is North Carolina University at Chapel Hill, North Carolina. Linked up with it is Paul Green and In Abraham's Bosom, and The Carolina Magazine whose next issue will establish the precedent of a white Southern magazine being given over to an issue of work by Negro writers. Recently during the Institute of Human Relations week, James Weldon Johnson lectured and held seminar courses at the University for a week. Exemplary of a changing Southern attitude is the following editorial from The Tar Heel, the University's official student paper: "Half a century ago an humble slave was janitor to North Carolina's State University students. His work was mean; his duties were lowly—for he was a janitor. And when George Moses Horton was not sweating to do the will of his young masters (many of whom he attended during illnesses due to both legitimate causes and unlawful wildness), he was their bard. He composed, at the behest of amorous students, many limericks and poems which won the favor of Southern sweethearts. Modern college students are astounded to learn that this bonded Negro composed excellent poems before he learnd to write. He was an author of short stories widely published and eagerly read. His literary talent won for him the admiration of Dr. Caldwell, Dr. Battle and Horace Greely, who printed some of his verse.

"Today the local scene is remarkably changed. George Horton no longer writes. But a national leader of his emancipated race, James Weldon Johnson, only a few weeks ago stood in dignity before white students, sat behind the professor's august desk, and read to them the poems of the slave Horton. Instead of a menial dormitory janitor, we now have before us a polished doctor of letters, a nationally recognized artist. Horton's posture was that of the bended knee. James Weldon Johnson has come with the majesty of an exalted leader.

"This is no lavish tribute to the liberality of our native state. The writer comes from a state where officers of the law are more successful in the apprehension of Sunday golfers than Negro-lynchers. But when he observes that 'Southern hospitality' and 'Southern chivalry,' once our chief virtues, have become relics of a moribund civilization—when he sees, as every one must, the pall of intolerance so nearly—he feels a huzzah should be raised to the glory of a liberal North Carolina. Your state university has acted her motto—Lux et libertas."

Without in the least deprecating the beauty of Negro spirituals or the undeniable fact that Negro singers do them, as it were, to the manner born, we have always resented the natural inclination of most white people to demand spirituals the moment it is known that a Negro is about to sing. So often the request has seemed to savor of the feeling that we could do this and this alone. It seems to me at this late date that spirituals are a matter of interpretation, as any other music is, and an open field for any competitor. It follows, of course, that we hold this same view about Negro singers and all other forms of music. Therefore we find the following excerpt from Burris Jenkins' column "The Drift of the Day" in the Kansas City (Mo.) Journal more than passingly interesting: "Recently I made a talk at the Negro High School in Kansas City, Kansas, and as always on such occasions I demanded that they pay me by singing for me. Some six or eight hundred students overpaid me. They first sang a folk tune, dating from before the Civil War, that I had never heard, with the refrain 'Way down by the riverside.' Then they sang The Miserere from Trovatore better than I had ever heard it sung on any stage by anybody. The sopranos, singing their part alone, went clear through me with their plaintive melody; then when the tenors and basses joined in, dividing on the parts in delicate harmony, the music fairly raised the little hair I've got left on my head. I never hope to hear that music sung so well again this side of the heavenly choir."

The list of the twelve most popular reserve books for the Harlem Branch library for the past month is as follows:

Fiction

Lewis: Elmer Gantry 36
Van Vechten: Nigger Heaven 32
Dreiser: American Tragedy 31
Erskine: Private Life of Helen of Troy 18
Peterkin: Black April 15
Erskine: Galahad 11
Deeping: Sorrell and Son 9

Non-fiction

Durant: Story of Philosophy 21
Vanderlook: Tom-Tom 11
Dorsey: Why we behave like Human Beings 10
Ripley: Main Street and Wall Street 4
Browne: This Believing World 4

Countee Cullen.

THE DARK TOWER

WITH the final decisions in this year's *Opportunity* Contest rendered and the prizes awarded, we should like, before the general tumult and shouting dies, to cast a reminiscent glance upon the section in which we were privileged to sit in judgment. Many of the poems entered in the contest served their only purpose after they had appeased their creator's urge to write something; they should then have been gently but firmly retired from the scene of action. Unfortunately, however, a proper sense of self criticism, lacking, to a large extent, even in the finest writers, seems absolutely unknown to the tyro. However, in spite of this the final reaction was that the entries augured well for poetry by Negroes; in fact one of our judges, Mr. Robert E. Kerlin, felt that the Negro is making a far from negligible conquest by his poetry.

But in the Alexander Pushkin section there was a more definite feeling of discontent with the poems entered. This is said with no disparagement to the winning poem, inasmuch as it received our vote for first place as well as the vote of the judge who was most disappointed in the Pushkin section. The announcement of the Alexander Pushkin prize plainly reads: "This section is expected to call forth the most ambitious and most mature work of the Negro poet, and it is requested that to this section only the best work be sent." Basing his reaction on the spirit of the announcement, Mr. Ridgley Torrence wrote: "In regard to the entries for the Pushkin Contest, I am extremely disappointed. They seem to me of a quality greatly inferior to those in the Holstein group." Surely contestants who entered quatrains and slight lyrics in this section gave little serious thought to the dignity of the prize offered and to the ennoblement of it through the name of Pushkin. We feel that it approximates a truthful observation to say that the prize poem is less often a poem of a moment's inspiration than it is one of endeavor and revision. Such in fairness to the Pushkin prize is it our hope to have entries in that section be, commensurate with the prize offered and the distinguished memory of Pushkin. Mr. Arna Bontemps has twice demonstrated his ability and inclination to work toward this end. With our next contest months away, it still is not too soon to urge others to begin even now to go and do likewise.

IT seems of no slight significance that those in places, if not intrinsically high, at least quite detached from our daily contact, are finding that some good can come out of Nazareth. *The Junior League Bulletin*, the readers of which are synonymous with a social structure built no less on money than on culture, has discovered and acclaimed Langston Hughes. We quote a portion of Katherine Garrison Chapin's review of *Fine Clothes to the Jew* in *The Junior League Bulletin* for June, 1927. "This book and its companion, *The Weary Blues*, published a year ago, are two volumes of poems of which we, as Americans, may be proud. Perhaps when Europe has again set its seal of approval on something native to us we will discover it: but by the time we are ready to give full honor to a Negro poet the need for giving that honor may have passed. Here is a young man who at the age of twenty-five has stepped out of the ranks where any social or racial discriminations might hold him, and walks easily among the best writers of his day. He is a poet, not merely a Negro poet . . . Perhaps we should take back what we said at the beginning. Langston Hughes *is* a Negro poet. It is a term of distinction."

SIMON AND SCHUSTER have added this month to their series of Pamphlet Poets in their endeavor to popularize poetry without demeaning it, *Four Negro Poets*, extracts from the work of Claude McKay, Langston Hughes, Jean Toomer, and Countee Cullen. The pamphlet is edited with an introduction by Alain Locke, and the poems are chosen to a large extent for their autochthonous value. Dr. Locke says: "Though their poetry ranges through all possible themes, it is no spiritual distortion or misrepresentation that their more racially distinctive poems have been selected for this little anthology. For the present-day Negro poet regards his racial heritage as a more precious endowment than his own personal genius, and to the common legacy of his art adds the peculiar experiences and emotions of his folk." As one, to a slight extent, in on the know of things, we have serious doubts that Negro poets feel themselves more strongly obligated to their race than to their own degree of personal talent. Two of the poets herein represented might subscribe to Dr. Locke's tenets; two we think are less racially altruistic.

THERE passed through our hands, for the briefest moment, on its way to a reviewer, *Congaree Sketches*, "Stories of Negro Life in Heaven, Hell, and the Congaree Swamps Way Down in South Carolina," by E. C. L. Adams, a white physician of Columbia, S. C. The contact was, however, long enough for us to feel the very able and unequivocal introduction which Paul Green contributed to the collection. Before this we had admired Mr. Green for many aspects of his work, yet never felt that we had sighted him clearly in the open. His introduction to these sketches makes us eat humble pie, and willingly. His words are severely weighed, but not with the guarded caution of the fence-straddler. We quote from him and ask if any Southern man has made himself more completely a target of liberality and common sense: "The Negro is crawling out of his ditch to stand on the bank with the white man. And the white man is reaching a hand to pull him up; but let it be a stronger hand and one that reaches farther than before. It may be they will stand in their separate place apart, but I doubt it. They have too much in common not to pass a word with one another after the gesture of brotherhood has been made. And in the light of such benefits to hand I can see no sense in the talk of segregation, back to Africa, and the like, which many of our politicians and faddist souls enjoy. It all seems beside the point. Even the movement going the rounds among some of the Negroes themselves for a separate racial culture and tradition, exemplified, say, in their upturning of native African art, likewise looks suspicious and outside the concrete demands of the case. Of course all such endeavors in uncovering racial heritage are valuable in establishing a point of view for growth and development. It is the familiar historical mind and method at work and is good for what it is, but not for an autonymity of the race as such. That can never be and we might as well recognize it. What can be and will be is a white and a thousand unconscious forces are at work for will. And it is most significant, I think, that black and many gifts of their race—their music and their song, and larger humanizing of the whole, an Americanizing, if you this larger humanity. * * * I am thankful for all the for their multitudinous services, whether noble or ignoble. They are a magnificent people and nothing can keep them little forebearance and imagination can aid so vastly in the and bend ears to the wind of too cheap expediency when a growing salvation of us all? And here I am not pleading for the Negro but for ourselves, the white man. For there is much worth the knowing and we're missing it, caught as we are in the lock-step of senseless conformity."

THE May issue of *The Carolina Magazine* is a number of historical importance in race relations in this country. For the first time, as it were, in the time of man, a Southern university magazine has given over one of its numbers to the work of Negro writers. No attempt has been made to inveigle the contributing writers into conformance to any preconceived notions of what should constitute work by Negroes. There is less of irony than of eventual justice in this phenomenon of a magazine the cover of which is decorated with the names of Poe, Cabell, Lanier, Harris, Page, O. Henry and Wilson, bearing on that cover an inset informative of the fact that within there is a brilliant article on *The Negro Enters Literature* by Charles S. Johnson, a reprint of *Symphonesque* by Arthur Huff Fauset and reproductions of the work of Aaron Douglas. . Other contributors to the number are Arna Bontemps, Helene Johnson, Waring Cuney, Eulalie Spence (represented by *The Hunch*, one of the prize plays in this year's *Opportunity* contest), Langston Hughes, Georgia Douglas Johnson, Edward Silvera, Donald Jeffrey Hayes, Angelina Grimke, Effie Lee Newsome, Nelson H. Nichols, Jr., Carrie W. Clifford, and Lewis Alexander, who served as honorary editor of the issue.

THE New York *Morning Telegraph* wishing to discover the best American actor and actress of the 1926-1927 season recently enlisted the aid of the drama reviewrs of New York. The resulting poll taken by eighteen reviewers acclaimed Pauline Lord and Alfred Lunt as the stellar thespians of the year. Mr. Percy Hammond, dramatic critic for the New York *Herald-Tribune*, gave his vote to Rose McClendon and Frank Wilson, who share the star roles in the year's Pulitzer Play, *In Abraham's Bosom*. Although Mr. Hammond's was the only vote cast for these actors, they tied with such distinguished colleagues as Helen Mencken, Lynne Fontanne, Jane Cowl, Ethel Barrymore, Blanche Yurka, Walter Huston and Morgan Farley, each of whom received one vote.

LEST the readers of this column should imagine that we believe the most interesting literature being written is that dealing with the Negro, we should like to recommend as constituting the most enjoyable reading we've done in many a day, the following books: *The King's Henchman* by Edna St. Vincent Millay, *Tristam* by Edwin Arlington Robinson, and *Go She Must* by David Garnett.

THE list of the twelve most popular reserve books at Harlem Branch Library for the past month is as follows:

Fiction:

Lewis—*Elmer Gantry*	30 reserves
Peterkin—*Black April*	14 reserves
Erskine:—*Helen of Troy*	9 reserves
Van Vechten—*Nigger Heaven*	8 reserves
Young—*Love Is Enough*	5 reserves
Erskine—*Galahad*	5 reserves
Norris—*The Sea Gull*	4 reserves
Dreiser—*An American Tragedy*	4 reserves
Deeping—*Sorrell and Son*	3 reserves

Non-Fiction:

Durant—*Story of Philosophy*	9 reserves
Bekker—*Story of Music*	6 reserves
Vandercook—*Tom-Tom*	3 reserves

Countee Cullen.

THE DARK TOWER

IF anything is calculated to give the South pause and make her consider the error of her ways toward her black citizens, it ought to be the stark dispassionate manner in which the color problem has been analyzed by André Siegfried, professor of economics in the Ecole Libre des Sciences Politiques of Paris, and published (through Harcourt, Brace and Co.) in his book *America Comes of Age*. The title is a most ironic misnomer, for in many respects America is the most infantile of countries, especially that section so thoroughly castigated by Professor Siegfried, castigated, however, in a manner not calculated to draw umbrage; for the professor has been a most detached reporter. But his evidence is damning. Taken for what it is worth, the unbiased observation of a scholar, the following information is enough to indict any country before an impartial court of justice:

"The best elements of the community often take part—society people, high officials, and even judges. Not only do they approve, but they make no attempt to hide their presence—they have told me this themselves! This explains the tragic undercurrent of anxiety and ferocity that is always present in this land of romance. The cordial, polished gentleman with whom you are talking is possibly a murderer who has gone into the wood at night to kill a man outnumbered a hundred to one; and thousands of others, your friends among them, may have been his accomplices. Outwardly, Texas, Georgia, and South Carolina are civilized States of the twentieth century, but in reality they should be classed along with the countries still guilty of pogroms."

"Where the color question is concerned, the white race has lost all sense of justice. Everything is permissible, even crime. Religion has no restraining influence, for the churches are divided into black and white; and the conscience of the Christian no longer suggests that he is doing wrong in maltreating the inferior race."

In recording what he has been vouchsafed as plausible explanations of certain southern conditions, the author has not allowed these extenuations to draw a film over his actual vision, as the following paragraph wil bear witness:

"In the old plantation days the masters used to take mistresses from among their slaves, and even today there are many middle-class men who keep a colored woman and have children by her. Therefore although the whites declare that the Negro is physically repulsive to them, you konw that it simply is not true. On the contrary, one of the most complex aspects of life in the South is this indescribable attraction of the black woman."

No millenium, where black and white shall, like the lion and the lamb of apocalyptic prophecy, lie down together, blurs on the horizon of the author not even in the most remote distance. Those of us who are putting our trust in a slowly evolving world that we hope may some day attain to a semblance of civilization, will find small encouragement in the doleful tone with which Professor Siegfried terminates his article:

"Is the regime of yesterday and today to carry on?"

"Yes," replies the South, "nothing else is possible."

"Why not suppress the insults, recognize the Negro as a man but maintain the separation of the races?"

"No!" answers the horror-stricken South. "This very contempt is the best possible barrier, and once this line of defence has been pierced, we should have a hideous confusion!"

Therefore, (and what person not a part of the situation would not feel the same way?) Professor Siegfried concludes:

"No matter which way we turn in the North or the South, there seems to be no solution. The color problem is an abyss into which we can only look with terror."

There are, however, those of us more vitally concerned with this problem whose hopes are more sanguine than Professor Siegfried's. Slowly but surely we see the hour glass running low with intolerance, bigotry and color oppression. And just often enough to keep us from cursing whatever gods there be, something happens that perks us up and gives the flagging heart a new rush of blood. We go somewhere, Canada, Europe, some place where the insidious seed of Nordic superiority has not been planted, and we get a glimpse of what we are striving for. We are treated not like anomolies of nature, but like mere men, than which we ask nothing more—merely treatment commensurate with our fitness to receive it. That glimpse is all we need to send us back determined, not to migrate to some country that has extended us its hospitality for a moment, but to work out our salvation here more by achievement than by fearing and trembling. And once in ever so many moons something will occur in this benighted land of ours to tell us that although the march of progress has halted for a while, its direction still is forward.

Just such a forward step do we consider the recent statement given out by the women of Mississippi. At last a group of southern women has grown weary of supplying the questionable excuse with which white men cover their brutality and mob violence. The white women of Mississippi have declared: "We place ourselves on record as unalterably opposed to mob murder. The barbaric practice of lynching arouses unchristian passions, violates the sovereignty of our state, brings Mississippi into disrepute in the eyes of the world, and brutalizes all those who come within its evil influence."

"As southern women we hold that no circumstances can ever justify mob action and that in no instance is it an exhibition of chivalric consideration for the honor of womanhood."

It would appear that the Lord's vacation from southern territory is drawing to an end in some sections and in some hearts.

———

APPROACHING her subject with an air as detached and as aloof as that of Professor Siegfried, although she herself is an inhabitant of the country whose problems she treats, Sarah Gertrude Millin, remembered for *God's Stepchildren*, her powerful novel of South African miscegenation, brings to her most recent book *The South Africans* (Boni and Liveright) an incisiveness that leaves the reader breathless with the thrill of the thing. She is a true vivesectionist, and the mighty heart of this dark country, dark in deed as well as in the complexion of those most indigenous to its ways, lies bleeding and bared, every vein alive and palpitant under the probing of a pen in a firm hand guided by a clear and piercing vision.

Hers is a moody tale of rapacity and greed, of the oppression of the weak by the strong, of the exploitation of the unlettered by the learned and cultured who have prostituted wisdom and pseudo-refinement to ends for which they were never devised. Gallantly and without comment she scrapes the surface clean as with a scapel and underneath the veneer of outward appearance one sees the festered bone of reality in this land where the black man is the lowest, cheapest adornment of the social order and any man with a white skin the highest achievement of deity. As the tale unfolds one cannot but blush for deity's masterpiece.

"Here we all are, a heterogenous collection of Europeans, an imported and established population of Asiatics, a man-created, rather than a God-created, nation of half-castes, a ghosthood of yellow aboriginals, and a flood— a strong and spreading flood—of dark-skinned African peoples . . . and the really important question is: how, since we are here together, we may live and develop with the least unhappiness and enmity." Such is the prime question and it is indicative of the author's hopes for its felicitous answering that it is asked negatively—*the least unhappiness and enmity—not the most happiness and concord.*

South Africa seems truly "the harlot of the nations" so many hands have been upon her, so many men have known her treasures and fought and bled for them; so many now sue with dubious legislation for the retention of her favors. It is a motley aggregate—Boer and Briton, Bantu, Bushman, Hottentot and Kaffir, Indian and Asiatic—and little love lost between them. The Boer and the Briton have been merged into what they term the true South African, although the despised Kaffir, their hewer of wood and drawer of water, might justly contest the claim. Consider the Kaffir: "The Kaffirs do nearly all the unskilled labor in South Africa. The latest legislation seeks to exclude them from competition with the whites. But in the mines, they, and not the miners, work on the stopes. On the farms, they, and not the farmers, do the planting and reaping and herding . . . Long before daylight they are at the housework. It is an utter shock to a South African when, on a ship going to England, he comes for the first time, upon a white man wiping the floors of cabins. Nor can he bear to see a white woman washing an English doorstep. In South Africa one does not see white men or white women working like that. A European has to be very poor indeed not to keep a Kaffir . . . . "

Yet in South Africa "when the Socialist and the Labour man speak of 'a chance in life for every man,' they do not mean the Kaffir."

A few aspects of the color situation in South Africa offer marked contrasts to the same situations in America. In South Africa the Cape man, or half-caste, is the only man of color toward whom the South African (white) feels any sympathy or obligation, recognizing to a certain extent his responsibility for the half caste's existence. In America it is safe to say that most Negroes of mixed blood, insofar as they are concerned with the mixture, depreciate the white portion; but in South Africa (sic Mrs. Millin) "it is not the author of his calamity that the Cape man abhors, not the man who deprived him of his heritage and sowed disaster in a clean land. Of his white blood he is terribly proud. It is the black man that calls up the bitterness in his heart, the reflection of the shamed, betrayed and desolate half within himself." Another distinction: "Socially, indeed, South Africa is kinder to the Eurafrican than is America. In South Africa a drop of black blood is, if possible—and despite all talk to the contrary—ignored. In America it is hunted out. South

Africa, in short, classes with the white any person who can conceivably pass as white, where America classes with the Negro any person who can conceivably pass as Negro."

For the most part, Mrs. Millin's observations are keen and her reactions sensible. At one point however, as far removed as we are from the South African scene, we think it wise to disagree with her. "There is one thing about a black man that the average South African cannot bear; and that is to see him well dressed in the European style." For this objection Mrs. Millin finds extenuations: "And he has reason for his intolerance. A Kaffir wearing the greys and blacks and browns of modern convention is aesthetically unsatisfactory. The sober colours make his brown-black skin look like mud. And, still worse, although he often has an imitatively sound and decorous taste in clothes that the European need not despise, he wears those clothes with a self-conscious air and swagger, which are not only amusing, but, if one does not look beneath the surface, also subtly offensive." Clothes have a fair share in the making of any man, and one may well imagine that the white man's objection to seeing his black compatriot in plus fours is not based upon anything as intelligent as aesthetics but is merely a white defence mechanism for keeping the Kaffir "in his place."

* * *

IF this column may vouchsafe the gratuitous recommendation of certain books to while away the time for those of its readers for whom summer is a season of leisure and play, our first vote is for Elizabeth Madox Roberts' *The Time of Man*, the faultless writing of which we have already paeaned and which, contrary to our ardent hopes, did not receive this year's Pulitzer award. *Early Autumn* by Louis Bromfied, which did receive the award we also recommend as a spirited piece of writing and an absorbing story. If the hot days preclude heavy reading for you, there is *Lolly Willowes* by Sylvia Townsend Warner, a last year's book which we continue to admire, the fascinating story of a spinster lady who found through actual contact that "the prince of darkness was a gentleman" and most suave and courteous at that. And if keen, rapier-sure satire that tears your dearest idol down with a laugh does not alarm you, an unbounded joy awaits you in the reading of this same author's latest opus: *Mr. Fortune's Maggot*—in which a missionary who went to seek and save the lost was himself found and converted to ways which if more heathenish than his own, also had more extenuations to offer. Add to these *Go She Must* by David Garnett who will be remembered for his delightful whimsey *A Man In the Zoo*, and *God's Trombones* by James Weldon Johnson, and your summer reading will be irreproachable. If you are prone to eschew the frivolities of the modern novel, try Sarah Gertrude Millin's masterly analysis of *The South Africans*. But we warn you that it is calculated to give such pleasure that you will find it reads more easily than many a novel, and holds your interest with a far tighter grip. Then there is Edwin Arlington Robinson's *Tristram* which many critics have crowned the one staunch beam holding up the tottering edifice of American poetry. Whether our poetic structure be crumbling or not—as indeed there is some question whether any such structure has ever been raised,—*Tristram* is a great poem, its nearest approach in our estimation being William Ellery Leonard's *Two Lives*. And in these months of sentiment when the fancies of both sexes, especially if they be incorporated in youth, turn to idle amours that for the space of a season seem so everlasting as the stars, we feel it an encumbent duty to ask that you carry away with you Dorothy Parker's poems *Enough Rope*, the most sparking collection of casual verse that we have read in many a day. Summer sentimentality will cause you no bruised organs with the coming of saner days of the year if you draw a magic circle around you with this book.   COUNTEE CULLEN.

THE DARK TOWER

A T this writing we are in a most festive and communicative mood. Our feelings approximate those which might have been Browning's when he wrote:

"I have a friend across the sea, ...
It all grew out of the books I write."

For no more appropriate reason than that one or two of our verses have pleased him, we have a friend as far away as Johannesburg, South Africa. His first letter is enough to win over any poor poet. He writes: "Will you accept this parcel, from an unknown African friend? You will notice that it is all African art. The Inkombe is a spoon from Shangaan, East Africa; the Intshengula is a snuff spoon from the Baca race, Cape Colony; the Isigaza are ear-rings worn by man with big holes in the ears, Zululand; the Ingawe is a pipe from the Ama Xosa tribe, Cape Colony; the Ketai ea di baga is a Becuana tie from British Becuana land; the mfanyefanye are rings for the legs worn by both women and men in Swaziland." The parcel hasn't come yet, but that letter has had a very disorganizing effect upon this department; what with our eyes glued to the door and our ears trying to meet the postman's tread halfway, there'll be no doing anything with us until that parcel comes. Maybe we'll be able to tell more about it in the next Tower.

Few of us when bored with the ennui of what we consider a trivial existence, or when unduly agitated about the individual inconveniences that we may be bent beneath, can adequately realize that nothing could ever be quite as exciting and interesting as being just what we are. Our familiarity with our own lives begets a contemptuous condescension in which we take a most unpardonable pride.

Florence Mills. By A. Stuart-Hill
(Sketch for a Portrait)

Just now I can really imagine nothing quite so emblazoned with interest as being a Negro. It is to be *a la mode*: and who would be the fashion should remember that in a slip shod world to be the vogue is also to be peculiar, and apart. The theatrical circles of three foreign capitals are acknowledging the magnetism of three colored comediennes; Ruth Bayton is teaching the Berliners a few racial steps; London has long since given its accolade to the inimitable Florence Mills, while Paris has scarcely a product not named after Josephine Baker. *Time*, that most invigorating digest of weekly news, recently carried a eulogy on Miss Baker. Two letters printed in the July 18 issue of *Time* are typical of two different kinds of reactions. From New York Miss Justine Agnes Clementine La Vie writes the editor: "My praise goes out to you for printing recently stories so complimentary and so fair to two of the loveliest women of my race in Paris, Miss Florence Jones and Miss Josephine Baker. But—ah!—why have you not mentioned the third?

"Just now all British society is admiring her portrait by A. Stuart Hill, which hangs in the recently opened Young Artists Exhibition. I visited the exhibition before leaving England, some ten days ago, and I noticed two Royal Dukes standing in admiration before this picture of—of course you know whom I mean — Miss Florence Mills."

Of quite a different tenor is the letter sent the editor of *Time* by George R. Carroll, an Atlanta, Ga., subscriber. The tribute to Miss Baker has cost *Time* the loss of one subscription, for Mr. Carroll writes: "I have been a double subscriber of *Time* for the past eight months, but I must now ask you to terminate that subscription which reaches my home. . . . . . .

"I do not deem it fit or proper that my wife or daughters should read such articles as that eulogy of the Negress dancer Josephine Baker of Paris which appeared in *Time*, July 4, I do not believe you can point out to me any other magazine read by white women which would have dared to publish such an item. . . . ."

The editor's note on the correspondence page of *Time* assures Mr. Carroll that "if Mrs. Carroll subscribes to the fashion magazine *Vigue*, let her turn to page 51 of Vogue's June 1 issue. There she will see a quarter-page sketch of a Negress black bottoming, and will read beneath: 'Josephine Baker is the Lulu Belle of Paris. . . . . Her graceful body is light seal-skin brown. . . . This woman is like a living drawing by Aubrey Beardsley. . . . One is struck by her great seductive allure.' "

Fame is a term that can well be modified and suffer the heights and depths of relativity; to be famed as the Lulu Belle of Paris and a deft interpreter of the black-bottom is one thing, and to be like a living drawing by Aubrey Beardsley quite another.

We never let pass an opportunity to witness a performance by Emil Jannings, to our mind the one incontestable genius of the screen. Our attendance upon his appearances has a punctuality that might well be spared for weightier things. Thus it was with a double interest that we recently shirked more serious obligations to see him portray that dark prince of tragedy, Othello. He brought to the role of the gullible Moor haunted by "the green-eyed monster which doth mock the meat it feeds on" his usual rare comprehension and skill. One suffered with him all the pangs and recriminations immortalized in that jealous protagonist.. But we consider it more of a sacrilege than an improvement that there should have been added to the scrip so naive an explanation of Othello's lineage. He is made to say, when defending his love for Desdemona: "I am the son of an Egyptian Prince and a Spanish Princess." Our text of *Othello* fails to disclose this singular

Ruth Bayton—the Josephine Baker of Berlin

revelation anywhere in its pages. "I fetch my life and being from men of royal seige," is a far more eloquent protestation, and incidentally Shakespeare. Shakespeare certainly leaves no room for cavil over Othello's complexion. Iago speaks of the Moor as "an old black ram," mentions him as "the thick-lips," drinks a measure to "the health of black Othello." Brabantio upbraiding Othello marvels that his daughter should "run from her guardage to the sooty bosom of such as thou." Desdemona even is constrained to justify her choice as having seen "Othello's visage in his mind." The Moor himself suffered no delusions concerning the hue that marked him apart. "For she had eyes and chose me" is his judicial defense of his marriage. And for Desdemona's apparent lapse of faithfulness he could find no more felicitous comparison than this:

> Her name, that was as fresh
> As Dian's visage is now begrimed and black
> As mine own face.

Was it necessary, then, to give him a royal geneology adding no cubits to the stature of a man whose sworn foe could say

> The Moor, howbeit that I endure him not,
> Is of a constant, loving, noble nature. . . .?

Desdemona loved him for the dangers he had passed. Was not that enough to establish a royal escutcheon for him?

Or was there the thought that this ebony visaged hero might be considered a Negro by the audience? Recourse to Webster might have reassured them, for there a Moor is defined as a "native of Morocco or neighboring North African states, of Arab or Berber blood, or a mixture of the two."

Suppose you already had a gridiron; in fact, after having exchanged to your satisfaction all the gridirons, which thoughtful friends, with a repetitious determination, had bestowed on you as wedding, birthday, and anniversary gifts, you still had two gridirons, and very little for us either; then suddenly, modern and sophisticated, with the sea salt still in his eyes and the ocean tang rolling on his tongue like a chewing man's favorite tobacco juice, Sinbad the sailor stood reincarnated before you, selling gridirons. Would you be wise? Would you buy, sensing the spirit of the Arabian nights and the shady side of a life mellow with rich happenings? If besides buying a needless gridiron, you were hospitable enough to invite your veteran peddler to a cup of tea, he might then a tale unfold such as Ethelreda Lewis heard from Trader Horn on the porch of her house in South Africa. It is no stranger that the Damocletian sword should depend from a thread than that *Trader Horn* (Simon and Schuster, New York) one of the most opulent recitals of adventure that we have read, should begin with a gridiron and a cup of tea.

No mere swashbuckler, no petty soldier of fortune, all brawn and a negligible brain, is this suave seaman of the West African Coast. Not a shade of sound or color, not a tribal custom that he has encountered but has left its mark of appreciation and comprehension upon him. Trader Horn is a philosopher of the first water; he would be the last to admit this, and he might resent the inference. But if a vigorous observation be the stuff of which the philosophical mind is made, some university might offer the trader a chair, and swell the popularity of its curriculum with a rarely stimulating course.

Some of us with weather-beaten ideas of places and peoples we have never seen may be dismayed at many of the trader's sentiments: "Cannibals . . . . . the most moral race on earth. The women chaste and the men faithful." . . . . . . "The black man's a fearful savage we say, when we see him crucify a man head down. Head down, and with one leg lower than the other. Then off with his head, and bowls set for the blood. Eighteen I might 'a' been. A lad receives a terrible imprint at eighteen, and Lancashire far from sight. . . . . But when we cry 'Savage!' we're forgetting the stone of sacrifice still standing on the hills of England on which white men and yellow-haired women were killed by white men for the benefit of religion. Cruel method, it was too,—breaking the spine across it like a stick against your shins."

There's something to a thought like this, this interpretation of the awful things of existence in terms of the small things of a man's career, on which even the orthodox may not entirely frown: "Aye, if we'd think of Death as the hand of nature it'd be no worse than lying down to sleep in a cornfield. It's when the parsons trick out a natural process with all sorts of common regalia like Heaven and Hell that it becomes something to fear."

For those, like us, who have no hope of ever seeing a herd of elephants trampling an African jungle in their fury, or to witness black magic in a native temple where death awaits the curious unitiate if discovered, or to encounter any of the thousand thrills that only the insatiable wanderer experiences, *Trader Horn* holds forth all the pleasure and none of the pain.

THE DARK TOWER

L EST one meandering columnist should bear down too severely on the patience of OPPORTUNITY's subscribers, the Tower for this month has been turned over to a guest conductor who will accomplish the double kindness of presenting our readers with a new personal angle on things, while at the same time permitting the usual wielder of this baton to limber up his fingers after a pleasant period of summer inactivity. . . . Introducing Mr. Richard Bruce, artist, poet, and for October 1927 impressario of The Dark Tower. . . .

"I have just looked over the proofs of *Caroling Dusk*, an anthology of verse by Negro poets, edited by Countee Cullen. It is going to be a beautiful book with a jacket by Aaron Douglas. Nearly all the Negro poets are represented: Langston Hughes, Georgia Douglas Johnson, Arna Bontemps, Angelina Grimké, Claude McKay, Paul Lawrence Dunbar, Alice Dunbar Nelson and W. E. B. Du Bois being among the best known. Albert Rice is represented by a few very lovely things. Mr. Rice is new to most of us. A very interesting feature is introduced in the auto-biographical sketches. Each artist has written his own except in three instances, in two of which the poet is dead and in the third too young. I shall get the first copy off the press. . . . And in connection with the proofs: I had taken them down to a friend's house to look over and discuss. It was in the middle of our discussion that she reminded me that there would be a demonstration such as I had never seen before in Union Square. So off we went to Union Square. We reached a vantage point just opposite *The Daily Worker's Bulletin*. As we took our places the bulletin read: "Japanese Workers Flood Streets Before U. S. Embassy Buildings." There was dead silence. Only a tenseness that we had first noticed. People talking in rather hushed tones. In Italian, Jewish and English. In French, Armenian, and Russian. Greenwich Village well represented by made-to-order suits and workingmen's shoes, patched suits and silk socks, sandles and smocks and long hair, cigarette holders and note books. And little Italy. By tight-fitting suits and patent-leather shoes. Corduroy trousers and well-shaven faces. Rough blue shirts and black hair. And Russia. By working clothes and florid faces. Haunted eyes and red hands. There was an overtone of hushed laughter and joking. But the merriment was a trifle forced, and artificial, and only tended to make the tense undercurrent more palpable. Strong individual and personal emotions vied with party emotions. A sense of helplessness and anxiety mixed with indignation seemed to pervade the crowd. People speaking in hushed tones. Smoking furtive cigarettes as though talking and smoking were forbidden. Whispered commonplaces spoken absently as all eyes shifted from time to time toward the bulletin board. An enormous crowd trying to appear individual and careless. Or grouped and defiant. Whispering. And we continued our conversation—in whispers. Speaking of the psychology of having each poet contribute his biographical sketch—of— the bulletin board again: "Fifteen Minutes To Live." The voices renewed their farce. And we. Mounted police kept a passage clear in the street, and patrolmen one clear on the sidewalks. The crowd divided. Part of it right, under the bulletin board. Then a line of mounted police. A clear streeet. More mounted police. A crowd, patrolmen, and a clear space; then patrolmen and the crowd. Filling the park and spilling out into Broadway and Seventeenth and Fourteenth Streets. Right in front of us a tall, dark boy with tangled

hair was offering silent prayer. A little blond girl with him kept her eyes glued to the board. There were excited movements in the office window next to the one displaying the bulletin. The window was thrown open. All sound ceased. The window swung to again. "Ten Minutes to Live." And the hum and buzz of the strained voices renewed. The false laughter and furtive smoking. Our conversation. Shifting. The bulletin again. "Sacco and Vanzetti Bravely Await Death." The crowd breathed again and shifted. It was becoming restless and a constant patrol by mounted police and patrolmen was necessary. The bulletin. "Witnesses to the Execution Begin to Arrive." The sound of shifting feet and nervous laughter became an accompaniment to the appearance on the bulletin. "They Enter the Death Room." Another bulletin. I could not see it. There was perfect silence. Then a scream. And another. And another. In front of me a young man was tearing his clothes, and giving voice to wordless cries. Some one screamed—*Assassini*. The word was put into his mouth. *Assassini—Assassini* . . . It was taken up by individuals. Tears and sobs and shouts. And cries of *assassini*. But the greater number was silent and motionless. The bulletin announcing Vanzetti's death was an anti-climax. Immediately the police attempted to disperse the crowds. Mounted police. Police in armored motorcycles. Patrolmen. And from the center of the park a woman's voice began the "Internationale." We were carried on the crest of the crowd. Down Fourteenth Street, singing, shouting, weeping, gesticulating. And police. At Second Avenue another attempt was made to disperse the crowds. Mounted police charged on the sidewalk. People scattered. We went down Second Avenue. At Twelfth Street a crowd suddenly overtook us. A charge of police in armored motorcycles scattered them. We ran behind the green lattice that protects the sidewalk tables at the "Royal." At the table were gathered most of the Jewish intelligentia. So we sat and sipped iced coffee and discussed the evening.

Next day was dark and rainy. Harlem was in gala attire. All the street lights were lighted. And thousands of red, green, and yellow lights strung across the streets. Banners and signs and flags. Elks heads and purple and white garbed people mingling with the already overcrowded streets. Someone shouted "They're coming!" All traffic was stopped; mounted police kept the streets clear. And with a blare of horns and drums the parade struck Seventh Avenue. People were hanging out of every window. Crowded every available foot of sidewalk and street. Passed by a white-dressed band. Pandemonium of cheers and personal greetings and shouts. A lady drum major strutted by clad in royal purple satin and yellow. Shod with golden slippers. As resplendent as Caius or Solomon. Banners, floats, pandemonium. And laughter. All beneath a heavy sky jewelled with string upon string of red, yellow, and green electric lights. No rain could wash away the purple or smiles or gold and laughter. And then night. Seventh Avenue resplendent. Beautiful. The electric lights given back again by the glassy streets. Laughter and gayety. Venders and hawkers. Corn puddin'; Virginia ham; corn bread; feasts for sale; and festivity. On and on into the night. Dark clothes and gala ties alternated with white clothes and purple ties . Dress. Red, white, yellow, and orange. Kaleidoscopic. And plumes, and feast and joy. And all around signs of welcome. Four days and nights in carnival attire.

I have just finished *Copper Sun* by Countee Cullen. It is very charmingly illustrated by Charles Cullen. Mr. Cullen's latest book of poems continues to fulfill his promise. It is replete with apt and beautiful imagery. One verse particularly stays with me as a perfect example of the possibilities for beauty and rhythm given a poet:

> I who employ a poet's tongue
> Would tell you how
> You are a golden damson hung
> Upon a silver bough.

It would be difficult to find four more beautiful lines. And those are merely an introduction to the poem itself.

———

Langston Hughes has returned to New York after having been south all summer. He has a number of very interesting tales to tell about the flood area and New Orleans. Strange tales about visiting voodoo gatherings where a "cunjer" woman put a protective charm upon Miss Zora Hurston and himself. And waters so calm and peaceful that one could hardly believe it was flood tide were it not for the houses jutting up like strange and melancholy water flowers. Were it not for the miles and miles of mud and ooze. Some of it hard and cracked like a bas-relief map—some of it soft and rich giving off colors of the rainbow under the sun. Were it not for the refugee camps, cluttered with bedding and pans and chairs and trinkets salvaged from the waters. Were it not for the thousands of congregated men and women and children. The laborers fortifying levees. The patrol of soldiers and the bustle to acclimate oneself to one's surroundings. Strange sights and weird streets in New Orleans. The vaults with their tier upon tier of tiny doors. Some ornamented, some plain. And Baton Rouge partly built on stilts. Out into the waters and swamps. And the flowers and steps growing right out of the water. And after all that New York again. Mr. Hughes should have much material for a number of new poems.

———

The Theatre Guild has been rehearsing for *Porgy* by Du Bose Heyward, which opens on the third of October. Frank Wilson plays the name part and the cast of principals includes Evelyn Ellis and Rose Maclendon. The play is very good, so far as I can see from rehearsals, Frank Wilson making an excellent cripple and Miss Ellis an excellent Bess. As for Miss Maclendon, her part as Robbins' wife gives her wide range for her powers. The atmosphere bits are done by local Negroes among whom you are certain to recognize a number of friends.

Richard Bruce.

THE DARK TOWER

In the Negro Cast of the Theatre Guild's Production of "Porgy"

Reproduced from the New York "World"

THE interest of the past month seems entirely to have been taken up by the theatre. Revivals, recastings and debuts have all played a part in a very mutatory month. Julius Blendsoe has been off on tour adding his interpretations of *The Emperor Jones* to the two illustrious impersonations already given us by Gilpin and Robeson. *In Abraham's Bosom* has profited liberally by its choice as the year's Pulitzer Play, so much so that a production which began probably as an aesthetic and esoteric venture has now entered the class of successful good plays. This play has made more stars than any show of Negro life that we have seen. Julius Bledsoe and Frank Wilson owe a large measure of their theatrical fame to the vehicle, while Abbie Mitchell's reputation, already established, was greatly enhanced by it. There have been so many changes of cast in Paul Green's opus that we have already made three pilgrimages to the Provincetown Theatre for the odious purpose of comparing the various character delineations. We sincerely hope the changes are at an end for a while, for three evenings given over to the unfortunate life of Abraham McCranie are all that we can stand in one year. Just now a very small part of the cast that originally made the play famous is still identified with it. Paul Green may well bear a bit of genial animus against his fellow Southerner Du Bose Heyward for this sad state of affairs; for into the current production of Heyward's *Porgy* has been poured the cream of Mr. Green's cast: Rose McClendon, Frank Wilson, and Richard Huey; while Abbie Mitchell has left to join the cast of *Coquette* in which, we understand, she will be given an opportunity to sing, something we think she ought to do in preference to all the acting in the world. She made of Muh Mack, a decidedly unlikeable old lady, a character which the audience applauded and accepted in spite of themselves. But if there is one thing this versatile person ought to do more than another, it is sing. Of the original cast of the Paul Green play, the one significant player still remaining with it is James Dunmore, who gives such a fine and artless performance as Puny Avery the turpentine hand.

Whether it was an off evening on which we last saw *In Abraham's Bosom* or whether the new players had not been playing long enough to get into the spirit of the production, we cannot say, but something seemed to have gone out of the play. If we had not already seen Bledsoe's fine acting, and Frank Wilson's finer, as Abraham McCranie, we would have considered Thomas Mosely adequate in the part; but he suffers in comparison. Doralyne Spence is in essence, we feel, a good actress, and she brought to the role of Goldie all the outward and physical expressions necessary; but her voice failed to catch the southern timbre and her dialect often wandered off into the correct speech which she is accustomed to use. It takes a person of parts, however, to wear the mantle of Rose McClendon, and Miss Spence, on the whole wears it well. Muh Mack as portrayed by Miss Mitchell was a spirited, vixenish old lady; Mrs. Frank Wilson, the new encumbent of the role makes her too lackadaisical to be convincing. Alston Burleigh as the no account son of McCranie leaves nothing to be desired.

In fear and trembling, and uttering many a silent prayer, we attended a dress rehearsal of the Guild production of *Porgy*. Having often witnessed the unholy hands with which the theatre has desecrated beautiful books in making them over into plays, we were apprehensive for the fate of one of our favorites. At the end of the performance, however, we were grateful for a play that has sincerely striven to be faithful to the original story. By a hair's breadth, but that is enough to redeem it, the play escapes being a musical production with some speaking thrown in. We are a singing people, no doubt, and that side of our nature has been given wide publicity, but I wonder if we just naturally must sing all the time, at work and at play, at funerals and at picnics, when we are happy and when we are afraid, when we feel religious and when we feel downright mean.

The musical part of this play does, as a compensation, introduce us to a fine new spiritual *Death ain't you got no shame?* while the importation of a part of the Jenkins Orphan Band from Charleston is a very happy injection of local color.

Evelyn Ellis and Rose McClendon have both gone far since they acted together in *Rose-Anne* a few years ago. It is difficult to say which of them is the star of *Porgy*. An arbitrary reference to the play itself would place Miss Ellis, who acts Bess superbly, alone in the firmament, but there is a dignity and a grace that Rose McClendon is capable of bringing to the most thankless role, and this capacity does not desert her in her portrayal of Serena. And one is convinced, seeing her sobbing grief-stricken over her murdered man in the first scene, that though the opportunities for effective and telling acting will all be Miss Ellis' throughout the remainder of the play, the odds at the final curtain will still be equal between these two actresses. To the belligerent role of Maria (and in Cat Fish Row they don't wait until you drop a hat to

fight; you merely have to twiddle it in your fingers)
Georgette Harvey brings a fine voice and a vehement piece
of character acting. Frank Wilson as Porgy and Jack
Carter as Crown bear up well.

Before the thought passes, we wonder why in the
production of plays dealing with Negroes the truth of
their multi-colored complexions is either unknown, overlooked or intentionally avoided. In recasting *In Abraham's
Bosom*, the part of one of the turpentine hands fell to
Mr. William White, a colored gentleman, although not
obviously so. He was toned down to an extent that
was ludicrous. The south is filled with light mulattoes,
and in a play dealing with a section of the country which
claims to be able to detect a Negro no matter how fair
he may be such an evasion of realism is out of place.
Jack Carter who plays Crown in *Porgy* is confessedly a
Negro, although one might not be struck with his racial
identity at the first casual glance. There is nothing in
Porgy as Mr. Heyward first wrote it to state that Crown,
although big and burly, is black. Mr. Heyward simply
wrote with that poetic economy which is an inseparable
part of his style: "Opposite Porgy, sitting upon his
haunches, and casting his dice in moody silence, was a
Negro called Crown. He was a stevedore, had the body
of a gladiator, and a bad name." Yet Mr. Carter is
shaded down to a black which while it is aesthetically
pleasing, we venture was not the result of aesthetic ex-
perimentaion.

Porgy has moments of thrill and suspense that ought to
insure its success and continuation long after the usual
six weeks' run to which a Guild production is entitled
has passed. The scene where Robbins is killed, that in
which his neighbors' contributions toawrd his funeral ex-
penses make him a "saucer-buried nigger", the storm scene,
are all impressive bits of theatre.

Of the current Broadway productions, one that appears
destined for a long run, is the bold, bawdy comedy with
the aphoristic title "Women Go On Forever". The part
of a colored maid in a play is generally negligible, but
Edna Thrower has been more generously dealt with in
Women Go on Forever, and makes of her slight role quite
a part.

Black Velvet, a play of adulterous miscegenation, lived
in New York one brief uneventful week. The colored
press of this metropolis were hardly moved to appropriate
diatribes against a play that had been so thoroughly denounced by the Negro press of Chicago. *Black Velvet*
died because it was a bad play, most of it being given over
to reminiscences of befo' de wah' between a southern
planter, General Darr, and his trusty black servitor and
childhood companion, Calhoun Darr—long speeches of
fond recollections halting the action of the play as long as
the General's extremely vivid memory persisted.

Had *Black Velvet* been a well constructed play, it might
have been successful with unfortunate results, for we
cannot recollect seeing any play more calculated to foster
and breed interracial 'misunderstanding. We do not
infer that this was the author's intention, for all the
objectionable speeches and viewpoints were in keeping
with ideas which we know are the stock in hand of the
type of characters represented. Acting that was indifferent at best hastened the play on to its early and happy
ending.

Countee Cullen.

THE DARK TOWER

Marguerita Fischer as "Eliza" and Arthur Edmund Carew as "George Harris" in Uncle Tom's Cabin"

*D*EATH, *ain't you got no shame?* This grief-born interrogation, darkly intoned by a wailing group of Catfish Row Negroes, might well be taken up as the sorrow song of a race that within the last month has lost two of the most valuable of its feminine luminaries. They moved in wholly different worlds, did Clarissa Scott Delany and Florence Mills, and in the main they probably spoke each a language from a different level of Babel. Death the terrible, that comes like a thief in the night or, if he wills to linger, with the stealthy but certain slowness of a malignant disease; Death, the irreverent disrespector of persons, sparing neither maid nor matron, celebrity nor nonentity; Death, the capricious, who takes the bride in the midst of her nuptial blushes and the dancer on her most applauded pirouette, in making them our common bereavement has drawn them into a juxtaposition life never suffered them to know. We lament them both, the one for that rare poise and simplicity of carriage which made us always think of her when it was a question of the perfect Negro woman, and for those artistic poentialities which we know were in her and which might have matured into an incalculable racial endowment; the other for the odds she had already braved and swept aside.

Inimitable is a word as tantalizing to the tongue as fire to a small and curious child. The tongue relishes the rhythm of it and has it ever on its tip. As chary as we should be of its use, never was it employed with better cause than when describing Florence Mills. Who will rear us up such another and when? is less an emotionally biased question than one inspired by a logical survey of our theatrical residue.

We met Florence Mills only twice, once when through the introduction accorded us by James Weldon Johnson she extended us a cool and casual hand at the DuBois Dinner in 1924. Still deeply imbued with some rather ancient ideas about actresses, we wondered at her being there, and what her reactions might be. From our seat at the speakers' table (because we had written a poem) between an eminent lady author and an actor of Shakesperian roles, whose presence we paradoxically took as natural, we watched her. There was about her none of that raucous air that membership in the Methodist church had taught us to expect of actresses. She was an agreeable disappointment, and one which we wanted to undergo further.

When we next met her, she and her husband were playing in Paris. One afternoon we were all members of a party that undertook to climb to the tower of Notre Dame for a close range view of the gargoyles. We had an opportunity then, through the short snatches of conversation we had with her, to learn about actresses from Florence Mills. She knew things; her interest ached beyond her own concerns, she knew what her people were doing in other life expressions. And she was heartily troubled at the rocky way they went. All too slender and slight for the bright vivacious flame of her being, she was a great personage, an artist of superior equipment.

We have silenced many a puritan lady, her mind and senses as laced and buttoned as her outmoded garments, by querying when she spoke, out of her cloistered ignorance, of the terrible obscenity of the Negro stage: "But have you seen Florence Mills?" If she hadn't seen her, the lady was silenced; if she had seen her, the lady invariably acknowledged our exception.

*C*ARL LAEMMLE, in his picturization of *Uncle Tom's Cabin*, has produced a film that may well go down as one of the great films of the year. Less Uncle Tom's story, in this vivid telling, than Eliza's and little Eva's, it still remains a stirring and deeply moving tale. Emotionally there is no hope for the man or woman who can sit through the heart-rending separation of Eliza and her husband George Harris, the incredible flight of Eliza across the ice-swollen river, her unavailing struggle to keep her little son Harry from being sold into Georgia, her entrance into the Legree household, and her discovery that Cassie, Legree's slave mistress, is her own mother, without a tug at his heart strings and lashes perilously near the point of tears. Sentimental and melodramatic as Mrs. Stowe's famous story undoubtedly is, it rises to superior worth as a sincere indictment against a monstrously iniquitous practice, even the memory of which is malodorous to the democratic spirit.

James B. Lowe as Uncle Tom is not vouchsafed much opportunity for histrionic display; his performance is more calm and cautious than vivid. The great moments are all Eliza's, in this case Miss Marguerita Fischer's. Topsy, as portrayed by Miss Mona Ray, charcoaled for the occasion, makes the most of one of the most memorable roles in the book, but due to the exigencies of economic film making, one extremely shortened in the picture. It is possible, however, that this Topsy is about as effective as is humanly possible, for much of the charm of this comic figure in the book is due to detailed descriptions that could not well be filmed without prolonging the picture interminably.

*W*E HAVE had *The Story of Philosophy* and in *This Believing World* the story of religion. The current tendency seems toward simplification (we disagree with those who think it an abasement) of knowledge for the benefit and better instruction of the layman. Now in *The Winged Horse* (Doubleday, Page & Co. $3.50) Joseph Auslander and Frank Ernest Hill have given us the story of poetry and the poets. Here is the truth about poetry, how it began, the grand role it played in the lives of the ancients, a sorrow at its decline to a minor importance with the advance of civilization, a prophesy of its rehabilitation. Not told that one who runs may read, but that any who reads may understand and more fully appreciate.

Mr. Auslander, than whom there is no American poet writing more vivid and breath-taking poetry, and Mr. Hill, a poet of acknowledged reputation, are both sympathetically equipped for their undertaking. The foot note crank may quarrel with the simplicity with which this story is

told, but the man who has always had, as most humans
have, a hankering after poetry as something he wanted
to know more intimately, yet something afar "from the
sphere of his sorrow," will bless that simplicity. The
whole story of poetry could not well be told in one volume
or ten, but the authors here have seized upon the high
spots in the various eras in poetry, in the lives and developments of the significant figures of each period. And what
good has a book done if something written in it does not
lead us on to another book? *The Winged Horse* will do
just that—set you flying off on the back of Bellerephon,
and where you end up is for you to say. There is no
doubt that this book will metamorphose many a sheepish
admirer of poetry into a brazen devotee.

J IM TULLY has never been accused of mincing his
words, or of bearing in special consideration the ven-
erated lares and penates of a Puritanic reading public. A spade has never been anything but black to him,
and fashioned for deep digging. *Circus Parade* (Albert
and Chas. Boni) is certainly a title to evoke all the fondest memories of brass bands, jovially and teutonically
blown, the big arena with a magic interminable spectacle too vast to be taken in by merely one pair of eyes;
and, of course, pink lemonade. But circus days as we
knew them, shellaced with gaiety and the mad capers of
the chalk-faced clowns, is not the same sort of parade
Jim Tully brought up the rear in. Chicanery and cruelty,
hypocrisy and deception, thievery and lust and betrayal,
human depravity at full tide, march in this carnal caval-
cade to a tune that only one who had been part and
parcel of the corps could play. This book will destroy
some illusions, but that is the natural function of truth.
Of the many characters, all memorably drawn, we carry
away our most vivid picture of three pathetic figures: the
strong woman deceived in her gullible hope that she had
finally found a man to love her four hundred corporal
pounds; the little Negro girl whose dark slim body became a pitiable temple of desecration, and, saddest of all,
Whiteface—born John Quincy, who became "a professional clown by accident." "He was a natural clown. People laughed at everything he did. Where he came from
no one knew. His features were aquiline. There were
traces of Ethiopian, Caucasian and Indian in him. But
in the South he was just another Negro." "There was an
eagle-like expression about his mouth and nose. In his
eyes was the meek love of a dove. His teeth were as even
as little old-fashioned tombstones in a row. He gave one
the impression of power gone to seed, of a ruined cannon
rusting in the sun, of a condor with broken wings."

His racial temperament may have accounted to some extent for Whiteface's effective clowning, as it surely accounted for the type of work alloted him under the big
tent: "He was made to assist in the smaller clown numbers. He took the brunt of physical jokes perpetrated in
the arena. He was always the clown upon whom the
bucket of water was thrown. It was John Quincy Adams
who was dragged by the trick runaway horse. It was his
great yellow body that stopped the majority of the slap-
sticks." Perhaps it was all in the work of a clown that
John Quincy Adams should have been mistaken for another Negro who had struck a white man, while playing in
a section of the South where he was "only another Negro".
Perhaps he was even symbolical of a more tragic Pag-
liacci going through his comic paces in a more extensive
circus.

Countee Cullen.

THE DARK TOWER

IF THERE is a poet in America with the true crusader's zeal and the ancient fighting spirit, he is E. Merrill Root, whose first book, *Lost Eden* (The Unicorn Press, New York), by its very title warns us that here is no rhymster of golden panegyrics to a world in which all is right because "God's in His heaven." Mr. Root has far too searching a vision not to see the worm in the wheat and the slithering coils that befoul the apple tree. And he is far too militant to make polite compromises. What, we wonder, do the black shirts think of that sonnet on *Il Duce*, ending with these scathing lines:

> The land of Francis, Dante, and Mazzini,
> Becomes today this good gorilla's home.
> Would Alighieri could come back to tell
> What cycle fits this Caesar's ape in Hell!

How the hearts of those few persons in Macon, Leaksville and Yazoo City, Mississippi; in Bragedocio, Missouri; and Paris, Tennessee—those capable of understanding it,—must swell with local pride in a deed well done when they read of the refined frolics that make up "Southern Holiday," niceties of torture to which those pictures of the Spanish Inquisition now on exhibition in this city are childish and vapid:

> Flame-acid ate his living flesh,
> His conscious flesh away.
> He tried to bend his fettered head
> And breathe the burning spray:
> The cool wires held him, and the mob
> Prodded him back in play.
> He freed one hand; he tried to snatch
> Live coals to eat and die;
> Men beat his blistered hands aside,
> And laughed to see him try.
> "Kill gently, now," they said, "and don't
> Let the damned nigger die!"

In "Suicide; Out of a Job," the poet flays our selfish indifference to poverty; "R. O. T. C." ridicules with an acid pen our peacetime preparations for war, scoring our famous cultural centres where

> Training to slit a human belly
> Can supplement a course in Shelley.

Animals owe a debt of gratitude to this poet; he seems to understand their language as no other poet does; and his observations whimsical, satirical, undeniable, would tend to establish a Darwinian kinship between us and these lesser members of the earthly family:

> We know we cannot breathe the aether:
> Fish know we cannot breathe the air.
> Fish doubt the earth as men doubt heaven:
> Fish see the cosmos bare and square.
> They know that sharks are hungry levin . . .
> Eaten is hell and eat is heaven . . .
> Love is a little lonely flare.

> . . . .
> Not fish alone, but we as well,
> Are carp that swim in heaven and hell—
> The little human fish of earth!

Mr. Root has an appreciable pity for that "bird of bronze lyrics once, who blazed and flew," and who, now tamed to the ways of man says, "Pretty Polly!" And his monkeys! Read them, and deny their consanguinity if you can.

One of the most mystic of all poets could love the simple things of earth enough to hope for nurseries in heaven;

to Mr. Root in "Earth is Enough" there are some things here which transplanted to that dim land might make it more attractive.

Eden might be restored to us if we were wise enough to be moved to action by this fine and glowing poetry.

IN HER endeavor to do for poetry what the Literary Guild and the Book of the Month Club are doing for prose, Miss Harriet Monroe, founder of the Poetry Clan, has made a wise selection in choosing as her first offering George Dillon's *Boy in the Wind*. Mr. Dillon cannot be dismissed, as most young poets are, as promising. "April's Amazing Meaning," one of his most delightful poems, is no less amazing than his own performance. His is an authentic and individual voice. There is about these poems so much perfection of technique and expression that an awkward line is wished for as a variant. The thoughts are the thoughts of youth, and they are not "long long thoughts," but poets of twenty-odd should not be expected to write with the topical experience of poets of forty. "Boy in the Wind" asks:

> Where will he ever come to rest,
> With that fire blowing in his brain,
> And that bird grieving in his breast?

So might we conjecture as to the future work of Mr. Dillon when we consider the high achievement of his first book. Who will describe ever again the languid descent of a fish now that he has told us of

> The sea where pallid fishes fall
> Like slow snow down the tall green gloom?

And who will attempt to improve in dimeter trochees on "The World Goes Turning"? Not even Elinor Wylie.

"WHAT Color is Your Co-operation?" asks *Co-operation*, a New York journal, in describing a recent essay contest sponsored by the Oklahoma Cotton Growers' Association. The subject for discussion was "The Marketing Contract of the Oklahoma Cotton Growers' Association," and there were white and colored prizes offered, one set for the best essay written by white children and one set for the best essay written by colored children. What color Co-operation? Also what color Democracy and likewise what color Christianity, to say nothing of what color Stupidity?

GOLDEN DAWN, a music drama to which New York has looked forward for the many weeks that the production has been on the road, has finally burst upon us in a lavish and opulent setting at the Hammerstein Theatre. The theatre itself is more like a small cathedral or oriental mosque with its domed roof and its stained glass windows flushed by lights that give a remarkable effect of sunlight streaming in. There is a pontifical elegance about the place that suits admirably the picturesque musical melodrama unfolded there. *Golden Dawn* has all the earmarks of popular appeal: the native African woman wronged and deserted by her white lover; her vow of vengeance culminating in the kidnapping for her lover's white child which she later learns to love as her own; her attempt to keep the child from the way of a man with a maid by dedicating her to the mystic bridal chamber of the native deity; the stock premise that blood will tell as the girl finds herself in love with an Englishman billeted during war time in her home. There is the final confession of the foster mother, the rage of the natives at their discovery that their goddess has been unfaithful to her imaginary spouse; their conversion from hatred to love of her and of the Christian church when before the gates of the Catholic nunnery rain, denied them for many a day of anguish and drought, falls in vindicating showers . . . the usual *mise en scéne* of a successful musical show. It ought to stay long on Broadway. And we mustn't forget the native villain, black and lowering; who looks with lustful eyes upon the white goddess. Incidentally this black counterpart of Simon Legree, played by Robert Chisholm, usurps the place of first honors from the star, Louise Hunter, even though she has a good voice and was recruited from the ranks of the Metropolitan Opera Company. In the entire play there is nothing quite so well done as the song in which Chisholm, as Shep Keyes, cracks his whip, to the terror of black and white alike, and thunders forth that in this old hell-hole in Africa he is the king. Special mention should be made of Jacques Cartier who, as a witch dancer, works into the play the African dance for which he is already famous.

Negroes in the cast play no important principal roles, but do their share toward contributing to a "musical ensemble that is worthy of the best opera traditions. We discerned among their ranks William Service Bell and Inez Clough, whose imperial figure and gait made her look more like a patrician than a mere African native.

THE Boston Evening Transcript for Oct. 6 takes Miss Ellen Glasgow to task in no uncertain terms for maintaining, in an article about her sent out by her publishers, a rather static and antedated idea about Negroes. Only an uncompromising state of warfare between her heart and her mind could have laid Miss Glasgow, assuredly one of the most brilliant novelists of the day, open to this attack in which we feel that the *Transcript* has most of the facts on its side: "If it be true that Miss Glasgow's honest belief is that men and women of African descent are merely children for whom she is profoundly sorry, we take the liberty of feeling quite as sorry for Miss Glasgow. . . . Has she considered with deliberation that remarkable novel by Jessie Redmon Fauset called *There Is Confusion*, which Boni and Liveright published three years ago? In America the position of women in the year 1900 was exactly what the position of the colored citizens of the United States is in 1927. Twenty-seven years ago women were gently derided if they wished to compete with men. They were assured that economic independence for them meant only earning a living wage in the most menial and monotonous occupations, and if they managed to rise to positions that required executive ability and independent judgment, they were told they were exceptionally gifted. Despite a multitude of handicaps, the women of this country have managed to accomplish a surprising amount. We rather suspect that the colored men and women, urged on by the spur of economic necessity, will do more than Miss Glasgow could ever imagine. At least they do not need either her compassion or her patronage." To which a fervent Amen.

Countée Cullen.

THE DARK TOWER

AS we took her extended hand and looked into the vivid animated face over which flitted those expressions associated with the polite and gracious hostess, we thought for the moment that she both saw and heard. But Helen Keller from birth had known neither of those pleasures; both as common and unmystical to the ordinary mortal as are the air he breathes and the sun that shines upon him. She had generously granted us an audience and we stood before her in that abashed and marveling attitude that all who, with sight and sound and unimpeded speech at their disposal, have done less than she with her lack of these, must in all justifiable humility adopt. And yet deficient in that vision which others enjoy, she talks of New York seen through the early evening mist shining like a diamond in the night. "There is," she says, "no limit to the sight of the spirit." Unable to hear, as we know hearing, yet through her interpreter she sees and hears the Irish Players in *The Plough and the Stars*, and is all eagerness when we tell her that *Porgy* is worth her attendance. Moving in a world which, save for the light of her will and the flaring torch of her spirit must be forever like a city of eternal night, she senses the approach of evening, and finds a curious joy in switching on the electric lights that others may see.

Her impediments have given her a kindred feeling for all oppressed peoples, for all in any way handicapped. She speaks of the people of the earth in a biblically symbolic way, telling us that Joseph's coat had many colors, all of which contributed to the beauty of that coveted mischief-working garment.

Strangely enough she was born in Alabama of people who felt the institution of slavery natural and heaven-condoned as they had dark servitors of their own. Her face glowed with the intensity of a cherished memory as she told of her indignation at the unjust treatment accorded her little colored playmate, Martha. Helen Keller, six years of age, had conceived and executed the idea of cutting off Martha's hair. Martha, being six and employing the logic of childhood, had retaliated in kind for which she was severely spanked when apprehended. Miss Killer, although vocally incapable of expressing herself, registered violent disapproval of such justice, and defense of her playmate by scratching and kicking the administrative hands and shins.

Our world is unconditionally hers. She has conquered it with more meagre weapons than most of us have at our command. Beyond that, there is her own world into which we may not pry, where we may only guess at the rich panarama floating before her veiled sight, the majestic symphonies beating their rhythms against her cloistered ears.

IN *The Spirit of St. Louis* (George H. Doran Company, $2) the poets pay their rapturous respects to Col. Charles Lindbergh. It would have been a sorry commentary indeed on the emotions of this age had there been evoked by the Colonel's matchless performance less than the reams of verse that were written. The poets have shown a proper and fitting sense of their obligation to a great deed and a brave and shining figure, but their collected encomiums have done little for the spirit of poetry. And surely this is not the Colonel's fault, for if ever there roamed abroad the spirit of romance, he seems that personification: Young, and with a carriage, brave in a humble self-effacing manner, wearing the spotlight of the world like a halo, and employing no ballyhoo to focus our at-

tention. The poets were apparently in haste to strike the red hot iron, with a prize in view. Aside from the three prize poems by Nathalia Crane, the youthful lady with the dazzling vocabulary, Thomas Hornsby Ferril, and Babette Deutsch, there are few others in the volume that transcend the poet's desire to chronicle a great event. The patriarchal Bliss Carman astounds us with a stanza like this:

> *With no fuss nor publicity-seeking*
> *Quietly with morning,*
> *With one or two loiterers standing by.*
> *He strolls down to his plane*
> *With a sandwich in his pocket,*
> *Steps in with a good bye*
> *And is off.*

Certainly that may be, if we consider veracity alone, an accurate and reportorial stanza, but it takes more than the bare truth to make a poem. Wherein the difference lies may be determined by comparing Mr. Carman's stanzas with Nathalia Crane's poem "The Wings of Lead", or with this final stanza from Mr. Ferril's poem "The Arrow of Acestes":

> *Then standing with his left leg on the world,*
> *He swung his right leg through a little arc,*
> *And pulled his left leg in and closed the door*
> *And arched the land and sea and day and dark.*

THE Negro as others see him appears in the collection *Negro Drawings* by Miguel Covarrubias (Alfred A. Knopf $7.50), and while the tribute is far from being aesthetically complimentary, it is an incisive commentary on Negrodom, mainly Harlem. This young Mexican has an uncanny feeling for the comical essence behind those characters that he chooses to portray; he does not choose to portray all, however, apparently finding his most interesting types in the cabarets. He is especially successful in capturing the illusion of motion: the drawings titled Charleston, Blues Singer, Rhapsody in Blue, in fact the entire stage section teems with action. Even in the still life drawing, Jazz Instruments, the various orchestral pieces seem about to blare forth a rhythmic cacophony of their own accord. To us the most interesting drawings in the book are The Negro Mother and The Three Cuban Women, especially La Negrita. In these honesty has not been subdued by caricature.

WHETHER one finds himself in accord or disagreement with Kathleen Coyle's conclusions, he cannot fail to find enjoyment in her latest novel *It Is Better To Tell* (E. P. Dutton & Company, $2.50). Miss Coyle undertakes to answer the question, "Is it better for a mother to tell her natural children about their father who is living his own life, or remain silent?" Lydia, the chief character of the book, finds that children have to be answered eventually, and that skeletons will rattle when the wind blows. This is the story of Lydia who had two children by Dion Tancred a foundering young playwright from whom she stole away one night taking her children with her because she felt that she hindered his progress. She leaves England and settles in Belgium, near Antwerp where she opens a toy shop and educates her two children. When they have matured to that point where separation from them would seem worse than death to her, Dion, their father, appears as a famous playwright invited to lecture in Antwerp to a group of young intellectuals of whom his own son is the leader. And he brings with him his mistress, Madame Lusitania (assuredly named after the ill-fated steamship) Argente, a French African lady who is quite the most devastating character in the book:

"She was wearing a pleated tomato-red crepe-de-chine

dress that exactly matched her turban-like hat. She did
not remove the hat. It fitted close over her ears. When
she stooped the diamond fringe of her solitary earring
swung out. The bright redness of her dress and hat
distracted one from her skin. And once . . . you had
recovered from the shock of that, you saw that she had
her own sort of beauty. Her nose was good although its
curve had that flat pressed look that broadened the nostrils. Her mouth was like a leaf, the centre vein where
her lips met very straight and the lips above and below
them very curved and full. She took off her shoes and
was peeling a pair of stockings off her legs.

Like her English hostess we too think Madame Argente's
remark why she wore two pairs of stockings delightful. She
explained, "I always have to wear two, the shadow shines
through."

Madame Argente is given to raising scenes and com-
mitting faux pas, critical reviews of which she always
attributed to the fact that she was black. Lydia, however,
felt that the reason was not purely ethnological, and that
had Madame Argente been an albino she would still have
had these receptions. And that, considering the Madame's
temperament, was no specious argument.

How Madame Argente loving Dion not at all, but wishing only to hold his interest in her until that of her own
wayward prize fighter husband should be revived, suspected him of falling in love with his own daughter
(the girl's kinship not having been revealed to Madame),
and how the tangles are all combed out make *It Is Better
To Tell* one of the most interesting books we've read in
some time.

*B*ALLADS FOR SALE, (Houghton, Mifflin Company), the latest posthumous book of verse to be
published for the late Amy Lowell, comes com-
mended as *fresh, new ballads, with the ink scarce dried
upon them.* Hawking her wares like a troubador Miss
Lowell goes by singing:

> *I am passing by your doors
> With sheets and sheets of songs,
> To tickle your tears and your laughter
> And set your feet a-jigging.*

But complaisant reader as we are, we neither weep,
nor burst buttons in our mirth, nor jig to the tune of
these poems. Perhaps the first poem in the volume with
this forbidding title, To a Gentleman Who Wanted to See
the First Drafts of My Poems in the Interests of Psychological Research into the Workings of the Creative Mind,
induced into us at once our mood of marvel and admiration at this lady whose interests were so large that almost
anything might form for her the subject of a poem. If
the Archduchess Anne "had great heart", Amy Lowell
had interests great enough to offer as an extenuation for
the fact that she actually wrote few real poems. There
is legerdemain of style and thought in these poems as
there as in everything she wrote; there is the impress of
a vivid and acquisitive mind for which nothing dwindles
too small for comment. But for the hungry heart to feed
upon, for the emotions to kindle and flame by, there is
little. Still, recalling a recent conversation which we had
with two young poets in Chicago, we remember that one
of the poets felt that it is not one grand epic, nor a few
flawless lyrics that make a poet great, but, in the main,
a diminutive amount of perfection bolstered up by a
vast amount of effort which might or might not be commonplace. If this contention be true, Miss Lowell's shade
walks with those whom posterity bears in mind; if it be
untrue, she still walks in that select company because
many are remembered for personality who might have
perished with their books.

COUNTEE CULLEN.

170

THE DARK TOWER

ROBERT BROWNING has a poem *House* in which he decries those poets who, especially in the sonnet sequences so much in vogue at the time, made a bleeding pageant of the heart, wearing it upon the sleeve for every careless passerby to prick and probe. So deep is the poet's dislike for what would seem a tendency toward indecent exposure that even Shakespeare does not escape his censure:

> *"With this same key*
> *Shakespeare unlocked his heart!*—Once more,
> *Did* Shakespeare? If so, the less Shakespeare he."

Browning advances his own attitude thus:

> Shall I sonnet-sing you about myself?
> Do I live in a house you would like to see?
>   *   *   *
> "For a ticket, apply to the Publisher."
> No: thanking the public I must decline.
> A peep through my window, if folk prefer;
> But, please you, no foot over threshold of mine!

Perhaps a bit of the Browning philosophy practiced by some of our present day Negro writers and journalists might improve race relations more than the wholesale betrayal of racial idiosyncracies and shortcoming which seems so rampant. Every house worthy of the name has an attic or a bin or an out-of-the-way closet where one may hide the inevitable family skeleton. But who inviting a prominent guest to tea, or dinner, and hoping to make even the slightest of good impressions, feels called upon to guide that guest sedulously through every nook and corner of the house, not omitting attic, bin, and the dusty retreat of the skeleton? In most well-regulated households one's guest would not get further than the parlor.

American life is so constituted, the wealth of power is so unequally distributed, that whether they relish the situation or not, Negroes should be concerned with making good impressions. They cannot do this by throwing wide every door of the racial entourage, to the wholesale gaze of the world at large. Decency demands that some things be kept secret; diplomacy demands it; the world loses its respect for violators of this code. Housecleaning is advisable, but one's neighbors are not apt to be the best helpers. Cleanliness should be a matter of personal concern.

The sins committed under shibboleths of art and truth are many, but we doubt if art and truth glibly flowing from the tongue are extenuating enough alibis. There is no more childish untruth than the axiom that the truth will set you free; in many cases it will merely free one from the concealments of facts which will later bind you hand and foot in ridicule and mockery. Let art portray things as they are, no matter what the consequences, no matter who is hurt, is a blind bit of philosophy. There are some things, some truths of Negro life and thought, of Negro inhibitions that all Negroes know, but take no pride in. To broadcast them to the world will but strengthen the bitterness of our enemies, and in some instances turn away the interest of our friends. Every phase of Negro life should not be the white man's concern. The parlor should be large enough for his entertainment and instruction. Browning can both point a moral and end one: *Put forward your best foot.*

THE dark thespian still struts upon Gotham's rialto; this month two new plays of Negro life came to swell the throng of productions which in some way or other touch Negro living, either directly or merely through the medium of an inconspicuous colored member of the cast. Both the new plays are in a way experimental, and neither can be laureled as wholly successful. Lester Walton in presenting at the Princess Theatre *Meek Mose*, a Comedy Drama of Negro life by Frank Wilson, who plays the title role in *Porgy*, has conjured up with unfortunate results shades of the old Lafayette Stock Company. But it is no longer the company we remember thrilling to as a boy when Inez Clough, Tom Brown, Abbie Mitchell and Mrs. Anderson caught and held week after week the changing tempos of *Within The Law, Resurrection, Madam X*, and other plays in their vast repertoire. Susie Sutton brings to her role in *Meek Mose* the same voice cadences, the same comic flutter of spirit, that marked those early days, but they do not fit a new day and time, and, more to the point, a new play. Sidney Kirkpatrick has old fashioned ideas of how a bad man should act, and carries on according to that misinformation. The one creditable performance of the play is that given by Laura Bowman as Josephine, wife of Meek Mose. In voice, gesture and all that goes to make a character delineation she gives a splendid performance. Hardly splendid enough, however, to raise to any considerable heights a wooden, amateurish play in which at intervals, apparently mathematically conceived, spirituals are indulged in for no good reason whatever, except that the action is on the wane.

Hoboken Blues or *The Black Rip Van Winkle*, Michael Gold's phantasy of Negro life first published in *The American Caravan*, and now presented at the New Playright's Theatre on Commerce Street, failed to rile us as it did the professional critics of this city. Certain crudities of expression and presentation, a too pronounced tendency to let the audience become identified with the cast, futuristic scenery that was at times disconcerting, all combined, did not make it fail of its mark as an entertaining spectacle. The play is modelled on the old Rip Van Winkle legend, only this shiftless hero is of color and answers to the call of Sam; his sleep and dream of twenty-five years do not occur in the Catskill Mountains; but in Hoboken; nor are they induced by the heady potency of any magic draught, but by the shock of a policeman's billy. The comedy and satire in the play are both done effectively, although it does occur to us that a Negro character who supplies his comedy through mispronunciation should by now be *persona non grata*. Having argued long and often that Negroes of ability should be allowed to read, write, or act whatever they are qualified for, we cannot properly deprecate the fact that the New Playwright group used white actors to portray colored characters. Acting mainly weak would not have been improved only if Negroes had been given the parts; they would have to be good actors. We thought the group, the ladies especially, used their make-up to good advantage, and to the further contention that colored ladies who are lovely are really that; indeed at one time we thought we saw the gracious and comely identities of Jessie Fauset and Doralyne Spence Jackson shouting hosannah in the revival scene, singing in a stately ladies' chorus, and dancing in the final cabaret movement—seriatim.

Countee Cullen.

THE DARK TOWER

ANY year that went by without William Stanley Braithwaite's annual survey of American Poetry would be marked by a pronounced hiatus in its record of progress. There is little save in the way of commendation that can be said of these annual appraisals of the American poetic output. Braithwaite's anthology still remains the devoted volume to a life long interest, and the final word in its field. The fifteenth annual issue containing those poems published in magazines during 1927 which Mr. Braithwaite considered among the year's finest is a splendid and patient piece of editing. Readers of this column will be especially interested to know that the following poets find representation in this year's collection: Lewis Alexander, Mae V. Cowdery, Gwendolyn Bennett, Sterling Brown, Helene Johnson, Langston Hughes, Georgia Douglas Johnson, and Anne Spencer. The list of magazines addicted to the publication of verse with their addresses should be especially helpful in aiding young poets in the disposition of their work.

We are almost tempted to renege on our feeling of the limitations of dialect for real poetic expression when we read in Braithwaite's anthology the two recent fine dialect poems by one Julia Johnson Davis, one of the poems *John* published first in *The Century Magazine*, the other poem *Peter* published in *Palms*. The dialect seems to transcend its little mould and to flow over into a fuller poetic pattern in this stanza from *Peter.*

Matthew is my staff what I cut f'om de ash,
  I leans on him at mah will,
Philip is mah arrow shootin' straight f'om de bow,
  Jeems is de candle on a hill.
John is mah lamp dey can' blow out,
  Shinin' jes' as steady as kin be,
But Peter is de one I count on mos',
  An' Peter is de changin' sea.

These poems invest dialect with a dignity and seriousness that are found in the poems of Burns, and we are anxious to observe what further and wider use Miss Davis will make of a language form heretofore, especially in Negro dialect, so limited.

WE journeyed late last month for the first time to the far South, passing with some slight tremors of the heart through Virginia, the Carolinas, Georgia and a bit of Alabama to Talledega, a fair college brimming with eager young Negroes intent on drinking at the Pierian well despite the indifference of their native states. We had our Pullman reservation from New York, and so were not made to change at Washington, although in the wash room next morning a young Georgian returning home from West Point without benefit of sheepskin informed us casually and somewhat proudly that he didn't think we could get a reservation on our way back. We thanked him.

As our train whirled deeper and deeper into what we could not help considering the fastnesses of a benighted country, we felt that the hand of the rioter had dug its nails deep into the soil of this land leaving it red and raw with welts of oppression. We thought of the neat orderly precision of the New England landscapes we had seen; we were far from these now, not so much in distance counted in miles as in distance of spirit and feeling; we were far from the genial, even if less carefully groomed, atmosphere of New York. We were in an untutored land among a proud folk who would not be taught. Strange incredible stories stirred to remembrance within us, and we shuddered at the sight of a charred bit of stick stretched like a slumbering snake along the road; we knew not of what insane rites it might have been part, what human torches it once might have served to light.

Save in the case of the Negroes, who are protected by their natural coloring, the brick-red Georgia and Alabama clay has a richer look than the faces of the people. The latter are inert, easy with life, listless with living, worn with the ardor of keeping others in their place. The Pullman porter a man who had lived in Birmingham all his life confided in us that there was "nothing good here but the climate." But if a man has a climate he loves, and a plot of ground he knows will answer to the caresses of the husbandman, why should that land, though it were a desert, not blossom like the rose? If only the South loved the Negro as he is capable of loving her—there is no end to what might be.

One finds emancipation in strange places, and in stranger forms. Our conductor was a bluff, hearty fellow, given to interspersing his remarks with quaint oaths from another world. While our berth was being made down, he invited us into the drawing room, which was unrented, for a smoke and a chat. We learned that he was a Southerner, a Georgian, a former showman, who knew and had toured with Dudley in his heyday, and had helped manage the career of Siserettu Jones. He was reminiscent and garrulous. His talk glowed with admiration for the late Henry Lincoln Johnson. "My mother," he said, "is a typical Georgia cracker, but if you want to make her fight, just say something against Henry Lincoln Johnson." We were amazed at this manner of taking us to his bosom, but grateful for the tribute to one of ours.

At Talledega we felt the presence and cordiality of the President's wife and of the students as a grateful benison to a stranger in a far country. These young men and women were eager and wide awake; they were growing culturally; they were not allowing their horizon to be limited by a little man made power; what could the white pool room straggler in their little town know of them, save what he failed to admit: that their presence in Talledega was its one claim to distinction. We slept well in Talledega, for the abiding things like the moon and the stars shine on all alike without fear or favor.

When leaving next morning, we had to ride a little way in the Jim Crow section, three hours before picking up our reservation at Atlanta. But what could the white man sitting in the coach in which we were not allowed know of the memories we had to keep us company? Three hours of enforced segregation pass all too soon when one can muse upon Tourgee Du Bose playing with infinite care and fondness his own composition *Intermezzo* that he sent us last year from Talledega to win one of the OPPORTUNITY prizes; when one can hear above the roar of the too intimate wheels the rich baritone of Frank Harrison singing *The Kashmiri Love Song;* when the eye of the mind can see, slender and lovely, the fingers of a slim brown girl as they ripple over black and white keys bringing sheer music out of such an inharmonious association. What could they know those people to whom we were as pariahs, of all this? And yet we wished they m'ght have known.

Countee Cullen

THE DARK TOWER

FROM Avignon (Vauclose) France, Walter White, who is nearly winding up his year abroad as a Guggenheim fellow sends us a page from *Candide*, one of the most exclusive and intellectual French journals to which none other than André Maurois, author of *Ariel and Disraeli*, has contributed an article on *Negro Poetry in the United States* for the issue of March 15. Any reaction M. Maurois might have to Negro work and life should be interesting to the readers of this column, and so we pass on to you this translation of his article:

André Siegfried in his fine book on the United States has shown that the Negro problem in that country is much less simple than a Frenchman, viewing it at a distance, imagines. The traveller then should guard against forming a moral judgment against the attitude of Americans in regard to their fellow citizens of the black race; but it is impossible for the novelist not to mark the feelings to which such an attitude must give birth.

——In America the black man even though cultured, though invested with diplomas, though wealthy, is held in contempt by white society. If he invades a section of the City (as was the case in Harlem in New York) the white man flees before the incursion; the value of property slumps with an astonishing rapidity until such a time as these immovable blacks combine to redeem it. When one enters Harlem, that section of New York comparable to others like the Plaine Monceau of Paris, he senses vividly that he has just passed a frontier. No longer is it a case of a few stray blacks; the merchants in the shops are black; the dentists, the doctors, are black; and the few whites who go by on the pavements hurry as though they are anxious to show that they are passing through Harlem but do not live there at all. In the South (which I did not visit) the barrier is still greater; the Negro is not admitted into the same trains with whites; he may not, at the railroad station, rest in the same waiting room.

To this treatment the average Negro is doubtless not extremely sensitive; I do not think that the railroad porters, all Negroes, all so fine looking under their red caps, consider themselves unfortunate. They gain a good livelihood; they form a closed group; doubtless they give little thought to white society. But the more cultured Negro suffers. There is at this moment in the United States quite a group of young Negro poets who express with much vigor and often with decided artistry the misfortune of their race. It is interesting in these short poems to note the poet's obsession with the contrast of these two colors which determine either his friends or his enemies. Night plays an important role with them, because the night in enveloping all visages in its shadow, leads back to a strange equality. One notices also a curious nostalgia for Africa, where the greater part of these Negroes have never been, and which, nevertheless, remains for them their fatherland, the country from which their ancestors came, that for which they were made, the country whose exotic scenery made them probably appear more natural and beautiful than the severe lines of an all mechanical and white civilization.

I have tried to translate a few of these poems. Here is one —

MORTE D'UNE JEAUNE FILLE NOIRE

Avec deux roses blanches sur ses seins,
Des chandelles blanches à sa tête, à ses pieds,
Sombre madone de la tombe, elle repose .
Sa Seigneurie la Morte l'a trouvée a son gout . . .
Sa mère a mis au clou sa bague de fiancailles
Pour pouvoir l' habiller en blanc.
Elle serait tellement fière quelle danserait et chanterait
Si elle pouvait se voir ce soir.

         Countee Cullen.   (*A Brown Girl Dead,*)
   And here are others:

LES TROPIQUES A NEW YORK

Des bananes mûres et vertes et des racines de gingembre.
Du cacao encore en graines et des poires d'alligator,
Des mandarines et des mangues, et encore des
     pamplemousses,
Tous fruits dignes, d'être primés à la foire de la paroisse.
Mes yeux devinrent troubles, je ne pouvais plus regarder,
Une vague de nostalgie traversa mon corps
Et, affamé du vieux pays familier,
Je me suis retourné, j'ai courbé la tête et j'ai pleuré.

       Claude MacKay (*The Tropics in New York*).

OBSESSION DE LA NUIT

Ouvrir tout grands mes bras à quelque place au soleil.
Et tourner, et danser, jusqu'à ce que soit achevé le jour
     brillant,
Puis se reposer dans le soir frais, sous un arbre élevé,
Tandis que la nuit vient doucement, la nuit aussi noire
     que moi.
Voila mon rêve.   *Ouvrir mes bras tout grands à la face*
     du soleil.
Danser! Tourner! Tourner! jusqu'à la fin du jour rapide,
Puis le repos au soir pale, un très grand arbre très mince,
Et la nuit venant tendrement, noire comme noi . . .

       Langston Hughes   (*Dream Variation*)

   And here is one by a woman:

LE DOIGT NOIR

Je viens de voir la plus belle des choses:
Mince et tranquille,
Sur un ciel d'or,
Un cypres noir et droit,
Sensible,
Exquis,
Doigt noir pointé vers le ciel. . .
Ah! pourquoi, doigt si beau, si tranquille, êtes-vous noir?
Et porquoi montrez-vous le ciel?

        Angelina Grimke. (*The Black Finger*)

It seems to me that the quality itself of such verses, the sensibility which they reveal, show to what degree the race problem is difficult. People who are capable of writing these poems and of writing them in a fascinating English of which my imperfect translation has been able to give only a feeble idea, must of necessity wish a share of culture with kindred spirits of the white race, and must experience a deep resentment when this equality is denied them.

Like everyone who comes to New York, M. Maurois saw *Porgy*, which drew from him the following comment:

In New York I went to see a play acted entirely by Negroes: Porgy. It is like Peer Gynt done in black. But the play was of value less for the drama itself than for the extraordinary quality of the actors. The scene rep-

resents the court yard of a great Southern tenement in Charleston, a house entirely occupied by Negro families and the teeming life of this tenement passes altogether to the accompaniment of violent musical rhythms, as if involuntary, rhythms which seem to burst out spontaneosly with the sensations and actions. At the beginning of an act, the household awakens; a woman thrusts her head out the window and begins to wash the glass with a definite rhythm; an old Negro woman comes down into the courtyard, begins to sweep and, having perceived the first woman, sweeps with the same rhythm; a third beats a carpet still on the same rhythm; men and children, all whatever may be their work or their play,seem, in spite of themselves, to enter into this rhythmical and spontaneous dance; and slowly, imperceptibly, with all the movements which seem to be in obedience to the baton of an invisible orchestra leader, there rises a chant, a chant at first confused, very low, then taken up from within the house by a hundred concealed voices, which finally swell to proportions such as to give the transported spectator the illusion that the entire universe is nothing more than a strong rhythm from which he is unable to escape. It is a spectacle of simple elementary grandeur, but I have seen few more beautiful.

In another scene one sees the entire household grouped around the deathbed of an old Negro. Men and women, squatting down, balance themselves, singing a meloepia which becomes stronger each time a new person enters the mortuary chamber. Then one begins to understand the words; it is a religious chant, an invocation to God. "O Lord, we need fifteen dollars to bury this poor man and we 've got only twelve dollars and twenty-five cents. Give us, O Lord, the two dollars and seventy-five cents which we need." The Negro who enters deposits an offering in the dish placed at the dead man's feet, and immediately the meloepia resumes "O Lord, we need fifteen dollars to bury this poor man and we still have only twelve dollars and fifty cents . . . Give us, O Lord, the two dollars and fifty cents which we need." The prayer mounts, rises up, the stooping figures straighten; one sees their giant shadows sway athwart the back of the room, music of the body supplementing music of the voice; and the white spectator, agitated, a bit troubled, experiences the confused feeling that this troup of black actors is perhaps nearer than himself to what were formerly the elementary sources of poetry and music.

S HOW CASES by Jaques Le Clerk (Macy-Masius Co., New York, $2.50) is an interesting collection of six delicately wrought stories of sex. They have about them in subject and style, in addition to an irritating propensity on the part of all the characters to show their familiarity with the French language, what is commonly considered a French flavor. This should not convey the insinuation that they are reprehensible, rather that they are frankly concerned wiuth sex problems which every one admits but which are spoken of only in private. The most interesting of the group are *The Case of Artemys Lynn, The Case of Bedrich Zatloukal,* and *The Case of Aristide de Saint Hemme. The Case of Fritz Lavater,* however, left a sour taste; there is something true to neither life nor art in the picture of a man who forces his intellect to supply him with briefs for justifying his continuation of an Oedipus situation.

Countee Cullen.

174

THE DARK TOWER

FROM San Antonio, Texas, a young white woman, a poet of fine and sensitive feeling, writes out of her slow convalescence from a six weeks' illness a note of sympathy and understanding, some parts of which we wish to quote:

"I cannot tell you how my heart goes out to your race. And how it goes out to everyone who must be crucified in a manner by the pedantic saying things . . . *I hate Niggers . . . Oh, just that Nigger . . . That damn Nigger.* Oh, people, can't you see the beauty of their stalwart brown bodies . . . their pain of heart . . . their beauty . . . their hunger after beauty . . . the struggle after the bare living . . . hurts coming every day . . . little hurts that callous their hearts toward beauty . . . that make it hard to reach them . . . poor hungry people . . . bleeding each day and singing plaintive songs at evening . . . while the little brown ones in the yards are so carefree. . . . I sat near the ten Negroes who went to hear Paderewski when he was here last month. . . . How hungry they were . . . how still they sat and listened . . . how people watched them with smiles on their faces, thinking that these few had gone only to look intelligent. . . . Did you not see the hunger of their brown faces . . . the old black, black one sitting so still and his night colored eyes drinking and drinking music. . . . Did you not see the little yellow girl about thirteen years old, as she sat entranced by the minor sounds. . . . Did you not see her beauty that was like some exotic tropic flower budding and fragrant and singing for youth and love. . . Oh, did you not see them and want to touch them . . . and say some word. . . . *Must* you laugh at them. . . . *Must you.* . . . I wanted so badly to put out my hand and say, *It was lovely wasn't it?* . . . I was going to. . . . But they went so quickly because their hearts were brimming and they wanted to forego stupid laughter. . . . My heart bled for them. . . . I felt their strength . . . their love of life . . . their right to happiness . . . all going for nothing . . . the laughter they must endure . . . endure . . . and forget because their hearts are all tangled with song . . . and all the stupid *Whites* there . . . the superior and ruling intellects . . . staring at the walls and coughing . . . shuffling programs . . . whispering. . . . How I hated them. . . . Of course there were a few. . . .

"I wish and wish that there was something I could do. . . . we are so limited . . . so very very small . . . our hearts bleed and we are silent . . . our hearts bleed and we are afraid of being misunderstood . . . especially in this southland . . . this Texas. . . . In Denver I used to go out to a newsstand and talk to Negroes. . . . I loved them . . . here one dares not talk to them, because they are so calloused against hurts . . . they almost hate you . . . they *do* despise you . . . and one can't blame them. . . . I smiled gently at one at the concert and she smiled a little ghost smile back, as if she were not seeing right . . . and then became painfully conscious. . . . We are so very small . . . so limited."

Viewed from afar with the aloof distaste of one whom rumor has induced to believe that the farther south one goes the worse things are for us, Texas has always appeared to us as a sort of earthly gehenna. Our poet's letter does not transport it into an elysium for us. And yet when we read at Mount Holyoke College last week at the invitation of another poet, Jeannette Marks, a gracious kindly person still bearing in her eyes the horror of the Sacco-Vanzetti case, the young lady who came to pilot us to the tea which *Blackstick*, the college literary society, was giving for us, mentioned casually and with no trace of consciousness that she was from Texas, and that she hoped we would go there some day to read. . . .

With patience to a large extent tinged with pride in the complimentary error we have these many months regretfully informed interested interrogators that Charles Cullen is neither our brother, uncle, cousin nor father. But we are constrained now to enter a more vigorous protest than ever when C. V. Bates, editor of the South African *Potschefstrom Herald*, writes in that paper of the striking drawings by our *son* Charles Cullen.

WHAT seems to us to be by far the most ambitious project yet undertaken by a Negro poet is Leslie Pinckney Hill's poetic drama *Toussaint L'Ouverture* (The Christopher Publishing House, Boston, $1.50). Design and research and a fine and sensitive appreciation of the uses of language all enter into the making and clothing of a pattern in the main highly successful. The foreword is an interesting document of open and candid intent: "I have also, in full view of all the risks, deliberately chosen blank verse as the only vehicle worthy of the dignity and elevation of my theme. We seem, as Mr. Trevelyan says, to have lost both the taste and tradition for this high medium. Serious and sensitive writers must undertake to restore both. I can only hope that patient hospitality may be accorded to that measure and rhythm most expressive of the power and cadence of our tongue." That is an artistic presumption which we heartily applaud, confident that it emerges from a determination which does not hold that the use of blank verse is a strictly English monopoly, most un-American and distinctly un-Negro.

Though not in so many actual words, this drama comes fully confessing a propagandistic impetus: "The Negro youth of the world has been taught that the black race has no great traditions, no characters of world importance, no record of substantial contribution to civilization. The withering moral and social effects of this teaching can hardly be computed. The creative literature now building up with such bright promise in Negro America must correct and counterbalance this falsehood of centuries. A worthy literature reared upon authentic records of achievement is the present spiritual need of the race."

If as Mr. Hill contends, the Negro "is still the world's accepted scaramouche", no brighter luminary than L'Ouverture could have been chosen to contest this ignominy,—Toussaint the black slave, who became Toussaint the liberator and the opener, dangerous enough to reduce the Corsican to the expediency of trickery in order to effect his capture.

Mr. Hill has attempted the grand manner of the great dramatic poets, and if here and there passages are reminiscent, they have the saving grace of calling up the masters. There are echoes in the voodoo scenes, which are admirably done in both structure and atmosphere, of the weird sisters in Macbeth, and though the mind reverts to the pale Prince of Denmark while reading Toussaint's strong soliloquy, this black chieftain's storm and stress constitute one of the finest pieces of sober writing yet done by one of our poets:

To be a leader! What is that to be?
To stand between a people and their foes
And earn suspicion for a recompense;
To care for men more than they care for themselves;
To keep a clear discriminating mind
Between the better counsel and the best;
To be a judge of men, that none may rank
In estimation higher than his worth,
Nor fail of scope to prove his quality;
To search the motive that explains the act
Before it is accounted good or bad;
To trust a man, and yet not be dismayed
To find him faithless, going on again
To trust another; to build failure up
Into the tedious structure of success;
To meet the subtle enemy within
As well as him without, and vanquish both;
To see the cause betrayed by those who pledge
The strictest loyalty; to overmatch
The envious with magnanimity;
To labor through the day, and through the night
To watch and plan and exorcise by prayer
The devil troop of doubts that tease the will;
To have a body that endures the strain
Of labor after labor, each in turn
Demanding more of nerve and hardihood;
To stand before your conscience offering
The utmost tithe of mortal sacrifice,
While selfish little critic parasites
Heckle and plot and spread malignant lies;
To walk through trouble with a heart that drips
The blood of agony, yet with a face
Of confidence and bright encouragement;
To do and do and die to raise a tribe
So robbed and bound and ignorantly weak
That God himself conceals their destiny—
To be a leader! God, that is the cost!

Mr. Hill is without a doubt practically aware of the poet's high calling.

———————

Lewis Alexander has again been accorded the privilege and the honor of editing a special issue of the Carolina Magazine of the University of North Carolina, the May issue being especially designated as a Negro Poetry issue. Alain Locke discusses The Message of the Negro Poets, while Charles S. Johnson writes on Jazz Poetry and the Blues. The poems are schematically divided into the following color sections: Jazz Notes and Blues Tones, Ebony Dreams, Black Shadows on Parnassus, Onyx Set With Pearls, Valhalla and Dawn. The blues section is by far the weakest; Langston Hughes remains the acknowledged master of that form, and Waring Cuney and Lewis Alexander are far too effective in their own way to content themselves with feebly echoing Hughes. We liked most in the issue "Old Man Buzzard" by Sterling Brown, "The Feast of Death" by Edward Silvera, "Episode" by Jessie Fauset, and the sonnets by Carrie W. Clifford. And we were especially pleased with the well-merited tribute paid by Editor Gardner to Editor Alexander.

———————

Minor Music, a book of verse by Henry Reich, Jr., is a slim tome of effective lyrics that stamp their author as a genuine poet. A too marked tendency to be cynically pert mars some of the poems, but that ambush is effectively shunned in Absolom, David, Traps, and Keats in Hades, the poems which appealed to us most.

———————

At the Liberty Theatre, the Blackbirds of 1928, the newest Negro review to reach Broadway, evokes memories of Florence Mills and ends as one more testimony to her utterly initimitable genius. Negro producers should by now realize that their problem is not to produce another Florence Mills, but to replace her. Slavish imitations of her particular affectations only serve in this instance to diminish the realy fine latent possibilities of Aida Ward and Adelaide Hall, the stars of this new edition of the blackbirds. While the review will offer no especial cerebral resistance, it is splendid eye and ear entertainment which might be made much better by several omissions, especially that of the ever present first scene extolling an inconceivable nostalgia for dear old Dixie, and of a graveyard scene that is centuries old. Also it would help a great deal if the program could be followed as printed. Of particular delight was the jazzing given the famous deathbed scene in Porgy, (although the song Porgy itself was quite insipid); a cornetist named Milton Crawley whose musical contortions left us breathless, and Bill Robinson a tap dancer whose evident pleasure in his vocation was as infectious as his performance.

THE DARK TOWER

WHILE in Cleveland about a month ago we had an opportunity to visit the Karamu Theatre, the playhouse of the Gilpin Players. Preparations were on for the production that afternoon of a phantasy, *Hilga and the White Peacock*, to be played by a group of children. We were unable to attend the play, but there was in the air a vibrant, enthusiastic eagerness that made one realize the seriousness with which this group was working out its particular vision. And now the Cleveland press for the past week has been lavishly encomiastic over the success of this little theatre cast in producing Paul Green's prize play, *In Abraham's Bosom*. The achievement is the more signal in that this is the first of our Negro art theatres to be taken from its local theatre and housed for a legitimate run in the popular theatrical district. Under the direction of Mr. and Mrs. R. W. Jelliffe, the Karamu Theatre since its inception eight years ago has presented sixty-four plays, culminating in the present run at the Little Theatre in Cleveland. The Cleveland press notices warrant the belief that their production of this famous play does not fall short of the memorable performances of Jules Bledsoe, Frank Wilson, Rose McClendon, Abbie Mitchell and others; and it would seem that new stars are swimming into our ken in the persons of Fitzhugh Woodford who plays Abraham McCranie and of Olive Hale who plays Goldie.

"A MAN trained as these Louisiana planters had been could have pointed out among the streaming crowd of blacks, the bossals, as the Negroes born in Africa were called, and could even have differentiated between the various tribes—here a Bambara turkey-thief with long blue tattoo marks, swollen in the middle, running from his temples down his neck, there an Arada, savage, avaricious and a voodoo; Agonas, Socos, and Fantins who have the qualities in common of being proud warriors, capricious and unafraid of death; bloodthirsty Judas; Mandingues, cannibalistic but good workers, their front teeth filed to points; Bissagots and Sosos who in their own land had carried shields of bullet-proof elephant hide and there made good hunters and watchmen for their masters; gentle intelligent Mozambiques very black and given to consumption, whose tribe in days gone by supplied Asia, Abyssinia and Arabia with their eunuchs; and Congoes, who gave their name to the Place Congo, gay gentle, eaters of bananas, quick-witted, thick-lipped and lubric, lovers of song and dancing and preferred over all others as house servants. . . . Black children of the Gold Coast, the Ivory Coast, the Grain Coast, the Pepper and the Malaguette Coasts had been ravished to form this crowd." . . .

From the above description of a company of slaves gathered for holiday making at the market place in New Orleans, the American Negro of today may gather some faint idea of the various branches on his ancestral tree. The paragraph comes from Edward Larocque Tinker's novel "Toucoutou" (Dodd Mead and Co.) Toucoutou is

the affectionate racial sobriquet which Clarcine a quadroon brought from Santo Domingo by her master during the slave rebellion there, and settled in New Orleans gives to her daughter and that of Bazile Bujac, her master. While in New Orleans Bazile succumbs a victim to the yellow fever plague that infests the city, and the rest of the story concerns Clarcine's efforts, supposedly prompted by a maternal desire to do her utmost for her child, to raise Toucootou, less familiarly known as Anastasie, white. Toucoutou is first sent to a convent school, the way to her entrance having been paved by Clarcine's sworn statement, abetted by a meretricious certificate, that Toucoutou is an orphaned white child left in her care. Toucoutou's days at the convent, however, are brief, for she fails to act like a lady (probably due to her Negro blood) and is carted back to Clarcine in complete disgrace. Then Toucoutou meets and falls in love with Placide Taquin, a young Creole merchant, who marries her believing her white. The air about them is sinister with heavy implications that one of Toucoutou's remote ancestors was black, and that Zozo, the little Taquin heir, is accordingly tainted. Finally, Toucoutou aggravated by a jealous neighbor is foolhardy enough to resort to a court trial to prove her white origin. The final chapter finds Toucoutou, having been judged a Negro in court. setting out with Placide and Zozo for Havana to begin life anew.

"Toucoutou" is a story of interesting atmosphere, and while some of its implications and assertions may rile the Negro reader, it is an artistically conceived and well written piece of work, which is far more praise than can justifiably be accorded to Frances Mocatta's "The Forbidden Woman" (G. Howard Watt, New York) in which a similar theme is treated. The latter book is a fantastic unreal tale of how Heloise Michard met Paul Dundas, a young Southerner in New York. married him and went to Paris, repented of her deception, revealed her blood, and then feigned suicide obliterating herself completely from her lover's life in her fear that the child she was about to bear would (this always strikes us as silly) be black. The child Annette Duval grows into a beautiful imperious woman whose one desire is to be considered white; and her preoccupation with this idea seems much beyond the point, because all she needed to do as described in the story was to go her way. Paul Dundas has in the meantime married a querulous insipid childhood sweetheart from Sandyville, Georgia, and has died leaving her with two children, Mary Lou (a delicious Southern name) and a younger daughter. The story at this point becomes acutely melodramatic in that Annette, made aware of her patrimony, threatens to expose her father's widow as not lawfully married to him, and her white half sisters as illegitimate. Mary Lou to save the honor of her family then does an amazing thing when one considers the Southern contention of an option on good manners, by palming Annette off as a white lady of quality on her and her mother's life long English friends, the Avondales. Annette unscrupulous and ambitious marries Lord Archie Avondale, the son, although all the affection she is capable of is centered in Cassius, a young mulatto concert singer, who is the one real character in the book, clinging to his black heritage ar something not to be denied but of which to prove the worth. The debacle ends with Lord Avondale's discovery and horror and with Annette's suicide. "The Forbidden Woman" is redolent with memories of Bertha Clay and Laura Jean Libbey in both content and style.

Countee Cullen.

THE DARK TOWER

THOSE few days that we were not shamelessly indisposed and confined to our cabin through sheer inability to rise from our couch lest we discover that the world was really falling part, and earth and sky accepting Shelley's famous adjuration to "mix and mingle" were spent in trying to learn why, according to Anita Loos, *Gentlemen Marry Brunettes*, in trying to ascertain why so many people call Ernest Hemingway the most exciting of contemporary writers of fiction (*The Sun Also Rises*, an excellent novel for those who don't care for any trimmings, was not the absolute revelation we had been told to expect), and in a vain endeavor to discover why Wallace Thurman continually makes out such a bad case for the Negro poets. Our moments in between, thanks to Arna Bontemps who let us take his copy of *The Closed Garden* by Julian Green on board ship, were given over to the thorough enjoyment of one of the most depressingly well written novels we have read.

Some good and influential friend of Mr. Thurman would do him an actual service by taking him aside and giving him a good heart to heart talking to, slyly and gently insinuating at the same time that now and then some good may actually come out of his race. This amiable and somewhat talented young gentleman represents an opposite as much to deplore as the man of color who finds that his race has an option on all the virtues and talents extant. We have no doubt that Mr. Thurman is his race's severest criitc, but that is not tantamount to calling him its greatest inspiration and friend. His article on "Negro Poets and Their Poetry" in the current *Bookman* surveys with little tolerance and much inadequacy of preparation the Negro poet's contribution to American literature from Jupiter Hammond to Helene Johnson. Many of Mr. Thurman's points of criticism are vitiated by an obvious desire on his part to be clever at the expense of being critically truthful, to say nothing of being socially truthful. It surprised us to learn that "Phillis Wheatley was exhibited at the Court of George III, and in the homes of the nobility much as the Negro poets of today are exhibited in New York drawing-rooms." Moreover, it is a thoroughly specious type of criticism which would divorce from James Weldon Johnson's "Fifty Years" what is probably and unfortunately the worst verse in a very fine poem, and on such inconsequential evidence damn so fine and noble a piece of work. The critic of poetry must bring to his task as much as he is inclined to take away, and key word knowledge of the art is not enough. We suspect that Mr. Thurman's evident horror of things academic is not the best recommendation one might wish.

We have been intending in more than one past column to recommend for vigorous and instructive reading Arthur Garfield Hays' challenging apostrophe *Let Freedom Ring* (Boni and Liveright, $2.50). Mr. Hays' many legal tilts in the interest of and toward the absiolute sensible emancipation of liberty, and his association with Clarence Darrow have made him a sort of St. George of the bar. His new brief for freedom consist of the recital of six trials *célèbres* involving Freedom of Education. Speech and Assemblage, Press, Residence, Stage, and Opinion. Although Negro readers may be more violently interested in the Chapter on Residence which concerns the trial of Dr. Ossian Sweet of Detroit (the Negro physician who is now residing in the home he was forced to protect so strenuously), the book as a whole should be of interest to every liberal minded person.

France has found time off from the stabilization of the franc and the other universal pursuits which the rest of the world labels typically French to take up the Negro in a literary way. Eugene Jolas in his *Anthologie de la Nouvelle Poésie Américaine*, in which translations have been made of the work of a hundred and twenty odd American poets, includes among them poems by Langston Hughes, Claude McKay, Jean Toomer, and the correspondent. In addition the most advertised book in Paris at the moment seems to be *Magie Noire* (Black Magic) by Paul Morand. Eugene Jolas undertook too large a party in his anthology to permit of the translation of more than one poem per poet. It is to be hoped that this infinitesimal extract from the large body of modern American verse will result in more anthologies or translations of some of the poets in their entirety. Many of the translations are admirable, retaining both the flavor and the substance of the original poems; yet equally as many could not be adequately transferred from the vigorous verse of Carl Sandburg, Vachel Lindsay, Robinson Jeffers and others into the gentler, more lyric idiom of the French. We are afraid that Langston Hughes also suffered in translation. In selecting a blues by which to portray Mr. Hughes' work the editor may have considered that he was giving the poet his ablest representation (and that was not true) but the Franch language is a sorry medium for a Negro blues. We scarcely recognize this verse from the Gallic equivalent of Po' Boy Blues:

> *Quand j'étais chez moi le*
> *Soleil semblait comme de l'or,*
> *Quand j'étais chez moi le*
> *Soleil semblait comme de l'or.*
> *Depuis que je suis ici au Nord tout*
> *La sacré monde est froid et mort.*

We have not yet had time to read *Magie Noire* in its entirety, for notwithstanding that the book is divided into the following chapters in the order named: Antilles, United States of America, and Africa, we immediately proceed to launch into the second chapter. M. Morand has undoubtedly visited the colored districts of the United States, among them being Harlem, and various southern sections, but along with a keen incisive observation he carried with him a fairly gullible spirit that allowed him to absorb some of the usual silly notions. His sketch *Excelsior* (the title is probably more allegorical than geographical) deals with a group of near white Negroes in Excelsior, Georgia. Their one ambition is to get away from the environment in which they are known as Negroes to some place where, unknown they may take a social and economic advantage of their fairness. This paragraph concerning their discussion of a suitable territory to which to migrate shows typical southern information: "In New York one is still not altogether sure of himself . . . there is Harlem . . . for although there are some intelligent Negroes who are proud to see one of their number pass the line, and others, with a sense of humor, who are enchanted at the idea of playing a trick on the whites, the majority of them are envious and furious. Or again when the location seems gained, one may fall under the implacable eye of an old Southerner who after having looked at your blue cornea and mauve-colored finger nails will sound the alarm." Although there are other naivites to which we have become accustomed, it is to M. Morand's credit that he did not allow his heroine to marry her Harvard boy and have a black baby!

BITTERS and sweets of an ever shifting and ever varying type are the accompaniments of a dark complexion wherever one may go, but it is a mixture that adds a zest and spice to what might otherwise prove a monotonous existence. . . . There was the bitter aloes on board the Isle de France of the little French boy who had been in America long enough to learn the ways of whites with blacks there, and who met my friend's overtures of friendliness, couched in questionable French perhaps, with a sharp stacatto cry of Nigger! But there was also on the same boat a group of social service workers on their way to the Paris Conference, among them several southerners who were gradually, certainly if slowly, casting aside the old outworn machinery of antebellum days for the modern equipment of mutual toleration and understanding. . . . Bitters again. . . . One decides to indulge, with no intention of taking an unsportsmanlike advantage of the low rate of French exchange, a luxury-loving proclivity that has long been held in check by the high cost of American opera . . . for forty francs, less than what Americans pay to see a mediocre movie, the doors and stalls of the magnificent Paris Opera House are thrown wide to the music lover . . . Tonight it is to be *Rigoletto*. We must go alone, because our companion, having a superior musical education, is amused at our ineradicable joy in florid arias and bel canto. . . . We have successfully passed the brilliantly arrayed guards at the opera entrance, our tickets have been taken and passed on by a gentleman in perfect evening attire, even to the high silk hat, and we have battled our way through legions of bespectacled ladies who serve as the French ushers, until finally we are ushered into our own red plush stall, and waved to a red plush chair. . . . Our spirits are buoyant for the moment; we are happy in having arrived before the tragedy of the king's buffoon begins . . . but only for a moment. Three of the other seven sharers of the box are visibly disturbed, and we note between them the fleeting passage of that expression of pained bewilderment always apparent when one of us intrudes upon the sacred aloofness of our fellow countrymen. . . .

Sweets! ! The moment of dejection changed into one of joy when after having each confided to the other that it would be pleasant to see a dark and remembered face in this rushing, gay Paris, we suddenly find ourselves sipping a tangy cold drink with Mrs. Noble Sissle as our vis-a-vis. We learn that the former member of the famous Shuffle Along quartet is now conducting a band at the Ambassadors, the most select night club in Paris. Wouldn't we love to hear a bit of jazz as we know those sable boys can play it? Bitters of another sort. The Ambassadors does not cater to poets and school teachers. . . . These moments of isolated pleasure rush into each other and

merge with a startling rapidity. Palmer Hayden, tall, dark, and looking more like an English gentleman than like the proverbial painter, shining out like a bit of ebony from among the other habitues of the Dome where most of the American artists can be found while in Paris. . . . Hale Woodruff just coming up smiling from a spell of sickness that has sent him to the American Hospital at Neuilly for ten days. . . . J. A. Rogers, European correspondent to a syndicate of American Negro papers, showing one those places of interest which the uninitiated generally miss. . . . Alain Locke, sage professor and dapper gentleman of two continents hailed and brought back to our table just as he is about to rush intently past the Dome.

A friend to whom we have confided our desire to hear some actual jazz suggests that the Bal Colonial is accessible in lieu of the Ambassadors, and is apt to prove as interesting as it is inexpensive. What is the Bal Colonial? Probably the most cosmopolitan and democratic dance hall in Paris, which may mean in the world. Speaking of it in general terms, one says it is a West Indian dance hall. It is the rendezvous of the Martiniquan Negroes of Paris. As the gesture of a fast-dying gallantry, ladies are admitted at half price which amounts to about fifteen cents. The music is probably as good as can be found in all Paris, and fame and fortune await the players should they ever decide to migrate to New York. It is a weird sort of playing, a melange or cross between modern jazz and the residue of old West Indian folk pieces. The most primitive notes of all are contributed by a player who shakes with varying modulations a leather box filled with pebbles.

The gathering is motley: West Indians from Martinique, French whites with whom they have intermarried or who are their friends, and the usual allotment of tourists. One senses immediately that all the fun is being had on the floor, not at the tables along the walls and along the balcony where congregate with half-amused yet half-intrigued faces the English and American tourists. The Anglo-Saxon, superior species, is in for a deep regretting when he realizes what natural joys he has allowed to decay and grow moth-ridden in his desire to maintain a condescending aloofness.

As an American Negro we are somewhat startled to find that our dark complexion avails us nought among these kindredly tinted people. Language must be the open sesame here, and it must be French. The Martiniquan lady whom we have had the temerity to ask to dance with us seems to sense an alien tongue in us, for she glides along amiably enough, but allows our painful attempts at conversation to languish gently. For the most part, as we survey the gliding, twisting panorama, we note that these Negroes have become Europeanized in dress and manner. The women are chic and smart in the Parisian way. Their hair, however, has undergone no chastening processes, but rises in shameless effrontery and fluffiness high above their heads. And, slanting back in mountainous fashion, the hair of many of the men rivals the length of that of the women.

The dancing for the most part is harsh and slightly reprehensible, faintly suggestive of the antics of some of the New York night clubs. In the midst of it all, however, one couple, as if disdaining such modern contortions, glides slowly along in an old Martiniquan step. Perhaps it is not strange that the woman is the only one who has not doffed her homeland costume, a one piece dress with a tightly fastened waist and a long flowing skirt, the whole brilliantly colored. And perched like a blazing star on her head she wears the old homeland turban. Her partner is dressed modern fashion, but there is a derisive curve to his lips and a mocking light in his eyes as he glides along, one hand upon his hip, the other gently supporting his companion. These two are like strong trees in a storm; they do not bend. They are perhaps the remnants of what the Bal Colonial was before the tourists discovered it, perhaps somewhat analogous to what the Harlem clubs were before downtown New York found them amusing.

We are on our way to Algiers. Green and blue at once, and mocking description the Mediterranean bears us on her bosom as though she were a vast billowy emerald. . . . Standing at the rail watching the water froth beneath the churning of the propellers, we suddenly note a slight brown figure at the other end of the boat. Surely an American colored girl, probably a school teacher on her vacation, we surmise. . . . Later, on forming Madame's acquaintance, in that easy democratic way of ships and trains, we discover that Madame speaks no English, that she is the mulatto offspring of a French and Algerian union, that she has been vacationing in Paris, and is on her way back to Algiers to join her husband and little son. . . . Attempts ot draw Madame into a discussion of black and white relations are futile. . . . Madame is French, and as such equal to any other of her countrywomen in their sight and the sight of her government . . . she has heard strange tales of America . . . are they true? We admit the validity of her information. Then, a natural question, why do we remain? We attempt reasons and extenuations . . . our birthplace, ours to share by right of toil, the home of our friends and relatives. . . . . Madame's hands go up in a typical French gesture of amazement and incomprehension that is at once a termination to the conversation. She cannot understand such reasoning . . . to her it is specious.

My friend and I lie in our bunks deciding what we are going to have Madame's husband look like. We are to be pardoned if we both decide that he is to be colored. It is fortunate that no stakes are attached to our prognostications for when we meet him next day, we learn that he is of French and Polish extraction, that he speaks nine languages and answers to the name of de Tymowski.

On the boat we have made the acquaintance of a young Frenchman whose home is in Algiers and who is just returning after a year of study in Paris. With the old world regard for some of those things which the new world holds as negligible and commonplace, he finds it pleasant to meet an American teacher and a poet. At our hotel that night we find a note from him asking if we will not come to his home for tea the next afternoon. We find that a pleasant rumor of our importance has preceded us, for many friends have been invited to meet the *professeur* and the poet. The young men present are mostly college youths, and America to them is a symbol of earthly greatness, a horn overflowing with peace and plenty. Then suddenly dark on the horizon looms a momentous question. One young man leans over to me, to whisper, as if half ashamed of such a silly question: "And do the American whites really dislike the blacks because of their color?" We would give anything to restore his wavering trust and faith in our land, for we know how the truth will hurt him. "I cannot understand it," he says, "Quelle betise!" What stupidity, indeed. Once more America has lost face in a foreign country.

We are back in our hotel . . . it is early morning . . . our room is high with a great circular balcony from which we can see in every direction Algiers spreading out like a large white fan, its white roofs shining and flashing in the early morning sun, the entire panorama one of bewildering beauty, if one could only forget the dirt and disease which stalks the Arab population. . . . Suddenly there is a knock at the door. We open to one of our boat companions, a young German aviator. In halting English he explains that he would like to indulge in a sun bath on our balcony in the hope that he might tan himself to what he really considers our marvelous complexion. . . . Will we allow him? My companion and I exchange smiles. No similar premium has ever been placed on our color where we came from. . . . Bitters and sweets, aloes and honeysuckle.

Countee Cullen,
Paris, August 3, 1928

+□+⸺+□+⸺+□+

The Literary Scene
Chronicle and Comment

By STERLING A. BROWN

ANNOUNCEMENT has reached the chronicler of the second appearance of *Folk-Say, A Regional Miscellany*. This annual is 'the first of the many movements to relate the American artist to his environment, which is founded upon a direct return to the folk. . . . Believing at the same time that the best art is universal, it holds that the universal is rooted in the provincial.' The question: "Who are the folk in America, and what can they contribute to American language and literature?" is answered by such authorities as Mary Austin, Barrett H. Clark, Percy MacKaye, Louise Pound and Carl Sandburg; there are articles on such subjects as "Folk Values in Recent Literature on the Negro," "The Blues as Folk Poetry," "Folk Values in a New Medium," "The Case Of The Folk Drama." Contributors well known to readers of these columns are Alain Locke, Langston Hughes, Waring Cuney, Lewis Alexander and the chronicler. The book, illustrated and beautifully done, is issued by the University of Oklahoma Press, Norman, Oklahoma.

Carl Carmer, in *Theatre Arts* for December, likewise sees great potentialities for art in the American scene and folk. His interesting essay, "Alabama-Mine For Dramatists," tells us of the untouched heaps of material waiting for the selecting, transforming hand of the dramatist. He tells us of the mountaineers; of the middle-people of the middlelands, where the white man who feels an inferiority can take it out on the blacks; of the *nouveaux riches;* of the college boys; of the Cajuns; and of the Negroes. Carl Carmer's thorough acquaintance with the South, has already been attested by the striking collection of poems, *Deep South*, published last year by Farrar and Rinehart. These convey excellently Alabama folk idioms and beliefs and ways of life. . . . Theatre Magazine has an article "Look Away, Dixieland," in which the author, John Anderson, is in agreement with Mr. Carmer, but believes the mine of material to extend over all the South. He says, "For here on our own doorstep is stuff no less touching and universal than the material Chekhov has wrought so superbly into his tear stained comedies" . . .

Mr. Anderson's belief that fiction has done

better by Southern material is further substantiated by Isa Glenn's *Short History of Julia* (Knopf) which continues the ironic appraisal of mildewed traditions she began so ably in *Southern Charm*. . . . *Po' Buckra* by Samuel Stoney and Gertrude Shelby (MacMillan) is a picture of the Southern tradition from another angle. Of interest in this book is the treatment of the "brass-ankles," people whose ancestry is Negro, Indian and English. This book is by the authors of *Black Genesis*, reviewed in the November OPPORTUNITY. . . . Another recent novel on characters of mixed blood, but running more to stereotype, is *Gulf Stream* by Marie Stanley (Coward McCann).

In *Strike!* by Mary Heaton Vorse, (Liveright) students of present economic problems, (and which of us can afford not to be?) will find a simply done, earnest novel based upon the industrial disturbances in Tennessee and the Carolinas. In *I'll Take My Stand* a group of young literati regret the passing of the old South. If any readers of *Chronicle and Comment* think that these books concern them little —'well, by your leave, ye're maybe wrong.'

Roark Bradford is creating a new John Henry myth in the Cosmopolitan Magazine; a new tall tale written out of wide acquaintance with Negro speech. It will probably stir controversy among the folk lorists, and dismay at some tea parties, not only in Boston.

In the *Age of Hate*, (Coward, McCann) George Fort Milton is said to have added an able volume to the creaking shelf on the Reconstruction. If any of these volumes succeed in crowding off Claude Bowers' *The Tragic Era*, well and good. Mr. Milton at least doesn't write a blood and tears melodrama, with angels and villains.

Tin Pan Alley, by Isaac Goldberg (John Day Co.) is a chronicle of the popular music racket. He pays due attention to the Negro's part, showing the influence of the slave songs, of the minstrel show, and of W. C. Handy. This book and *Black Manhattan* are somewhat supplementary.

So runs a merely partial list. . . . But where, or where is the Negro author. . . .

The Literary Scene
Chronicle and Comment
By STERLING A. BROWN

WE are not as yet a reading people. Explain it how we may, the fact remains. To a group in economic duress, the insistence that we read more might seem counsel to fiddle while Rome burns. What help in books for an increasing breadline? Perhaps it seems naivete, but the chronicler believes that there is a great deal of help. If there is a way out of this morass, it is only by intelligent concentration and not by table thumping that one shall find it. Books for the idle hour in a rushing time permitting few idle hours, books for escape, books for narcotics, may well be frowned upon by the mature thinker. But books for tools, books for indications, books for revelations, have been and will be absolute necessities. Yes, in times like these. Even more in times like these.

And of course, since we don't read books, we don't buy them. This seems to be another sad proof of the dictum of Prof. Kelly Miller that the Negro pays for what he wants, and begs for what he needs. True, too true. . . .

Perhaps our practical man, often self made, and often admirably so, distrusts mere book learning as a useless appendage. But since with all of his practicality he finds things generally in a pretty sorry mess, he might supplement his pragmatic wisdom with something of the book wisdom of the world. He has turned to so many other helps. And if he should, he would find himself in the good company of men like Bacon, Newton, Voltaire, Rousseau, Jefferson, Lincoln, Marx, Lenin, Einstein and Gandhi. (In that list he should find somebody he respects).

It is probably a shameful platitude—but the Negro must, because of his greatly disadvantaged state, *learn to use books as tools*. It *is* a platitude. But it needs acceptance, rather than lip service.

The chronicler's task is to bring before the reader of OPPORTUNITY a list of whatever books and articles he is able to find that bear directly or indirectly upon our concerns. These books and articles are of course not only those by Negro authors (indeed from the first indications, not even mainly so), and not entirely upon Negro subjects. But the chronicler believes that most of them do have a bearing upon

the Negro. He would be the last one even to intimate that these should be the sole reading matter of our audience. But there are already so many valuable indices to the current output of books of general interest, that it is his belief that for a special group a special index might be made.

Abram Harris, in a provocative essay, "The Prospects of Black Bourgeoisie," published in *Ebony and Topaz*, concluded by saying, "But even if theoreticians existed in the Negro population, their profoundest formulations, however rational, when contrary to popular assumptions would be futile speculation to a racial group that is looking for solutions and is impatient of theory." In a book *The Black Worker*, just off the press, Dr. Harris and his collaborator, Dr. Sterling Spero, have given us an acute, thorough, ably written study of the Negro in his relationships to the American labor movement. The book is preeminently one of those that could be used as 'tools'; it is the type of work sorely needed at a critical period. Since our journals, our churches, our public meetings are crowded with economic advice both hit or miss and intelligent, the work is assuredly timely. One hopes that it reaches more than the experts; one hopes that it reaches even that part of "our population impatient of theory." It seems to the chronicler, who admits his ineptitude in economics, that a mere shouting for an economic backbone is not enough. It takes a good head to find a good backbone. We certainly can't develop economic power merely by wishing for it. Unless "happy days are here again—" the happy days of Horatio Alger and Cinderella. . . .

The book will in all likelihood stir controversy. But as the mature work of one of our best minds it should be carefully considered.

The Repertory Players of Washington, D. C., started their career with an excellent presentation December 27th of *John Ferguson* by St. John Ervine. Outstanding performers —not easy to select from such a talented cast— were Mrs. Louise Cook Hill, as Mrs. Ferguson, and Samuel Popel as Clutie John. The play showed the able and careful directing of Miss Mary Burrill. The group will not confine itself to plays dealing with Negro life.

Abraham Lincoln has finally reached Washington. The show seen by the chronicler was only sparsely attended, but since two of the other movie houses were showing rather warm love stories, wrestling matches according to the posters, with not even 'strangleholts' barred, one could understand where the people were. The picture was satisfactory, and may help redeem David W. Griffith. One did get a sweep of titanic forces, and the drama of the period. The 'middle passage' was graphic. One might have wished to see more of the slavery background;—Stephen Vincent Benet could have done well with this if we may judge from *John Brown's Body.* Certainly the two Aframericans "kicking up sand, Jonah's band," when the boys in gray stomped past to the tune of Dixie, might have been more supplemented by other scenes than it was. And a bit of Hollywood crept into the backwoods. But it was a good picture, and one shouldn't ask for miracles. And Sheridan did do a tall piece of riding, didn't he?

George Schuyler's novel *Black No More* (Macaulay) will probably be off the press by the time this is printed. The book promises a few shocks, if advance information is true, and if Mr. Schuyler follows his usual manner. . . . Paul Morand's *New York* contains as one might expect a section on Harlem; Monsieur Morand is a seeker after the exotic wherever it may be found and sometimes where it cannot. (Cf. *Black Magic*). . . . At the opposite pole from his book would be Rossa B. Cooley's *School Acres* (Yale University Press, illustrated by Winold Reiss). The author of this book has already written about these same Negroes of St. Helena Island, in a volume entitled *Homes of the Freed* (Republic Dollar Book Series). Duke University Press has just announced *Tambo and Bones* by Carl Wittke, a book on the rise of Negro minstrelsy. This book should be supplementary to Spaeth's *Gentlemen, Be Seated* and Goldberg's *Tin Pan Alley* (John Day). . . . The Literary Associates, Incorporated, have recently published Dr. John Louis Hill's *Negro: A National Asset or Liability.*—Well, if you are still curious, there the answer is. Dr. Hill is an ex-Southern minister. The Laurel Publishers announce the publication of *Make Way For Happiness*, a book of poems, by Alpheus Butler, who recently edited *The Parnassian.*

Paul Robeson is now on tour, after his European successes in concerts and on the stage. Perhaps all who rush to hear him do not know that his life has been interestingly written by Mrs. Robeson in *Paul Robeson, Negro.* (Harper and Bros.) Mr. Robeson, in a recent interview with Richard Reagan in the New York Herald-Tribune tells something of his future plans, most of which the chronicler hopes will be carried out; attacks second generation respectability; expresses his grief over the death of another great actor, Wesley Hill, the "Gabe" of Green Pastures; insists on his aversion to those who would make of him a sophisticate, and promises "to penetrate the bush of Africa eventually and drink his fill of savage emotions."—All of this is interesting, although why one needs to go to Africa for savage emotions puzzles the chronicler.

Current magazines contain many articles worthy of comment. In *Harper's* for January Walter White tells the highly interesting narrative of Parker's defeat. ("The Negro and the Supreme Court.") In the *Modern Quarterly*, a fair Confederate tells of her gradual emancipation from the prejudices of her homeland, and of her marriage to a Negro intellectual. ("The Fall of a Fair Confederate.") *The Nation* of December 24 published an article by Raymond Leslie Buell called "Slavery and Forced Labor." This uncovered many of the disgraceful practises still in vogue in backward lands of the world. The article is pertinent, disturbing; it should be pondered deeply.

Though it may be lese-majesty to state it, when Winston Churchill is one of the writers, still one must admit that the series of "If" articles running in *Scribner's* is a tedious business. The first one 'debunked' reconstruction; the December article, "If Lee had not won Gettysburg" by Winston Churchill, assumes that Lee won Gettysburg, and that therefore all was well with the world; an English Speaking Association was formed, which by some mystical power brought it about that the Russian bear and the German lion lay down together and got up again; the danger of world war was averted; and 'bliss was it in that day to be alive.' If Lee had won! But Lee lost; hence no English Speaking Association; no European unity:—no second paradise on earth. . . . Historians with their Ifs! If. . . .

The Literary Scene
Chronicle and Comment
By STERLING A. BROWN

THE psychologist will probably be interested in *Race Psychology*, by Thomas R. Garth (McGraw-Hill) ; the economist in *Racial Factors in American Industry,* by Herman Feldman (Harper and Bros.) ; *The Negro Wage Earner*, by Lorenzo Green and Carter G. Woodson (Associated Publishers), and *The Negro in Modern Industrial Society*, by Dean Dutcher (published by the author). These books, however, should not be considered the province of the scientist only, for as their direct bearing upon our concerns is great, so would our casual passing them by be either foolhardy or stupid.

Books of a similar scientific import are *African View*, by Julius Huxley (Harper and Bros.), a selection of the Scientific Book Club, and *Caliban in Africa*, by Leonard Barnes (Lippincott). These deal with white-black relationships in Africa; the first book dealing with British East Africa, and the second with South Africa. If, as one of our leading thinkers has stated, the problem of the twentieth century is the problem of the color line, we who are so much involved had best attend to the ramifications of this problem in places where it is fully as acute as here.

Jungle Ways, by William B. Seabrook (Harcourt, Brace), is an African book with a difference. According to the publishers, "this new book will further mark him as a writer about the primitive and ecstatic elements of life." . . . It deals largely with sorcery and magic and strange religions, and will probably do for the Ivory Coast what *Magic Island* did for Haiti. The spring book list of Harcourt, Brace has many other items of interest for readers of these columns: *The Black Napoleon* (the story of Toussaint), by Percy Waxman; *Oklahoma Town*, by George Milburn, which, to judge from excerpts printed in the American Mercury, promises to be mordant, and veracious to anyone knowing the frontier South; a new revised edition of James Weldon Johnson's *American Negro Poetry*, the pioneering venture in anthologies of Negro poetry; and *God Sends Sunday*, by Arna Bontemps. This last is a novel in a new genre, dealing with a Negro jockey and his adventures in the nineties. It is by a young man familiar to *Opportunity* readers, who has already evinced high artistic caliber in his sincere and quietly musical poetry.

The Southwest Review, Winter 1931, contains "Negro Suffrage and the South," by James Samuel Stemons, author of *The Key; A Tangible Solution of the Negro Problem* (Neale, 1916). Food for thought just as sustaining is to be found in the current Journal of Negro History. This, of course, is to be expected. From the choice list these might be selected: Prof. W. O. Brown's *Racial Inequality: Fact or Myth*, and Prof. Newbell N. Puckett's *Religious Folk-Beliefs of Whites and Negroes*. The first of these essays is a very valuable index to the pros and cons, as well as a cogent presentation of his own views; it is a valuable exposition to have on hand. Prof. Puckett's article is as interesting as we should expect of the author of *Folk Beliefs of the Southern Negro*, and sheds new light on the so-called "race" characteristics, and on the Negro's heaven. James Weldon Johnson's heaven in "Saint Peter Relates an Incident of the Resurrection Day" uses this heaven in its essentials. . . . The University of North Carolina announces Mary Grissom's *The Negro Sings a New Heaven*, a book which the reviewer has not yet seen. Even *Fine Prints of the Year*, 1930 (Minton, Balch) contains a print "Nigger Heaven," as well as many excellent prints dealing with Negro subjects. The volume, all in all, is a treasure.

Of the earthly paradise which Caucasian dwellers below the Potomac and Ohio Rivers insisted was synonymous with home, and burnt cork dwellers along East River yearned for mournfully, Gerald Johnson speaks less worshipfully in "No More Excuses" in February Harper's and Howard Mumford Jones, more politely (since he's a Northern visitor) in the Southwestern Review.

Golden Tales From the South, edited by May Lamberton Becker (Dodd, Mead), might be supposed to glorify the Old South, but it does not completely. It is likely, however, that these do: *Limestone Tree* (Knopf), by Joseph Hergesheimer (the lover of swords and roses) ; Opie Read's *I Remember* (Richard R. Smith), Willson Whitman's *Contradance* (Bobb, Merrill), and Frances Tinker's and Edward Larocque Tinker's *Old New Orleans*. Appleton is bringing out the last publication in four volumes just as it brought out Edith Wharton's *Old New York*. Whether these books defend the old South or not, it is certain that *I'll Take My Stand*, by Twelve Southerners, does more than defend (Harper's). The book is a dirge over the passing of the old South; the chronicler believes that a companion book might as justifiably be written, entitled *Hooray, Hooray*, by Twelve Who Were Never Fooled by a Dreamland Dixie. An extended exposition upon this book, necessary and probably revelatory of the new enlightenment below the Mason Dixon line, is promised for the next Chronicle and Comment. If you have tears to shed, shed them then.

THE LITERARY SCENE
CHRONICLE AND COMMENT

A Romantic Defense

By STERLING A. BROWN

I'LL TAKE MY STAND, by Twelve Southerners is a romantic defense of the agrarian tradition. These twelve articles, all of them ably written, would have served well enough for magazines, but cohering in a book they don't seem to be nearly so epochal as some would have us believe. In the last analysis, they are all fairly old stuff. At their worst they are Thomas Nelson Page; at their infrequent best they are Emerson (a 'damyank'), and diluted Matthew Arnold.

The thesis of this book is that in our mechanized age there is a great deal lacking. That is, what has been the common intellectual property from Ruskin and Carlyle down to Van Wyck Brooks, Randolph Bourne, Sinclair Lewis, and John Dewey, (to mention only a few names), has now crossed the Potomac and reached Tennessee. Industrialism being a curse, it follows logically(?) that the only escape is a return to the blessing dispensed unto man in the shape of the Old South. Graciousness and culture and art and individual liberty are indigenous to agrarianism; the South was agrarian, and our only way out of perplexity therefore is a reassumption of the Southern way of life.

But just what *was* the Southern way of life is not so explicit as the Neo-confederate distrust of the machine. The contributors who are confident of what it was hand out many underripe assertions. Thus, 'the South has been non-acquisitive.' (With an oligarchy of planters ruining the past and future of their section!) 'It has been leisurely (praises be for euphemism), kindly, serene.' So we have heard Southerners insist heatedly and long. 'Only recently Northern interests have opened up the South to industry.' (The Birmingham of the last century is forgotten). The frontier qualities of the Old South don't fit into the picture and artistically (or artfully) are left out. Old wives' tales, and gentlemanly colonels musing over mint juleps, are better sources than the other Page, (Walter H.), Broadus Mitchell, T. S. Stribling, and Francis Pendleton Gaines.

God made the country (and in this case Dixie,—page Al Jolson) and man—the Damyank—made the town. And its oh for the loss of the poor white's folk art! says the author who deals with the South's "forgotten man." He was happy once, whether hill billy or independent yoeman, or poor white trash; but now shades of the factory descend. Perhaps. But while it takes no perspicuity to

see the present evils of industrialization, it does take a great imagination to see this peasant's paradise just as it does to see the whole mythical Arcadia—unless, of course, one happens to be an ancestor worshipper.

The chronicler suspected all along that there would be hidden somewhere the unreconstructed Southerner's attitude to the Negro—the proverbial African woodcarving in the lumber yard. One contributor Donald Davidson had written (italics mine)

"Black man, . . . Though I am no longer
A child, *and you perhaps unfortunately*
Are no longer a child, we still understand
Better maybe than others. . . .
. . . But now I cannot
Forget that I was master, and you can hardly
Forget that you were slave.
Let us not bruise our foreheads on the wall."

The suspicion based on the earlier writings of these twelve is justified. In "The Briar Patch" Mr. Warren, with all the metaphysics of his breed, and using all the connotations of the title,—tells the world about the Negro's place in that world. "Money has trickled down from the North to be invested in the negro's education. Southern states have doled out money from their all too inadequate educational funds. . . . For what is the negro to be educated? . . . . Are most negroes to be taught to read and write, and then turned back on society with only that talent as a guaranty of their safety or prosperity? Are some others, far fewer in number, to be taught their little French and less Latin, and then sent packing about their business? The most urgent need was to make the ordinary negro into a competent workman or artisan and a decent citizen. . . . This remains, it seems, the most urgent need. . . . The Southern white man . . . wishes the negro well; he wishes to see crime, genial irresponsibility, ignorance and oppression replaced by an informed and productive negro community. . . . Let the negro sit beneath his own vine and fig tree. The relation of the two will not immediately escape friction and difference, but there is no reason to despair of their fate."

The white man's burden. Oh the pity of it, Iago. A separate community the ideal,—"Under his own vine and fig tree." (Which is a 'cultured' euphemism for ghetto).—It seems to the chronicler that he's heard all of this, somewhere, before. . . .

An American Epoch

By STERLING A. BROWN

THE list of books by Prof. Howard Odum on the social conditions of the South is a long and honorable one. If report be credited, he has repudiated an early book of his which dealt with racial characteristics in rather sweeping fashion. Since then his works have been characterized by candor, scholarship, and interpretative power. In addition he writes in a manner unlike that of many of his fellows in the social sciences; it is obvious that he is a poetic craftsman as well as a social observer.

An American Epoch, Southern Portraiture in the National Picture, dedicated aptly enough to "The Next Generation," is a thoroughly documented but entirely readable story of the Old South and the New. It is not written to the tune of Dixie; it is no intransigent crying from the last ditch; but it is just as heroic. Instead of the Confederate yell, there comes the calm voice of understanding; instead of waving the bloody shirt, there is the waving of the pointer—"just here and there we (The South) missed the mark, or exceeded it; and just here and there we did well." This book gives more hope for the New South than *I'll Take My Stand,* which, in some of its papers, partook of the recalcitrance of "I'm as good a man as any other man, any day, yessir, and by Gard a long sight better."

Prof. Odum, though a son of the South, and proud of his birthplace, is no chauvinist. Having spoken pleasurably enough of "The Glory That Was the South," he speaks as truthfully in the next chapter of "The Grandeur That Was Not." The feudal aristocracy he recognizes for what it was; it is worthy of note that the protagonists of the book are Uncle John, a respectable yeoman, and the old Major (not the Maxwell House Colonel or General, praises be!) who has himself risen from yeoman stock. That a special breed of men were set under Southern skies by a special dispensation of God is not the burden of this book. For the settlement and development of the Southern States was first of all an American story. . . . "The South was anything but homogeneous at any time." . . . "It was not surprising that the North, East, West or Europe did not understand the South, nor that the South was sadly unacquainted with itself."

Those who linger in twilight dreams of a plantation Arcadia might do well to ponder these statements: "Mass pictures of the Old South based upon romantic developments from individual incidences of beauty and glory, pictures that never were on land or sea or earth or sky." . . . "Any who criticized the old order or brought to light facts not conducive to its glorification were either not patriots or else uncultured. . . ." ". . . The lovely women of the South had tried to project an atmosphere of gentility, beauty, and glory through an over-weening pride, bitterness and narrowness." Side by side with the Dumas episode of a bride, confronted by Union soldiers concealing a diamond in her mouth, is the Molière farce of "a family having distinguished company to dine, assigning one of the girls to blacken her face and hands and bring in the dinner in high fashion."

Certain truths about slavery that are tabu below the Mason Dixon line Prof. Odum candidly states; attacking the "extra-familial relationships of master with the women slaves," the professed morality and practiced immorality; white men, college boys, kidnapping Negro girls; the disintegration of the Negro family; and cruelty to slaves, driving and beating and putting in chains. "How much of this pattern remains today in the mob brutality and white man defense of mob murder no man can measure." There was, of course, kindliness and loyalty, and Prof. Odum pays these full due. And there was in these slaves earnest of a splendid future. "There was Tom-Jim . . . one of whose grandchildren was to achieve distinction in the musical world. Some (of the descendants of slaves) were destined to achieve strange lives, some in travel and attainments, some in the tragedies of race conflict. Some of the grandchildren of the slaves would outdistance some of the grandchildren of Uncle John and the old Major. There were to be descendants of the old slaves and of the old officer destined to distinguish themselves in inter-racial amity; and there were other descendants of the slaves destined to die through mob action of the descendants of Uncle John and the old Major."

Anyone interested in the past of the South, or its future, should read this book. The same author's *Cold Blue Moon,* slated for subsequent review in *Opportunity,* is a fictionalized treatment of certain aspects of the Old South, done in the manner of *Rainbow Round My Shoulder.* It is poetically conceived, and of course authentically documented.

Two other books dealing with the same period and worthy of careful attention are T. S. Stribling's *The Forge,* and John Peale Bishop's *Many Thousands Go.*

As To "Jungle Ways"

By STERLING A. BROWN

ALTHOUGH the chronicler has been no nearer to Africa than Old Point Comfort, still he has read many romantic books. It requires no undue temerity then for him to comment upon *Jungle Ways,* or what the publishers call "Seabrook's Book Out of Africa." This book is romantic with a vengeance—as one might expect when one remembers the same author's *Magic Island* and sees the dedication to Paul Morand. Terming the book romantic does not in the least call into question the accuracy of the reporting. Many of the episodes are of the "believe it or not" variety, but all have— the ring of candor and truth. But Mr. Seabrook carried to Africa the baggage of his earlier trips to Arabia and Haiti; a gusto for discovering strange truths in out of the way places; for delving into mysteries of the black art, and of generally unexplored religions; and for describing graphically his discoveries.

"When others ask what it is that drives me away from the asphalt, draws me towards deserts and jungles, I answer so sensibly with fine, fair, honest words which sound so well: love of travel, desire to see a strange thing, to learn more perhaps of savage customs, a sincere liking for primitive people—and, if I am pricked to be even more honest, the subsequent vain pleasure of seeing my name spread about in bookshops, and on the tables of my friends." There the author announces himself: the wanderer, the seeker, the romantic twentieth century Don Juan—Childe Harold. And, like these two, he reveals not only an interesting pilgrimage—but also his own interesting personality.

"When one writes of adventure there is a tendency to gloss the parts that were not adventurous. But looking back, it seems to me that a full third of the time I have spent intimately among primitive groups . . . has been spent in sitting." These lines are surprising; Mr. Seabrook's exploits seem to have left little time for 'sitting.' It is amazing what the man saw in his comparatively short stay.

The first part deals with the forest people, with Wamba, queen of jungle magic, and travelling companion de luxe; with the sword jugglers who impaled two children, piercing them through and through, and who later showed the children still alive and well; with a bridge that obligingly responded to mumbo-jumbo and rose out of the Cavally River. Mr. Seabrook does not attempt to explain all of this, but he denies a belief in miracles and on the other hand insists that a hypothesis of charlatan trickery will not hold.

With the Guéré cannibals the author is able to satisfy 'a long standing personal curiosity.' Believing all earlier commentators on cannibalism to be blowers off of hot air, he seeks, and dines upon a meal of human flesh. He contributes to anthropology the discovery that human flesh tastes more like veal than like pork. He is a zestful raconteur in this section,—getting obviously a big kick out of the experience.

One of the most interesting episodes was the Timbuctoo interlude, wherein he meets Père Yakouba, a noted French student of African language and customs, with whom the author raises and quenches a Sahara-like thirst. Père Yakouba steps forth from the page like one of the giants of great fiction. A French monk, he had taken to his bosom a native wife, who bore him thirty sons and daughters. . . . The last section deals with the Habbe, a tribe of phallic worshipping cliff dwellers, whose social customs read like a chapter out of *Erehwon.*

All of this is told engagingly by a man who plainly knows how to write. The style varies from the sprightly humorous to the melancholy mannered prose of the last century. There are shrewd satiric thrusts at arm-chair ethnologists, at American shams, at human nature in general. Mr. Seabrook's gift is more than the seeing eye. He has likewise an ability to understand. He honestly attempts not to condescend; he is free of certain prejudices he might have been expected to have.

And yet. . . . Well there are many Africas, and of course many diverse ways to write of them. The obvious way for complacent Main Streeters is to show the striking local peculiarities. That which is different from us is thereby a screaming joke for us. Mr. Seabrook speaks out against this. None the less, his book is likely to be widely read on Main Street. Much of it has already appeared in one of the ladies' magazines; one of its facts— that in certain tribes a girl can't be betrothed until she has had a baby—has been appropriately decked out as an excruciating joke in a widely circulated weekly.

When the chronicler was a boy, he pored over a page in *Heroes of the Dark Continent,* illustrating African superstitions: the black Cyclops with his baleful glaring one eye, the man whose head was

(Continued on page 221)

AS TO "JUNGLE WAYS"

(Continued from page 219)

below his shoulders, and the reclining beauty whose foot was longer than he was tall, and very flat to boot. . . . In the total, though not in the item, *Jungle Ways* was a throwback to that page. There was something vaguely reminiscent. And then, during the past year, there came to one of the theatres a movie, whose posters (we were allowed to see those) screamed the sensational facts about Africa: tribal marriages to gorillas, and African women with platform lower lips, the color of liver, and the size of heavy saucers. . . . Main Street must have got an eyeful. One doesn't wish to classify Mr. Seabrook's book with this Africa concocted by Hollywood for Main Street. But Main Street unfortunately has its use for Mr. Seabrook. And there's the rub.

For since it is Main Street, it will skip all the harsh things he has to say of America, and rush to the rest of the book. And the rest is Freud's plenty. There's enough for the titillation of all the reading clubs: weird ceremonies, bloodletting, phallic worship, all kinds of manifestations of sex. The book is destined for a large plurality: literati, semi-literati, and illiterati. Well, they certainly ought to get a big kick out of it.

"Caroling Softly Souls of Slavery"

By Sterling A. Brown

THE chronicler, in rummaging about the attic, discovered a modestly bound, modestly printed small volume, published in 1897. This dusty relic was *Thirty Years a Slave*, the life story of one Louis C. Hughes. It served as the assembly call for many thoughts that have heretofore been even more scattered than they appear to be on this page.

Prof. William Dodd in *The Cotton Kingdom* says of the slaves: "Willingly or unwillingly, they increased its solidarity and lent enchantment to the life of the planter. They boasted of the limitless lands of their masters, of the incomparable horses of "ol' massa", of the riches of "ol' massa's" table and the elegancies of "ol' massa's great house". *What their inmost thoughts were is not likely ever to be known.*" From *Thirty Years A Slave* these inmost thoughts are still not to be learned. The subtitle of this autobiography *From Bondage to Freedom, The Institution of Slavery As Seen On The Plantation and In The Home Of The Planter* would indicate of course that the book deals with generalities rather than particularities. The author doesn't take us inside with him. We learn from what so many of the "Bondage and Freedom" narratives we have already learned: the size of the cabins, the differences between house and field servants, preparing cotton for markets, etc. E.g. "The overseer was a man hired to look after the farm and whip the slaves." "There was a section of the plantation known as 'the quarters' where were situated the cabins of the slaves." —These are the type of comments; fellow slaves go unnamed, uncharacterized, almost unmentioned. And all the time how much these things would have meant to us!—the things he actually saw and did, the 'real' things that fixed themselves forever in his mind—what he thought in those long hours hidden in the hold of the steamboat, what separation from his mother meant to him and what the whipping of his wife meant to him, what the joyous band on safely escaping from the plantation said to each other in the days of Jubilo.

It would be more than ungrateful to blame for sins of omission a gentleman who afforded one a quiet meditative vista into days nearly forgotten now, and put away by so many, forever. The chronicler realized well enough, on picking out the book, that this new friend was not likely to be a Douglass, in either life or letters. To expect the analyst, the register, the artist, of this hard pressed struggler for subsistence, decency, self respect and a fair measure of happiness would be foolish, of course; to expect more than what he gave from a man disclaiming in his preface any of the "adjuncts of literary adornment" would be futile.

But there's the rub. The chronicler realizes that this must be so—but the pity of it remains. If only! If only instead of an oft repeated generalized treatment the man had told us what he really *knew*. One fears that this narrative was recollected in too much tranquillity. The drama, the emotion, the personality what one feels to be the essential truth is somehow missing.

Mr. Hughes' life certainly contained material enough. Cities and men he knew: Richmond slave mart, Mississippi plantations, Memphis big houses, Cincinnati, Milwaukee, Detroit in days after the war; life on plantation, in house service, on steamboats, in Federal and Confederate camps; the separation of families, frustrated breaks for freedom, courtship, marriage, running picket lines, self education, escaping slavery, working in hotels, in his own laundry business: much had he seen and known. He could have told us so much. Instead, and I quote his preface, "the narrator presents his story in compliance with the suggestion of friends, and hopes that it may add something of accurate information regarding the character and influence of an institution which for two hundred years, etc. etc." With all of his disclaimers one believes that he had too much of an eye on "literary adjuncts": he wanted to be important, and he should have been himself. In his portrait, which shows a kindly faced man with alert eyes and a humorous mouth—he wears the old styled coat—the "jim-swinger". Too many of his pages are "jim-swinger".

If only the impossible could have happened, that from this man's brothers and sisters there could have come simple, unvarnished accounts of what they *knew*. There it seems is a great loss to the full chronicling of American life, that this people—"leaving, soon gone" should have been either enforcedly silent or unable to reveal in terms that would stay alive what slavery really was to the slave. To an understanding of antebellum, civil war, and reconstruction days some of the finest talent in American literature has applied itself. Certainly the Negro artist could well follow, for an epic theme, where Evelyn Scott and Stephen Vincent Benet have led the way. There is room for a complement to the *Wave* done with the same integrity and artistry. In lieu of this treatment of course, there always remains the prime testimony of the spirituals—and of course for those who will have it—and one fears they are many—the picture vouched for by slaveowners of the perpetual and glorious holiday that antebellum life was.

But those artists, seeking as Jean Toomer once sought to "catch the plaintive soul, leaving, soon gone," will find that few and far between now are those who once could have told so much. And even with them—there is the slow, inevitable—and after all, not to be deplored—erasure of the years. Not to be deplored. . . . For the chronicler remembers his persistence in the face of an old gentleman's studied avoidance of pointed questions about cruelty. Finally, the old man said, "Was dey evah cruel? Certainly dey was cruel. But I don't want to talk about dat". And he closed his eyes. . . .

Concerning Negro Drama

By STERLING A. BROWN

NOW that with the end of August *The Green Pastures* leaves New York, and 'de Lawd wawks 'round de rest uh de country lak a nachal man; and advanced reports of the new ventures come in, one wonders what will be the Negro dramatic success for the coming year. It is a safe enough bet that there will be one, if the hospitable past repeats itself. Paul Green, according to vague rumor, is working on a version of "John Henry," and various other plays of Negro life are in rehearsal. What with the inevitable song and dance shows, there opens up something of promise for the Negro actor. One fears, however, that the Negro playwright won't be there.

Passing in review *The Emperor Jones*, *Porgy*, *In Abraham's Bosom* and *The Green Pastures*, one is struck by two facts: one, the hardy longevity of these plays upon the stage, and the other, the absence of the Negro playwright from the list of authors. The second of these facts is more striking than the first, for the artistic stature of Paul Green, DuBose Heyward, Marc Connelly, and Eugene O'Neill is ample warrant for the tenacity with which their plays have held the boards. The absence of the Negro playwright is more noticeable.

The lag of the Negro artist, inevitably bound up with his social conditions, is more obvious in drama than in other branches of writings. The easy explanation—too easy, one believes—is that only a caricatured stereotype is acceptable to the powers that be on Broadway, and that 'since the self-respecting Negro playwright refuses to create his characters after the fashion of Daddy Rice's Jim Crow and the Christy minstrels, Broadway will have none of him. This complaint would have carried more weight in the first part of the century, when such an artist as Bert Williams could bear witness to the pressure of the stock tradition. But after *Porgy*, and Brutus Jones, and the Jim of *All God's Chillen Got Wings*, and Abraham McCranie, and the glorious ensemble of saints and sinners

in *The Green Pastures*, one must realize that the mould is broken.

Those who still see nothing but a stereotype in character as diverse as these lay themselves open as suspect. One fears that for them the dramatic ideal is race glorification, and any portraiture of Negroes means the betrayal of a race. Unless the world is shown that Negroes too have a Babbitry, absolutely faithful to its white model, smugly going through its paces to a happy ending, the producer is perpetuating the old libels.

The guess of one obtuse person is as good as that of another. It is the chronicler's guess that no army of aspirant Negro playwrights has besieged Broadway. It is his further guess that if any Negro author offered Broadway a play about Negroes that his play would be considered on his merits, and whatever his play said about Negro life whether new or old, would be accepted, *providing that it was dramatically well said.* Of course producers are for the most part in the show business for the same reason that men go into the shoe business, or in bootlegging, i. e. for money. But with the encroachments of the talkies and the revues, the legitimate stage has found that it must interest a smaller but more critical audience and that therefore well written plays are good investments. Moreover there are the experimentalists. The New Playwrights have already shown their beliefs in the fruitful possibilities of Negro life for drama. To conclude the guesswork, one doesn't believe that there couldn't be found in New York some producer who would be willing to stage a well written play by a Negro, however courageous, or subversive of the typical American credo on things racial. After such plays *The Last Mile*, *Once In A Lifetime* and *Roar China* it is hard to believe the New York producer to be nothing but a timid sheep following the ram public opinion over the same old fences.

The chronicler attributes the failure of the

(Continued on page 288)

CHRONICLE AND COMMENT

(Continued from page 284)

Negro dramatist to emerge to the simple fact of the tremendous difficulty of dramatic craftmanship. A man may have ability at characterization, at dialogue, a wide knowledge of life, a deep and sincere humanity and still be a dramatic flop. There is so much of technique to be learned; so arduous an apprenticeship to go through. Obviously a first hand knowledge of the stage is essential—often an absolute prerequisite. To this of course must be added a knowledge of the underlying laws of dramatic construction. A big order obviously.

So far even New York gives our embryonic playwright little enough opportunity for actual contact with the stage. And survey courses of the drama from Aeschylus to Pirandello, or courses on the influence of Beaumont and Fletcher on Restoration drama don't teach technique, whatever else may be their value. The typical audience of our small towns has a confused idea of drama as compounded of a church pageant, a fashion show, and an object lesson in etiquette, and that of our larger towns is sold to Hollywood. Neither furnishes much sustaining interest for the aspirant Ibsen.

The greatest hope lies in the little theatre movements springing up all over the country. Cleveland, New York, and Washington are among the cities boasting community dramatic enterprises; almost every college has its little theatre group. If these will only sponsor the creative efforts of young dramatists as well as the established successes, something of value may come out of them. Eugene O'Neill, Paul Green, according to report, started from such humble (?) beginnings. Lynn Riggs, setting out from a little theatre movement in the Southwest, finally struck Broadway with *Green Grow*

The Lilacs in his saddlebags.— The little theatres should serve as laboratories for the Negro dramatist. But they must demand as careful workmanship as they think Broadway demands, or else they will defeat their own end. And Mrs. Grundy and Pollyanna should be locked out. No dramatist has ever got much done with them forever snooping around.

Poor Whites

By STERLING A. BROWN

ANYONE interested in modern developments in American literature, might profitably read *American Earth* by Erskine Caldwell (Scribner's $2.50), *God In The Straw Pen* by John Fort, (Dodd Mead $2.50) and *Oklahoma Town* by George Millburn (Harcourt Brace $2.00) books dealing with the poor white people of the South who are often known generically as "crackers." Two other types of readers to whom these books are recommended are first, the white reader who uses instances of sensuality, "primitiveness" and crime, found in books dealing let us say with Cat-fish Row or with Black Belt cotton plantations, as justifications for certain preconceptions about "Negro characteristics"; and second, the Negro reader who reads into such books an intention on the part of the author to libel all negroes.

Paul Green's *The Man Who Died At Twelve O'Clock*, a play which I have heard indignant friends berate because of the liquor drinking old Negro, and other details which they considered unsavory, was originally a short story about white characters, called "The First Death," found in the volume *Wide Fields*. A note reads, *"Uncle January Evans—the worst reprobate in Little Bethel. A play was written about him, in which he was characterized as a Negro. He heard of it and threatened 'to git the law on them writing folks at Chapel Hill.' "* Having changed the color of the characters, Mr. Green did little else other than change a more rambling short story into a closely knitted play. Dialect and characterization remained the same. Reading this story after the play, I was struck anew by the interchangeability of qualities erroneously considered as belonging to one special group. Even a casual reading of books dealing with the poor whites of the South would substantiate the belief in this interchangeability of traits—if one's personal experience weren't enough. *Teeftallow* and *This Bright Metal* by T. S. Stribling, *Angel* by Du Bose Heyward, many of Paul Green's plays are easily procured evidence that the lives of poor white and poor black folk in the South conform broadly to the same pattern. Superstitions, moonshining, camp meeting debaucheries, illiteracy, dialect—none of these are inalienable monopolies of either group. Of course within the outline there are differences, some subtle and some obvious. For instance, most of the studies of poor whites reveal more dourness, more cruelty and less humor than those of poor Negroes. On the other hand the Negroes have to do without the joys of mob violence; and one type of regalia they

do not wear is the nightgown on horseback. But the broad outlines remain the same; and there is a interchangeability of many features.

And now strength is added to this belief from new sources. *God In The Straw Pen* is a graphic account of a Methodist revival in the hills of Georgia in 1830. An emotionally starved frontier settlement is visited by an evangelist, who differing from Bishop Grace in certain particulars, produces the same result in his straw pen, where terrified sinners writhe and moan, get happy, wallow in ecstasy, and occasionally fall easy prey, after the fashion of Burn's *Holy Fair*, to those onlookers whose minds are fixed more on sex than on religion. The book has many excellencies; one of them is that it will serve as an interesting gap filler in the literary recreation of the South of the past. The descendents of these Georgians, together with other folk of the South, are shown in the first part of *American Earth* by Erskine Caldwell. These stories, anecdotal in manner, deceptively simple, run all the way from the idyllic to the grim. "Saturday Afternoon" and "Savannah River Pay-day" show the cracker in his dealings with Negroes. They are, as might be expected, gruesome tales; they are told matter-of-factedly and therefore over-whelmingly. The same detachment is to be seen in George Milburn's *Oklahoma Town*. In this book another young Southern writer reveals what he knows of life among the religious hypocrites, the Ku-Kluckers, the Negro-baiters, the semi-barbaric yokels, the flaming youth of a town only halfway won over from the frontier.

Should the Man from Mars read these stories, after a session with the tomes of learned commentators on "racial characteristics," he would probably believe that the characters were Negroes. Religious hysteria, lechery, petty gambling, what Prof. James Truslow Adams calls "Negro sensuality," murder, criminality, dialect, illiteracy—all of the sorry total of afflictions that the Negro brought over with him when he invaded America in the slave ships are here in abundance. Only when the Man from Mars happens to read the accounts of favorite Southern sports such as torturing Negroes (the account in *God In The Straw Pen* is especially well done) or of burning Negroes at the stake, will he be given pause in his classification. The Man from Mars however, since things must be ordered better up there, would probably be too sensible to swallow the theorizing about "racial qualities" in the first place.

(Continued on Page 320)

CHRONICLE AND COMMENT

(Continued from page 317)

Should the hypersensitive Negro reader, who cannot enjoy *Green Pastures* for fear that the play will be considered typical of all Negroes, practice what he believes others do, he would see here a complete picture of white America. That is, if he were logical. Unable to go in for such an absurdity, he might say, however, that here is Crackerdom—and all crackers are religiously hysterical, illiterate, lustful and criminal—a generalization he probably already believes. And of course again he would be wrong. Because as the work of such diverse observers as T. S. Stribling and Edith Madox Roberts, and Maristan Chapman, and William Faulkner, to name only a few authors, would show—there are many varieties of "crackers." What the three books under consideration show is not Crackerdom but the observations of highly individual artists about the lives of individual poor whites, set against a fairly definite social background. All Crackerdom is not revealed here, nor will ever be anywhere—not even in the collected works of these authors.

What these books reveal, is the awakened interest of modern authors in what Walter Hines Page called the "South's forgotten man." They show the farces and tragedies in the lives of underprivileged people living under conditions which may safely be called frontier. They show these unflatteringly; which is as it should be. It would take a great liar to cast a roseate hue over the lives of these folk. For they live in a land, arid and bitter for any people, whether they be white or black, who, like them, have committed the terrible crime of being poor.

The Point of View

By Sterling A. Brown

THE difference between tragedy and comedy lies very often in the point of view. As Pat replied to Mike's praise of the new jail's magnificence—'it dipends on where ye're standin' to look at it.' A situation may resolve itself into comedy or tragedy according to whether you're outside or in. Even the fat man falling upon the ice, a comic standby, dating surely from pleistocene days, can be tragic if the fat man's point of view be taken. The stuttering child is not only the comic thing which his schoolmates, whose tongues waggle more easily, make of him. The stupid fellow withered by some brilliant schoolmaster's sarcasm is not purely and simply cause for hilarity. And those who in race, background, culture, nationality, or whatever other accident, differ from the established 100 per cent norm, are not always as amusing as from one point of view, they may appear.

Shift the point of view, and Ford's jealousy, which helps to make *The Merry Wives of Windsor* the riproaring comedy it is, becomes the terrible perplexity of Othello. Shylock, seen from the point of view of a Jew-baiting audience is a different character indeed from the one portrayed in Ludwig Lewisohn's *The Last Days of Shylock*. And even in *The Merchant of Venice* it is entirely possible to see a tragic Jew, sinned against as much as sinning, especially for an audience acquainted with sufferings similar to his.

One does not wish to be either sentimental or hypersensitive about this. There is certainly a large place for the free, robust spirit of comedy. Genial satire of extremes, merry realization of life's incongruities—these are godsends. There is laughing *with*, as well as laughing *at*. It is hardly possible to identify oneself with everything that man has found laughable, and by doing so to see only the tragic side. And yet one must realize that too often things are made comic that are merely unfortunate parallels to the child's stammering, and the man's falling. When comedy makes copy out of injustice and wretchedness by disguising these, or being blind to them, it exceeds its prerogative.

As a case in point, the Negro, from the time when Daddy Rice's "Jim Crow" first kicked up his heels in 1832, has been one of the prime ingredients of American humor. The list of his comic attributes, and the situations in which he finds himself is a long and familiar one. He appears often as the errant husband wedded to the Amazon, often as the wife-beating, razor-toting bad man. The chronicler remembers the Howard Theatre of yesterday, where the hero would brandish his huge "razzor" to the gleeful delight of the audience. It was a dreamworld razor, as innocuous as Mutt's club, or the brick that lays poor Krazy Kat low. We in the gallery knew that such delightful weapons didn't cut, although the alleys at the stage doors, and perhaps a neighbor two seats off could have informed us differently.

Octavus Roy Cohen, Arthur Akers, and the minstrel stage have furthered the dream. In one of the widely read short story magazines there is the picture of a huge Negro swinging a wicked blade at the departing part of a man who had done him wrong. The artist must have been highly amused at his conception.

As a decided and valuable contrast, William Faulkner's "That Evening Sun Go Down" in a collection of stories, *These Thirteen* (Cape and Smith, $2.50), might be read. This story is a masterpiece of suspense and terror. It is not complimentary to the Negroes who appear in it, but that has nothing to do with its value. It shows what the difference in point of view can do. The razor-toting husband, the domestic difficulty, the threats, the fears, all are here, but *seen from within*. What is a ridiculous situation in the hands of burlesquers becomes harsh and terrifying as in reality it is. This is the way *people* are affected by these things, you say; these are not corked puppets in a dream world where razors don't cut, and death, being averted at the story's end, is funny.

The story is of one Nancy, who is waiting for her husband Jubah, a Negro with a razor cut down his face, and a bitterness in his heart, to come and kill her. The story is told by a child, who with his sister Caddy and brother Jason (characters in that remarkable novel *The Sound and the Fury*) does not understand exactly what is happening. The story builds up with little strokes here and there a picture of the brutal life of the community. But more than this, it shows the gradual increasing of the doomed woman's terror, while the children prattle on about inconsequentials. It is a technical masterpiece, but more important, it is a marvel of understanding. And it is because Mr. Faulkner looks upon Nancy as a woman with the fear of death upon her, and not as an immortal

(Continued on Page 350)

CHRONICLE AND COMMENT
(Continued from Page 347)
clown that literature rather than tedious slapstick results.

This is very different from John Henry's fight with Stacker Lee in Roark Bradford's book. Stacker Lee shoots off John Henry's shoestrings, buttons, hatband, necktie, and belt. And so our hero slapped Stacker Lee in the river, and then slapped him so hard that it dried out his clothes. Now *John Henry* purports frankly enough to be a tall tale, about people and lands that never were, and perhaps we shouldn't ask for anything more than momentary amusement. But when this is called interpretation of the Negro! And without Mr. Bradford's comic genius, the other writers on this comical darker brother who has no troubles because razors don't cut and bullets don't wound, etc., etc., fall pretty flat.

Because seen from within, DuBose Heyward's treatment of Hagar's superstition becomes literature rather than the tittering of one who knows so much better. For the same reason *The Half Pint Flask* succeeds, and *Green Thursday*; and *The Green Pastures* rises far, far above *Ol' Man Adam and His Chillen.* For the same reason— but one could go on forever. . . . So much depends upon the point of view.

Pride and Pathos

By STERLING A. BROWN

THIS* is a book of high praise for the low country. Written by South Carolinians who united to preserve Negro Spirituals and Folksongs and to educate 'the rising generation in their character and rendition,' it is an expression of the glamour of the coast country of 'The Carolinas,' and of a nostaglia for 'the days that are no more.' There are essays by Augustine T. Smythe, Herbert Ravenel Sass, Alfred Huger, Thomas R. Waring, Archibald Rutledge, DuBose Heyward and Robert W. Gordon; poems by Beatrice Ravenel and Josephine Pinckney; a collection of spirituals, and illustrations by several artists who have caught the undeniable physical beauty of the section.

The authors are agreed in their worship of South Carolina's achievement, and fill up a roster with proud names. Francis Marion, Calhoun, Haynes, the Pinckneys, the Rutledges, the Heywards, Wade Hampton, these and many more are here; to Charleston came James Monroe to dance at a St. Cecilia ball, and Edgar Allen Poe to serve as a private soldier in the harbor fortifications, and Thackeray to learn a lesson in manners. Lafayette stopped at one of the baronies. The story of the low country is a dramatic one, with its wars between the Spaniards, the French, and the English, between the colonists and the Yemassees, the British and the Continentals, the Confederates and the Federals; with Denmark Vesey's tragic stroke for liberty, the oratory of Haynes, and the Reconstruction episodes. In this book a story already romantic is told by arch-romantics, who are convinced that the like of South Carolina has never been seen on the face of God's earth, and never will be seen.

There is a graciousness in the writing, although the adulatory tone approaches the 'purple' (which is the 'epic colour' in the setting), and at times goes definitely over into lushness. These twentieth century artists, born too late, stand in awe of the marvelous resemblance of South Carolina to the England of the 18th Century, and to feudal Europe. In the beauty of the swamps, the decadence of the plantations, the baronial manors, and the architecture of Charleston they find a supernal loveliness indescribable in words.

Archibald Rutledge writes of the outcome of the

* *The Carolina Low Country,* by Members of the Society for the Preservation of the Spirituals. Macmillan $5.00.

'War for Southern Independence': "In 1860 there perished by the sword of misunderstanding the gentlest, the most humane, the most chivalric civilization that America has ever known. . . . That the plantation people of our Low-Country practised a religion pure and undefiled we may judge from the gentleness and the serenity of their lives: their faith in the ancient virtues, their utter devotion to home and family; their compassion to their slaves. . . . I know not where else to look for an existence more humane, affectionate, and sunny hearted than the life of the old time Carolina planter." This essay is nearer to Burbling Bob's than the others; still, we find Mr. Sass writing: "Inevitably, too, it is a gallant past that comes back, sweet (perhaps too sweet, but this may be forgiven)with the scent of roses. He narrates the obligatory scene of the 100% Southern belle beautiful in her wide silk dress cut low to reveal her smooth shoulders, bejeweled, gliding into the shadows of the high, pillared portico, to meet in the evening's cool a young man, wide shouldered and slim-waisted in his tight-fitting broadcloth coat, his eyes alight with exultant joy. . . . He bends and kisses the tips of her fingers; then together they fade into the shadows." Lastly, Mr. Dooley writes (but in another book): "He did not boast iv his section iv th' country. A thrue Southerner niver does. It wud ill become him to suggest that th' South is anything thin th' fairest spot of Gawd's footstoll, inhabited by th' bravest men, and th' loveliest and most varchous women, th' most toothsome booze, and th' fastest ponies in th' wurruld."

The authors at times do recognize a minor flaw; Archibald Rutledge in "Plantation Lights and Shadows" in order to prove that old plantation days had their 'shadows' tells how a girl caught the yellow fever, and died. But that's about the only one.

DuBose Heyward's essay "The Negro In the Low Country" is the best in the book. He insists that between the Abolitionist's and the defensive Southerner's 'the real Negro slave must stand.' And yet his essay partakes of the nature of the rest of the book more than one might have suspected. Although he admits that the mutual affection existing between master and slave has been 'sentimentalized ad nauseam,' he does insist that the Negro was 'temperamentally ideally suited to make his own way in a state of slavery,' that the

(Continued on Page 384)

the Negro, compared with his earlier happiness, a melancholy business. There is more of Thomas Nelson Page in the other contributors. M ͟ass says that the Negro, in lower Carolina, is 'one of the happiest mortals, take him all in all, to be found anywhere on earth.' He cites another variant of the old story 'Tell Mars Linkum to tek his freedom back,' telling of Old Aleck who on being freed asseverated "Miss I don' want no wagis." "God bless you, old Aleck," says Mr. Sass. The regretful refrain of all the essays is 'There are no Negroes singing in the fields.' The verb is never 'working.' Mr. Rutledge envies the plantation slaves, who spent their lives "in pastimes praised by Walton and Shakespeare (fishing and hunting) for which millionaires of our times are willing to make a princely outlay!"

The best features of the book are the spirituals and the illustrations. The spirituals, many of them unfamiliar, carry the burden of the rebuked and scorned, who have as recompense not the idyllic content ascribed them by their interpreters, but a rich vein of melancholy poetry. Robert W. Gordon writes an interesting, if not strikingly original essay, "The Negro Spiritual." He follows Newman I. White in his insistence that the vocabulary of slavery and freedom that the Negro used refers to 'spiritual' slavery and not to physical. He is in company with other southern white men who interpret for the world, the Negro included, what the Negro's songs really mean. He traces resemblances in diction and structure to old Methodist revival hymns. He denies that the spiritual is entirely or exclusively the work of the Negro, although he admits its genuine individuality in spite of its borrowings. One of his colleagues states that out of the radiant antebellum life came the spirituals—'which belong to neither race but to both races.' It is not so strange that today the whites should claim half of the credit for the spirituals. They do so with justice. These songs of suffering *do* owe equally to both slaves and masters: the first produced the song, and the second produced the sufferings.

The chronicler was nearly wooed by the lovely etchings and paintings and the Tennysonian descriptions to leave on the next train for Charleston. But he realized soon enough that, for him, there is no train running to this Xanadu. He wonders if this dream world has ever been visited by anyone: if the record of its past is not the epic of Lost Atlantis. He will remain in a gray northern city perforce, momentarily exiled from a South whose physical beauty he too loves. And in this exile he will have to read his other books on South Carolina: E. C. L. Adams', DuBose Heyward's, when he is more of the artist and less the apologist; Julia Peterkin's; *Bancroft's Slave Trading in the Old South*. After *The Carolina Low Country* he feels a need for "Ol' Man Hildebrand" and "The Slave Barn" by E. C. L. Adams, and the description of the Charleston belle in Paul Green's *House of Connelly*.

Pride and Pathos
(Continued from Page 381)

Gullahs ran away because they were stupid and easily led, and that to contemplate the future of

Truth Will Out

By STERLING A. BROWN

IT is an ironic coincidence that many of the proud names catalogued in *The Carolina Low Country** are in this book,** too, appearing in all their glory as barterers in human flesh, or as ardent apologists for that calling. A Rutledge of Low Country fame said of the slave traffic: "Religion and humanity have nothing to do with this question. Interest alone is the governing principle with nations." Louis D. De Saussure, Thomas Norman Gadsden and many other members of old Charleston families appear among Mr. Bancroft's slave traders, in company with fellow grandees in Richmond, Memphis, New Orleans, etc. An obvious contrast between *The Carolina Low Country* and this work could take as its starting point this remark of Mr. Bancroft's: "The Old Exchange or Customhouse . . . is the most historic building in perhaps all the South. The Sons of the Revolution in South Carolina have placed on it a bronze tablet with an eloquent inscription . . . ; here George Washington in 1791 was entertained. . . . With no less historical importance they might have added: From colonial days until after the middle of the nineteenth century from several hundred to many thousand slaves were annually sold to the highest bidders. . . ."

In striking contrast, too, are the lovely paintings and etchings of the romantic book beside the photographs and contemporary drawings of the history. These latter show a semi-frontier civilization whose brutishness is thrown into even more shocking relief because of the occasional psuedo-elegance. In *The Carolina Low Country* mention of slave-trading (which *was* a major industry) is conspicuously absent. Slave-trading may not be history, after all. Perhaps only exquisite amours, chivalry, and derring do are history.

There has been such a Hallelujah chorus for the glories of antebellum days that even the cautious hints that all of slavery may not have been paradisal, were once warmly received as revolutionary, especially if the opinions were delivered below the Potomac. Occasionally commentators mentioned a few abuses, cancelled them with a few humanitarian incidents, and left slavery a'straddling the fence. Some of us, however, could never accept slavery as a fifty-fifty proposition. The chronicler is convinced, upon reading the book, of an earlier opinion: that slavery had its good side, that it even had its best, and that at its best it was hell.

The apostles' creed handed down by Dew, Harper, Thomas Nelson Page and Thomas Dixon to their disciples The Revisionists (!) should now be silenced forever. Mr. Bancroft demolishes many more than the following ten pronouncements. (1) "The Old South scorned acquisitiveness. (Damyank money grubbing.)" In reality the great extent of slave trading and its defense grew out of the fact that it was so lucrative. The foundations of many great fortunes lay in slave trading. One could make up for extravagance and poor management by selling a few slaves. As John Jay Chapman says, "Slavery was always commerce." Even before the "negro fever" an annual average involved in slave trading amounted to $64,999,600. (2) "Charges of antebellum sexual immorality are libellous." Mr. Bancroft does not have to point to the cloud of witnesses about, but gives proofs of the fancy prices paid for "fancy girls," a fancy name for concubines. (3) "The South would have abolished slavery in its own time (true) and way." The facts are that just before the Civil War "the negro fever" was raging, and attempts were made to reopen the African slave trade. Free Negroes were often in jeopardy of being sold. (4) "Negroes were contented with their lot, and (5) were happy even when sold." Mr. Bancroft gives the records of the many Negroes sold as 'criminal,' i.e., intractable. He tells us of the many suicides, attempted and committed by the newly sold slaves. (6) "Negroes were so clumsily unskilled that good hoes weren't allowed to them, etc." The records afford extensive evidence of the slave's skill as artisan. It would be better to consider separately the last four particulars of the creed: (7) "Families were not broken up," (8) "children were not sold separately," (9) "There was no slave breeding," (10) "Slave traders were ostracized."

Mr. Bancroft does not set out to refute, but to present the truth. When he does find falsehood parading, however, he strips off the regalia with obvious joy. Speaking of the separation of families, which has been minimized, he says: "Interested persons easily satisfied themselves that slaves were almost indifferent to separations. This was refuted by the use of handcuffs by new purchasers, by the chain-gangs of the interstate traders and

---

*Reviewed in last month's "Chronicle and Comment."
**Slave Trading in the Old South, by Frederic Bancroft, Baltimore: J. H. Hurst Co., $4.00.

by thousands of advertisements telling that run-aways were supposed to have returned to their old homes or gone to kindred from whom they had been parted. And because separations were too notorious to be denied, it was often undertaken to palliate them by saying that they were no worse than those among white persons. . . . Any favorable sophistry or sanctimonious mummery was welcomed and hailed as a complete defense."

Of one of the statements of Ulrich Phillips who has come to be considered the authority on slavery, Mr. Bancroft writes: " 'Hardly ever sold separately!' On the contrary, they were hardly less than a staple in the trade. . . . It may be worth while to heap to overflowing the measure of indisputable facts." And he does heap it with a vengeance. Nor is this the only place where he believes refutation of Prof. Phillips is needed, and easily accomplished. About 'slave breeding,' DuBose Heyward, in *The Carolina Low Country* writes: "The ridiculous accusation that stocks were bred up by the forced mating of particularly fine specimens finds not the slightest corroboration in fact." If, quibbling aside, this means that there was no 'slave breeding,' Mr. Heyward joins the group which Mr. Bancroft, by cold statistics and keen logic, completely overthrows. A Charleston advertisement reads: " . . . [These Negroes] are prime, their present Owner, with great trouble and expense, selected them out of many for several years past. They were purchased for stock and breeding Negroes, and to any Planter who particularly wanted them for that purpose, they are a very choice and desirable gang." The proceeds from slave rearing filled the coffers of the border states of Virginia, Kentucky and Missouri. Fecundity was at a premium; "a rattlin' good breeder," "a young girl who would breed like a cat," "too old for breeding" were familiar expressions in chivalric parlance. Women past childbearing were drugs on the market.

The 'social ostracism of the slave trader' Mr. Bancroft proves to be another figment of the imagination. He shows the most eminent luminaries of church and state engaged in the traffic. It paid, hence it was respectable. Of course, there were gradations. The socially prominent preferred to be known as 'brokers' while the lesser fry were often still 'livery stable keepers.' But the greatest difference was that the socially prominent 'brokers' sold more slaves and made more money than the riffraff traders. And thereon hangs a moral.

The book is overwhelming in more senses than one. It is documented from all sources: from travellers' accounts, memoirs, unwritten recollections (properly checked up) and especially from what is uncontrovertible evidence: court records and slave traders' own advertisements and accounts. It covers exhaustively a territory extending from Washington to Missouri and all points South. It is done in the best tradition of scholarship, with pertinent anecdotes and occasional gleams of irony. Some of his narratives have the climactic force of the best short stories; among these is the story of what Mackay saw at Gadsden's patriarchal plantation, and what dire things happened there shortly after.

This excellent book should be in the home of every intelligent American. One fears, however, that some of our own 'literati' will consider it too 'harrowing,' and that the Southern 'revisionists' damning it as later generation abolitionism, unfortunately won't read it. It happens, however, that here, as in so many other cases, *facts are abolitionist*. *Slave Trading In The Old South* may be swept over and covered by another avalanche of sentimental nonsense about the Old South's grandeur and her 'peculiar institution.' Let the avalanche come. This book is a solid rock, not to be moved. It is *here* and *will be* here, when time has swept all of the loose dirt away.

"Never No More"

By STERLING A. BROWN

NEVER NO MORE. By James Knox Millen. A play in Three Acts. Produced at The Hudson Theatre, by Robert Sparks. Settings by Jo Mielziner.

This play, a frontal attack upon lynching, is the culmination of two honorable lines: the plays of social protest such as *Roar China*, *The Last Mile*, *Precedent* and *1931*, and the best plays of Negro life, such as *The Emperor Jones*, *Porgy*, *In Abraham's Bosom*, and *The Green Pastures*. Its merits, whether from the standpoint of playwriting, acting, direction, truth to life, or dramatic power, make its position in those groups high and secure. Whatever its run at the Hudson Theatre, it must be considered one of the important plays in American dramatic history.

The author, James Knox Millen, a Yale graduate, and an ex-cotton planter, is brother to Gilmore Millen, parts of whose novel *Sweet Man* could hardly have been relished in their native Memphis, and cousin to Roark Bradford, famous for his burlesques of Negro life. According to an interview reported in The New York *Times*, Mr. Millen's grandmother, on her deathbed, said to him, "If you are unhappy on the plantation, try your lot at writing. Roark has done right well." We hasten to add, he has never done so well as this. One evening, Mr. Millen, leaving in disgust his unremunerative 4,000 acres, stumbled across an orgy of the South. A Negro was being burned at the stake. "All that night he sat on the stump of a tree, turning the horrors of the ghastly spectacle over and over in his mind. In the morning he had two acts of a play."

The curtain rises on an appealing, genuine idyll. We are introduced to a stoical family, presided over by a strong, lovable mother. They have come the long, hard road, but they forget that now, happy because of the bales they have made, their "blue" mules, the corn for the winter, and the large neatly stacked pile of ash wood cut in stove lengths. The two daughters gleefully scan a mail order catalogue, Ike, the feeble-minded son, is fixing up (unknown to his mother) a forbidden contraption to dynamite fish, the older boys are happy at their harvest, Big Tom's Susie is carrying his child. Mammy, herself, would be at peace except for worrying about the apple of her eye, Solomon, who threatens to turn out badly.

Her fears are well enough grounded. Solomon has got into trouble, has killed a white girl. The mob is on his trail. It is not long before they

have caught him, and (although interminably long in the theatre) before they burn him on the pile of wood in his own yard. The mob then seeks to satiate its bloodlust upon his household. The children determine to shoot it out with the mob, but Mammy, by threatening to drop dynamite into a fire bucket and blow her house, family and tormentors to bits, forces the defenders of American civilization to skulk homeward. The curtain falls as the two brothers go out to get the charred remains of Solomon, while Mammy slowly lays out his dressy Sunday suit for his burial.

This is a terrible play about a terrible subject. When the cries of the mob, mingled with the boy's pleading, filled the theatre, and the lurid glow of the fire flared through the heavy covering over the window, the tension was almost unbearable. In its impact, *Never No More* is very much like *The Last Mile*. Like that play, too, it ran the risk of anticlimax. After the gruesome ending of the second act, one wondered what could follow. Mr. Millen shows his skilled craftsmanship, however, by giving a third act as gripping, if less horrible. After all, this play is not solely the staging of a lynching. It is just as much a study of the effect of lynching upon the innocent and deserving, of the precariousness of the Negro's hold upon peace and happiness, and of the great power of hate to turn hard won content into misery. Nor does the ending of the play bring any solution. One is forced to ask, what of tomorrow? And that is a question worth our asking.

Never No More is a play of character and background as well as of action, powerful and absorbing though that action may be. There is no savage rhythm to the lives of these folk. Instead of the beating of tom-toms, literal or figurative, there is a more ominous sound, the deep baying of bloodhounds, and the yells of the mob. "I ain't never talked back to a white man in my life," whimpers Ike, as a shotgun is forced into his hands. But the daughter-in-law is proud and scornful. "They ain't got no color now; they'se killers." And Joe, easy going as he may be, is of stern stuff. His mild humor becomes sardonic, he knows what he knows. "Can't God see out there?" asks one of the besieged. "God's gone somewheres else tonight." There is a deep religion in the lives of these people, a fatalistic submissiveness. But there is a courage, too. And they are not being fooled.

It does one's heart good to see the name of Rose McClendon in the lights over the theatre entrance,

The role of the dignified matriarch seems to be cut out for her. Those who object to her restraint are probably influenced by ancient stereotypes, or by what, in New York purlieus, they think a mammy should be. She is convincing; anyone acquainted with the Negro folk could recall numerous prototypes for her. In her execution of the part, Miss McClendon is not only faithful to Mr. Millen's creation; she is inspired. When she appears at the door of her cabin, when she crawls on her knees across the stage to the fire, when she defies the mob, she gives added proof to the belief held by many for a long time, that here is one of America's leading actresses. She is very ably sustained by a sincere and powerful cast.

Among the many objections to the play, one voiced frequently is that the boy should be innocent. A reply to that is couched in the question, "If the lynching of a guilty person is such a terrible thing, what must the lynching of an innocent person be?" Some hypersensitive critics have explained their dislike to the play, by insisting that it succeeds as a shocker, but not as drama. This specious criticism might be directed at any tragedy from *Oedipus* to Ibsen's *Ghosts*. But if the control of characterization, background, dialogue, situation, suspense, and the stirring of pity and terror in this first tragedy are not drama, and do not augur well for the dramatic future of Mr. Millen, one wonders at the capriciousness of the gods who dispense the dramatic laurels.

This play is not for whites who nurse their prejudices, nor for sentimental Negroes who, like the ostrich, bury their heads in the sand. Mr. Millen is of the group of contemporary artists, who, with Thomas Hardy, hold

"That if way to the Better there be,
it exacts a full look at the Worst."

We are grateful that such a sympathetic and powerful dramatist as Mr. Millen has taken this full look. And American literature should be grateful for another fine play.

Weep Some More My Lady

By Sterling A. Brown

IN Louis Untermeyer's *American Poetry: From the Beginning to Whitman*, which is as indispensable as his *Modern American Poetry*, there are critical essays on Negro spirituals, blues, work-songs and "Negroid" melodies. They afford an instance of the truism that a poet can best get at the heart of poetry. It is Mr. Untermeyer's consideration of the "Negroid" melodies, however, with which the chronicler has immediate concern. Speaking of Stephen Foster, he says: "His Negro evocations are less true to the plantation than to the proscenium. . . . We accept the songs with their mixture of pathos and bathos, uncritically, immediately."

Certain it is that the acceptance of the Foster melodies and their countless brood has been uncritical, immediate but longlasting, and wide. America, since Foster, has been set clamoring for idyllic content beneath Carolina skies, in the sleepy hills of Tennessee, where one may tuck oneself to sleep in his old Tucky home while the Mississippi—that lazy river—rolls on and Dandy Jim strums chords to Lucinda in the canebrake. Cleverly aware of the possibilities in the furore, a Jewish comedian evolved the supreme gesture: he corked his face, and sinking to one knee, extended his white-gloved hands and wailed variations of "Mammy" and "Sonny-Boy." And America took him to her sentimental bosom. Tin Pan Alley, most of whose dwellers had been no farther south than Perth Amboy, frantically sought rhymes for the southern states, cheered over the startling rediscovery of Albammy and Miami for their key word Mammy, and of Dinah for Carolina.

We have had the epidemic with us for a long time, and are likely to have it always. It is stimulated, however, at certain economically advantageous periods. Sardonic observers noticed that a flood of songs about going back to Alabama appeared coincidentally with the cramming of northbound jim-crow cars. The vogue of the spirituals stimulated the market. One of the most illuminating contrasts between the genuine and the shoddy is furnished by *Dear Old Southland*, a jazzed up version plus a dash of Foster, of the spiritual *Deep River*. The first is an insincere, pitiful yearning for a Dixie Arcadia, written by a Negro who stays in London; the second is an expression of the real tragedy of Negro experience in a real South.

One of the most recent (though one should qualify 'recent' since yesterday's hit on Tin Pan Alley is as remote today as Yankee Doodle) contains these lines:

When Poets write, they love to write
About the Southland. . . .
Whatever they write, whatever they say
Is not exaggeration,
It's not imagination.
If you want to see the moon in all its splendor,
If you want to see the stars can shine,
Spend an evenin' in Caroline.

The chronicler doubted whether bathos could go farther, until he picked up one of the latest effusions of George White's Scandals which is 'chiseling in' on some of the earning power of *Green Pastures*. It departs slightly from the homesickness of its brothers and sisters, but compensates by a liberal dash of biological, ethnological, and teleological wisdom. This gem is called *That's Why Darkies Were Born*. After such orthodox Dixie precepts as 'Someone left the work to the colored man; what must be, must be, so accept your destiny'; it prattles on

Someone had to pick the cotton
Someone had to hoe the corn
Someone had to slave and be able to sing
That's why Darkies were born.
'Someone had to laugh at trouble,
Someone had to be contented with any old thing,
So sing! sing! . . .
That's why Darkies were born.'

After this, what can be said? Better critics than the chronicler have inveighed against the imbecilities of the lyrics ground out in Tin Pan Alley. The appearance of the words in cold print, away from the seduction of saxophone and cornet, should be their downfall, but unfortunately isn't. The fake Negro song, nearly as moronic as this last one, has robustly survived so long. What does the mob-mind care that it is bald-faced lying? The mob-mind wishes it, will have it so. One can do no more than register a horse-laugh at the obvious Americanism of setting up sham in place of unpleasant truth, and at the Negro's easy complaisance in accepting a stereotype, and reaping his own shekels by perpetuating it. One can only turn the record over from *Sleepy Time Down South* and listen, for blessed relief from the languishing sweetness, to the ribald, fantastic Louis Armstrong blurt raucously:

'I'll be glad when you're dead, you rascal, you!'

Joel Chandler Harris

By STERLING A. BROWN

JOEL CHANDLER HARRIS: EDITOR AND ESSAYIST. Edited by Julia Collier Harris. Chapel Hill: University of North Carolina Press, $4.00.

In this book the daughter-in-law of Joel Chandler Harris has collected his less known personal, literary, and political essays and has edited them with a valuable commentary upon the man and his times. The essays range from appreciations of the Georgian countryside to lengthy discussions of the Negro problem.

Although not pretentious, Harris's literary essays are sensible, and could furnish food for thought even in our own days. The following is a creed he trusted to with fine results: "The very spice of all literature, the very marrow and essence of literary art, is its localism. No literary artist can lack for materials in this section. They are here all around him, untouched, undeveloped, undisturbed, unique and original. . . . But they must be mined. . . . You may be sure that the man who does it will not care one copper whether he is developing. . . . Southern or Northern literature, and he will feel that his work is considerably belittled if it be claimed by either on the score of sectionalism." Change the words Southern and Northern to Negro and the word sectionalism to racialism, and the statement is worthy of study by those interested in the truthful portraiture and interpretation of Negro life. Harris's preference of 'localism' (i.e., a loving study of the artist's own background, written with standards of artistic integrity) to 'sectionalism' (i.e., a chauvinistic worship of sectional peculiarities) explains why the work of Joel Chandler Harris is so far superior to that of Thomas Nelson Page.

Harris, on the strength of his presentation of Uncle Remus, was in great demand as a spokesman for the Negro's past, present and future. His major beliefs about the Negro are elusive. At times, one feels sure that he is nothing but a defender of the 'plantation tradition'; and then an occasional gleam of liberalism lights up the picture. The suspicion remains, however, that Harris's attitude is largely that of a paternalistic master, kindly but condescending. After all, these thoughts were largely for a rural Southern audience, spoken generally through the mouth of a 'Sage of Snap Bean Farm,' or of 'Uncle Remus,' or of 'Billy Sanders,' cracker-box philosopher for crackers.

In a day and in a section noted for pessimism about the Negro's prospects, Joel Chandler Harris showed his common sense by being an optimist. The educated Negro was no bugbear to Harris, and to offset the 'shiftless' Negro, he presented to his readers the taxpayer. He asked that the race be judged by its best; having Billy Sanders say: "Let a bow-legged nigger come along and do his devilment, an' right straight we lay the responsibility of the crime on the whole nigger race." Lynching was roundly condemned throughout Harris's career, as "a demoralizing and dangerous form of barbarism." He has his philosopher of Shady Dale say: "When you-all up here let a lot of thirty cent loafers whirl in and kill innocent niggers, I folded my two han's an 'vowed that kinder things neither looked nor smelt like Southern chivalry."

But in this last quotation something is amiss, as there is in much of the social thinking of the book. There is too much of the 'folding my two hands,' of invoking the spirit of a Southern chivalry that Harris wishes to believe in. The quotation continues: "I was sorry for the poor niggers, but lots sorrier for the white people—an' it depends on the way you do herearter whether I ever git over my sorrow." Being a good-hearted man, Harris trusts implicitly to the good-heartedness of his neighbors. He insists, without belligerency, but firmly, that the Southerner must be allowed to solve this problem, unhindered, and that enough beams exist in the eye of the North, to make the Negro problem in the South a mere mote. All of this is a familiar line. It reveals that Mr. Harris could not entirely escape sectionalism. He says that whatever of value the past has afforded the Negro is a result of Southern efforts, passing entirely over such catalytic agents as Sumner and Schurz, Lincoln and Grant, *Uncle Tom's Cabin* and the March to the Sea. As for the Negro, all he needs to do is work hard and live right. "In this republic property is the best protection a man can have, whether he be black or white," says Harris, sharing the delusion common to his day, and in some quarters even to ours, that in our great land, property grows like apples on wayside trees and asks only the picking.

In spite of his condemnation of lynching, Mr. Harris writes this: "There have been among the Negroes manifestations of brutality unparalleled, so far as I know, since the dawn of civilization, and the reprisals that have been made are but the natural result of the horror that must fill the bosoms of the best men who are brought sharply face to face with such cruelty and bestiality." This is revelatory, as is his comment that Booker Washington "is the only capable leader (the Negro race) has ever had," with its omission of Douglas. Social equality makes him fold his hands; "it exists nowhere," so why should he worry? The presence of Negro leaders in politics, "is unfortunate because there are so many ways in which they could benefit their race." "Whatever form of injustice (the Negro) has been made the victim of has been almost entirely due to the unwise and unnecessary crusade inaugurated in his behalf by the politicians of the North."

Although Harris attacked Jefferson Davis for belated fire-eating, as well as "Southern strutters," and easily irritated editors who earned for the South the sobriquet of the 'galled jade,' he was a true son of the South, ready to defend it from outside charges, and to see its excellences, even where they never existed. Slavery for him was "in some of its aspects . . . far more beautiful and inspiring than any of the relations between employers and the employed in this day. . . ." "In Middle Georgia the relations between master and slave were as perfect as they could be under the circumstances." *"Uncle Tom's Cabin"* was in reality "a defense of American slavery" and its moral was "that the realities of slavery, under the

best and happiest conditions, possess a . . . beauty and tenderness all their own." Harris chose to remember only the best and happiest conditions. He extolled the Mammy and the "Old Darky," and lamented the passing of the plantation in elegies as sad as those of Archibald Rutledge.

We have, revealed in this book, a mild, kindly disposed romantic, more at home in cultivating his garden, or lingering in memories of a faithful, well-loved "Uncle," than in mixing with harsh realities. He believed that merely exhorting good will toward men would accomplish wonders. He had a faith in the South unwarranted in these later years, and the chronicler is forced to believe, just as unwarranted in his own day. He remains the inspired amanuensis of the Negro folk-imagination; deserving high praise because he had the insight to see the importance of Uncle Remus, and the artistry to recreate him. He is too much the child of his age, and of his state, to be considered a liberal in his discussion of the South's peculiar problem. In fairness towards the Negro, he did not go as far as Cable, who was chased out of the South for his views. But let us have some of the charity that he himself manifested. He did go, in Uncle Remus' parlance, "a short piece down de road." And that is a great deal farther than most of his Georgian contemporaries ever went; and if the truth be known, farther than most of those living there now would go.

THE LITERARY SCENE
CHRONICLE AND COMMENT

A Literary Parallel

By STERLING A. BROWN

"A STRANGE PEOPLE!—merry 'mid their misery,—laughing through their tears, like the sun shining through the rain. Yet what simple philosophers they! They tread life's path as if 'twere strewn with roses devoid of thorns, and make the most of life with natures of sunshine and song!" This sounds strikingly familiar, and might be taken for one of the glib characterizations of the Negro which filled so many pro-slavery and reconstruction attempts at "racial understanding." But, oddly enough, it is no such thing. It comes from a poor melodrama about Irish life, *The Shamrock and The Rose*, and is spoken by an Englishman, whose soldiers are overrunning the land.

Its sham elegance should not mislead us. It is about the people whose degradation wrung from Swift this bitter protest: "It is a melancholy object to those who walk through this great town or travel in the country, when they see the streets, the roads, and cabin doors, crowded with beggars of the female sex, followed by three, four, or six children, all in rags and importuning every passenger for alms. These mothers, instead of being able to work for their honest livelihood, are forced to employ all their time in strolling to beg sustenance for their helpless infants, who as they grow up either turn thieves for want of work . . . or sell themselves to the Barbadoes . . . The old are every day dying and rotting by cold and famine, and filth and vermin, as fast as can be reasonably expected. And as to the young laborers . . . they cannot get work, and consequently pine away from want of nourishment . . ." Any history of Ireland will reveal that the social conditions which Swift denounced in the eighteenth century have prevailed in the main until our own day. Yet the concept of the happy Irishman dominated them, and has its power even now. We have here an excellent illustration of the formula which serves for the literary treatment of submerged peoples. The harsher their afflictions, the happier their dispositions. Sunshine through the rain!

The Negro, the Jew, the Irishman—comic standbys, enormously amusing. What difference does it make that theirs is a history of servitude, of persecution, of insult and shame? Let Cohen come out with his shrug and his loose garments; let Casey, bellicose and bibulous, with his clay pipe and shillelah, roar out his brogue; let Sambo, as in *If Booth Had Missed* smack his lips over "fried eels"; and then we can easily forget the wretchedness and the wrongs. These are not so difficult to forget, anyway, when seen from the outside by, let us say, one hundred per cent Americans.

One of the by-products of exploitation is the development in literature of a stereotyped character of the exploited, which guards the equanimity of the "superiors" and influences even the "inferiors" when they are unwary. This is one parallel that might be drawn from a consideration of the literature about the Negro, the Irishman, and the Jew. How one group, the Irish, set out to solve its literary problem might be worthy of our study.

Yeats writes that the dramatic movement he did so much to create belongs with those having for their purpose "the making articulate of all the dumb classes each with its own knowledge of the world, its own dignity." Such was necessary for Ireland. The Irish caricature had gone the rounds; a comic Paddy with a bare hint of truth in externals but a great deal of falsity in essentials, had been created by outsiders and copied by second-rate insiders to such an extent that he was taken for the real thing. He existed for the delectation of an English audience. His brogue, a mere phonetic distortion, not the true dialect, flattered their sense of grammatical superiority; his rags and odd garments, their sartorial correctness; his ignorance, their intelligence; his drunkenness, their sobriety; his freakishness, their normalcy. His mirth, his racial "laughter in spite of misery," did more than flatter, it soothed any whisperings of conscience. And his laziness did most—it justified their abuses.

Such writers as Yeats, Lady Gregory, and Synge set themselves to drive this figure off the boards. Yeats stated in his critical work that Ireland, a country largely of peasants, needed to have its peasantry understood rather than caricatured, explored rather than exploited. Lady Gregory stored up the folk-lore, saw the raciness and beauty of the folk-speech, and realized that instead of its being a thing for the culturally *parvenu* to ridicule, it could be fashioned into an instrument of marvelous literary effects. And Synge, fed up with the arty-art of Paris, having travelled with open eyes over the continent, came back to Ireland, recognizing that what had seemed *Irish* unkempt freakishness was not without cause, "nor did it prove the people freakish or inept; for other countries whose stories were similar were not different." He went into the huts of the people and lived with them; from this collaboration the literature of the world is the gainer, Synge developed from an imitative second-rater into a great artist, and Ireland has another star in her crown.

These pioneers had no suitable playhouse. The halls they were forced to use were without proper lighting for the stage, almost without dressing rooms, and with level floors preventing all but the people in the front rows from seeing properly. Their works were misunderstood by the people whose true character they wanted to show, and whose latent geniuses they wished to arouse and sustain. Riots were frequent when in contradistinction to the stereotype of the vaudeville stage they refused to set up plaster-of-paris saints. Friends were lost as well as won; government pressure was at times brought to bear upon them. But they had their own quiet heroism; they persevered; and today the players they trained, the plays they wrote, make up a cultural embassy from the Irish Free State to the world. Indirectly, for they believed that the creation of a literature was their calling more than the creation of propaganda, they advanced Ireland politically; certain it is that culturally their movement went step by step with Ireland's advance to independence.

Today, because of their efforts, and those of the young men they fostered, the world, except for such benighted sections as the audiences of vaudeville shows, recognizes the Irish, not as jumping jacks for childish laughter but as people with the same blunders, the same triumphs, the same farces, the same tragedies, the same ignorance and the same aspirations as the rest of humanity. It is one of life's ironies that this humanity ever had to be pointed out. But life seems to have a liking for such ironies. Masterpieces of Irish life belong now with the masterpieces of the world; Irish writers can now devote themselves to the search for truth about the Irish scene and the Irish people; men with the powers of Goldsmith, Sheridan, and Shaw do not need to feel now that only in London and in English literature is there any home for their abilities.

Differences between the histories of these two submerged peoples, the Irish and the Negro, are of course manifold and obvious. But one of their problems ran parallel to one of our own, and their solution deserves our deep attention. All of our philistines to the contrary, the reinterpretation of the Negro character in literature is not one of our least concerns.

More Odds

By STERLING A. BROWN

MR. EMBREE'S *A Few Portraits* present a range of Negro character; gamins on Canal Street (embryonic Mills brothers); the tenant farmer, Uncle Jeb, relic of antebellum and reconstruction days; Jake, on the larry gang in a cokeyard; hotel workers so graphically represented in Langston Hughes' *Brass Spittoons*; Prof. Burrus, the well beloved scholar of Fisk University; and Horace Mann Bond, the young intellectual, belonging to a new order of pioneers. Reading these sympathetic sketches when they appeared in the *Atlantic Monthly*, the chronicler hopefully looked forward to *Brown America's* including many more. This hope was not realized, but a rereading of these portraits together with "Odds Against The Nigger" has been of great suggestiveness.

> The Negro's life has flowed full and strong. In spite of toil and torment he has not wasted away nor become exhausted. Always there has been abundant energy, flowing over in spirituals and field songs, in laughter and dance, in sharp furious hates and loves, even in loud rhythmic moaning in sorrow. This exuberance, which has flowed so richly into folk art, is now beginning to find expression in more recondite forms: literature, drama, music, painting, all aspects of what are called the fine arts.
>
> From *Brown America*,
> by Edwin R. Embree

It suggests that to Mr. Embree's list of "Odds" there may be added another. And where as this is less immediate, less tragic than Mr. Embree's odds of disease, poverty, illiteracy, and crime, it is nevertheless far reaching in importance and deserving of attention. It is the odds against the Negro artist, who, according to Mr. Embree's "Soul and Soil" must interpret the life and the spirit of brown Americans. Remembering from the recent history of China, Ireland, Germany, and Russia, that a vigorous literary movement is part and parcel of social change, the chronicler does not feel that he must apologize for bringing in literary matters in crucial times.

The difficulties confronting the Negro artist are not those, thrice-told, of caged genius, ineffectual and sensitive, beating his wings against the bars of a cruel world. The Negro artist, like the artist of many minority groups, is betrayed often by what is false within. The hardship he faces is an alienation from Negro life, largely self-directed, although helped along by miseducation and social pressure. The danger he risks for this alienation is artistic aridity.

One Southern author, widely known for his composite pictures of peasant Negro life and character, stated to a literary group that he could get more material from the Negro folk than an educated Negro could. According to him, the condescension of the educated Negro, his collegiate accent and mannerisms build up suspicion and jealousy among the folk.

The chronicler interposes a demurrer to this now just as he did when he heard it. He believes that the final interpretation of Negro life must come from within, in spite of the evidence of excellent books about the Negro done by white socioogists, novelists and dramatists. He believes that the accent be it Harvard or Oxford can be easily discarded, that the mannerisms are seldom more than superficial, and that whatever sympathy a white author can bring to a collaboration can be equalled and increased by a Negro who *desires* the collaboration. Reception by the folk is not nearly so difficult as the desire to be received. But just there is the rub. All too frequently the Negro "intellectual" with one eye on the Nordic Babbitt, and the other on Babbitt's darker brother, doesn't wish to be "received." He is often like the singer who preferred Spanish folk-songs to Negro; who called the song of the Volga boatman a classic whereas Water-Boy was beneath contempt. He was so far removed from Water-Boy, he said.

The periodical punishments for being Negro that some of our intellectuals receive on Northern college campuses, the tabus that others meet with in our own schools, develop in them a snobbish disdain for the underprivileged and ignorant. Negro society often reenforces this. The Negro thinker and artist learns to sneer and gird at what he considers peculiarly "Negro," whereas any sort of perspective would reveal that these peculiarities can be found in any people similarly placed, and that they have *definite causes that must be understood.*

Reeducation, so necessary for us all, may serve as a corrective for our suicidal short-sightedness. It may bring about a consciousness of the common past of all Negroes, and our common destiny. Mr. Embree insists that the white world must dispense with its indifference to the "odds against the nigger." *Brown America* is a good step towards this. It is even more essential that the Negro should not add to these grievous odds by stupidly accepting at face value the contempt to be learned in certain sections of white America.

This is not a brief for folk-literature, or proletarian literature. But none of our artists even when they write of our upper middle class can afford an "aristocratic" disdain of our masses. After all, though it may be *lese majeste*

to say so, our elite is only one remove—even our "ritziest" only one and a half removes—from our masses. Nor does the chronicler believe that he is calling for a sentimentalizing of the Negro masses. What we need is not exploitation, but exploring; not idealizing but revelation. Finally, the chronicler recognizes the integrity and courage of many of our writers who *have* braved the Babbittry in interpreting the folk. But *their* strength is not the rule; and they are comparatively few in number. In the meanwhile our folk-lore and songs are being assiduously collected by white editors, and plays and novels about Negro life by white authors stir America and win Pulitzer prizes. Material in abundance exists; do our artists believe it to be so far beneath their notice? Has it been so easy, then, for school and society to fix in us a savage contempt for the rock whence we were hewn?

Local Color or Interpretation

By STERLING A. BROWN

JULIA PETERKIN has set herself the task of the literary cultivation of a specific locale. In four books and occasional articles she has recorded the folkways of the Gullah Negroes living on Blue Brook Plantation or its environs. There is no doubt of her sympathy with these people. "I like them," she says. "They are my friends and I have learned so much from them." And in *Living Philosophies* she repeats an admiration for their approach to life. There is no doubt of her deep knowledge of folk speech and lore. Guy Johnson writes that *Black April* might almost be called a source book of the folk beliefs of the South Carolina low country Negroes. Nor is there any doubt of her literary skill. The simplicity, seeming artlessness, and ability to get a milieu within the covers of a book, have all been highly and justly praised, and, when *Scarlet Sister Mary* appeared, won for her the Pulitzer Prize. She has been unhurried; she started writing in her maturity, and in a period of about seven years has given to the public only four books.

Her latest, *Bright Skin,* takes its name from a mulatto girl, the daughter of a white "gentleman" and one of the women of the plantation. But just as *Black April* was not so much about the character April as about the boy Breeze, so here the central character is not Cricket, the "bright skin," but the boy Blue. He is brought by his father, who is running away from his unfaithful wife, to the home of Cun Fred, overseer of the plantation. The initiation of Blue into the life of the section gives the author a great chance for some delightful local color. Fishing experiences, schooling, and country parties are described at some length, and seem the most interesting portions of the book. Blue falls in love with his bright-skinned cousin, saves her from "disgracement" when her mulatto groom does not show up for her wedding, and allows himself to be considered the father of her child, which is born out of due season. But the monotony of the place wears on Cricket. She has always yearned for the city. "*If I stay on here,* Blue, nothin ain' ahead for me but to dry up an' get sour like Aun' Missie. I'm a bright skin, Blue. People here holds it against me. Cooch says bright skin people stands well in town." When Blue goes to Charleston, Cricket follows, but coincidentally they do not meet. Cricket waits in Charleston for money from Blue; not receiving it, she goes on to Harlem. There she finds her cousin Man Jay, who runs a gambling joint, and her grandfather Reverend Africa, who runs a huge church and a cabaret on the side. Cricket becomes a famous cabaret dancer, "Princess Kazoola." Blue solaces himself on the dull plantation with Cooch. The converted Harlemites return to the plantation to get a "deevoce" so that Man Jay and Cricket may marry. Blue must give up his love. " 'Good-by, lil Cricket,' he whispered softly. 'Good-by, my lil star lily.' "

There are passages of genuine beauty, of humor, of melancholy, and of tragedy. But at times one wonders if there is not too highly selective an artist working on the material, with too great a fondness for the startling, the bizarre, the primitive, the *different.* One reader at least is apprehensive, fearing that beneath all of this there lurks some thesis. These items, in all probability, are true, just as the Harlem reports, in all possibility, may be. But whether the total picture is the truth, whether Blue Brook, or any other plantation, is like *this,* is still a question. At any rate the chronicler feels that the characters are not *all there.* Their motivation at their crises is scanty; and in general they approximate types. Sympathetic as this plantation owner may be to her folk, reportorial as she may be about their words and actions, one wonders how far inside her characters she can really get.

One does not wish Mrs. Peterkin to abandon her chosen region for a section which she can never know one-tenth so well. What she has gleaned from that field is a rich yield. One merely has the uncomfortable suspicion that she has harvested what she preferred, and that there are teeming fields still waiting the sickle. Selection is surely her prerogative, as an artist. But critics must be wary about saying that her harvest is the full yield. "Mrs. Peterkin knows the Negro" is the familiar dictum. It would be more accurate to say that she has carefully studied a certain section of Negro life, restricted in scope and in character, and that she has revealed skillfully and beautifully and from a single point of view the results of her study. That is about all one artist can do. Nevertheless, the point of view often determines the degree of understanding. And one is not always sure that Mrs. Peterkin has surmounted the difficulty of being a plantation owner.

Finally, it must be said, that any artist, in one book or in half-a-dozen, shows that he knows "the Negro" is of course a patent absurdity. "The Negro" does not exist; and he never did.

THE LITERARY SCENE
CHRONICLE AND COMMENT

A Poet and His Prose

By STERLING A. BROWN

THE poetry of Claude McKay belongs with the very best work produced by recent Negro authors. When his poems first appeared in this country he became, that which is most difficult, something of a poet of· the people. The chronicler has run across enthusiasts for his poems in as unexpected places as a hotel kitchen in Jefferson City and a barber shop in Nashville. The intelligentsia welcomed him as a harbinger. His poetry combined easy control of the most rigorous forms with independent and virile thinking. Here was no idle singer of an idle day, but a man deeply concerned with the bite and tang of actuality. Such a poem as "Two-An-Six" showed winningly the peasant life of his native Jamaica; "Flame-Heart" expressed beautifully the nostalgia for tropic scents and sounds and ways of life. But, in spite of his homesickness and although America "fed him bread of bitterness," he was fascinated by his new home. In "the ugly corners of the Negro belt" he found poetry, catching in poems like "Harlem Shadows" and "The Harlem Dancer" something of the Harlem that later exploiters left out. The social protest that aligned him with the old *Masses* and the *Liberator* gave power to "Tired" and "On The Road" and "America." The specialized oppression of his blood brothers he expressed in poems like "The White City," "In Bondage" and "The Lynching." And the much quoted "If We Must Die" was a stirring assembly-call, phrasing the Negro's growing rebelliousness and stimulating it to militancy.

The Harlem stories have a dispassionate objectivity that turns what might have been tragedy in *The Prince of Porto Rico* into a wry irony. The Gingertown* stories show greater sympathy. And whereas some are still chronicles of easy lovers and easy love the stories as a whole do give what one believes to be a composite picture of village and rural life in Jamaica. They are all leisurely narrative, without much dialogue, or dramatic twists, resembling the biographical style. One of these, *When I Pounded The Pavements*, the interesting tale

Gingertown, by Claude McKay. New York: Harper and Bros. 1932: Price, $2.50.

of a peasant lad who served on the constabulary but was unwilling to make an arrest is probably autobiographical. *The Agricultural Show*, rich in local color, is an unhurried picture of the social stratification of Gingertown. *Crazy Mary* tells the tragedy of the little sewing-mistress of the village, pretty and idealistic, lonely and frustrated. *The Strange Burial of Sue* deals with Miss Mary's antithesis, a Gingertown Scarlet Sister Mary who for all of her "free-loving" left behind her a reputation for kindliness. For all of the book's ·title and bookjacket, these are all of the Gingertown stories. The chronicler wishes that there were more. Not so dramatic as Walrond's, nor so colorful, nor with so sharp a sense of dialogue, they are nevertheless rich and warm, and give a rounded picture that helps one to understand why McKay is called the Burns of his island.

Nigger Lover is in the vein of *Banjo*. The scene is a southern port where yellow, brown, white, and black, Far Orient, Occident, African, and Mediterranean mingle. The sketch is of a white prostitute who, after her first affair with a Negro sailor where she finds kindliness instead of the brutality she was accustomed to, becomes enamored of Negroes.

Claude McKay is a· sensitive artist, and his prose is colorful and pleasing. He has brooded over the follies and the devotions of humankind with pity and understanding. If the high points of his fiction do not approach those of his poetry, he is still not an inconsiderable prose-writer. It is not difficult, however, for an admirer of his poetry to believe that as yet his work in fiction is not an adequate representation of his great abilities. Whether he should use these in depicting Harlem, or the well-beloved, understood peasant life of Gingertown, or the waterfront of Marseilles, or some new setting, or all of these combined, is up to Mr. McKay alone. But if he should select Harlem, let him be assured ʹthat he need never limit himself to those strait purlieus that he and others staked off in the rush, and worked exhaustively. There is other gold in other hills, thereabouts.

Signs of Promise

By STERLING A. BROWN

LENNOX ROBINSON, director of the Abbey Theatre, and himself a product of the greatest little theatre of them all, writes in his preface to the *University of Michigan Plays*.* "I have been this winter in the West, in Washington and Oregon, and have spoken in universities and colleges and normal schools which had classes in drama with very able insructors. . . . These universities, colleges and normal schools are making for themselves beautifully equipped theatres. They are beginning to create their own plays and players. . . . America is very proud of Paul Green who is a pupil of Professor Koch of the University of North Carolina. Professor Rowe's class in Ann Arbor, though it has not yet discovered its Paul Green, is doing as important work."

Three of the plays in the book thus prefaced deal with Negro life; and two of them, the work of Doris D. Price, have been presented by the Delta Sigma Theta Sorority. Both deal with folk-life in the South, and have a moving quality, one of them being singled out for praise by Mr. Robinson. The chronicler cannot always hear the dialect as Miss Price transcribes it, but he is perfectly ready to lay the blame upon his ear.

From a course at Illinois similar to Prof. Rowe's at Ann Arbor, there came two comedies of Negro life by James Butcher, a student under Professor Hillebrand, the author of one of the most practicable of manuals, *Writing The One Act Play*. Both of these are well handled and genuinely amusing. *Milk and Honey* has a delicate fancy and originality, and some of our little theatres could do far worse than try it out on the boards.

Courses in our own colleges may in time come to mean what Harvard's English 47 has meant to some American playwrights. Of course it is a moot question how much college courses can do for aspirant authors. Perhaps as one professor has said: "All that this course can teach

University of Michigan Plays, edited by Kenneth T. Rowe. George Wahr, Ann Arbor, Mich., 1932.

is the immense difficulty of writing anything well. "But if a course in writing teaches what *not* to do it has done something. There can be plays and stories as wrong as an eleven line sonnet—and it is essential, it seems, that some of us learn that.

Our colleges have not always been favorable to courses in writing. Within the not too distant past, the chronicler has known educators whose idea of literature was a concoction of Emily Post, the Boy Scouts handbook, and somebody's cyclopedia of quotations, and who knew that the *only* authors were dead authors and since his students were alive, authorship was out of the question, etc., etc. It is a sign of some progress, therefore, when colleges like Fisk and Howard endow chairs in creative composition. From Fisk has come the first *Miscellany: Selections from Work Done in the Course of Creative Literature*, which, as Professor James Weldon Johnson says, is "an earnest effort of artistic and creative powers." At Howard, the Stylus, founded long ago by Professors Alain Locke and Montgomery Gregory, has published a literary supplement which has its high points.

The least that may come from such collegiate interest in writing is a much needed group of recruits to a much needed literary audience; the best is a group of interpreters of our racial life. If only these young students will ponder what Lennox Robinson urges in the before cited preface: "how we owed our existence to the enthusiasm and hard unselfish work of a few people who passionately wanted something on the stage which the theatre of commerce did not give them; . . . how not to be afraid to write about poor people; not to be afraid of accent and dialect; how the materials of the American play were the sticks and stones lying outside the American door; how the Negro is part of their subject matter, or life in the Kentucky hills, or in some cottage by the sea, or in a tenement in New York or Chicago. . . ." Change the word play to story or poem or novel; the value of the lesson is the same.

THE LITERARY SCENE

CHRONICLE AND COMMENT

Amber Satyr

By STERLING A. BROWN

ROY FLANNAGAN is one of the newer Southern realists. An earlier novel of his, *The Whipp'ng*, was capably done, recording with a sardonic directness a vastly different South from that of the moonlight and magnolia legend. The same high qualities of accurate observation, irony and courage are to be found in this novel.* He has dealt here with a new theme, not only for him but for white novelists. He narrates, with matter-of-fact plausibility what up until now has been unwritten history—but history just the same—the importunate desire of a Southern white woman for a Negro, with the sequel that histories do record. It is likely that the shades of Thomas Nelson Page suffered agues when the book came off the press; Thomas Dixon, should he ever read it, would probably call back into service the Ku Klux Klan. But *Amber Satyr* does not rely on sensationalism; it is a quietly told, simple story, shot through with wry humor, and concluded with a tragedy unforcedly described.

Sarah Sprouse, married to a sickly irritating "cracker," is thrown into daily contact with Luther Harris, who does the chores upon her place. Luther is a stalwart, handsome bronze mulatto, part Indian; industrious, ambitous for his daughter, and nursing illusions of being considered better than a Negro because of his Indian blood. Sarah conveys her great desire for Luther by hints that grow almost into demands. Luther knows too much of the history of such relationships, however, and cannily avoids the lovesick Sarah. When finaly, on a stormy night, she comes to his house with a basket of victuals, a pint of liquor, and inclinations to stay, he rushes out—"into the night"—authors of very different seduction plots would have said.

The situation is fraught with tragedy, Luther flees to Richmond where he joins a group of Negro-Indians lobbying for recognition of their kinship to Pocahontas, jockeyed into doing so by smart white lawyers. We have here good journalistic reporting of some of the farrago of the attempted "race purity" bill. Luther tires of the waste of time and money, and in spite of

Amber Satyr, by Roy Flannagan. Doubleday Doran: Price $2.00.

certain insistencies decides to get back to see his daughter in the kind of place he knows. "*We ain't got no business down here makin' out like we's Indians. We ought to be home mindin' our business 'stead of mess'n' round up here in 'e city.*"

So he goes home although danger lurks there, attested by the love letters from the disappointed Sarah—letters which he cannot read. He recognizes the danger but he cannot stay away from home. And perhaps he can still dodge Sarah's advances.

But Sarah is not his only complication. She has been indiscreet about writing letters in a community where letter writing seems to be a state occasion. Her brother-in-law, Benjo, one of the most repulsive of the "crackers" in the novel (and in all the literature of crackerdom) has been doing a bit of backwoods sleuthing, starting it because of his lust for Sarah. He puts two and two together and gets three and one-half. Therefore, when Luther returns home, Benjo, and a third brother, the county sheriff, catch him at the train, search him, and find the incriminating letters. There is, of course, only one thing to do. They take the handcuffed Luther for a ride, and pump lead into him. The newspaper, in reporting the lynching, said: "Harris had been arrested on charges involving an unnamed white woman, and was being taken to the county seat from East Point station when the mob confronted the officer."

While brief, *Amber Satyr* still gives a remarkable picture of a social background. The squalor and shiftlessness of such "crackers" as the Sprouses (Sarah's letters are pitiful, ridiculous documents on the ignorance of the section) the defenselessness of the poor catspaw Negroes who are not allowed even to stick to their own rows in peace—all of these things are forcibly shown.

That a Southern white man has the courage to show this miserable state of affairs unflinchingly is one of the few things keeping this bitterness from going over into despair. It was not always so; perhaps the fact that intelligent realists are now recording these wrongs is a sign that they cannot go forever unrighted.

In Memoriam: Charles W. Chesnutt
By Sterling A. Brown

THE death of Charles W. Chesnutt on November 15th removes a figure from our midst who was as much a pioneer to our writers of fiction as was Dunbar to our poets.

Charles W. Chesnutt was born in Cleveland in 1858, and spent his childhood in that city. For a long time he lived in North Carolina, where he received his schooling, taught school, and stored up material he was later to use. After a brief journalistic career in New York, he returned to Cleveland in 1887, passing the bar and becoming a court stenographer. In 1927 he was awarded the Spingarn Medal for his "pioneer work as a literary artist depicting the life and struggle of Americans of Negro descent."

Mr. Chesnutt was the author of six books and several uncollected stories. He wrote a short biography of Frederick Douglass; two volumes of short stories: *The Conjure Woman* and *The Wife of His Youth*, and *Other Stories of the Color Line*; and three novels: *The House Behind the Cedars, The Marrow of Tradition,* and *The Colonel's Dream*. Of these the only easily available works are *The Conjure Woman*, recently issued by Houghton Mifflin (a story from which appeared in Calverton's Anthology) and the story *The Wife of His Youth* included in Cromwell, Dykes, and Turner: *Readings From Negro Authors*. The date of his last book is 1905.

As one who knows the vagaries of the critical mind might suspect, the name of Mr. Chesnutt is conspicuously absent from the books purporting to deal with American literature at the turn of the century. Professor Pattee's three comprehensive volumes on literature since 1870, the Newer American Literature, and the American Short Story, each of which has an index resembling a directory, do not mention Mr. Chesnutt, although Octavus Roy Cohen and Edgar Guest receive space. Even two other histories, noteworthy for their treatment of Negro authors as American, do not mention his name.

Against these omissions might be set the high critical praise of Mr. Chesnutt from such estimable critics as William Dean Howells, Joel E. Spingarn, and John Chamberlain. Carl Van Vechten has his character Byron say of Chesnutt: "This man had surveyed the problems of his race from an Olympian height and had turned them into living and artistic drama. Nothing seemed to have escaped his attention. He had surveyed the entire field, calmly setting down what he saw, what he thought and felt about it." Professor Spingarn writes: "He was the first Negro novelist, and he is still the best."

The Conjure Woman, stories from which appeared in "The Atlantic Monthly" is a book of folklore, done in the vein of Joel Chandler Harris and Thomas Nelson Page, but with its own individual excellences. Mr. Chesnutt's more representative work is in his novels. Here he shows the turbulency of Reconstruction times, with Hydra-headed prejudice raising its head throughout the land. The wrongs of the "prostrate South," and the glories of Ku Kluxery were the themes of the melodramas of Thomas Page and Thomas Dixon. Chesnutt is one of the few novelists who protested against their propaganda, presenting, often melodramatically it must be admitted, but always powerfully, the wrongs suffered by the new freedmen. The position of the octoroon in the South is charted in *The House Behind the Cedars*, the relationships between a white girl and her mulatto sister in *The Marrow of Tradition*, and another reconstruction "fool's errand" to reform the South in *The Colonel's Dream*. Mr. Chesnutt revealed the color prejudice within the group in *The Wife of His Youth*.

His ultimate position is indicated in this comment of John Chamberlain: "He pressed on to more tragic materials, and handled them as no white novelist could have succeeded at the time in doing. And before he lapsed into silence all the materials of the Negro novel and short story as a vehicle for dramatizing racial problems had made their appearance, either explicitly or through adumbration in his work."

He wrought well; and although his days of producing seemed already regrettably in the past, his death comes as a real loss to our literature. Another pioneer, and an able one, is gone.

215

THE LITERARY SCENE

CHRONICLE AND COMMENT

A New Trend
By STERLING A. BROWN

THE four books to be considered have already been reviewed in Opportunity, but the chronicler feels that since they illustrate an arising and important tendency in recent fiction of Negro life, they are worth further comment. They show an awareness of a different type of Negro from the pet of most of those who have turned to the interpretation of the Negro. A newcomer has been admitted to the gallery; now, in addition to those characters over whom cabaret hangers-on might murmur "how dionysiac," "how bacchanalian," and the local colorists "how odd, how quaintly amusing," there steps in the class, doubly oppressed because of his race. He has always been there to be studied, but until recently, literature took the cue from life and passed him by. In contrast to the fabulous eater of hog-jowl and greens, the happy-go-lucky come day, go day buffoon, there appears the tenant farmer, hardworking, but doomed to poverty,—bewildered and forgotten. With all of their differing emphasis, these four books agree on the wretchedness of his state, and the viciousness of the circle he must tread.

Inchin' Along deals with the tribulations of Dink Britt, a Negro farmer of Alabama. His enterprise and endurance, which set him apart from the thriftless, browbeaten Negroes and the shiftless crackers of the section, avail him little. His mulatto wife gives birth to the child of a young white aristocrat, and goes blind. The more hard-earned dollars Dink saves, the more he is hated by the white farmers. He conceives of buying land as the best use for his money. This is a dangerous example to the other Negroes; the tenant system must be preserved; and Dink is therefore disastrously tricked into buying some useless swamp land. This does not stop his "inchin' along." His unpopularity increases until he narrowly escapes being lynched. Dink's hardships in the main are a necessary result of the tenant system. A provident, independent Negro is an anomaly in a society whose motto, instead of the Latin upon state-houses, seems to be:

"Aught is a aught, figguh is a figguh,
All fo' de white man, and none fo' de nigguh."

Amber Satyr is in fundamental agreement with *Inchin' Along* in its showing the Negro to be a goat for the whites to ride. The lynching of a Negro because he struck the fancy of a white woman, while his daughter could with impunity be the plaything of the woman's brother-in-law, shows another of the bitter irregularities of present day race-relations. Luther, like Dink Britt, hoes his own row and tended to his own business, but that

was not enough. He, too, found that being poor and being a Negro carry their own penalties.

Free Born is a companion volume to Scott Nearing's *Black America*. It is a bitter novel setting forth the thesis of the exploitation of the Negro. There is irony in the title. Like *Inchin' Along*, *Free Born* suffers in that the enormous list of wrongs heaped upon the hero strains credence, but the propagandist might insist that only so can injustice be made sufficiently striking. What is certain is that the broad social picture is accurate and convincing. The story focuses attention where attention is needed. That the novel was unpublishable is significant; that it should remain unread would be a misfortune.

If *Free-Born* is the new *Uncle Tom's Cabin* of the new (?) slavery, *Georgia Nigger* is the *J'Accuse* of some of the principal features of that slavery. John L. Spivak has turned a searchlight on the darkness of peonage, the convict labor system, and prison conditions. They have been attacked before, but here, in the guise of a novel, we probably have a more powerful weapon than other factual, sociological studies. It is not that the book isn't factual; it is, but it concentrates its attack in a work of undeniable emotional power. David Jackson is a mere pawn in a desperate game. For a trifling misdemeanor he experiences the horrors of the chain gang and of peonage. Escaping from peonage, he is arrested, for vagrancy, although he has money in his pocket and is on his way to a job. The state and the planters both need cheap labor. He chooses the state's chain gang in preference to working out his time for another planter. It was an escape from hell to hell.

Arthur Brisbane, who generally teaches the man in the street what the man in the street already believes, has recently commented apropos of the Negroe's unfortunate environment: "This seems to offer an opportunity for missionary work more important to the Negro race than any mere effort to convince the colored man that he is as good as the white man or better." These books, which might be considered prescribed anti-toxin for such naivete, would probably state that if missionary work is to be done, the imposers of these conditions need it even more than the sufferers, and that one absolute necessity of any improvement is the overthrow of dogmas of inequality. But since keeping Negroes in wretched conditions, and propagating the belief that they belong there, have paid so well in the past, one might wonder at the efficacy, in these times, of even the best intentioned missionaries.

216

Alas the Poor Mulatto

By STERLING A. BROWN

GEOFFREY BARNES, in *Dark Lustre** writes another of the seemingly endless disquisitions on the tragedy of the poor, poor mulatto.

Aline, of the darkly lustrous body—darkly used in that comparative sense, since she is nearly always mistaken for white—is the child of a Southern aristocrat and a Negro servant (described as a pretty young girl on one page, and a sooty crone on the next). She has left the stupidity of Lexington, Kentucky, for Harlem, where, after restlessly trying job after job, and man after man, she becomes a model for Peter Brant, a sculptress. Aline sees in Peter the type of woman she longs to be and fancies herself Peter's *alter ego.* Therefore, when Peter's beloved Alan turns up, Aline realizes that he is the golden god she has been tormenting herself to find. Peter and Alan are timorous about marriage; Peter runs off to Bermuda to clarify her mind, and Alan rides up to Harlem to pacify his. At a cabaret he meets Aline; the liaison is not long in beginning. The return of Peter complicates the situation. The lovers are aghast, but there is no confession until in a very theatrical scene Alan is. forced by Peter to hold the nude model in his arms for a pose. Then Peter learns everything. But forgiveness for Alan follows. He and Peter decide to marry—so timed by the author that the wedding takes place the day Aline is confined to bear Alan's child. The melodrama is solved by Peter's last minute escape from the honeymoon suite on a liner, and by Aline's dying in the hospital, having given birth to another girl to continue the "cycle of Pain." The philosophical doctor, however, insists that "in time (probably through such liaisons) the stain will be absorbed." And there you are.

The wise-cracking Hemingway dialogue, and the hardboiled situations cannot disguise the melodrama and sentimentality of the book. Alan loses and regains his wealth opportunely, and Peter appears and disappears according to the needs of the story. Aline's pregnancy is

Dark Lustre. By Geoffrey Barnes. Alfred H. King, Inc. $2.00.

timed to concur with the desertion in the best tradition of tearful nineteenth century fiction. Alan and Peter are fairly plausible representatives of the self-worshipful wastrels of near-artistic Bohemians. There are proofs that the author knows something of Negro life: the porter 'spots' Aline as a Negro, the typical Harlemites are truculent toward the "Ofays," Negro artists are introduced by name in the story, and probably from some acquaintance. The attack upon Southern hypocrisy seems somewhat first-hand, although it was news to the chronicler that Negro and white children study in the same class-rooms in Kentucky.

Where the book absolutely falls down, of course is in its wild generalizing about the mulatto. The author says: "Her body was hybrid, nearly white, and beautiful. Her mind was hybrid, and too good for it . . . handed down by the Bassetts (her father's tribe). The more drinks Aline takes in the cabaret, the deeper she sinks into self-pity. Neither black nor white, she insists that she is nothing. She yearns to be either like one of the black harlots she sees, or like the white goddess Peter Brant. The old familiar mathematical formula is here —half-white, reason; half black, emotion. When Aline is driven by lust, it is the black uppermost; when sacrificial, and thoughtful, the white is triumphing. So runs the refrain. The chronicler submits that it is all nonsense.

There may be Alines, worshipful of narcissistic whites, torn by a disgust at their Negro blood. Perhaps a number do yearn for the heaven of white leisure class dilettantism. But to generalize from a weak sentimentalist, from an obvious "sport" such as Aline, about the millions of mulattoes (and our author has done this) is as sensible as to generalize from Peter Brant and say that all white women run away from marriages, and that therefore the white race is doomed to extinction. Dark Lustre merely repeats the hackneyed 'tragic mulatto,' stereotype, without any added insight. But it may serve its purpose; it does cater to the conceit of a dominant group, which for all of its self-assurance seems to have great need of flattery.

Time For A New Deal

By Sterling A. Brown

BOOKS like *I am a Fugitive* and *Cabin in the Cotton*, movies taken from them, or illustrating similar material, Faulkner's works and Caldwell's are today focusing attention upon the impoverishment, backwardness, and wrongs of the poor whites in the South; Spivak's *Georgia Nigger* and Nearing's *Free Born* have concentrated upon the even more prevalent inhumanity to the Negroes. *The Southern Oligarchy* by William H. Skaggs* goes a long way towards explaining much of what these books have illuminated. The book is as timely now as when it was written; the menace to America's boasted democracy is by no means quieted, and the prophecies implicit then are today direly coming to pass. *The Southern Oligarchy* is well worth immediate and serious concern.

Mr. Skaggs, an Alabaman, imputes the gross evils of the South, whether historic or contemporary to an "oligarchy," which rides roughshod over the masses of the people. This oligarchy, in antebellum days, was composed of the slave-owning aristocracy, of whom Lincoln wrote: "The slave-breeders and slave-traders are a small, odious, and detested class among you; and yet in politics they dictate the course of all of you. . . ." In the Reconstruction, the oligarchy was composed by venal opportunists who used the "bugaboo of Negro domination" to bring about a Solid South. Today, the oligarchy is composed of "bankers, landlords, and lawyer-politicians" all of them, to Mr. Skaggs, parallel to the "kings, nobles, and priests" who "literally devoured the common people" before the French Revolution.

The results of the shrewd scheming of this oligarchy are disastrous. With a wealth of detail, Mr. Skaggs presents the shameful record of illiteracy, squalor, political corruption, the fee system, convict labor, peonage, the Ku Klux Klan, appalling crimes in general, and lynchings in particular. This is a familiar account to most Negroes, since they are so deeply involved, but to see a native Southerner writing

*"The Southern Oligarchy," by William H. Skaggs. The Devon-Adair Company. $4.50.

of it is unfamiliar. Moreover, his laying the responsibility for these evils squarely upon the shoulders of the "oligarchy" is important. No longer can apologists blame the shiftlessness of their section finally upon the poor whites, for these have been kept poor and shiftless for a definite reason; and the white man's burden, which the Negro is supposed to be, is discovered by Mr. Skaggs to be resting where most white men's burdens—less figurative—generally rest—on the Negro's back.

The naive notions of an idealistic South introduced to corrupt politics in the Reconstruction are exploded in this book. In the early nineteenth century all sorts of venality were practised, e. g. grounds allocated for state schools, were parcelled off and sold for the benefit of "oligarchs," Tillman, Vardaman, Cole Blease, the Kingfish, are not phenomena peculiar to our day; they are in a long line of legitimate descent from the giants of "more cultured" days. There was, in those days too, blatancy, vulgarity, cheapness, and crookedness. To effect certain ends, all oligarchs, whatever their period, adopt certain means. If the people suffer, well, what else are the people for?

Mr. Skaggs is sympathetic to the Negro's sufferings and struggles. He attacks racial proscription, viewing this largely as the oligarchy's playing upon deep-seated fears which earlier oligarchs had instilled, in order to regiment a Solid South. In all of Mr. Skaggs' long catalogue of abuses, the wronged Negro has, as facts would naturally dictate, a prominent place. He shows abuses running from educational disadvantages, daily ignominy, peonage, injustice in the courts, and deprivation of rights to mob violence. *"Two generations in the South have been taught that Uncle Tom's Cabin was a wicked libel on the Southern people, and yet nothing related in the writings of Mrs. Stowe is as horrible and as atrocious as numerous crimes that have been committed in the Southern States every year for the past forty years."* Mr. Skaggs does not mean us to

(Continued on page 126)

TIME FOR A NEW DEAL
(Continued from page 122)

infer, however, that "lynching" is a product of Reconstruction; he gives proof of its vicious presence in antebellum days as well. Mr. Skaggs insists moreover, upon a fact not usually presented in the South: that less than one-fourth of the lynchings are due to assaults upon women.

Mr. Skaggs frequently points out that the South has no monopoly upon corruption, crime, and "man's inhumanity to man." For a Harlan, or Gastonia, there is of course a Detroit. But he does warn us that the abuses are more general, and more acute in the South, and penalties for speaking out against them are greater. At the end of his book, Mr. Skaggs seems to see something of promise, quoting, "Let the people know the truth and the country is safe." One is not completely convinced. In 1921, Governor Dorsey of Georgia wrote: "If conditions indicated by these charges should continue, both God and man would justly condemn Georgia more severely than . . . Belgium and Leopold for Congo atrocities." But, in spite of these courageous words, the atrocities have continued. Mr. Skaggs wrote his provocative book, revealing a great menace in 1924. It must have done good in awakening the public conscience then; it will assuredly do good now. But, in the meanwhile there are still peonage, Harlan, and Scottsboro. Is the "oligarchy" forever to remain in the saddle?

Smartness Goes Traveling

By STERLING A. BROWN

EVELYN Waugh, of a literary family, is one of the clever post-war English novelists. From novels of sophisticated London life, done with cynical flippancy, he now turns to the charting of little known countries and peoples. The ultra-civilized brings the Oxford-Piccadilly manner to bear upon East Africa. The incongruities to be expected are recorded in full measure in *They Were Still Dancing** and *Black Mischief.*** That the books are amusing is, of course, natural; it is likewise natural and unfortunate that their general tone should be one of cocksureness—the blase aesthetes have so very little to learn—and of ridicule mixed with disdain.

They Were Still Dancing recounts Mr. Waugh's experiences in Abyssinia at the time of the late coronation, and in neighboring countries such as Zanzibar and Kenya. Three of the five sections of the book are labelled "nightmares," but all of them produce a sort of Alice-in-Wonderland effect. The telling is graphic, with a liberal injection of malice. Purporting to tell the truth about the coronation in contrast to the lies of other correspondents, Mr. Waugh concentrates upon discomforts, dirt, jumble, bad architecture, mishaps, trains off schedule, appointments never kept, and loss of luggage. For all of its occasional social analysis the book is in the comic vein; some of its passages being farce, and most of them irony-directed at potentates, natives and "august gate-crashers" who graced the ceremony for purposes of commerce or political advantage.

This is said, by Mr. Waugh's publishers and himself, to be the "perfect travel book." It is undeniably skillful, but if one asks that a travel-book interpret a nation and the people as well as reveal the traveller's personality and vicissitudes, one could hardly consider *They Were Still Dancing* to be perfect. As a case in point, the soldiers of Mr. Waugh, with their bandoliers filled with empty shells and cartridges that do not fit the guns they carry, with their general rag-tail, bob-tail aspect, re-

*They Were Still Dancing, by Evelyn Waugh. Farrar and Rinehart, $2.50.
**Black Mischief, by Evelyn Waugh. Farrar and Rinehart. $2.50.

semble very little the soldiers, who at Adowa, in 1896 severely defeated an Italian army of 10,000 trained soldiers, and who over the many years have played a considerable part in keeping their nation the "last of free Africa." The curious fact of Abyssinia's Christianity, while it does call forth from Mr. Waugh a comment similar to Gordon MacCreagh's that here is probably an example of what primitive Christianity was like, is scantily treated in order that Mr. Waugh may stay at the center of the picture. A typical wise-crack occurs when Mr. Waugh annotates the "Ghiz" in this way: "The ecclesiastical language, unintelligible to all the laity and *most of the priesthood.* It is written in Amharic characters."

The book has its share, too, of Kipling's "white man's burden" brought up-to-date. Apologizing for the appropriation of Kenya by Britishers, Mr. Waugh writes: *"It is barely possible to explain to North Europeans the reality of race antagonism. . . . The fear of Indians, negroes, Japanese or Chinese obsesses one or other of all the branches of the Nordic race who . . . have exposed themselves to these strangers. Anglo-Saxons are perhaps worse than any. It is easy enough for Anglo-Saxons in London whose only contact with colored people is to hear gramophone records of spirituals or occasionally share a bus with a polite, brown student to be reasonable about the matter and laugh at the snobbery of their cousins in India or shudder at the atrocities of their more distant cousins in Virginia, but the moment they put on a topee, their sanity gently oozes away. . . . It is not a matter one can be censorious about. Gentle Reader, you would behave in just the same way yourself after a year in the tropics. . . . It is just worth considering the possibility that there may be something valuable behind the indefensible and inexplicable assumption of superiority by the Anglo-Saxon race."*

Mr. Waugh's *Black Mischief* can be understood in the light of the preceding passage. For in this book the natives are cast either in the roles of clowns performing hilarious antics in a *comedie bouffe,* or as bloodthirsty
(Continued on page 158)

Smartness Goes Traveling
(Continued from page 154)

cannibals producing a climax so horrible that its grotesqueness seems in line with the earlier farce. The book is diabolically clever. But it is another Alice-in-Wonderland story. Perhaps that removes the tragedy from real horror.

Like Paul Morand, Evelyn Waugh seeks out exotic lands and peoples and makes literary copy of them. Cosmopolitan in experience, talented, superficially ironic and advanced, nevertheless, his point of view is essentially that of the poor stay-at-home who in his snug domesticity mumbles nightly as the chief article of his creed: "Oh Lord, what a swell fellow am I!"

THE LITERARY SCENE
CHRONICLE AND COMMENT

John Brown: God's Angry Man

By Sterling A. Brown

TO the chronicler, *God's Angry Man** superbly justifies what, by its abuse, has been open to attack: the novelists' interpretative re-creation of biography and history. Here we have what we believe to be the essential John Brown. The magnetism of John Brown, while alive, drew the youthful dreamer, the rebel, the cynic, the marauder, the churchman, the soldier of fortune, the scholar; and now even though he is dead, his magnetism draws the minds of men. In this portrait, more nearly life-size than Benets' admirable characterization, we get something—a great deal—of the thrill that Thoreau and Kagi knew, that electrified Watson and Oliver Brown to give up cherished wives and children, that even J. E. B. Stuart and Lee must have recognized at Harper's Ferry.

The man of this book differs greatly from the horse stealing, homicidal fanatic in the latest biography of Brown, done by Robert Penn Warren. Yet Leonard Ehrlich's Brown is not conceived in the spirit of blind hero-worship. The horrors of Bloody Kansas are not palliated; Mahala Doyle, wife of one of Brown's first victims is as sympathetically interpreted as poor Mary Brown—Jason Brown the lover of peace as much as Owen Brown the blind devotee of his father. There is no undue partisanship. But there is deep understanding. The tragic events of a confused period: the eye-for-an-eye ethics of the border, the sufferings of the women whose hopes of security and happiness were shattered against the flint-like logic of an old man's dream, the irony of the fact that the first victim of Brown's raid to free Negroes was the free Negro, Hayward, the failure on the part of Negroes to join the man whose attempt to free them was to lead him to the gibbet—all are here, in graphic, vigorous and beautiful prose. But above them all towers, as in real life he towered, the figure of John Brown, a mystic who believed in a God-given task and relentlessly pursued it to its

*God's Angry Man, by Leonard Ehrlich. New York: Simon and Schuster, 1932. $2.50.

end—sacrificing for its achievement what men call blessed — driven by the dominant belief that slavery was evil, and that only blood could wipe away its wrongs.

"All this bloodshed, then, this violence, how in Heaven's name do you justify it?" (asked the governor at his trial.)

"Upon the Golden Rule, sir. I pity the poor in bondage that had none to help them. That's why I am here. Not to gratify any personal revenge or vindictive spirit. It's my sympathy with the oppressed and the wronged, that are as good as you and as precious in His sight. And I want you to understand, gentlemen"— here the old man raised himself a little—"I want you to understand that I respect the rights of the poorest and weakest of colored people oppressed by the slave system, as much as I do those of the most wealthy and powerful. . . . Ay, let me say furthermore, that you had better, all you people of the South, prepare yourself for a settlement of that question. . . . You may dispose of me very easily. I'm nearly disposed of now. But this question is still to be settled. This Negro question, I mean. The end of that is not yet."

The portraiture of the subsidiary characters is brilliantly executed: Kagi, for whom the gaunt avenger supplies the need for something to believe in; Oliver, fretting against the tyranny of his father and yet drawn to him; Higginson, the bearded abolitionist, refusing to flinch when most of the cautious Northerners fled; Thoreau, who saw in Brown the embodiment of his philosophy of anarchy. The Negro characters are done with fine sympathy. These are some of them: Frederick Douglass, willing to use violence against slavers but not against a government arsenal, realizing the bitter fact that too many Negroes, broken by slavery, wanted only "hot yams and a roof and not to be beaten"; Harriet Tubman the splendid, nearest to John Brown in character, a Moses, wanted "dead or alive, and ten thousand dollars would be paid for the body";

(Continued on Page 187)

JOHN BROWN: GOD'S ANGRY MAN

(Continued from Page 186)

William Still, who knew more about the "Underground" than any man in the land, who said to Brown, "You free them; I'll lead them out"; John Anthony Copeland, mulatto student at Oberlin, who left his garret lamp of learning for an even finer light; Dangerfield Newby, whose wife in the far South was never to be redeemed; and finally 'Emperor' Green, who after the night-long argument, between Douglass and Brown said only, "I b'lieve I go wid de ole man."

This is a moving book about a great subject. For the modern timorous mind, it is difficult to believe that men such as John Brown ever existed, or acted from the motives that were theirs. Therefore, biographers have tried to explain Brown as a maniac, or an egotist, whose chief desire was to be 'head of the heap.' Such a discounting of the motive of burning resentment at oppression, a resentment not satisfied with mere humanitarian well-wishing is an indictment of our days. It is just because John Brown did have such a resentment that today, for all appearances to the contrary, "his soul goes marching on. . ."

THE LITERARY SCENE
CHRONICLE AND COMMENT

Banana Bottom

By Sterling A. Brown

CLAUDE McKAY'S poems interpreting Jamaican life, such as "Two An' Six" and those revealing a nostalgia for that life such as "Flame-Heart" are probably not so well known as his militant challenges, but they undoubtedly belong with the best of his poetry. In *Gingertown*, a book of short stories published last year, the sketches of Mr. McKay's native island were, to one reader at least, the most richly rewarding of the volume. Now Mr. McKay returns to Jamaican subject matter in his third and most successful novel. A quiet story, quietly told, *Banana Bottom* really approaches originality more than his Harlem fiction did. Mr. McKay seems really at home in this province; it is hardly likely that any novelist would be more so.

Banana Bottom is a novel of character and setting. The plot is of the simplest. And although there is a motivating idea, it is not unduly stressed. There is nothing of the preachments that, in *Banjo*, edged uncomfortably close to the Messianic. The book is written in a leisurely manner suiting the life portrayed better than the staccato rhythms of *Home to Harlem* would have done.

Bita Plant as a child was raped by a troubadour of the island, Crazy Bow, half-crazy but a musical genius. To lessen disgrace, Bita was adopted by the Reverend Malcolm Craig and his wife Priscilla, and when old enough, was sent to England to be educated. We see her life traced from the time when "wearing a long princess gown, and with her hair fixed up in style" she returned to Jamaica—an excellent musician and a developed personality. Her education, strangely to her religious sponsors and to even some of her own people, opened her eyes to the rich quality of her native life. Her perception was quickened by Squire Gensir who was an enthusiastic student of Jamaican folk-ways. The Craigs selected Herald Newton, a theological student, for Bita's husband, hoping all the time that Bita could be made a replica of themselves. Newton, detected in a disgraceful aberration, fled the scene. But the chance solution of this problem did not end

the conflict between the Craigs' soft domineering and Bita's intention to be herself. Finally when the outlines of the straitjacket became too visible, Bita rebelled and returned to her parents. Out of pique at the restrictions of life at the mission, Bita had taken up with one Hopping Dick Delgado, a peacock of the district, and finally believed herself in love with him. Her canny parents quickly showed her the real quality of the peacock, and the book closes with Bita's marrying Jubban, a steady, hardworking, upstanding peasant of a stock which Mr. McKay obviously respects.

This plot exists more as a framework for the characterization of many interesting folk figures than in its own right. We see Sister Phibby Patroll, sharp-tongued gossip and trouble-mixer; Anty Nommy and Jordan Plant, Bita's parents; Yoni Legge, who out of desire for a fine wedding postpones the ceremony until after her child is born; Belle Black, whose fine voice is raised as a church singer, but who likes her "tea-parties" quite as well; Squire Gensir, one of the few whites of the island who got to know the people because of his uncondescending admiration for them; Hopping Dick and Tack Tally, lady killers; and last but not least Crazy Bow. All of these are ably sketched. Mr. McKay insists that all of them are imaginary, but they all have the ring of real life.

The picture of the folkways of the people is similarly convincing. Life on this island seems a quiet pastoral. Occasionally sensational incidents break the easy tenor of life in *Banana Bottom*—Tack Tally's suicide, the obeah-man, and the fall from grace of Herald Newton being examples—but, for the most part things seem to flow easily. Mr. McKay describes, with what seems remarkable memory since, according to reports, he has been away from Jamaica a long time, the dances, revivals, the marketing, the small town gossip, the school affairs, the color complications, the folkways such as the hawking of ballads, the ordinary life of the villagers and farmers. The dialect sounds true;

(Continued on Page 222)

BANANA BOTTOM

(Continued from Page 217)

in places it is rich in humor and shrewd wisdom.
The flowers, fruits, and garden produce of the
rich bottom-land are described frequently and
with a great deal of charm.

But against this idyllic background, Mr.
McKay does impose one problem: how far
should the "missionary" attitude toward
Negroes be allowed to go. Bita did have a
great deal to thank the Reverend and Mrs.
Craig for. She realized the value of the education and development they had made possible
for her. The question arises: should gratitude
for those values mean the abnegation of one's
own personality? To this question Bita, and
Mr. McKay, answer firmly in the negative.

From The Southwest
By Sterling A. Brown

TONE *The Bell Easy* (Texas Folk-Lore Society, Austin, Texas, $2.00) is the tenth annual publication of the Texas Folk-Lore Society. The editor is J. Frank Dobie, author of *Coronado's Children* and other authoritative books on the Southwest.

Besides having two articles devoted to him, the southwestern Negro bobs his head up unexpectedly throughout the book which includes legends of southwestern heroes, witch tales, and studies of folk cures, surviving British Ballads, and white camp-meeting spirituals. In "Old-Time White Camp Meeting Spirituals, Samuel E. Asbury and Henry E. Meyer align themselves with such critics as George Pullen Jackson who insist that the little known white spirituals are the melodic, harmonic, and textual sources of the Negro spiritual. Mr. Asbury says this does not mean that the white spiritual is equal or superior to the Negro spiritual, although he finds two white spirituals more beautiful than most Negro spirituals and the equal of "Deep River" and "Motherless Child." He adds: "But the words of the best white spirituals cannot compare as poetry with the words of the best Negro spirituals." This is borne out partly by a song, "Jesus Gonna Make Up My Dyin' Bed," included by Martha Emmons in "Dyin' Easy" an article dealing with the folk-Negro's attitude to death. From this song the title of the volume is taken.

The longest contribution is a collection of slave tales "Juneteenth" by J. Mason Brewer, a professor at Samuel Huston College. The word "Juneteenth" stands for the nineteenth of June, Emancipation Day in the Southwest. "Squirming Out" is a group of tales showing the slave's artful dodging, "At the Prayer Tree" his comic misadventures when he took to his knees, "Bear and Other Boogies" when he took to his heels from bears and graveyards, and "Jes' Lak A Fool Niggah" his grotesquely fatal misunderstandings. Variants of many of these stories are to be found in Pickens's *American Aesop, Cold Blue Moon*, dialect poems, and probably around urban and rural barber-chairs. There is an abundance of watermelon and chicken stealing. As Mr. Dobie points out they smack of Thomas Nelson Page; as a witness to the relationships between master and slave the chronicler conceives them to be unreliable, as a group of jokes must be. There is a store of folk-tales of slavery which do not so unfailingly dwell on the jocund; the chronicler has heard some even from Brazos Bottom.

Mr. Brewer seems somewhat exercised over the vogue of "Harlem realism." His insistence that "the Harlem representation of the Negro is false to the Negroes of the South and Southwest" would gain the eager assent, I imagine, of the "Harlem realists." To say that Harlem Negroes are "false to" Brazos Bottom Negroes is to say no more than that the latter are "false to" Pittsburgh Negroes. So what? Surely Mr. Brewer does not wish us to infer that the Negroes he portrays approximate more closely that mythical non-entity "*the* Negro." As large as Texas may be, there are still fifty-six other varieties of Negroes for the asking.

In *Negrito* (San Antonio: Naylor Co., $1.50) Mr. Brewer attempts a cross section of Negro life in Brazos Bottom. The work is in dialect, rendered painstakingly. Barbershop, poolroom, lodge meeting, Rosenwald school, 'Juneteenth' celebrations, County meets, barbecues, etc., are grist to Mr. Brewer's mill. He obviously knows thoroughly the life of which he writes. One doubts, however, that he has made it artistically his own; there is too great a reliance on Dunbar. The tone is unconvincingly comic-pastoral. The harsh edges that life in Brazos Bottom *does* have are smoothed over by a native son's optimism. At their best they are amusing, as were the slave stories, and contain some shrewd cracks; but occasionally they seem to miss their point. The book is prefaced by one Dr. L. W. Payne, Jr., professor of English in the University of Texas, who, according to the publisher's announcement, "is ample authority for Professor Brewer's qualifications to depict the Negro." The Chronicler is puzzled over that sentence; not about the "qualifications of Professor Brewer," but about the "ample authority" part. He knows what the words mean, but he can't make any sense out of them. He just can't.

THE LITERARY SCENE
CHRONICLE AND COMMENT

Kingdom Coming

By STERLING A. BROWN

WITH the best intentions, blurbists often are enemies to the books which they blurb. The bookjacket to *Kingdom Coming** promises "*a side of the Civil War never before seen. We see New Orleans now invested with Union troops and at one end a huge concentration camp of 'freed negroes.' It is the story of these waifs of freedom that Roark Bradford tells.*" All of this is misleading, to say the least. The Civil War is one of the minor concerns of this book, and the side never before seen is not clear. A Red River antebellum plantation is the locale of the best part of the narrative, New Orleans being dragged in as a mere backdrop for an unconvincing theatrical ending. These are not quibbles. Checking up on inaccuracies like these might cause reviewers to be wary of such wide statements as "Mr. Bradford has written the true story of slavery and the true story of freedom." To ask that any book of three hundred and seventeen pages should tell the true story of slavery and of freedom when there are millions of such stories, each equally true, is to make an order on Mr. Bradford, that, with all of his ability, he cannot fill.

Throughout all of Mr. Bradford's works we have had skillful reporting and interpreting and arranging, from a narrowly specialized point of view, of selected features of a segment of Negro life. *The* Negro has never been there, any more than he has been in the books of Mr. Bradford's talented fellow authors. It is careless thinking to consider *Kingdom Coming* a wide canvas showing finally "the" Negro of slavery and of freedom. *Kingdom Coming* is, thankfully, no such ambitious work. It tells the story, quiet mainly until the discordant blare at the end, of *a* Negro family, set only casually against a background of slavery and emancipation.

Messenger, with his horse racing and coach-driving days behind him, is exiled from New Orleans to Wilkins Bend Plantation, there to oversee the horses and mules. He is accompa-

*Kingdom Coming, by Roark Bradford, Harper & Bros., $2.50.

nied by Telegram, his son and pride, and Crimp, his wife, who is carrying a second child. Unknown to Messenger, Crimp's condition is the cause of his banishment; his master does not want any "light-skinned" babies born in his aristocratic house, and he suspects that Crimp's second child is his grandchild. When the mulatto baby is born, Messenger's deep fondness for his wife turns to hatred. Dissuaded from murder and even wife-beating by Aunt Free Dahlia, he turns to a relief he has postponed, and takes to the "underground." In his case, the "underground" is "blind," and he is killed by the unscrupulous agents, who were stealing off slaves to resell them. Telegram is left to the tutelage of Aunt Free. He becomes the best teamster of the quarters. But tragedy stalks him as well. He marries Penny, takes her to New Orleans when the war breaks up the plantation, and loses her to a voodoo cult. She changes swiftly from a likeable "Penny" to a sinister voodoo queen—"Madame Mo-ree," and for sacrificial purposes, kills her own baby. The melodrama here is pretty bad. Messenger avenges his son, kills Penny with a brick, and, refusing to talk, is executed by a Yankee firing squad. He doesn't understand what is being done to him. "*Henry had said the Yankees mumbled words over Negroes when they set them free. . . . Then the soldier with the pistol said the last word of the charm that set Grammy free. He heard a rumble and roar . . . and he landed squarely in the middle of Free Heaven, right on the lap of the Sweet God A'mighty King Jesus.*"

This closing passage might be disregarded, were its implications not supported throughout by Aunt Free, who having bought her freedom, doesn't want it, urging that only in Heaven can true freedom be found—"When de good Lawd sets you free." We are supposed to believe, according to some reviewers, that because one Negro, under peculiar circumstances, is shot by a firing squad, freedom for the Negro is a tragedy. This is silly, and if Mr. Bradford intends his book to be allegorical in this fashion, he invalidates a work that does have elements of truth and beauty. Nullify freedom, because some "waifs of freedom," unadjusted in a detention camp, turn to voodoo practise, is like nullifying the colonizing of America because the witches sabbath had devotees in New England, or like suggesting that the whites of Mr. Bradford's native state be enslaved because faith healing prospers there. *Kingdom Coming* is better read as a good story, spoiled at the end, of two fine, though simple souls, who happened to be married to the wrong women.

The book does not break new ground. Stribling's *The Store* and *The Forge*, Evelyn Scott's *The Wave*, and Ehrlich's *God's Angry Man* are to the reviewer more comprehensive, less particularized, pictures of slavery and freedom. The "blind underground," supposed to be a different feature has received fuller attention in Christopher Ward's *The Strange Adventures of Jonathan Drew*. Slavery, in Mr. Bradford's version, is for the most part easygoing, and heaven knows this isn't new. Some callousness is seen, and some cruelty; almost all of the slaves desire freedom, "The North Star" being their symbol of hope. But they do not understand it, and there is the suggestion that true freedom for them is unattainable, because of their own deficiencies. Concubinage is frequent, but even its admission doesn't keep the book from veering at times perilously close to the "antebellum Arcadia" stereotype.

All in all, Mr. Bradford's slave plantation doesn't differ greatly from his contemporary levees and cotton farms. The scenes don't seem to be historically set; a few uniforms and swords aren't enough to make this a period novel. Mr. Bradford might mean this to prove that the freed Negro is no better off than the slave. In certain sections, especially those Mr. Bradford knows so well, this is near to the truth. But the corollary, that these "poor waifs" are not ready for freedom, hardly follows. Instead of the Negro's unfitness, what such a condition proves is the South's unwillingness to grant freedom in fact, and *its* unfitness to serve as guardian for "poor waifs."

Kenneth Burke, in an interesting essay, has distinguished between the Negro as symbol of "contented indigence" and the Negro as symbol of power. The first, "naive, good-natured, easily put upon" is endearing, and elicits "white warmth," having the "loveableness of the incompetent." The second is more troubling, more perplexing. Mr. Bradford is a pastmaster at the portraiture of the first. Knowing folk-speech and folk-ways (his handling of mules in this book is as expert as Telegram's) with the genius of a humorist, and in this case, a new willingness to see deeper than laughter, he has nevertheless confined himself to one type of the Negro. There were many others, even on Red River plantations. Before Mr. Bradford can be considered a historian of "the" Negro in slavery or in freedom, before he can be called the author who "knows the blacks of the deep South better than perhaps anybody else writing today" he must repair his omissions. There were not only bewildered Telegrams and otherworldly Aunt Frees on these plantations; Frederick Douglass had brothers there, Harriet Tubman sisters, who did not have the chances to escape, but who kept their spirit unbroken. And freedom for such as these was no tragedy.

Arcadia, South Carolina
By STERLING A. BROWN

ROLL, Jordan, Roll is the work of two well known collaborators, Doris Ulmann, the photographer, and Julia Peterkin, the novelist. From over one thousand studies of the American Negro done by Doris Ulmann, seventy full page photographs have been selected for the book, Julia Peterkin says of her accompanying text: "I have tried to put down here things which will give as full a picture of Negro life in the South as I am able to give, matters which I want to see in print before they are forgotten." The publishers insist that *Roll, Jordan, Roll* is a powerful picturization of *the* Southern Negro; doing for the Southern Negro what *Humanity Uprooted* does for the modern Russian. Their insistence does not persuade.

Julia Peterkin's "Negro life in the South" needs greater explicitness; the section she deals with is very much in need of definition. At times she mentions a "county," and one imagines her to be writing again of Blue Brook plantation and its environs. At other times she speaks generically of the Southern Negro. Perhaps for "Southern" Mrs. Peterkin wishes "South Carolinian." Yet even this view cannot be supported entirely, for in her narrative of "The Dreamer," she repeats, with only minor changes, the legend which Carl Carmer published in *Opportunity* for March, 1932 under the title "The Prophetess of Eutaw." According to Mr. Carmer the setting of this legend is around Eutaw and Demopolis, Alabama. The reader of *Roll, Jordan, Roll* is perplexed as to his whereabouts; signposts would be much in order. As it stands it is risky: for the unwary, who may be misled, and for the knowing, who may be startled.

Yet even if we place this River Jordan geographically, setting it in the part of South Carolina that Mrs. Peterkin obviously knows, we do not believe a "full picture" of Negro life of the vicinity has been given—not if the word full has any suggestion of completeness. The types shown are for the most part simplified: loyal, fatalistically resigned Uncles and Aun-

* Roll, Jordan, Roll, by Julia Peterkin and Doris Ulmann. Robert Ballou, Publisher. New York. $3.50.

ties, mistrusting civilization as much as Mrs. Peterkin herself, suspicious of the printed word; the old share cropper who had thirty 'yard' children with an indeterminate number of others; the old auntie who forgot how many children she had had but remembered, by their given names, every one of the many white children she had nursed; the young servant who worships his chivalrous master; the wild bucks, the girls who slash or conjur their errant lovers. These primitive folk "*do not build or run machines, they have no books or newspapers . . . radios or moving pictures . . . but they have leisure to develop faculties of mind and heart and to acquire the ancient wisdom of their race.*" . . . "Better to be poor and black and contented with whatever God sends than be 'vast-rich and white and unrestless,' " runs their philosophy.

All of these items are demonstrably true, but that does not mean that Mrs. Peterkin's picturization is full. And so it is with her generalizations about Negro character. 'The children are precocious up to fourteen, then they lose their aptness.' Mrs. Peterkin might tell us something of their opportunities for schooling at that age. To her, the Negro has a 'short memory for sorrow' and is endowed with a blessed lightheartedness. It is possible that in their cabins at night, when the lady of the big house is not around, they remember their grief. What might be the underlying causes of Negro character as she expounds it, other than divine *fiat*, she does not tell. When Mrs. Peterkin started writing, she was expected to go beyond Thomas Nelson Page.

What are the omissions, the underemphases in this book? Mrs. Peterkin writes: "Few of the old slaves are alive now, but they like to talk about the glories of past days. The hardships of slavery have faded from their memories and they often express a wish for its advantages." Other dwellers in this Arcadia have heard ex-slaves say the exact opposite. Which is the truth. Perhaps the same ex-slave could say both, his answer depending upon his hearer's wishes. Doris Ulmann has included some excellent pictures of the chain-gang. But Mrs.

Peterkin avoids discussion of this. She writes: "Fear of the law and the chain gang is extreme . . . although courtesy and kindliness are the law of the land." Let us assume that the land is Mrs. Peterkin's neighborhood. In the Congaree section of the same state, not so far away, E. C. L. Adams has recorded the monstrous perversions of Southern justice and the Negroes' cynical knowledge of them (cf. *Nigger to Nigger*); DuBose Heyward has dealt with the same (cf. *Mamba's Daughters*); across the state line is the scene of Spivak's *Georgia Nigger;* a little farther to the west is Scottsboro. Certainly 'this land,' wherever it is, is not representative of the South.

The bookjacket promises a tale of Uncle Mose, "well over ninety years old, captured in the African bush . . . brought to America . . . in the stinking hold of a slave ship." My copy of the book must be defective, for I cannot find Uncle Mose. Instead I find another Uncle, one hundred and eleven years old, archtype of all hat-in-hand Uncle Toms; jeering at the Yankees, whom he blames for slavery; calling Abraham Lincoln 'poor white trash' whose Civil War was based on jealousy of the 'bredded' Southern whites; seeing cause for his own abjectness in Noah's curse on Ham; subscribing in short to all the beliefs of his fellow revisionists of Southern history. Such a substitution for Uncle Mose's "stinking slave ship" is indicative.

Poverty is lightly touched upon. Negro "field hands are pitifully improvident and wasteful"; one of them, accustomed to going barefoot, wears his shoes all day Monday because of his love of display! One of the good workers "expects good pay (!) and asks nine cents an hour for himself and the same price for his mule and cart." . . . One does not believe Mrs. Peterkin to be ironic here. "Free school starts after all the crops are gathered, and ends when field work starts in the spring"; that is four or five months at best. Mrs. Peterkin is not indignant; perhaps she believes this is as it should be. Should be for whom? Occasionally Mrs. Peterkin mentions the hard lot of Negro life in the South. But the cause of hardship is always left vague. "Plantation days may be hard sometimes if *the moon gets contrary* and causes trouble in the world, but they are never monotonous to these people who love life too well ever to find it dull." "Their struggle for existence has been unrelenting and their stories and songs teach the children to look for victory from the disadvantages *to which life has sentenced them, when death takes their souls to*

heaven." Life alone, or the moon, is to blame; never exploitation, never injustice. There is hope, but only in bright mansions above. *"In return for faithful work and loyalty they expect the white owners to help them settle their difficulties, provide them with land and with homes, and protect them from injustice whenever the law threatens them with punishment for wrongdoing."* The word "owners" is exact. At last we have located our Arcadia. It is the slave-holding section of the present day South.

The pictures in the book are lovely, and reveal a great deal of the beauty of the country, and the dignity and character of the folk. Looking upon Doris Ulmann's selections, one realizes the difficulty facing an artist in words who wishes to get at the essential truth of the lives of these people. Comprehensive understanding only can do them justice; Mrs. Peterkin's selection of incidents and types is more rigorously narrowed than Miss Ulmann's. Mrs. Peterkin's descriptive catalogues of superstitions, nature-craft, and folk cures are the most authoritative part of her contribution; her short stories probably the best; but her direct exposition of Negro character and the milieu is far less secure. She undoubtedly loves the ancient wisdom and beauty of these primitives who are out of touch with the machine age, and she can convey this love. The happiness she feels at gazing on the picture, however, makes her transmit a happier quality to the picture than others might see. In her personal dealings with the people on her plantation she is in all likelihood a kindly mistress. But kindliness is not enough. These people pay for their quaintness by their—at best—semi-enslavement. And even for quaintness, this is too much to ask.

John Davis, recently returned from a trip to the South, brought back another group of photographs. These tell a harsh story, not so much of divorce from the machine age, as of ignorance, squalor, injustice, exploitation. One of them, especially, is of pertinence here. Its locale is Arcadia, South Carolina; the chief character is named "Gentle" Woodson. The picture is of a shack with six children on the steps, and two women in the doorway. The legend reads: "This is the family of Gentle Woodson, together with his sister-in-law. No one works but Gentle, who gets twenty cents an hour; but has work on the average of thirty hours a week. He supports everyone in the picture on his earnings." Obviously to other dwellers in this section, or visitors to it, there is something in this Gilead other than balm.

Satire of Imperialism
By STERLING A. BROWN

*MANDOA, MANDOA!** by Winifred Holt-by, is a delightful book. Subtitled "A Comedy of Irrelevance"—and it is rich in humor and irrelevance—it is nevertheless a great deal more. Its appraisal of two contrasted ways of life is not only sparkling but trenchant as well, and its gayety is frequently not very far from tragedy. It is superficially similar in plot to Evelyn Waugh's *Black Mischief*, reviewed earlier in *Opportunity*. But it lacks the smart assumption of superiority of that book, and is both wittier and wiser. Its confessed irrelevances are after all very relevant to us, and set forth though they are sometimes in brilliant paradox, and sometimes with absurdity, they still deserve our closest pondering.

Mandoa is a mythical kingdom, in Eastern Africa, near to, and resembling Abyssinia in topography, racial makeup, and social and political organization. Since it did not exist, Winifred Holtby had to discover it for her engaging modern descendant of *Gulliver's Travels* and *Candide*. In this "Catholic Colony of Abyssinia" she discovers a strange monarchy: a queen always rules (nominally) and the succession falls to a daughter. The father of the daughter is selected from a college of archbishops. If he is the father of a son, he is done away with, if of a daughter, he becomes Arch-archbishop. The ruling caste is Ethiopian-Portuguese; beneath them are freedmen and enslaved Dinkas, Gallas, Somalis, and Sudanese. Slave-trading is the most lucrative pursuit. Mandoans "never, never shall be slaves."

A wandering English schoolmaster had introduced Safi Talal, the Lord Chamberlain, and other Mandoans to the glories of Western civilization. A trip to Addis-Ababa the Abyssinian coronation converted Talal to the religion of telephones, handkerchiefs, victrolas, aeroplanes, cocktail shakers, and bathtubs. Then an American movie company was stranded in Mandoa. When, departing, it left behind it four specimen reels, "Hollywood Parade," "Diamond-set Divorce," "College Girls Must

Mandoa, Mandoa! by Winifred Holtby. The Macmillan Co. $2.50.

Love," and "Red-Hot Mamma," Talal's worship was fanned to white heat. He would civilize Mandoa. He had allies; the speech of Mandoa went Hollywood; archbishops and slaves alike replied "O. K., chief" and "I don't say mebbe" on all and sundry occasions. "College cuties, blonde sweeties, weeping stars in closeups with immense tears on their synthetic lashes, enraptured half Mandoa." Mary Pickford became even more of a goddess than she has been in America.

Talal's fight against barbarism was unexpectedly aided by Sir Joseph Prince, of Prince's Tours, Ltd. of London, who supplied jaded Europeans with new travel thrills. He sent Bill Durrant, a brilliant but war-shocked misfit, as an agent to Mandoa, to prepare the way for English travellers. Durrant and Talal planned a marriage between the Mandoan princess and an Abyssinian prince, a ceremony threatening to eclipse the Abyssinian coronation. Engineers came out; aerodromes, roads, a Prince's hotel were constructed. To tell how the well laid plans go astray would be unfair to the story, in which the surprises are delightful. Suffice it to say that all reckoned without Safi Malrita, chief of the council, who, having seen the Hollywood movies, was determined to preserve his native-land from Western contamination. A crafty, cruel diplomat, he showed the effete intellectuals who flocked to Mandoa enough genuine savagery to shock them. He kept Mandoa still Mandoa, and brought Talal into temporary disgrace. But Talal at the end of the book, is still irrepressible. He plans a long trip to Europe and America, and then on his return, expects to hoodwink the League of Nations on the slavery question. Then, he foresees a great city of elevators and factories and electric cars. In the meanwhile huge fungoid growths are choking the city of his first experiment.

Mandoa, Mandoa! is an exciting adventure story, with slave raids, African ceremonies, abductions, aeroplane rescues, and intrigue piled on intrigue. It presents admirably two settings, both described from wide and deep knowledge. Contemporary England with its unemployment, elections, liberals of every dye, its perplexed uneasiness, its crisis, is presented as interestingly as Mandoa. The characterization of major and minor personages is more than adequate: Bill and Maurice Durrant, Jean Stansbury, Rollett, Safi Talal and Safi Malrita, are not going to be easy to forget. The comedy is rich; especially hilarious are the code of etiquette submitted to Mandoan nobles for the protection of the sensibilities of Europeans, and the scene in which Talal rejects the advances of Felicia Cardover, who rightly considered herself irresistible to Europeans. To Talal, alas, she is too skinny; her scarlet claws and the strange scent of her expensive Parisian perfume are obnoxious. Miss Holtby's banter covers a wide field: the post-war lost generation, ineffectual liberals, Victorians, ambitious politicians, dog-in-the-manger editors, fashionable seekers after the new *frisson*, hypocritical humanitarians—all are satirized—though never with caricature, and always with understanding. *"Negro rhythm exploited by a Polish songplugger, with American words, sung by a Canadian-Jew ,and reproduced on a German record —and that's our civilization,"* growls Fanshawe, a thirster after the exotic.

Most important, however, it seems to the reviewer, is what the author has to say about Africa. *"You would prefer to keep us quaint . . . You would always wish to spoil our culture. I have heard that many times. . . . You are very clever, artistic, cultivated men. But you know nothing about us, nothing. Since you came, you have all the time said. . . . 'How fine to be isolated, unique, primitive'. . . . To be isolated means to be poor. No trade, no travel, no cultural contact. To be unique means to be lonely. To be primitive means to sleep in dirty huts, to ride on donkeys, to do the same things day after day. It means to live in a very little world where nothing changes, to suffer from droughts and diseases and tapeworm and lice. . ."* To Miss Holtby, Mandoan nobles are not "noble savages." She sees their bloodthirstiness, oppression, backwardness; she knows that in Mandoa disease, squalor, poverty, and slavery are too frequently the rule. But she is never unmindful that if Mandoa is cruel, so is England: that the slave trade and other Mandoan abuses have their civilized parallels. In short she sees two different ways of life and presents them, siding with neither. And she understands imperialism. She knows that it is important for England that Mandoa be civilized so that rails can come from Sheffield and engines from Doncaster. She knows that much of the concern over slavery is imperialistic policy in the sheep's clothing of humanitarianism. She knows that a chief Anglo-Saxon tabu is "putting ideas into Negroes' heads." She knows a very great deal about a number of things. And her knowledge, while informing a gay, witty novel, is a little bit scornful, and a little bid sad. *Mandoa, Mandoa!* is a wise book; it should be read with care.

Six Plays for a Negro Theatre

By STERLING A. BROWN

PROFESSOR KOCH, in a foreword to this book of plays* states truly that Randolph Edmonds is foremost in the new dramatic awakening in our colleges. The Negro Intercollegiate Dramatic Association owes its inception to him, and modelled upon it, other associations are springing up over the South. Before the founding of this association, collegiate dramatics had sporadically risen, thrived, and declined. Now there are exchange programs, tournaments, valuable inter-change of ideas, and instead of the haphazard annual performance, a veritable repertory of plays given during the year. While first rate dramatic work is being done at colleges unconnected with any association, notably (to the chronicler's knowledge) at Lincoln under Joseph N. Hill and at Atlanta under Anne Cooke, it can safely be asserted that the vision and diligence of Randolph Edmonds are responsible for a great deal of the advance. The success of Professor Edmonds' Morgan Players did give harassed directors exhibit A to point out, in overcoming official inertia. And the admirable *esprit de corps* of the Morgan Players is a fine ideal for any group of rising actors.

Randolph Edmonds has set himself, as a director and playwright must do, patiently to study the vagaries of the audiences of our plays. As an article in the *Afro-American* showed, he is aware that racial audiences, after the fashion of minorities, is on a strict defensive when any aspects of its life are presented. In the preface to these plays he writes: "It has long been my opinion, however, that it is not the crude expressions of the peasant characters that contribute to this dislike; but rather the repelling atmosphere and 'psychology of the inferior' that somehow creep into the peasant plays of even the most unbiased authors of other racial groups." He attempts in this book to supply plays of a different sort, by combining "worthwhile themes, sharply drawn conflict, positive characters (i.e. those who fight heroically in their losing struggle) and a melodramatic plot." The

*Six Plays For A Negro Theatre, by Randolph Edmonds. Walter H. Baker Co., Boston. $.75.

sharply drawn conflict and the melodrama are concessions to an audience limited in its experience with plays.

All six of these plays are serious; all except one end tragically. Nat Turner and Breeders are set in slavery days; in the first we have the dramatizing of the historic insurrection of the wild prophet of the Great Dismal. Breeders likewise shows the rebellious slave: Ruth prefers poison to being mated to a big buck noted for breeding. *Old Man Pete* turns on the theme of filial ingratitude. Pete's children, Harlem-wise, insult the old man and pass him around until his spirit will stand no more, and he and his old woman go out to Central Park and freeze to death. *Bad Man* shows the renovation of a killer, and his sacrifice of himself to a mob. *Bleeding Hearts,* dealing with the misery of a farm-tenant, promises heroism, although the last determination of the long suffering Joggison is merely to leave the section. *The New Window* is another treatment of the bad man, unregenerate this time, one Bullock, bootlegger, who is killed in a strange backwoods duel by the brother of one of his victims.

Summarizing plays in one sentence hardly does justice to them, and Mr. Edmonds has somewhat disarmed criticism by his avowed purpose to use melodrama to carry the plays across. Mr. Edmonds is too astute theatrically, however, not to know that melodrama can be both expert and inexpert in its cogency. To the chronicler such melodrama as the death of David, in *Breeders* by falling on his own razor and cutting his throat, is incredible; and the old couple's death by freezing in Central Park smacks too much of the blood and tears of the old shockers. In the two plays of slavery occasionally the diction and psychology seem anachronistic. The plays show at times too facile a solution of structural problems; the *entracte* of *Nat Turner* designed to give an impression of three days fighting does not and cannot accomplish any such purpose, and the final scene of *Old Man Pete* seems tagged on.

But simple themes, unpretentiously worked out

233

and occasionally crossing over into the sentimental and melodramatic, are still what the average audience takes to its bosom. And his choice of characters, almost all of them with backbone and willing to go down fighting is fortunate, coinciding with the growing militancy of our times. Mr. Edmonds has wisely realized that a supine protagonist cannot be a tragic hero. The settings are well chosen and well conveyed; sawmill camp, bootlegger's hangout, Harlem flat, and tenant cabin, all ring true and seem to have been observed closely. Although the dialogue lacks the lift and quotableness of such a writer as Zora Neale Hurston, and has occasional lapses, it is adequate and forthright. The action is swift and exciting, true to the types of life shown. The work has freshness, and, if reminiscent of any plays, recalls those of the long honored dramatic tradition.

Our little theatre movement has long suffered from a dearth of plays about Negro life and these plays will be welcome in their supplying of an important demand. They are easy to stage and produce, and require no great outlay of money. Most important of all, probably, to Mr. Edmonds, is the fact that, on the stage, these plays *take*. Two of them have been prize winners in collegiate tournaments. The chronicler was fortunate enough to see *Nat Turner* on the stage in a southern town. There was no doubt about its moving power; the audience was transported, the applause was stentorian.

(Sterling Brown directed the Howard Players last year.)

Stars Fell on Alabama*

By STERLING A. BROWN

SOME of us do not need Carl Carmer's word that this book was a long time in the writing. The reviewer is among those who have been waiting for it. Carl Carmer's occasional descriptions of Negro folk and their ways in Theatre Arts, in Opportunity; his score or so of poems in *Deep South* dealing with the legends and superstitions of Alabama poor whites; all were evidence that here was a writer with an interesting terrain to work, and the skill to work it. Few will be disappointed in *Stars Fell on Alabama,* which appears at long last.

Stars Fall on Alabama is a poet's book. Many of the poems from *Deep South* he has amplified in this narrative; and the principle of selection of his poetry is apparent in his prose. He favors the grotesque, the original; his method is that of the romantic realists. His title suggests that; over the Alabama he has chosen to write about there is a spell of enchantment. He plays with the fantasy that an intangible net of sorcery encompasses the "hill-billies and niggers, poor whites, and planters, Cajans and Lintheads." Open-eyed with wonder at the new and exotic, he looks upon Alabama as a 'state-that-is-another-land.' "The Congo is not more different from Massachusetts or Kansas or California," he writes; as a professor at the state University his affirmation of a similar idea to his students was attended with some hazard. One reader feels that the protest of the Alabama collegians was correct. Alabama must have its own brand, the contrasts in its culture are striking, and Mr. Carmer in his six years stay there did observe both widely and closely, but it is not completely unique. At any rate the testimony Mr. Carmer adduces does not differentiate the state so much from its next door neighbors, Georgia and Mississippi. His Red Hills are not so different from the Ozarks, and his Cajans are to be found not only in Alabama.

Mr. Carmer vividly, with gleams of humor, irony and affection, sets before us the way of life of Alabama. He stresses the semi-tropical

*Stars Fell On Alabama, by Carl Carmer. Farrar and Rinehart, $3.00.

dawdling, the lazy rhythm now quickened by passion and violence, the accepted contrasts of worship of chastity and practise of lechery, of moonshining and the Bible belt, of sentimentality and cruelty, of grandeur and shame. The strange juxtaposition of opposites is clear in the host of River Falls; friendly and hospitable, a horse-fancier, he has in a locked room one of the most complete collections of opera records in the world, and he exploits convict labor in his sawmills. Mr. Carmer takes us from the Red Hills section in which Scottsboro is located through the Foothills, The Black Belt, Conjure Country (in which is Tuskegee) down to Cajan Country, and Mobile Bay. The vegetation, the soil, the weather are recorded sensitively; the changes in the human scene are charted as carefully.

Folk-lore is one of Mr. Carmer's major concerns. Among the hill-billies he collects folk-signs, folk-cures, and 'ballats'; he attends 'all-day sings' in which two thousand or more people gather and, by singing *mi, fa, sol, la,* produce what Mr. Carmer calls "a fearsome hodge podge of sound, an outlandish gibberish," he goes to fiddling contests and square dances, and watches the hardshells go through their ritual of foot-washing. He is always on the alert for the picturesque custom of revelatory phrase; he knows how to mingle and is soon accepted by the people he wants to get into his book. In cabins and on the porches of the big houses he collects his tales of famous outlaws such as Steve Renfroe, the Simsite brethren, and Rube Barrow, the Robin Hood of Alabama. He listens to plantation tales, strange compounds of honor and treachery, which have hidden away in them implications of the tragedy of slavery that he does not otherwise write about. Strange pages of history, semi-legendary, he hands down to us: accounts of the German settlement from St. Louis, the French refugees who attempted to found a new 'Plaisant Pays de France' with grape vines and olive trees, one nobleman ending as a ferryman, while his wife, a former marchioness, cooked flapjacks on the river-bank.

235

One of the best tales is of Two-Toe Tom, the man and mule eating alligator, still an unconquered crawling menace.

The Negro characters he deals with are for the most part 'originals'; their ways of life are exotic, pageant-like. The story of Railroad Bill is here in full. To the oppressed Negroes of Alabama his wild courage and impudence in braving the law are regarded with superstitious reverence and furtive pride. John Henry is here, talking of the Central Georgia now instead of the C. & O. The "Prophetess of Eutaw" who was first met by the reviewer in Opportunity and then in Julia Peterkin's *Roll, Jordan, Roll* is here, as are two "White-Man's Niggers." One of these, Antimo, catches rattlesnakes and coons, and has been pleasing white men all of his life; the other, Wade Finley is a "bad nigger" to Negroes because he kills "upstart niggers," but is therefore a "good nigger"—in fact the country's best—to the whites. Strange fertility rites, jungle-like religious services and dances, and a catalogue of love charms and folk signs from the Conjure woman show that he has explored Negro folk-lore as well as white. He records a few Uncle Remus tales, and one anecdote of Jim "the stud nigger," (the rest being too Rabelaisian for even this frank book). Mr. Carmer is aware of the brutality that Negroes may expect in Alabama, and touches upon it here and there. He describes the community turmoil during a lynching, and is impressed by the fatalism of the Negroes at a church service afterwards. The Negroes of present day Alabama according to his picture are a dispirited lot, to whom Mr. Carmer extends sympathy in passing to more picturesque sets. He goes to Decatur on the day for trying Heywood Patterson; he registers the constant attitude of natives of varying social levels: a white woman has spoken, Patterson must die. He does not stay to the trial, and gives rather short shrift, it must be said, to the whole affair.

And just there one feels is the chief limitation of the book. Alabama is approached too frequently as *sui generis,* as a spectacle for wonder, as a romantic other-world, and not often enough as a subject for analysis, and as a realistic place established too firmly in the here and now. By concentrating on exoticism, on strange survivals, on romantic pageantry—things present no doubt in the total scene, and ably set down as they may be—there are too many gaps left. The chronicler realizes that one of the cardinal sins of reviewing is to talk about a book the reviewer wishes the author had written, rather than the book he did write. But one must run the risk. Here goes: Mr. Carmer has done a graphic introduction to an interesting state, a book worthy of the fine illustrations of Cyrus Le Roy Baldridge; and that is high praise. A Northerner went South and brought back a sympathetic account, far above local color. But this reviewer holds that the account was too sympathetic, that a gentleman was too responsive to hospitality. The enchantment, undeniable as it is, exerted too much power. We wish he could have had the 'spell untricked', and could have told us with the same skill more about the lintheads, the poor whites, the Negro sharecroppers on their less picturesque and more workaday side. We wish that, excellent poet though he is, that he would explain in some other way than the falling of the stars why the good folk down there do not miss a hanging, and why in spite of glamorous variety, such a large part of the natives, both black and white, lead lives of unenchanted misery.

Mississippi—Old Style*

By STERLING A. BROWN

SO RED THE ROSE is one of the leaders among the best sellers. This is not only because of the skill of the narration, the fluent prose, and the able weaving of history, legend, and first rate talk. But it conforms to a literary pattern dear for over a century to the American reading public: an ideal plantation, peopled with feudal lords (pirated from Walter Scott) living a life of leisure, beauty, and *noblesse oblige,* graciously condescending to the adoration of black serfs, called servants never slaves, untroubled by grief, unacquainted with wrong, until the cruel Civil War—pardon, the War Between the States. Then our old Kentucky home (Mississippi in this case)—good night! So runs an American dream of frequent recurrence.

Stark Young has devoted novels and essays to the defense of the gracious way of life of the Old South. In *So Red the Rose,* to set forth his thesis he uses two families, the McGehees and the Bedfords, between whose gentility, sweetness, aristocratic connections, and all the other attributes of perfection, there is nothing to choose. Thoroughly patrician in his preferences, Mr. Young writes: "It had not taken long for the settlers pouring over the Southern States to find their level and divide. There were the adventurers, the drifters, the scum, and wreckage of life in the older colonies and abroad; they lingered, dropped lower. . . . There were those who wished to make homes, to own land. . . . At the same time, scattered here and there . . . were certain communities that from the very start had been made up of a special class who in their turn drew others like them." With the first two classes, the poor whites and the "yeomen," Mr. Young is as cavalier as his aristocrats —who kept these at their doorsteps, forbidden even the spacious porch, untouchables. The life of the planters is presented as "a simple gra-

*So Red the Rose, by Stark Young, New York. Charles Scribner's Sons. $2.50.

cious system of living that has seldom seen its equal."

At Montrose plantation near Natchez, the McGehees live out their idyll; at Portobello, the Bedfords live theirs. It is a fine, pretty world, my masters. There is a deep sense of family tradition, which, Mr. Young infers, is peculiarly Southern; there are frequent parties, dances, sessions of excellent talk, alternating between brilliance and sentiment; handsome cavaliers are beloved of charming heroines; and libraries of many thousands of books serve as hunting ground for the Latin quotations that spangle social converse, or make endurable the bivouac. The planters do not believe in secession, and, though quiet it may be kept, do not believe in slavery. The planters did not like slavery, but it had been inherited, and nothing could be done about it—except to make the most of it by sitting down and being cultivated ladies and gentlemen, and attacking abolitionism as "fetid New England Puritan old maid idealism." And when the War Between the States came, planters of the Bedford, McGehee stripe fought because their fair land was invaded, and not—oh, forbear to think it—because their property was threatened. Mr. Young is, of course, one of the leading stylists of modern writing. The picture he draws is lovely.

But the Civil War (War Between the States) comes, blown along by windbags North and South, and the gracious way of life is disturbed, and then nearly destroyed. Edward McGehee, grave, admirable, promising, is killed at Shiloh; Malcolm Bedford comes back from Vicksburg, spent, and dies of typhoid. His son, Duncan, after a career of gallantry and hardship, finally returns, to recover, in spite of the devastation, something of happiness in the lovely arms of Valette. But the melancholy of the book is inescapable. Mr. Young heightens the terror of a terrible war that needs no heightening, and in that, I believe, he strikes a false note. The incident of the bomb's crashing "through a bed of pinks" and then over a too curious pigeon before heartbroken children, is a case in point. Sometimes Mr. Young seems to imply that the tragedy of the Civil War lay in its bringing an end to some fine conversations and to the leisurely cutting of roses.

So Red the Rose is a masterpiece of special pleading. The planters are less people than personifications of ideals; as such they are only superficially distinguishable. The Southern ladies, whether "My Dumplin' " or "Darlin'," are still—Southern ladies, i.e. ideally charming, except Miss Mary Cherry, the best character in the book. Northern enemies are frequently caricatured; the history levied upon is chiefly of the sort of "Beast" Butler's insult to the ladies of New Orleans, General Grant's false teeth and drunkenness, and Mrs. Grant's *parvenu* inclinations. Sherman comes off better, but then he spent many years in the South, and was anti-abolitionist. The South should be judged by its stated ideals, not its actualities, urges Mr. Young; whereas the North, because its practice did not always hew to the line of its principles, is hypocritical. All of this is more or less suavely done, but it is there.

The Negro characters are more allegorical here than in some of Mr. Young's sketches. William Veal went to the battlefield of Shiloh and in the dark felt the hair of all the dead men "till he found Edward, he knew him by his hair; you know how fine it was." He buried the Montrose silver from marauding Yankees, and, for reward, gets a black coat with a tail and satin lapels, and a gold watch and chain from his masters, his picture on the bookjacket from the publishers, and his due meed from Stark Young. Slavery certainly paid Mr. Veal. Most of the other Negroes are ingrates, who though they had nothing to do before the war, ran off to the Yankees, and died like flies in concen-

tration camps. The Negroes upon whose backs the leisure and culture of Montrose and Porto-bello were founded do not appear, any more than the thousands of bales that went into the thousands of books. During the war, Negro soldiers are almost entirely referred to as grog-filled burners and looters. In Reconstruction, when the "bottom-rail came on top," the state of affairs was unspeakable; the thing was a shame. And it is a shame for a man as intelligent as Mr. Young, despite his adulation of the planter oligarchy, to go the way of Claude Bowers and Tom Dixon.

Mr. Young has a perfect right to compose an idealized account of Southern aristocracy, and, embittered by memories, to engage in ancestor worship. He is correct in believing that the likes of these people are not to be seen today. That they were no more to be seen yesterday is a possible belief, but one not invalidating his novel, *as* novel. To generalize about the ante-bellum South from this highly selected group of exquisites, however, or even about the planters is a dubious proceeding. And that is what reviewers, critics, and the publishers have rushed to do. One can understand the chauvinism of Southern reviewers who claim that *So Red the Rose* shatters the false fictional stereotype of the planter. But it does not. It says about the planter, in more skillful manner, what *Swallow Barn* said in 1832 and Thomas Nelson Page said in the Reconstruction. For this to be the Old South, too many important elements are missing. The tragic aspects of Southern life, except for the Civil War's affecting the élite, are skirted gingerly. We are asked to accept a master of special pleading, a known advocate of the defendant, as an impartial judge. We are asked to concur in a grandson's judgment of a worshipped grandfather. This is too much to ask; this is easy only for those who have already declared the defendant "not guilty," and have already composed hosannas to his name.

Mississippi, Albama: New Style

By STERLING A. BROWN

IN *Look Homeward, Angel,* one of the best of the recent novels of the South, Thomas Wolfe decries "the romantic halo that his school history cast over the section . . . the whole fantastic distortion of that period where people were said to live in 'mansions', and slavery was a benevolent institution, conducted to a constant banjo-strumming, the strewn largesses of the colonel and the shuffle-dance of his happy dependents, where all women were pure, gentle, and beautiful, all men chivalrous and brave, and the Rebel horde a company of swagger, death mocking cavaliers. Years later, when he could no longer think of the barren spiritual wilderness, the hostile and murderous intrenchment against all new life—when their cheap mythology, their legend of the charm of their manner, the aristocratic culture of their lives, the quaint sweetness of their drawl, made him writhe—when he could think of no return to their life and its swarming superstition, without weariness and horror, so great was his fear of the legend, his fear of their antagonism, that he still pretended the most fantastic devotion to them, excusing his Northern residence on grounds of necessity rather than desire."

There is at present a group of Southern writers who are convinced of the "barren spiritual wilderness" of their native section, and have no hesitancy in repudiating the romantic legend. Unlike Stark Young, they are more concerned with the twentieth century South than with the ante-bellum, but they do know the past, and their comments upon it are hardly elegies for the lost Eden. William Faulkner in a series of highly original novels has stripped off cherished illusion after illusion. Thomas Wolfe's *Look, Homeward, Angel* has already been cited. William March and T. S. Stribling in the two novels for review add powerful voices to a chorus that must be heard.

Come In at the Door (Smith & Haas, $2.00), is a worthy successor to William March's *Company K*, one of the best war novels. Its structure is unique; imaginative sketches each repeating a motif of the novel, and excerpts from the diary of a Southern gentlewoman, spinsterish

and sentimental, are interpolated in the narrative of a boy's conditioning and growth. Robert Hurry, scion of one of the old families, goes to seed in the waste land of the Mobile delta country. Frustrated and soured, he repulses his motherless son Chester, who falls back upon the Negro servants for guidance and companionship. Chester's tutor, Baptiste, an educated Creole mulatto, is hanged partly because of the child's inadvertence; the impression made by the spectacle on the sensitive child was to be ineradicable though not always comprehended. Chester's later life is one of disillusionment and futility. Though primarily a psychological study, *Come In At The Door* persuasively shows a milieu and its effect upon character. Most of the characters are divested of their haloes; Chester's favorite uncle is married to a harlot, his aunt is an arriviste, his wife a frantic candidate for Babbittry. The bewildered Chester, his kindhearted Uncle Bush, his Aunt Bessie who repudiates the South and goes "left," and at times his broken shell of a father, win sympathy, but defeat is the dominant note that is struck. And during it all, as a quavering obbligato, the great aunt Sarah raises hymns to the lost glory of the days that are no more.

The book takes its title from a Negro spiritual. Mr. March's Negro characters are, like the rest of his people, well understood and portrayed. Baptiste the vagabond, a bantering but keenly alert philosopher, is a hauntingly tragic figure. He alone could be Robert Hurry's intellectual comrade, but the *mores* of the wasteland forbid Robert's stooping. Mitty, who becomes Robert's mistress and bears him six children, is a new type of mammy. Wily but superstitious, loyal but self-centered, illiterate but managerial, kindhearted but capable of fierce hate, she is definitely a complex, unstereotyped person. Aunt Hattie and Jim show good observation of folk Negroes; Jim with his coon Buck is delightful. The hardship encountered by Negroes is implicit throughout the work.

T. S. Stribling's *Unfinished Cathedral* (Doubleday, Doran, $2.50) is the third volume of his trilogy on a family's history in the old and new

South. The Vaiden family is not the conventional choice for a Southern novel; its origins were lower middle class, and although Miltiades Vaiden is now a wealthy, respected, legitimate 'colonel,' lost in dreams of vanished splendor before the Yankees came, he is still a long ways from being a Maxwell House Coffee advertisement. His wealth, based upon a theft, has made him a key man of the Florence boom. This boom fails, and the cathedral of which he had been the chief financial support remains unfinished. His family is broken up; at the time when orators are spouting about the purity of white womanhood, his daughter is seduced by a Florence dolt. The mulatto side of his family, throughout the trilogy, has had a hard road to travel. In the second novel of the series, *The Store,* Miltiades' son by his half sister, Gracie Vaiden, was lynched because he refused to be browbeaten by Colonel Milt, whom he did not know as his father. In *Unfinished Cathedral,* Gracie's grandson is one of the Negro boys hustled off of a train into a framed rape case.

As might be apparent, Mr. Stribling stretches the long arm of coincidence too far, but the novel is extremely valuable for its careful working in of the social background. Light is shed where until recently there had been darkness: on the relationship of the clergy, bankers, realtors, sheriffs, and judges to the lynching mobs. The New South is here with its new lust for sudden wealth, and its old disregard of human values; with its rebellious youth, and its strivers seeking to arrive with the aid of genealogical charts and lip service to the Lost Cause. Least pleasant to contemplate is the indecency of treatment of Negroes, an indecency upon which the better educated are in substantial unanimity with the hoodlums. Mr. Stribling has a frame up in Florence very similar to the Scottsboro case; suggestive of the Crawford case, a Northern governor refuses to extradite one of the escaped prisoners. Mr. Stribling does not hesitate to show intelligent, militant Negroes; and even beneath the grotesque robes of some of the lodge brothers he shows us guns. "White educated Southerners are completely cut off from black educated Southerners by the inherited attitudes of master and slave, and the one really does not know that the other exists," writes Mr. Stribling. But Mr. Stribling is not so cut off, and that is why this latest novel of his, improbable as it may seem in one or two coincidences, is nevertheless one of the truest, most honest, and most courageous novels to come out of the present day South.

Genealogists concerned with the family trees of the cavalier South might ponder Gracie's words: "Colored relations! What colored relations? I was born to my mother, old Hannah, long after Old Pap sold off her husband Jericho! I'm not white for nothing! Aunt Creasy told me long ago that my father was Old Pap, the same as yours! Toussaint, the son I had by you, was nothing but a Vaiden on both sides. The child Lucy had by Toussaint, the son you hanged, I named Marcia; and Marcia's boy you're holding in jail this minute is named James Vaiden Hodge. Who would my grandchild come back to see except white people, Miltiades?" . . . And to these words, the old Colonel, in his majesty replies: "Shame on you, Gracie, coming here and talking disrespectfully like this!"

THE LITERARY SCENE
CHRONICLE AND COMMENT.

Imitation of Life: Once A Pancake

By Sterling A. Brown

IMITATION OF LIFE,* by Fannie Hurst, first appeared as *Sugar House* in The *Pictorial Review*. It was another American success story. Bea Pullman, a hard working, motherless girl, with a paralyzed father, forges her way, after her husband is killed in a railroad accident, from drab poverty, to Duncan Phyfe, Heppelwhite and Sheraton prosperity. She is grateful to life for her talent to "provide people with a few moments of creature enjoyment" in the shape of succulent waffles and maple syrup; she should be grateful to Delilah, upon whose broad shoulders she rode pickaback to affluence. Delilah, whose recipe and skill are the makings of the world famous enterprise, wants little but the chance, since she is full of "a rambunctious capacity for devotion," to be mammy to the whole world, and especially to Miss Bea. Her greatest trouble is her fair daughter Peola, who wants to be white in the worst way, and finally marries a young blond engineer, who, coincidentally, was never to know that he had called his mother-in-law "mammy" over a stack of wheats. Peola and husband disappear into Bolivia; Delilah obligingly dies after the business is established and Miss Bea, free at last for love, finds that it is too late, that her beloved has been swept away by her daughter, Jessie. It is, in the main, a tearful story.

Those who have seen the picture will recognize the differences in plot. The characterization and ideas, however, are little changed. Delilah, "vast monument of a woman," "her huge smile the glowing heart of a furnace," "her round black moon face shining above an Alps of bosom" is essentially the same, with her passion for rubbing "dem white little dead beat feet," the inebriation of her language, too designedly picturesque, her unintelligible character, now infantile, now mature, now cataloguing folk-beliefs of the Southern Negro, and now cracking contemporary witticisms. Her baby talk to the white child partakes too much of maple sugar; to her own, too much of mustard.

*"Imitation of Life," by Fannie Hurst. Harper & Bros. $2.50.

Delilah's visions of going to glory recur in the book. To the reviewer they are not true folk-eloquence. "I'm paying lodge-dues an' I'm savin' mah own pennies for to be sent home and delivered to de glory of de Lawd wid plumes and trumpets blowin' louder dan rhubarb would make growin'." There is a great deal of talk on the text: "Never the Twain Shall Meet." Delilah is completely black, and therefore contented: "Lovers of de Lawd an' willin' servers is my race, filled with de blessings of humility" . . . "Glory be to Gawd, I's glad I's one of his black chillun, 'cause, sho' as heaven, his heart will bleed fust wid pity and wid mercy for his lowdown ones." Peola, near white, but with "not a half moon to her finger nails" is unhappy. *"It's de white horses dat's wild, a'swimmin' in de blood of mah chile. . . . I wants to drown dem white horses plungin' in mah baby's blood."* Can one reader be forgiven, if during such passages, there runs into his mind something unmistakably like a wild horse laugh?

Remembering the book I was unprepared to believe that the theatregoers and critics who urged the novelty, the breaking away from old patterns of the picture. Of course they had reasons. It is true that the picture is a departure from Stepin Fetchit. There is less of Octavus Roy Cohen in the film than in the book (perhaps the intrinsic dignity of Louise Beavers kept down the clowning.) The bandana has been exchanged for a white chef's cap. There is a warm mutual affection between the two mothers; kindheartedness meets up with gratitude. Important roles, of some seriousness, were given to Louise Beavers and Fredi Washington, who are certainly deserving actresses. If their names on the screen were not quite in the largest type, they were still high up on the list, and will be remembered because of first rate performances. Moreover, Lelilah is a preternaturally good woman, except for a little breadth of diction, and Peola's morality, in spite of her bitterness, is unimpeachable. Cabins and cottonfields are a long way from the suite (downstairs) of Delilah. Both Delilah and Peola can dress up,

241

after a fashion. Poverty is back in the past, due to Miss Bea's midas-like touch (?) and her generosity (!) "Ain't you made life a white padded cell for Delilah?" The word "nigger" is not once used, even in places where logically it should occur. Minor problems are touched upon. All of these things are undoubtedly gladdening to our bourgeois hearts. But that doesn't make them new. However novel in Hollywood, they are old in literature. It requires no searching analysis to see in *Imitation of Life* the old stereotype of the contented Mammy, and the tragic mulatto; and the ancient ideas about the mixture of the races.

Delilah is straight out of Southern fiction. Less abject than in the novel, she is still more concerned with the white Jessie than with Peola. She has little faith in Peola's capacities: "We all starts out smart; we don't get dumb till later on." Resignation to injustice is her creed; God knows best, we can't be telling Him his business; mixed bloods who want to be white must learn to take it, must not beat their fists against life; she doesn't rightly know where the blame lies. When she refuses her twenty per cent (not because it was too little) she is the old slave refusing freedom: "My own house? You gonna send me away? Don't do that to me? How I gonna take care of you and Miss Jessie if I's away? I's yo' cook. You kin have it; I make you a present of it." She finally consents for some money to be put aside against a funeral. *"Once a pancake, always a pancake."* The "passing" episodes are as unbelievable. She is ignorant of the school attended by her daughter (in Atlantic City of segregated schools); she naively gives Peola away, insisting that she did not intend to. Later, finding her daughter passing as a cashier she announces, "I'se yo' mammy, Peola," although she could have spared the girl embarrassment by sending in Miss Bea. She is canny about the ways of men and women where Miss Bea is concerned; but when her daughter is yearning for music and parties, she says, "Come on, honey, I'll dance with you." The director would not even let Delilah die in peace. She must speak, in a tragic scene, well acted, comic lines about "colored folks' eyes budging out," and "not liking the smell of gasoline." Her idiom is good only in spots; I have heard dialect all my life, but I have yet to hear such a line as "She am an angel."

Peola, wistfully hearing the music upstairs, searching the mirror for proof of her whiteness, crying out her hatred of life, her vexation at her black mother, is the tragic octoroon, familiar to novels more than to life. She, too ,is at

times hard to believe in. For she never quite gets a grasp of the true problem. There was a chance for real bitterness when Miss Bea stops her as she is finally leaving her mother. But the tirade does not come, although Peola must have seen through the condescension and the gentle exploitation. It would be refreshing to have heard what a girl like Peola would really have said; I believe Miss Washington could have risen to heights in its delivery. There is a scene where Miss Bea goes upstairs while Delilah goes down. It is symbolic of many things. One is, that in *Imitation of Life* where Claudette Colbert has a role to bring out all that there is in her, both Miss Beavers and Miss Washington have, so to speak, to go downstairs; Miss Beavers to a much greater childishness, and Miss Washington to a much greater bewilderment than they would recognize in real life. But so Hollywood would have it; and so Hollywood gets something less artistic and less true.

To the reviewer the shots nearest to truth are the Harlem funeral scenes; the most memorable is the flash of the electric sign after the death of Delilah. The good old heart-broken soul dies, having made Miss Bea's road an easy one, for little more return than comfort and affection; Miss Bea goes on to wealth, love, and happiness, and Delilah gets her dubious immortality as an electrified trademark. The music of the quartette is stirring, although it is unfortunately synchronized with Delilah's dying, and is another instance of Hollywood's poor imitation of life. One of the worst shots is the renunciation finale in the romantic garden, with the lights on the river reminiscent of Venice.

It goes without saying that the picture has its moments of truth to American life. It is true, for instance, that in such a partnership, the white member, whose contributions were mild flirtations for business support, and energy, and "brains," would give the real power behind the enterprise a paltry twenty per cent. It is true that the white partner would most likely live upstairs, the black down; and that they would not ride side by side in the same automobile. It is true that after the death of the dearly beloved Mammy, the lost daughter, finding her friends again, would be gently comforted, and placed in the family car up front with the chauffeur. And it is true that for Jessie, business success would mean horse-shows, Switzerland, and finishing schools, where she could learn to stretch her eyes and simper, whereas for Peola it would mean a precarious future, remorseridden and threatening. All of this is true to the ways of America. But it hardly seems anything to cheer about.

THE LITERARY SCENE
CHRONICLE AND COMMENT.

Miss Fannie Hurst, internationally known novelist, takes exception to the review of "Imitation of Life" by Sterling A. Brown, published in the March OPPORTUNITY. Mr. Brown, author of "Southern Road" and many articles on Negro folklore, graduate of Williams, Phi Beta Kappa, and Master of Arts, Harvard, who regularly conducts Chronicle and Comment, makes reply.

Miss Fannie Hurst

Editor "Opportunity"
1133 Broadway
New York, N. Y.

Dear Sir:-

I am in receipt of a copy of "Opportunity" containing a review of the picture "Imitation of Life."

I realize, of course, how merciless any race is in its interpretation of itself by an outsider, and to an extent, I realize the inevitability of its attitude. I do, however, regret the fact that the thinking Negro can permit his point of view to be obscured behind such detail as characterized in the article you carry in "Opportunity."

As the author of the novel from which this picture is made, there are many aspects of it that fall short or deviate or even malign my original theme. But for purposes of what I have to say, that is beside the point.

I do think however, that instead of the carping, petty angles of criticism presented by your reviewer, there is a much larger view of this picture which he has overlooked. In other words, he did not see the woods for the trees.

The important social value of this picture is that it practically inaugurates into the important medium of the motion-picture, a consideration of the Negro as part of the social pattern of American life.

Instead of concerning himself with the superficialities of idiom, and the shape of the cook's cap, it does seem to me that your reviewer might have been awake to the larger social values of a picture such as "Imitation of Life."

The attitude is ungrateful, but what is much more important, it is also unintelligent.

Sincerely yours,

FANNIE HURST

Mr. Sterling A. Brown

To the Editor of "Opportunity":
Dear Sir:-

My attitude toward *Imitation of Life* was not part of some racial "mercilessness" toward interpretation by an "outsider." I believe, and have stated time and again that "outsiders" have contributed some of the very best interpretations of Negro life. But I do not consider Miss Hurst's book, or the picture, to belong with these.

Moreover, I have insisted, and still do insist, upon the right of the artist to deal with highly exceptional characters, and with improbable situations, provided that he does not ask us to generalize from these about the normal run of humanity, or the currents of human behavior. I felt, and the preceding letter supports me in this, that Miss Hurst did intend the story of Delilah and Peola to be considered somewhat typical of Negro life and character, in the twentieth century. I do not believe Delilah and Peola to be typical, I consider them highly romanticized, and I consider a large part of the story to be incredible.

It was of such criticism that the review was compounded, rather than of minutiae such as the shape of the cook's cap. This detail was one of many introduced to show the superficial points of divergence from the old pattern. I believe that if Miss Hurst were to reread the review she would see that this was hardly one of my major concerns. Be that as it may: I concede to Miss Hurst its unimportance, I gladly surrender the chef's cap; but I believe the argument remains substantially the same. I cannot agree that the matter of idiom is superficial: in a book or talking picture depending so largely upon Delilah's verbiage, I believe that accuracy is important.

My review was a decided failure if it did not reveal that the social implications of the book and picture were uppermost in my—let us call it thinking. I am well aware, and indicated, that there was a warmth of emotion in the mutual-affection situations. I realize that, as one movie critic put it, the picture mystified some who were "used to having their color on the screen in the guise of low comedy" and then discover "that this was tragedy and they were not supposed to laugh." They did laugh, of course, in some incongruous places, but in the main, they came to be amused, and remained to weep.

But pity is not enough; sentimentality is not enough. This picture breaks no new ground. The beloved mammy is a long familiar darling in the American consciousness; vaudeville headliners, song-pluggers, after-dinner speakers (especially Southern), moving pictures, and novels have placed her there. The tragic mulatto, who adds to the cross borne by the long suffering saintly mammy, is likewise a fixture. She is so woe-begone that she is a walking argument against miscegenation; her struggling differentiates her unpleasantly from the self-abnegation of the mammy; her cheap yearning to be white is a contemptible surrender of integrity. Like her mammy, she contributes to Anglo-Saxon self-esteem. It is not easy to see any "social value" in perpetuating these stock characters.

It seems to the reviewer that *Imitation of Life* does not "inaugurate" into moving pictures, a true "consideration of the Negro as part of the pattern of American life"; rather it reenforces stereotypes that Hollywood holds to firmly, and I understand profitably. I am glad that Miss Washington and Miss Beavers had chance to show their remarkable talents; I think their performances were first-rate, but other roles could have called forth even better acting. Opening serious roles in Hollywood for these actresses, however, and truthfully portraying Negro life and character are two greatly different things. Very little of Negro life gets into the picture; Delilah's meteoric career is almost fantastic, and very few Negroes, I feel, resemble the two extremists, Delilah and Peola. To me the social value of this picture is still suggested by the subtitle of the review: "*Once a pancake, always a pancake.*" And I submit that if Hollywood can only be opened to pictures of Negro life that convey such theses, it may as well remain closed. In the publishing world, fortunately, there is here and there, greater courage and social vision.

Concerning my unintelligence, I am perfectly willing, since Miss Hurst has pronounced upon the matter with finality, that her judgment be considered final; far be it from me to dispute such a trivial point with a lady. Concerning my ungratefulness, let me cheerfully acknowledge this degree of unintelligence: that I cannot imagine what in the world I have to be grateful for, either to Universal Pictures or to Miss Hurst.

Yours truly,
(Signed) STERLING A. BROWN

Come Day, Go Day

By Sterling A. Brown

ROARK Bradford's new book, *Let the Band Play Dixie* (Harpers, $2.00) is a collection of his best stories, published over a period of eight years or more. Mr. Bradford's fantasy, humor, mastery of dialogue and local color are present, but the book will hardly increase his stature. There is repetitiousness: "The same thing that . . . had warned Cooter not to step over a fallen tree and on the back of the rattlesnake that lay coiled there," (p. 98) becomes in a story about Ruby something "that told her not to step over a fallen tree and on the back of a cottonmouth moccasin that lay coiled there," (p. 171); the type of snake at least is changed. What is more important the characters are frequently repetitious, going through the same antics, and speaking the same drolleries.

With six books and several uncollected stories of Mr. Bradford's before us, we can state, with show of proof, certain generalities about him. Mr. Bradford is not at his best in characterization. His idea about the character of *the* Negro (for Mr. Bradford in a well known preface does not limit his blanket generalizations to the delta Negroes whom he knows so well) are ideas to be expected of a Louisianian, however affectionate he may be to his subjects. It goes without saying that Mr. Bradford has distinctive excellences. His plots are ingenious and frequently original, although the demand of large sale magazines may cause his work to run thin and repeat itself. His knowledge of folk-lore, mule-lore, and steamboatin' is enviable. His prose is simple, lucid, and conveys definitely a sense of place. When he comments on human nature he can be compassionate and wise, wiser than when he goes in for ethnology. And when he laughs, he is in the great tradition of Mark Twain. But all of these are still not enough.

"Child of God," the O. Henry Prize winning story for 1927, and "Cold Death" are stories related to *The Green Pastures* in tenderness. In the first, a kindly Lord God Jehovah allows a hanged Negro to return to earth; in "Cold Death" an old woman, firm in her love of children and God, dies, and without any intermission, even in Heaven, goes on about her caring for babies. The title story of a feud between two old Negroes, one Confederate and one Federal, is easy laughter. Many of the stories deal with the riverfront and New Orleans. Of the steamboatin' tales, "The Final Run of Hopper Joe Wiley" is a delightful folk-tale, and "Three for a Nickel," a good farce. "Old Average Lightning" is a first-rate bit of mule-lore, from the cotton fields. More savage and truculent riverfront life is to be seen in "The Razor Man," "Cooter," and "Blue Steel's Eva." The casual lovemaking of the levee and plantation appears often; generally, however, ending in lovers' meetings, happily.

One story, "Come Day, Go Day," dealing with a roustabout, Bugaboo Jones, seems to set the tone of the volume. The life of this irresponsible, harmless playboy is one long round of hard but happy work from Saturday until Thursday; Thursday for ecstasy, Friday for repentance; and then the week starts again. So it is with most of the people in the book, though on a different daily schedule. It is a quaint pastoral life, especially in the cotton fields and on steamboat decks and levees. Violence flares up now and again: the river-witch calls, or Africa surges: "Raw gin, the intermingling odors of smoke and cheap perfume, and the 'devil in the drums' was too much for that other one-eighth of Eva Paul's blood . . . with an animal-like shriek she tore at her flimsy clothing." But on the whole, there is very little of exploitation, or injustice and almost nothing of bitterness.

And therefore, in spite of Mr. Bradford's affectionate familiarity with his material, his picture, even for these few characters and along this limited front, is incomplete and in some important respects, unreliable.

* * * * *

Don't You Weep, Don't You Moan, by Richard Coleman (Macmillan, $2.50) is likewise a partial story. It purports to be a novel of "social value," covering a great deal of Negro Charleston: the aristocratic "Sacred Ground," where old families maintain "their Negroes," the teeming streets of the Negro ghetto. Since Mr. Coleman charts all of this in less than three hundred pages, besides hopping over to the sea islands, it is obvious that he must omit a great deal. What his imagination gleans as worth saving from the ruck of impressions shows his bent. He is the traveller to a strange country, cherishing the incident of picturesque local color and the exotically primitive character. This novel would pass current as realism only with those who hold that some accuracy of speech, costume, custom and setting is enough to balance very unusual people in unbelievable carryings on. Recalling Heyward and Julia Peterkin and even Roark Bradford, he does not equal their portraiture.

The narrative follows closely the love-life of the heroine Lasses, brown and 'beautageous' and of the siren, Crissy, near-white and villainous. Both take lovers with equal alacrity, regularity, and casualness, although Lasses is kept the ingenue, and Crissy the hussy. Tater is in love with Lasses, but keeps liason with Crissy. Crissy always sends for him when Lasses is with some presentable rival; Tater, despising Crissy always goes, and Lasses is as free as she is willing to gather more lovers. But after Froggy Lesesne is cut to ribbons by a jealous swain over another girl, and the Gadfly has killed Day-dey on account of Lasses, and Tater (à la Rudolph Fisher's *Blades of Steel*) has gashed Gadfly's face with a razor blade, and black Cupid of the Sea Islands renounced Lasses, and Tater has lost status as a "whuh-folks nigger" for cutting (and one reader has become weary of the cute names and longs for a plain old Sam and Annie)— then Lasses and Tater go back to the soil to live out their destiny.

Mr. Coleman went to Charleston in 1932; he is only twenty-seven years old. But, more Roman than the Romans themselves, *he knows his Ne-*

groes! Thus: Lasses' "eyes were bright and intelligent. But thetre the manifestation of white blooded ended." "Crissy's father had been the lightest Negro in Charleston. His eyes were gray and intelligent. He swept over the mulatto women in town like a plague." Tater, a citybred servant, son of servants *"stooped and picked up a soft clod of the black earth . . . felt a strange feeling of contentment . . . he did not understand. He did not know that to the black man whose roots were torn from Africa and embedded deep in this new land of the South that 'a garden and a cabin and a cotton field' are his simple and ultimate goal. They are his black heritage." "A nigger like de sweat pourin' off him, and like de cotton fiel' bettuh den any othuh place in de worl'."* Sure. That's why darkies were born.

Mr. Bradford's publishers: *"By birth, environment and education, Roark Bradford is perhaps better fitted to write of the Southern Negro than anyone in the United States. . . . No one interprets the mercurial moods of the careless, happy, colored people of the South as vividly and sympathetically."* Mr. Coleman's publishers: *"The true Southern Negro. . . . All the superstition, the primitive fanaticism, the sensuality, lightheartedness, easy humor and violence of the black man."* The masters have no quarrel; they agree in what is there. They also agree in forgetting to mention insult, brutality, deprivation of opportunity, injustice, and exploitation. Well, I guess they know what they are doing; maybe these things aren't really there; these literary masters are white folks, they ought to know.

WHEN THE NEGRO WAS IN VOGUE

The 1920's were the years of Manhattan's black Renaissance. It began with *Shuffle Along, Running Wild,* and the Charleston. Perhaps some people would say even with *The Emperor Jones,* Charles Gilpin, and the tom-toms at the Provincetown. But certainly it was the musical revue, *Shuffle Along,* that gave a scintillating send-off to that Negro vogue in Manhattan, which reached its peak just before the crash of 1929, the crash that sent Negroes, white folks, and all rolling down the hill toward the Works Progress Administration.

Shuffle Along was a honey of a show. Swift, bright, funny, rollicking, and gay, with a dozen danceable, singable tunes. Besides, look who were in it: The now famous choir director, Hall Johnson, and the composer, William Grant Still, were a part of the orchestra. Eubie Blake and Noble Sissle wrote the music and played and acted in the show. Miller and Lyles were the comics. Florence Mills skyrocketed to fame in the second act. Trixie Smith sang "He May Be Your Man But He Comes to See Me Sometimes." And Caterina Jarboro, now a European prima

223

donna, and the internationally celebrated Josephine Baker
were merely in the chorus. Everybody was in the audience
—including me. People came back to see it innumerable
times. It was always packed.

To see *Shuffle Along* was the main reason I wanted to
go to Columbia. When I saw it, I was thrilled and de-
lighted. From then on I was in the gallery of the Cort
Theatre every time I got a chance. That year, too, I saw
Katharine Cornell in *A Bill of Divorcement*, Margaret
Wycherly in *The Verge*, Maugham's *The Circle* with Mrs.
Leslie Carter, and the Theatre Guild production of
Kaiser's *From Morn Till Midnight*. But I remember
Shuffle Along best of all. It gave just the proper push—a
pre-Charleston kick—to that Negro vogue of the 20's, that
spread to books, African sculpture, music, and dancing.

Put down the 1920's for the rise of Roland Hayes, who
packed Carnegie Hall, the rise of Paul Robeson in New
York and London, of Florence Mills over two continents,
of Rose McClendon in Broadway parts that never measured up to her, the booming voice of Bessie Smith and the
low moan of Clara on thousands of records, and the rise
of that grand comedienne of song, Ethel Waters, singing:
"Charlie's elected now! He's in right for sure!" Put down
the 1920's for Louis Armstrong and Gladys Bentley and
Josephine Baker.

White people began to come to Harlem in droves. For
several years they packed the expensive Cotton Club on
Lenox Avenue. But I was never there, because the Cotton Club was a Jim Crow club for gangsters and monied
whites. They were not cordial to Negro patronage, unless
you were a celebrity like Bojangles. So Harlem Negroes
did not like the Cotton Club and never appreciated its Jim

Crow policy in the very heart of their dark community. Nor did ordinary Negroes like the growing influx of whites toward Harlem after sundown, flooding the little cabarets and bars where formerly only colored people laughed and sang, and where now the strangers were given the best ringside tables to sit and stare at the Negro customers—like amusing animals in a zoo.

The Negroes said: "We can't go downtown and sit and stare at you in your clubs. You won't even let us in your clubs." But they didn't say it out loud—for Negroes are practically never rude to white people. So thousands of whites came to Harlem night after night, thinking the Negroes loved to have them there, and firmly believing that all Harlemites left their houses at sundown to sing and dance in cabarets, because most of the whites saw nothing but the cabarets, not the houses.

Some of the owners of Harlem clubs, delighted at the flood of white patronage, made the grievous error of barring their own race, after the manner of the famous Cotton Club. But most of these quickly lost business and folded up, because they failed to realize that a large part of the Harlem attraction for downtown New Yorkers lay in simply watching the colored customers amuse themselves. And the smaller clubs, of course, had no big floor shows or a name band like the Cotton Club, where Duke Ellington usually held forth, so, without black patronage, they were not amusing at all.

Some of the small clubs, however, had people like Gladys Bentley, who was something worth discovering in those days, before she got famous, acquired an accompanist, specially written material, and conscious vulgarity. But for two or three amazing years, Miss Bentley sat, and played a big piano all night long, literally all night, without stopping—singing songs like "The St. James Infirmary," from ten in the evening until dawn, with scarcely a break between the notes, sliding from one song to another, with a powerful and continuous underbeat of jungle rhythm. Miss Bentley was an amazing exhibition of musical energy —a large, dark, masculine lady, whose feet pounded the floor while her fingers pounded the keyboard—a perfect piece of African sculpture, animated by her own rhythm.

But when the place where she played became too well known, she began to sing with an accompanist, became a star, moved to a larger place, then downtown, and is now in Hollywood. The old magic of the woman and the piano and the night and the rhythm being one is gone. But everything goes, one way or another. The '20's are gone and lots of fine things in Harlem night life have disappeared like snow in the sun—since it became utterly commercial, planned for the downtown tourist trade, and therefore dull.

The lindy-hoppers at the Savoy even began to practise acrobatic routines, and to do absurd things for the entertainment of the whites, that probably never would have entered their heads to attempt merely for their own effortless amusement. Some of the lindy-hoppers had cards printed with their names on them and became dance professors teaching the tourists. Then Harlem nights became show nights for the Nordics.

Some critics say that that is what happened to certain Negro writers, too—that they ceased to write to amuse themselves and began to write to amuse and entertain white people, and in so doing distorted and over-colored their material, and left out a great many things they thought would offend their American brothers of a lighter complexion. Maybe—since Negroes have writer-racketeers, as has any other race. But I have known almost all of them, and most of the good ones have tried to be honest, write honestly, and express their world as they saw it.

All of us know that the gay and sparkling life of the so-called Negro Renaissance of the '20's was not so gay and sparkling beneath the surface as it looked. Carl Van Vechten, in the character of Byron in *Nigger Heaven*, captured some of the bitterness and frustration of literary Harlem that Wallace Thurman later so effectively poured into his *Infants of the Spring*—the only novel by a Negro about that fantastic period when Harlem was in vogue.

It was a period when, at almost every Harlem upper-crust dance or party, one would be introduced to various distinguished white celebrities there as guests. It was a period when almost any Harlem Negro of any social importance at all would be likely to say casually: "As I was remarking the other day to Heywood—," meaning Heywood Broun. Or: "As I said to George—," referring to George Gershwin. It was a period when local and visiting royalty were not at all uncommon in Harlem. And when the parties of A'Lelia Walker, the Negro heiress, were filled with guests whose names would turn any Nordic social climber green with envy. It was a period when Harold Jackman, a handsome young Harlem school teacher of modest means, calmly announced one day that he was sailing for the Riviera for a fortnight, to attend Princess Murat's yachting party. It was a period when Charleston preachers opened up shouting churches as sideshows for white tourists. It was a period when at least one charming colored chorus girl, amber enough to pass for a Latin American, was living in a pent house, with all her bills paid by a gentleman whose name was

251

banker's magic on Wall Street. It was a period when every season there was at least one hit play on Broadway acted by a Negro cast. And when books by Negro authors were being published with much greater frequency and much more publicity than ever before or since in history. It was a period when white writers wrote about Negroes more successfully (commercially speaking) than Negroes did about themselves. It was the period (God help us!) when Ethel Barrymore appeared in blackface in *Scarlet Sister Mary!* It was the period when the Negro was in vogue.

I was there. I had a swell time while it lasted. But I thought it wouldn't last long. (I remember the vogue for things Russian, the season the Chauve-Souris first came to town.) For how could a large and enthusiastic number of people be crazy about Negroes forever? But some Harlemites thought the millennium had come. They thought the race problem had at last been solved through Art plus Gladys Bentley. They were sure the New Negro would lead a new life from then on in green pastures of tolerance created by Countee Cullen, Ethel Waters, Claude McKay, Duke Ellington, Bojangles, and Alain Locke.

I don't know what made any Negroes think that—except that they were mostly intellectuals doing the thinking. The ordinary Negroes hadn't heard of the Negro Renaissance. And if they had, it hadn't raised their wages any. As for all those white folks in the speakeasies and night clubs of Harlem—well, maybe a colored man could find *some* place to have a drink that the tourists hadn't yet discovered.

Then it was that house-rent parties began to flourish—and not always to raise the rent either. But, as often as not, to have a get-together of one's own, where you could do the black-bottom with no stranger behind you trying to do it, too. Non-theatrical, non-intellectual Harlem was an unwilling victim of its own vogue. It didn't like to be stared at by white folks. But perhaps the downtowners never knew this—for the cabaret owners, the entertainers, and the speakeasy proprietors treated them fine—as long as they paid.

The Saturday night rent parties that I attended were often more amusing than any night club, in small apartments where God knows who lived—because the guests seldom did—but where the piano would often be augmented by a guitar, or an odd cornet, or somebody with a pair of drums walking in off the street. And where awful bootleg whiskey and good fried fish or steaming chitterling were sold at very low prices. And the dancing and singing and impromptu entertaining went on until dawn came in at the windows.

These parties, often termed whist parties or dances, were usually announced by brightly colored cards stuck in the grille of apartment house elevators. Some of the cards were highly entertaining in themselves:

We got yellow girls, we've got black and tan
Will you have a good time? - YEAH MAN !

A Social Whist Party

—GIVEN BY—

MARY WINSTON

147 West 145th Street   Apt. 5

SATURDAY EVE., MARCH 19th, 1932

GOOD MUSIC   REFRESHMENTS

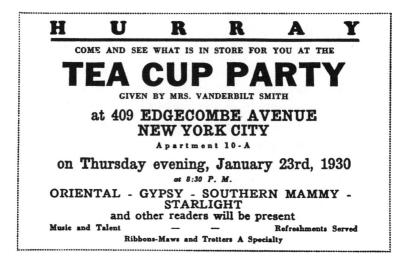

H U R R A Y

COME AND SEE WHAT IS IN STORE FOR YOU AT THE

TEA CUP PARTY

GIVEN BY MRS. VANDERBILT SMITH

at 409 EDGECOMBE AVENUE
NEW YORK CITY

Apartment 10-A

on Thursday evening, January 23rd, 1930

at 8:30 P. M.

ORIENTAL - GYPSY - SOUTHERN MAMMY -
STARLIGHT
and other readers will be present

Music and Talent   —   —   Refreshments Served

Ribbons-Maws and Trotters A Specialty

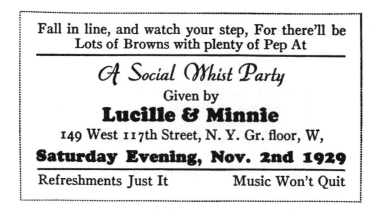

Fall in line, and watch your step, For there'll be
Lots of Browns with plenty of Pep At

A Social Whist Party

Given by

Lucille & Minnie

149 West 117th Street, N. Y. Gr. floor, W,

Saturday Evening, Nov. 2nd 1929

Refreshments Just It   Music Won't Quit

If Sweet Mamma is running wild, and you are looking
for a Do-right child, just come around and
linger awhile at a

SOCIAL WHIST PARTY

GIVEN BY

PINKNEY & EPPS

260 West 129th Street   Apartment 10

SATURDAY EVENING, JUNE 9, 1928

GOOD MUSIC   REFRESHMENTS

Railroad Men's Ball

AT CANDY'S PLACE

FRIDAY, SATURDAY & SUNDAY,

April 29-30, May 1, 1927

Black Wax, says change your mind and say they
do and he will give you a hearing, while MEAT
HOUSE SLIM, laying in the bin
killing all good men.

L. A. VAUGH, *President*

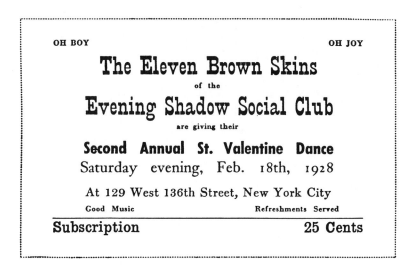

OH BOY   OH JOY

The Eleven Brown Skins

of the

Evening Shadow Social Club

are giving their

Second Annual St. Valentine Dance

Saturday evening, Feb. 18th, 1928

At 129 West 136th Street, New York City

Good Music   Refreshments Served

Subscription   25 Cents

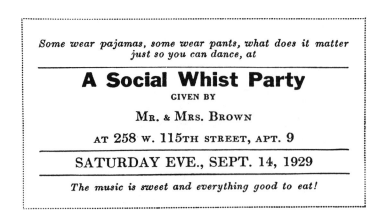

*Some wear pajamas, some wear pants, what does it matter
just so you can dance, at*

A Social Whist Party

GIVEN BY

Mr. & Mrs. Brown

AT 258 W. 115TH STREET, APT. 9

SATURDAY EVE., SEPT. 14, 1929

The music is sweet and everything good to eat!

Almost every Saturday night when I was in Harlem I went to a house-rent party. I wrote lots of poems about house-rent parties, and ate thereat many a fried fish and pig's foot—with liquid refreshments on the side. I met ladies' maids and truck drivers, laundry workers and shoe shine boys, seamstresses and porters. I can still hear their laughter in my ears, hear the soft slow music, and feel the floor shaking as the dancers danced.

HARLEM LITERATI

The summer of 1926, I lived in a rooming house on 137th Street, where Wallace Thurman and Harcourt Tynes also lived. Thurman was then managing editor of the *Messenger*, a Negro magazine that had a curious career. It began by being very radical, racial, and socialistic, just after the war. I believe it received a grant from the Garland Fund in its early days. Then it later became a kind of Negro society magazine and a plugger for Negro business, with photographs of prominent colored ladies and their nice homes in it. A. Phillip Randolph, now President of the Brotherhood of Sleeping Car Porters, Chandler Owen, and George S. Schuyler were connected with it. Schuyler's editorials, à la Mencken, were the most interesting things in the magazine, verbal brickbats that said sometimes one thing, sometimes another, but always vigorously. I asked Thurman what kind of magazine the *Messenger* was, and he said it reflected the policy of whoever paid off best at the time.

Anyway, the *Messenger* bought my first short stories.
They paid me ten dollars a story. Wallace Thurman
wrote me that they were very bad stories, but better than
any others they could find, so he published them.

Thurman had recently come from California to New
York. He was a strangely brilliant black boy, who had
read everything, and whose critical mind could find something wrong with everything he read. I have no critical
mind, so I usually either like a book or don't. But I am
not capable of liking a book and then finding a million
things wrong with it, too—as Thurman was capable of
doing.

Thurman had read so many books because he could read
eleven lines at a time. He would get from the library a
great pile of volumes that would have taken me a year to
read. But he would go through them in less than a week,
and be able to discuss each one at great length with anybody. That was why, I suppose, he was later given a job as
a reader at Macaulay's—the only Negro reader, so far as I
know, to be employed by any of the larger publishing
firms.

Later Thurman became a ghost writer for *True Story*,
and other publications, writing under all sorts of fantastic
names, like Ethel Belle Mandrake or Patrick Casey. He
did Irish and Jewish and Catholic "true confessions." He
collaborated with William Jordan Rapp on plays and
novels. Later he ghosted books. In fact, this quite dark
young Negro is said to have written *Men, Women, and
Checks*.

Wallace Thurman wanted to be a great writer, but none
of his own work ever made him happy. *The Blacker the
Berry*, his first book, was an important novel on a subject

little dwelt upon in Negro fiction—the plight of the very dark Negro woman, who encounters in some communities a double wall of color prejudice within and without the race. His play, *Harlem,* considerably distorted for box office purposes, was, nevertheless, a compelling study—and the only one in the theater—of the impact of Harlem on a Negro family fresh from the South. And his *Infants of the Spring,* a superb and bitter study of the bohemian fringe of Harlem's literary and artistic life, is a compelling book.

But none of these things pleased Wallace Thurman. He wanted to be a *very* great writer, like Gorki or Thomas Mann, and he felt that he was merely a journalistic writer. His critical mind, comparing his pages to the thousands of other pages he had read, by Proust, Melville, Tolstoy, Galsworthy, Dostoyevski, Henry James, Sainte-Beauve, Taine, Anatole France, found his own pages vastly wanting. So he contented himself by writing a great deal for money, laughing bitterly at his fabulously concocted "true stories," creating two bad motion pictures of the "Adults Only" type for Hollywood, drinking more and more gin, and then threatening to jump out of windows at people's parties and kill himself.

During the summer of 1926, Wallace Thurman, Zora Neale Hurston, Aaron Douglas, John P. Davis, Bruce Nugent, Gwendolyn Bennett, and I decided to publish "a Negro quarterly of the arts" to be called *Fire*—the idea being that it would burn up a lot of the old, dead conventional Negro-white ideas of the past, *épater le bourgeois* into a realization of the existence of the younger Negro writers and artists, and provide us with an outlet for publication not available in the limited pages of the small Negro magazines then existing, the *Crisis, Opportunity,*

and the *Messenger*—the first two being house organs of
inter-racial organizations, and the latter being God knows
what.

Sweltering summer evenings we met to plan *Fire*. Each
of the seven of us agreed to give fifty dollars to finance the
first issue. Thurman was to edit it, John P. Davis to handle
the business end, and Bruce Nugent to take charge of dis-
tribution. The rest of us were to serve as an editorial
board to collect material, contribute our own work, and
act in any useful way that we could. For artists and writers,
we got along fine and there were no quarrels. But October
came before we were ready to go to press. I had to return
to Lincoln, John Davis to Law School at Harvard, Zora
Hurston to her studies at Barnard, from whence she went
about Harlem with an anthropologist's ruler, measuring
heads for Franz Boas.

Only three of the seven had contributed their fifty dollars, but the others faithfully promised to send theirs out of
tuition checks, wages, or begging. Thurman went on with
the work of preparing the magazine. He got a printer.
He planned the layout. It had to be on good paper, he
said, worthy of the drawings of Aaron Douglas. It had
to have beautiful type, worthy of the first Negro art
quarterly. It had to be what we seven young Negroes
dreamed our magazine would be—so in the end it cost
almost a thousand dollars, and nobody could pay the
bills.

I don't know how Thurman persuaded the printer to
let us have all the copies to distribute, but he did. I think
Alain Locke, among others, signed notes guaranteeing
payments. But since Thurman was the only one of the
seven of us with a regular job, for the next three or four
years his checks were constantly being attached and his

income seized to pay for *Fire*. And whenever I sold a poem, mine went there, too—to *Fire*.

None of the older Negro intellectuals would have anything to do with *Fire*. Dr. DuBois in the *Crisis* roasted it. The Negro press called it all sorts of bad names, largely because of a green and purple story by Bruce Nugent, in the Oscar Wilde tradition, which we had included. Rean Graves, the critic for the *Baltimore Afro-American*, began his review by saying: "I have just tossed the first issue of *Fire* into the fire." Commenting upon various of our contributors, he said: "Aaron Douglas who, in spite of himself and the meaningless grotesqueness of his creations, has gained a reputation as an artist, is permitted to spoil three perfectly good pages and a cover with his pen and ink hudge pudge. Countee Cullen has written a beautiful poem in his 'From a Dark Tower,' but tries his best to obscure the thought in superfluous sentences. Langston Hughes displays his usual ability to say nothing in many words."

So *Fire* had plenty of cold water thrown on it by the colored critics. The white critics (except for an excellent editorial in the *Bookman* for November, 1926) scarcely noticed it at all. We had no way of getting it distributed to bookstands or news stands. Bruce Nugent took it around New York on foot and some of the Greenwich Village bookshops put it on display, and sold it for us. But then Bruce, who had no job, would collect the money and, on account of salary, eat it up before he got back to Harlem.

Finally, irony of ironies, several hundred copies of *Fire* were stored in the basement of an apartment where an actual fire occurred and the bulk of the whole issue was burned up. Even after that Thurman had to go on paying the printer.

Now *Fire* is a collector's item, and very difficult to get, being mostly ashes.

That taught me a lesson about little magazines. But since white folks had them, we Negroes thought we could have one, too. But we didn't have the money.

Wallace Thurman laughed a long bitter laugh. He was a strange kind of fellow, who liked to drink gin, but *didn't* like to drink gin; who liked being a Negro, but felt it a great handicap; who adored bohemianism, but thought it wrong to be a bohemian. He liked to waste a lot of time, but he always felt guilty wasting time. He loathed crowds, yet he hated to be alone. He almost always felt bad, yet he didn't write poetry.

Once I told him if I could feel as bad as he did *all* the time, I would surely produce wonderful books. But he said you had to know how to *write*, as well as how to feel bad. I said I didn't have to know how to feel bad, because, every so often, the blues just naturally overtook me, like a blind beggar with an old guitar:

> *You don't know,*
> *You don't know my mind—*
> *When you see me laughin',*
> *I'm laughin' to keep from cryin'.*

About the future of Negro literature Thurman was very pessimistic. He thought the Negro vogue had made us all too conscious of ourselves, had flattered and spoiled us, and had provided too many easy opportunities for some of us to drink gin and more gin, on which he thought we would always be drunk. With his bitter sense of humor, he called the Harlem literati, the "niggerati."

Of this "niggerati," Zora Neale Hurston was certainly the most amusing. Only to reach a wider audience, need she ever write books—because she is a perfect book of entertainment in herself. In her youth she was always getting scholarships and things from wealthy white people, some of whom simply paid her just to sit around and represent the Negro race for them, she did it in such a racy fashion. She was full of side-splitting anecdotes, humorous tales, and tragicomic stories, remembered out of her life in the South as a daughter of a travelling minister of God. She could make you laugh one minute and cry the next. To many of her white friends, no doubt, she was a perfect "darkie," in the nice meaning they give the term—that is a naïve, childlike, sweet, humorous, and highly colored Negro.

But Miss Hurston was clever, too—a student who didn't let college give her a broad *a* and who had great scorn for all pretensions, academic or otherwise. That is why she was such a fine folk-lore collector, able to go among the people and never act as if she had been to school at all. Almost nobody else could stop the average Harlemite on Lenox Avenue and measure his head with a strange-looking, anthropological device and not get bawled out for the attempt, except Zora, who used to stop anyone whose head looked interesting, and measure it.

When Miss Hurston graduated from Barnard she took an apartment in West 66th Street near the park, in that row of Negro houses there. She moved in with no furniture at all and no money, but in a few days friends had given her everything, from decorative silver birds, perched atop the linen cabinet, down to a footstool. And on Saturday night, to christen the place, she had a *hand*-chicken dinner, since she had forgotten to say she needed forks.

She seemed to know almost everybody in New York. She had been a secretary to Fannie Hurst, and had met dozens of celebrities whose friendship she retained. Yet she was always having terrific ups-and-downs about money. She tells this story on herself, about needing a nickel to go downtown one day and wondering where on earth she would get it. As she approached the subway, she was stopped by a blind beggar holding out his cup.

"Please help the blind! Help the blind! A nickel for the blind!"

"I need money worse than you today," said Miss Hurston, taking five cents out of his cup. "Lend me this! Next time, I'll give it back." And she went on downtown.

Harlem was like a great magnet for the Negro intellectual, pulling him from everywhere. Or perhaps the magnet was New York—but once in New York, he had to live in Harlem, for rooms were hardly to be found elsewhere unless one could pass for white or Mexican or Eurasian and perhaps live in the Village—which always seemed to me a very arty locale, in spite of the many real artists and writers who lived there. Only a few of the New Negroes lived in the Village, Harlem being their real stamping ground.

The wittiest of these New Negroes of Harlem, whose tongue was flavored with the sharpest and saltiest humor, was Rudolph Fisher, whose stories appeared in the *Atlantic Monthly*. His novel, *Walls of Jericho*, captures but slightly the raciness of his own conversation. He was a young medical doctor and X-ray specialist, who always frightened me a little, because he could think of the most incisively clever things to say—and I could never think of anything to answer. He and Alain Locke together were great for intellectual wise-cracking. The two would fling big and witty words about with such swift and punning innuendo that an ordinary mortal just sat and looked wary for fear of being caught in a net of witticisms beyond his cultural ken. I used to wish I could talk like Rudolph Fisher. Besides being a good writer, he was an excellent singer, and had sung with Paul Robeson during their college days. But I guess Fisher was too brilliant and too talented to stay long on this earth. During the same week, in December, 1934, he and Wallace Thurman both died.

Thurman died of tuberculosis in the charity ward at Bellevue Hospital, having just flown back to New York from Hollywood.

GURDJIEFF IN HARLEM

One of the most talented of the Negro writers, Jean Toomer, went to Paris to become a follower and disciple of Gurdjieff's at Fontainebleau, where Katherine Mansfield died. He returned to Harlem, having achieved awareness, to impart his precepts to the literati. Wallace Thurman and Dorothy Peterson, Aaron Douglas, and Nella Larsen, not to speak of a number of lesser known Harlemites of the literary and social world, became ardent neophytes of the word brought from Fontainebleau by this handsome young olive-skinned bearer of Gurdjieff's message to upper Manhattan.

But the trouble with such a life-pattern in Harlem was that practically everybody had to work all day to make a living, and the cult of Gurdjieff demanded not only study and application, but a large amount of inner observation and silent concentration as well. So while some

of Mr. Toomer's best disciples were sitting long hours concentrating, unaware of time, unfortunately they lost their
jobs, and could no longer pay the handsome young teacher
for his instructions. Others had so little time to concentrate, if they wanted to live and eat, that their advance toward cosmic consciousness was slow and their hope of
achieving awareness distant indeed. So Jean Toomer
shortly left his Harlem group and went downtown to drop
the seeds of Gurdjieff in less dark and poverty-stricken
fields.

They liked him downtown because he was better-look-
ing than Krishnamurti, some said. He had an evolved
soul, and that soul made him feel that nothing else mat-
tered, not even writing. From downtown New York,
Toomer carried Gurdjieff to Chicago's Gold Coast—and
the Negroes lost one of the most talented of all their
writers—the author of the beautiful book of prose and
verse, *Cane*.

The next thing Harlem heard of Jean Toomer was that
he had married Margery Latimer, a talented white
novelist, and maintained to the newspapers that he was
no more colored than white—as certainly his complexion
indicated. When the late James Weldon Johnson wrote
him for permission to use some of his poems in the *Book
of American Negro Poetry*, Mr. Johnson reported that the
poet, who, a few years before, was "caroling softly souls
of slavery" now refused to permit his poems to appear in
an anthology of *Negro* verse—which put all the critics,
white and colored, in a great dilemma. How should they
class the author of *Cane* in their lists and summaries? With
Dubose Heyward and Julia Peterkin? Or with Claude
McKay and Countee Cullen? Nobody knew exactly, it being a case of black blood and white blood having met and

the individual deciding, after Paris and Gurdjieff, to be merely American.

One can't blame him for that. Certainly nobody in Harlem could afford to pay for Gurdjieff. And very few there have evolved souls.

Now Mr. Toomer is married to a lady of means—his second wife—of New York and Santa Fe, and is never seen on Lenox Avenue any more. Harlem is sorry he stopped writing. He was a fine American writer. But when we get as democratic in America as we pretend we are on days when we wish to shame Hitler, nobody will bother much about anybody else's race anyway. Why should Mr. Toomer live in Harlem if he doesn't care to? Democracy is democracy, isn't it?

PARTIES

In those days of the late 1920's, there were a great many parties, in Harlem and out, to which various members of the New Negro group were invited. These parties, when given by important Harlemites (or Carl Van Vechten) were reported in full in the society pages of the Harlem press, but best in the sparkling Harlemese of Geraldyn Dismond who wrote for the *Interstate Tattler*. On one of Taylor Gordon's fiestas she reports as follows:

What a crowd! All classes and colors met face to face, ultra aristocrats, Bourgeois, Communists, Park Avenuers galore, bookers, publishers, Broadway celebs, and Harlemites giving each other the once over. The social revolution was on. And yes, Lady Nancy Cunard was there all in black (she would) with 12 of her grand bracelets. . . . And was the entertainment on the up and up! Into swell dance music was injected African drums that played havoc with blood pressure. Jimmy Daniels sang his gigolo hits. Gus Simons, the Harlem crooner, made the River Stay Away From His Door and Taylor himself brought out everything from "Hot Dog" to "Bravo" when he made high C.

A'Lelia Walker was the then great Harlem party giver, although Mrs. Bernia Austin fell but little behind. And at the Seventh Avenue apartment of Jessie Fauset, literary soirées with much poetry and but little to drink were the order of the day. The same was true of Lillian Alexander's, where the older intellectuals gathered.

A'Lelia Walker, however, big-hearted, night-dark, hair-straightening heiress, made no pretense at being intellectual or exclusive. At her "at homes" Negro poets and Negro number bankers mingled with downtown poets and seat-on-the-stock-exchange racketeers. Countee Cullen would be there and Witter Bynner, Muriel Draper and Nora Holt, Andy Razaf and Taylor Gordon. And a good time was had by all.

A'Lelia Walker had an apartment that held perhaps a hundred people. She would usually issue several hundred invitations to each party. Unless you went early there was no possible way of getting in. Her parties were as crowded as the New York subway at the rush hour—entrance, lobby, steps, hallway, and apartment a milling crush of guests, with everybody seeming to enjoy the crowding. Once, some royal personage arrived, a Scandinavian prince, I believe, but his equerry saw no way of getting him through the crowded entrance hall and into the party, so word was sent in to A'Lelia Walker that His Highness, the Prince, was waiting without. A'Lelia sent word back that she saw no way of getting His Highness in, either, nor could she herself get out through the crowd to greet him. But she offered to send refreshments downstairs to the Prince's car.

A'Lelia Walker was a gorgeous dark Amazon, in a silver turban. She had a town house in New York (also an apartment where she preferred to live) and a country mansion at Irvington-on-the-Hudson, with pipe organ programs each morning to awaken her guests gently. Her mother made a great fortune from the Madame Walker Hair Straightening Process, which had worked wonders on unruly Negro hair in the early nineteen hundreds—and which continues to work wonders today. The daughter used much of that money for fun. A'Lelia Walker was the joy-goddess of Harlem's 1920's.

She had been very much in love with her first husband, from whom she was divorced. Once at one of her parties she began to cry about him. She retired to her boudoir and wept. Some of her friends went in to comfort her, and found her clutching a memento of their broken romance.

"The only thing I have left that he gave me," she sobbed, "it's all I have left of him!"

It was a gold shoehorn.

When A'Lelia Walker died in 1931, she had a grand funeral. It was by invitation only. But, just as for her parties, a great many more invitations had been issued than the small but exclusive Seventh Avenue funeral parlor could provide for. Hours before the funeral, the street in front of the undertaker's chapel was crowded. The doors were not opened until the cortège arrived— and the cortège was late. When it came, there were almost enough family mourners, attendants, and honorary pall-bearers in the procession to fill the room; as well as the representatives of the various Walker beauty parlors throughout the country. And there were still hundreds of friends outside, waving their white, engraved invitations aloft in the vain hope of entering.

Once the last honorary pallbearers had marched in, there was a great crush at the doors. Muriel Draper, Rita Romilly, Mrs. Roy Sheldon, and I were among the fortunate few who achieved an entrance.

We were startled to find De Lawd standing over A'Lelia's casket. It was a truly amazing illusion. At that time *The Green Pastures* was at the height of its fame, and there stood De Lawd in the person of Rev. E. Clayton Powell, a Harlem minister, who looked exactly like Richard B. Harrison in the famous role in the play. He had the same white hair and kind face, and was later offered the part of De Lawd in the film version of the drama. Now, he stood there motionless in the dim light behind the silver casket of A'Lelia Walker.

Soft music played and it was very solemn. When we were seated and the chapel became dead silent, De Lawd said: "The Four Bon Bons will now sing."

A night club quartette that had often performed at A'Lelia's parties arose and sang for her. They sang Noel Coward's "I'll See You Again," and they swung it slightly, as she might have liked it. It was a grand funeral and very much like a party. Mrs. Mary McCleod Bethune spoke in that great deep voice of hers, as only she can speak. She recalled the poor mother of A'Lelia Walker in old clothes, who had labored to bring the gift of beauty to Negro womanhood, and had taught them the care of their skin and their hair, and had built up a great business and a great fortune to the pride and glory of the Negro race—and then had given it all to her daughter, A'Lelia.

Then a poem of mine was read by Edward Perry, "To

A'Lelia." And after that the girls from the various Walker beauty shops throughout America brought their flowers and laid them on the bier.

That was really the end of the gay times of the New Negro era in Harlem, the period that had begun to reach its end when the crash came in 1929 and the white people had much less money to spend on themselves, and practically none to spend on Negroes, for the depression brought everybody down a peg or two. And the Negroes had but few pegs to fall.

But in those pre-crash days there were parties and parties. At the novelist, Jessie Fauset's, parties there was always quite a different atmosphere from that at most other Harlem good-time gatherings. At Miss Fauset's, a good time was shared by talking literature and reading poetry aloud and perhaps enjoying some conversation in French. White people were seldom present there unless they were very distinguished white people, because Jessie Fauset did not feel like opening her home to mere sightseers, or faddists momentarily in love with Negro life. At her house one would usually meet editors and students, writers and social workers, and serious people who liked books and the British Museum, and had perhaps been to Florence. (Italy, not Alabama.)

I remember, one night at her home there was a gathering in honor of Salvador de Madariaga, the Spanish diplomat and savant, which somehow became a rather self-conscious gathering, with all the Harlem writers called upon to recite their poems and speak their pieces. But afterwards, Charles S. Johnson and I invited Mr. Madariaga to Small's Paradise where we had a "ball" until the dawn came up and forced us from the club.

In those days, 409 Edgecombe, Harlem's tallest and

most exclusive apartment house, was quite a party center. The Walter Whites and the Aaron Douglases, among others, lived and entertained there. Walter White was a jovial and cultured host, with a sprightly mind, and an apartment overlooking the Hudson. He had the most beautiful wife in Harlem, and they were always hospitable to hungry literati like me.

At the Aaron Douglases', although he was a painter, more young writers were found than painters. Usually everybody would chip in and go dutch on the refreshments, calling down to the nearest bootlegger for a bottle of whatever it was that was drunk in those days, when labels made no difference at all in the liquid content—Scotch, bourbon, rye, and gin being the same except for coloring matter.

Arna Bontemps, poet and coming novelist, quiet and scholarly, looking like a young edition of Dr. DuBois, was the mysterious member of the Harlem literati, in that we knew he had recently married, but none of us had ever seen his wife. All the writers wondered who she was and what she looked like. He never brought her with him to any of the parties, so she remained the mystery of the New Negro Renaissance. But I went with him once to his apartment to meet her, and found her a shy and charming girl, holding a golden baby on her lap. A year or two later there was another golden baby. And every time I went away to Haiti or Mexico or Europe and came back, there would be a new golden baby, each prettier than the last—so that was why the literati never saw Mrs. Bontemps.

Toward the end of the New Negro era, E. Simms Campbell came to Harlem from St. Louis, and began to try to sell cartoons to the *New Yorker*. My first memory of him is at a party at Gwendolyn Bennett's on Long Island. In the midst of the party, the young lady Mr. Campbell had brought, Constance Willis, whom he later married, began to put on her hat and coat and gloves. The hostess asked her if she was going home. She said: "No, only taking Elmer outside to straighten him out." What indiscretion he had committed at the party I never knew, perhaps flirting with some other girl, or taking a drink too many. But when we looked out, there was Constance giving Elmer an all-around talking-to on the sidewalk. And she must have straightened him out, because he was a very nice young man at parties ever after.

At the James Weldon Johnson parties and gumbo suppers, one met solid people like Clarence and Mrs. Darrow. At the Dr. Alexander's, you met the upper crust Negro intellectuals like Dr. DuBois. At Wallace Thurman's, you met the bohemians of both Harlem and the Village. And in the gin mills and speakeasies and night clubs between 125th and 145th, Eighth Avenue and Lenox, you met everybody from Buddy de Silva to Theodore Dreiser, Ann Pennington to the first Mrs. Eugene O'Neill. In the days when Harlem was in vogue, Amanda Randolph was at the Alhambra, Jimmy Walker was mayor of New York, and Louise sang at the old New World.

DOWNTOWN

Downtown there were many interesting parties in those days, too, to which I was sometimes bidden. I remember one at Florine Stettheimer's, another at V. F. Calverton's, and another at Bob Chandler's, where the walls were hung with paintings and Louise Helstrom served the drinks. Paul Haakon, who was a kid then whom Louise had "discovered" somewhere, danced and everybody Oh'ed and Ah'ed, and said what a beautiful young artist! What an artist! But later when nobody was listening, Paul Haakon said to me: "Some baloney—I'm no artist. I'm in vaudeville!"

I remember also a party at Jake Baker's, somewhere on the lower East Side near the river, where I do not recall any whites being present except Mr. Baker himself. Jake Baker then had one of the largest erotic libraries in New York, ranging from the ancient to the modern, the classic to the vulgar, the *Kama Sutra* to T. R. Smith's anthology of *Poetica Erotica*. But since Harlemites are not very familiar with erotic books, Mr. Baker was never able to get the party started. His gathering took on the atmosphere of the main reading room at the public library with everybody hunched over a book—trying to find out what white folks say about love when they really come to the point.

I remember also a big cocktail party for Ernestine Evans at the Ritz, when she had got a new job with some publishing firm and they were celebrating her addition to the staff. Josephine Herbst was there and we had a long talk near the hors-d'œuvres, and I liked Josephine Herbst very much. Also I recall a dinner party for Claire Spencer at Colin McPhee's and Jane Belo's in the village, where Claire Spencer told about a thrilling night flight over Manhattan Island in a monoplane and also another party in the Fifties for Rebecca West, who knew a lot of highly amusing gossip about the Queen of Rumania. I remember well, too, my first party after a Broadway opening, the one Horace Liveright gave for Paul Robeson and Fredi

Washington, following the premiere of Jim Tully's *Black Boy*. And there was one grand New Year's Eve fête at the Alfred A. Knopf's on Fifth Avenue, where I met Ethel Barrymore and Jascha Heifetz, and everybody was in tails but me, and all I had on was a blue serge suit—which didn't seem to matter to anyone—for Fifth Avenue was not nearly so snooty about clothes as Washington's Negro society.

Downtown at Charlie Studin's parties, at Arthur and Mrs. Spingarn's, Eddie Wasserman's, at Muriel Draper's, or Rita Romilly's, one would often meet almost as many Negro guests as in Harlem. But only Carl Van Vechten's parties were *so* Negro that they were reported as a matter of course in the colored society columns, just as though they occurred in Harlem instead of West 55th Street, where he and Fania Marinoff then lived in a Peter Whiffle apartment, full of silver fishes and colored glass balls and ceiling-high shelves of gaily-bound books.

Not only were there interesting Negroes at Carl Van Vechten's parties, ranging from famous writers to famous tap dancers, but there were always many other celebrities of various colors and kinds, old ones and new ones from Hollywood, Broadway, London, Paris or Harlem. I remember one party when Chief Long Lance of the cinema did an Indian war dance, while Adelaide Hall of *Blackbirds* played the drums, and an international assemblage crowded around to cheer.

At another of Mr. Van Vechten's parties, Bessie Smith sang the blues. And when she finished, Margarita D'Alvarez of the Metropolitan Opera arose and sang an aria. Bessie Smith did not know D'Alvarez, but, liking her voice, she went up to her when she had ceased and cried: "Don't let nobody tell you you can't sing!"

Carl Van Vechten and A'Lelia Walker were great

friends, and at each of their parties many of the same people were to be seen, but more writers were present at Carl Van Vechten's. At cocktail time, or in the evening, I first met at his house Somerset Maugham, Hugh Walpole, Fannie Hurst, Witter Bynner, Isa Glenn, Emily Clark, William Seabrook, Arthur Davison Ficke, Louis Untermeyer, and George Sylvester Viereck.

Mr. Viereck cured me of a very bad habit I used to have of thinking I had to say something nice to every writer I met concerning his work. Upon being introduced to Mr. Viereck, I said, "I like your books."

He demanded: "Which one?"

And I couldn't think of a single one.

Of course, at Mr. Van Vechten's parties there were always many others who were not writers: Lawrence Langner and Armina Marshall of the Theatre Guild, Eugene Goossens, Jane Belo, who married Colin McPhee and went to Bali to live, beautiful Rose Rolanda, who married Miguel Covarrubias, Lilyan Tashman, who died, Horace Liveright, Blanche Dunn, Ruben Mamoulian, Marie Doro, Nicholas Muray, Madame Helena Rubinstein, Richmond Barthe, Salvador Dali, Waldo Frank, Dudley Murphy, and often Dorothy Peterson, a charming colored girl who had grown up mostly in Puerto Rico, and who moved with such poise among these colorful celebrities that I thought when I first met her she was a white girl of the grande monde, slightly sun-tanned. But she was a Negro teacher of French and Spanish, who later got a leave of absence from her school work to play Cain's Gal in *The Green Pastures*.

Being interested in the Negro problem in various parts of the world, Dorothy Peterson once asked Dali if he knew anything about Negroes.

"Everything!" Dali answered. "I've met Nancy Cunard!"

Speaking of celebrities, one night as one of Carl Van Vechten's parties was drawing to a close, Rudolph Valentino called, saying that he was on his way. That was the only time I have ever seen the genial Van Vechten hospitality waver. He told Mr. Valentino the party was over. It seems that our host was slightly perturbed at the thought of so celebrated a guest coming into a party that had passed its peak. Besides, he told the rest of us, movie stars usually expect a lot of attention—and it was too late in the evening for such extended solicitude now.

Carl Van Vechten once wrote a book called *Parties*. But it is not nearly so amusing as his own parties. Once he gave a gossip party, where everybody was at liberty to go around the room repeating the worst things they could make up or recall about each other to their friends on opposite sides of the room—who were sure to go right over and tell them all about it.

At another party of his (but this was incidental) the guests were kept in a constant state of frightful expectancy by a lady standing in the hall outside Mr. Van Vechten's door, who announced that she was waiting for her husband to emerge from the opposite apartment, where he was visiting another woman. When I came to the party, I saw her standing grimly there. It was her full intention to kill her husband, she said. And she displayed to Mrs. Van Vechten's maids the pistol in her handbag.

At intervals during the evening, the woman in the hall would receive coffee from the Van Vechten party to help her maintain her vigil. But the suspense was not pleasant. I kept feeling goose pimples on my body and hearing a gun in my mind. Finally someone suggested phoning the

277

apartment across the way to inform the erring husband of the fate awaiting him if he came out. Perhaps this was done. I don't know. But I learned later that the woman waited until dawn and then went home. No husband emerged from the silent door, so her gun was not fired.

Once when Mr. Van Vechten gave a bon voyage party in the Prince of Wales suite aboard the Cunarder on which he was sailing, as the champagne flowed, Nora Holt, the scintillating Negro blonde entertainer de luxe from Nevada, sang a ribald ditty called, "My Daddy Rocks Me With One Steady Roll." As she ceased, a well-known New York matron cried ecstatically, with tears in her eyes: "My dear! Oh, my dear! How beautifully you sing Negro spirituals!"

Carl Van Vechten moved about filling glasses and playing host with the greatest of zest at his parties, while his tiny wife, Fania Marinoff, looking always very pretty and very gay, when the evening grew late would sometimes take Mr. Van Vechten severely to task for his drinking—before bidding the remaining guests good night and retiring to her bed.

Now, Mr. Van Vechten has entirely given up drinking (as well as writing books and smoking cigarettes) in favor of photography. Although his parties are still gaily liquid for those who wish it, he himself is sober as a judge, but not as solemn.

For several pleasant years, he gave an annual birthday party for James Weldon Johnson, young Alfred A. Knopf, Jr., and himself, for their birthdays fall on the same day. At the last of these parties the year before Mr. Johnson died, on the Van Vechten table there were three cakes, one red, one white, and one blue—the colors of our flag. They honored a Gentile, a Negro, and a Jew—friends and fellow-

Americans. But the differences of race did not occur to me until days later, when I thought back about the three colors and the three men.

Carl Van Vechten is like that party. He never talks grandiloquently about democracy or Americanism. Nor makes a fetish of those qualities. But he lives them with sincerity—and humor.

Perhaps that is why *his* parties were reported in the Harlem press.

SHOWS

During the *Fire* summer, I earned my living by writing lyrics and sketches for an intimate musical revue for Caroline Dudley (then Mrs. Reagan), sister of Dorothy Dudley, who wrote a fine study of Theodore Dreiser, and who introduced the Italian poet Carnevali to America.

Mrs. Reagan lived in an apartment in an old house in, I believe, West 11th Street, with a courtyard garden in the rear. And the apartment was all aflurry with excitement over the prospect of an intimate Negro revue, to star Paul Robeson, and to include the sparkling Nora Holt. And to present many of the then unexploited Negro folk-songs. All the material, music, and sketches were to be by Negro writers. I was helping Mrs. Reagan plan the revue, and later Rudolph Fisher came in on some of the skits. The house was alive with the continual comings and goings of Negro artists having auditions, tap dancers in one room, tramp bands in another, the ear-splitting voice of George Dewey Washington bursting the walls of the parlor, and comedians looking dumb in the courtyard.

In the midst of it all, Dorothy Dudley, who had suffered a broken toe, lay on a chaise longue, looking very pretty and bird-like, taking it all in, making charming comments, and waiting for her husband, Henry Harvey, to come home from his office. Then, if we were still working in the early evening, Mrs. Reagan would send out for a chicken or two, some peas and beans and cucumbers, and put them all in a grilling pan and run them in the oven, where everything cooked at once and automatically came out tasting very good, while everybody went on talking about the revue and writing things down and only looking once or twice in the oven to see what the chicken and cucumbers and peas were doing. And they would be doing very nicely, and would be eaten in the midst of writing, talking, and singing.

I continued to come up to New York from college weekends most of the winter to work on the revue. But meanwhile, Paul Robeson had gone to London to appear in *Showboat*. He made such a tremendous hit there that he refused to come back, although he was under contract to Mrs. Reagan, so Mrs. Reagan went to law. Paul's wife, Essie Robeson, came back to New York, but could not settle the matter, it seems, and was forced to flee over the Harlem roof tops with baby Paul in her arms, like Eliza in *Uncle Tom's Cabin*, in order to escape the clutches of Mrs. Reagan's process servers. But Essie Robeson got to the boat, escaped, and was off to England again. So then Mrs. Reagan went to London and sued Paul Robeson there. She won her case and got several thousand pounds, so it was said in Harlem, where the people Mrs. Reagan had under contract were paid what was due them on her return.

But the revue never went on. Delay and trouble broke

it up. So Mrs. Reagan went to Paris and married a French poet and lived in the south of France and no longer worried about show business.

Mrs. Reagan had bad luck with Negro shows. It was she who took *La Revue Nègre* to Paris, with Maude Russell, Claude Hopkins, settings by Miguel Covarrubias, and the then unknown Josephine Baker. Miss Baker, with her Charleston and her verve, stole the show from the more veteran Negro performers and overnight became the hit of Paris, stepping immediately from the chorus to stardom.

There is a story about Josephine Baker's first month in Paris, which the Parisians find very amusing. They say a wealthy and distinguished old Frenchman was so entranced with Miss Baker that he came every night to see *La Revue Nègre*. He sent daily bouquets of flowers to the dusky youngster from St. Louis, who could fling her limbs about in such amazing directions to the rhythm of Harlem music. He even went so far as to insist that Miss Baker accept the use of one of his town cars and a chauffeur in uniform. All of which Miss Baker accepted—but still paid the wealthy and elderly gentleman no mind. Finally, he asked her, in the best English that he could muster, just why she did not find his attentions to her liking.

Miss Baker naïvely replied: "But, monsieur, I thought you said you gave me all these things because you loved my art!"

Of course, after that she no longer had the town car nor the chauffeur nor the flowers from the same monsieur. But she did have many bids for her appearances in the various large theaters of Europe. She accepted one of these offers and left the American show to go to Berlin. And because she was under age, Mrs. Reagan could not prevent her going. With Josephine lost, the show was forced to close.

And that was the end of *La Revue Nègre*.

In those days, most of Harlem's actors were kept busy either on the Broadway stage, in night clubs, or in London or Paris. Aubrey Lyles, the comedian, rode up and down Seventh Avenue in a long red car with solid ivory trimmings. It was the first car Harlem had seen that could be turned into a sort of Pullman sleeper at will, the back seats sliding out to make a bed.

Another car that excited the colored world was that of Jules Bledsoe, who originated "Old Man River" in *Show Boat*. One day he appeared in the streets of Harlem with an expensive, high-powered motor, driven by a white chauffeur in livery. Mr. Bledsoe, who is dark, explained to the delight of Harlem that he had a white-uniformed chauffeur so that the public could tell which was the chauffeur and which the owner of the car.

Somewhat later, I recall a sincere but unfortunate attempt on Jules Bledsoe's part to bring "Art" to Harlem. He appeared in Eugene O'Neill's *The Emperor Jones* at the old Lincoln Theater on 135th Street, a theater that had, for all its noble name, been devoted largely to ribald, but highly entertaining, vaudeville of the "Butterbeans and Susie" type. The audience didn't know what to make of *The Emperor Jones* on a stage where "Shake That Thing" was formerly the rage. And when the Emperor started running naked through the forest, hearing the Little Frightened Fears, naturally they howled with laughter.

"Them ain't no ghosts, fool!" the spectators cried from the orchestra. "Why don't you come on out o' that jungle—back to Harlem where you belong?"

In the manner of Stokowski hearing a cough at the Academy of Music, Jules Bledsoe stopped dead in his tracks, advanced to the footlights, and proceeded to lecture his audience on manners in the theater. But the audience wanted none of *The Emperor Jones*. And their manners had been all right at all the other shows at the Lincoln, where they took part in the performances at will. So when Brutus continued his flight, the audience again howled with laughter. And that was the end of *The Emperor Jones* on 135th Street.

In those days Ethel Waters was the girl who could thrill Harlem. Butterbeans and Susie could lay them in the aisles. Jackie Mably could stop any show. Snakehips was a permanent "solid sender," and Louis Armstrong a killer!

But who wanted *The Emperor Jones* running through the jungles?

Not Harlem!

POETRY

I think it was at a party at 17 Gay Street in the Village, where Dorothy and Jimmy Harris lived, that I first heard people talking about New Mexico and Taos, and about writers and artists heading west to the desert and the Indians. It was about that time, too, that I first met Genevieve Taggard, Robert Wolf, and Ernestine Evans. And heard Eli Siegel read "Hot Afternoons There Have Been in Montana."

I met a lot of very exotic and jittery writers and artists of that period, too. And the more exotic and jittery they were, the more they talked of heading for Taos and the desert and the Indians. So I began to wonder what the Indians would think about their coming and if they would drink as much in Taos as they did in the Village. When

I got back to Washington, after one of my prize-money trips to New York, I was walking home from work one night when this poem came to me. I named it "A House in Taos."

RAIN

Thunder of the Rain God:
   And we three
   Smitten by beauty.

Thunder of the Rain God:
   And we three
   Weary, weary.

Thunder of the Rain God:
   And you, she and I
   Waiting for nothingness.

Do you understand the stillness
Of this house in Taos
Under the thunder of the Rain God?

SUN

That there should be a barren garden
About this house in Taos
Is not so strange,
But that there should be three barren hearts
In this one house in Taos—
Who carries ugly things to show the sun?

MOON

Did you ask for the beaten brass of the moon?
We can buy lovely things with money,

You, she and I,
Yet you seek,
As though you could keep,
This unbought loveliness of moon.

WIND

Touch our bodies, wind.
Our bodies are separate, individual things.
Touch our bodies, wind,
But blow quickly
Through the red, white, yellow skins
Of our bodies
To the terrible snarl,
Not mine,
Not yours,
Not hers,
But all one snarl of souls.
Blow quickly, wind,
Before we run back into the windlessness—
With our bodies—
Into the windlessness
Of our house in Taos.

It was a strange poem for me to be writing in a period when I was writing mostly blues and spirituals. I do not know why it came to me in just that way, but I made hardly a change in it after I put it down.

A year or so later from Lincoln University, during my first term there, I submitted the poem to *Palms,* as an entry in Witter Bynner's Intercollegiate Undergraduate Poetry Contest. It was given the First Award of one hundred and fifty dollars and published in *Palms* in 1927. Then amusing things began to happen. I did not know anybody in Taos, nor had I ever been there, but the Greenwich Villagers all seemed to know people there and even houses that the poem fitted, and I received a number of gossipy and amusing letters about it from folks I had never met. In one letter there was even a series of snapshots of what the writer claimed to be the very house of my poem—Mabel Dodge Luhan's house in Taos.

At that time, I had never heard Mrs. Luhan's name, nor did I know she had married an Indian, or that Jean Toomer had been a guest in her home. The red, yellow, and white of my poem came from the Indian corn colors of the desert. Three was a mystic number. The rain, sun, moon, and other nature words I used in contrast with the art-houses being built by the exotics from the Village.

Years later, when I met Mrs. Luhan in Carmel, the first thing she said to me was: "My house is not a bit like that." And she invited me to come and see for myself.

In New York in the summer of 1926, I wrote a poem called "Mulatto" which was published in the *Saturday Review of Literature*. I worked harder on that poem than on any other that I have ever written. Almost every night that summer I would take it out of the table drawer and retype it and work on it, and change it. When I read it one night at a gathering at James Weldon Johnson's, Clarence Darrow said it was more moving than any other poem of mine he had read. It was a poem about white fathers and Negro mothers in the South.

From the time when, as a small child in rompers in Lawrence, I had played with a little, golden-haired boy whose mother was colored and whose father, the old folks whispered, was white, and when, as this boy grew up, he went over into the white world altogether, I had been intrigued with the problem of those so-called "Negroes" of immediate white-and-black blood, whether they were light enough to pass for white or not. One of my earliest poems was:

CROSS

My old man's a white old man
And my old mother's black.
If ever I cursed my white old man
I take my curses back.

If ever I cursed my black old mother
And wished she were in hell,
I'm sorry for that evil wish
And now I wish her well.

My old man died in a fine big house.
My ma died in a shack.
I wonder where I'm gonna die,
Being neither white nor black?

The problem of mixed blood in America is, to be sure, a minor problem, but a very dramatic one—one parent in the pale of the black ghetto and the other able to take advantage of all the opportunities of American democracy. Later I presented one phase of this problem in my play, *Mulatto,* on Broadway. And I have written several short stories about it.

My second book of poems, *Fine Clothes to the Jew,* I felt was a better book than my first, because it was more impersonal, more about other people than myself, and because it made use of the Negro folk-song forms, and included poems about work and the problems of finding work, that are always so pressing with the Negro people.

I called it *Fine Clothes to the Jew,* because the first poem, "Hard Luck," a blues, was about a man who was often so broke he had no recourse but to pawn his clothes—to take them, as the Negroes say, to "the Jew's" or to "Uncle's." Since the whole book was largely about people like that, workers, roustabouts, and singers, and job hunters on Lenox Avenue in New York, or Seventh Street in Washington or South State in Chicago—people up to-day and down tomorrow, working this week and fired the next, beaten and baffled, but determined not to be wholly beaten, buying furniture on the installment plan, filling the house with roomers to help pay the rent, hoping to get a new suit for Easter—and pawning that suit before the Fourth of July—that was why I called my book *Fine Clothes to the Jew.*

But it was a bad title, because it was confusing and many Jewish people did not like it. I do not know why the Knopfs let me use it, since they were very helpful in their advice about sorting out the bad poems from the good, but they said nothing about the title. I might just as well have called the book *Brass Spittoons,* which is one of the poems I like best:

BRASS SPITTOONS

Clean the spittoons, boy!
    Detroit,
    Chicago,
    Atlantic City,
    Palm Beach.
Clean the spittoons.
The steam in hotel kitchens,
And the smoke in hotel lobbies,
And the slime in hotel spittoons:
Part of my life.
    Hey, boy!

A nickel,
A dime,
A dollar,
Two dollars a day.
   Hey, boy!
   A nickel,
   A dime,
   A dollar,
   Two dollars
Buys shoes for the baby.
House rent to pay.
Gin on Saturday,
Church on Sunday.
   My God!
Babies and gin and church
and women and Sunday
all mixed up with dimes and
dollars and clean spittoons
and house rent to pay.
   Hey, boy!
A bright bowl of brass is beautiful to the Lord.
Bright polished brass like the cymbals
Of King David's dancers,
Like the wine cups of Solomon.
   Hey, boy!
A clean spittoon on the altar of the Lord,
A clean bright spittoon all newly polished—
At least I can offer that.
   Com'mere, boy!

Fine Clothes to the Jew was well received by the literary magazines and the white press, but the Negro critics did not like it at all. The Pittsburgh *Courier* ran a big headline across the top of the page, *LANGSTON HUGHES' BOOK OF POEMS TRASH*. The headline in the New York *Amsterdam News* was *LANGSTON HUGHES—THE SEWER DWELLER*. The Chicago *Whip* characterized me as "The poet lowrate of Harlem." Others called the book a disgrace to the race, a return to the dialect tradition, and a parading of all our racial defects before the public. An ironic poem like "Red Silk Stockings" they took for literal advice:

> Put on yo' red silk stockings,
> Black gal.
> Go out and let the white boys
> Look at yo' legs.
>
> Ain't nothin' to do for you, nohow,
> Round this town—
> You's too pretty.
> Put on yo' red silk stockings, gal,
> An' tomorrow's chile'll
> Be a high yaller.
>
> Go out an' let de white boys
> Look at yo' legs.

Benjamin Brawley, our most respectable critic, later wrote: "It would have been just as well, perhaps better, if the book had never been published. No other ever issued reflects more fully the abandon and the vulgarity of its age." In the Negro papers, I believe, only Dewey Jones of the Chicago *Defender* and Alice Dunbar-Nelson of the Washington *Eagle* gave it a sympathetic review.

The Negro critics and many of the intellectuals were very sensitive about their race in books. (And still are.) In anything that white people were likely to read, they wanted to put their best foot forward, their politely polished and cultural foot—and only that foot. There was a reason for it, of course. They had seen their race laughed at and caricatured so often in stories like those by Octavus Roy Cohen, maligned and abused so often in books like Thomas Dixon's, made a servant or a clown always in the movies, and forever defeated on the Broadway stage, that when Negroes wrote books they wanted them to be books in which only good Negroes, clean and cultured and not-funny Negroes, beautiful and nice and upper class were presented. Jessie Fauset's novels they loved, because they were always about the educated Negro—but my poems, or Claude McKay's *Home to Harlem* they did not like, sincere though we might be.

For every Negro intellectual like James Weldon Johnson, there were dozens like Eustace Gay, who wrote in the Philadelphia *Tribune,* of February 5, 1927, concerning my *Fine Clothes to the Jew*: "It does not matter to me whether every poem in the book is true to life. Why should it be paraded before the American public by a Negro author as being typical or representative of the Negro? Bad enough to have white authors holding up our imperfections to public gaze. Our aim ought to be to present to the general public, already mis-informed both by well-meaning and malicious writers, our higher aims and aspirations, and our better selves."

I sympathized deeply with those critics and those intellectuals, and I saw clearly the need for some of the kinds of books they wanted. But I did not see how they could expect every Negro author to write such books. Certainly, I personally knew very few people anywhere who were wholly beautiful and wholly good. Besides I felt that the masses of our people had as much in their lives to put into books as did those more fortunate ones who had been born with some means and the ability to work up to a master's degree at a Northern college. Anyway, I didn't know the upper class Negroes well enough to write much about them. I knew only the people I had grown up with, and they weren't people whose shoes were always shined, who had been to Harvard, or who had heard of Bach. But they seemed to me good people, too.

So I didn't pay any attention to the critics who railed against the subject matter of my poems, nor did I write them protesting letters, nor in any way attempt to defend my book. Curiously enough, a short ten years later, many of those very poems in *Fine Clothes to the Jew* were being used in Negro schools and colleges.

NIGGER HEAVEN

The strange inability on the part of many of the Negro critics to understand irony, or satire—except the obvious satire of George S. Schuyler's *Black No More*—partially explains the phenomenon of that violent outburst of rage that stirred the Negro press for months after the appearance of Carl Van Vechten's *Nigger Heaven*.

The use of the word *nigger* in the title explains the rest of it. The word *nigger* to colored people of high and low degree is like a red rag to a bull. Used rightly or wrongly, ironically or seriously, of necessity for the sake of realism, or impishly for the sake of comedy, it doesn't matter. Negroes do not like it in any book or play whatsoever, be the book or play ever so sympathetic in its treatment of the basic problems of the race. Even though the book or play is written by a Negro, they still do not like it.

The word *nigger*, you see, sums up for us who are colored all the bitter years of insult and struggle in America: the slave-beatings of yesterday, the lynchings of today, the Jim Crow cars, the only movie show in town with its sign up FOR WHITES ONLY, the restaurants where you may not eat, the jobs you may not have, the unions you cannot join. The word *nigger* in the mouths of little white boys at school, the word *nigger* in the mouths of foremen on the job, the word *nigger* across the whole face of America! *Nigger! Nigger!* Like the word *Jew* in Hitler's Germany.

Countee Cullen's poem "Incident" [1] captures with great power the meaning of *nigger* for most black Americans—except that that meaning extends far beyond the child world, as the poem indicates. Cullen says:

> *Once riding in old Baltimore,*
> *Heart-filled, head-filled with glee,*
> *I saw a Baltimorean*
> *Keep looking straight at me.*
>
> *Now I was eight and very small,*
> *And he was no whit bigger,*
> *And so I smiled, but he poked out*
> *His tongue and called me, "Nigger."*
>
> *I saw the whole of Baltimore*
> *From May until December:*
> *Of all the things that happened there*
> *That's all that I remember.*

[1] From *Color,* by Countee Cullen (New York: Harper & Brothers).

So, when the novel *Nigger Heaven* came out, Negroes did not read it to get mad. They got mad as soon as they heard of it. And after that, many of them never did read it at all. Or if they did, they put a paper cover over it and read it surreptitiously as though it were a dirty book— to keep their friends from knowing they were reading it. And they held meetings to denounce it all across America. At one meeting in the Harlem Public Library, the crowd saw a large white-haired old gentleman in the back they thought was Carl Van Vechten. They turned on him in verbal fury. Astonished, the old gentleman arose stammering in amazement: "Why, I'm not Carl Van Vechten."

Carl Van Vechten was distressed at the reactions his book provoked in the Negro press. He had not expected colored people to dislike it. Certainly in the novel he had treated the Negroes of Harlem much better, for instance, than he had treated his own home folks in *The Tattooed Countess*. But I doubt if any of the more vociferous of the Negro critics had ever read *The Tattooed Countess*, so, naturally, they didn't know that. I doubt if any of those critics had ever read any book of Mr. Van Vechten's at all, or knew anything about his style. If they had they could not then have written so stupidly about *Nigger Heaven*.

Perhaps, like my *Fine Clothes to the Jew*, Mr. Van Vechten's title was an unfortunate choice. A great many colored people never did discover that the title was an ironical title, applying to segregated, poverty-stricken Harlem the words used to designate in many American cities the upper gallery in a theater, which is usually the only place where Negroes may buy tickets to see the show —the *nigger heaven*. To Mr. Van Vechten, Harlem was like that, a segregated gallery in the theater, the only place where Negroes could see or stage their own show, and a not very satisfactory place at that, for in his novel Mr. Van Vechten presents many of the problems of the Negroes of Harlem, and he writes of the people of culture as well as the people of the night clubs. He presents the problem of a young Negro novelist faced with the discriminations of the white editorial offices. And he writes sympathetically and amusingly and well about a whole rainbow of life above 110th Street that had never before been put into the color of words.

But Mr. Van Vechten became the goat of the New Negro Renaissance, the he-who-gets-slapped. The critics of the left, like the Negroes of the right, proceeded to light on Mr. Van Vechten, and he was accused of ruining, distorting, polluting, and corrupting every Negro writer from then on, who was ever known to have shaken hands with him, or to have used the word *nigger* in his writings, or to have been in a cabaret.

Some of the colored critics, evidently thinking I did not know my mind, accused Mr. Van Vechten of having brought about what they felt were the various defects of my *Fine Clothes to the Jew*. But the truth of the matter was that many of the poems in the book had been written before I had heard of or met Mr. Van Vechten, and they were not included in my *Weary Blues*, because scarcely any dialect or folk-poems were included in the *Weary Blues*. And, although I did shake hands with Mr. Van Vechten once upon being introduced to him at the N.A.A.C.P. party in 1924, it was many months before I saw him again. The blues, spirituals, shouts, and work poems of my second book were written while I was dragging bags of wet wash laundry about or toting trays of dirty dishes to the dumb-waiter of the Wardman Park Hotel in Washington.

Margaret Larkin in *Opportunity* was the first critic to term my work proletarian, in her review of *Fine Clothes*. Since high school days I had been writing poems about workers and the problems of workers—in reality poems about myself and my own problems. And, contrary to the accusations of the critics, after I came to know Carl Van Vechten, I never heard him say: "Don't write poems about workers." Or in any way try to influence me in my writing.

What Carl Van Vechten did for me was to submit my first book of poems to Alfred A. Knopf, put me in contact with the editors of *Vanity Fair,* who bought my first poems sold to a magazine, caused me to meet many editors and writers who were friendly and helpful to me, encouraged me in my efforts to help publicize the Scottsboro case, cheered me on in the writing of my first short stories, and otherwise aided in making life for me more profitable and entertaining.

Many others of the Negroes in the arts, from Paul Robeson to Ethel Waters, Walter White to Richmond Barthe, will offer the same testimony as to the interest Van Vechten has displayed toward Negro creators in the fields of writing, plastic arts, and popular entertainment. To say that Carl Van Vechten has harmed Negro creative activities is sheer poppycock. The bad Negro writers were bad long before *Nigger Heaven* appeared on the scene. And would have been bad anyway, had Mr. Van Vechten never been born.

IX

A Wife, a Book, and a Hospital

In 1922 two things happened to me which have been important factors in everything which has followed. The first and most important was my marriage on February 15th to Leah Gladys Powell, who for two years previous to that had been (from my point of view at least) much the most interesting member of the NAACP staff. The second was Jim Johnson's casual invitation to go along with him to an appointment with H. L. Mencken, then editor of *The Smart Set*.

Shortly after meeting Mencken I received one of his characteristically terse and salty notes asking what I thought of *Birthright*, a novel about the Negro by T. S. Stribling of Tennessee. Flattered, I wrote a lengthy and painfully erudite criticism of the book pointing out that the novel had courage in depicting Negroes as human beings instead of as menials or buffoons, but that it obviously was written from the outside looking in. I said that Stribling's depiction of Negro servants was not too bad, but that he fell down badly in his portrayal of what educated Negroes feel and think. Mencken replied, "Why don't you do the right kind of novel? You could do it, and it would create a sensation."

Such an idea was at first preposterous. I had never even thought of attempting to write fiction. Mencken, Jim, and I talked over the notion as they both tried to convince me that the variety of experiences which my appearance made possible by permitting me to talk with white people as a white man and with my own people as a Negro gave me a unique vantage point. Mary White Ovington generously joined the conspiracy by offering Gladys and me the

65

use of her cottage "Riverbank" at Great Barrington, Massachusetts. We took the train with typewriter, paper, pencils, and little other equipment—and certainly no clearly thought out plot for a novel. I had a rather misty notion of using as my central character a Negro doctor, trained in a first-class Northern medical school and returned to his native Georgia small town, but what would happen to him was not thought out at all.

I started to write and found that many of the characters seemed to rise up begging to be described, and creating their own story. I wrote feverishly and incessantly for twelve days and parts of twelve nights, stopping only when complete fatigue made it physically and mentally impossible to write another word. On the twelfth day the novel was finished and I dropped on a near-by couch and slept for hours.

Back in New York I ran into John Farrar, now a publisher but at that time editor of *The Bookman*, scholarly monthly of the arts published by George H. Doran and Company. In answer to his friendly query as to how I had spent the summer I hesitantly confessed I had written a novel. John asked to see it, but I demurred until I had rewritten it and corrected at least the more glaring deficiencies in writing with which I knew the manuscript was filled.

John insisted that I let him see the novel before it was rewritten: he could determine better if I had any ability as a fiction writer from the first draft, he assured me, than from a later version which might have some of its strength removed by attempts at "elegant writing." Somewhat dubiously, because I had reread parts of the manuscript, I sent the novel to John's office the next morning.

Not long afterward I received from Mr. Doran the most exciting —the most deliriously exciting—letter I had ever received in my life. We like your novel, he wrote, and will publish it after a few changes have been made which we wish to discuss with you.

To say that I walked on air between the receipt of the letter and the day of my appointment with Mr. Doran is a gross understatement. The famous publisher greeted me warmly and introduced me to Eugene Saxton, then one of his associate editors. John Farrar was naturally there too. Mr. Doran warmly congratulated me but I noticed that John and Eugene Saxton appeared to be somewhat uncomfortable. I learned the reason a few minutes later.

"Your novel has great drama and power," Mr. Doran told me. "But there are some changes we want you to make. Your Negro characters—uh, uh—are not what readers expect. I'm sure you will be willing to make the necessary changes," he added somewhat lamely, as he noticed my expression.

We talked for an hour or more, and it became increasingly clear that someone had convinced Mr. Doran that even though there were Negro college graduates who talked correct English instead of dialect, the number of such Negroes was too small to justify their being written of as educated and normal human beings. I learned some time later that Mr. Doran had submitted my novel to Irvin S. Cobb, the Kentucky humorist, who had been so shocked by its outspokenness that he had advised against its publication, fearing that it would cause race riots in the South.

Disheartened and disillusioned, I sent the manuscript to Mencken, who replied almost by return mail, "I have read *The Fire in the Flint.* There is not one episode in it which has not been duplicated in real life over and over again. I suggest that you send it to Alfred Knopf."

Knopf published the novel in 1924, and reaction to it was gratifyingly prompt and vigorous. It told of a Negro doctor who, after graduation from a Northern medical school, returned to his home in Georgia filled with idealistic zeal and determined to devote himself to raising the deplorable health conditions among his people. He was equally determined to avoid involvement in the race question. He soon learned, however, that for a Negro a life devoted to pure science is impossible, and becomes involved more and more in the problems which his people face. Because his medical education is superior to that of any white doctor in the town, he is called upon to operate on and save the life of the daughter of a prominent white citizen. In the meantime he has been active in organizing a cooperative movement among Negroes which brings upon him the organized hostility of local merchants and landlords and of the Ku Klux Klan. The story ends dramatically—perhaps melodramatically would be more accurate—when the doctor is lynched. But while it ends in personal tragedy and death for the hero, one senses that the spirit of revolt against bigotry which he symbolizes will be accelerated rather than diminished by his death.

The first review of the book was written by Laurence Stallings, at that time literary editor of the *New York World,* who, in collaboration with Maxwell Anderson, had achieved phenomenal success as a playwright with the famous play *What Price Glory.* Stallings said that the Central City of *The Fire in the Flint* was the most accurate portrayal of a small town in his native Georgia that he had ever read, and that the characters and plot were the truest of any novel written about the South to date. A columnist, Coleman Hill, on the *Macon Daily Telegraph* in Stallings' home town, reprinted his review and expressed agreement with it. The newspaper was swamped with denunciatory letters, telephone calls, and other expressions of disapproval. To set itself clear with its readers and subscribers, the *Daily Telegraph* published several editorials denouncing Stallings and Hill and, even more vigorously, myself. Heywood Broun took up the cudgels for the three of us in his famous column in the *New York World.* As a result the novel was catapulted into the gratifying position of being a modest best-seller, far beyond its literary merits. The novel went through several editions and was published in England and, in translation, in France, Denmark, Russia, Japan, and Germany. It received the honor of being one of the books burned in Germany after Hitler came into power.

Two interesting experiences attended publication of *The Fire in the Flint* in Russia and Japan. During the height of world-wide agitation over the Scottsboro Case, a newspaper correspondent friend of mine was present at a huge demonstration in a Moscow park at which I was bitterly denounced by the Communists, who had persuaded the Scottsboro defendants to dismiss the NAACP from the case and turn its direction over to the Communists. At the Moscow meeting I was savagely attacked as "a tool of the capitalists" and "an ally of the lyncher forces." Walking away from the meeting, the newspaper correspondent passed the state publishing company, where he saw a display of translations of *The Fire in the Flint* —which, at the time, was enjoying a considerable sale as a picture of what a "capitalist" nation like the United States does to its minorities.

Unwittingly and unwillingly, I was also utilized through the medium of *The Fire in the Flint* in Japan. The novel was first published in translation there under its original title and enjoyed a modest sale. Later, when American indignation over Japan's invasion of China mounted, a new Japanese edition, with the title changed to *Lynching*, was brought out. The new edition sold in fantastic numbers, due to a publicity campaign by the Japanese government pointing out that the novel pictured the kind of barbarities which were tolerated and even encouraged in the democracy which had the temerity to criticize Japan for her acts in China. I am glad to say that I never received royalties from either the Japanese or Russian translations, for I wouldn't have liked that money.

These years, however, were not all devoted to work and tragedies. Jim and Grace, his beautiful and charming wife, were responsible more than any others for the so-called Negro Renaissance of the early twenties. Frequently their apartment was the gathering place of writers, poets, singers, and men and women of the theater. Many an evening we talked until long after midnight. The color line was never drawn at Jim's. It was there that many who were later to do much in wiping out the color line learned to know each other as fellow human beings and fellow artists without consciousness of race.

Sometimes there would be parties at my house or at the homes of one or another of those I met at Jim's. Heywood Broun, Claude McKay, Fania Marinoff, and Carl Van Vechten (who later established the invaluable James Weldon Johnson Memorial Collection at Yale University), Langston Hughes, Eva and Newman Levy, Ruth Hale, Countee Cullen, Carl and Irita Van Doren, Marie Doro, Edna St. Vincent Millay, Sinclair Lewis, George Gershwin, Mary Ellis, Willa Cather, Blanche and Alfred Knopf, Walter Wanger, Joan Bennett, and many others who then enjoyed fame or were destined to achieve distinction in the arts, letters, or human relations were among those I was privileged to know.

THE HARLEM INTELLIGENTSIA

I had departed from America just after achieving some notoriety as a poet, and before I had become acquainted with the Negro intellectuals. When I got the job of assistant editor on *The Liberator*, Hubert Harrison, the Harlem street-corner lecturer and agitator, came down to Fourteenth Street to offer his congratulations.

I introduced him to Robert Minor, who was interested in the activities of the advanced Negro radicals. Harrison suggested a little meeting that would include the rest of the black Reds. It was arranged to take place at the *Liberator* office, and besides Harrison there were Grace Campbell, one of the pioneer Negro members of the Socialist Party; Richard Moore and W. A. Domingo, who edited *The Emancipator,* a radical Harlem weekly; Cyril Briggs, the founder of the African Blood Brotherhood and editor of the monthy magazine, *The Crusader;* Mr. Fanning, who owned the only Negro cigar store in Harlem; and one Otto Huiswood, who hailed from Curaçao, the birthplace of Daniel Deleon. Perhaps there were others whom I don't remember. The real object of the meeting, I think, was to discuss the possibility of making the Garvey Back-to-Africa Movement (officially called the Universal Negro Improvement Association) more class-conscious.

I remember that just as we ended our discussion, Max Eastman unexpectedly popped in to see how the *Liberator* office was running. Jokingly he said: "Ah, you conspirators," and everybody laughed except Robert Minor. Minor had recently renounced his anarchism for Communism and he was as austere-looking as a gaunt Spanish priest.

It was interesting to meet also some of the more conservative Negro leaders, such as the officials of the National Association for the Advancement of Colored People. Dr. W. E. B. DuBois, the author of *The Souls of Black Folk* and editor of *The Crisis,* had me to luncheon at the Civic Club. Of Dr. DuBois I knew nothing until I came to America. It was a white woman, my English teacher at the Kansas State

College, who mentioned *The Souls of Black Folk* to me, I think. I found it in the public library in Topeka. The book shook me like an earthquake. Dr DuBois stands on a pedestal illuminated in my mind. And the light that shines there comes from my first reading of *The Souls of Black Folk* and also from the *Crisis* editorial, "Returning Soldiers," which he published when he reurned from Europe in the spring of 1919.

Yet meeting DuBois was something of a personal disappointment. He seemed possessed of a cold, acid hauteur of spirit, which is not lessened even when he vouchsafes a smile. Negroes say that Dr. DuBois is naturally unfriendly and selfish. I did not feel any magnetism in his personality. But I do in his writings, which is more important. DuBois is a great passionate polemic, and America should honor and exalt him even if it disagrees with his views. For his passion is genuine, and contemporary polemics is so destitute of the pure flame of passion that the nation should be proud of a man who has made of it a great art.

Walter White, the present secretary of the National Association for the Advancement of Colored People, possessed a charming personality, ingratiating as a Y. M. C. A. secretary. One felt a strange, even comic, feeling at the sound of his name and the sight of his extremely white complexion while hearing him described as a Negro.

The White stories of passing white among the crackers were delightful. To me the most delectable was one illustrating the finger-nail theory of telling a near-white from a pure-white. White was traveling on a train on his way to investigate a lynching in the South. The cracker said, "There are many yaller niggers who look white, but I can tell them every time."

"Can you really?" Walter White asked.

"Oh sure, just by looking at their finger nails." And taking White's hand, he said, "Now if you had nigger blood, it would show here on your half-moons."

That story excited me by its paradox as much as had the name and complexion of Walter White. It seemed altogether fantastic that whites in the South should call him a "nigger" and whites in the North, a Negro. It violates my feeling of words as pictures conveying color and meaning. For whenever I am in Walter White's company my eyes compose him and my emotions respond exactly as they do in the case of any friendly so-called "white" man. When a white person speaks of Walter White as a Negro, as if that made him a being physically different from a white, I get a weird and impish feeling of the unreality of phenomena. And when a colored person refers to Walter White as colored, in a tone that implies him to be physically different from and inferior to the "pure" white person, I feel that life is sublimely funny. For to me a type like Walter White is Negroid simply because he closely identifies himself with the Negro group— just as a Teuton becomes a Moslem if he embraces Islam. White is whiter than many Europeans—even biologically. I cannot see the difference in the way that most of the whites and most of the blacks seem to see it. Perhaps what is reality for them is fantasy for me.

James Weldon Johnson, song writer, poet, journalist, diplomat and professor, was my favorite among the N. A. A. C. P. officials. I liked his poise, suavity, diplomacy and gentlemanliness. His career reveals surprises of achievement and reads like a success story. When a Negro makes an honorable fight for a decent living and succeeds, I think all Negroes should feel proud. Perhaps a day will come when, under a different social set-up, competent Negroes will be summoned like other Americans to serve their country in diplomatic posts. When that time comes Negroes may proudly cite as a precedent the record of James Weldon Johnson, Negro pioneer of the American diplomatic service, who performed his duties conscientiously and efficiently under unusually difficult conditions.

Jessie Fauset was assistant editor of *The Crisis* when I met her. She very generously assisted at the Harlem evening of one of our *Liberator* prayer meetings and was the one fine feature of a bad show. She was prim, pretty and well-dressed, and talked fluently and intelligently. All the radicals liked her, although in her social viewpoint she was away over on the other side of the fence. She belonged to that closed decorous circle of Negro society, which consists of persons who live proudly like the better class of conventional whites, except that they do so on much less money. To give a concrete idea of their status one might compare them to the expropriated and defeated Russian intelligentsia in exile.

Miss Fauset has written many novels about the people in her circle. Some white and some black critics consider these people not interesting enough to write about. I think all people are interesting to write about. It depends on the writer's ability to bring them out alive. Could there be a more commendable prescription for the souls of colored Americans than the bitter black imitation of white life? Not a Fannie Hurst syrup-and-pancake hash, but the real meat.

But Miss Fauset is prim and dainty as a primrose, and her novels are quite as fastidious and precious. Primroses are pretty. I remember the primroses where I lived in Morocco, that lovely melancholy land of autumn and summer and mysterious veiled brown women. When the primroses spread themselves across the barren hillsides before the sudden summer blazed over the hot land, I often thought of Jessie Fauset and her novels.

What Mary White Ovington, the godmother of the N. A. A. C. P., thought of me was more piquant to me perhaps than to herself. Her personality radiated a quiet silver shaft of white charm which is lovely when it's real. She was gracious, almost sweet, when she dropped in on *The Liberator*. But as I listened to her talking in a gentle subjective way I realized that she was emphatic as a seal and possessed of a resolute will.

She told me about her reaction to Booker T. Washington, the officially recognized national leader of the Negroes. Miss Ovington had visited Tuskegee informally. Booker T. Washington had disregarded her, apparently under the impression that she was a poor-white social worker. When he was informed that she originated from a family of high-ups, he became obsequious to her. But she responded coldly. By her austere abolitionist standard she had already taken the measure of the universally popular and idolized Negroid leader.

I repeated the story to my friend Hubert Harrison. He exploded in his large sugary black African way, which sounded like the rustling of dry bamboo leaves agitated by the wind. Hubert Harrison had himself criticized the Negro policy of Booker T. Washington in powerful volcanic English, and subsequently, by some mysterious grapevine chicanery, he had lost his little government job. He joined the Socialist Party. He left it. And finally came to the conculsion that out of the purgatory of their own social confusion, Negroes would sooner or later have to develop their own leaders, independent of white control.

Harrison had a personal resentment against the N. A. A. C. P., and nick-named it the "National Association for the

Advancement of Certain People." His sense of humor was ebony hard, and he remarked that it was exciting to think that the N. A. A. C. P. was the progeny of black snobbery and white pride, and had developed into a great organization, with DuBois like a wasp in Booker Washington's hide until the day of his death.

And now that I was legging limpingly along with the intellectual gang, Harlem for me did not hold quite the same thrill and glamor as before. Where formerly in saloons and cabarets and along the streets I received impressions like arrows piercing my nerves and distilled poetry from them, now I was often pointed out as an author. I lost the rare feeling of a vagabond feeding upon secret music singing in me.

I was invited to meetings in Harlem. I had to sit on a platform and pretend to enjoy being introduced and praised. I had to respond pleasantly. Hubert Harrison said that I owed it to my race. Standing up like an actor to repeat my poems and kindle them with second-hand emotions. For it was not so easy to light up within me again the spontaneous flames of original creative efforts for expectant audiences. Poets and novelists should let good actors perform for them.

Once I was invited to the Harlem Eclectic Club by its president, William Service Bell. Mr. Bell was a cultivated artistic New England Negro, who personally was very nice. He was precious as a jewel. The Eclectic Club turned out in rich array to hear me: ladies and gentlemen in *tenue de rigueur*. I had no dress suit to wear, and so, a little nervous, I stood on the platform and humbly said my pieces.

What the Eclectics thought of my poems I never heard. But what they thought of me I did. They were affronted that I did not put on a dress suit to appear before them. They thought I intended to insult their elegance because I was a radical.

The idea that I am an enemy of polite Negro society is fixed in the mind of the Negro élite. But the idea is wrong. I have never had the slightest desire to insult Harlem society or Negro society anywhere, because I happen not to be of it. But ever since I had to tog myself out in a dress suit every evening when I worked as a butler, I have abhorred that damnable uniform. God only knows why it was invented. My esthetic sense must be pretty bad, for I can find no beauty in it, either for white or colored persons. I admire women in bright evening clothes. But men! Blacks in stiff-starched white façades and black uniforms like a flock of crows, imagining they are elegant—oh no!

XIII

"Harlem Shadows"

•

MEANWHILE I was full and overflowing with singing and I sang in all moods, wild, sweet and bitter. I was steadfastly pursuing one object: the publication of an American book of verse. I desired to see "If We Must Die," the sonnet I had omitted in the London volume, inside of a book.

I gathered together my sheaf of songs and sent them to Professor Spingarn. He was connected with a new publishing firm. Many years before I had read with relish his little book, entitled *Creative Criticism*. I wrote to him then. He introduced me to James Oppenheim and Waldo Frank of *The Seven Arts,* and they published a couple of my poems under a nom de plume. That was way back in 1917. Now, five years later, I asked Professor Spingarn to find me a publisher.

I had traveled over many other ways besides the railroad since those days. Professor Spingarn was appreciative of me as a Negro poet, but he did not appreciate my radicalism, such as it was! Paradoxically, Professor Spingarn supported and advocated Negro racial radicalism and abhorred social radicalism. Professor Spingarn preferred my racial jeremiads to my other poems. Well, I was blunt enough to tell Professor Spingarn that he was a bourgeois. He didn't like it. Nevertheless he found me a publisher.

When I told a Yankee radical about myself and Professor Spingarn, this radical said that it was impossible for any man to be pro-Negro and anti-radical. He said, he believed that Professor Spingarn was pro-Negro not from broad social

147

and humanitarian motives, but because he was a Jew, baffled and bitter. I said, "But Oswald Garrison Villard is also pro-Negro, and he is not a radical nor a Jew." The radical said, "Oh, Villard is an abolitionist by tradition." And I said, "Isn't it possible that Professor Spingarn is also an abolitionist, and by even a greater tradition?"

If only individual motives were as easy to categorize and analyze as they appear to be! Anyway, Professor Spingarn got Harcourt Brace and Company to accept my poems. Max Eastman wrote a splendid preface, and the book was published in the spring of 1922.

Harlem Shadows was a *succès d'estime*. The reviews were appreciative, some flattering, flattering enough to make a fellow feel conceited about being a poet. But I was too broke and hungry and anxious about the future to cultivate conceit. However, I was not discouraged. The publication of my first American book uplifted me with the greatest joy of my life experience. When my first book was published in Jamaica, I had the happy, giddy feeling of a young goat frolicking over the tropical hills. The English edition of my poems had merely been a stimulant to get out an American book. For to me America was the great, difficult, hard world. I had gone a long, apparently roundabout way, but at least I had achieved my main purpose.

The last *Liberator* affair in which I actively participated was an international dance. The winter had been cold on our spirits and our feelings warmed currently to celebrate the spring. We trumpeted abroad our international frolic and the response was exhilarating. All shades of radicals responded, pink and black and red; Left liberals, Socialists, Anarchists, Communists, Mayflower Americans and hyphenated Americans, Hindus, Chinese, Negroes. The spirit of *The Liberator* magnetized that motley throng. There was a large freedom and tolerance about *The Liberator* which made such a mixing possible. (How regrettable that nothing like the old *Liberator* exists today! Social thinking is still elastic, even chaotic, in America. Class lines and ideas here are not crystallized to such an extent as to make impossible friendly contact between the different radical groups.)

Our spring frolic brought that international-minded multitude into Forty-second Street. But the metropolitan police resented the invasion. They were aghast at the spectacle of colored persons mixed with white in a free fraternal revel. So they plunged in and broke it up, hushed the saxophones, turned the crowd out of the hall, and threw protesting persons downstairs, lamming them with their billies.

* * * * * * * *

X

Research

Research is formalized curiosity. It is poking and prying with a purpose. It is a seeking that he who wishes may know the cosmic secrets of the world and they that dwell therein.

I was extremely proud that Papa Franz felt like sending me on that folklore search. As is well known, Dr. Franz Boas of the Department of Anthropology of Columbia University, is the greatest anthropologist alive, for two reasons. The first is his insatiable hunger for knowledge and then more knowledge; and the second is his genius for pure objectivity. He has no pet wishes to prove. His instructions are to go out and find what is there. He outlines his theory, but if the facts do not agree with it, he would not warp a jot or dot of the findings to save his theory. So knowing all this, I was proud that he trusted me. I went off in a vehicle made out of corona stuff.

My first six months were disappointing. I found out later that it was not because I had no talents for research, but because I did not have the right approach. The glamor of Barnard College was still upon me. I dwelt in marble halls. I knew where the material was all right. But, I went about asking, in carefully accented Barnardese, "Pardon me, but do you know any folk-tales or folk-songs?" The men and women who had whole treasuries of material just seeping through their pores looked at me and shook their heads. No, they had never heard of anything like that around there. Maybe it was over in the next county. Why didn't I try over there? I did, and got the selfsame answer. Oh, I got a few little items. But compared with what I did later, not enough to make a flea a waltzing jacket. Considering the mood of my going south, I went back to New York with my heart beneath my knees and my knees in some lonesome valley.

I stood before Papa Franz and cried salty tears. He gave me a good going over, but later I found that he was not as disappointed as he let me think. He knew I was green and feeling my oats, and that only bitter disappointment was going to purge me. It did.

What I learned from him then and later, stood me in good stead when Godmother, Mrs. R. Osgood Mason, set aside two hundred dollars a month for a two-year period for me to work.

My relations with Godmother were curious. Laugh if you will, but there was and is a psychic bond between us. She could read my mind, not only when I was in her presence, but thousands of miles away. Both Max Eastman and Richmond Barthe have told me that she could do the same with them. But, the thing that delighted her was the fact that I was her only Godchild who could read her thoughts at a distance. Her old fingers were cramped and she could not write, but in her friend Cornelia Chapin's exact script, a letter would find me in Alabama, or Florida, or in the Bahama Islands and lay me by the heels for what I was *thinking*. "You have broken the law," it would accuse sternly. "You are dissipating your powers in things that have no real meaning," and go on to lacerate me. "Keep silent. Does a child in the womb speak?"

She was just as pagan as I. She had lived for years among the Plains Indians and had collected a beautiful book of Indian lore. Often when she wished to impress upon me my garrulity, she would take this book from the shelf and read me something of Indian beauty and restraint. Sometimes, I would feel like a rabbit at a dog convention. She would invite me to dinner at her apartment, 399 Park Avenue, and then she, Cornelia Chapin, and Miss Chapin's sister, Mrs. Katherine Garrison Biddle would all hem me up and give me what for. When they had given me a proper straightening, and they felt that I saw the light, all the sternness would vanish, and I would be wrapped in love. A present of money from Godmother, a coat from Miss Chapin, a dress from Mrs. Biddle. We had a great deal to talk about because Cornelia Chapin was a sculptor, Katherine Biddle, a poet, and Godmother, an earnest patron of the arts.

Then too, she was Godmother to Miguel Covarrubias and Langston Hughes. Sometimes all of us were there. She has several paintings by Covarrubias on her walls. She summoned us when one or the other of us returned from our labors. Miguel and I would exhibit our movies, and Godmother and the Chapin family, including brother Paul Chapin, would praise us and pan us, according as we had done. Godmother could be as tender as mother-love when she felt that you had been right spiritually. But anything in you, however clever, that felt like insincerity to her, called forth her well-known "That is nothing! It has no soul in it. You have broken the law!" Her tongue was a knout, cutting off your outer pretenses, and bleeding your vanity like a rusty nail. She was merciless to a lie, spoken, acted or insinuated.

She was extremely human. There she was sitting up there at the table over capon, caviar and gleaming silver, eager to hear every word on every phase of life on a saw-mill "job." I must tell the tales, sing the songs, do the dances, and repeat the raucous sayings and doings of the Negro farthest down. She is altogether in sympathy with them, because she says truthfully they are utterly sincere in living.

XI

Books and Things

While I was in the research field in 1929, the idea of "Jonah's Gourd Vine" came to me. I had written a few short stories, but the idea of attempting a book seemed so big, that I gazed at it in the quiet of the night, but hid it away from even myself in daylight.

For one thing, it seemed off-key. What I wanted to tell was a story about a man, and from what I had read and heard, Negroes were supposed to write about the Race Problem. I was and am thoroughly sick of the subject. My interest lies in what makes a man or a woman do such-and-so, regardless of his color. It seemed to me that the human beings I met reacted pretty much the same to the same stimuli. Different idioms, yes. Circumstances and conditions having power to influence, yes. Inherent difference, no. But I said to myself that that was not what was expected of me, so I was afraid to tell a story the way I wanted, or rather the way the story told itself to me. So I went on that way for three years.

Something else held my attention for a while. As I told you before, I had been pitched head-foremost into the Baptist Church when I was born. I had heard the singing, the preaching and the prayers. They were a part of me. But on the concert stage, I always heard songs called spirituals sung and applauded as Negro music, and I wondered what would happen if a white audience ever heard a real spiritual. To me, what the Negroes did in Macedonia Baptist Church was finer than anything that any trained composer had done to the folk-songs.

I had collected a mass of work-songs, blues and spirituals in the course of my years of research. After offering them to two Negro composers and having them refused on the ground that white audiences would not listen to anything but highly arranged spirituals, I decided to see if that was true. I doubted it because I had seen groups of white people in my father's church as early as I could remember. They had come to hear the singing, and certainly there was no distinguished composer in Zion Hope Baptist Church. The congregation just got hold of the tune and arranged as they went along as the spirit moved them. And any musician, I don't care if he stayed at a conservatory until his teeth were gone and he smelled like old-folks, could never even approach what those untrained singers could do. LET THE PEOPLE SING, was and is my motto, and finally I resolved to see what would happen.

So on money I had borrowed, I put on a show at the John Golden Theater on January 10, 1932, and tried out my theory. The performance was well received by both the audience and the critics. Because I know that music without motion is not natural with my people, I did not have the singers stand in a stiff group and reach for the high note. I told them to just imagine that they were in Macedonia and go ahead. One critic said that he did not believe that the concert was rehearsed, it looked so natural. I had dramatized a working day on a railroad camp, from the shack-rouser waking up the camp at dawn until the primitive dance in the deep woods at night.

While I did not lose any money, I did not make much. But I am satisfied that I proved my point. I have seen the effects of that concert in all the Negro singing groups since then. Primitive Negro dancing has been given tremendous impetus. Work-songs have taken on. In that performance I introduced West Indian songs and dances and they have come to take an important place in America. I am not upset by the fact that others have made something out of the things I pointed out. Rather I am glad if I have called any beauty to the attention of those who can use it.

In May, 1932, the depression did away with money for research so far as I was concerned. So I took my nerve in my hand and decided to try to write the story I had been carrying around in me. Back in my native village, I wrote first "Mules and Men." That is, I edited the huge mass of material I had, arranged it in some sequence and laid it aside. It was published after my first novel. Mr. Robert Wunsch and Dr. John Rice were both on the faculty at Rollins College, at Winter Park, which is three miles from Eatonville. Dr. Edwin Osgood Grover, Dr. Hamilton Holt, President of Rollins, together with Rice and Wunsch, were interested in me. I gave three folk concerts at the college under their urging.

Then I wrote a short story, "The Gilded Six-Bits," which Bob Wunsch read to his class in creative writing before he sent it off to *Story Magazine*. Thus I came to know Martha Foley and her husband, Whit Burnett, the editors of *Story*. They bought the story and it was published in the August issue, 1933. They never told me, but it is my belief that they did some missionary work among publishers in my behalf, because four publishers wrote me and asked if I had anything of book-length. One of the editors of the J. B. Lippincott Company, was among these. He wrote a gentle-like letter and so I was not afraid of him. Exposing my efforts did not seem so rash to me after reading his letter. I wrote him and said that I was writing a book. Mind you, not the first word was on paper when I wrote him that letter. But the very next week I moved up to Sanford where I was not so much at home as at Eatonville, and could concentrate more and sat down to write "Jonah's Gourd Vine."

I rented a house with a bed and stove in it for $1.50 a week. I paid two weeks and then my money ran out. My cousin, Willie Lee Hurston, was working and making $3.50 per week, and she always gave me the fifty cents to buy groceries with. In about three months, I finished the book. The problem of getting it typed was then upon me. Municipal Judge S. A. B. Wilkinson asked his secretary, Mildred Knight, if she would not do it for me and wait on the money. I explained to her that the book might not even be taken by Lippincott. I had been working on a hope. She took the manuscript home with her and read it. Then she offered to type it for me. She said, "It is going to be accepted, all right. I'll type it. Even if the first publisher does not take it, somebody will." So between them, they bought the paper and carbon and the book was typed.

I took it down to the American Express office to mail it and found that it cost $1.83 cents to mail, and I did not have it. So I went to see Mrs. John Leonardi, a most capable woman lawyer, and wife of the County Prosecutor. She did not have the money at the moment, but she was the treasurer of the local Daughter Elks. She "borrowed" $2.00 from the treasury and gave it to me to mail my book. That was on October 3, 1933. On October 16th, I had an acceptance by wire.

But it did not come so simply as that. I had been hired by the Seminole County Chamber of Commerce to entertain the business district of Sanford with my concert group for that day. I was very glad to get the work, because my landlord was pressing me for the back rent. I now owed $18. I was to receive $25 for the day, so I saw my way clear to pay up my rent, and have a little over. It was not to be that way, however. At eight o'clock of October 16th, my landlady came and told me to get out. I told her that I could pay her that day, but she said she didn't believe that I would ever have that much money. No, she preferred the house. So I took my card table and my clothes up to my Uncle Isaiah's house and went off to entertain the city at eleven o'clock. The sound truck went up and down the streets and my boys sang. That afternoon while I was still on the sound truck, a Western Union messenger handed me a wire. Naturally I did not open it there. We were through at three o'clock. The Chamber of Commerce not only paid us, we were all given an order which we could take to any store we wanted and get what we chose. I needed shoes, so I took mine to a shoe store. My heart was weighing as much as cord-wood, and so I forgot the wire until I was having the shoes fitted. When I opened it and read that "Jonah's Gourd Vine" was accepted and that Lippincott was offering me $200 advance, I tore out of that place with one old shoe and one new one on and ran to the Western Union office. Lippincott had asked for an answer by wire and they got it! Terms accepted. I never expect to have a greater thrill than that wire gave me. You know the feeling when you found your first pubic hair. Greater than that. When Producer Arthur Hornblow took me to lunch at Lucey's and hired me at Paramount, it was nice—very nice. I was most elated. But I had had five books accepted then, been a Guggenheim Fellow twice, spoken at three book fairs with all the literary greats of America and some from abroad, and so I was a little more used to things. So you see why that editor is *Colonel* to me. When the Negroes in the South name a white man a colonel, it means CLASS. Something like a monarch, only bigger and better. And when the colored population in the South confer a title, the white people recognize it because the Negroes are never wrong. They may flatter an ordinary bossman by calling him "Cap'n" but when they say "Colonel," "General" and "Governor" they are recognizing something internal. It is there, and it is accepted because it can be seen.

I wrote "Their Eyes Were Watching God" in Haiti. It was dammed up in me, and I wrote it under internal pressure in seven weeks. I wish that I could write it again. In fact, I regret all of my books. It is one of the tragedies of life that one cannot have all the wisdom one is ever to possess in the beginning. Perhaps, it is just as well to be rash and foolish for a while. If writers were too wise, perhaps no books would be written at all. It might be better to ask yourself "Why?" afterwards than before. Anyway, the force from somewhere in Space which commands you to write in the first place, gives you no choice. You take up the pen when you are told, and write what is commanded. There is no agony like bearing an untold story inside you. You have all heard of the Spartan youth with the fox under his cloak.

"Dust Tracks on a Road" is being written in California where I did not expect to be at this time.

I did not come out here to California to write about the state. I did not come to get into the movies. I came because my good friend, Katharane Edson Mershon, invited me out here to rest and have a good time. However, I have written a book here, and gone to work in the movies. This surprises me because I did not think that I would live long enough to do anything out here but die. Friend Katharane Mershon is a mountain goat while I am a lowland turtle. I want to rock along on level ground. She can't look at a mountain without leaping on it. I think she is ashamed if she ever catches both of her feet on the same level. She cries "Excelsior!" in her sleep. Jack, her husband, told me that the reason he has that sort of smoothed-off look was because she dragged him up a mountain the next day after they got married and he has never been able to get his right shape back again. Well, 1941 was a hard year for me, too. She showed me California. Before it was over, I felt like I had spent two months walking a cross-cut saw. The minute I get to be governor of California, I mean to get me an over-sized plane and a spirit-level and fix this state so it can be looked at without rearing back. EPIC nothing! LEVEL! Level California! And I do mean L E V E L !!!

Harlem Vista

Harlem: Negro Capital of the Nation is the title of a column which appears in a large bloc of the nation's Aframerican weeklies. But critics in other cities have challenged the claim with facetious taunts and jabs at Harlem. Some jeer at Harlem as the capital of clowns whose fame rests upon cults and cabarets. They say that Harlem is a vast circus in which the people seem satisfied with an army of noise makers who swing in the dance halls and sing wildly in peace kingdoms; that they love spectacular parades of drums and uniforms, and prancing on the pavements by day and jiving in the honkey-tonks by night.

These critics do not regard Harlem as a typical American Negro community, such as exists in Chicago, New Orleans, Atlanta and Durham. Such communities are more sober and balanced than Harlem, which is hectic and fluid. Harlem *is* lacking in group solidarity and the high seriousness of other Aframerican communities. Even intellectually, Harlem is backward, some contend, although it has more well-paid teachers and excellent schools, libraries and librarians than any other black belt. For the widely circulated national Negro weeklies are not located in Harlem. They are published in Pittsburgh, Chicago and Baltimore, and in comparison with them the Harlem weeklies are provincial.

There is plenty of truth in the arguments made by the critics of Harlem. Harlem is a piece of New York. And exactly as New York is not the typical American city, similar to one in the Middle West or the Southeast, so Harlem is no black Chicago or Durham, N. C. But as the metropolis of New York attracts America and the rest of the world, so

15

does Harlem, in a lesser sense, make its appeal to the Negroes of America and of the world.

Harlem is the queen of black belts, drawing Aframericans together into a vast humming hive. They have swarmed in from the different states, from the islands of the Caribbean and from Africa. And they still are coming in spite of the grim misery that lurks behind the inviting façades. Over-crowded tenements, the harsh Northern climate and unemployment do not daunt them. Harlem remains the magnet.

Harlem is more than the Negro capital of the nation. It is the Negro capital of the world. And as New York is the most glorious experiment on earth of different races and divers groups of humanity struggling and scrambling to live together, so Harlem is the most interesting sample of black humanity marching along with white humanity. Sometimes it lags behind, but nevertheless it is impelled and carried along by the irresistible strength of the movement of the white world.

Like a flock of luxuriant, large-lipped orchids spreading over the side of a towering rock, the color of African life has boldly splashed itself upon the north end of Manhattan. From the nucleus of a comparatively few years ago it has grown like an expansive tropical garden, springing naturally from the Northern soil.

Four decades ago the artistic and social expression of Aframerican life was centered in West 53rd Street. Musicians, actors and journalists established clubs there. There they socialized among themselves, with other professional persons of their group and with white friends, mainly stage folk.

The black masses then resided in the thirties in the area around the Pennsylvania Railroad station. In San Juan Hill large numbers were wedged in among the Irish population. But Brooklyn was preferred by the respectable and exclusive families. There homes were bought or leased by the old Negro butlers of Knickerbocker families, the reliable bank messengers, caterers and head waiters of downtown clubs and hotels. Brooklyn had this advantage over Manhattan: there Aframericans were not herded together in a single quarter.

And the houses had spacious backyards and gardens in which their children could play.

In Manhattan the Aframericans always led a cramped existence. Even the 53rd Street district was not a congenial quarter. Day and night a thunderous racket came from the elevated trains overhead. And only its proximity to Broadway made residence there tolerable. The blocks around the Pennsylvania Station were overflowing with blacks. And San Juan Hill was notorious for the interracial strife between Aframericans and Irish.

The black people had to expand somewhere in Manhattan. Any realtor who could find a new location would make money. Scouting for an opening, an enterprising Negro realtor, Phillip A. Payton, discovered that there was ample room in Harlem, where many new apartment houses were standing empty.

White Manhattanites in increasing numbers were moving farther northwards and a building boom was under way. But the section of Harlem spotted by the black realtor did not quite suit the better class of whites. It was like the tangible boundary between the East Side and the West Side.

The first apartment house rented to colored tenants was located in 134th Street near Fifth Avenue. It was immediately filled up. Other houses were allotted. And like a pebble making ripples in a pool, the Aframericans began spreading away from that first block into others. But they went westwards among the middle classes of respectable whites.

As the Aframericans pushed forward from Fifth towards Seventh Avenue, the black invasion alarmed the white residents. They feared the permanent quartering of an army of them in the highly desirable section of Upper Manhattan. Patriotic old residents banded together to stem the onrushing black tide. They attempted to buy out houses occupied by colored tenants and have them vacated. They strove to prevent white realtors from selling or renting to black folk. They sought to evoke city ordinances as quarantine measures.

But certain social factors worked in favor of the blacks. Most potent was the power of money. The blacks willingly paid from a hundred to two hundred per cent more than did the whites. And they paid promptly in those days. They were eager to prove themselves good tenants, worthy of living in a better residental district. Penned in the gangster-ruled blocks of lower Manhattan, they were bound to expand or explode. Already there were indications of serious inter-racial trouble growing out of savage incidents in Hell's Kitchen, the Tenderloin and San Juan Hill.

Faced with opposition, the Aframerican realtors resorted to stratagem to develop Negro Harlem. They got "fronts" to make certain contacts and deals. The fair-skinned members of the group were used as decoys. Posing as whites, they achieved better bargains. A Chinaman doing business in the neighborhood was a "front" for many years in acquiring property for Aframericans. Other factors helped. Sometimes a Jewish landlord, affronted by gentiles, retaliated by selling or leasing to Negroes. And when white tenants proved unreliable, a colored family accommodated in the building would frighten them into leaving.

The Aframericans paid a formidable price, however, to obtain and consolidate the new territory. In the lowest bracket of wage earners, they were living in houses beyond their means. They were compelled to do considerable doubling up to pay that rent and otherwise exist. Two and three families rented an apartment together. And all families rented rooms. Every space was utilized—sometimes bathrooms were improvised as bedrooms—to meet the rent. Dignified private houses were made over into rooming houses.

The black masses were attracted from everywhere by the greater living space of Harlem. And soon the churches followed. In the beginning of the movement to Harlem most of the churches were concentrated in the Pennsylvania Station section. Chapels in Harlem were temporarily established in front rooms of private houses. When the migration became an exodus the churches began adjusting themselves to the shift of population. Between 1910 and 1922 all the large churches disposed of their property downtown and moved to Harlem, where white people's churches were bought and a few new churches built.

Even before the arrival of the Aframericans, Harlem was a place of innumerable churches, Presbyterian, Lutheran, Baptist, Methodist, Adventist, Roman Catholic, Jewish and Congregational. The white residents retreated far westward and northward, but their churches remained for a time. And one of the curious spectacles of the earlier settlement of Harlem with Aframericans was the processions of white congregations that returned each Sunday to Harlem to worship God. This unusual Sunday feature came to an end when colored congregations purchased the white churches. Often the transaction was made by a colored congregation's taking over the white church of its own faith. There still remain a few white churches in the midst of the blacks, but the public seem hardly aware of them.

It was the fact that the churches followed the masses that induced conservative colored families to consider Harlem a proper residential section. Hitherto the "quality" Negroes in Harlem were mainly members of the theatrical and cabaret sets. The cabarets were the first establishments to move from downtown to Harlem. And they attracted that theatrical and bohemian set of whites who were *aficionados* of Negro entertainment. The leading cabaretiers of the period, Conners, Barron Wilkins, Leroy Wilkins and Edmonds, operated large and extravagantly decorated places. And soon Harlem became more than locally famous as an amusement center.

The World War brought great waves of southern Negroes to the industrial centers of the North. And many settled in Harlem. At the end of the war the Aframerican population was limited to the district between 130th and 143rd Street, from Fifth to Eighth Avenue. But this quarter had become extremely congested and the residents were cautiously pushing down to 125th Street and over beyond Eighth Avenue.

Suddenly national attention was focussed on Harlem. A grandiose pan-African movement started there by the

West Indian, Marcus Aurelius Garvey, stirred American and West Indian Negroes to wild enthusiasm. Mammoth meetings and enthusiastic parades glittering with gorgeous uniforms were organized in Harlem. Branches quickly spread throughout the states. The movement's slogan was, "Africa for Africans." Its general programme aimed at political, cultural, and commercial relationship between Africans and Negroes abroad, and an Africa freed from European domination.

It was African Zionism. And it received an amazing acclaim from Aframericans. The idea was conceived of a Black Star Line of ships. A stock company was promoted and thousands of shares sold. Aframericans had benefited by plenty of work and higher wages during the war. And they poured their money into the stupendous scheme of African redemption.

As headquarters of the movement, Harlem became nationally and internationally famous.

When the Garvey movement first attracted world attention, 1918-1919, the solid Black Belt extended from 127th to 145th Street between Fifth and Eighth Avenues. From 125th Street to 110th Street, Jews dominated. The breaking of the boundaries coincided with the rise of the pan-African movement. Also the influx of the darker-hued Puerto Ricans and other Latin Americans speeded the change. The Puerto Ricans began penetrating lower Harlem from 110th Street up. And as they pushed up and over from the East Side, the Aframericans surged down to meet them.

The Negro Quarter Grows Up

Vastly different is the Negro Harlem of today from what it was when the First World War ended. Central Park now forms its Southern frontier. It stretches from Morningside Avenue to Lexington and, sweeping up from 110th Street and skirting the Harlem River, it abruptly takes the hill and extends to 164th Street. Then coming down Amsterdam Avenue, it embraces Convent Avenue to 141st Street and turns off, dropping down under the high terrace of the College of the City of New York. It follows the margin of Harlem-under-the-hill up to 129th Street. Then it strikes across further west and zigzags in and out among white houses and almost seems lost. But hard by the Lincoln school fronting the park at 123rd Street it captures Morningside Avenue and runs down under Columbia University Heights to 110th Street.

Holding the handle of Manhattan, this special African-American area is like no other in New York. It lacks the oppressive drabness of the East Side. It is more comparable with Chinatown, which, although it has slum features, does not exude the atmosphere of the slums. Harlem is like the glorified servant quarters of a vast estate. It has that appearance, perhaps, because the majority of Aframericans are domestics, who live in imitation of their white employers, although upon a lower level. The distinction of Harlem is unlike the huddle of European minorities in New York. The essential quality of the latter is the magic of foreign languages and particular national traits which are emphasized in everyday living. But as Aframericans express themselves in the common American idiom and have shed all the ex-

21

ternals of African traits, the distinguishing characteristic of Harlem lies in the varied features and the African color of its residents.

Perhaps it is easier for the eye to appreciate Harlem than for the heart to understand. Harlem is noisy and its noises strike the eye as loudly as they do the ear. Because the district is congested, the street corners and bars provide an outlet as forums and clubs. Children swarm in the streets, although the new playgrounds are full of them.

Groups of children persistently practise the Lindy Hop all over Harlem, as if they were all training to be expert dancers. The allure and longevity of the Lindy Hop are prodigious. Countless other dances of the jazz age have been created and highly publicized, and have tickled the people's feet. But after a hectic time they have been discarded, forgotten. But the Lindy Hop has remained in Harlem, competing for life everlasting with the fox-trot and tango. With its pattern, Harlem's children make fantasy on the pavement. When a new piece is put in the nickelodeon of a bar and it lilts to the Lindy Hop, the kids come together on the pavement to dance. Since they are not permitted to enter, they sometimes ask adults to put coins in the machine to give them music. Utterly oblivious of oldsters passing or watching, they dance with an eagerness and freshness that is even rustic. They put a magic in the Lindy Hop that it does not possess as an exhibition dance, which primarily it is. They make a folk dance of it.

Visually, Harlem creates the impression of a mass of people all existing on the same plane. Even the natives are generally unaware of the prestige of their own notables. The pace-makers who, fashionably dressed, flash along the avenue in splendid cars have mostly been identified with the racketeering class of numbers "kings" and "queens," bootleggers, hot stuff fences, and the rest. Downtown, a gentleman wearing a top hat or a lady in a mink coat may stir the casual observer to imagine a big banker or industrialist or a dowager or debutante of the exclusive hundreds. But to the average Harlemite, and also to the white police, the top-hatted gentleman and his lady might be a Pullman porter with his lady going to a formal dance at the Renaissance or just a big time procurer.

The first thought of the casual onlooker is not that the gentleman of color may be a professional person or a wealthy realtor. There are many such in Harlem with dinner coats and tails, but there is no opera, no Waldorf Astoria where they may go. There is no other minority group in New York having such an extraordinary diversity of individuals of achievement and wealth who are compelled to live in the midst of the mass. Inexorably the individual is identified with the mass and measured by its standards.

The efforts of the Harlem élite to create an oasis of respectability within the boundaries of Aframerica is strenuous and pathetic. Their number is considerable; doctors and dentists, lawyers and politicians, businessmen, teachers, nurses, successful actors and musicians, government employees and the large corps of social workers. Quite a group of them, but not large enough to establish an exclusive residential district. Wherever they move, the common people follow and threaten to submerge them.

They have succeeded, but just a little, in making a few blocks slightly more desirable than the rest of Harlem. The best result is the block of buildings in 139th Street, between 7th and 8th Avenues, which was designed by the celebrated Stanford White. The houses are private, and when the whites decided to move out, in 1920, a colored group banded together to buy them and keep the section exclusive. The tree-shaded block still retains some of its quiet air of respectability. But it lacks much of the elegance of its lily-white days. The Negroes rent rooms there as they do in every other block in Harlem. And the spacious back alleys with gardens, attesting to Stanford White's fine idea of city planning, are now dilapidated and garbage-strewn. The residents keep a sharp lookout for undesirable intruders. Recently the Colored Fraternal Order of Elks was compelled to vacate its premises in the block, because it was considered a nuisance. But Father Divine immediately set up a kingdom there. The residents attempted to oust him. But Father Divine fought back and declared that God was no respecter of persons. So Striver's Row had to make its peace with the "kingdom" of Heaven. Adjusting itself to the dignity of the block, the "kingdom" is a very decorous place. No heavy stomping or cacophonous shouting is heard there. And daily it dispenses ten-cent meals to many respectable Negroes in need.

Long famed for creating an atmosphere of sylvan retreat in the heart of Manhattan, the Block Beautiful—130th Street between Lenox and Fifth Avenue—has not, like Striver's Row, managed to keep its end up. It still bravely exhibits the little lawn patches before the low porticoed brick houses and the row of luxuriant trees, which gave it the appearance of a nice corner of a German garden town. But its perfect trimness has disappeared. The neat fences are broken, the gates unhinged and leaning awry, the sidewalk unkempt.

The original congregation of the massive grey pile of the Presbyterian Church of the Puritans, at the Northeast corner, held the church for many years after the block was ceded to the blacks. What a tale that block could tell of the strange dark-hued horde sweeping down upon it! But it stood almost virginal white while the Negroes milled around it and headed towards 125th Street. Then in 1922 a Negro bought the first house in the block. Gradually the others went black. And by 1925 the block was entirely colored, excepting the mansion of the Widow MacLean. The Church of the Puritans remained white until 1933. Then it became Aframerican Saint Ambrose Episcopal with a West Indian preacher, a majority of West Indian worshippers and a ritual closely following the Church of England.

The last white landmark of the block, the mansion of the Widow MacLean, disappeared in the spring of 1937. The house was adjacent to the Church of the Puritans and the grounds covered between 130th and 131st Street. The owner had lived in the great establishment 53 years. When finally the Block Beautiful capitulated to the dark invasion and all the white residents had fled, she refused to sell and remained the only white survivor. With a retinue of servants, she maintained the place in grand style, and it suggested a medieval castle with poor retainers squatting in the surrounding land. She became reconciled to the presence of the newcomers and was friendly and charitable to the poor among them.

It was Park Commissioner Moses' idea that the place could be turned into an excellent playground for the poor children of the neighborhood. He persuaded the Widow MacLean at the age of 80 to dispose of the property for that purpose. She agreed and the structure was quickly demolished and the plot transformed into a splendid playground. Now the colored children are joyfully romping on the grounds where the Widow MacLean so recently walked in stately loneliness.

Facing Central Park, the littoral of 110th Street between Fifth and Eighth Avenues is desirable, but not so exclusive as Striver's Row. It was the last residential stronghold of the better class Jews in Harlem. Swarthy Harlemites pushed through to it only five years ago. 110th Street has a particular significance, perhaps mainly symbolic, as a frontier between the white world and the Negro group. It is not by any means a straight clear line, not exactly a color line. Mayor La Guardia, who resides at the corner of 109th Street and Fifth Avenue, may get a pretty good view of Harlem over the border. But his residence is a landmark behind which flows the movement of an entirely different world. The extraordinary social importance of this part of Harlem, its significance to New York and also to America, will be seen as the picture of Harlem unfolds.

From the half lot at 138th Street, between St. Nicholas and Edgecombe Avenue, where the elegant buffstone Dorrance Brooks building, with gloved and smartly uniformed doorman, marks a conspicuous new departure, Harlem climbs up to the hill,—up to the Sugar Hill famous in tune and tale. This is the district which became Aframerican with a resounding theatrical BANG! Like the strangest of orchids upon the broken stem of prosperity, it flowered wildly. It was in

1929 that the Aframericans surged up from the Harlem valley to the heights, commanding a panoramic view of the Bronx. The new expansion was not a people's movement, like that from downtown to Harlem, nor the irrepressible mass elbowing-out of post-war years which accompanied the development of the Back-To-Africa project. It was mainly an operation springing from the urge of Aframerican intelligentsia and élite to create an exclusive residential area.

The build-up of a fashionable and artistic Harlem became the newest fad of Manhattanites in the middle nineteen twenties. And the propaganda in favor of it was astoundingly out of proportion to the economic potentiality of a Harlem smart set and the actual artistic and intellectual achievement. New Yorkers had discovered the existence of a fashionable clique, and an artistic and literary set in Harlem. The big racket which crepitated from this discovery resulted in an enormously abnormal advertisement of bohemian Harlem. And even solid real estate values were affected by the fluid idealistic art values of Harlem.

Sugar Hill has the reputation of being the romping ground of the fashionable set. But the vast majority of its residents are also ordinary Harlemites like those living under the hill. Most of the propertied Harlemites reside under the hill. The houses on the hill are more modern, but rents are exorbitant.

Sugar Hill faces the problem of any other fairly desirable residential quarter of Harlem. The fashionable set cannot keep it exclusive, for it is infinitesimal. Families double up in apartments as elsewhere in Harlem. And racketeers of clandestine professions also set the pace. They are the people who can afford the extortionate rents without caring.

No. 409 Edgecombe Avenue is the best-known building in Sugar Hill. It is supposed to be an exclusive residential house tenanted by some of the prosperous professional persons of the group and high-salaried state and municipal employees. But many of the tenants there also belong to the ordinary working mass of Aframerica. And, too, there are "Rooms to Rent" in these apartments. "409" has something of the atmosphere of a European resort hotel for smart people with small incomes.   When a Harlemite says, "I live in '409,' " one imagines that he belongs, or is trying to belong to the Smart Set.

One's imagination is not so easily excited by the Rockefeller colony of houses under the hill, embracing the whole block between Seventh and Eighth Avenue from 149th to 150th Street.   These houses, with their lovely, spacious gardens, were built at the same time the smarter set among the Aframericans began the climb to Sugar Hill.   And they were designed primarily for the respectable workingman and his family.   But the average black worker could not afford the cost of living in them and they were occupied by members of the white-color group—professional persons and city employees and their families.   These houses also presaged a new era in the urban existence of Aframericans as typified by New York.   Optimistically, a bank was opened in 135th Street and a branch established in the Rockefeller houses.   But the project proved a financial loss.   The bank was closed and in 1938 the Rockefeller estate sold the houses. This housing project is a brief but enlightening news reel of what actually happens when the Aframerican group moves into better districts.

Sugar Hill is vinegar sour to many of its residents pinching themselves to meet the high rent.   Its identification with the hectic pseudo-renaissance period of the Aframerican élite was not an economic asset.   If its development had been less spectacular, it might have registered a less dubious social advantage to the group.   But the rapacious landlord sharks of Harlem were hungrily waiting on the hill for the disorderly black rush into their jaws.   Where white tenants formerly paid reasonable rentals, the blacks were charged up to four times as much.   The idea of a miraculous Negro cultural life, although based upon no reasonable group economy, was nationally touted.   And the landlords profited by the black credulity and primitive hankering after ostentation.

Excepting the privileged few, the majority of families up there in sweet Sugar Hill are packed together like sardines.

The prohibitive rent makes the unit of private family life the rarest thing. Almost all families take in lodgers. All available space must be occupied. Rooms, rooms and more rooms to let. Adequate clothing and even vital food must be sacrificed to meet the high cost of housing. That exclusive Sugar Hill society of the white writer's imagination is simply a café society. And café society, it is true, is more important in Sugar Hill than in any part of Harlem. The bars up there are more elaborate than those under the hill. During prohibition, following the scramble up the hill, the Italians planted a few well-appointed speakeasies. And spick and span, with blazing lights and comfortable lounges, they came up from underground with Repeal. The Italian bars set the tone for others, both white and colored, which were opened later. As Sugar Hill has precious few of the petty businesses which flourish under the hill, such as grocery stores, candy stores, drug stores, and the rest, its cafés are more attractive in their setting than those under the hill. Cabaret and theater artistes and their friends comprise the major portion of the clientèle with a considerable collegiate leaven. Also, out-of-town visitors favor the hill for its light divertissement. There is not much dancing up there, no cabaret extravaganza. For hot amusement the Sugar Hillies go under the hill on Seventh and Lenox Avenues to the Lido, Renaissance, Smalls', Jimmie Daniels' and Savoy. And they trek to 125th Street where the Apollo specializes in the rich variety of its glorification of the Aframerican brown girl.

Dubbing all of Harlem a vast slum would be offensive to the upper class of Aframericans who must needs make their lives worth living there. It is their tragedy that externally their individuality is almost effaced in the rough scramble of the mass. Slum dwellers do not always see themselves as others see them. Little foxes leap and fleas jump. But both must live in holes and nests. The elastic lump of Harlem below 116th Street has something of the aspect of a flea market. It is the alluring borderline of every type, where all species of humanity mix pell mell. It has something of the quality of the Vieux Port of Marseille, only it is minus the flotsam and jetsam of the immediate waves with the ships arriving and departing.

African, Mongolian, European—all the types of all the races indiscriminately flung together have created a jungle of colors in which pullulate all the imaginable shades of white and black, red, brown, yellow: indigo, chestnut, slate, amber, olive, canary, mauve, orange, ruby and the indefinable. An unaware interracial and international movement dominates the thickly crowded atmosphere. Puerto Ricans and other Latin Americans have tenanted buildings whose façades are still engraved with double triangles and over five thousand years of figures which proclaim their original Jewish occupancy. "Unamerican" signs—*bodega, tienda, carneceria, dulceria, fonda* and *imprenta* are spread across the fronts of stores. Italian Americans have pushed over from the East Side, competing with the Spanish Americans. They have reached up from coal shops and fruit stands to grab and monopolize the lucrative business of bars in Harlem. Greeks have come out from the stinking fried fish joints to install nice restaurants and become the only rivals of Jews in the grocery business. And lastly Negroes are breaking into the candy and cigar stores and express moving business.

World-famed for their promenading ritual, the Spanish have given a special éclat to the tempo of the street. The Aframericans have always delighted in the strut and shuffle. And crossing and mingling steps with the Spanish, together they are making a new movement in lower Harlem.

But it is not wholly a sentimental picture. This patchwork of humanity was planned by no expert mind. It did not evolve from any blue print of interracial and international adjustment. It is a crude, bold offspring of necessity. And it has its sinister side. Around the subway at Lenox and 116th Street, when the sun goes down, there is the feeling in the atmosphere of an apache-dominated quarter of Paris. The bright lights of the cluster of little drinking places and eating joints draw the wasps buzzing together.

The odor of reefers hangs in the air. At any moment the switch blade may flash. The young muggers are on the *qui vive*.

It is mostly in this neighborhood that some of the stupidest crimes in Harlem occur. Like hawks the muggers watch out to rob the men bemused by liquor, going home from the bars. Here too, the pants trick is mercilessly played. Victims are mostly white; imagining they are being introduced to a hot party, they are whisked up to the roof. There they are divested of money—and then their pants to impede their getting emergency help from the police. The exploits of the muggers were so detrimental to the amusement business of Harlem that two years ago it was rumored that the procurers of the borderline had organized to curb the muggers and protect the clients of their ladies.

From the nature of its soil and the arrangement of its fences, wheat and tares will continue to grow together in Harlem. Its Aframerican minority has no counterpart in any other of America's black belts. And it is fundamentally different from the other minorities that have contributed to the making of America's composite. Usually language or religion is the basic bond of other minorities. But in Harlem it is that common yet strange and elusive chemical of nature called color.

Within it are the Ishmaelite remnants of other groups, the nondescripts of miscegenation. From the Caribbean islands of the French, the Dutch, the Danes, the British, they came. From Central America and South America. Each brought something of the characteristic of the dominant European nation, but all bore the common mark of Africa. There are brown North Africans, swarthy East Africans speaking Arabic and ebon-black West Africans wearing their tribal stigmata. All have been forced into the ranks of the original Aframerican group.

Some critics within the group believe that it is doomed to remain an unwieldly, inert and invertebrate mass, precisely because it is a conglomerate color group. Because it lacks a religion or language of its own upon which it may build its self-respect. But the group is a group nevertheless and perhaps it may be to its advantage that it has not the impediment of a separate language and religion with which to contend. The children and grand children of the foreign Negroes are all good Americans. There is no difference between them and those of the original American Negro stock.

The larger problem is the adjustment of the Aframerican as a minority to fit into the frame of the American composite. Probably an examination of the mass movements of Harlem may yield an indication of the trend and direction of the group as a whole.

The Business of Numbers

Playing numbers is the most flourishing clandestine industry in Harlem. It is the first and foremost of the rackets and the oldest. Exciting the masses' imagination to easy "hits" by the placement of tiny stakes with glittering quick returns, it squeezes Harlem in its powerful grip. To the Negro operators it is not so enormously profitable today as in its halcyon period, when its foundations were laid and it spread with impunity, not fearing white competitors and the action of the law. At that time the operators ("kings" and "queens" as they were called) each had a turnover of a quarter of a million dollars yearly. But after a span of unbelievably fabulous, gold-years, the law of the land at last became aware of them and Federal and Municipal investigations compelled well-known operators to retire to private, comfortable and even luxurious lives. Through fear or careless management the business of some slipped from their hands and they were reduced to penury. And others were driven from the field by white overlords.

Through all the changes Harlemites have played the game increasingly and apparently will as long as Harlem exists. Numbers is a people's game, a community pastime in which old and young, literate and illiterate, the neediest folk and the well-to-do all participate. Harlemites seem altogether lacking in comprehension of the moral attitude of the white world towards its beloved racket.

In its early years these whites in and around Harlem who were aware of the game were tolerantly amused, and contemptuously called it "the nigger pool," or "nigger pennies"! "Numbers" was the only game on which a penny

101

could be put up as a wager. But a lucky penny makes 6 dollars for the player, minus the small percentage for the collector who places the bet. The white world never imagined that the pennies of Harlem's humble folk were creating fortunes of thousands of dollars and "kings" and "queens" in Harlem.

But suddenly in 1928 the nation became aware of the state of affairs when a wealthy Harlem Negro, Caspar Holstein, was kidnaped and held for $50,000 ransom. Holstein was considered to be worth half a million dollars. He was outstanding and upstanding in the community. He operated the Turf Club, which was the rendezvous of Harlem's fastest set. He owned the premises. Prominent in Negro Elkdom, he was exalted ruler of one of the best lodges. He was known as Harlem's philanthropist—the only one! He donated money to Negro colleges and charitable institutions. He provided scholarships for brilliant Negro students, who were too poor to enter high school and college. Through his club he tided needy individuals and families over difficult times. And although he used his personal income, he did not attach his name to such gifts.

There was also an artistic side to Holstein's extraordinary activity. He was *persona grata* among Harlem's élite. And he gave pecuniary assistance to struggling and aspiring writers and artists. In collaboration with the Negro magazine, OPPORTUNITY, he set up a fund for literary prizes. He did not exclude white organizations from his generosity and thus he contributed donations to the League for Mutual Aid. Holstein was born in the Virgin Islands and when the island of St. Thomas was devastated by an earthquake, he gave a large sum of money, organized relief, shipped food and clothing to the victims, and lumber and skilled workmen to rebuild the houses.

Locally Holstein dealt in real estate, but everybody was aware of his real business as a race-track broker and a numbers banker. He was one of the big six among the numbers bankers. He was liked, he was respected, he was trusted.

Sometimes faced with the payment of unusually large sums to winners, some numbers bankers defaulted and fled Harlem. But Holstein was renowned for his reliability. He paid fully the heaviest winnings. His fame spread and his business increased.

The kidnaping occurred on the night of September 21, when Holstein was leaving a friend's house in 146th Street. A white man approached, flashed a detective badge and said that Holstein was wanted at police headquarters in Harlem. Holstein replied that he would go willingly, although he knew of no reason why the police should want him. Another white man came up and between them they walked Holstein to a waiting car. In the car a third accomplice was sitting beside the chauffeur. All were white. Holstein was roughly shoved in. The car started, but instead of turning south toward the police station, it headed north to the Bronx. Aware then that he was tricked, Holstein struggled with his captors. They covered him with their guns, overpowered and blindfolded him and drove to a hideout in the Bronx.

The gangsters had reasoned that Holstein, carrying on an illegal business, was just another gangster who would gladly toss them a large sum and hush up the affair. But Holstein enjoyed being munificent voluntarily; otherwise he was a very stubborn man. He insisted that his property was in collateral and that he did not possess any considerable amount of negotiable funds. Ascertaining that Holstein dealt regularly with the Chelsea bank in Harlem, the kidnapers telephoned there to ask if Holstein's cheque would be honored for a large sum. But already the bank was notified that Holstein had disappeared in a suspicious manner, and it gave a non-committal reply. Holstein's close associates had telephoned the bank. They were worried by his absence even for a short while, without any of them being informed of where he was. For his affairs demanded his constant personal attention.

Soon Harlem was agitated by the rumor of Holstein's kidnaping. Some thought that rival numbers bankers had had him "taken for a ride." But a message was received at the Turf Club demanding a payment of $50,000 for his release. The police started hot on the trail. The Negro sergeant (now Lieutenant Battles) was then the glamor boy of the police in the eyes of Harlemites, at a time when Negroes on the police force were a rarity and none was an officer. Battles was a friend of the kidnaped man and knew the places in which the right information could be picked up. A bootleg basement spot in 125th Street yielded the clue.

It put the police on the trail of one Michael Bernstein, a beer runner of the Bronx. Scenting the police on their heels, the kidnapers released Holstein on the fourth day of his detention. But upon his return to Harlem, Holstein pretended that he did not know who were his kidnapers or where he had been held. He said that he was blindfolded when he was taken and could not identify his captors or his environment. The police intensified their activity and within a few hours Michael Bernstein and his accomplices, Peter Donohoe, Anthony Dagustino and Moe Schubert were apprehended. But in court Holstein still refused to identify the men. His attitude was evasive. He admitted that he had been beaten and tortured to reveal the extent of his bank account, but said he had not been permitted to see his captors. Holstein's reticence fed the gossip that his kidnaping was perhaps a hoax engineered by himself.

But he was not the type of man who would foolishly give his clandestine business a sensational publicity which finally helped to ruin it. Always he was extremely reserved about his affairs. Had he desired, he might have allowed his vanity to feed and inflate itself upon his charitable acts, but many of his large gifts were covered under anonymity. Often when he gave donations under his name to respectable institutions he suggested that it should not be published, because he was averse to placing such institutions in a compromising position. Many "innocents" among the respectability of Harlem were quite unaware of his real business affiliations. Although he was one of the fabulous six of Harlem's numbers operators, he never paraded his prosperity in the flashy big-shot-of Harlem way of the "kings" and "queens." He was very conservative in his appearance and his habits. He dressed quietly, like a dignified broker, and abstained from drinking liquor and smoking. To obtain his release, he made a deal (which was eventually confirmed) not to squeal on his kidnapers.

The Holstein case hit the front page and won national notoriety. It was the first time a wealthy Negro was kidnaped and held for ransom. It made the world aware of another phase of Harlem. For ten years Harlem was nationally advertised as the headquarters of the Garvey Black-Star-Back-To-Africa movement. And carried forward by the impetus of the ascendant literary and artistic bohemianism of New York, the Negro renaissance spurt of the latter nineteen twenties had stimulated national interest in the creative possibilities of Harlem. But Holstein's kidnaping flashed the searchlight on a Harlem underworld, different from the drab ugly tenements nauseating with odors of fried pork chops and rot-gut gin. This was an underworld comparable within its dimensions to the dazzling dynamic underworld of the whites, a world in which the shrewd enterprising members of the Negro minority chiseled out a way to social superiority by the exploitation of the potentialities of their own people. That "nigger-pool" was not such a contemptible thing after all. And it was destined amazingly to stimulate the speculative propensities of the Negroes and establish itself as the new game of the white and black masses of all the United States.

And now others besides the big racket monopolists of the white underworld discovered an interest in the Harlem game. Federal agents ferreted out information about the "kings" and "queens" of the black masses, who paid no income taxes. And as they probed, they uncovered startling facts. The secret "nigger-pool" was no child's play. But, disarming as black laughter in Harlem, albeit loosely organized, it was a formidable parasitic growth within the social body of the blacks.

And the great black bottomless pool had spawned independent auxiliaries. The avid playing of numbers enormously multiplied the appetites of the credulous in the science of numerology. Harlem was set upon a perpetual hunt for lucky numbers. House numbers, car numbers, letters, telegrams, laundry, suits, shoes, hats, every conceivable object could carry a lucky number. Any casual thing might become unusual with the possibility of being endowed with a lucky number: a horse in the street, the first person you meet, an automobile accident, a fire, a fight, a butterfly fluttering on the air, a funeral, even a dog posing against a wall! And dreams! Harlem is haunted by numbers.

Dreaming of numbers is an inevitable condition of the blissful state of sleeping. And so the obsession of signs and portents in dreams as interpreted by numbers created a business for local numerologists. They compiled books of dreams interpreted by playing numbers. Dream books of numbers were published by Prince Ali, Madame Fu Futtam, Professor Konje, Red Witch, Moses Magical and many others. Such are the best sellers of Harlem.

"Hot" lucky numbers are peddled on the streets. Some are offered with a phial of oil or a box of incense to elude the curiosity of the police. But many are brazenly sold in a little piece of folded paper. And the occult chapels have multiplied and increased their following by interpreting dreams by numbers and evoking messages from the dead with numbers attached to the messages and by figuring out signs and portents by numbers.

The religious playing of numbers naturally increases the development of mysticism in Harlem. The numbers must be guessed and played at hazard. When such numbers do not win, the addicts of the game will readily resort to those psychic types of persons who profess to be mediums of numbers. It may be crudely manifested in Harlem, but this mystical abnegation is not a Negroid monopoly. It exists among the international gamblers of Monte Carlo as well as the *aficionados* of the Spanish lottery. In fact I have been amused in foreign parts by some gamblers taking me as a kind of fetich and touching my skin before placing a bet.

The early history of the founding and growth of the numbers industry in Harlem is unknown to the millions who ardently participate in the game today. It has a Mediterranean background and might parallel the story of a small smuggler in Spain or Sicily building himself up to great power by the active cooperation and admiration of the common people.

In the first decade of the Negroes' big trek to Harlem, 1910–1920, a few Puerto Ricans and Cubans joined them and established barber shops in the black belt. They had a large patronage, chiefly among the British West Indians, many of whom had worked in Cuba and Central and South America, before coming to the United States, and thus were familiar with Latin-American customs. Then the Spanish-American colony did not border on the Negro district as it does today, but was concentrated in the east nineties.

The numbers game had its first start in these Spanish barber shops. Originally it was known as *bolita* or *paquerita*. The British West Indians called it "numbers" and popularized it. It was introduced to Harlem by a Spaniard from Cataluña, who was nicknamed Catalan by the Spanish-speaking Harlemites. Catalan devised his system of playing the numbers from the financial figures of the Stock Exchange. Familiar as he must have been with the method of the Spanish lottery, this could not have been a difficult job. The playing number was deduced from the totals of domestic and foreign sales. Its computation was not mathematical. Figures were arbitrarily chosen and put together to make a unit of three. To the uninitiated it was an extremely puzzling thing; to the players who were given the key, it was simple. As the financial figures printed in the newspapers are exact, there could be no trickery.

The numbers game has gripped all of Harlem precisely because there is no obvious trickery in it. It is an open, simple and inexpensive game of chance. Any winner gets an enormously sweet profit. Who would not thrill to a Cinderella penny placed on a number, say 391 and bringing the player 6 dollars? Make it 10 cents and it is 60 dollars, if you win.   And the average Harlemite reasons that he may as well invest a dime on a lucky number as he might in a glass of beer or a piece of candy.

Of course the operator of the numbers game is more fully insured against loss than the moguls who run the gambling Bank of Monte Carlo.   For a thousand different numbers are played every day and only one can win.   And there is only one chance in a thousand of a person winning. Yet not a day passes but somebody does win.   The stakes may be small or big, more often small, but still that is a great incentive for everybody to play.

Catalan was the sole numbers operator in Harlem for many years.   The barbers gathered up the numbers slips and the money for him and he hired a few collectors to pick up numbers here and there.   Nobody knew the extent of his wealth.   He was unassuming and lived modestly.   Once he went to Spain and it was rumored that he purchased there a fine piece of property.   But shortly after the ending of the World War he returned to Spain again to settle down.

Before leaving he made over his business in Harlem to a Cuban Negro named Messalino, who was his chief aide and confidant.   Messalino was quite a different type of man. He was flashy, amiable, man-about-town.   As lieutenant to Catalan, his flair for extravagance was checked by the latter's thriftiness and simplicity of living.   But when Catalan made his exit, deeding to Messalino the Harlem field, the latter splashed forth gorgeously.   He bought a big car and hired a chauffeur in uniform.   He entertained lavishly.   Catalan had checked accounts and paid winners from his small apartment.   Messalino rented an office and installed clerks with adding machines and typewriters.   He expanded the game, exciting community interest and making all Harlem numbers-minded.   He was the first of the dazzling line of numbers kings.

With the speculative propensities of the simple people aroused, other Negroes became aware of the huge operating profits and Messalino was challenged by rival numbers bankers.   The post-war expansion of Harlem brought the considerable Puerto Rican colony to the border of the black belt. And new rival bankers sprang from their group. The common people became enchanted by lucky numbers and Harlem a huge factory humming with the alluring activity of the game.

The operation of the game became more complex with its hectic spread. An army of collectors was organized to solicit players. Over the collectors were controllers, who received the money with the slips, which they turned over to the bankers. Each collector was remunerated with 10% of monies collected. And from any client who played the lucky number he was entitled to 10% of his win. The controller's reward was 5% of the total sum turned over to the banker. A competent controller is a powerful asset in the setup and may have as many as 50 collectors in charge.

The chances of winning were increased by the combination plan of six ways of playing a number. No. 915 could be played thus:

$$915$$
$$519$$
$$159$$
$$195$$
$$591$$
$$951$$

A player might put six cents on this number, alloting one cent to each component.

The magnetism of the game was heightened by its illegitimate link to the Stock Exchange. Harlem folk thought that they too had a little part in the ramifications of the stock market. The widespread playing and the increase and rivalry of bankers had brought into existence a type known as the tipster. The tipster made it his business to discover the lucky number prior to the publication of the financial reports in the newspapers. This was done by establishing contact with minor employees of the Stock Exchange, who perhaps were not aware of the purpose for which the figures were used.

The tipster played the number himself and also informed a few confidential persons, who agreed to share their winnings with him. The tipster did not always receive full advance information, sometimes he could give only the first and second figures of the lucky number. At other times his lead was wrong, as the earlier Stock Exchange reports were subject to correction before final publication.

However, the tipster idea was a profitable one, and in the dizzying era of Prohibition the tipster was a mighty man in the numbers business. One ingenious Harlemite actually rigged up an office in the Wall Street district and was highly regarded as "the Negro with a office in Wall Street." He organized a syndicate to play his tips. The bankers were afraid of him, as his tips were generally good winners. Sometimes he played both ends against the middle by tipping off bankers and players. The informed bankers held in their collectors on such occasions and remunerated the tipster. Sometimes the method was employed to break the smaller competing bankers and run them out of the racket. In the hectic Harlem of the late nineteen twenties, "the Negro in Wall Street" became an affluent Harlemite. He purchased a yacht, upon which he played host to members of Harlem's smart set. His prosperous reign continued until the Seabury investigations of 1931, when the Stock Exchange discontinued the publication of the Clearing House reports from which the lucky numbers were computed.

·   ·   ·   ·   ·   ·   ·

RACIAL GROUPS

Herbert R. Bruce is a West Indian and an orphan. Born in the Barbadoes, he was brought to New York when he was 5 years old. He was educated in the Public schools and grew up in Harlem. There is a sharp struggle for place and elbow room between the educated West Indians and native-born Negroes. It is not keen among the ordinary types of both groups. The natives call the West Indians "monkey-chasers" and the West Indians call them "coons" and they fight or laugh over it. But they work together, play together, marry one another and share equally the joys and sorrows of the group.

The educated American Negro is brought up in the old tradition of special protection and patronage for the talented members of his group. He regards the West Indian as an outsider, who should not share in the special patronage. But the native-born Negro is perhaps not so keenly aware of the subtle changes and shifts in the social system as is the West Indian.

I think the same state obtains among European immigrants, who are often quicker than some white native-born to appreciate the new currents and opportunities in the social set-up. The educated native Negroes resent the aggressiveness of the foreign-born Negroes, especially in politics. The first Negro Democratic Presidential elector, Dr. Godfrey Nurse, is a West Indian. And that the first Democratic District Leader should be also a West Indian! It was natural that the exclusive tenth among the native-born would be a little resentful.

Mr. Mal Frazier, boss of the Mimo Club, was put up as candidate to oppose Bruce. Bruce was pictured as a West Indian provincial, using his leadership to protect West Indians only! A forged letter was sent out over his signature requesting West Indians to vote for him because he was one of them! Despite this propaganda the voters went to the polls and gave Bruce an overwhelming vote of confidence.

It was amazing because, as his opponents said, 90 per cent of the Harlem vote is American Negro.

The rivalry between West Indians and native born is more amusing than tragic. They both are subject to the same discriminatory practices as a minority group. The American-born Negro derives great fun out of the West Indian accent. This accent is a colonial variant of Scotch and Irish, in Jamaica a curious hybrid Cockney. Strangely enough, the native born Negro does not appear to find funny the accent of South-Eastern Europeans and Levantines who may be his employers, and of the Irish policemen and political bosses who lord it over him. Yet some of these accents are hard as a fist in one's face in comparison to the liquid dialect of the West Indians.

An influential white person told me of a young Negro who was seeking his help to secure an important appointment. The Negro was well educated and fitted for the position. But before approval of his application, the white person sought to learn something of the applicant's character from a distinguished Harlemite. The Harlemite replied that the young man was of good character, but he was a West Indian. The white man was puzzled, for he was not aware that there were any sharp differences between West Indian and native-born Negroes and desired to know why. His informant said that it was because the West Indians were taking good jobs away from the native-born Negroes. This feeling of resentment against the West Indian immigrant does not seem to extend to the European immigrant.

The West Indians might find consolation in the fact that immigrants in all countries are more or less resented and patronized by the native-born. But they are more inclined to think of Aframericans as Negroes like themselves than as native-born Americans! In France, for example, the considerable colonies of Spanish, Corsican and Italian that concentrate in the Midi are tolerated but never quite accepted by the French. Yet they are all Latins. The first generation of immigrants are precisely in the same dilemma as the West Indians in Harlem.

Prejudice against first-generation immigrants may be stupid, but it is a universal human trait. And it must be said that the West Indians are largely responsible for their unpopularity among the educated Afro-Americans. Many of them lack the bonhomie of the natives and are considered too serious-minded by the latter. There also is too much pretense among West Indians. They boast irritatingly of better social conditions for Negroes in the islands, which cannot hold under analysis. The English do not have laws against intermarriage; they do not have Jim-Crow laws separating Negroes from whites in public places and conveyances; they do not disfranchise Negroes; they do not establish a rule of refusal to serve them in hotels, bars, etc. But in reality all such restrictions more or less obtain in the islands. This is easy. The large masses of Negroes live in such a poverty-stricken condition that they cannot aspire to the better life of the British aristocracy of the military and high government officials. Only the members of the entailed mulatto aristocracy can afford to intrude in the privileged area. This mulatto group of wealthy landed proprietors and business men is the controlling factor in the political and industrial life of the islands. It has in the United States no counterpart that could be cited in comparison.

West Indian masses do not eat the same food nor enjoy the same amusements as do the white aristocracy. There are no poor whites except the regiments of English soldiers, who live in camp apart from the natives. Here in the United States there are poor whites, rich whites and poor Negroes and wealthy Negroes. Rich and poor, white and black, all alike eat ham and eggs and potatoes and cornflakes and white bread. The bootblack rubs shoulders with the bank clerk at a hot-dog counter. That doesn't happen in the West Indies.

Unlike the West Indian, the American Negro is a minority in the midst of the white man's activities. His wages may be much lower than white wages, but it is incomparably higher than West Indian wages. It affords him the privilege of participating in the ordinary creature comforts of American life, just as the white bootblack. But he is often barred from such because of his complexion. It creates a resentment of which the average West Indian is oblivious until he lands in this country and participates in the life of the Negro minority.

Again, the West Indians are incredibly addicted to the waving of the Union Jack in the face of their American cousins. Of all the various peoples who migrate to America, the West Indians may be classed as the most patriotic to their homeland. All immigrants come to America to seek an opportunity for better life. They may come seeking employment or education; whichever it is, they seek something that is denied to them in their native land.

The Irish came with a hatred of the English who oppressed and exploited them. Poles and Russians fled from the mailed fist of Russian imperialism. Jews fled persecution. They all came incensed against the social orders which degraded them. But the West Indians seem strangely lacking in this spirit of resentment. They remain romantic about the régime that oppressed them. Yet they are black and suffer even so much more than white immigrants of the same category.

. . . .

In Harlem there is a miniature Chinatown at the bottom of Lenox Avenue. And there are Japanese who run the neat Sandwich Shops, which feature American and Chinese, but no Japanese food. There is a small colony of Haitians and a pocket of Martinique Negroids.

But the Spanish element, predominantly Puerto Rican, is the most important and provocative bloc of people in relation to the Negro group. It is of special and complicated interest because of the considerable numbers of Negroids within its fold. This Spanish-speaking mass embraces the area from 110th Street to 116th Street, between Lexington and Seventh Avenues. Some of them live beyond Seventh Avenue and above 116th Street and extend on the East Side as far down as 96th Street. But the popular movement of their life pulses in the first-named section.

Puerto Rico is one of the rare Caribbean islands where color has never been a major problem. Extensive miscegenation has occurred there. And here in Harlem the white and the yellow and the brown Puerto Ricans (there are not so many black ones) insouciantly mingle on equal terms. Nevertheless the pressure of American mores is having its effect upon them. The American Negro cannot comprehend the brown Puerto Rican rejecting the appellation, "Negro," and preferring to remain Puerto Rican. He is resentful of what he considers to be the superior attitude of the Negroid Puerto Rican. He is not aware that basically it is also a matter of language, that in Spanish Negro is the word for black and therefore brown cannot be black. The Aframerican also holds to the popular notion that all West Indians are colored and imagines that the white Puerto Rican or other white West Indian is merely the Caribbean counterpart of the near-white colored American.

Besides his natural adherence to his own language group, the colored Puerto Rican is motivated by economic necessity. By insisting that he is Puerto Rican and Spanish, he may, like the swarthy Sicilian, escape a little from that stigma which fixes the American Negro in a specific position in the social set-up. For the Puerto Ricans also have their social problems. Their avenues of employment are limited, as are the Negroes in the same field. Housing conditions are bad, often worse than among Aframericans, and are a menace to health. And politically the Puerto Ricans are not so flexible as Aframericans in party-politics and in winning favors from influential politicians. Of recent years, however, there has developed a strong movement for political cooperation between the two groups.

The community life of the Puerto Ricans, with the rest of the Spanish-speaking group, is more compact and purposeful than the Aframerican. The Aframerican efforts towards social adjustment in Harlem have been handicapped by invidious notoriety. The Puerto Ricans also have had a grim experience in establishing themselves in Harlem, but it was unaccompanied by spectacular publicity. The Puerto

Ricans concentrated their energy in building up a bulwark of small business. The Negroes have centered theirs upon moving into big and costlier apartment houses. In replacing the former residents and businesses the Spanish group encountered strenuous opposition. There were disputes and bloody fights, and much difficulty in renting shops.

Today the Spanish quarter in Harlem is as definitely Spanish as the Italian quarter is Italian. Unlike the Negro quarter it does not consist of a large professional stratum at the top and masses of laborers at the bottom with a void between. The Spanish group contains a bulging belly of middlemen—traders. There are 300 grocery stores, 200 restaurants, 50 dry goods stores, and cigar stores, laundries, tailor-shops, shoe-repair shops, pharmacies, bakeries, bars, dancing halls, two theaters and many bookstores. The casual observer may imagine that there are far too many. But competition is keen within the Spanish group itself. The word *"barato"* has infinite nuances to the Puerto Ricans, for it means so much to their group economy. Its equivalent, "cheap" or "good bargain," is of far less significance to the Negro group.

The Puerto Ricans will not pay the exorbitant rents that are exacted from the Aframericans. Therefore, apartments are much cheaper in their quarter. Some Harlem landlords have a rule of not renting to them. They consider the Negroes better tenants. In many instances the Spanish-speaking tenants of a house have been evicted and Negroes installed at higher rentals.

The Puerto Ricans unwittingly aided the Negroes in their expansion below 116th Street. When white Puerto Ricans moved into a house, the brown ones followed and that inevitably opened the doors to the Aframericans. However, until quite recently there were houses in 110th Street facing Central Park that had dark Puerto Ricans as tenants but refused Aframericans. When the landlords gave the signal and they became "houses for colored tenants" the rents went up. Harlem has many such interesting contradictions. Quite a number of native whites still live in the Negro quarter in isolated houses carrying signs: "Apartments for Whites Only."   When some open up to Negro tenants the signs are changed: "Apartments for Respectable Colored."   There are even colored landlords who rent only to whites and hang out signs: "For Whites Only."

A singular aspect of the Spanish scene, which appears imitative of the Aframerican, is the diversity of "store-front" churches.   For a Roman Catholic people this is an arresting development, for all such churches are Protestant.   There are Pentecostal, Evangelical, Church of God, Adventist, Jehovah's Witness and other churches.   I have not yet come across the Spanish Church of Christ, Scientist.   The worshipers in these places are as noisy as Aframericans in theirs. There are, in addition various occult or spiritualist chapels, redolent with incense and aromatic oils and burning colored candles.

But there are other aspects which give obvious distinction to the quarter.   The cafés have introduced a new spirit of social amenity in the life of Harlem.   They are the nearest approach to popular men's clubs in the community.   There men come together after dinner and engage in long conversations over cups of coffee or glasses of wine.   These cafés have no equivalent in the Aframerican bars, where customers are expected to spend the time imbibing one drink after another and not in conversation.

As elsewhere there is in the Spanish quarter, the inevitable petty criminal element.   It was one of its juvenile members who ignited the fuse that exploded the Harlem riots of March, 1935.   But it is interesting to note that the notorious gangsters and public enemies among Latin Americans do not belong to the Spanish-speaking group.   In Harlem its crimes are mainly misdemeanors.   Often the offenders are unjustly treated and nourish resentment for being held in jail for days because there are no Spanish interpreters.

In the congested blocks prostitution is rampant and brazen with apache overtones, and must naturally be repugnant to native Americans.   But it is also objectionable to respectable Spanish-speaking residents and especially to the business people. *Chulos* and *cabrons* on the street corners spit aloud the filthiest epithets, especially when women are passing by. Perhaps this exhibition is a corruption of the ancient Spanish custom of the right of males to flirt with females on the promenade. In Spanish Harlem it has degenerated into an extremely obnoxious practice. It could easily be checked if there were Spanish-speaking policemen on the beat. Unfortunately there are none. And the English-speaking policemen have no comprehension of what is being said and done around them.

Signs of literary culture are more evident in the Puerto Rican than in the Aframerican quarter. A number of book stores are stocked with Spanish classics and contemporary literature, and also English books. Negro Harlem has one only and that recently established: the Blyden Bookstore owned by Dr. Willis Huggins.

As far back as 1921, the 135th Street branch librarian, Ernestine Rose, remarking the infiltration of Spanish-speaking persons into Aframerican Harlem, recommended and obtained the appointment of a Spanish-speaking assistant. But the Spanish-speaking population, enormously increasing in Harlem about 1925, settled in the 116th Street section. The assistant, Miss Pura Belpré was transferred to the 115th Street branch library. Under the direction of Head Librarian Leah Lewinson the branch accumulated a collection of Spanish literature. It contains 2,600 volumes and is extensively used by Harlem's Spanish readers.

Perhaps the most distinctive contribution of Puerto Rico to the literary culture of Harlem is the Arthur A. Schomburg collection of books and manuscripts which, although housed in the Negro Division of the 135th Street Library, is pertinent to any discussion of the Spanish-speaking group of Negro Harlem. The Schomburg collection is the most important library of books by and about Negroes in the world. It consists of 10,000 volumes and 3,000 manuscripts of letters, poems, addresses, sermons, historical documents, etc., written by or about well-known and little-known persons of the Negro group. Many of the volumes are extremely rare.

There are books in all the major occidental languages: Spanish, Portugese, French, Italian, German, Russian and Latin.

Through the active interest of Branch Librarian Ernestine Rose, cooperating with the officials of the National Urban League, the Schomburg Collection was purchased by the Carnegie Corporation in 1926 and turned over to the New York Public Library. The directors of the Library established a Negro Division in the 135th Street branch and the collection was there installed. In 1932 Mr. Schomburg was appointed curator. The collection is accessible to readers and research workers and is extensively used. Ironically, this priceless affirmation of the culture of the Negro group has been disparaged by some of its intellectuals as a segregated institution.

The story behind this incomparable collection is as remarkable as the collection itself. Arthur Schomburg came from Puerto Rico to this country at the age of 23, seven years before the United States acquired the island of Puerto Rico. In appearance he was like an Andalusian gypsy, olive-complexioned and curly-haired, and he might easily have become merged in that considerable class of foreigners who exist on the fringe of the white world. But because of his African blood, he chose to identify himself with the Aframerican group, and soon he was married to an Aframerican woman. He worked at various "Negro" jobs, such as bell-hop and elevator boy. After he had gained experience in New York he obtained a position as messenger for the Bankers' Trust Company. His excellent command of Spanish earned him promotion to the Latin-American Mail Department. Finally he became head of the bank's mailing department.

In the Negro colony he was attracted to a circle of eager-minded intellectuals, Aframerican and West Indian. The leading members were John Edward Bruce, a prominent Freemason, David Fulton, Dr. York Russell, eminent physician, the Rev. Dr. Charles D. Martin of Harlem's Moravian Church and William Ernest Braxton, a remarkable painter.

They founded in 1911 the Negro Society of Historical Research. Schomburg was elected secretary and librarian. Lewanika, King of Basutoland, South Africa, was the Honorary President. The membership included Negroes from the Barbadoes, Brazil, Capetown, Costa Rica, Cuba, Gold Coast, Lagos, Liberia, London, Panama, Puerto Rico, Sierra Leone. The aim of the Society was to create in New York a cultural center for the promoting of research work and the collecting of literary and historical items of the Negro race. Within a year of its formation the Society acquired 300 books and pamphlets.

These founding members also began collecting individually: John Edward Bruce, Arthur Schomburg, The Rev. Dr. Charles D. Martin and Henry P. Slaughter of Washington, who at present possesses the finest private collection. Schomburg's Spanish background was a priceless asset to the Society in its research work. It helped him to unravel the threads of that African Negro contribution to modern civilization, which came by way of Spain, through its conquest and 700 years' domination by the Moroccans. One of his invaluable finds was the rare volumes of the Negro Juan Latino, famous Latin scholar and professor of poetry at the University of Granada in the 16th Century.

Yet Schomburg was not typically literary. His private taste in books was inclined to the esoterically erotic. But he possessed a bloodhound's nose in tracing any literary item about Negroes. He could not discourse like a scholar, but he could delve deep and bring up nuggets for a scholar which had baffled discovery.

When he received $10,000 for his collection from the Carnegie Foundation he must have been highly gratified. But the honor of being rewarded for a noble work must have meant even more to him, for when he became obsessed with the urge to buy Negro books, often denying himself creature comforts, so that out of his moderate salary he might acquire a rare item, he was not actuated by the possibility of pecuniary profit. Nor were any of his colleagues. There was no national interest in Negro books, and Negro writers

were a liability.   But they were hoodooed by the strange
magic of one special branch of literature, which was greater
than they had imagined.

Schomburg's first thought after disposing of the collection
was to travel to Spain and visit the libraries of Seville and
the Escorial and search through antique books and manuscripts for more material about the Negro.   Perhaps a psychologist might have been interested in plumbing him to
discover whether the Spanish-European or the African-West
Indian was uppermost in his character.   Intellectually he
was proud of his Spanish heritage and fond of Puerto Rico,
yet he cultivated no social contact with Harlem's Puerto
Ricans.   He strangely combined a simple, disarming exterior
and obscure inner complexes.   And his emphatic character
and lusty appetite for life were amazing.   He had large, expressive eyes and the body and energy of a powerful Spanish
bull.   He was thrice married, each time to an American
Negro woman, and he reared 7 children.   He was full of
wonderful love and admiration and hate, positively liking his
friends and positively disliking his foes.   He died in 1938.

Marcus Aurelius Garvey

The movement of Marcus Garvey in Harlem was glorious with romance and riotous, clashing emotions. Like the wise men of the ancient world, this peacock-parading Negro of the New World, hoodooed by the "Negromancy" of Africa, followed a star—a Black Star. A weaver of dreams, he translated into a fantastic pattern of reality the gaudy strands of the vicarious desires of the submerged members of the Negro race.

There has never been a Negro leader like Garvey. None ever enjoyed a fraction of his universal popularity. He winged his way into the firmament of the white world holding aloft a black star and exhorting the Negro people to gaze upon and follow it. His aspiration to reach dizzy heights and dazzle the vision of the Negro world does not remain monumental, like the rugged path of the pioneer or of the hard, calculating, practical builder. But it survives in the memory like the spectacular swath of an unforgettable comet.

Leaving the Caribbean island of Jamaica, Marcus Garvey arrived in New York in March, 1916. He did not come as "a Numidian lion" (as he was once described by Mr. William Pickens of the National Association for the Advancement of Colored People) to lead the Negro people. He came as a humble disciple of the late Booker T. Washington, Founder of Tuskegee Institute. Garvey had hoped to establish in Jamaica an institution similar to Tuskegee. He corresponded with Booker T. Washington about his plan and was invited to visit Tuskegee. But the Founder of Tuskegee died suddenly before Garvey's arrival in the United States. Garvey then planned to raise funds and return to Jamaica

143

to establish his institution.   There, in 1914, he had organized the Universal Negro Improvement Association, which failed.

Marcus Garvey was born in 1887 in the village-town of the most beautiful region of Jamaica, called locally The Garden of Jamaica.   His father was not a peasant, but an artisan, a carpenter who, during Garvey's early years, lived comfortably by his work.   Garvey was given an excellent common school education.   Modeled on the English plan, the elementary school system of Jamaica is sound.   And Garvey received extra education, presumably the pupil-teachers' course of training, which, depending on the ability of the student, may be very thorough.   Garvey has stated that he studied at the University of London, but the truth of this statement is doubted by persons who knew something of his earlier life and his enormous capacity for exaggeration.   However, by substantial, catholic reading and traveling, Garvey provided himself with a higher education, perhaps greater than he might have derived from an institution.

Like all ambitious provincials, Garvey was attracted to Kingston, the capital of Jamaica.   There he went as a lad to learn the trade of printing.   He was so proficient that at twenty he became a master printer and foreman of one of the largest local firms.   This was no easy achievement.   Indeed it was extraordinary.   Printing is a first-class trade in Jamaica and some of the foremen of the big plants were imported from Britain and Canada.

A mere youth, the youngest foreman printer in Kingston, Garvey held down this position of responsibility and authority until in 1909 a printers' strike took place in Kingston. All the rank and file printers were native blacks and mulattoes.   Being foreman of his plant, Garvey had not been informed of the strike and the walkout of his men took him unawares.

Nevertheless, he was a native son himself; he understood the grievances of the strikers and voluntarily supported their demands for better wages and shorter hours.   The strikers welcomed Garvey and he quit his job to join them.   He was the only foreman who did.   Grateful, the strikers elected him to lead the strike. He did the job efficiently, organized public meetings and for the first time demonstrated those extraordinary oratorical talents which were to magnetize the Negro people and stir the world.

The employers finally won the strike. They broke it by introducing the linotype machine and importing key printers from abroad. Most of the men compromised and returned to their jobs. But as the one foreman who joined the strikers, Marcus Garvey was boycotted by all the employers, who were white, and nevermore could he obtain another job as a printer in Jamaica. It was probably this bitter experience which later made him contemptuous of workers' organizations and the labor movement in general. And when he was able, as a universal leader, to sway thousands of Negroes, he ignored all efforts that were made by various quarters to bring about an understanding or working agreement between the forces of labor and his racial mass movement.

The following year, after the strike, Garvey established a periodical called *Garvey's Watchman*. Also he organized an annual Elocution Contest. The Elocution Contest was a success and still is conducted in Jamaica. But the newspaper failed. Garvey emigrated to Central America. He tried to establish another paper in Costa Rica, where there is a considerable population of English-speaking West Indians. This venture failed, precipitating difficulties, and it is said that he was arrested and deported from Costa Rica.

Next Garvey is discovered in London in 1912 or 1913. There he became associated with an Egyptian author, Duse Mohammed Ali, who published the monthly *African Times and Orient Review*. He visited the British Museum and contemplated the relics of the culture of ancient Egypt. He studied the tribal cultures of West Africa and South Africa. He read many books about native West African empires, such as the Empire of Benin, which became extinct. He studied the colonization system of Africa. Duse Mohammed introduced him to other Africans in London: cocoa and copra and palm oil merchants and their student sons.

In July, 1914, just before the outbreak of the World War,

Garvey returned to Jamaica. His head was big with the idea of an African Redemption and Colonization scheme. Garvey had been quite irritated by the complacency of the Africans in London. They appeared to him to be apologetic black Englishmen rather than Africans proud of their race and country. Garvey believed that the Africans should be awakened with new ideas and a world outlook. And he had proposed to Duse Mohammed the plan of an international organization of Africans and Negroes of the New World.

Back again in Jamaica, he founded the Universal Negro Improvement Association. The native intelligentsia did not respond to Garvey's efforts. The majority of educated British West Indians are more conservative in their patriotism than many Britons and feel little kinship with the natives of Africa. The Jamaica intelligentsia ridiculed Garvey's pan-African dream.

But the common people were receptive. So Garvey preached to them. But he felt that if the common people were to grasp fully the significance of his movement, they needed a wider education. There were no facilities in the West Indies for the education of such people. So Garvey planned to establish an institution similar to Tuskegee and accordingly corresponded with Booker T. Washington. The Universal Association had already failed from lack of public support when Garvey left Jamaica for the United States.

Garvey had been converted to the Roman Catholic faith in his youth and he carried letters from members of the Catholic hierarchy in Jamaica commending his work. His first public meeting in New York was held in the annex of St. Marks Roman Catholic church in Harlem. The meeting was not a success. A majority of his audience who were mostly West Indians, were aware of the opposition Garvey had encountered in Jamaica and were hostile to his pan-African dream. And they made the evening hot for Garvey.

Garvey was not prepossessing in that first New York appearance. By purely Negroid standards he is an ugly man.

As a boy in Jamaica he had been nicknamed "Ugly Mug."
He was short and ungainly, built something in the shape of
a puncheon. He had not yet cultivated that stern domineering manner which later distinguished him. The audience
listened attentively enough when he outlined his plan of
establishing a school for the underprivileged children of
Jamaica. But when he aired his pan-African ideas he was
heckled and booed. In the confusion Garvey fell off the
platform, hurting himself slightly, and the meeting broke
up. Later, hostile critics said that his fall from the platform had been deliberate, to win the sympathy of the
audience.

Subsequently Garvey was persuaded to join a group of
street speakers of radical-racial ideas. And from 1916 on-
wards he harangued crowds on the sidewalks of Harlem.

A few persons who believed in him prevailed upon him
to establish his Universal Negro organization in New York.
They convinced him that New York was a world center, from
which it would be possible for him to reach and influence
more Negroes than anywhere else.

In 1917 Garvey organized in Harlem the Universal Negro
Improvement Association. He had as a nucleus an intelligent
group of men who belonged to a long established History
Club, which specialized in the Negro people's ancient past.
Auspiciously Garvey started off on a lecture tour, which
covered a majority of the States that had a considerable
Negro population. He was warmly welcomed and received
large contributions of money.

Garvey was establishing himself. But he still faced serious
opposition in Harlem. Towards the end of 1917 one of
his opponents received a letter from Garvey's former associate in London, Duse Mohammed, which discredited Garvey and made serious charges against his character. The
recipient of the letter read it at an open meeting. It exploded like a well-timed bomb and broke up the organization. But Garvey, determined, started again to build another organization. In the first month of 1918 the *Negro*

World, its weekly organ, was launched.   Disseminating the pan-African ideas of Garvey, this newspaper in a few months established itself as the leading national Negro weekly.

Africa for the Africans!   Renaissance of the Negro Race! Back to Africa!   A Black Star Line!   These were the slogans Garvey broadcast in a thousand different ways to move the mind of the Negro people.   There was magic in his method. It worked miraculously.   The Negro masses acclaimed the new leader.   The black belts clamored to hear his voice and competed with one another for his lectures.   Money poured in for subscriptions to the *Negro World,* money that would help establish the Black Star Line and set in motion the Redemption of Africa.   Garvey struck African Redemption medals.   A bronze cross was bestowed upon subscribers of from $50 to $100, a silver cross for subscribers of from $100 to $500 and a gold cross for donors of $500 to $1000.

Now, after many vicissitudes, Garvey was successfully launched on his career of world leadership of the Negroes. Evidently Garvey himself was astounded by the overwhelming acclaim he received in the United States.   After extensive traveling he was convinced that the advance guard of the Negro race was in America.   The Negroes, discovering in him the inspired prophet of their group, kept him here and lifted him to the dizzying pinnacle of fame.

There were other worthy organizations and leaders of the period.   The National Association for the Advancement of Colored People and the Equal Rights League had fought for nearly a decade for the human and legal rights of Negroes. But Dr. DuBois and Monroe Trotter, the outstanding personalities of these organizations, respectively, were highly educated and refined men.

And the times were auspicious for a popular leader.   The whole world was in the midst of war.   Negroes from the United States, the West Indies and Africa were fighting the battle of Europe in France and the Near East.   And there was no leader who was giving voice to the thoughts of these common Negro soldiers and their kinsfolk at home. Negroes were segregated as soldiers.   In America there was a conflict raging within the group whether Negroes should participate in the war. Some held that Negroes should fight as other citizens: others maintained that Negroes were not as other citizens. In 1917, when America entered the war, there were frightful outbreaks and riots between whites and blacks, notably in Houston, Texas. A considerable body of Southern whites deplored the Negroes' participation in the war. The Negro minority lacked an authoritative voice of leadership.

The supply of cheap European labor was cut off by the World War. Southern Negro workers were available. The mills and factories of Northern industrialists were whirring with war orders. They dispatched agents to the South to round up Negro workers. The South was alarmed over losing the brawn and sinews of its mistreated minority. It didn't care to let the "unwanted" Negroes go. Every effort was used to restrain them. The Northern agents were intimidated. Negro migrants were pulled off trains and driven to the plantations with shotguns poking their backs. Still the Negroes contrived to elude their jailers and pour into the centers of Northern industry. The black migration increased industrial conflicts and race riots, of which the bloody massacre of East St. Louis was the most appalling.

The liberal spirit of the entire nation was outraged. Negro and white organizations demanded that the corrupt authorities of East St. Louis should protect the Negro citizens. But the American Federation of Labor president, Samuel Gompers, released a statement in which he justified the mob of white workers in their attacks upon the Negro workers, because the latter were imported to compete with the whites. Yet the Negroes were not strike-breakers. They were merely filling a gap that the United States war efforts had opened. The political horizon for the Negro was as full of foreboding as was the industrial horizon. The 1916 national election had returned another Democratic Administration. The men who controlled the destinies of the Republican Party were alarmed. There was a proposal to reform the electoral vote of the Southern States: either Negro citizens should vote, or their potential voting strength should not be misused to increase the power of the Southern political bloc. The entire block of Southern States and their sympathizers in the North were aroused to combat the idea. New York's leading Democratic organ came out flatly with this statement: "The white man will rule his land."

The statement was reprinted and commented upon by all the important Negro newspapers. Some of the most loyal meliorists of the Booker T. Washington political school were stirred to join up with the radicals. There was a general feeling abroad that the Negro, however loyal, would never be permitted to call America his land. However much property he acquired he would have no voice in the control of it and would remain at the mercy of white political sharks.

In the midst of this crisis Marcus Garvey appeared with his Negro Improvement and Back-to-Africa programme. He thundered phrases that were authoritative if not wise. But the Negro people were ripe for such a prophet. Girding for a supreme war effort, America had little time to devote to the growing problems of its large Negro minority. Harassed in the South and rebuffed in the North, the southern Negroes eagerly swallowed the sayings and the projects of Garvey.

Marcus Garvey became the mouthpiece of these southern and West Indian migrants to the northern centers of industry. Whether they worked in Jersey or Pennsylvania, Connecticut or Massachusetts, Harlem was their Mecca. They gave Garvey all the money he needed to institute his programme. But only an infinitesimal few of these people really desired to go—BACK TO AFRICA. And obviously Marcus Garvey himself had no intention of going back to live in some corner of the vast land of his ancestors. But Back-to-Africa on a Black Star Line was magical propaganda. American Negroes had never beheld a steamship with a Negro crew and owned and officered by Negroes. Even the smallest excursion boat chartered by a church for a summer's day vacation was owned and officered by whites. Garvey declared that it could be otherwise. His disciples desired to see.

Inspired by the response of the masses, Garvey outlined a programme for a planned Negro economy. He exhorted Negroes to trade among themselves, to make contacts for trading with Negroes abroad, to start a real Negro Church based upon African religion, build Negro schools and a society of Negro people. He wanted to create a Negro society according to the European plan, with royalty, nobility, laity, priests, workers.

.   .   .   .

At first Garvey's mighty plans did not appeal to the educated Negroes. Apparently they were no more than grandiloquently spoken and printed words which could never be translated into action. But certain individuals, leaders, would-be leaders and practical politicians were disturbed by the man's magnetic influence over the masses.

Just a few months after the founding of his organization, Garvey was involved in disputes with his most prominent officials. He ousted some of them. Already Garvey was accused of misappropriation of funds which he had collected. Early in 1919 he was nearly assassinated by one George Tyler, who shot him three times in the arms and leg. He was saved by his secretary, Miss Amy Ashwood, who threw herself between him and his antagonist. The would-be assassin committed suicide the following day by leaping from the fourth-story window of the jail.

The attempt on Garvey's life, besides his arrest sky-rocketed his stock. He incorporated the Black Star Line, capitalized at ten million dollars. Shares sold at five dollars each. The drive started for funds to purchase and launch that year the first ship of the Black Star Line. "Up, you mighty race!" cried Garvey. And the race rose up. Garvey spoke and the Negro masses were transformed. "Negro, Black, and Africa," the magic words repeated again and again made Negroes delirious with ecstasy. Wherever Garvey led they were

ready to follow.   He was the modern Moses, the black savior.
His message reached Negroes everywhere.   From the plantation of the deep South, they hearkened to his voice, in the
islands of the Caribbean they were moved as never before,
now that the voice of Marcus Garvey was broadcast from
New York.   Across the Atlantic, in the heart of the Congo,
Negroes talked of the black Messiah.

No wonder Garvey thought himself invested with godlike
attributes.   The Negro people pushed him up on a pedestal
and seated him upon a throne.   They were overwhelmed by
waves of emotion, subterranean waves rising and sweeping
over them, waves which might have frightened Garvey himself.   Hitherto their enormous store of energy and emotion
had swept along the channels of religion.   But for the first
time since Emancipation, they were touched by a momentous
social awakening.   Could Garvey rule this swelling ocean of
enthusiasm?   As it rolled along, carrying him on its heaving
bosom, Garvey, in gaudy paraphernalia and with a symbolic
sword, shouted gorgeous words, words spinning like bullets,
words falling like bombs, sharp words, like poisoned daggers,
thundering words and phrases lit with all the hues of the
rainbow to match the wild approving roar of his people.
And the words seemed sufficient, apparently of greater value
even than the little action which resulted from them.

The pan-African empire which he builded in Harlem was
a fantastic realm.   But it flourished, extending its power
over a mighty host.   To the innumerable black subjects it
was a real empire.   The Garvey-created nobility were a
serious ruling caste.   The dukes and lords and ladies had
special duties to perform as leaders of sections.   They took
precedence over the masses and were obliged to set an
example of higher living.   And it is interesting to observe
that some of these titled personages of the dream empire
came from the élite of Aframericans.   The Duke of the
Nile was Emmett J. Scott, a light mulatto, Registrar of
Howard University, former Secretary of Tuskegee Institute,
close associate of Booker T. Washington and friend of some
high ranking leaders of the Republican Party.   Lady Hen-

rietta Vinton Davis was one of the finest elocutionists of the Negro group and a very sensitive interpreter of Shakespearean roles at home and abroad.

The Black Legion, in its dark-blue uniform and red stripes, was as imposing as the Black Guard of the Sultan of Morocco. The Black Cross nurse appeared as chic and competent as any one of the unit of colored girls in a New York hospital. The Black Star choristers chanted melodiously of the Empire land. Harlem became the provisional capital of the empire. And it carried an allure, a peacock pride at being the center of a colossal movement.

As thousands of dollars were rained down on Garvey for the founding of the Black Star Line and the glorification of his dream of African empire, other Negro leaders, less spectacular, showed serious concern about this waste of the earnings of the Negro masses. Standing aloof and extremely critical, few of the Negro intellectuals had any faith in the operation of a Black Star Line of ships.

A Negro ship! Master, officers and crew all Negro! Hostile Negro newspapers demanded to know where Marcus Garvey would find a Negro captain. If one could not be found in America, Garvey knew that specimens existed in the West Indies, where wealthy Negroids owned their own coastwise vessels, officered and manned by Negroes.

And so while leading Harlem Negroes were instigating an investigation of Garvey's financial ventures, he ran a series of articles in the *Negro World,* picturing the glories of the Black Star Line and the moral and material benefits that Negroes could get from running their own ships.

In the latter part of 1919, while the pundits of the Negro minority were still proving by mathematical manipulation that Negroes by themselves could not operate a line of ships, Marcus Garvey announced that the Black Star Line had acquired its first boat. There was consternation in the camp of his opponents, while the masses of Black Dixie shouted hosannas. Garvey also had the master of his ship in the person of Captain Joshua Cockburn, who had actually served with the British Merchant Fleet during the First

World War. Negro mates, first and second, and a Negro crew were also on hand.

There was a wild invasion of Harlem by Negroes from every black quarter of America. Hordes of disciples came with more dollars to buy more shares. The boat was moored at the pier with its all-Negro crew. And the common people gladly paid half a dollar to go aboard and look over the miracle. Loudly talking and gesturing, they inspected the ship, singing the praises of Marcus Garvey. Summer after summer most of them had taken excursion trips, organized by churches or clubs. But it was always a "white" boat and not always were they treated considerately and politely by officers and crew.

Now, in this first boat of the Black Star Line, owned by the Universal Negro Improvement Association, they saw something different. They saw themselves sailing without making any apology for being passengers. It was their own ship, a Negro ship. It was their money that had bought it. But it had required a black leader to show them how they could do it.

That night Liberty Hall was jammed with Negroes. Hundreds could not get in and the sidewalks overflowed with spectators between Lenox Avenue and Seventh Avenue. Marcus Garvey transformed the great audience into a waving, shouting, frenzied host as he cried: "Up, you mighty race, you can accomplish what you will."

The price of the boat was said to be $165,000. It was sent on goodwill trips to coastwise ports and enthusiastic supporters were sold hundreds of shares in the Negro line. Early in 1920 the boat sailed on its first voyage to the West Indies, carrying a cargo of liquor. It proved to be almost unseaworthy and foundered at Newport News. The trip did not enhance the prestige of the Black Star Line. The crew became undisciplined, raided the cargo and went on a boozers' holiday.

But if the Black Star did not shine so brilliantly at sea, Garvey's individual star, nevertheless, rose wonderfully. Towards the end of 1919, he married his secretary Miss Amy

Ashwood, who had flung herself between him and his would-be assassin.   She too was from Jamaica, where she had graduated from the Westwood High School.

In 1920 Marcus Garvey staged the first Universal Negro Convention in Harlem.   This was the dramatic occasion that made the City of New York fully aware of the movement in Harlem.   The convention went over with theatrical éclat. During the hard years of organization, Garvey had lived simply and dressed modestly.   His exuberant attitude toward life had been held under control in Jamaica.   But in Harlem Garvey could let himself go.   His speech could be as decorative as arabesques and his raiment as rich as an Eastern potentate's.   The common people would pay him still greater homage, for Harlem adores colorful, colossal demonstrations.   Garvey borrowed generously from cult manifestations and fraternal rituals in painting his political mission in gay colors.

And so a most gorgeous show was organized by Garvey in 1920.   Delegates arrived from Africa, Brazil, Colombia, Panama and other Central American countries, and from the islands of the West Indies.   Every State of the Union was represented.   Harlem blinked at the dazzling splendor of that wonderful parade.   Garvey wore a magnificent uniform of purple, green and black, and a plumed hat.   He stood in his car and saluted the cheering crowds that jammed the sidewalks.   Behind him in full regalia rode the nobility and the notables of the Universal Negro Association, brilliant sashes denoting their rank.   The African Legion filed past, stiff, erect, left, right, left, right, and all the auxiliaries of the association and the enormous mass of the rank and file.

The following evening, Garvey packed Madison Square Garden with his followers and admirers.   In a long speech he exhorted the Negroes to unite and work for the redemption of Africa.   He recited the history of the organization, giving details of what had been accomplished.   He told the people that they had done everything and could do greater things.   Resolutions were passed and messages sent to United States government officials, to the Empress of

Ethiopia and the President of Liberia.   Most significant of all was the message of sympathy and support sent to Eamon de Valera, Provisional President in Exile of the Irish Republic. That message was duly noted in certain London newspapers. The Irish struggle against Britain was most acute at that time.   And if the British government had never heard of a British subject named Marcus Garvey in London and Jamaica, perhaps they became aware of him now in New York.

.   .   .   .

In the fall of 1921 Garvey boldly took a position on the Negro's place in American politics, and thus arrayed against him the radical element of Negro leaders.   President Harding had visited Birmingham, where he delivered a significant speech on the Negro's part in politics.   There was an echo of Booker T. Washington's famous Atlanta speech in what the President had to say.   He said that racial amalgamation there could not be, but partnership of the races there must be: "I wish that both the tradition of a solid Democratic South and the tradition of a solidly Republican black race might be broken up. . . .   Let the black man vote when he is fit to vote, prohibit the white man from voting when he is unfit to vote."

The South was not too enthusiastic over the President's speech.   And the northern Negroes were non-committal. Politically, the Negro minority was at that time in a dilemma. Dissatisfied with President Taft's administration and displeased with Theodore Roosevelt's stand on the Negroes in 1912, thousands had been led by their leaders to vote for President Wilson and The New Freedom.   But politically the group had fared worse under the Democratic Administration than under any Republican Administration since Lincoln.   The Negroes were demoralized, not knowing to which party they should turn.   Booker T. Washington, although resident in the South, had always been a Republican and a strong influence among the conservative Negroes.   But he had died during President Wilson's first term and no other Negro leader had forged forward to take his place.

Marcus Garvey sent a telegram of endorsement to President Harding, in which he said: "All true Negroes are against Social Equality, believing that all Negroes should develop along their own social lines. . . . The New Negro will join hands with those who are desirous of keeping the two opposite races socially pure and work together for the industrial, educational and political liberation of all peoples. The Negro peoples of the world expect the South to give the Negroes a fair chance. Long live America. Long live President Harding in his manly advocacy of Social Justice."

It is not recorded what effect this telegram had upon President Harding and his entourage. The Republicans were badly in need of a leader of national proportions, who could combine the shrewdness and sagacity of Booker T. Washington in dealing with the white North and the white South, while commanding the respect of the conservative majority of Negroes. Perhaps if Garvey were less bombastic and had apprenticed himself to learn more of the mechanism of American politics, he might have been that leader. There was no other Negro in sight for the job (there has not yet been one) and Garvey had the Negro masses in the hollow of his hand.

But Garvey had stumbled headlong into the hornet's nest of the Northern Negro intelligentsia. For 75 years "Social Equality" has been the red sign of danger between the white world and the Negro. Southern whites interpret it to mean, mainly, intimate social intercourse between whites and blacks, with resultant miscegenation. The Northern Negro intelligentsia challenge this interpretation. They interpret Social Equality to mean equal opportunity for Negro Americans under the American system of economy: equal opportunity in the industrial, educational, political and other avenues of American life.

In the West Indies, Social Equality is generally used in the careless way of the Southern whites. And so it meant the same thing to Marcus Garvey as it did to them. In his excessive group and racial pride Garvey held that social intercourse should not become an acute political issue between the colored minority and the whites in America. He was too proud and self-confident to imagine that the Negro was inferior. Garvey always preached to his followers the potential equality of the Negro with the white person.

Garvey was a fervent admirer of Booker T. Washington's marvellous skill in building up and holding together a modern all-Negro institution. He was a partisan of the Tuskegee school of politics. And this school was especially detested by that northern Negro group led by the powerful National Association for the Advancement, of Colored People of New York and the Equal Rights Association of Boston. They accused Garvey of advocating Segregation and of pandering to the worst prejudices of Southern whites. Opposition was erected against him. This opposition was joined by the small but intelligent and influential group of Negroes affiliated with the Labor and Radical movements. And doubtlessly it was this powerful combination of the Negro intelligentsia, aided by wealthy white supporters, which finally brought about Garvey's downfall.

The Negro masses throughout the nation backed Garvey. And as the opposition of the Negro intelligentsia gained in strength, the masses demonstrated their greater loyalty. At a stupendous mass meeting in Harlem, Garvey was presented with a new broom to sweep the opposition away. In every State, loyalty meetings of the Universal Negro Improvement Association were held. And resolutions were passed, pledging the loyalty of the Negro people to Garvey. He journeyed triumphantly to the populous centers to show his appreciation and stir the people with his magnetic oratory. Liberally they contributed with donations or purchases of shares.

Garvey's invasion of the South, the acclamation of the Black Belts and the attitude of the Southern whites presented a puzzle to northern Negro intellectuals. Garvey had announced previously that he was going South to talk to his own people and that the white man should leave him alone.

Now many Northern blacks and whites had been manhandled and run out of the South for attempting to hold peaceful meetings with colored people! A Mr. Shillady, the white Secretary of the National Association of Colored People, was obnoxiously insulted, beaten and driven out of the South, when he attempted to meet with colored persons. Booker T. Washington was always extremely cautious in his spoken and written words.

But in Louisiana and Alabama, notably, Garvey succeeded in holding some extremely boisterous and enthusiastic meetings and getting away without a scratch. Of course, he had his way of doing it. He employed a special technique. He thundered, "Africa for the Africans," and shouted at the white South in a semi-religious harangue, "Let my people go!"

The South permitted Marcus Garvey to talk that way to cheering multitudes of Negroes. Northern Negro critics maintained that the South gave Garvey leeway because he was not a challenge: the South wanted to get rid of the Negro and approved Garvey's slogan, "Let my people go." But Garvey *was* a challenge and the South did *not* want to get rid of its black serfs. During the World War and the years immediately following, when labor manpower was a problem, the South had desperately tried to keep its Negroes from migrating North.

Probably there was some truth in the report that Garvey had made a secret deal with the Ku Klux Klan that his meetings should not be molested. The Ku Klux Klan undoubtedly possessed the power and perhaps the Kleagle secretly admired a Negro who could organize the blacks on a grand scale, employing the same tactics by which the Klan had organized the whites.

Meanwhile, the Federal government had undertaken an investigation of Garvey. In January, 1922, he was arrested on a charge of using the mails to defraud. He was indicted with three high officials of his organization. The charge was that Garvey had used the mails to solicit funds for a Black Star Line which was not established. He was released on bail of $2500.

At the same time a vigorous campaign was launched

against Garvey by the Friends of Negro Freedom, a group composed of officials of the National Association for the Advancement of Colored People, and labor leaders, editors and ministers.   But Garvey's loyal followers organized larger meetings and he received hundreds of telegrams pledging support.   The Universal Negro Improvement Association released an open letter appealing to the White Race to let the Black Race manage its own affairs.

The prosecution of Marcus Garvey was not rushed.   This delay aroused his opponents.   Meetings were called and resolutions passed demanding his speedy prosecution.   The resolutions were telegraphed to the Department of Justice. But it appeared as if the authorities were in no hurry to proceed.   Perhaps Garvey had friends in high places of whom he was not even aware: he was too egotistic to care.

For the balance of the year he remained unmolested, and organized in Harlem one of his grandest conventions.   From every State in the union, from the West Indies, from Central and South America, from Europe and Africa, an inspiring deputation of delegates converged upon Harlem.   It was the greatest swarm since Garvey started his movement.   They brought gifts to Garvey: special contributions to defend his case, sums for African Redemption and thousands of subscriptions to reorganize the Black Star Line.   It was during this time that a delegate from Central America drafted a new will bequeathing to Garvey's organization his estate, valued at over $300,000.   At that convention Garvey generously increased the strength of his nobility.   Among the new titles were Duke of Nigeria and Overlord of Uganda. To the tremendous tributes he responded as befitted a grand potentate.   The ribbons and braids of his gleaming satin robe were richer than ever, his plumes were as long as the leaves of the Guinea grass and as white as snow; seated in his car as upon a throne, he received the ovations and salutes of Harlem.

It was not until the following year, near the middle of 1923, that Garvey's trial began.   It lasted a month.   And it was a real show, one of the amusement features of the great city of New York. The government's case was weak and everything seemed in Garvey's favor. First, there was apparently official reluctance in prosecuting. The evidence for prosecution was flimsy. There was no letter to prove that the Black Star Line had directly sold shares through the mails. Only an envelope was offered as evidence. Although the Black Star Line was not actually in operation, since its ships were old and broken down and lacked personnel, it was not altogether bankrupt. Above all, the Garvey organization remained intact and its multitudes of members demonstrated implicit faith in their leader, supported him morally and materially. Garvey also had an asset in the Metropolitan press. It was always indulgent, perhaps because he provided such exciting and diverting items for the edification of the reading public. Sometimes Garvey and his antics crowded a lynching off the front page!

But as the trial progressed, it appeared as if Garvey was determined to jail himself. This acknowledged leader of millions of Negroes was extremely fond of litigation. Probably as a youth he had desired to become an attorney in Jamaica, an ambition which might have remained. Here was a chance to gratify this ambition. And upon such a stage! A Federal courtroom in the great city of New York.

Garvey had in Mr. Henry Lincoln Johnson an able Negro lawyer. But when the case started he dispensed with his services and announced that he would be his own attorney. For a month Garvey had a magnificent time indeed in that Federal courtroom. In his role as attorney for the defendant, he had such fun with the witnesses arrayed against him that he appeared to forget entirely the gravity of the charge. He corrected the witnesses' English, instructed them how they should answer his question, declared that the British government was behind his prosecution; he was frequently at loggerheads with the judge. Yet he had some strong points in his favor. He proved that his Black Star Line was not merely a fabrication of his imagination. He had been duped into buying rotten ships. The boat for which he paid $165,000 had made only one trip before it fell apart.

It was sold as junk for $1650. But Joseph H. Philbin, sales-manager of the United States Shipping Board, testified that the Board held $22,500, which the Garvey organization had deposited on the purchase of a ship.

Garvey gloried in his day in court. He proved to his myriad of faithful followers that he was literally the Great Advocate. Perhaps in his self-conceit that was adequate consolation for his sentence of five years in prison and a fine of $1,000. The sentence was appealed. Garvey's prestige rose with his conviction. New recruits flocked to his African standard and he received strong support from West Africa. Africans were seriously listening to the words and pondering the plans of the American Negro Liberator. Consequently the *Negro World,* the organ of the Garvey movement, was banned in the colonies of British West Africa.

.   .   .   .

Breaking away from the Roman Catholic Church, Garvey launched out in a new field. He established the African Orthodox Church as an adjunct to his organization. This was a bold stroke which excited the imagination of his followers. They would have their own church. But it was not so exciting to the Negro clergy. The majority of the Garvey following were members of ordinary Negro churches and the ministers were alarmed lest their flocks should desert them for the new church.

As protagonist of the new church, Garvey obtained a fine figure of a man. This was the Rev. George Alexander McGuire, a minister of the Episcopalian Church. Mr. Mc-Guire had served under Bishop Brown of Arkansas, who achieved national notoriety as a convert to and fearless advocate of Communism. But the Rev. McGuire had quarreled with his bishop, accusing him of race prejudice. Mr. McGuire was called to a church in Boston where he won the respect of the most influential white and colored people.

The Reverend McGuire was one of the many intellectuals of the Negro minority who joined the Garvey movement after the highly publicized maiden voyage of the first ship of the Black Star Line in 1920. His adherence to the movement was a sensational gesture. He had a marvelous voice for the tribune, much more cultured than Garvey's. His character was impeccable. His English education was excellent. He was a black gentleman who fiercely lived up to the high moral standard of the white world. Often in his sermons he tiraded against the laxity and shiftlessness of the Negroes. He denounced charlatans and buffoons who held up the Negro race to ridicule. And when he enlisted in the Garvey movement, he immeasurably increased its prestige among the skeptical intelligentsia and silenced many of its enemies. The Rev. George Alexander McGuire became the first archbishop of the African Orthodox Church. He was consecrated by an archbishop of the Greek church.

Garvey had established relationship with Liberia. His representatives there were two former high officials, ex-presidents Barclay and Howard. The Liberian government was almost without funds and unable to obtain more loans in Europe or America. Had Garvey been a little discreet and willing to make a secret deal with one of the major American political parties, he might have put over something concrete for the benefit of the post-war American Negro and the West African Negro. But Garvey was too self-confident and bombastic to understand practical hints. He did not even seem aware of the deep anxiety that his movement gave to certain European governments. He did not know that his contacts and understanding with Liberian officials were a matter of concern in European chancelleries. Yet it was public rumor that the Liberian government was using his movement to wring concessions out of European countries.

The annual convention of the Negro Improvement Association was attended by Gabriel Johnson, Mayor of Monrovia, capital of Liberia. The Mayor of Liberia was duly impressed. He saw with his own eyes that Marcus Garvey was indeed a mighty person not only in the Negro city of Harlem, but in New York at large. His meeting at

Madison Square Garden brought out a veritable army of white policemen to guard him.   Why, the President of Liberia had no such honor accorded to him when he visited Paris and London.   His visit would barely be chronicled in an obscure corner of the newspapers.

The Mayor of Monrovia, Liberia, was highly pleased to accept the grander title of High Potentate of Africa, conferred upon him by Marcus Garvey, Provisional President of the Empire of Africa.   He was also voted a salary of $12,000 a year, almost as much as the salary of the President of Liberia. The Mayor of Monrovia returned to Liberia wearing his new Universal Improvement and Back-To-Africa regalia and insignia.   The Mayor of Monrovia so seriously considered his new title of High Potentate of Africa that he demanded that he should take precedence over the President of Liberia at state functions!   The black aristocracy of Liberia was outraged and the poor mayor was nearly lynched.

A delegation consisting of three members of the Universal Negro organization was dispatched to Liberia.   Miss Henrietta Vinton Davis was a member of the delegation and its chairman was Robert L. Poston, the husband of the Negro sculptress, Augusta Savage.   Marcus Garvey announced that $50,000 had been used in the purchase of materials towards establishing a colony in Liberia.

The Black Star Line was reorganized as the Black Cross, and the *General Goethals,* a boat of over four thousand tons, was purchased from the government.   The first members of the colony were scheduled to sail in 1924.   But trouble broke in Liberia.   It was said that the Garvey party there was using the world-wide influence of the Universal Negro Organization to overthrow the government.

The opponents of Marcus Garvey were deeply troubled by the man's increasing power.   Despite his romantic theory of an African empire, he was becoming more elastic in his methods.   His plan for a ship of Negro officers and crew had failed.   He had quarreled with his first Negro captain and there were not enough trained Negro officers to meet the demands of the Black Star Line.   Therefore he put white

officers and a black crew on the new boat. He started flirting, too, with white politicians. At an overflow Madison
Square mass meeting held in March, 1924, one of the prominent speakers was Surrogate John P. O'Brien. At last
Marcus Garvey was taking his American lessons.

The common people humbly worshiped the man. They
bowed down when he passed by them in his Lord High
Potentate's robes. Wherever he went he was guarded by
his personal guard. At mass meetings members of the
African Legion lined the way in serried ranks as he strode
to the platform. His people believed that his enemies were
seeking to do him harm. His conviction had increased
his prestige a thousandfold. He wore his prison sentence
like a martyr's crown.

The August, 1924, convention of the Universal Negro
and Black Cross was designed as a monster farewell party to
the Negroes who were to leave for Liberia in the fall.
Bearing splendid gifts of household goods and special sums
of money, thousands of Universalites swarmed into Harlem.
Those who were chosen to go were religiously regarded as
angels of the New Heaven, Marcus Garvey's promised land,
the Negro Zion.

The Archbishop of the African Orthodox Church, the
Right Reverend C. A. McGuire, in his robes of state, pronounced a blessing upon the convention, said a special prayer
for Marcus Garvey and the Universal Negroes who were the
first to have elected to return to Africa. The Archbishop
discoursed on the past. He pictured the ruins of African
empires and of the dispersion of the Negro peoples. He
traced the beginning of the slave trade in America, described
the slave ship riding the Atlantic with the first cargo of
slaves. He told of the early lives of the slaves in the West
Indies and in the United States, of the rise of the Abolitionist
movement and the Emancipation. The Negroes came to
this land with bound hands and feet, he said. But their
children were returning with gifts to Africa and as brothers
of the children of Africa to build a new Africa. The children of the African Orthodox Church must return to the

bosom of the motherland. "You must forget the white gods," he said. "Erase the white gods from your hearts. We must go back to the native church, to our own true God."

Inspired, inflamed, the mighty assembly rose and cheered the Archbishop for many minutes, shouting, "Hallelujah, God save Africa, Hallelujah!"

Goodwill messages were sent to President King of Liberia, President Coolidge, the President of Haiti, the Empress of Ethiopia, the President of the Irish Free State, Kemal Pasha, Dictator of Turkey, Abdel Krim, the rebel leader of Spanish Morocco, Mahatma Gandhi and other internationally known personages who were more or less engaged in the battle of liberty.

But in the midst of the thirty-day convention, the Liberian government issued a statement repudiating the Universal Negro organization, and refusing to recognize its advance delegates. Some were actually arrested. It also protested to the American Administration against the activities of the Garvey organization in Liberia.

Marcus Garvey was stupefied—for a while. His followers were dismayed. He accused President King of treachery, declaring that the Universal Negro Association had already invested $50,000 in Liberia. He charged that European governments were intriguing in Africa against his organization. And the American Negro enemies of Africa were attempting again to sell the Negro race into slavery. He rallied his followers at mighty mass meetings, pledging his life to redeem the black man. He declared that with the secret magic of ancient Africa, he would reconquer the land for the Negro.

But while some of his obeah-minded and Voodoo-enchanted followers applauded, believing in Garvey's knowledge of deadly magic, he resorted to other means to discredit the Liberian government among the Negro peoples. In 1920 Garvey had sent Eli Garcia, his Secretary-General and formerly a Haitian official, to survey the Liberian field. Upon his return to the United States, Garcia presented a confidential report to his chief, which contained a strong indictment of the Liberian governmental group.

Garcia said that the American-Liberians, because of their "white" education, were vain, conceited and overbearing toward the autochthonous people. The American-Liberians called themselves "the Whites" and the tribes "the Natives." All American-Liberians competed with one another for government jobs, in which they are in a position to lord it over the tribes. Yet, they did nothing to improve the standard of the natives, nothing to better their primitive standard of living, nothing to exploit the vast, rich agricultural lands.

Rice, the staple food, was imported and sold so dearly that the common people were undernourished. The primitive tribal economy was not sufficient to support the ruling caste in the high European style of living. Therefore the tribes were sullen and in some parts of the country revolted against the government. Garcia charged that the ruling Negroids countenanced the practice of slavery. Young native girls were sold at from $20 to $30 per head.

Garcia said that by sounding out unofficial persons he was convinced that the ruling clique of Liberians were opposed to any considerable number of American Negroes emigrating to Liberia to start a model colony. They were unprogressive and opposed to any plan that would introduce new blood and modern ideas into the so-called black republic.

Now Garvey released this grave report. And it certainly injured the cause of the Liberians among the Negro peoples of the world. In the early nineteen thirties, the League of Nations, notably Britain and France, presented substantially the same charges against Liberia during its border troubles against the revolting tribes. And they were a serious threat to the independence of the Monrovian administration.

Obviously Liberian officials had used the Marcus Garvey colonization scheme to bargain with white governments and capitalists for loans. They thought perhaps that the few thousand dollars collected from the black folk could scarcely compete with millions of white dollars. So the black visionary lost his preliminary investments in Africa, and the golden faith of his myriad of disciples, even as he was doomed to lose in America. Marcus Garvey had dreamed of a vast model colony in Liberia. But it was Harvey Firestone who realized the dream with his extensive rubber plantations.

However, if Marcus Garvey felt his movement betrayed by the American-Liberian aristocracy, he and his following were inspirited and uplifted by a significant event. That year the Prince Kogo Honeou Tovalou of Dahomey made his first voyage to America. Prince Kogo, as a royal native potentate, was honored with a picturesque reception at Liberty Hall, where all the colors of God's fertile imagination were assembled in his honor. He made a speech full of praise for the work of the Universal Negro Association and saluted Marcus Garvey as the leader of the Negro people of the world. Prince Kogo was appointed representative of the Association for France and her colonies.

Probably Prince Kogo, overwhelmed by the wonderful reception, was not fully conscious of the political significance of his act. He was no African clown prince. He was an authentic member of the family of Behanzin, the deposed King of Dahomey. Behanzin was exiled by the French to Algeria, where he had died and was buried. His son, Prince Behanzin, lived in France and was in close touch with his cousin, Prince Kogo.

Kogo was a fine figure of an African, tall and as handsome and smooth and shiny as ebony. He was educated in Europe and was fluent in French, English and German. In Paris he was the mignon of bohemian artistic circles. Among his friends there were titled French persons, officers of the navy and army, actors and actresses, painters, singers. Hitherto he had not identified himself with politics, especially African. But these were early post-war years. There were many changes in Africa and the African responds quickly to the influences of change. Germany had lost her colonies. There was friction in mandated colonies. BATOUALA, *Prix Goncourt* novel by the Negro René Maran, had exploded like a bomb in intellectual and political circles, and had challenged new interest in Africa.

And above all there was Garvey's Universal Negro propaganda. Its repercussion in Africa was greater than the American Back-to-Africa devotees realized. In the interior of West Africa new legends arose of an African who had been lost in America, but would return to save his people. And there were sporadic demonstrations against the local administrations. In 1924 there was a countrywide strike of men and women in Nigeria against the administration. Stevedores in the ports refused to load the ships.

Kogo's princely act in acknowledging Garvey's leadership came as an inspiration to the movement at that critical time. But Kogo later paid dearly for it. In those days it was not considered good taste to mix political issues with smart bohemianism, at least not in Allied lands. It was the time when James Joyce and Marcel Proust and T. S. Eliot were the intellectual gods. It was ten years before the Popular Front brought about a democratic marriage between Dilettantism and Bolshevism. And so when Prince Kogo returned to Paris as representative of the Universal Negro, he was no more *persona grata* in ultra-chic circles. Later he was ignominiously humiliated. One of the largest Paris dailies published a report on his personal affairs. It stated that Kogo was a swindler and a faker. He was not truly a prince. Posing as a prince of Dahomey he had borrowed large sums of money from people which had never been repaid. Gallant as he was, and certainly spoiled by the sophisticated Parisian circles, to whom an educated and suave African like Kogo was something like a rare piece of primitive African sculpture, perhaps Kogo was no worse than the whites of that same circle. But he *was* a prince of Dahomey, recognized by Behanzin, the son of the dethroned king. And when the latter died a few years later, his South American wife put herself under the protection of Kogo as the next of kin in France.

• • • • • • • •

Enemies black and white were constantly badgering Garvey and reminding the authorities of his menacing existence. His appeal slowly dragged along its course. The following Negroes, in a signed petition to the Department of Justice, demanded his imprisonment and deportation: George W. Harris, prominent politician, editor of New York (Harlem) *News,* Robert S. Abbott, editor-publisher of the Chicago *Defender,* John E. Nail, wealthy realtor, William Pickens and Robert W. Bagnall, officials of the National Association for the Advancement of Colored People; Chandler Owen, editor of the *Messenger* magazine, Harry H. Price and Dr. Julia P. Coleman. Finally, in 1925, the appeal was rejected by the United States Supreme Court. In February, 1925, Marcus Garvey entered Atlanta Federal Penitentiary to serve a five-year term of imprisonment.

But in prison he was perhaps as powerful as he was when free. His message to his followers appeared every week on the front page of the *Negro World.* Often it read like an epistle of one of the Apostles. While he was on trial, the prosecuting attorney referred to him as "The Tiger." And when he was at last convicted, his former editor and countryman, now turned enemy, Mr. W. A. Domingo, telegraphed congratulations to the United States Attorney-General that the Tiger was caged. The Garvey people delighted in the phrase and said, "They put our Tiger in the cage, but we will never rest until we get him out." They fought hard to free Garvey. His lawyer released a memorandum showing that the chief count upon which Garvey was convicted was untenable. Petitions were sent to the President of the United States. The jury that convicted him came out with a statement in favor of his release. Metropolitan newspapers, such as the *Daily News,* which has a large circulation in Harlem, demanded that Garvey be pardoned. He was turned loose in November, 1927, and deported to Jamaica.

Delegations of his increased multitude of followers made the pilgrimage to New Orleans to bid him farewell. Garvey was profoundly moved by the unflagging demonstration of loyalty. His people declared that they would follow him wherever he went, in spirit at least, if it were impossible in the flesh. And Garvey promised that he would always fight for them. He declared that wherever he was, his one aim in life would be the welfare of the Universal Negroes. His address to them from the deck of the SS. Saramacca, just before sailing, is one of the finest episodes of his life.

Thus Garvey was returned to the island of Jamaica. It was over a decade since he had sailed away to the United States unheralded. But a vast multitude was awaiting his return. The Jamaica natives, disciplined in British reserve and restraint, let themselves go to welcome the man. From the plains and the hills the peasants swarmed along the roads to join the city folk and hail the leader who had lifted up the Negro race with his voice and carried it round the world. Even if he had wanted to, Garvey could not escape from the movement that he had started. The man had that magic in him by which the Negro masses were bewitched.

From Jamaica he continued to conduct his world-wide propaganda. Every week his message cabled to New York was printed in large type on the front page of the *Negro World*. His family (second wife and two children) had joined him there with a staff of workers from the New York office. The program of the Universal Negro Association remained the same.

Marcus Garvey had promised his people to take his propaganda in person to Europe. And he was only a few months in Jamaica before he made his plans to go. He arrived in England in May, 1928. He rented Albert Hall in London for a mass meeting, but merely a handful of people attended. The English press was not so indulgent to him as had been the American.

Garvey had better luck in Paris. He addressed the French intellectuals at the Club du Faubourg and received a remarkable reception. His style was something that the French could appreciate more than the English. He visited the League of Nations, to which he had previously sent delegations from the Universal Negro Association. But there was very little he could do in Europe. He yearned to see something of that African land to the redemption of which he had dedicated his life, but British authority kept him out. He was never to see the Promised Land.

In the fall he landed in Canada. It was the year of the Hoover election. Garvey sent out an appeal to Negroes advising them to vote for Governor Smith. The Canadian authorities objected to his political activities and he was ordered to leave the country.

Back he went to the suffocating island prison. The members of the organization had to decide upon the vexing issue as to whether New York or the island of Jamaica should be their headquarters. Many preferred New York because it was a great world center, but Garvey felt that the center of the world was wherever Garvey resided. He announced that "the Greatest Assembly of Negroes Since Creation," would meet in Jamaica in 1929. And the future of the Universal Negro organization would be decided at that convention. In his enthusiasm, Garvey acted the part of a tourist barker for the island of Jamaica. He invited the delegates to "come and see the beautiful tropics: make a tour of Jamaica, the most beautiful island in the world."

And indeed it was a gigantic convention, the greatest international group of visitors that ever landed in Jamaica. Speaking English, Spanish, French and Portuguese and coming from Africa, Central and South America, the other West Indies and the United States, the delegates, accompanied by relatives and friends, descended on Jamaica. These delegates from abroad were incomparably superior, socially and intellectually, to the majority of the peasant followers of Garvey in Jamaica. And so Garvey received the coveted homage of the Jamaica élite, who honored the delegates. The mayor, members of the Legislature and other politicians and leading citizens attended the great reception. At last the King, Garvey the Great, was fully honored in his own country.

The Garvey folk staged a monster parade through the

streets of Kingston. Over 25,000 people were estimated to be in the procession. Garvey and his delegates in uniform and costume captured the tropical scene. More than a hundred and twenty-five of the delegates came from the United States. They were nearly all American Negroes. Some were students, others were in business. The Madame C. J. Walker Manufacturing Company sent a special New York representative. Doctors and lawyers were there. At least two of the student delegates are at present responsible Federal employees. The Communist Party sent its international carpet-bagger, Otto Huiswoud, who challenged Garvey to debate whether Negroes should join the Comintern. Garvey took up the challenge and, speaking on the negative side, won overwhelmingly.

Marcus Garvey became the most popular personage in Jamaica. But the British government was vigilantly watching him. During the first week of the convention (it lasted a month) he was humiliated with arrest for contempt of court, because he had said uncomplimentary things against Jamaica justice and judges in his daily newspaper. The Chief Justice fined him $500. The delegates paid the fine. The convention projected a grand plan for the rehabilitation of the movement. Millions of dollars were to be raised to start the Black Star Line again and carry trade forward between the Negro peoples. As the West Indies and Africa were entirely agricultural lands, the delegates agreed that the United States should be the industrial center of the Negro movement. But Garvey was determined to reorganize the Universal Association with Jamaica as Chief Headquarters. This plan hurt the pride of the American delegates. They held that as the association was founded in New York and had there grown to international fame, the headquarters should there abide. Garvey curried favor with the delegates and played them against one another. Finally he won and organized the Parent Body of the Association in Jamaica. But that stratagem split the movement and a rival group was started in the United States with headquarters in New York. That was the beginning of the breakup of Garvey's vast organization. Eventually Garvey's highhandedness resulted in his forfeiting a $300,000 estate, which, although bequeathed by a wealthy Central American Negro to the Universal Negro Association, was primarily intended to be at his disposal. In the long, exciting litigation which ensued, it was finally ruled by the highest English court that Garvey's claim to the estate as the head of the "Parent Body" in Jamaica was illegal, and it was allocated to the original New York organization.

Garvey soon lost much of his popularity in Jamaica. Not contented with living as an exalted exiled ruler, he became active in local politics. Again he attacked the Jamaica courts and again he was fined and this time sentenced to three months in prison by three judges of the High Court. Dramatically Garvey declared in court: "I will be an everlasting flea in the collar of my enemies."

Jamaica, the more-English-than-the-English little England of the West Indies, was gradually subduing and demoralizing the great Garvey. When a man is sent to prison in a British colony, even for a political offense, he loses prestige among the common people. It is not like going to prison for a political offense in America. While Garvey was in prison the people elected him to the City Council. His seat was voided by the municipal government. But immediately upon his release the people re-elected him by popular vote.

Garvey served for a year. But he was naturally uncomfortable in a city councillor's little seat in the tight island of Jamaica. He organized a People's Party. But the local politicians united to block his way to power. They told Garvey that they would make it harder for him in Jamaica than in America. At one of his mass meetings a heckler baited him and said Garvey thought he was a great man, but he could make him look like a foolish boy. Immediately Garvey challenged him to do it. Advising Garvey's American bodyguard to stand aside, the strapping peasant rushed Garvey, knocked him down on the platform and ripped his pants off. There was no more meeting. Deprived of his pants, Garvey was hastily wrapped in a blanket, hurried to his car and quickly driven away.

Shortly afterwards he left Jamaica for Europe. He took up residence in London. Intermittently he published a magazine entitled *The Black Man*. But, broken into disunited fragments, the Universal Negro Association lost its irresistible international appeal.

His leadership was finally eclipsed by the Ethiopian conflict. In the early days of the Italian invasion he made the cause of the Emperor of Ethiopia his own and exhorted the remnants of his followers to organize to help Ethiopia. He denounced Mussolini. He turned to exercise his hand at a Martin Tupper-like kind of didactic verse. And one of his contributions to *The Black Man* was a poem entitled "The Smell of Mussolini," and one couplet ran:

> We hate the smell of Mussolini,
> We'll lay quite low the violent Roman hog.

But the Emperor of Ethiopia was forced to flee his country, leaving it in the hands of Mussolini, to seek refuge in Europe.

When the Emperor of Ethiopia and Lion of Judah arrived in London he avoided all contact with Marcus Garvey, "Highest Potentate of the Negro World and Lion of Numidia." A delegation of colored folk in London attempted to present the Emperor of Ethiopia with an address when he arrived, but could not come near his high person. It had been published abroad that the emperor did not desire any contact with "Negroes."

All during the Ethiopian crisis such rumors had persisted. As soon as agitation over Italy's designs on Ethiopia began stirring the Africans and Aframericans, the English-speaking press took to publishing articles which said that the Ethiopians were not Negroes. So American Negroes queried whether the Ethiopians were Europeans and white. Aframericans are not generally aware that many other Africans besides Ethiopians object to being called Negroes, because they regard it as a name fit for black slaves. The Ethiopians will not even allow themselves to be designated as Abyssinians, because it is Arabic for slave.   Yet because of this propaganda against the Ethiopians, many Aframericans refused to identify themselves with the Help Ethiopia movement.

Garvey struck out in his magazine, *The Blackman*, and bluntly denounced the emperor as a coward and a traitor to desert his people and run away from his country.   Garvey said the emperor was prouder of being the descendant of Solomon than the ruler of a black land, that he had played a "white" game all during his reign and trusted white advisors only, and that they had betrayed him in his hour of need.   Garvey wrote: "Haile Selassie is the ruler of a country where black men are chained and flogged. . . . He proved the incompetence of the Negro for political authority. . . . The emperor's usefulness is at an end.   He will go down in history as a great coward who ran away from his country."

But Garvey's denunciation did not swing his people.   To the emotional masses of the American Negro church the Ethiopia of today is the wonderful Ethiopia of the Bible. In a religious sense it is far more real to them than the West African lands, from which it is assumed that most of the ancestors of Aframericans came.   They were happy that the emperor had escaped alive.   As an ex-ruler he remained a symbol of authority over the Negro state of their imagination.

Ex-Emperor Haile Selassie wisely sent his personal emissary, the native Ethiopian, Dr. Malaku Bayen,* to represent him in Harlem.   In Dr. Bayen's charming presence Aframericans could be convinced that Ethiopians are not white or Mongolians, but authentic native Africans, even if, like thousands of educated Aframericans, they reject the word "Negro."

When Dr. Malaku Bayen arrived here in 1936, Harlem gave him a grand welcome.   On the day of his arrival with his Aframerican wife, Dorothy, and their young son, he attempted to establish temporary residence in a modest downtown hotel (there is not one decent family hotel in Harlem) but owing

* Recently deceased.

to the conspicuousness of his Ethiopian skin, he was unceremoniously shunted up to the inconvenience of Harlem.

The direction of the Harlem United Aid to Ethiopia was
turned over to Dr. Bayen and the name was changed to the
"Ethiopian World Federation." The Federation established a weekly organ, the *Voice of Ethiopia* (in which
the word "Negro" is proscribed), and conducts propaganda
meetings in New York and other cities. It draws its supporters from the same common people that gave power to
the Garvey movement. Many were once members of the
Garvey Universal Negro organization. One of the principal
animators, Mr. Rudolph Smith, was formerly a top figure
and sparkling orator of the Back-To-Africa movement.

Marcus Garvey's influence over Aframericans, native
Africans and people of African descent everywhere was vast.
Whether that influence was positive or pervasive and in-
direct, Negroes of all classes were stirred to a finer feeling
of racial consciousness. The intellectual Negro's hostility
to and criticism of Garvey were also motivated by a spirit
of resentment that the amazing energy and will to uplift
awakened in the Negroes by Garvey were not harnessed to
the purpose of a practical, constructive industrial project.

Garvey assembled an exhibition of Negro accomplishment
in all the skilled crafts, and art work produced by exhibitors
from all the Americas and Africa, which were revelations to
Harlem of what the Negro people were capable of achieving.

The vivid, albeit crude, paintings of the Black Christ and
the Black Virgin of the African Orthodox Church were
startling omens of the Negro Renaissance movement of the
nineteen twenties, which whipped up the appetite of literary
and artistic America for a season. The flowering of Harlem's
creative life came in the Garvey era. The anthology, THE
NEW NEGRO, which orientated the debut of the Renaissance
writers, was printed in 1925. If Marcus Garvey did not
originate the phrase, New Negro, he at least made it popular.
First novels by Harlem writers were published in that period:
Jessie Fauset's THERE IS CONFUSION, Walter White's THE FIRE
IN THE FLINT, Nella Larsen's QUICKSAND, Rudolph Fisher's

THE WALLS OF JERICHO and Wallace Thurman's THE BLACKER
THE BERRY. Eric Walrond, who was author of TROPIC DEATH,
was the literary editor of the Garvey organ, the *Negro World*.

The sweet singer of Harlem, Countee Cullen, plaintively
cried in *Heritage*:*

> What is Africa to me:
> Copper sun or scarlet sea,
> Jungle star or jungle track,
> Strong bronzed men, or regal black . . .
> *One three centuries removed*
> *From the scenes his fathers loved,*
> *Spicy grove, cinnamon tree.*
> *What is Africa to me?*

Another contemporary poet, Langston Hughes,† chanted:

> All the tom-toms of the jungle beat in my blood,
> And all the wild hot moons of the jungles shine
>   in my soul.
> I am afraid of this civilization—
>   So hard,
>   So strong,
>   So cold.

The "Black Tiger" and "President-General" of the Negro
World, Marcus Garvey, died in London on June 10, 1940.
At the time of his death he still was revered as their greatest
leader by the American Negro masses. His prestige remains
higher among Americans than among West Indian Negroes.
No ordinary Negro, and only a few intellectual Negroes,
believe that Garvey appropriated to his personal use the
enormous sums which were dissipated by his Universal
Negro-Back-To-Africa movement. And the hostility of the
intellectuals has undergone a striking change since the Great
Depression. They say now that Garvey's ideas were sounder

* Reprinted by courtesy of the publishers, Harper & Bros. from Cullen's
book, COLOR.
† Reprinted from THE WEARY BLUES. Copyright 1927 by Alfred A.
Knopf.

than his methods. The Communists again tried to woo him during their Popular Front Five-Year plan. But even though they were formidably powerful, operating under the good will of the democratic forces of Europe and America, Garvey, poor and in exile, still rejected them. Although something of a dictator himself, to the last he preferred government under Democracy to government under Fascism. Many of the Garveyites compare Garvey with Hitler, to the latter's disadvantage. They say that Hitler's torrential flood of rhetoric, with its direct appeal to primitive mass emotions, is similar to the Garvey oratory, but that Hitler perverted Garvey's racial philosophy and proclaimed the superiority of the German over all other races, while Garvey tried to lift up and convince the Negro that it was basically the equal of other races.

Editorially commenting upon his death, the New York *Times* estimates: "He no more represented the Negro race in this country than Mr. Capone or Mr. Hauptmann the white race." This is a strange and cryptic comparison to Negro readers, for although Marcus Garvey was a demagogue, he was not a common criminal, a bandit ambushing and blackmailing the unwary wealthy, or a kidnaper and murderer of babies. Garvey was no violator of the flower of the human spirit; he was more obsessed with the idea that the spirit of humanity should flower more universally.

The late James Weldon Johnson, who was the most diplomatic and distinguished representative of the Negro élite, and also endowed with the shrewdest mind among contemporary Negroes, has this penetrating estimate of Garvey in BLACK MANHATTAN,* published in 1930. "Garvey failed; yet he might have succeeded with more than moderate success. He had energy and daring. . . . He stirred the imagination of the Negro masses as no Negro ever had. He raised more money in a few years than any other Negro organization ever dreamed of. He had great power and great possibilities within his grasp. But his deficiencies as a leader outweighed his abilities. . . . Garvey made several vital blunders, which,

* Reprinted through the courtesy of Alfred A. Knopf, the publishers.

with any intelligent advice, he might have avoided. . . . He made the mistake of ignoring or looking with disdain upon the technique of the American Negro in dealing with his problems of race. . . . To this man came an opportunity such as comes to few men, and he clutched greedily at the glitter and let the substance slip from his fingers."

.   .   .   .

The launching of the Popular Front simultaneously with the setting up of the New Deal's W. P. A. gave the Communists that vast influence among colored professional groups which they could not succeed in wielding among the masses. The W. P. A. gave hundreds of college-bred Negroes their first opportunity at clerical jobs. And their attitude was different from that of many white workers who had held better positions before the depression and regarded W. P. A. as a stop-gap only. As the Communists were the most efficient organizers of the W. P. A. workers it was natural that they should make headway among the Negro white-collars who, unlike many whites, had no previous radical affiliations.

Under the aegis of the Popular Front, the Help Ethiopia and the Negro Aid for Spanish Democracy groups enlisted leading Negro ministers, doctors, nurses, teachers, actors and the rest of the Negro intelligentsia. The black bohemians of the pre-depression era were influenced by white friends, many of whom became seriously social-minded after 1929, visited Soviet Russia and were enlisted under the banner of the Popular Front.

The Communists actively organized the Emergency Relief Bureau Workers. But soon a militant nucleus of colored workers generated opposition to the Communists. They complained that the white comrades, while mouthing fraternity and equality and promoting interracial affairs, were taking all the best jobs for themselves. The discontented nucleus organized a majority of Negro workers of the ERB into an association called the Metropolitan Guild. It proposed to take steps directly to protect the members against Communist intrigue and to win promotions. The Communists were opposed to the Guild and denounced it as a segregated group whose aim was to separate the Negroes from their white comrades. But the Guild was supported by non-Communist whites. Father Mulvoy of St. Mark's Roman Catholic Church was one of its most active supporters.

An almost similar situation arose among Negroes on the Federal Writers' Project. The New York Project set up groups of several nationalities—Italian, Jewish, Negro and others—who were engaged in special work pertaining to these groups. But as soon as the writers became organized the Communists started a whispering campaign to the effect that the Negro writers were segregated on the project. There was no truth in the accusation. Many Negroes on the project were engaged on other assignments and were working with white writers. But the Negro group was doing special research work and some of us preferred it, because the facts we unearthed were of intrinsic value to those of us who were writing about Negro life in our off-project time.

All of us went in at the same door, used the same sanitary conveniences and signed the same time sheets, and there was friendly contact between these white and colored workers, who felt they had something in common. Into this atmosphere the Communists injected the poison of Segregation. Then, strangely enough, a Negro Writers' Guild was organized in Harlem. Most of its members were little known in Harlem as writers, but they were on the project and were putty in the hands of the Communists. None of us who had any reputation as writers was asked to join, but the assistant director of the New York Federal Writers' Project and the white supervisor of the Negro group were invited to their meeting. The assistant director was said to be a former Communist Party member who had resigned when he was appointed to the high administrative post. But those who understood the inside methods of the Communists asserted that the resignation was not real but a blind, as the Communists did not want members who held important positions to be known as party members.

Two of Harlem's most expert journalists were on the project—Mr. Henry Lee Moon, who contributed occasional articles to the New York *Times* and Mr. Theodore Poston, the New York *Post's* Harlem reporter. They had recently lost their jobs on a Harlem weekly because of their Newspaper Guild and strike activities. I spoke to them about the Negro Writers' Guild and said we ought to join and checkmate the Communists. But Moon and Poston refused because they were jealous of their craft standards and did not rate the members of the Guild as first-class journalists. I joined up.

Soon afterwards the famous Federal writers' sit-down strike was sprung. It had been whispered for some two weeks that a strike was due. Certain of the Communists said they had "inside information" from Washington. That "inside information" trick was played by the comrades to the extreme note. They always knew before the rest of us when administrative changes were going to occur, when there was to be a lay-off of workers (even the names of those who would be laid off), when promotions would take place and who would be promoted. Naturally, then, it appeared to everyone that the Communists controlled the Writers' Project, and all the motley gang of careerists who wanted advancement or some consideration were submissive to and fawned upon them.

When we learned about the strike, we who were not on the inside called it a "company" strike. And it certainly was. It was a strike in which the rank and file paraded and starved for the benefit of the little bosses. It was a kind of strike that any real labor leader would be ashamed of and of which only Communists could be proud. It lasted a week. On the second day all the supervisors passed through the picket line and signed the time sheets. We of the rank and file were amazed. Why should the supervisors, whose wages were double and treble our own, be allowed to scab on the rank and file? Yet the few members of the rank and file who decided to pass through the picket line and sign in were booed and pilloried.

We demanded to know why this was, and were told that the supervisors were being organized and the Communists desired to placate them so that they might be easier to organize! Thus they were allowed to break through the picket line, and each supervisor agreed to contribute a day's pay to the strike fund. A meeting of the supervisors was held to discuss the issue. Some of the members belonged to the Newspaper Guild unit. At this meeting the Harlem journalists Moon and Poston were the only persons who protested against the supervisors' passing the picket line. They contended that this practice was having a bad effect on the rank and file workers, that, if anything, the supervisors should be setting an example of solidarity with these workers by staying away from the office. A few of the supervisors who had not shed all ideas of manly decency, despite contact with Communists, were sympathetic. But soon it was whispered around that the supervisors' action was entirely approved by the Communist Party unit, and Moon and Poston were squelched.

The supervisors received their week's salary and donated a day's pay to the strike fund, most of which, it was rumored, found its way to the coffers of the Communist Party. The Administration tried to soften the effects of the strike for the rank and file and sent out forms for the workers to sign in place of the time sheets. It was a purely nominal thing, which would have insured the payment of the week's wages lost. But the Communist leaders of the strike advised all the employees not to sign. And they posted pickets to spy upon all who did. It was all right for the rank and file to lose a week's wages and tighten their belts in the interest of Communist Party discipline. But not the supervisors! It was a heyday for the Popular Front when the Communists were so careful not to offend the sensibilities of the better people.

The two strange creatures of backward Harlem who tried to teach the Communists a lesson in human decency, Henry

Moon and Theodore Poston, paid the penalty of their audacity. The Communists, active in supporting and financing Harlem's *Amsterdam News* strike, had expected that Moon and Poston would show gratitude at least and become good "fellow travellers." For these two Harlemites had been chalked up on the Communist blacklist for over five years— ever since they did their part in exposing the ruthless opportunism of the red apostles of idealism!

It all happened in that historic period of 1932-33, when Franklin Delano Roosevelt and Adolf Hitler rose to the leadership of two great nations. Up until then the Kremlin was still ostensibly the pretended champion of the working people, suppressed minorities and the rest. And as a part of its world program, a group of American Negroes were summoned to Moscow to make a documentary film of Negro life in the United States. The idea first took form in the Scottsboro year of 1931. The group of some twenty persons was headed by the poet and storyteller, Langston Hughes, and Moon, Poston and other prominent persons of the outmoded Negro Renaissance set were members. They arrived in Moscow towards the end of 1932.

But before anything could be done on the film project, Hitler, now at the helm of the German nation, was already directing his flaming threats against the mighty seat of Bolshevism. And the Kremlin, seeking allies, was hastily editing its idea of white America towards its black minority. Among other things of major importance, so infinitesimal an item as the Russian projection of a film of American Negro life was abandoned.

Limited and confined to the provincial theater of Harlem, few of the members of the troupe were aware that they were minor actors in a vast drama in which the idea of a red film of black oppression in America was less than a blade of seaweed washed up on the shore of the mighty ocean.

The Negro Film Group was extravagantly entertained in a series of receptions by Moscow politicians and cultural groups. They met big men of the Russian Film industry and there were perfunctory conversations about the Negro picture. But weeks petered out and there was no action preparatory to the making of the film. At last the Negro troupe was informed that because of inadequate material and technical difficulties the decision was taken to scrap the project.

Nearly all the members of the company accepted the decision without protest. They had had a fine trip and the Russians had given them a good time in the lavish Russian manner, as they do when they desire to woo people. But the newspapermen, Moon and Poston, remained dissatisfied. Attracted to the Communists mainly by the Scottsboro case, they had given up their positions on the Harlem weekly to go to Moscow with the one purpose of making a Negro film. Ferreting out the real reasons why the film was not to be made, they discovered that the Kremlin was already angling for United States recognition of the Soviet government. And the Negro picture which Moscow intended to make was such a trenchant indictment of American civilization that it could not have contributed to friendly relations between the two nations. Moon and Poston released their findings to foreign correspondents in Moscow and the story was sent around the world.

It enraged not only the Moscow Communist hierarchy, but the entire Comintern. They denied the assertions and declared that the Negro picture was abandoned for purely cultural and technical reasons, which were non-political. As if there is anything in the Communist conception of life that is not political! Through its leading Negro spokesman, James W. Ford, the American Communist Party published a refutation of the accusation and castigated the two obstreperous Negro journalists. Speaking for the rest of the company, Mr. Langston Hughes said that "the newspaper reports of the Film group are absolutely untrue," and that the film would be made in the spring. But that spring Moscow was busy baiting its hook for much bigger fish than the Negro. And in the spring the Kremlin shed its proletarian red shirt and donned a stiff white front to enter the democratic League of Nations.

Following this incident, Moon and Poston were having a hard time among the "redskins" of Moscow and were glad to get away and back to America with their black skins intact. Reprimanding Mr. Moon for releasing private Communist items to bourgeois newspapers, a big red official said: "You would not be so bold if you were in Georgia." Mr. Moon replied that when he published the facts, he had not imagined that a Negro should feel afraid in the utopian metropolis of Moscow. If it were not for the publicity they obtained through the bourgeois press, Moon and Poston might have landed in an "utopian" jail.

Thus, the two Harlem journalists earned themselves a place on the red blacklist. And when they returned to America, many Communist-inspired innuendoes were printed about their character. Indeed, the Harlem comrades were hostile to almost the entire film group. They were often referred to as "moral degenerates"—that delectable phrase which Moscow reserves for "the enemies of the Soviets."

However Moon and Poston were the most capable newspapermen in Harlem, and with the launching of the Popular Front and the National Negro Congress their friendly cooperation might have been invaluable to the Communists. But the young journalists would respond to no more blandishments. And now again, during the Federal Writers' strike, they had dared to expose the Communist double-crossing of the rank-and-file writers. The result was that immediately after the strike they were summarily expelled from the company of the supervisors and reduced to rank-and-file status. The administrative excuse for this act was that the junior assistant supervisorship, or master writer's rank, which they held, had been abolished. But for many succeeding months other writers of that rank were carried on the payroll.

The Negro Writers' Guild had received front-page notice as one of the units. At the first meeting that was held after the strike, I told the members that such front-page publicity was of no material benefit to the Negro group on the project. And since the guild was recognized as representing the Negroes among the Federal Writers, they should de-

mand something concrete from the union. I submitted
that the guild should ask the union to recommend the
promotion of capable Negro writers to the post of supervisor. The three supervisors of the Negro group were all
white, enjoying nice salaries. I thought that if the fraternity-
and-solidarity always flaunted by the comrades in the union
was something real, it should be translated into something
substantial.

But instead of acting on the question of Negro supervisors, the Communists again agitated against the segregation
of Negroes within the group. Nothing was said about segregation of the other racial groups in the project. The red
heart was bleeding for the poor Negro. Why not? If there
were no Negro group, the Harlem Guild might not be
demanding Negro supervisors! The next step in the comedy
was to plant a number of white writers among the Negro
group. Down at the union hall and at Communist meetings
there always were notices drawing the attention of members to the Negro minority as a special field in which to
gather material for literary and theatrical innovations. But
there never was any appeal to Negro writers and artists
to explore the white field.

When the Negro Writers' Guild convened again, a Negro
Communist came with a white woman whom he proposed
for membership. For many years this woman had been interested in Negro uplift and she devoted much of her time
to the cause. She had undertaken special investigations for
the National Association for the Advancement of Colored
People and acquitted herself brilliantly. She published
articles about the Negro in distinguished magazines. Her
work in the interest of fairness and justice to the Negro
minority was purely unselfish and so ardent and incautious
that she had paid dearly for it. She was a staff worker on
one of our great charitable organizations which, although
considered to be above all prejudice, had followed a secret
policy of discrimination against the Negro. She divulged
the fact that it cost her her job.

The Negro Communist brought this woman to our Guild

meeting and sprang her candidacy on the members without previously consulting them. She desired to join because she considered herself a friend of the Negro minority. That was her qualification for joining a Negro guild. The situation was embarrassing, just the kind that intriguing Communists delight in. None of us there who were opposed to a white person's joining a Negro guild had any desire to wound the sensibilities of this fine-spirited woman. But the unpleasant thing had to be done and we had to inform her that we wanted the guild to remain Negro.

She could not understand this. She taunted us with condoning the Jim Crow policy and segregating ourselves. The Negro Communists sided with her. A non-Communist member said the Communists were trying to break up the guild by forcing in a white person as member. The white woman informed the meeting that she was not a Communist and was opposed to some Communist measures. But it was precisely because she was not a Communist that the situation was so confused. She was a left liberal of Abolitionist tradition. Perhaps she was not even aware that the Communists were using her to disrupt our group, precisely as they had done with liberal groups in promoting their innumerable "front" organizations. The very thing we feared now occurred. The Communists got enough of their members to swing the vote in favor of admitting a white person as member. However, the officers of our organization were opposed to a white person's becoming a member of a Negro Guild. They quit with the records, and left the rump of the Negro Guild to the Communists. It died. In releasing the incident to the Negro newspapers, those who opposed the candidacy of the white woman were made to appear as advocates of Negro Segregation.

A few of us tried to bring the Negro writers together in an organization with the late James Weldon Johnson as President. There are about twelve creative writers of some distinction in Harlem and an equal number of journalists. No one could accuse James Weldon Johnson of believing in any kind of Segregation. He was a member of numerous white cultural and artistic organizations, and his prestige then meant much in setting up a group, especially as he was a lecturer on Negro culture at New York University. He was the perfect person around whom we could organize— well balanced, a meliorist in his attitude towards race relations.

A representative group of us came together: Miss Zora Neale Hurston, Mrs. Jessie Fauset Harris, novelist of the Negro intelligentsia and teacher of French at DeWitt Clinton High School, Mrs. Regina Andrews, Head.Librarian of the 115th Street Library, Mrs. Catherine Latimer, Reference Librarian at the 135th Street Library, Miss Marcia Prendergast, the late Arthur Schomburg, curator of the Negro Division at the 135th Street Library, Mr. Earl Brown, Editor of the *Amsterdam News*, Henry Lee Moon, Theodore Poston, Bruce Nugent, M. Casseus, a Haitian writer, Countee Cullen and myself.

At an initial meeting James Weldon Johnson pointed out that he could see no segregation in Negroes having their own all-Negro groups. It was something like a man organizing his own household and running it in his own way. He could have his neighbors in as guests, and they could cooperate on general lines, but they could not be members. Negroes had the same larger human interests as white people, but also they had peculiar interests which could be worked out only among themselves. For example, any group of Negroes who are freely discussing relations between colored and white persons will say things they never would if a white person were present, unless they intended to be rude.

However, Negro intellectuals among themselves, even more than the masses, are hard to organize. The Harlem renaissance movement of the antic nineteen twenties was really inspired and kept alive by the interest and presence of white bohemians. It faded out when they became tired of the new plaything. And so even the prestige of James Weldon Johnson was of no avail. Most of the Negro intellectuals were directly or indirectly hypnotized by the propaganda of the Popular Front. Anathema to them was any idea of an exclusive Negro organization.   It was not merely segregationist: a new label was made, isolationist.   The League of American Writers was open to every Negro who professed to be a writer, and its propaganda was active in Harlem. Any insignificant coterie of whites could get the proudest of the Harlem élite scampering downtown to a meeting.   Suddenly, tragically, James Weldon Johnson was killed in the spring of 1938.   And the group of Negro writers came together for the last time at his funeral.

·   ·   ·   ·   ·   ·   ·

XI

NIGGERATTI MANOR was in a ferment. It seemed as if everyone in the house on this particular day was unusually active. From the basement came the lugubrious wailings of Eustace as he finally began the serious practice of spirituals. His conversion had been slow. It had necessitated much cajoling, flattery and diplomatic argument, but he had finally been won over. His piano was now cleared of his beloved classic music which he had tenderly wrapped in luxurious packets of green velvet and laid away in a cedar chest. The time for his audition was approaching rapidly.

Eloquently had he announced his plans to Raymond.

"Yes, I'll sing spirituals. And I'll also astound them with the rest of my repertoire. I'll make them appreciate my talent. And I'll sing the classics so

113

much better than spirituals that they'll realize which is my metier."

Then with a grimace of distaste he had set about learning *Ezekiel Saw the Wheel.*

Raymond was busy writing a magazine article. He had locked his door and dared anyone to interrupt him. Paul remained downstairs with Eustace, amusing himself by conceiving a series of designs to illustrate Carl Van Vechten's *Nigger Heaven.* Stephen was away from home, working at the library, collecting data for his doctor's thesis.

Pelham meanwhile was putting the finishing touches on his *magnum opus,* a portrait of two girls, daughters of the lady who lived in the rear room on the third floor. This lady professed to be an actress, but so far her appearances had been confined to Harlem church socials and lodge benefits. She took her histrionic career quite seriously, so seriously in fact that she refused to do any other type of work and somehow managed to support herself and her two daughters on the small weekly pittance she received from her estranged husband.

No one in the house, except Pelham, ever had much traffic with the lady, outside of the conventional greeting should they happen to meet either her or her offspring on the stairs. She had made overtures of friendship and had even crashed certain of their parties, but they had always treated her like a complete outsider. She made no appeal to any of them either as a person or as an artist. Consequently they ignored her.

Pelham was different. He was always giving her a portion of the cakes or pies he constantly made. He would also cut out paper animals and color them for the adolescent girls. Hardly a day passed that they did not invade his room to watch him work. It was inevitable that he should finally suggest painting their portraits, for Pelham was eternally in search of new models, and having used Raymond, Stephen, Eustace and Paul again and again, he was eager for fresh subjects.

There also lived on the third floor a mysterious, witch-like person, labeled the Pig Woman by Raymond, because of her resemblance to an outstanding character in a contemporary *cause celebre*. She was aged, wrinkled and black. Her torso was the shape of an arc, and she limped as she walked along mumbling to herself. It was not known how long she had been living in the house. Euphoria had found her there. She still remained. Three times per week she left home at six in the morning and she always returned exactly twelve hours later. The other days she remained at home, unheard, unseen—a silent mysterious person who held converse with no one in the house except herself. Nor was she ever known to have visitors.

Raymond remembered vividly his first glimpse of her. He had just moved into the house. He, Paul, Eustace and Pelham were arranging the furniture in his room and hanging pictures on the wall. Suddenly their ears had been ravaged by a series of hoarse, guttural shrieks as if coming from the throat of a wounded parrot. Frightened, they had rushed into the hall, where they had seen the Pig Woman leaning over the banisters wildly gesticulating. They had run up the stairs, eager to know the cause of the disturbance. With palsied fingers she had pointed to a stray bat blindly beating itself against the ceiling. Pelham had run for a broom. Eustace had leaned back against the wall, gathering the folds of his green dressing gown tightly about him. Raymond had tried to silence the old lady. Paul had stood by and laughed.

In a few moments Pelham had returned with the broom and after a wild scurry succeeded in knocking the blind intruder to the floor. Paul had wrapped it tightly in newspaper and, taking the parcel to the cellar, burned it in the furnace.

The Pig Woman had been distraught.

"Evil spirits, I tell you. Evil spirits. Dat's bad luck. Dis house is doomed. De people in it are damned."

And she had stumbled into her room eerily sobbing to herself.

Before nightfall of this singularly hard-working day, Pelham had completed his masterpiece. So elated was he over what he declared to be a remarkable resemblance to his subjects, and a crafty blending of colors, that he bounced around the house like a rubber ball, exhibiting his canvas to all within. The picture was atrocious, but no one was heartless enough to disillusion him. No one told him that there was not even the slightest resemblance between portrait and subject. No one winced openly at the blurred features, or at the hideously colored and highly incongruous background. Neither did anyone, save the girls and their mother, praise his handiwork. Being used to the reticence of the others, he accepted it as suppressed appreciation.

His joy was complete when the mother of the girls asked him to give her the picture and also to pen her an accompanying poem. Anxious to make the poem a fitting complement to the portraits, he announced that he would be unable to prepare dinner that night. The muse must function this one time uninterrupted by menial duties. He then shut himself up in his studio, and the eavesdropper could hear the scratch of his pen and the occasional crumpling of unsatisfactory sheets of paper.

It fell to Paul to cook the dinner. Raymond had not expected him to volunteer, but he had, and had asked only that he be left alone. He was to prepare meat balls and spaghetti and a lettuce and tomato salad. This he did in a surprisingly short time, and his announcement of the meal was eloquent.

Three times Eustace went for Pelham before he could be persuaded to come to dinner, and, when he did arrive, he brought his manuscript to the table, ignoring the food placed before him while he continued to work. Even the uproar occasioned by Stephen's asking why the spaghetti was sweet and Paul's admitting that he had poured the contents of the sugar bowl into the kettle, failed to divert Pelham from his chosen creative task. The poem must be finished and it must be good. The lady had promised to present both the poem and the portrait of her daughters to her art club, and she was certain that many of her friends would commission him to do their portraits, and that the club would request him to design and write verses for Christmas cards, programs and reception favors. The cognoscenti might scoff or remain enviously silent. The public would acclaim, and he would at last reap the fruit of his sowing.

George Jones, for that was Pelham's real name, did not remember either his father or his mother. He remembered only a woman he called grandmother and with whom he had migrated from Virginia to New Jersey with a family of white people while still an infant. This grandmother had been a servant in the house since her birth in slavery. Her parents before her had served the same family. They were the type of Negro who had refused freedom and who had remained with "ole miss" and "ole master" until their death. Grandmother Mack had lived, too, only to serve the children of her parents' master. And when one of the younger girls had married and moved north, Grandmother Mack had come, too, determined to see that her mistress' daughter did not suffer for want of care.

George was not her grandson, nor was he any relation to her whatsoever. He was a stray pickaninny whom no one claimed and for whom she had developed an affection because, as she phrased it, "he was so consarned black." No one objected to her adopting the apparently parentless pickaninny, nor had her white folks objected when she brought him north with her.

In his youth, George knew nothing but the kitchen, the backyard, the basement and the alleyway. He ran errands for his white folk and for Grandma Mack. He also assisted the old lady in the kitchen and in the laundry room, and, as he grew older, he was promoted to waiting upon the table, making up the beds, washing the windows, sweeping the floors, dusting the furniture, and ironing the flat work.

He went to school only because his white folk insisted upon it. Grandma Mack had no patience with those hifalutin' niggers who tried to emulate white folks. Niggers were made to be servants. God had willed it. And only through a life of servitude could they hope to obtain an entry into heaven. They were the sons of Ham who had been cursed for looking upon his father's nakedness. They were also the children of Cain who had been cursed and made black for murdering his brother, Abel. Schools were for white folk. These modern niggers made Grandma Mack angry, always talking about education, prating about social equality, criticizing the superior pale face. If they remained in their places, accepted the menial positions to which they were entitled instead of trying to usurp the parlor, they would not have to worry about being lynched, jim-crowed and otherwise put in their place. Grandma Mack had never forgiven Abraham Lincoln for freeing the slaves. Nor could she forgive him for sending hordes of uncouth Yankees into the South-land to rape, pillory and otherwise molest the only truly genteel folk in the United States. Venomously did she regard northern whites, and savagely did she denounce northern blacks.

In this atmosphere had George continued his en-forced schooling. His home work always remained undone, because his home duties were so numerous. Grandma Mack was older now, almost too old and infirm of limb to do much else besides cook and supervise George. It was amazing the amount of work her diminutive black charge managed to do.

When George was fourteen an older son of the house had been sent to Europe. He was going to be an artist, a portrait painter. After a year abroad he had returned home, laden down with lithographic reproductions of the old masters, and almost daily he received copies of art magazines from continental capitals. These latter items eventually became George's property. He mulled over them constantly, and was stirred by the brilliant colors and voluptuous figures which decorated some of the pages. George also took great pride in cleaning up his young master's attic studio. He would linger there under pretense of being busy, finger the brushes, the paint pots, the canvases, and, when he was certain of not being interrupted, would often posture in front of a mirror with a palette.

He was going to be an artist. Taking toilet paper he would place it over the pictures in the various magazines and use it for tracing paper, later transferring the copied reproduction on to smoothed out sheets of wrapping paper or maltreated paper bags.

He was going to be an artist. His school books were defaced with malodorous pictures of his fellow students, all of whom, according to their delineator, were possessed of well-rounded bodies, prominent nostrils, slit eyes, and perpendicular ears. At home he formed fantastic designs in his soapy dish water. When he washed windows he used Bon Ami so that he might trace figures on the surface of the glass as he rubbed it clean. And the peeling of potatoes or apples was a constant exercise in fancy carving.

When he was twenty years of age, Grandma Mack had died. Her white folks had her savings account transferred to one for George. They also deposited to this account the small sum she had coming from a Metropolitan Life Insurance policy which they had taken out for her. George obtained his bank book by stealth, withdrew the money, and boarded a ferry boat bound for New York. He had decided to risk all in order to gain fame and fortune as an artist.

Native intuition saved him from immediate disaster. Promptly upon arriving, he sought a job, and obtained one as valet to an actor. In this position he was most happy, being able congenially to combine his two professions. He lived in his employer's apartment, attended to all his wants, and continued the painting of pictures and the writing of verse in his spare time. All was well until he happened across Euphoria Blake's advertisement in the *Harlem News* announcing "congenial studios for Negro artists." That was what he wanted. He telephoned Euphoria immediately, reserved a studio, stocked up with paints, charcoal, modeling clay, brushes, scalpels, palettes, easels, water colors, and everything else the clerk in the art store suggested he might need, changed his name to Pelham Gaylord, and dedicated his life to the serious business of being an artist.

He was overjoyed when Raymond moved into

the house. For it had been bruited about that he was soon to emerge as one of the black hopes of Negro literature. George also knew that most of Raymond's friends were in some measure known to the public for their poems, stories or drawings. Their names were often mentioned in magazine and newspaper articles. This was just the group he needed to know, just the people he should cultivate. To be in such company was Pelham's conception of heaven. He considered them as gods far up the Mount Olympus he himself was trying to scale. After knowing them, he was frankly ill at ease in their company, quite often shocked by their conversation, and obviously disturbed by the presence of their white friends whom they accepted so casually. Nevertheless he was determined to learn, determined to observe and assimilate. He must be like them.

It came to be a matter of routine that he should clean their studios, prepare the communal meals, wash the dishes, and act as a servant when they had company. Raymond, Eustace and Paul accepted this service, politely encouraged him in his art, and kept a straight face when without warning he would burst in upon them, black face wreathed in smiles, proudly to exhibit a new picture or a new poem. Dutifully did they sit for him to do their portraits.

The extent of his ineptitude was abysmal. Quietly they suggested that he attend an art school, then immediately knew they had said the wrong thing, for Pelham had native talent, which he himself was going to develop. Artists were not made in schools. A phrase of their own was flung at them triumphantly. Paul told him he was a Dadaist. Eustace, Raymond and Euphoria acquiesced. Only Stephen scoffed, and his scoffing was discounted by Pelham, because Stephen was white, and white people would naturally resent a black genius.

By the time all had finished eating, Pelham had finally finished his poem. Triumphantly he threw his fountain pen into his plate of untouched food, and waved his piece of paper before them. No one encouraged him to read what he had written and he remained impervious to the covert conversation of mischievous eyes. He accepted their silence as a request for an immediate rendition. Gleefully, he read:

"I paint on canvas
And on paper
Charms of girlhood
Youthful bloom,
Beauteous maidens
All a-flutter
On life's threshold.

"You who charm the artist's brush
You who guide his fountain pen
You who bring the spirit solace
With your trusting innocence.

"Beauteous maidens, gracious mother,
E'en the sun don't always shine.
Life is real, and fate is earnest.
God will guide you to his shrine
Of eternal happiness."

He finished and beamed at his audience. They sheepishly avoided his gaze and earnestly tried to think of something appropriate to say. No one laughed. No one even felt the urge to snicker. It was impossible to ridicule when his voice was so tender, his eyes so bright, his smile so pleased and ingratiating. There was complete silence. The eyes no longer conversed. Pelham's black face shone with satisfaction. His audience had been stirred, moved, affected by the pathos and beauty of his poem. But he was not concerned with them. He must rush to those for whom it was intended. Still beaming, he pushed his chair back from the table, and hastened from the kitchen. They could hear him noisily running up the stairs.

Everyone was saddened. Even Paul was pensive. Conversation was desultory and lagged. Stephen was surly. Eustace hurried to his studio and could soon be heard softly singing *Water Boy*. Raymond struck a match to light a cigarette, and burned his lip before he realized that the cigarette was still lying on the table, where he had placed it while he found the matches. But even this performance elicited no comment, realized no audience. Stephen muttered something about the damn dishes and went out of the room. A moment later the front door slammed. Paul and Raymond stacked the dishes in the sink, conversing meanwhile in subdued tones about the multiplying cockroaches. Their task finished they both went out into the street. Paul to roam the avenue. Raymond to meet Lucille. And on the top floor, in the little coffin shaped studio, Pelham read and reread his poem to an appreciative audience.

XII

WHEN Raymond arrived at the subway kiosk where they had planned to meet, Lucille was already there. She rushed forward to meet him, a trim tailored figure with a mischievous gleam in her sparkling eyes.

"Gee, Ray. I haven't seen you in a coon's age."

"Your fault, my dear."

"Not so sure. Where do we go . . . to your house?"

"Not yet. Let's have a drink."

After a short walk, they were soon seated in the rear room of their favorite speakeasy, which stood on the corner, one half black removed from Nigger-atti Manor. They ordered gin rickies. Lucille noted Ray's depression.

"What are you in the dumps about?"

"Nothing, I suppose, yet everything. I guess that damn house is getting on my nerves."

128

"Too much whoopee?"

"No, not particularly. Too much everything, and particularly too much Pelham. I can't laugh at him any more and it hurts."

"Why don't you be frank with him?" Then as Raymond sipped his drink she answered her own question. "No . . . you couldn't be. He wouldn't believe you anyhow."

"People like him should be exterminated."

"He's happier than you."

"I wonder. That's what Tony says . . . to be dumb is to be happy, but to be that dumb!!!!!"

They both laughed.

"That's probably not the kind of dumbness Tony meant; after all there is a difference between being dumb and being stupid."

"Right you are and there is also a difference in being . . . Oh, hell! let's forget it."

Raymond drained his glass and rang for the bartender.

"Let's have another."

"Sure."

The bartender acknowledged their signal.

"What have you been doing, 'Cile?"

"Falling in love."

She giggled as she said it.

"Good God," Raymond shouted. "If another woman tells me that, I'm gonna commit murder."

Lucille remained silent as she drained her glass.

"And who, if I may ask, is your beloved?"

"Bull."

"Bull!!"

"Yes, Bull."

"Well, I'll be damned."

"I knew you'd be surprised."

He stared at her unbelievingly, assured that she was joking. He hunted for a gleam of mischief in her eye. There was none.

"When did this begin?"

"Well, I met him at your house a couple of times. He took me home one night when you couldn't be pried away from Barbara."

"Is this retaliation?"

"Not at all. Why should it be?"

"So that's why Bull's been so irrepressible lately."

"Me too."

"But Bull," he advanced weakly, then rang for another rickey. "It's preposterous." For the first time he laughed. "Come on, let's drink." They gulped down their rickies. The bartender was summoned again.

"Now, quit kidding."

"I mean it, Ray. I'm mad about him."

"As Stephen would say, 'Horse Collar.'"

"I admit it's surprising, but after all I have to have my fling sometime or other. I always knew I'd fall for a man of that type."

"Attraction of opposites, I suppose."

"Maybe so, and maybe not, but Bull does represent something I have needed in my life. Damn it all, Ray, there's something in me which revolts against the even, stodgy, prim life I have to lead. I'm sick of being constantly surrounded by sterile white people, and of having to associate with Negroes who are also sterile and pseudo-white. I suppose I find the same thing in Bull that white women claim to find in a man like Jack Johnson. That's the price I pay, evidently, for becoming civilized."

"I think you're as full of hooey as a backyard telephone booth. Jesus, does one ever know one's friends? Must we be treated to these constant surprises? There's Janet gettin' hysterical 'cause she can't have a crack at Stephen an' 'cause her chum beat her to the first white man she ever wanted. An' here's you falling for an ignorant braggart 'cause he's virile. Are you the girl who told me sex meant little to you? Are you still frigid?"

The bartender brought them another pair of rickies. It was his treat.

"Don't be nasty, Ray."

"Maybe I'm jealous."

"Nonsense."

"Why is it nonsense? I ain't human, I guess."

"Sure, you're human, plenty much. And maybe you're jealous, but not from the accepted causes."

"Oh, no-oo?"

"No. You're too much in love with yourself ever to love anyone. You're jealous only because so much has happened without your knowledge. Had I made you believe you engineered the thing you'd be happy."

"Didn't you tell me not to be nasty?" Raymond forced a smile. Lucille had touched a vulnerable spot. "Nevertheless, you can't blame me for being upset. Prim Yankee maiden falls for Harlem bruiser. Educated girl gives self to burly roustabout." He began to laugh. "Jesus, this is good."

Lucille was still self-possessed.

"Bull may be ignorant, a roustabout, and a bruiser, but at least he's a man, and knows how to get what he wants."

The bartender stood over their table. Lucille

ordered another pair of rickies. There was an incisive, angry gleam in Raymond's eyes.

"What do you mean by that?" he asked when they were alone again.

"Forget it. Let's go to the house."

"I ain't goin' nowhere till you 'splain."

"An' I ain't gonna 'splain."

"Dammit all, 'Cile . . ." The bartender returned before he could finish. Lucille handed him a five dollar bill, then swiftly downing her drink, got up from the table and crossed the room to a mirror, adjusted her hat, powdered her face, received her change, and started from the room. Raymond staggered slightly as he rose to follow her.

A few minutes later they stumbled noisily into Raymond's studio. Paul was there, indolently coloring a series of voluptuous geometric designs which he characterized as spirit portraits. Stephen and Aline were curled up on a corner of the daybed, heads together, intimately whispering. Barbara was on the floor beside Paul, watching and admiring his deft and easy brush manipulations. Samuel was sitting as usual, bolt upright in one of the wicker chairs, solemn of countenance, frowning at the couple on the bed. Eustace and Janet were sharing the other wicker chair, reading from *Fine Clothes to the Jew*, Langston Hughes' latest book of poems. Behind their chair was Bull, his bulky shadow darkening the book's pages. Pelham was in the kitchenette, mixing drinks.

"Hi, everybody," Lucille and Raymond shouted in unison. "We're high as kites."

Bull frowned as Lucille swayed toward him. He took her in his arms and guided her way to the couch. They sat down in the corner opposite from the one occupied by Aline and Stephen. Raymond watched them jealously.

"Why in the hell don't someone make some noise? Start the victrola, Samuel."

"Pipe down, son," Bull growled. Lucille's head slumped to his shoulder.

"I want music, I tell you," Raymond continued shrilly. "I must have music. The world's crazy. I want jazz, crazy as the world."

He stood in the center of the room, dishevelled, gesticulating, shouting:

> "Drink gin, drink gin.
> Drink gin with me goddam.
> I don't give a damn
> For no damn man
> Who won't drink gin with me, goddam.
> Go to hell.
> Sonofabitch—Oh———"

Barbara got up from the floor and started toward him. He pushed her away, staggered into the alcove, gulped down one of the drinks Pelham had prepared, then lurched back into the room and flopped himself down beside Paul. Barbara joined him. Pelham passed the drinks. Raymond giggled:

"Paul's gone phallic again. Hey, Sam, seen this?"

Barbara drew his head into her lap. Paul's brush continued its swift strokes. Lucille had gone to sleep on Bull's shoulder. The others drained their glasses.

"Read out loud, Eustace," Barbara commanded. Eustace arched his eyebrows and in his best theatrical manner intoned Langston Hughes' poem:

> "I am your son, white man!
> Georgia dusk
> And the turpentine woods,
> One of the pillars of the temple fell.
> You are my son!
> Like hell!

> "The moon over the turpentine woods
> The southern night
> Full of stars
> Great big yellow stars.

> "Juicy bodies
> Of nigger wenches
> Blue black
> Against black fences
> O, you little bastard boy
> What's a body but a toy?

"The scent of pine wood in the evening air

"A nigger night,
A nigger joy,
A little yellow
Bastard boy."

"Marvelous," Barbara exclaimed.

"Disgusting," Samuel shot through compressed lips.

Raymond was aroused. "How d' y' figure disgusting?"

"It's an insult to any self respecting Negro."

"How come?" Raymond's head abruptly left Barbara's lap. He sat on his haunches as if ready to spring, glaring directly into Samuel's face. "How come, I say?"

"It's vulgar. Moreover why should one of your poets prate publicly about your yellow bastard boys? You ought to be ashamed of them."

"How come?" Raymond reiterated defiantly.

"Shut up, both of you." Stephen knew that Raymond was drunk. "Fix us another drink, Pelham."

"Ain't gonna shut up. Gonna make Samuel tell me what he means. I'm sick of his *ex 'thedra* 'nouncements 'bout the race. I don't think he knows a damn thing 'bout it."

"All right, we agree," Stephen interpolated.

Raymond continued stubbornly. "Yeah. He's a misfit white tryin' to become a latter day ab'lishionist. He's makin' a career of Negroes. He comes here to direct and patronize. He knows so much more 'bout what we ought to do an' feel cause he's white an' he's read soshology."

"Hush, sweet," Barbara pleaded and placed her hands on his shoulders.

"Ain't gonna hush. Gonna tell him what I think. Gonna say what I think 'bout all these meddlin' whites. They oughta stay outa Harlem."

"Are you becoming a race purist?" Stephen sought to draw Raymond's attention to him.

"Hell, no. But that's what Samuel thinks I oughta be. He frowns at you an' Aline. He scowls at me an' Barbara. He tells me privately Barbara ain't nothin' but a common hussy. Then he gets her an' lectures 'bout her losin' self respect bein' intimate with Negroes."

Samuel flushed more deeply than before.

"You're drunk and damn insulting."

"I ain't drunk. An' I'm jes tellin' you the truth. You can't stand to see a Negro and a white woman friends, can you? You believe in social equality. Oh, yes. You'd even marry a colored girl if one'd have a nincompoop like you. But white women are sacred.

441

You're a pukin' hypocrite. If you can't stand the gaff you oughta get out for good."

Samuel leaped to his feet. His face was brick red. His eyes cold and angry. His lips quivered.

"That's what I say about you Negroes. You don't know a friend when you have one. You don't know how to treat decent white people who mean you good. You'd rather lick the boots of trash."

"You want me to lick your boots, don't you? You goddamned sonofabitch." Raymond dashed the contents of his half empty glass into Samuel's face. Samuel's foot shot into the air and kicked Raymond on the side of his head. The room was in an uproar. Bull pushed Lucille's head from his shoulder and started for Samuel. Stephen attempted to hold him back. Lucille slumped unconscious to the couch. Aline and Janet screamed. Eustace sat perched on the edge of his chair, twiddling the book he held, murmuring: "Mercy, mercy," over and over again. Pelham stood transfixed against the door, a tray of empty glasses in his hand. Paul made a desperate, futile effort to rescue his drawings as Samuel was floored by Bull's fist.

"Kick 'im, will ya?" Bull was raving mad. "You lousy white trash, I'll stomp your dirty guts out."

Only Stephen's tackle of his legs prevented Bull from carrying out this ghastly threat.

XIII

Y OU made rather an ass out of yourself last night."

"To the contrary, I would say I made asses out of the rest of you." Raymond was irritable and mordant. Stephen sat on the side of the bed examining red bruises on his arms and legs. "I didn't want to fight. I didn't ask the rest of you to fight."

"That's why you threw your liquor in Samuel's face. Just a friendly gesture, eh?"

"He deserved it. Damn it all, my patience with him is fretted out. I was probably woozily illogical last night, but, as I remember, I gave him a much deserved tongue lashing. Don't you realize what a pest he and his type are? Zora Hurston has named them Negrotarians, which when analyzed is most apt. They are as bad as those eloquent, oleaginous Negro crusaders and men of God, who sit in mahogany office chairs or else stand behind pulpits and

139

thunder invective to Negroes against whites. The Negrotarians have a formula, too. They have regimented their sympathies and fawn around Negroes with a cry in their heart and a superiority bug in their head. It's a new way to get a thrill, a new way to merit distinction in the community . . . this cultivating Negroes. It's a sure way to bolster up their own weak ego and cut a figure. Negroes being what they are make this sort of person possible."

"Which means?"

Raymond replied sharply: "That ninety-nine and ninety-nine hundredths per cent of the Negro race is patiently possessed and motivated by an inferiority complex. Being a slave race actuated by slave morality, what else could you expect? Within themselves and by their every action they subscribe to the doctrine of Nordic superiority and the louder they cry against it the more they mark themselves inferiors. Of course they are flattered by whites like Samuel, flattered to be verbally accepted as equals by someone who mayhap mentally is their inferior. But as long as he has a white skin it's all right. In the white world what is Samuel? A nonentity who doesn't count. Among Negroes . . . my God, he's a king, looked up to, pursued. And look at Barbara, absolutely down and out until she chanced to come to Harlem. Now every male in the respectable Negro middle class she has invaded longs to possess her. And yourself . . ."

"What about me?"

"Don't play dumb. You know. You can't help but be aware of the eager subservience they proffer you, both men and women."

"Aren't you generalizing?"

"I said a little while ago . . . ninety-nine and ninety-nine hundredths per cent."

"And that remaining one hundredths per cent?"

"You know as well as I do who it is in this crowd. Lucille, myself, and sometimes Paul. And you also know that we are the only ones around here with whom you can feel natural. The rest force a certain psychological reaction."

"But Bull . . ."

"Is so afraid of the white man," Raymond snapped angrily, "that his only recourse is to floor one at every opportunity and on any pretext. Should one suddenly turn the tables and smash him back he'd run away like a cowed dog."

Stephen laughed. "What's to be done about it?"

"What's to be done about anything? Nothing. Negroes are a slave race and a slave race they'll remain until assimilated. Individuals will arise and escape on the ascending ladder of their own individuality. The others will remain what they are. Their superficial progress means nothing. Instinctively they are still the servile progeny of servile ancestors."

"God, but you love your race this morning. You haven't been so eloquent in weeks."

"Oh, I know they can't help it. I don't condemn. Why should I? They have no free will . . . no choice but to be what their environment and nature has made them. Fifty per cent of them never think about it. They go about their business, happy in their menial jobs, enjoying themselves while and as they may. The rest . . . the educated minority and middle class have that memorable American urge to keep up with the Joneses. Well, let them. But why not face reality and admit what they are? Why invest themselves with possibilities beyond their reach? No intelligent person subscribes to the doctrine of Nordic superiority, but everyone can realize that now the white man has both the power and the money. His star is almost at the zenith of its ascendancy. There are signs of an impending eclipse, but meanwhile he holds the whip. The rest of the races have to dance and imitate. And we all know that this whip is not held by the white masses although the world has been made safe for democracy. The white masses and the black masses must all cater to the masters who hold the money bags. The white masses seemingly have the edge only because of their closer kinship to those in power."

"I don't follow you altogether, Ray. You seem confused. Is this Communism you're preaching?"

"Hell, no. I preach nothing. I don't give a good god damn what becomes of any mass. Communism can no more change their status than democracy, although for the moment we might have the pleasure of seeing our enshrined bourgeoisie lose their valued heads."

"And if that should happen?"

"I'd stand by enjoying the carnage, then pessimistically await the emergence of a similar bunch of dolts to take the places of the deceased."

Stephen finished putting on his clothes.

"You've learned your lessons well."

"What?"

"I say, you've learned your lessons well. Good schoolmasters you've had, too, *n'est-ce pas?*"

He smiled benignly and left the room, before Raymond's confused mind could digest his words or formulate a fitting retort.

447

XXI

AFTER Stephen's unexpected visit and their long conversation together, Raymond seemed to have developed a new store of energy. For three days and nights, he had secluded himself in his room, and devoted all his time to the continuance of his novel. For three years it had remained a project. Now he was making rapid progress. The ease with which he could work once he set himself to it amazed him, and at the same time he was suspicious of this unexpected facility. Nevertheless, his novel was progressing, and he intended to let nothing check him.

In line with this resolution, he insisted that Paul and Eustace hold their nightly gin parties without his presence, and they were also abjured to steer all company clear of his studio.

Stephen had gone upstate on a tutoring job.

226

Lucille had not been in evidence since the donation party, and Raymond had made no attempt to get in touch with her. There was no one else in whom he had any interest. Aline and Janet he had dismissed from his mind, although Eustace and Paul had spent an entire dinner hour telling him of their latest adventures. Both had now left Aline's mother's house and were being supported by some white man, whom Aline had met at a downtown motion picture theater. They had an apartment in which they entertained groups of young colored boys on the nights their white protector was not in evidence.

Having withdrawn from every activity connected with Niggeratti Manor, Raymond had also forgotten that Dr. Parkes had promised to communicate with him, concerning some mysterious idea, and he was taken by surprise when Eustace came into the room one morning, bearing a letter from Dr. Parkes.

"Well, I'm plucked," Raymond exclaimed.

"What's the matter?" Eustace queried.

"Will you listen to this?" He read the letter aloud.

"My dear Raymond:

I will be in New York on Thursday night. I want you to do me a favor. It seems to me that with the

449

ever increasing number of younger Negro artists and intellectuals gathering in Harlem, some effort should be made to establish what well might become a distinguished salon. All of you engaged in creative work, should, I believe, welcome the chance to meet together once every fortnight, for the purpose of exchanging ideas and expressing and criticizing individual theories. This might prove to be both stimulating and profitable. And it might also bring into active being a concerted movement which would establish the younger Negro talent once and for all as a vital artistic force. With this in mind, I would appreciate your inviting as many of your colleagues as possible to your studio on Thursday evening. I will be there to preside. I hope you are intrigued by the idea and willing to coöperate. Please wire me your answer. Collect, of course.

Very sincerely yours,

Dr. A. L. Parkes."

"Are you any more good?" Raymond asked as he finished reading.

"Sounds like a great idea," Eustace replied enthusiastically.

"It *is* great. Too great to miss," Raymond acquiesced mischievously. "Come on, let's get busy on the telephone."

Thursday night came and so did the young hopefuls. The first to arrive was Sweetie May Carr. Sweetie May was a short story writer, more noted for her ribald wit and personal effervescence than for any actual literary work. She was a great favorite among those whites who went in for Negro prodigies. Mainly because she lived up to their conception of what a typical Negro should be. It seldom occurred to any of her patrons that she did this with tongue in cheek. Given a paleface audience, Sweetie May would launch forth into a saga of the little all-colored Mississippi town where she claimed to have been born. Her repertoire of tales was earthy, vulgar and funny. Her darkies always smiled through their tears, sang spirituals on the slightest provocation, and performed buck dances when they should have been working. Sweetie May was a master of southern dialect, and an able raconteur, but she was too indifferent to literary creation to transfer to paper that which she told so well. The intricacies of writing bored her, and her written work was for the most part turgid and unpolished. But Sweetie May knew her white folks.

"It's like this," she had told Raymond. "I have to eat. I also wish to finish my education. Being a Negro writer these days is a racket and I'm going to make the most of it while it lasts. Sure I cut the fool. But I enjoy it, too. I don't know a tinker's damn about art. I care less about it. My ultimate ambition, as you know, is to become a gynecologist. And the only way I can live easily until I have the requisite training is to pose as a writer of potential ability. *Voila!* I get my tuition paid at Columbia. I rent an apartment and have all the furniture contributed by kind hearted o'fays. I receive bundles of groceries from various sources several times a week . . . all accomplished by dropping a discreet hint during an evening's festivities. I find queer places for whites to go in Harlem . . . out of the way primitive churches, sidestreet speakeasies. They fall for it. About twice a year I manage to sell a story. It is acclaimed. I am a genius in the making. Thank God for this Negro literary renaissance! Long may it flourish!"

Sweetie May was accompanied by two young girls, recently emigrated from Boston. They were the latest to be hailed as incipient immortals. Their names were Doris Westmore and Hazel Jamison. Doris wrote short stories. Hazel wrote poetry. Both had become known through a literary contest fostered by one of the leading Negro magazines. Raymond liked them more than he did most of the younger recruits to the movement. For one thing, they were characterized by a freshness and naïveté which he and his cronies had lost. And, surprisingly enough for Negro prodigies, they actually gave promise of possessing literary talent. He was most pleased to see them. He was also amused by their interest and excitement. A salon! A literary gathering! It was one of the civilized institutions they had dreamed of finding in New York, one of the things they had longed and hoped for.

As time passed, others came in. Tony Crews, smiling and self-effacing, a mischievous boy, grateful for the chance to slip away from the backwoods college he attended. Raymond had never been able to analyze this young poet. His work was interesting and unusual. It was also spotty. Spasmodically he gave promise of developing into a first rate poet. Already he had published two volumes, prematurely, Raymond thought. Both had been excessively praised by whites and universally damned by Negroes. Considering the nature of his work this was to be expected. The only unknown quantity was the poet himself. Would he or would he not fulfill the prom-

ise exemplified in some of his work? Raymond had
no way of knowing and even an intimate friendship
with Tony himself had failed to enlighten him. For
Tony was the most close-mouthed and cagey individual Raymond had ever known when it came to
personal matters. He fended off every attempt to
probe into his inner self and did this with such an
unconscious and naïve air that the prober soon came
to one of two conclusions: Either Tony had no depth
whatsoever, or else he was too deep for plumbing
by ordinary mortals.

DeWitt Clinton, the Negro poet laureate, was
there, too, accompanied, as usual, by his *fideles
achates*, David Holloway. David had been acclaimed the most handsome Negro in Harlem by a
certain group of whites. He was in great demand
by artists who wished to paint him. He had become
a much touted romantic figure. In reality he was a
fairly intelligent school teacher, quite circumspect
in his habits, a rather timid beau, who imagined
himself to be bored with life.

Dr. Parkes finally arrived, accompanied by Carl
Denny, the artist, and Carl's wife, Annette. Next
to arrive was Cedric Williams, a West Indian,
whose first book, a collection of short stories with
a Caribbean background, in Raymond's opinion,

marked him as one of the three Negroes writing who actually had something to say, and also some concrete idea of style. Cedric was followed by Austin Brown, a portrait painter whom Raymond personally despised, a Dr. Manfred Trout, who practiced medicine and also wrote exceptionally good short stories, Glenn Madison, who was a Communist, and a long, lean professorial person, Allen Fenderson, who taught school and had ambitions to become a crusader modeled after W. E. B. Du Bois.

The roster was now complete. There was an hour of small talk and drinking of mild cocktails in order to induce ease and allow the various guests to become acquainted and voluble. Finally, Dr. Parkes ensconced himself in Raymond's favorite chair, where he could get a good view of all in the room, and clucked for order.

Raymond observed the professor closely. Paul's description never seemed more apt. He was a mother hen clucking at her chicks. Small, dapper, with sensitive features, graying hair, a dominating head, and restless hands and feet, he smiled benevolently at his brood. Then, in his best continental manner, which he had acquired during four years at European Universities, he began to speak.

"You are," he perorated, "the outstanding personalities in a new generation. On you depends the future of your race. You are not, as were your predecessors, concerned with donning armor, and clashing swords with the enemy in the public square. You are finding both an escape and a weapon in beauty, which beauty when created by you will cause the American white man to reëstimate the Negro's value to his civilization, cause him to realize that the American black man is too valuable, too potential of utilitarian accomplishment, to be kept downtrodden and segregated.

"Because of your concerted storming up Parnassus, new vistas will be spread open to the entire race. The Negro in the south will no more know peonage, Jim Crowism, or loss of the ballot, and the Negro everywhere in America will know complete freedom and equality.

"But," and here his voice took on a more serious tone, "to accomplish this, your pursuit of beauty must be vital and lasting. I am somewhat fearful of the decadent strain which seems to have filtered into most of your work. Oh, yes, I know you are children of the age and all that, but you must not, like your paleface contemporaries, wallow in the mire of post-Victorian license. You have too much at stake. You must have ideals. You should become . . .

well, let me suggest your going back to your racial roots, and cultivating a healthy paganism based on African traditions.

"For the moment that is all I wish to say. I now want you all to give expression to your own ideas. Perhaps we can reach a happy mean for guidance."

He cleared his throat and leaned contentedly back in his chair. No one said a word. Raymond was full of contradictions, which threatened to ooze forth despite his efforts to remain silent. But he knew that once the ooze began there would be no stopping the flood, and he was anxious to hear what some of the others might have to say.

However, a glance at the rest of the people in the room assured him that most of them had not the slightest understanding of what had been said, nor any ideas on the subject, whatsoever. Once more Dr. Parkes clucked for discussion. No one ventured a word. Raymond could see that Cedric, like himself, was full of argument, and also like him, did not wish to appear contentious at such an early stage in the discussion. Tony winked at Raymond when he caught his eye, but the expression on his face was as inscrutable as ever. Sweetie May giggled behind her handkerchief. Paul amused himself by sketching the various people in the room. The rest were blank.

"Come, come, now," Dr. Parkes urged somewhat impatiently, "I'm not to do all the talking. What have you to say, DeWitt?"

All eyes sought out the so-called Negro poet laureate. For a moment he stirred uncomfortably in his chair, then in a high pitched, nasal voice proceeded to speak.

"I think, Dr. Parkes, that you have said all there is to say. I agree with you. The young Negro artist must go back to his pagan heritage for inspiration and to the old masters for form."

Raymond could not suppress a snort. For De-Witt's few words had given him a vivid mental picture of that poet's creative hours—eyes on a page of Keats, fingers on typewriter, mind frantically conjuring African scenes. And there would of course be a Bible nearby.

Paul had ceased being intent on his drawing long enough to hear "pagan heritage," and when DeWitt finished he inquired inelegantly:

"What old black pagan heritage?"

DeWitt gasped, surprised and incredulous.

"Why, from your ancestors."

"Which ones?" Paul pursued dumbly.

"Your African ones, of course." DeWitt's voice was full of disdain.

"What about the rest?"

"What rest?" He was irritated now.

"My German, English and Indian ancestors," Paul answered willingly. "How can I go back to African ancestors when their blood is so diluted and their country and times so far away? I have no conscious affinity for them at all."

Dr. Parkes intervened: "I think you've missed the point, Paul."

"And I," Raymond was surprised at the suddenness with which he joined in the argument, "think he has hit the nail right on the head. Is there really any reason why *all* Negro artists should consciously and deliberately dig into African soil for inspiration and material unless they actually wish to do so?"

"I don't mean that. I mean you should develop your inherited spirit."

DeWitt beamed. The doctor had expressed his own hazy theory. Raymond was about to speak again, when Paul once more took the bit between his own teeth.

"I ain't got no African spirit."

Sweetie May giggled openly at this, as did Carl Denny's wife, Annette. The rest looked appropriately sober, save for Tony, whose eyes continued to telegraph mischievously to Raymond. Dr. Parkes

459

tried to squelch Paul with a frown. He should have known better.

"I'm not an African," the culprit continued. "I'm an American and a perfect product of the melting pot."

"That's nothing to brag about." Cedric spoke for the first time.

"And I think you're all on the wrong track." All eyes were turned toward this new speaker, Allen Fenderson. "Dr. Du Bois has shown us the way. We must be militant fighters. We must not hide away in ivory towers and prate of beauty. We must fashion cudgels and bludgeons rather than sensitive plants. We must excoriate the white man, and make him grant us justice. We must fight for complete social and political and economic equality."

"What we ought to do," Glenn Madison growled intensely, "is to join hands with the workers of the world and overthrow the present capitalistic régime. We are of the proletariat and must fight our battles allied with them, rather than singly and selfishly."

"All of us?" Raymond inquired quietly.

"All of us who have a trace of manhood and are more interested in the rights of human beings than in gin parties and neurotic capitalists."

"I hope you're squelched," Paul stage whispered to Raymond.

"And how!" Raymond laughed. Several joined in. Dr. Parkes spoke quickly to Fenderson, ignoring the remarks of the Communist.

"But, Fenderson . . . this is a new generation and must make use of new weapons. Some of us will continue to fight in the old way, but there are other things to be considered, too. Remember, a beautiful sonnet can be as effectual, nay even more effectual, than a rigorous hymn of hate."

"The man who would understand and be moved by a hymn of hate would not bother to read your sonnet and, even if he did, he would not know what it was all about."

"I don't agree. Your progress must be a boring in from the top, not a battle from the bottom. Convert the higher beings and the lower orders will automatically follow."

"Spoken like a true capitalistic minion," Glenn Madison muttered angrily.

Fenderson prepared to continue his argument, but be was forestalled by Cedric.

"What does it matter," he inquired diffidently, "what any of you do so long as you remain true to yourselves? There is no necessity for this movement becoming standardized. There is ample room for everyone to follow his own individual track. Dr. Parkes wants us all to go back to Africa and resurrect our pagan heritage, become atavistic. In this he is supported by Mr. Clinton. Fenderson here wants us all to be propagandists and yell at the top of our lungs at every conceivable injustice. Madison wants us all to take a cue from Leninism and fight the capitalistic bogey. Well . . . why not let each young hopeful choose his own path? Only in that way will anything at all be achieved."

"Which is just what I say," Raymond smiled gratefully at Cedric. "One cannot make movements nor can one plot their course. When the work of a given number of individuals during a given period is looked at in retrospect, then one can identify a movement and evaluate its distinguishing characteristics. Individuality is what we should strive for. Let each seek his own salvation. To me, a wholesale flight back to Africa or a wholesale allegiance to Communism or a wholesale adherence to an antiquated and for the most part ridiculous propagandistic program are all equally futile and unintelligent."

Dr. Parkes gasped and sought for an answer. Cedric forestalled him.

"To talk of an African heritage among American Negroes *is* unintelligent. It is only in the West Indies that you can find direct descendents from African ancestors. Your primitive instincts among all but the extreme proletariat have been ironed out. You're standardized Americans."

"Oh, no," Carl Denny interrupted suddenly. "You're wrong. It's in our blood. It's . . ." he fumbled for a word, "fixed. Why . . ." he stammered again, "remember Cullen's poem, *Heritage:*

> " 'So I lie who find no peace
> Night or day, no slight release
> From the unremittant beat
> Made by cruel padded feet
> Walking through my body's street.
> Up and down they go, and back,
> Treading out a jungle track.'

"We're all like that. Negroes are the only people in America not standardized. The feel of the African jungle is in their blood. Its rhythms surge through their bodies. Look how Negroes laugh and dance and sing, all spontaneous and individual."

"Exactly," Dr. Parkes and DeWitt nodded assent.

"I have yet to see an intelligent or middle class American Negro laugh and sing and dance spontaneously. That's an illusion, a pretty sentimental fiction. Moreover your songs and dances are not individual. Your spirituals are mediocre folk songs, ignorantly culled from Methodist hymn books. There are white men who can sing them just as well as Negroes, if not better, should they happen to be untrained vocalists like Robeson, rather than highly trained technicians like Hayes. And as for dancing spontaneously and feeling the rhythms of the jungle . . . humph!"

Sweetie May jumped into the breach.

"I can do the Charleston better than any white person."

"I particularly stressed . . . intelligent people. The lower orders of any race have more vim and vitality than the illuminated tenth."

Sweetie May leaped to her feet.

"Why, you West Indian . . ."

"Sweetie, Sweetie," Dr. Parkes was shocked by her polysyllabic expletive.

Pandemonium reigned. The master of ceremonies could not cope with the situation. Cedric called Sweetie an illiterate southern hussy. She called him all types of profane West Indian monkey chasers. DeWitt and David were shocked and showed it. The literary doctor, the Communist and Fenderson moved uneasily around the room. Annette and Paul giggled. The two child prodigies from Boston looked on wide-eyed, utterly bewildered and dismayed. Raymond leaned back in his chair, puffing on a cigarette, detached and amused. Austin, the portrait painter, audibly repeated over and over to himself: "Just like niggers . . . just like niggers." Carl Denny interposed himself between Cedric and Sweetie May. Dr. Parkes clucked for civilized behavior, which came only when Cedric stalked angrily out of the room.

After the alien had been routed and peace restored, Raymond passed a soothing cocktail. Meanwhile Austin and Carl had begun arguing about painting. Carl did not possess a facile tongue. He always had difficulty formulating in words the multitude of ideas which seethed in his mind. Austin, to quote Raymond, was an illiterate cad. Having examined one of Carl's pictures on Raymond's wall, he had disparaged it. Raymond listened attentively to their argument. He despised Austin mainly because he spent most of his time imploring noted white people to give him a break by posing for a portrait. Having the gift of making himself pitiable, and having a glib tongue when it came to expatiating on the trials and tribulations of being a Negro, he found many sitters, all of whom thought they were encouraging a handicapped Negro genius. After one glimpse at the completed portrait, they invariably changed their minds.

"I tell you," he shouted, "your pictures are distorted and grotesque. Art is art, I say. And art holds a mirror up to nature. No mirror would reflect a man composed of angles. God did not make man that way. Look at Sargent's portraits. He was an artist."

"But he wasn't," Carl expostulated. "We . . . we of this age . . . we must look at Matisse, Gauguin, Picasso and Renoir for guidance. They get the feel of the age. . . . They . . ."

"Are all crazy and so are you," Austin countered before Carl could proceed.

Paul rushed to Carl's rescue. He quoted Wilde in rebuttal: Nature imitates art, then went on to blaspheme Sargent. Carl, having found some words to express a new idea fermenting in his brain, forgot the argument at hand, went off on a tangent and began telling the dazed Dr. Parkes about the Negroid quality in his drawings. DeWitt yawned and consulted his watch. Raymond mused that he probably resented having missed the prayer meeting which he attended every Thursday night. In another corner of the room the Communist and Fenderson had locked horns over the ultimate solution of the Negro problem. In loud voices each contended for his own particular solution. Karl Marx and Lenin were pitted against Du Bois and his disciples. The writing doctor, bored to death, slipped quietly from the room without announcing his departure or even saying good night. Being more intelligent than most of the others, he had wisely kept silent. Tony and Sweetie May had taken adjoining chairs, and were soon engaged in comparing their versions of original verses to the St. James Infirmary, which Tony contended was soon to become as epical as the St. Louis Blues. Annette and Howard began gossiping about various outside personalities. The child prodigies looked from one to the other, silent, perplexed, uncomfortable, not knowing what to do or say. Dr. Parkes visibly recoiled from Carl's incoherent expository barrage, and wilted in his chair, willing but unable to effect a courteous exit. Raymond sauntered around the room, dispensing cocktails, chuckling to himself.

Such was the first and last salon.

Acknowledgments

FIRE!! 1 (November 1926): 1–48.

Harlem: A Forum of Negro Life (November 1928): 1–45.

Bennett, Gwendolyn. "The Ebony Flute." *Opportunity* (August 1926–May 1928)

    Opportunity 4 (August 1926): 241, 260–61.

    Opportunity 4 (September 1926): 292–93.

    Opportunity 4 (October 1926): 322–23.

    Opportunity 4 (November 1926): 356–58.

    Opportunity 4 (December 1926): 391.

    Opportunity 5 (January 1927): 28–29.

    Opportunity 5 (March 1927): 90–91.

    Opportunity 5 (April 1927): 122–23.

    Opportunity 5 (June 1927): 182–83.

    Opportunity 5 (July 1927): 212–13.

    Opportunity 5 (August 1927): 242–43.

    Opportunity 5 (September 1927): 276–77.

    Opportunity 5 (October 1927): 308–9.

    Opportunity 5 (November 1927): 339–40.

    Opportunity 5 (December 1927): 376.

    Opportunity 6 (January 1928): 24.

    Opportunity 6 (February 1928): 55–56.

    Opportunity 6 (April 1928): 122.

    Opportunity 6 (May 1928): 153.

Cullen, Countee. "The Dark Tower." *Opportunity* (November 1926–September 1927)

    Opportunity 4 (November 1926): 337.

    Opportunity 4 (December 1926): 388–90.

    Opportunity 5 (January 1927): 24–25.

    Opportunity 5 (February 1927): 53–54.

    Opportunity 5 (March 1927): 86–87.

    Opportunity 5 (April 1927): 118–19.

    Opportunity 5 (May 1927): 149–50.

    Opportunity 5 (June 1927): 180–81.

    Opportunity 5 (July 1927): 210–11.

Opportunity 5 (August 1927): 240–41.

Opportunity 5 (September 1927): 272–73.

Bruce, Richard. "The Dark Tower." *Opportunity* 5 (October 1927): 305–6.

Cullen, Countee. " The Dark Tower." *Opportunity* (November 1927–September 1928)

Opportunity 5 (November 1927): 336–37.

Opportunity 5 (December 1927): 373–74.

Opportunity 6 (January 1928): 20–21.

Opportunity 6 (February 1928): 52–53.

Opportunity 6 (March 1928): 90.

Opportunity 6 (April 1928): 120.

Opportunity 6 (May 1928): 146–47.

Opportunity 6 (June 1928): 178–79.

Opportunity 6 (July 1928): 210.

Opportunity 6 (September 1928): 271–73.

Brown, Sterling A. "The Literary Scene: Chronicle and Comment." *Opportunity* (January 1931–September 1935)

"The Literary Scene: Chronicle and Comment." *Opportunity* 9 (January 1931): 20.

"The Literary Scene: Chronicle and Comment." *Opportunity* 9 (February 1931): 53–54.

"The Literary Scene: Chronicle and Comment." *Opportunity* 9 (March 1931): 87.

"A Romantic Defense." *Opportunity* 9 (April 1931): 118.

"An American Epoch." *Opportunity* 9 (June 1931): 187.

"As to 'Jungle Ways.'" *Opportunity* 9 (July 1931): 219, 221.

"Caroling Softly Souls of Slavery." *Opportunity* 9 (August 1931): 251–52.

"Concerning Negro Drama." *Opportunity* 9 (September 1931): 284, 288.

"Poor Whites." *Opportunity* 9 (October 1931): 317, 320.

"The Point of View." *Opportunity* 9 (November 1931): 347, 350.

"Pride and Pathos." *Opportunity* 9 (December 1931): 381, 384.

"Truth Will Out." *Opportunity* 10 (January 1932): 23–24.

"Never No More." *Opportunity* 10 (February 1932): 55–56.

"Weep Some More My Lady." *Opportunity* 10 (March 1932): 87.

"Joel Chandler Harris." *Opportunity* 10 (April 1932): 119–20.

"A Literary Parallel." *Opportunity* 10 (May 1932): 152–53.

"More Odds." *Opportunity* 10 (June 1932): 188–89.

"Local Color or Interpretation." *Opportunity* 10 (July 1932): 223.

"A Poet and His Prose." *Opportunity* 10 (August 1932): 256.

"Signs of Promise." *Opportunity* 10 (September 1932): 287.

"Amber Satyr." *Opportunity* 10 (November 1932): 352.

"In Memoriam: Charles W. Chesnutt." *Opportunity* 10 (December 1932): 387.

"A New Trend." *Opportunity* 11 (February 1933): 56.

"Alas the Poor Mulatto." *Opportunity* 11 (March 1933): 91.

"Time For A New Deal." *Opportunity* 11 (April 1933): 122, 126.

"Smartness Goes Traveling." *Opportunity* 11 (May 1933): 154, 158.

"John Brown: God's Angry Man." *Opportunity* 11 (June 1933): 186–87.

"Banana Bottom." *Opportunity* 11 (July 1933): 217, 222.

"From the Southwest." *Opportunity* 11 (October 1933): 313.

"Kingdom Coming." *Opportunity* 11 (December 1933): 382–83. Reprinted with the permission of the National Urban League.

"Arcadia, South Carolina." *Opportunity* 12 (February 1934): 59–60. Reprinted with the permission of the National Urban League.

"Satire of Imperialism." *Opportunity* 12 (March 1934): 89–90. Reprinted with the permission of the National Urban League.

"Six Plays for a Negro Theatre." *Opportunity* 12 (September 1934): 280–81. Reprinted with the permission of the National Urban League.

"Stars Fell on Alabama." *Opportunity* 12 (October 1934): 312–13. Reprinted with the permission of the National Urban League.

"Mississippi—Old Style." *Opportunity* 12 (December 1934): 377–78. Reprinted with the permission of the National Urban League.

"Mississippi, Alabama: New Style." *Opportunity* 13 (February 1935): 55–56. Reprinted with the permission of the National Urban League.

"Imitation of Life: Once a Pancake." *Opportunity* 13 (March 1935): 87–88. Reprinted with the permission of the National Urban League.

"Miss Fannie Hurst"; "Mr. Sterling A. Brown." *Opportunity* 13 (April 1935): 121–22. Reprinted with the permission of the National Urban League.

"Come Day, Go Day." *Opportunity* 13 (September 1935): 279–80. Reprinted with the permission of the National Urban League.

Hughes, Langston. Excerpt from *The Big Sea* (New York: Hill and Wang, 1993): 223–72. Copyright 1940 by Langston Hughes. Copyright renewed 1968 by Arna Bontemps and George Houston Bass. Reprinted by permission of Hill and Wang, a division of Farrar, Straus & Giroux, Inc.

White, Walter. Excerpt from *A Man Called White: The Autobiography of Walter White* (New York: Arno Press, 1969): 65–69, 43. Reprinted with the permission of Jane White Viazzi.

McKay, Claude. Excerpt from *A Long Way From Home* (New York: Arno Press, 1969): 108–15, 147–49. Reprinted with the permission of Harcourt Brace & Company.

Hurston, Zora Neale. Excerpt from *Dust Tracks on a Road: An Autobiography* (Philadelphia: J.B. Lippincott Company, 1942): 182–85, 214–22. Reprinted with the permission of Virago Press Ltd.

McKay, Claude. Excerpt from *Harlem: Negro Metropolis* (New York: E.P. Dutton & Company, Inc., 1940): 15–31, 101–10, 132–80, 239–49.

Thurman, Wallace. Excerpt from *Infants of the Spring* (Carbondale: Southern Illinois University Press, 1979): 113–43, 226–45. Reprinted with the permission of Southern Illinois University Press.